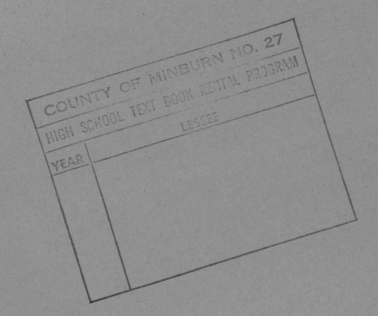

AMERICAN HOME AND FAMILY SERIES

ABOUT THE AUTHORS

Dorothy E. Shank, formerly Food and Nutrition Editor of *What's New in Home Economics* Magazine, was Director of Research Kitchens of the American Stove Company, and Head of the Food Section, Nutrition Division of the Bureau of Home Economics, U. S. Department of Agriculture. She taught at Lasell Junior College in Massachusetts and at Douglass College in New Jersey.

Natalie K. Fitch, Professor Emeritus in Home Economics, Columbia University, was formerly Instructor in Foods at Russell Sage College, New York, and Associate in Foods, University of Illinois. She is co-author of the college textbook *Foods and Principles of Cookery.*

Pauline A. Chapman, Chairman of the Home Economics Department of the Abraham Lincoln High School, Philadelphia, formerly taught in a vocational high school in Chester County, Pennsylvania, and in junior and senior high schools of Philadelphia.

Mary Suzanne Sickler, Director of Home Economics in the West Orange, N.J. school system—kindergarten through high school—was formerly on the Agricultural Extension staff in Pennsylvania. She is author of the New Jersey State Guide, *Homemaking in the Elementary Schools.*

Canadian edition adapted by R. Meryl Ballantyne, Nutritional Consultant

Guide

*Drawings by MAXINE FIELD KRAMER
and MARY GIBSON*

to Modern Meals

CANADIAN EDITION

Dorothy F. Shank

Natalie K. Fitch

Pauline A. Chapman

Mary Suzanne Sickler

**McGRAW-HILL COMPANY
OF CANADA LIMITED**

Toronto   Montreal   New York   London   Sydney

Johannesburg   Mexico   Panama   Dusseldorf

GUIDE TO MODERN MEALS,
Canadian Edition

ISBN 0-07-092784-7

456789 EP-70 9876543

Printed and Bound in Canada

Acknowledgment is made to the following for photographs appearing on chapter opening pages:

Ch. 1, p. 2: Betty Crocker of General Mills. Ch. 2, p. 13: Florida Citrus Commission. Ch. 3, p. 34: National Canners Association. Ch. 4, p. 48: Johan E. Phragmén. Ch. 5, p. 72: School District of Philadelphia. Ch. 6, p. 94: General Electric Company. Ch. 7, p. 120: Towle Silversmiths. Ch. 8, p. 137: Corning Glass Works. Ch. 9, p. 149: Poultry and Egg National Board. Ch. 10, p. 159: International Silver Company. Ch. 11, p. 173: Oneida, Ltd. Ch. 12, p. 186: Towle Silversmiths. Ch. 13, p. 206: United Fruit Company. Ch. 14, p. 215: Wheat Flour Institute. Ch. 15, p. 225: The Nestlé Company. Ch. 16, p. 234: Poultry and Egg National Board. Ch. 17, p. 247: Armour and Company. Ch. 18, p. 253: Wesson Oil Company. Ch. 19, p. 261: Armour and Company. Ch. 20, p. 279: Poultry and Egg National Board. Ch. 22, p. 298: Western Growers Association. Ch. 23, p. 308: West Bend Aluminum Company. Ch. 24, p. 317: Standard Brands. Ch. 25, p. 333: Ewing Galloway. Ch. 26, p. 345: National Association of Margarine Manufacturers. Ch. 27, p. 349: Ann Pillsbury's Home Service Center. Ch. 28, p. 357: The Nestlé Company. Ch. 29, p. 367: National Biscuit Company. Ch. 30, p. 373: Sealtest. Ch. 31, p. 379: Western Growers Association. Ch. 32, p. 389: American Institute of Baking. Ch. 33, p. 399: "Better Homes and Gardens." Ch. 34, p. 405: Ball Brothers Company.

Credit for cover photo:
Robert E. Coates

Preface to the Teacher

Each day we see further evidence of the complexity of our way of life and of the need to prepare to live in a world that will remain in a state of constant change. It is an exciting time for those of us who like to see man use all the resources of his environment to improve his way of living. It is a time of great responsibility for us in education as we try to plan a curriculum that will prepare our present generation of boys and girls to live their adult lives in a world about which we know little except that it will be different.

Research has shown us that as long as man lives he will have need for food, clothing, and shelter, and for the ability to get along with himself and other people. As life becomes more complex, so do the procedures for satisfying basic needs increase in complexity with greater emphasis being directed toward improving relationships with our fellowmen. Food, the most basic of our needs, has long been recognized for its role as the important source of nutrients required by the body for life. It is only within the past few years that greater recognition has been given to the nonnutritional significance of food and its role in the personal relationships among men.

Everyone eats, and most people find pleasure in eating in a family or social group. All families and social groups have many things in common, but each group is also different in character from every other group. Each family has its own cultural traditions and customs, its own patterns of living, and its own social and economic standards. Meals may differ among families because of differences in nationality backgrounds, religious backgrounds, sections of the country, economic conditions, and the occupations and ages of the family members. Habits and attitudes of individual members also have an influence on the kinds of meals the family has and when they are served.

If mealtime in the family is to be an occasion that brings pleasure and satisfaction to all members (as well as helping them to develop the ability to use food to improve their personal relationships), then boys and girls must receive the knowledge and skill necessary to accomplish these goals. The planning of a menu, the way the time and work are managed, how the food money is spent, and the way the food is prepared and served are all important. Information on all these topics, as well as information about foods, the kitchen and its equipment, and how to select and use recipes are given in this book.

The Purpose

It is our belief that good meals make a vital contribution to good family life and eventually to good community life. To this end, we present *Guide to Modern Meals* as our contribution to preparing boys and girls to live in a world of change. The planning, preparing,

v

z of nutritious, appetizing meals in-
owledge of basic concepts concerning
s well as the management of time, ef-
money, and equipment resources.

Young people, engaged in the study of foods,
will acquire the following kinds of information,
experiences, skills, and values that will be of
use today and in the future:

An appreciation of the contributions mealtime
can make to family and community life.
An understanding of the relation of food to
health, that is, some knowledge of the chem-
istry of food and its relation to the physi-
ology of the body.
Experience in dealing with all phases of management problems of family meals and how
to obtain the most food value for the family
dollar.
Some skill in the preparation and serving of
meals.
An opportunity to exercise creative talents.
A means for becoming self-reliant when preparing meals alone or cooperative when
working in a group.
An opportunity to learn accepted habits of
conduct at the table and so gain the poise
that such good habits bring.

Basic Understandings and the Curriculum

With the great potential for change that lies
ahead and the explosion of knowledge that is
occurring daily, it is imperative that our curriculum be based on broad generalizations
rather than on specific subject matter. The
provincial departments of education have provided leadership in developing a conceptual
framework for home economics education
that makes this type of curriculum possible.

Guide to Modern Meals has been revised to
take advantage of this new approach to curriculum development. To help teachers in
developing their foods curriculum, the conceptual framework that is used is given below.
It includes the basic concept for Parts I, II,
and III, and the supporting generalizations
for the different chapters in these parts. The

broad generalizations, given on the title pages
of Parts I, II, and III, are not repeated here.
The framework corresponds in sequence to
the subject matter of the text.

Conceptual Framework—Guide to Modern Meals

Part I. *Meals Are Better When Carefully Planned*

Chapter 1—Planning Meals for the Family
Supporting Generalizations:
A. Planning meals in advance will result
in more efficient use of the homemaker's
and family's resources to achieve goals
related to food, and will allow for creativity and personal satisfaction on the
part of the homemaker.
B. More healthful and attractive meals will
result when menus are based on a good
food guide and follow meal patterns
that best suit the family's way of life.
C. Nutritionally adequate diets may be attained with many combinations of foods
commonly available throughout the
world even though no single food guide
or meal pattern is followed.
D. Selecting foods for meals involves de-
cision-making in regard to personal
preferences, ease of handling, cost, and
purposes for which food is to be used.
E. Plans for good meal management should
be simple, complete, flexible, and work-
able.
F. The ability to evaluate food articles and
advertisements and to make use of good
buying practices can save time, work,
and money.

Chapter 2—Planning Meals for Health
Supporting Generalizations:
A. The personal appearance of an individual is affected by food patterns and eating habits because of the beneficial
influence these have on the personal
characteristics that indicate good health.

vi

B. Foods supply the nutrients needed by the body to build new tissues and replace worn tissues, to provide work energy for body activities and heat energy for body warmth, and to regulate body processes. Foods vary in the quantity and quality of the nutrients they contain.

C. An individual's knowledge of the nutrients, their sources in many foods, and appropriate patterns of combining the foods into balanced meals contribute to a wider freedom of choice among foods in attaining good nutritional health.

D. The amounts and kinds of nutrients needed by individuals vary and are influenced by age, sex, size, activity, climate, and physical and emotional states.

E. The kinds of foods, the ways they are prepared, their grouping in meals, and even the manner in which they are served and eaten constitute the food customs that are characteristic of a country or region. Although these customs differ widely, they can meet nutrient needs equally well.

F. The well-balanced distribution of foods among the daily meals and snacks is easy to adjust to individual family needs and to different situations.

G. The optimum frequency of eating in relation either to physiological comfort or to utilization of nutrients is not known and may differ with individuals and situations, but the occurrence of hunger in all individuals is affected by the time lapse since the last intake of food, the amount and composition of food eaten, and the activities of the individual.

H. People are likely to accept a wide variety of foods if they have wide experiences, knowledge, and appreciation of foods, and if their environment reinforces positive rather than negative attitudes.

I. Wide acceptance of food by an in ual can mean easier adaptability varied social situations and differe economic circumstances, and increased likelihood of obtaining adequate nutrition and pleasure from foods and meals.

Chapter 3—Planning Meals for Variety and Attractiveness
Supporting Generalizations:

A. Variety in meals can be obtained through the use of different foods and different methods of preparation and service.

B. Identification of a food and its ultimate acceptance or rejection depends largely upon the sensory qualities of flavor, texture, and appearance, all of which are influenced by the physical and chemical properties of the food.

C. Prepared foods will be attractive and appetizing when the underlying principles of cookery preparation are followed.

D. The appearance of the table and the manner of serving the food can make eating a pleasant experience.

Part II. *Meals Are Better When Family Resources Are Carefully Managed*
Chapter 4—Managing Meals to Save Time and Effort
Supporting Generalizations:

A. The forms of food selected, the methods of preparation, and the way the meal is served will influence the amount of time and effort needed to prepare and serve a meal.

B. Organization of work and time for meal preparation will contribute to gracious family living.

C. A work-and-time schedule should be flexible, since differences in individuals, in kitchens, in kinds and arrangement of equipment, in numbers of persons preparing the meal, and in numbers persons being served will all affect the schedule.

D. The arrangement of the kitchen and its equipment and the work habits used will influence the amount of time and energy used in preparing family meals.

E. When safety is emphasized in the selection, placement, installation, and use of household equipment, a saving in time and energy will result and the possibility of physical injury to occupants and damage to property is reduced.

F. The methods used for preparing and serving food, and for clearing away after the meal, will depend on the type of equipment available, the arrangement of the sink and working surfaces, and the placement of storage facilities for dishes and utensils.

Chapter 5—Managing Meals to Get Your Money's Worth
Supporting Generalizations:

A. The amount of money allotted to food in the budget differs among families, but in all families it should be spent to obtain maximum nutritional value and appetite appeal.

B. Family food costs will vary with the size and composition of the family, the value placed on food, the resources available, and the special needs of family members.

C. A careful homemaker can reduce the amount of money spent for food by choosing less expensive foods from each of the five groups of Canada's Food Guide; however, there is a practical minimum below which it becomes increasingly difficult to acquire adequate nutrition and to provide culturally accepted variety in foods.

D. The careful food shopper plans in advance for the kind, quantity, and quality of food needed and where and when to buy for cost advantage.

E. An intelligent consumer is aware of government laws that regulate the production, processing, and marketing of the food supply and uses these laws when buying food.

F. When there is evidence that the addition of a particular nutrient or other non-nutrient additive to a food serves a useful purpose, the government defines and regulates such additions and requires their declaration on the package label.

G. Information on labels and in advertising is useful as a basis for choosing products, especially as rational choices among the very large number of foods in the markets become ever more difficult.

H. The proper handling, storage, preparation, and serving of food, and the skillful use of leftover food will help the family obtain the greatest value for the money spent.

Chapter 6—Management in the Kitchen
Supporting Generalizations:

A. Family composition, values, goals, and patterns of living, as well as available space and money, influence the kitchen plans and the kind and quantity of equipment acquired by an individual family.

B. Efficiency and comfort in the kitchen are dependent upon the types and arrangement of work centers, the organization of the necessary equipment and supplies in each center, and the lighting, ventilation, and background in the room.

C. Equipment should be selected for efficiency, durability, ease of operation, frequency of use, and safety features as well as for design and cost.

D. The types of storage cabinets, as well as the arrangement of equipment and supplies in them, influence the expenditures of time, motion, and energy needed in kitchen tasks.

E. Small appliances, when correctly used, save time and money and may take the place of major appliances.

F. Safety in the use of electrical equipment is conditioned by the safety in wiring, location and suitability of outlets, condition of insulation within appliances and cords, and precautions in the use of equipment.

G. An understanding of the meaning and reliability of available seals of approval is useful in the buying and safe use of electrical and gas equipment.

H. Food preparation is simplified through the selection of appropriate tools for the tasks, many of which tools serve multiple uses and can be adapted to varying situations.

I. Consideration of the size, shape, materials, construction, and efficiency of equipment for food preparation is valuable in its selection, use, care, and repair.

Part III. *Meals Are Better When Carefully Prepared and Served*

Chapter 7—Table Setting and Etiquette

Supporting Generalizations:

A. Mealtime is an important family activity which requires careful planning of time and space if family interaction is to occur.

B. Changing modes of living, space arrangements in modern kitchens, and new kinds of equipment create new applications of basic principles of serving meals. In all families the mealtime pattern followed will be determined by the values held and by the work activities of the family members.

C. Selection of table appointments depends upon their suitability to the types of meals customarily served and on the manner of serving the meals.

D. Knowledge of kinds, cost, va. uses, and principles of design wi. the individual to make an intellig selection of table equipment.

E. Rules for table setting, based on convenience and best appearance, can be adjusted to the menu, table appointments available, and comfort of the family.

F. Rules for the different types of table service, like those for table setting, are based on the convenience and comfort of those at the table. The type of service followed, in any case, is governed by the values held by the family in regard to mealtime in the home.

G. Rules for table etiquette are essentially the same in any situation. Observing the customs that are generally considered acceptable contributes to an individual's poise in any social situation and reflects consideration of others.

Chapter 8—Preparing Meals

Supporting Generalizations:

A. Good management in meal preparation involves organizing procedures, following recipes correctly, and observing good grooming and sanitary habits.

B. Performance of routine tasks, according to a basic plan designed for repeated use, facilitates planning, preparing, and serving meals, and increases satisfaction, even though different meals and situations require adjustments in the basic plans.

C. Success in the use of recipes and creativity in food preparation are dependent upon the ability to measure accurately, a familiarity with terms used, an understanding of the reasons for methods given in recipe directions, and a mastery of the basic techniques called for in the directions.

D. Directions for obtaining a product of given characteristics are reliable only when they take into account the nature the original food or food mixture and the effect of the physical or chemical processes to which it is subjected.

E. Some processes involved in food preparation may result in little change, while others modify the food in appearance, texture, consistency, and flavor, and even in food value.

F. Procedures for preparing food products are based on principles of cookery, with the particular principles depending upon the ingredients in a recipe. In some cases a single nutrient in one of the ingredients will be the determining factor as to the principle involved.

G. Following the principles of cookery applies science to food preparation. Giving thought also to the appearance of food when it is ready for serving will apply artistic values. These two factors ensure products of high standards of quality.

Chapters 9, 10, 11—Preparing and Serving Breakfast, Lunch, Supper, and Dinner

Supporting Generalizations:

A. Efficiency in the preparation and service of meals should result in fewer people missing a meal because of time limitation.

B. Cooperative planning, creation of routine procedures, coordination of activities, and clear understanding of individual roles should result in successful group work.

C. An evaluation of the planning, preparation, and serving of a meal can result in suggestions for improving the procedure for future meals.

D. The use of convenience foods reduces the amount of time and effort necessary for preparing a meal without influencing the way of serving it.

E. The special foods selected, the skill of the cook in using them, and the manner in which the foods are served will influence the expenditures of the resources and the attractiveness of the meals.

F. The specific details of any meal plan will depend upon the decisions of the group regarding the form of the various foods to use and the manner of serving the meal.

Chapter 12—Entertaining

Supporting Generalizations:

A. Social gatherings require preliminary organization including: plans for the refreshments to be served; procedures for preparing and serving the refreshments; and plans for the entertainment of the guests and their social interaction.

B. The principles of food preparation remain the same, whether the refreshments are light or elaborate and whether they are to be cooked outdoors or in. The same careful attention should be given to setting the table and serving the food.

The Organization

For ease and clarity of discussion *Guide to Modern Meals* has been organized into six parts. The first three parts deal with the development of basic concepts and supporting and broad generalizations.

Part IV is a subject-matter section. It covers a study of individual foods, considering their use in meals, how to select and store them, the principles of cookery, and how these principles influence the methods of preparing foods. An understanding of this basic information will help the homemaker now and in the future to be prepared to take advantage of any technological changes in food processing and equipment development for preparing meals for the family.

Part V contains an introductory section on using recipes, the necessary tables and directions for measuring ingredients, and approximately 300 recipes. The recipes have been selected to illustrate the material of the book.

Although there are many ways to write recipes, the one used has been found to be the most easily followed by students inexperienced in food preparation. The ingredients are listed in order of use and the method of preparation is in numbered steps. Standards are given for some products where the characteristics of high quality are definite and are generally accepted.

Part VI contains a 25-page table of common foods and their nutrients as adapted from a publication of the Canada Department of Agriculture. This should prove of value in planning meals and in determining nutrients in the diet as research reveals new data on individual food requirements.

A selected list of books and the latest Government pamphlets follows Part VI. The books have been chosen to serve both teachers and students at various levels of learning.

A special feature of *Guide to Modern Meals* is the placing of the recipes at the back of the book rather than dispersed throughout the subject matter section. In this way the student has available a good basic recipe book in addition to a book on foods subject matter. Thus the teacher is able to use the same textbook for either of two approaches: prepare the product first and then study the principle of cookery or study the principle of cookery first and then apply it in the laboratory.

The Supplements to the Text

Questions for Summarizing and Review and Experiences for Applying Your Knowledge are given at the end of Parts I, II, and III. They have been developed to help the student formulate basic concepts as they relate to a specific topic and to gain experience in applying them to everyday home and community living. In general, the experiences included in each part are based on information found in that part. Yet, in each case there are exper-

iences for which background materials from another part are essential. Some experiences draw on the initiative of the student for original ideas, but all make use of the knowledge gained from the book. There are no questions or experiences at the end of Part IV because these chapters are informational in scope; however, subject matter found in this part is called on for carrying out the experiences given at the end of the first three parts.

Much of the text material of a technical or directional nature has been placed in chart form with headings for clarity of presentation, quick comprehension, and easy reference. Tables are placed throughout the book where it is thought they will be most helpful. The illustrations, both photographs and drawings, have been chosen for their instructional qualities. Some are useful in helping students visualize the manner in which a result is obtained; some show processes in individual steps; some show how a finished product will look; some depict the setting of the table, ways of serving, and correct ways to eat; and some give ideas for arranging and garnishing food. In Chapters 7–12 drawings are used to illustrate certain of the techniques and procedures used in preparing and serving meals.

The Sequence

A good text should provide basic subject matter in sufficient depth to be of help to any foods teacher. The teacher, rather than the text, should determine the focus she will use with her individual students and classes. Her choice of basic concepts and generalizations will determine the subject matter and learning experiences needed to teach for the specific understandings of her students.

While there is merit in studying the subject matter in each part of the book separately, it is not necessary that the different parts be studied in sequence. Rather, it might be more effective to integrate the material from several parts of the book and teach for a broad generalization. For example, in a study of the nutritional status of family members, the broad generalization and basic subject matter are given in Part I, but a detailed discussion of the main points is deferred to the chapters in Part IV where the nutritive value and selection of specific foods are discussed; cookery procedures are explained briefly in Part III but in greater detail under the principles of preparation in the various chapters of Part IV, and the principles are applied in the recipes of Part V.

It is our hope that *Guide to Modern Meals* will aid the teacher in helping boys and girls to see how fascinating and rewarding the study of foods can be as they use their knowledge to cope with the feeding problems that continue to evolve in a world of constant change.

NATALIE K. FITCH
PAULINE A. CHAPMAN
MARY SUZANNE SICKLER

Acknowledgments

During the time since publication of the First Edition of *Guide to Modern Meals* the authors have kept in close touch with authoritative sources for information which has enabled them to present current and factual subject matter in the many areas allied to the subject of food, and therefore, they wish to express their sincere appreciation to the following people and organizations who supplied information and help in the preparation of the manuscript for the First Edition and the production of the Second Edition:

Those who have patiently and unstintingly responded to frequent requests for the latest information and pertinent up-to-date subject matter in a specific area of home economics as concerned with the different aspects of food study included in the text

Those who, from the inception of this book to its publication, have supplied constant editorial supervision and practical advice in its preparation and publication

The many commercial companies, magazines, trade associations, and government agencies for their discriminating cooperation in supplying photographs, transparencies, and other illustrative materials

To the following administrators and teachers of home economics in the School District of Philadelphia, Pennsylvania, who assisted in the application of the manuscript to classroom use:

Miss M. Esther Hill, formerly Director of the Division of Home Economics Education

Miss Dorothy J. Showers, Assistant Director of the Division of Home Economics Education

Miss Josephine Dillingham, formerly Supervisor of the Division

Miss Anne M. Frye, homemaking teacher, Mastbaum Technical High School

Mrs. Norma G. Hutchings, formerly homemaking teacher, West Philadelphia High School

Miss Ruth E. Wilson, homemaking teacher, Frankford High School

The authors wish to express appreciation also to the following people who reviewed the outline for the manuscript:

Miss C. Aileen Ericksen, State Specialist, Utah State Board of Education, Salt Lake City, Utah

Dr. Frances M. Hettler, Dean, College of Home Economics, South Dakota State University, Brookings, South Dakota

Miss Georgia Oldham, formerly Associate Professor of Foods and Chairman of the Foods Department, Pratt Institute, Brooklyn, New York

Miss Myrtle G. Temple, formerly City Supervisor of Home Economics, North Adams, Massachusetts

Mrs. Elizabeth L. Wichert, Department of Home Economics, New Mexico State University, University Park, New Mexico

To the following people who reviewed parts or all of the manuscript:

Mrs. Nell M. Arnold, Vocational Counselor, Russellville High School, Russellville, Alabama

Dr. Elizabeth W. Crandall, Chairman, Department of Home Management, College of Home Economics, University of Rhode Island, Kingston, Rhode Island

Miss Mildred Deischer, Home Economics Field Representative, Salem Technical Vocational College, Salem, Oregon

Miss Adrienne M. DeLisle, Director of Home Economics Education, Hamden, Connecticut

Dr. Marietta Eichelberger, Food and Nutrition Consultant, Chicago, Illinois

Mrs. Gertrude Evanoff, Department of Home Economics Chairman, Woodrow Wilson High School, Los Angeles, California

Mrs. Gene Greenwood, homemaker, Claremont, California

Dr. Frances M. Hettler, Dean, College of Home Economics, South Dakota State University, Brookings, South Dakota

Sister Mary Renee, B.V.M., Head of English Department, Mount Carmel Academy, Wichita, Kansas

Mrs. Eugene D. Swift, homemaker, Rogers, Arkansas

Mrs. Elizabeth L. Wichert, Department of Home Economics, New Mexico State University, University Park, New Mexico

NATALIE K. FITCH
PAULINE A. CHAPMAN
MARY SUZANNE SICKLER

Contents

PART I...

Meals Are Better When Carefully Planned

1

Planning Meals for the Family

■ PLANNING for anything is thinking ahead and deciding what to do about a situation. To plan meals, then, is to think ahead and decide what to have for them. In most homes the homemaker serves three meals a day, or twenty-one meals a week. It involves a great deal of money, time, and effort to produce these twenty-one meals to the enjoyment and satisfaction of everyone. With so much at stake, it seems only sensible to think ahead and plan meals for several days, or preferably for a week, in advance rather than to leave the choice to a last-minute decision to be made three times every day in the week.

The homemaker who does not plan meals beforehand finds herself at a great disadvantage. She becomes tense and fatigued as she keeps wondering what to have

for the next meal. Then confusion results because she starts meal preparation only to find that there is too little time to prepare the food, that there is too much to do at one time, or that some essential food item is lacking. Perhaps she may rush to the market and then buy impulsively and unwisely, selecting food that is quick and easy to prepare without regard to its cost or appropriateness to the other meals of the day. She is apt to neglect to include those foods that are so necessary to the health of her family. She may resort to the preparation of some foods so often that her meals become monotonous. She is often wasteful because she ignores or forgets to make use of food left from a previous meal, which, with planning, could be made into an appetizing dish.

Advantages of Planning

The homemaker who plans her meals ahead of time has these advantages over the one who does not make plans:

1. She can take into consideration her family's nutritional needs.
2. She can consider her family's food likes and prejudices.
3. She can make her meals varied and attractive.
4. She can save time and effort in buying, preparing, and serving meals.
5. She can save money.
6. She will experience less tension.

How to Plan

There are many things a homemaker must know if she is to profit from all the advantages of planning meals ahead. She must have some knowledge of the right foods to select for her family's health and of the reasons why these foods are important. She must know how to distribute these foods among the three meals of the day so her family will be satisfied with both the amounts and kinds of foods and with the appetizing quality of each meal. She must know what foods are available in the markets and their approximate cost. As she plans, she must have some knowledge also of ways to organize her work so her plans can be carried out efficiently later on. An experienced homemaker thinks of all these points more or less at the same time, but for someone less experienced it is a good idea to consider each point separately. Help with the problems of meal planning is given in this chapter, while in Chapter 8, "Preparing Meals," there are suggestions for carrying out plans in actual meal preparation.

● If you plan menus for several days or for a week in advance, meal preparation will go more smoothly and family needs and preferences can be considered.

Follow Planning Guides

Two kinds of guides are helpful in planning meals: (1) a daily food guide based on the nutritive contribution of foods to the diet, and (2) meal patterns based on courses in a meal (see page 4). There are a number of daily food guides and meal patterns. The ones followed are a matter of personal choice. Meals planned with these guides, adjusted to family preferences for foods, are sure to be nutritious and pleasing.

Canada's Food Guide. The guide followed in this text is published by the Department of National Health and Welfare (pages 10 to 12). It gives information on the nutritive value of foods by classifying foods into groups according to their nutritive content. For good health, the body needs substances called "nutrients"—carbohydrates, proteins, fats, minerals, vitamins, and water. Nutrients are present in foods, but no one food contains

Courtesy School District of Philadelphia

● In making menus, follow meal patterns such as those in the chart below.

MEAL PATTERNS

	PATTERN I	PATTERN II	PATTERN III	PATTERN IV
Breakfast	Fruit Cereal and Milk Bread Beverage	Fruit Main Dish Bread Beverage	Fruit Cereal and Milk Main Dish Bread Beverage	
Lunch	Soup Sandwich Beverage	Soup Salad Bread Beverage	Salad Bread or Sandwich Dessert Beverage	Main Dish Vegetable and/or Salad Bread Dessert Beverage
Dinner	Main Dish Vegetables Bread Dessert Beverage	Main Dish Vegetables Salad Bread Dessert Beverage	Appetizer Main Dish Vegetables Bread Dessert Beverage	Appetizer Main Dish Vegetables Salad Bread Dessert Beverage

all of them. Moreover, these nutrients are present in different amounts in different kinds of foods—fruits, vegetables, and meats, for example—and it is this fact on which the classification of foods in Canada's Food Guide is based. The Guide lists five groups of foods: Milk, Fruit, Vegetables, Bread and Cereals, Meat and Fish. In addition, it gives for each group (1) some representative foods, (2) the special nutrient contribution of foods in this group, and (3) recommendations for the amounts of these foods that should be eaten every day and Vitamin D.

Meal-pattern guides. These guides are helpful because Canada's Food Guide does not include information on planning the three individual meals of the day among which the needed foods are distributed. A meal pattern is something like an outline, for it lists the parts of a meal. These parts are called "courses." A meal pattern also suggests the kinds of foods that make up each course. There are a number of possible patterns for each meal. Meal patterns for any one of the three daily meals differ from one another in the number or kind of courses served. Which pattern is selected will depend on such things as types of activity and ages of family members, time available for preparation of meals, how family meals are served, and the amount of money which can be spent for food.

Examples of patterns for breakfast, lunch, and dinner are given at the left. A breakfast planned according to Pattern I is nutritionally adequate, provided the servings are ample. In fact, it is considered to be a "minimum adequate breakfast." However, a breakfast following either Patterns II or III would be more satisfying, especially to active and rapidly growing teen-agers. These breakfasts would go further toward meeting their nutritional needs than the breakfast in Pattern I. (See Chapter 2, "Planning Meals for Health.") A lunch such as the one suggested in Pattern I is a light lunch, and it may not include foods from as many of the groups in Canada's Food Guide as is desirable. The other lunch patterns are more adequate because they give an opportunity to use foods from more of the groups in Canada's Food Guide. Dinners following Patterns I and II are light meals, and those following Patterns III and IV are more elaborate and more suitable for a hearty dinner.

Make Menus

A menu is a list of specific foods, or "dishes" as they are sometimes called, to fit the meal pattern selected. If, in planning menus, you use for each day any combination of meal patterns for breakfast, lunch, and dinner and include in your menus foods from all the groups as recommended in Canada's Food Guide, you will have good, healthful meals. For example, for one day you may decide to follow breakfast Pattern II, lunch Pattern III, and dinner Pattern I. Then for the menus you will choose specific foods for each course in each meal pattern. To illustrate this suggestion: Using breakfast Pattern II, you could choose grapefruit juice from among the fruits listed in the Fruit Group of Canada's Food Guide, from the Meat and Fish Group have scrambled eggs as the main dish, from the Bread and Cereal Group, select buttered toast, and from the Milk Group you could have cocoa as the beverage. With a little imagination, you can make your meals varied and attractive. (See Chapter 3, "Planning Meals for Variety and Attractiveness.") Whatever selections of foods you make for meal patterns, you

● Consider the advertisements in newspapers.

● Consider the nutritional needs.

● Consider the members of the family.

● Consider the amount of money available.

should keep in mind family preferences for foods and ways to make meals appetizing.

When you fit the menus into meal patterns and think of specific foods, you also must think of recipes for preparing these foods. Recipes play an important part in meal planning. Some recipes are simple and easy to prepare, while others are more

PLANNING MEALS

● Consider the foods on hand.

● Consider the time needed.

● Consider the best form of food.

● Consider the method of preparation.

complicated. Your choice of recipes may depend on the amount of preparation time needed, your experience in cooking, the availability of ingredients and their cost.

The spending of money for food is the business end of meal planning, and, of course, it too must be considered. Whether the amount of money available for food is large or small, it should be spent wisely if full money's worth is to be obtained with no sacrifice of goodness or nutritive quality. (See Chapter 5, "Managing Meals to Get Your Money's Worth.")

As you make your menus, it is important to keep the cost of food in mind. Some foods always cost more than others. Out-of-season foods, some cuts of meat, meats of the highest quality, and top-quality canned fruits and vegetables are relatively expensive. There is also a variation in price of the same food, depending on the form in which it is sold. For example, whether a fruit or vegetable is fresh, canned, frozen, or dried may make a wide difference in cost.

Food columns in some newspapers carry a paragraph once a week on the best buys. There are also food advertisements in the newspapers, as well as on TV and radio, which tell about specially priced foods. By making a practice of considering these sources of information, you can plan to use some less-expensive foods in your menus. In addition, when the foods advertised are staples, you may save money by buying in quantity. Perishable foods, of course, must be bought for early use. However, by planning menus for several days ahead, you can see more clearly when it is an advantage to buy one or more foods in quantity for use in several meals. Such a practice may save you time, work, and money.

Ways to save time and effort in meal preparation should be kept in mind also as you plan menus. You can save time and effort in the following ways: (1) Use foods in a form that will save the most labor in preparation, such as frozen or canned peas instead of fresh. (2) Avoid having too many foods requiring last-minute attention, such

● After you have planned your meals, or made your menus, make a market order. Organize your list according to the kinds of food or the section of the store where the food is located. In making out your market order, you will need to check the recipes you will use for the meals planned and the supplies that you already have on hand. (See page 76.)

as hot cereal, hot toast, and bacon and eggs for breakfast. (3) Use foods that can be made ready well ahead of time, such as fruit gelatin, which must be made early in the day or even the day ahead. (4) Have foods that require a minimum number of serving and cooking dishes, such as a meat and vegetable casserole for the main dinner dish. (See Chapter 4, "Managing Meals to Save Time and Effort.")

Suggestions for menus for four days will be found on the opposite page. In these menus, variety and attractiveness of meals have been considered, as well as health, economy, and amount of time and work needed for preparation.

SUGGESTED MENUS

DAY 1

Breakfast
Honeydew Melon
Pancakes   Maple Syrup
Milk   Coffee

Lunch
Cream Cheese and Jelly Sandwich
Fresh Pineapple
Cookies
Milk   Tea

Dinner
Vegetable Soup   Cheese Crackers
Fried Chicken   Gravy
Candied Sweetpotatoes   Peas
Cranberry-Orange Relish
Tossed Salad
Chocolate Ice Cream
Milk   Coffee

DAY 2

Breakfast
Orange Slices
Cold Cereal   Top Milk
Poached Egg on Toast
Milk   Coffee

Lunch
Cream of Corn Soup
Chicken Salad Sandwich
(Made with chicken left over from
yesterday's dinner)
Milk   Tea

Dinner
Tomato Juice
Veal Paprika   Buttered Noodles
Glazed Carrots   Sweet Pickles
Peach Shortcake
Milk   Coffee

DAY 3

Breakfast
Stewed Prunes with Lemon
Hot Cereal   Top Milk
Buttered Toast
Milk   Coffee

Lunch
Tuna Fish and Egg Salad
Buttered Toast
Canned Cherries   Peanut-butter Cookies
Cocoa

Dinner
Pot Roast
(Potatoes-Carrots-Onions)
Green Cabbage Slaw   Quick Dressing
Whole-wheat Bread
Fresh Fruit Cup   Butterscotch Cookies
Milk   Coffee

DAY 4

Breakfast
Grapefruit Juice
Cold Cereal   Top Milk
Scrambled Eggs   Cinnamon Toast
Milk   Coffee

Lunch
Grilled Cheese,
Tomato and Bacon Sandwich
Celery and Carrot Sticks
Canned Plums
Milk   Tea

Dinner
Baked Stuffed Pepper   Tomato Sauce
(Made with meat left over from pot roast)
Parsley Potatoes
Asparagus   Mock Hollandaise Sauce
Deep-dish Apple Pie   Cream
Milk   Coffee

Plan for Buying

The making of a market order completes the work of meal planning. To make a market order, you need to do the following: (1) Get out the recipes you will need. (2) List the ingredients in the recipes and all other foods in the menus. (3) Check the foods on the list with those already in the kitchen. (4) Make a new list of the foods you must buy.

If you have followed the plan of making menus for several days in advance, you will have a large market order. But a large market order should prove to be an economy of time, since one trip to the market will take care of food supplies for several days. This is good meal-planning management.

Whatever plans you make for meals or marketing should be flexible, for circumstances may make it advisable or even necessary to change your plans. You may have an opportunity to buy some food at a very good price that is not on the menus, or the arrival of unexpected guests may require more food or a different selection of food than you originally planned.

CANADA'S FOOD GUIDE*

MILK GROUP

Contribution to Diet

Milk is our leading source of calcium which helps to build and maintain bones and teeth. It also provides high-quality protein, riboflavin and many other nutrients. Whole milk and its products are good sources of vitamin A. Check to see if vitamin D has been added to your milk.

Amounts Recommended

Children (up to 11 years)	2½ cups (20 fl. ounces)
Adolescents	4 cups (32 fl. ounces)
Adults	1½ cups (12 fl. ounces)
Expectant and nursing mothers	4 cups (32 fl. ounces)

Photo courtesy National Dairy Council

Milk can be fluid whole, skim, 2 percent or buttermilk. Evaporated, condensed and whole or skim powdered milk can also be used.

The calcium content of many foods made from milk is similar. Milk can be eaten in the following amounts for equivalent calcium intake:

½ cup milk	6 ounces cottage cheese
⅔ ounce cheddar cheese	¾ ounce processed cheese
1 cup ice cream	½ cup cream soup
½ cup milk pudding	

FRUIT GROUP

Contribution to Diet

Fruits such as citrus fruits are main sources of vitamin C. Vitamin C is needed to develop and maintain bones, teeth and gums. Vitamin A which is needed for growth, normal vision and healthy skin comes from some yellow fruits. Fruits also supply other vitamins, minerals and bulk.

Photo courtesy Department of National Health and Welfare

*From—Good Eating with Canada's Food Guide—Department of National Health and Welfare, 1967

Amounts Recommended

Two servings of fruit or juice including a satisfactory source of vitamin C (ascorbic acid) such as oranges, tomatoes, vitaminized apple juice.

A satisfactory source of vitamin C can supply enough vitamin C to meet your daily requirements. Examples are: 3 ounces vitaminized apple juice, ¼ cantaloupe, ½ grapefruit, 1 small orange, 3 ounces orange juice, 5 large fresh strawberries, 6 ounces tomato juice.

The vitamin A content of apricots, cantaloupe, and fresh peaches is worthwhile.

VEGETABLE GROUP

Contribution to Diet

Vegetables are valuable as sources of vitamins A and C, minerals and bulk. Green and yellow vegetables and tomatoes are sources of vitamin A. Some raw and carefully cooked vegetables can be sources of vitamin C. Most green vegetables supply iron which is needed to prevent iron deficiency anemia.

Photo courtesy Department of National Health and Welfare

Amounts Recommended

One serving of potatoes.

Two servings of other vegetables, preferably yellow or green, and often raw.

The following vegetables contain sufficient vitamin C to meet the day's requirements. (Please remember that vitamin C is easily destroyed and care must be taken in vegetable preparation.): 1 large potato cooked in skin, ¾ cup canned tomatoes, ¼ cup cooked broccoli, ½ cup cauliflower, ¾ cup cooked spinach, ½ cup raw turnip.

The following vegetables are good sources of vitamin A: beet greens, broccoli, carrots, celery, sweet potatoes, spinach and winter squash.

BREAD AND CEREALS GROUP

Contribution to Diet

Bread and cereals contribute worthwhile amounts of food energy, minerals and protein. When they are enriched or whole-grain products, they are also important sources of iron, niacin, thiamine, and riboflavin.

Photo courtesy National Dairy Council

Amounts Recommended

Bread (with butter or fortified margarine).

One serving of whole-grain cereal.

Unless they are enriched, refined breads will have less nutrient value than whole-grain or enriched breads such as whole-wheat and enriched white bread.

Whole-grain cereals are whole-wheat or bran flakes products, shredded wheats, and various hot cereals such as rolled oats. Enriched noodles, macaroni and spaghetti are available. Whole-grain cereals can also be used in making cookies, muffins and desserts. Check to see if the flour you are using is whole-grain or enriched flour.

MEAT AND FISH GROUP

Contribution to Diet

Meat, fish, poultry, eggs, cheese, dried beans or peas contribute protein, iron, thiamine, riboflavin, niacin and vitamin A to the diet. Liver is a particularly good source of all these nutrients.

Protein is essential for growth and repair of body tissues and protein of the highest quality is obtained from animal products including eggs and cheese. Although the quality of protein from dried beans and peas is less, these foods are economical and important in the diet.

Photo courtesy National Dairy Council

Amounts Recommended

One serving of meat, fish or poultry.

Eat liver occasionally.

Eggs, cheese, dried beans or peas may be used in place of meat.

In addition, three servings per week of each of eggs and cheese.

Examples of a serving of meat, fish, poultry, or other foods in this group are: 3 to 4 ounces of cooked meat such as roast beef, 2 lamb chops, 1 cup baked beans, 1 chicken breast, 2 eggs, 4 ounces of salmon.

Vitamin D

Vitamin D is not found in most foods: therefore, a vitamin D preparation or fluid milk with vitamin D added or a similar source should be taken daily by all growing persons and expectant and nursing mothers in order to supply 400 International Units.

2

Planning Meals for Health

■ YOU can have a lot of fun and do a great many worthwhile things when you are healthy. Good health brings vitality— the quality that makes you interested in the things you do and an interesting companion to your friends. How can you determine whether or not you are healthy? Here are some characteristics. You are healthy if you have...

...good body posture when you stand, sit, walk, and run.

...an absence of any aches, pains, or ailments.

...a complexion that is clear and free from blemishes.

...eyes that are bright.

...hair that is shiny.

...sound teeth and gums.

...good appetite and an enjoyment of food.

...good digestion and elimination.

...steady growth.

...weight that is approximately right for your sex, age, and height. (See table on page 19.)

...a high resistance to infection.

Do you have all these qualities? If you have, you will want to know what you can do to keep them. The chances are, though, that you do not have all of them and will want to know what you can do to acquire them.

First of all, you must always get plenty of rest and take plenty of outdoor exercise. Then, and of great importance, you must eat the right kind and the right amount of

BODY ACTIVITY INFLUENCES ENERGY EXPENDITURE

Sybil Shelton from Monkmeyer

● When you sit quietly playing a game, you spend relatively little energy.

John Rees from Black Star

● In washing and drying dishes, you spend somewhat more energy.

Courtesy Lincoln High School, Philadelphia

● Dancing requires the expenditure of a large amount of energy.

Fritz Henle from Monkmeyer

● Swimming is one of the strenuous sports in which you spend the most energy.

food because food nourishes the body by providing it with the materials that it needs.

Food and Health

Your body is a wonderful mechanism in which many activities are going on all the time. As you walk and as you play, your muscles are working. As the various organs of your body carry on their special processes, they are working too. Also, your body maintains a more or less constant temperature. Both work and heat are forms of energy, and the food you eat supplies the body with this energy. Food contains substances which give this energy by being burned—or, in chemical terms, oxidized—in the body cells. In addition to providing energy, food contributes materials that regulate body processes and, in so doing, keeps the internal condition of your body in a proper and therefore healthy balance.

Then, too, your body is growing and constantly forming new tissues—muscles, bones and teeth, blood and nerves, and connective tissues. Food supplies materials for building new tissues for all these parts of your body. Also, as you grow, and even when you are fully grown, some tissues are worn down each day and must be renewed. The same materials in food that build new tissues also repair these worn tissues.

Because food makes all these activities possible, food performs the following three functions:

1. It furnishes energy.
2. It builds and renews body tissues.
3. It regulates body processes that keep all parts of the body in good working order.

The Nutrients in Our Foods

The substances in foods that carry on these functions are the nutrients. These are, as you learned in Chapter 1, carbohydrates, proteins, fats, minerals, vitamins,

NUTRIENT CLASS—CARBOHYDRATES

Composition: Carbon, hydrogen, and oxygen

Function: To give work energy for body activities
To give heat energy for maintenance of body temperature

Kinds: Starch   Lactose
Sugar   Cellulose

Food sources: Starch—Grains and their products; potatoes
Sugar—Table sugar; sirups; fruits
Lactose—Milk
Cellulose—Whole-grain products; fruits; vegetables, especially stem and leafy kinds

NOTES

1. The elements that make up carbohydrates are the same as those in fats, but in carbohydrates, they are combined in different amounts and in different ways.
2. Cellulose, unlike other carbohydrates, is not digested in the body and therefore does not supply energy. Its value lies in the fact that it gives bulk to food in the digestive system and so aids in digestion and elimination.

and water. Each one of these nutrients is responsible for one or more of the functions. It follows, then, that a food can perform a function only if that food contains the right nutrient for that function. Let us take proteins as an illustration. The chief function of this nutrient is to build and renew body tissues. Milk, meat, and eggs are among the foods rich in protein; therefore, they are valuable as tissue-building foods. Canada's Food Guide, discussed in Chapter 1, is based on the fact that different foods are especially rich in different nutri-

ents and as a result are especially valuable for a given function. When you follow a guide like this in planning your meals, you can be sure that the foods in your diet are giving you all the nutrients.

Although there are six nutrients, there are several kinds of each nutrient except water. For this reason it is convenient to speak of classes of nutrients—carbohydrates, proteins, fats, minerals, vitamins, and water.

The first step in the making of the nutrients in food takes place in green plants.

NUTRIENT CLASS—PROTEINS

Composition: Carbon, hydrogen, oxygen, nitrogen, and sulfur

Functions: To build and renew body tissues
To supply energy

Kinds: Complete proteins[1]
Incomplete proteins
Partially incomplete proteins

Food sources: Complete proteins—Milk; cheese; eggs, meat; fish; poultry; some nuts; soybeans; whole-grain products (small amounts)
Incomplete proteins—Gelatin
Partially incomplete proteins—Grains and their products; dry beans and dry peas

NOTES

1. The elements that make up proteins are first combined to make amino acids, of which there are about twenty-one. The amino acids are then combined, in different numbers and ways, to make the proteins, of which there are many.
2. The protein that is used to give energy for body activities and maintenance of body temperature is that in excess of the amount needed for building and renewing tissues.
3. Complete proteins contain certain ones of the amino acids which are called "essential amino acids." These amino acids are required by the body to build and renew body tissues and must be in the food eaten. Complete proteins can build new tissues as well as tissues worn in daily activities.
4. Incomplete proteins do not contain all the essential amino acids. They cannot build new tissues nor renew worn tissues.
5. Partially incomplete proteins contain all the essential amino acids, but some of them are in too small amounts to build new body tissues. They can renew worn tissues.

[1] "High-quality proteins."

● In planning family meals, use meal patterns (page 4) and Canada's Food Guide (pages 10 to 12) so meals will be healthful and appetizing. Use variety in the menu, the method of preparation, and the manner of serving to prevent monotony.

● Attractive platter arrangements can be achieved by serving the main dish with the other foods of the meal for contrast in color, shape, and texture. Such an arrangement also makes fewer serving dishes necessary. The hot meat loaf at the top of the page on the left is made colorful by being surrounded with stuffed baked potatoes and peas on broiled tomatoes. The cold meat loaf mold at the bottom is filled with beets and onion rings and encircled with deviled eggs and whole green beans. The corned beef above is nested on a platter with the foods which were cooked with it—onions, cabbage, and carrots.

Yeast breads, whether plain or fancy, are the staple foods in the day's meals. With its high food value, and its eye and appetite appeal, bread should be used in variety depending on the occasion and the meal at which it is served.

Robert E. Coates

● Vegetables and fruits generally have more flavor, are more appealing, and, in season, are less expensive when fresh than in any other form. To obtain the best value in fresh vegetables and fruits, buy them in season, learn to recognize good quality, and make your selection in person.

A good lunch should be nutritious, colorful, interesting, and varied in the kinds of foods used and the way in which they are combined. The serving of a bowl of hot soup with a hearty sandwich gives variety of temperature, texture, and flavor to the meal.

● Cheese is a valuable, nutritious, versatile food. Noted chiefly for its complete proteins, cheese is used in a myriad of ways: as an appetizer or a dessert, in hot or cold sandwiches, as an accompaniment to a salad or a piece of pie, as a topping, or in the making of many prepared dishes.

● The many colors and shapes of fruit used in any combination make it an especially appealing food for a salad. Fruit ranks high in healthful qualities; when served with cheese and nuts it is an excellent choice as a main luncheon dish.

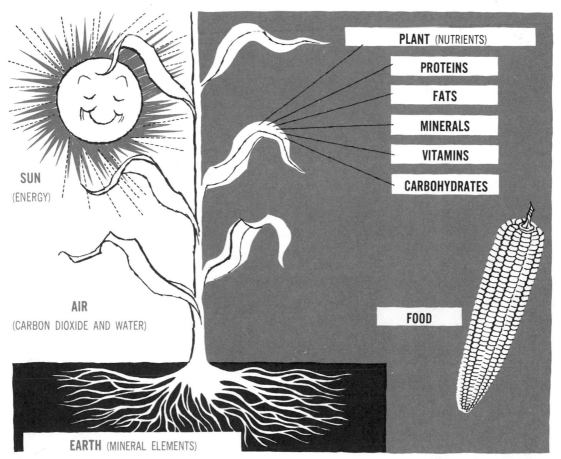

SUN
(ENERGY)

AIR
(CARBON DIOXIDE AND WATER)

EARTH (MINERAL ELEMENTS)

PLANT (NUTRIENTS)

PROTEINS

FATS

MINERALS

VITAMINS

CARBOHYDRATES

FOOD

● Plants make nutrients by a complex process. The plant takes minerals and water from the earth and carbon dioxide and water from the air, and, by means of the sun's energy, transforms these into nutrients.

Green plants take water and minerals from the soil and water and carbon dioxide from the air and, under the influence of the energy of the sun, build them into the nutrients. Then people and animals eat the plants and obtain the nutrients from them. Because people eat some animal foods too, they also get the nutrients which the animals have obtained from the plants.

After a person eats the foods, each nutrient in them must be made ready to perform its function in the body. This preparation process takes place in the digestive tract where the nutrients are changed into simple forms. Then these simple forms are transported to the various body cells where each carries on its special function.

From this discussion you can see that it is really the nutrients on which the selection of foods for a good diet is based. In Chapter 8, "Preparing Meals," you will find that many of the ways in which foods are prepared are also determined by the nutrients in them. For example, eggs are cooked as they are because of the protein in them; that is true also of meats. Vege-

RECOMMENDED NUTRIENT INTAKES FOR CANADIANS[1], REVISED 1968*
These intakes are considered to be adequate for the maintenance of health among the majority of Canadians

	Age (Years)	Weight (Lb.)[2]	Activity Category[3]	Calories	Protein gm.[4]	Calcium gm.	Iron mg.	Vitamin A I.U.[5]	Vitamin D I.U.	Ascorbic Acid mg.	Thiamine mg.	Riboflavin mg.	Niacin mg.
Men	25	158	A	2850	48	0.5	6	3700	—	30	0.9	1.4	9
	45	158	A	2645	48	0.5	6	3700	—	30	0.8	1.3	8
	65	158	A	2460	48	0.5	6	3700	—	30	0.7	1.2	7
Women	25	124	A	2400	39	0.5	10	3700	—	30	0.7	1.2	7
	45	124	A	2230	39	0.5	10	3700	—	30	0.7	1.1	7
	65	124	A	2075	39	0.5	10	3700	—	30	0.6	1.0	6
Pregnancy—during 3rd trimester, add up to				500	9	0.7	3	500	400	10	0.15	.25	1.5
Lactating—add to			1000	500	23	0.7	3	1500	400	20	0.3	0.5	3
Children	0–1	7–20	Usual	360–900	7–13	0.5	5	1000	400	20	0.3	0.5	3
	1–2	20–26	Usual	900–1200	12–16	0.7	5	1000	400	20	0.4	0.6	4
	2–3	31	Usual	1400	17	0.7	5	1000	400	20	0.4	0.7	4
	4–6	40	Usual	1700	20	0.7	5	1000	400	20	0.5	0.9	5
	7–9	57	Usual	2100	24	1.0	5	1500	400	30	0.7	1.1	8
	10–12	77	Usual	2500	30	1.2	12	2000	400	30	0.8	1.3	8
Boys	13–15	108	Usual	3100	40	1.2	12	2700	400	30	0.9	1.6	9
	16–17	136	B[6]	3700	45	1.2	12	3200	400	30	1.1	1.9	11
	18–19	144	B[6]	3800	47	0.9	6	3200	400	30	1.1	1.9	11
Girls	13–15	108	A[7]	2600	39	1.2	12	2700	400	30	0.8	1.3	8
	16–17	120	A[7]	2400	41	1.2	12	3200	400	30	0.7	1.2	7
	18–19	124	A[7]	2450	41	0.9	10	3200	400	30	0.7	1.2	7

[1] The allowance levels are intended to cover individual variations among most normal persons as they live in Canada under most environmental stresses. The recommended nutrients can be attained with a variety of common foods, providing other nutrients for which human requirements have been less well defined.

[2] Weights include indoor clothing without shoes.

[3] Activity has an important bearing on caloric requirements. In Canada so many people fall within the A classification that it may be considered typical and therefore is the one used in this table. B classification is considered typical of more active teen-age boys.

[4] Protein recommendation is based on normal mixed Canadian diet. Vegetarian diets may require a higher protein content.

[5] Vitamin A is based on the mixed Canadian diet supplying both Vitamin A and carotene. As the preformed Vitamin A the suggested intake would be about ⅔ of that indicated.

[6] Expenditure assessed as being 113% of that of a man of same weight and engaged in same degree of activity.

[7] Expenditure assessed as being 104% of that of a woman of the same weight and the same degree of activity.

* From "Dietary Standard for Canada." *Canadian Bulletin on Nutrition*, Vol. 6, No. 1, 1964, revised 1968.

NUTRIENT CLASS—FATS

Composition: Carbon, hydrogen, and oxygen

Functions: To give work energy for body activities
To give heat energy for maintenance of body temperature

Food sources: Butter; margarine; lard; salad oils; vegetable shortenings; milk, cream, and ice cream; cheese; meat; fish; poultry; eggs

NOTE
The elements that make up fats are the same as those in carbohydrates, but in fats, they are combined in different amounts and in different ways.

WEIGHT–HEIGHT–AGE TABLE FOR BOYS AND GIRLS OF SCHOOL AGE*

| | Boys | | | | | Girls | | | |
Age (years)	Average Weight (pounds)	Range in Weight (pounds)	Average Height (inches)	Range in Height (inches)	Age (years)	Average Weight (pounds)	Range in Weight (pounds)	Average Height (inches)	Range in Height (inches)
4	38.2	33.7– 42.7	40.9	39.0–42.8	4	37.3	32.5– 42.1	40.9	39.0–42.8
5	43.2	37.7– 48.7	43.9	41.9–45.9	5	42.0	36.1– 47.9	43.6	41.6–45.6
6	47.6	41.3– 53.9	46.1	44.0–48.2	6	46.4	39.6– 53.2	45.8	43.7–47.9
7	52.5	45.4– 59.6	48.2	46.0–50.4	7	51.2	43.7– 58.7	47.9	45.7–50.1
8	58.2	49.5– 66.9	50.4	48.1–52.7	8	56.9	47.5– 66.3	50.0	47.7–52.3
9	64.4	54.6– 74.2	52.4	50.0–54.8	9	63.0	51.9– 74.1	52.0	49.6–54.4
10	70.7	59.2– 82.2	54.3	51.8–56.8	10	70.3	57.1– 83.5	54.2	51.6–56.8
11	77.6	64.5– 90.7	56.2	53.6–58.8	11	79.0	63.5– 94.5	56.5	53.7–59.3
12	85.6	69.8–101.4	58.2	55.3–61.1	12	89.7	71.9–107.5	59.0	56.1–61.9
13	95.6	77.4–113.8	60.5	57.3–63.7	13	100.3	82.3–118.3	60.6	58.0–63.2
14	107.9	87.8–128.0	63.0	59.6–66.4	14	108.5	91.3–125.7	62.3	59.9–64.7
15	121.7	101.1–142.3	65.6	62.5–68.7	15	115.0	98.8–131.2	63.2	60.9–65.5
16	131.9	113.0–150.8	67.3	64.5–70.1	16	117.6	101.7–133.5	63.5	61.3–65.7
17	138.3	119.5–157.1	68.2	65.6–70.8	17	119.0	103.5–134.5	63.6	61.4–65.8

* From *Basic Body Measurements of School Age Children*, Office of Education, U.S. Department of Health, Education, and Welfare, 1953.

tables are cooked as they are because of their content of minerals and vitamins. There are many other examples of a similar kind which you will meet in your study of food preparation.

Since the nutrients play such an important role in planning and preparing meals, it is clear that a knowledge of the nutrients is a fundamental part of the study of foods. In the charts on pages 15 to 25 you will find information about the composition of the nutrients, what they do for you, and some important food sources of them. In the chapters in Part IV you will find how the nutrients influence cooking procedures. The recipes in Part V apply these procedures.

Quantities of Nutrients in Daily Meals

It is not known exactly how much of each nutrient is needed in the daily meals of any one person. However, as a result of research, quantities which are considered desirable for many of the nutrients have been established. These quantities are suggested for people of different age and sex groups. They are called "Recommended Daily Dietary Allowances" and will be found in the table on the opposite page.

In this table the columns are headed by the names of the various nutrients, except those for carbohydrate and fat. Instead, for these two nutrients, the column is headed "Calories." The reason for this is that carbohydrates and fats have the common function of supplying the body with work and heat energy. The convenient unit for measuring energy is the unit that measures quantities of heat. This unit is the calorie.[1]

[1] A calorie is the amount of heat required to raise the temperature of one gram of water one degree centigrade. This is the small calorie and the one you have studied about in your science class. In the science of nutrition, the calorie used for measuring energy is the large calorie which is 1,000

(Continued on page 20)

NUTRIENT CLASS—MINERALS

Composition: All the elements in foods that are in addition to those in carbohydrates, proteins, and fats

Minerals	Functions	Food Sources
Calcium	To build and renew bones, teeth, and other tissues To regulate the activity of the muscles, heart, and nerves To control the clotting of the blood	Milk and milk products except butter; oranges; dark-green vegetables (see Note 1 below)
Iron	To build and renew hemoglobin (see Note 2 below) To make part of the nucleus of every body cell	Eggs; meat, especially liver and kidney; deep-yellow and dark-green vegetables; potatoes; fruits; whole-grain products; enriched flour, bread, and breakfast cereals
Iodine	To enable the thyroid gland to perform its function of controlling the oxidation of foods in the cells at the proper rate	Fish obtained from the sea; some plant foods grown near the sea-shore; table salt fortified with iodine, so-called "iodized salt"
Phosphorus	To build and renew bones and teeth To influence the oxidation of foods in the body cells	Eggs; cheese; oat cereals and whole-wheat products; dry beans and dry peas; meat; fish; poultry; nuts

NOTES

1. There are a few dark-green vegetables which cannot be counted on for calcium because they contain oxalic acid, which prevents the utilization of their calcium by the body. These vegetables include spinach, beet greens, and Swiss chard.
2. Hemoglobin is the red pigment in the blood which has the special function of carrying oxygen from the lungs to the cells, where it oxidizes the fuel nutrients; hemoglobin also carries carbon dioxide, which is made in the oxidation process, from the cells to the lungs to be expired. Copper is needed for the formation of hemoglobin and aids in the oxidation process. Foods that make a good diet can be relied upon to furnish adequate amounts of copper.

The number of calories that are recommended for your daily meals depends on your age and sex. You can determine the number of calories by referring to the table on page 18, but your activity will affect this recommended calorie allowance. If you are very active, you spend extra energy and will need more calories than the number given in the table. Your weight is somewhat of an indication of whether or not you are getting the right number of calories. If you maintain a weight that is near that

times greater than the small calorie. It is the measure of the amount of heat that will raise the temperature of 1,000 grams of water one degree centigrade or four pounds of water one degree Fahrenheit. You will sometimes see the large calorie written with a capital C. This practice, however, is not generally followed in the study of nutrition.

DIFFERENCES IN DAILY CALORIE REQUIREMENTS BY AGE AND SEX

Boy or girl, 2 to 3 years of age:
1400 calories

Boy or girl, 4 to 12 years of age:
4 to 6: 1700 calories
7 to 9: 2100 calories
10 to 12: 2500 calories

Girl, 13 to 19 years of age:
13 to 15: 2600 calories
16 to 17: 2400 calories
18 to 19: 2450 calories

Boy, 13 to 19 years of age:
13 to 15: 3100 calories
16 to 17: 3700 calories
18 to 19: 3800 calories

Adult woman, 25 years of age and over:
25 to 44: 2400 calories
45 to 64: 2230 calories
65 plus: 2075 calories

Adult man, 25 years of age and over:
25 to 44: 2850 calories
45 to 64: 2645 calories
65 plus: 2460 calories

which is average for a person of your age, sex, and height, you may be sure your calorie intake is about right for you. If your weight is much above the average, your food is giving more calories than you need and, as a result, fat is deposited in your tissues. On the other hand, if your weight is below the average, you need more calories because your body is using some of its own tissues to supply the energy you are spending. The table on page 19 gives average weights for boys and girls of different age and height.

Since the figures in this table are for average weights, you can tell only approximately what you should weigh. Size of body frame and muscle development are factors which make you vary from the average. Thus you may weigh more or less than the tables state, depending on whether your frame is large or small and on your muscular development. A difference in weight that is within 10 percent either above or below the average is not considered significant. Your calorie intake will still be right for you.

If your weight is 10 percent above or below the average, it is time for you to consider making adjustments in your daily diet. You can do this by counting the number of calories in the food you eat each day. The calorie values of many foods have been determined, and they are listed in the table "Nutritive Values of the Edible Part of Foods" given on pages 532 to 556. If you keep a record of the kinds and the amounts of the foods you eat every day, you can easily calculate the calorie value of your daily meals. Then you can follow the suggestions given in the chart at the right if your weight is not as near the average as you would like.

TO CORRECT YOUR WEIGHT

OVERWEIGHT

1. Decrease your calorie intake.

2. Eat only the amount of food at each meal that satisfies you.

3. Eat preferably only at mealtime, or if you take a snack, eat low-calorie foods.

4. Eat liberally of milk (skim milk is good), eggs, lean meat, fish, poultry, fruits, and vegetables.

5. Limit foods that are largely carbohydrate, and eat sparingly of fat-rich foods.[1]

6. Increase your daily exercise.

UNDERWEIGHT

1. Increase your calorie intake.

2. Eat as liberally at each meal as you can with comfort.

3. Make a between-meal snack a habit. Have it consist of foods such as milk, cocoa, milk shakes, or malted milk, and not of soft drinks. A bedtime snack is good.

4. Stress calorie-rich foods, but be sure they carry other nutrients as well—for example, macaroni and cheese, cereal with cream, butter or margarine on bread, and ice cream.

[1] Specially prepared low-calorie foods are available in food markets for those who are dieting. Preserves, canned fruits, and prepared desserts sweetened with a noncaloric sweetener, as well as fruits canned without sugar and low-calorie salad dressings, are only a few of the many kinds to be found. All such special foods should be used with understanding, since much misinformation is given out concerning the use of so-called "reducing foods." It is always best to follow Canada's Food Guide (pages 10 to 12) as a measure of your food requirements.

NUTRIENT CLASS—VITAMINS

Composition: Carbon, hydrogen, oxygen, nitrogen, and sulfur

Vitamins	Functions	Food Sources
Thiamine (vitamin B₁)	To maintain a healthy condition of the nerves To foster a good appetite To influence the oxidation of carbohydrates in the body cells	Fruits and vegetables; whole-grain products and enriched grain products; meats, especially pork, liver, and kidney; dry beans and dry peas
Riboflavin (vitamin B₂)	To keep skin, mouth, and eyes in a healthy condition To maintain a state of resistance to infection To prolong the span of active adult life	Milk; cheese; eggs; meat, especially liver and kidney; dry beans and dry peas; whole-grain and enriched grain products; fruits and vegetables, especially the dark-green vegetables
Niacin (nicotinic acid)	To influence oxidation of carbohydrates in the body cells To prevent pellagra, working along with other ingredients (see Note 1 on page 24)	Milk; cheese; meat; fish; poultry; eggs; peanuts; dark-green vegetables; whole-grain products and enriched grain products
Vitamin C (ascorbic acid)	To act like cement between body cells and so help them to work together to carry on their special functions To maintain a sound condition of teeth and gums To increase resistance to infections	Citrus fruits—especially oranges and grapefruit—cantaloup and strawberries; tomatoes, raw onions, cabbage, and green and sweet red peppers; dark-green vegetables; other vegetables and fruits
Vitamin A (see Note 2 on page 24)	To prolong the span of active adult life To prevent night blindness (see Note 3 on page 24) To ensure a healthy condition of the hair and skin To maintain a state of resistance to infection of eyes, mouth, and the respiratory and digestive tracts	Dark-green and deep-yellow vegetables; apricots, cantaloup; milk; cheese; eggs; meat organs, especially liver and kidney; fortified margarine; butter; fish-liver oils

(Continued)

Vitamins	Functions	Food Sources
Vitamin D (see Note 4 below)	To enable the growing body to use the minerals calcium and phosphorus in a normal way in building sound bones and teeth (see Note 5 below)	Eggs; vitamin D milk (see page 226); fish-liver oils
Other vitamins	These have various and important functions in maintaining health. It is believed that when liberal quantities of foods containing the vitamins described above are in the diet, these other vitamins will be supplied as well.	

NOTES

1. Pellagra is a disease common among people living on a diet poor in quality, such as one made up largely of corn and very little of protein-rich foods from animal sources.
2. Vitamin A exists in two forms: (1) in plants as carotene, often called "provitamin A," which is changed in the animal body to vitamin A; and (2) in animals as vitamin A, into which the carotene of the food has been changed. Some carotene also is in animal foods.
3. When eyes do not adjust normally to lower levels of light, a person is said to have "night blindness."
4. There is a substance in the skin that the sun's rays change into vitamin D, and therefore this vitamin is sometimes called the "sunshine vitamin."
5. When the body does not use calcium and phosphorus in a normal way, a disease known as "rickets" occurs.

Only the primary function of protein (that of building and renewing body tissues) is considered in determining the protein allowance. The allowance is based on the assumption that energy needs will be satisfied by carbohydrate and fat. The table on page 18 shows that the protein allowance for girls between fourteen and eighteen years of age is less than the protein allowance for boys of this age. This is because boys, as a rule, reach larger size than girls. Note that the protein allowance for girls of fourteen years and older equals that for women, while the allowance for boys is less than the allowance for men. Protein needs are high during pregnancy and lactation.

The suggested allowances of certain nutrients other than protein reflect the value of adequate supplies of them in the diets of young people for general health purposes and for good bone, tooth, and blood development. Larger amounts of calcium are recommended for both boys and girls in the ten-to-eighteen year-old groups than for adults. The iron allowance for boys in the twelve-to-eighteen year-old groups exceeds that for men; and for girls of this

NUTRIENT CLASS—WATER

Composition: Hydrogen and oxygen

Functions: To regulate body processes
To aid in regulating body temperature
To carry nutrients to body cells and waste products away from them

Food sources: Drinking water; beverages; all foods except those made up of a single nutrient, as sugar and some fats

NOTES

1. The approximate amount of water needed in one day is 10 glasses.
2. The work done by the body and the weather are influencing factors in the amount of water necessary to perform its functions.

age it equals the allowance for women. The amounts of vitamin C and riboflavin recommended for young people are less than for adults, while those for thiamin and niacin are greater. The allowance for vitamin A for both groups is similar. Vitamin D is recommended to the age of twenty-two. It is necessary for efficient use of calcium and phosphorus in building strong bones and teeth.

Meals and Health

When your meals contain the right amounts of nutritious foods, you will have good nutrition and possess those characteristics that are signs of good health. On the other hand, if your diet is not a good one, you will show some signs of poor health. Among these may be slow growth, poor teeth, poor complexion, a susceptibility to infections, and a constant feeling of fatigue.

The usual Canadian custom is to have three meals regularly every day. In some families, especially those with young people, snacks are quite customary. When

there are snacks, they must be considered as a part of the daily diet just as other meals are.

The Regular Meals of the Day

Although the custom is to have three regular meals, the time of day when they are eaten, the intervals between them, and their heartiness are different among families. Breakfast is normally the first of the three meals. Whether the noon meal is a lunch followed by a heartier meal at night or the reverse depends on which plan for these two meals fits the family situation.

Breakfast. Breakfast is the most important meal of the day. Between breakfast and the evening meal of the day before there is a longer interval of time than between any of the other meals. In the morning the stomach is empty and the body is in need of nutrients for the activities of the morning. Breakfasts may be light or hearty, but no matter what the type, there are three standards a breakfast must meet if it is nutritionally adequate:

1. It must supply from one-fourth to one-third of a person's daily calorie needs.

25

NUTRITIOUS MEALS FOR A DAY

● Breakfast

Courtesy National Dairy Council

● Lunch

Courtesy National Dairy Council

●Dinner

Courtesy National Dairy Council

REASONS FOR IMPORTANCE OF AN ADEQUATE BREAKFAST

1. If one-fourth to one-third of your calorie requirement is taken care of at breakfast, it will be easier for you to get the remainder of your calorie requirement in the other two meals.

2. The protein allowance of teen-agers is large. Your body seems to use protein most efficiently in building tissues if the total amount of protein is divided more or less evenly over three meals.

3. The blood contains sugar, and a breakfast adequate in calories and protein keeps sugar at the proper level. With such a level of sugar in your blood, you will have a better chance of being mentally alert and of doing more work during the morning. There is also less danger of your becoming tired before lunchtime.

4. You will have a greater resistance to colds and other infections.

5. You are more certain of having a generally sound nutritional condition. Unfortunately, there are many people, including teen-agers, who omit breakfast altogether or eat an inadequate one. Why is this? Some people use as an excuse that they do not have the time for breakfast. This is not really an excuse because time can be made by getting up a few minutes earlier. Some people say they are not hungry in the morning and for this reason skip breakfast. Not being hungry is a condition which probably has been acquired by the habit of omitting breakfast. The stomach gets used to being without food, and it does not report the sensation of hunger. But, just as easily, the habit of being hungry in the morning can be acquired. If you eat breakfast every morning, your stomach will be comfortable only if food is in it. Without food you will feel hunger pangs.

2. It should include about one-fourth to one-third of the recommended protein allowance.

3. It should make a start toward filling the mineral and vitamin quotas of the day.

If you make it a practice to eat breakfasts that follow the breakfast patterns which are listed in Chapter 1 on page 4, you may be sure that your breakfasts will meet these standards. For some of the benefits of eating a good breakfast, see the chart on the opposite page.

Lunch. The noonday meal is lunch, and the name customarily implies a light meal. However, when everyone is home at noon, the family may prefer to have their hearty meal then. In this case, the noonday meal is generally called dinner. There is really no definite or even general rule for the names applied to meals. Family custom sets the rule in each home.

But no matter what it may be called, a good meal at noon is important. Some people skip this meal, which is a very bad practice. The body needs more food by noontime, and the feeling of hunger then is normal. The time when hunger strikes depends on the time when breakfast is eaten, on the heartiness of that meal, and on the work or other activity done in the morning.

Whatever the kind of meal your family likes at noon, it must make its contribution to the daily allowances of nutrients for all members. Canada's Food Guide and the meal patterns for lunch and dinner that are given in Chapter 1 will help you in making a good choice of foods.

Dinner or supper. The evening meal is the last regular meal of the day and provides the last opportunity to complete the food needs. Usually the main dish is one of

H. Armstrong Roberts

● Remember that food eaten for snacks is also counted in the day's food intake.

meat, poultry, fish, cheese, or eggs. Vegetables and some kind of bread accompany the main dish, and a dessert ends the meal. An appetizer, such as soup, a fruit cup, or a vegetable or fruit juice, and a salad are included as desired. With these usual kinds of foods at dinner, it is not hard to supplement, where necessary, the food groups already represented in breakfast and lunch. The patterns for dinner that you will find on page 4 give suggestions for ways in which these several kinds of foods may be grouped together in the dinner meal.

Sometimes there are days when foods from all the food groups have been included in breakfast and lunch and in the main course of the dinner. This is the time, then, for a special treat—maybe a generously frosted cake, a rich pudding, or pie à la mode. You do eat for good nutrition but you also eat for enjoyment.

Between-meal snacks. Active, growing young people spend a lot of energy and may require more food than they can eat comfortably at the regular meals. To give this extra energy, between-meal food may

27

● A carefully planned and packed carried lunch can be as nutritious as a lunch at home.

be eaten. If you are very active—a basket-ball or tennis player, for example—an afterschool snack of nutritious food, or one at bedtime, can supply the extra energy. However, you should be careful not to make eating between meals a habit or let it interfere with your regular meals. It is best to have a period of activity after an afternoon snack so that you will have an appetite for dinner. When you and your friends get together after school, eating is generally a part of your activity. It is all right to have a snack, provided you recognize the fact that it is part of the food intake for the day.

Special Meals

In almost every family, situations some-times arise that call for changes in the regu-lar mealtime program. In such situations, extra meals or meals of a different kind than usual seem desirable or even neces-sary. The more knowledge you have about nutrition in relation to all kinds of meals, the better able you will be to meet these special problems.

Lunch in the school cafeteria. Lunches are eaten very often in the school cafeteria or in a nearby restaurant. Here you make your own selection of foods and so have an opportunity to apply your knowledge of food values. You should make these noon-time meals supply their quotas of essential foods.

When you "eat out," you should con-sider the sanitary aspects of the place. You can be sure of the school cafeteria in this respect. Often there are small lunchrooms near schools that do not measure up to very high standards of cleanliness. As a usual practice, it is better to carry a lunch or to select one in the school cafeteria where you can be sure of getting good food in clean and pleasant surroundings.

The carried lunch. The same care should be observed in planning and preparing a carried lunch as is given to the noon meal when eaten at home. Since this lunch is the regular noonday meal, foods representing several of the food groups should be included.

It is easy to let the carried lunch become monotonous. For example, sandwiches, which are easy to make and to pack, lose their appeal when used too often as the main part of the lunch. Instead, an attractive salad, packed in a covered carton, might be the main part of the lunch. Celery, wrapped in moisture-resistant paper, instead of lettuce, which is apt to wilt, will add a crisp touch to the salad. Differences,

too, in color, flavor, and texture may be obtained with raw fruit, pickles and olives, carrot strips, sweet-pepper strips, or some other raw vegetable. A vacuum bottle of hot soup or cocoa or of cold milk or other cold drinks is always a good accompaniment to a carried lunch. And so, with a little thought, the carried lunch can be a meal to be looked forward to rather than something to be eaten only to satisfy hunger. It can be just as nutritious as a lunch eaten at home.

Packing the carried lunch does not need to be a problem when the necessary equipment for packing it is kept ready at hand. If possible, a special place in one of the kitchen cabinets can be devoted to a supply of suitable containers, wrapping papers, paper napkins, paper plates, and forks and spoons.

Meals for the sick. Meals are sometimes a problem when a member of the family is sick or recovering from an illness. Certain kinds of illness require special diets that are prescribed by the doctor in charge, and these may continue through convalescence. Unless this is the case, meals for the person who is either sick or convalescent are usually similar to those that are normally eaten—that is, meals that meet the daily food allowances for the age and sex of the person. It is important to have plenty of milk in the meals because of its excellent value in protein and calcium. Also, foods rich in vitamins and minerals should be well represented.

Because an ill or convalescent person is more or less inactive, the amounts of food served should be adjusted to the appetite. It is advisable also to prepare foods simply and to avoid rich cakes, pastries, and many highly seasoned foods. Care should be

● The doctor decides on the formula for the baby, but the baby-sitter or mother should learn how to hold the baby when feeding him the formula.

H. Armstrong Roberts

taken to make the patient's meals appetizing and to have the tray daintily set with the nicest appointments the household affords. Sometimes a flower from the garden, a pretty picture, or a small favor on the tray brings cheer to the shut-in. In Chapter 10, "Preparing and Serving Lunch or Supper," pages 171 and 172, there are some suggestions for serving a tray meal.

Meals during pregnancy. The meals for a woman during pregnancy must be planned on the basis of providing an adequate diet for the prospective mother and, in addition, the needed nourishment for the new life so that there will be no sacrifice of the mother's health.

If you examine the table "Recommended Nutrient Intakes for Canadians," page 18, you will find that, during pregnancy and lactation, larger allowances are suggested for calories and for all of the nutrients listed in the table except iron. An allowance for vitamin D is given as well. In order to obtain these larger quantities of nutrients, it may be necessary to increase either the size of the individual servings or the number of servings of some foods. If it is difficult to take all the milk at regular meals, milk may be taken between meals. Meals such as these provide for the usual and satisfactory diet for a pregnant woman. The physician in charge will advise a diet in any unusual situation.

Infant feeding. During the first year of a baby's life he makes very rapid growth. Feeding the baby properly is so important to getting him started on a healthy life that it is usually directed either by a private physician or through a baby clinic. At first, milk is the chief food in the baby's diet, since it provides the right amount of proteins and minerals needed for the growing body. Nature's way—that is, by breast feeding—is simple and, unless there are reasons to prevent it, will most probably be the way recommended by the doctor. If the mother nurses the baby, her meals must supply enough food for her own needs, for those of the growing child, and for the work of producing milk. The diet pattern described above for the latter months of pregnancy may be followed, but the foods should be eaten in even larger amounts. It is recommended also that four or more cups of milk be included in the daily diet.

When breast feeding is not possible, the doctor will plan a feeding formula for the baby. The basic ingredient will be milk. Dried milk, evaporated milk, or pasteurized bottled milk may be used. Homogenized milk, fortified with vitamin D, is considered excellent because vitamin D is essential for the infant's use of calcium and phosphorus in building normal bones and teeth. Pasteurized and homogenized milks must be brought to boiling before they are used for making the formula. Evaporated milk need not be boiled, but the water used to dilute it should be boiled. Milk and water are boiled as a sanitary precaution. The baby's formula need not be warmed before feeding, however, since recent research indicates that infants accept cold milk and thrive as well on it as on warm milk.

When the baby is about two weeks old, he will need more vitamin D and vitamin C than he can get from milk. For vitamin D, cod-liver oil or another source of the vitamin may be recommended by the doctor. He will also prescribe the amount to use as well as the manner in which vitamin D is given to the baby. Orange juice is used to supply the baby's vitamin C needs.

30

Courtesy Gerber Products Company

● Soon the baby begins to eat solid foods in addition to milk and fruit juices—with the father's or mother's help of course.

When orange juice is given, either strained fresh juice or canned or frozen is suitable. Frozen juice is diluted in the regular manner. Some infants are allergic to orange juice, so here too the doctor will prescribe the form of vitamin C to use. Instead of orange juice, either grapefruit juice or strained tomato juice may be used. However, larger amounts of tomato juice would be necessary, for tomatoes are less rich in vitamin C than is orange juice.

Soon the baby will need other foods in addition to milk and fruit juices. As he becomes increasingly active, he spends more energy. For this reason he requires more calories than can be supplied by milk. Also, his digestive tract is getting ready to take care of solid foods. These foods will include, at first, finely divided cooked cereals and cooked egg yolk; then a little later, strained green and yellow vegetables, mild-flavored fruits, whole egg, and meat, fish, and poultry. The doctor will decide in each individual case when such foods should be started and which kinds they should be. When new foods are introduced, the amounts should be small, say a teaspoonful or less, and then gradually increased as the infant gets used to them. The foods should be thin in consistency and smooth—strained vegetables and fruits at first, and either chopped or mashed later. If a new food is refused, it may be made acceptable by mixing it with another familiar food that the child already likes.

Meals for young children. After the first year, children are more independent, and habits as well as diet are an important aspect of a mealtime program. The child eats increasingly larger amounts of food to take care of a growing body and greater activity. Milk is still important, with at least two or three cupfuls needed each day. By the time the child is nine years old, more than three cupfuls of milk are recommended. Milk can be used in foods like cream soups and creamed dishes and in milk desserts such as custards and puddings. A citrus fruit or another source of vitamin C is necessary in the diet. Vegetables, especially the dark-green and deep-yellow ones, continue to be important. One egg and a serving of lean meat, fish, or poultry should be provided each day. The vegetables and meats should be chopped to make them more easily digested until such time as the child has learned how to chew. Since all parts of the child's body are growing, complete proteins, minerals (especially calcium, phosphorus, and iron), and the vitamins must all be in his diet in liberal amounts. If care is taken that the foods mentioned here are included every day as basic to the rest of his diet,

Courtesy Gerber Products Company

● Children like to feed themselves, but they have to learn how to eat and how to drink.

which makes up his needed calories, the child will have an excellent chance of developing a healthy body. If extra meals are necessary or advisable to meet the calorie requirement, they should be regularly scheduled and should consist of nutritious foods, such as more milk, a fruit juice, or some cooked fruit and a cookie. Concentrated sweets, eaten as between-meal snacks, contribute little other than calories and are apt to dull the appetite for the next regular meal.

The acceptance of practically all foods on the part of any individual is a safeguard against illness. It is also a social asset when a person is old enough to go about among people for meals in restaurants or as a guest in someone's home. Here courtesy demands that a guest eat the foods offered him. Therefore, part of mealtime training in childhood is to provide an opportunity for the child to become acquainted with many foods and to learn to like them. It is best to introduce a new food more or less casually together with other familiar foods and to give it in a small portion. Also, the grown-up members of the family should set a good example by eating the food with enjoyment.

When there are young children in the home, time in meal planning and preparation can be saved by the use of foods that are suitable for children as well as adults. Here are some suggestions:

1. Make foods simple. For example, instead of making a mixed-vegetable salad, serve the vegetables separately, as a strip of carrot, celery, or a floweret of cauliflower.
2. Have desserts that use milk, eggs, and fruits, such as rennet pudding, custard, tapioca cream, fruit tapioca, stewed prunes or apricots, applesauce, or baked apples. These desserts are good for everyone, even better probably than rich puddings and pies.
3. Make the beverage milk, cocoa, or a milk shake. Serve coffee or tea if the adults wish it.
4. Avoid frying as a means for cooking meats, fish, and poultry. Instead, bake, pan-broil, or broil them.

Meals for older people. When there are older people in the family, just as when there are very young members, meal plans will need some adjustment. The problem is not a difficult one, provided the older persons do not have some physical condition that requires a diet prescribed by a physician.

For the normal person in later years, a good diet can be planned according to Canada's Food Guide. However, it should be remembered that activity among older people is usually less than in their younger years. As a result, their energy expenditure is less and the calorie value of their diet should be relatively lower. When meals are planned on this low-calorie basis, special care is necessary to include foods rich in other nutrients, as it is believed that the protein and mineral needs, and those of most of the vitamins, should not be reduced in advancing years. Such nutritious foods can be used in adequate quantities if such calorie-rich foods as gravies and sauces, those garnished with whipped cream or mixed with salad dressings, and rich pastry or cake desserts are used sparingly. Serving smaller amounts of breads and cereals is also helpful.

If the older people are overweight, restriction in foods high in calorie value will need to be even greater. On the other hand, if it is a question of being underweight, such foods may be included, or if preferred, between-meal snacks used instead. With older people it is often necessary to serve foods that can be digested easily, and for this reason foods containing much fat may cause trouble. Then milk or fruit juice with a cookie make better snacks than do calorie-rich foods. A cup of warm milk at bedtime adds calories and also is thought to be helpful to sleep.

Often older members of the family feel that they have lost their usefulness in the family group. Such an idea is likely to be emphasized unless adjustments in the food prepared are made unobtrusively. Diets good for older people in normal health are diets good for other people. Therefore, the same meals can be prepared for all the family, of course excluding the baby.

● Elderly people who dislike milk should eat ice cream and other dairy foods.

3

Planning Meals for Variety and Attractiveness

■ MEALS are most satisfying and enjoyable when they include a variety of foods from meal to meal and from day to day and when they are attractive in appearance. Meals are attractive when they are pleasing to look at and when they are enjoyed as they are eaten.

There are two good reasons why variety in family meals is important: (1) It is only by the use of many different foods that good nutrition can be secured. (2) Variety in meals avoids monotony, and an adventurous spirit in eating different foods leads to a keener interest in meals.

There are also two good reasons why meals should be attractive: (1) Food that looks and tastes good stimulates the appetite. (2) Food that looks good is eaten with relish.

How Meals Can Be Varied

Meals that are planned by the use of a food group guide and meal patterns, as explained in Chapter 1, may be fundamentally alike; yet it is possible to avoid monotony by including different foods in your menus, by using different methods of preparing them, and by serving them in different ways. Of course there is some merit in repeating certain menus occasionally when they include foods that are particularly popular with the family. Then, too, a familiar meal can be prepared quickly if, perhaps, time is short, since a work schedule will already have been established for its preparation. (See Chapter 4, "Managing Meals to Save Time and Effort.") Furthermore, when guests are expected, it is reassuring to prepare a familiar meal. Preparation can be carried on with the knowledge that each dish will be a success and will be ready on time.

Vary the Patterns for Menus

One good way in which you may be sure of obtaining variety in meals is to vary the meal patterns you follow when making menus. To illustrate: If you are planning dinner menus for the family for a week, you will succeed in making this meal more interesting if you use several different patterns, or at least two of them, during the seven days. If you use Pattern II during the week, then use either Patterns III or IV on Sunday, usually the most leisurely day of the week.

Vary the Kinds of Foods in the Menus

As you plan menus for any meal, instead of using different patterns on different days, you can vary the choice of foods within the same pattern. In many families breakfast, of necessity, may follow a given pattern. In such an event, if we assume that breakfast is planned according to Pattern III, a selection of different kinds of foods in each course on different days will bring variety into the meal. Breakfast Pattern III consists of fruit, cereal with milk, a main dish, bread, and a beverage. Among the many possibilities for varying the foods in each course, as well as for different ways of preparing them, are those given in the chart on page 37.

Vary the Methods of Preparation

Variety may also be brought into meals when methods of preparing the same food are changed. If foods such as apples are in season, and so are abundant and reasonable in price, it is a good idea to serve them frequently. Since there are so many ways to prepare apples, their use two times a day, or even more, need not be monotonous. Apples are good when "eaten out of hand," and applesauce and apple salads

● Cookbooks, magazines, newspapers, radio, and television are usually good sources for ideas on preparing, serving, and varying meals. With a little imagination and good judgment, you can apply these ideas to your own family's requirements to prevent meals from becoming monotonous.

Courtesy United Fruit Company

● The use of different kinds of bread is one way to give variety to meals from day to day.

Courtesy Processed Apples Institute, Inc.

● Using apples to top a pudding is a change from the more familiar ways of preparing them.

Courtesy Stokely-Van Camp, Inc.

● A fruit sauce poured over dessert pancakes is a different way of serving a familiar food.

are popular. Apples are good, too, when baked, stewed, or fried. They may be used in fruit cups as an appetizer at the beginning of lunch or dinner, or they may be used as the dessert at the end of either meal. They may also be served as apple dumplings or apple brown Betty; in pies, tarts, or cobblers; or in apple tapioca pudding.

Ground beef—always a family favorite—is often made into patties that are pan-fried, broiled, or baked. But there are other savory ways to prepare them that should not be neglected. You can plan to make the ground meat into a meat loaf—one large one or enough individual loaves for each member of the family. You can cream ground meat, serving it over toast, or you can use it in many dishes with noodles, rice, spaghetti, or beans.

From such examples you can see that it is not difficult to get variety into your menus when you change from time to time the method of preparing the same food. A spirit of adventure and a willingness to try new and unfamiliar recipes are valuable assets.

Vary the Ways of Serving Foods

There is yet another way to make meals seem different. This way is to serve a food in a different manner at different meals. You can serve a salad on individual plates one time, and at another time from a large salad bowl at the table. You can serve a creamed food over toast, in toast cups, or over cooked rice or noodles. You can bring an electric frying pan to the table and from it serve such a dish as a stew. You can plan a dinner which may be served either on in-

Courtesy Cereal Institute, Inc.

● A salmon loaf topped with a sauce and surrounded by broccoli and sliced tomatoes gives the meal a pleasing color contrast.

WAYS TO GET VARIETY IN BREAKFAST MENUS

FRUIT

Oranges or grapefruit,[1] halved, sectioned, sliced, or as juice
Vitaminized apple juice[1]
Tomato juice[1]
Cantaloupe,[1] halved or in balls or slices
Strawberries[1]

Apples, fresh, baked, or as sauce
Apricots, fresh, canned, or stewed dried
Prunes, fresh, canned, or stewed dried
Bananas, sliced, or split and broiled
Peaches, fresh, canned, or frozen
Pears, fresh or canned

CEREAL WITH MILK

Oatmeal and corn meal, hot
Oat cereal, a ready-to-eat kind
Wheat cereal, hot or a ready-to-eat kind
Rice cereal, a ready-to-eat kind
Corn cereal, a ready-to-eat kind

MAIN DISH

Eggs, soft- or hard-cooked, baked, poached, fried, scrambled, or omelet
Bacon, pan-broiled or broiled

[1] These fruits are all high in vitamin C.

Sausage, pan-broiled or broiled
Ham, pan-broiled or broiled
Creamed dried beef
Creamed codfish
Codfish cakes

BREAD

Bread, white, whole wheat, or rye, plain or as toast
Rolls, plain or sweet, white or whole wheat
Coffeecake
Crumb cake
Biscuits
Muffins, plain, whole wheat, corn meal, blueberry, or date
Doughnuts
Waffles
Pancakes
English muffins, toasted

BEVERAGE

Milk
Cocoa or chocolate
Coffee
Tea

dividual plates from the kitchen or from a platter and serving dishes at the table. These are only a few suggestions for various ways of serving foods. You will undoubtedly find many more in cookbooks, newspapers, and magazines and as you prepare meals.

How Meals Can Be Made Attractive

"Eye appeal" in meals is necessary if they are to be eaten with enjoyment. Attractive meals appeal to the aesthetic sense of the family and contribute to a feeling of satisfaction and well-being. Such meals also stimulate the appetite, as the aroma and sight of tempting food help to start the flow of digestive fluids and increase a feeling of hunger. Perhaps you can recall a time when you were not especially hungry but as you smelled food cooking and then saw how tempting it looked on the table you quickly developed an appetite and were able to eat heartily. Or you may recall an experience that is just the reverse when you lost your appetite because the food looked unattractive and so did not appeal to you.

Color Combinations of Foods

One secret of making meals attractive is to select foods that look well together as they will be seen on the table. With so many pleasingly colored foods it should not be difficult for you to choose those that will make attractive color combinations. For example, vegetable plates are colorful, as are salads, either fruit or vegetable. Many desserts present opportunities to select harmonious color combinations and to demonstrate your artistic ability. Lack of color, too much repetition of the same color, or colors that clash with one another or with

the dishes on which they are served detract from a meal's appearance. For example, a main course of white meat of chicken, mashed white potatoes, and creamed cauliflower—although all good to taste—is colorless. On the other hand, mashed sweetpotatoes and green peas served with the chicken make good color contrasts and are appetite-provoking. Repetition of a color served in the same course, such as the green of kale or spinach with either snap beans or lima beans, is not so pleasing as when there is a contrast. A yellow vegetable, such as yellow squash, served with the spinach would make a more interesting combination. As another example, baked stuffed tomatoes served with red cabbage slaw gives an inharmonious color note which can be avoided if a green or a yellow vegetable accompanied either the tomatoes or the red cabbage.

One good way to get color into meals is by the use of a garnish. An edible garnish, such as the slice of lemon so frequently served with fish, is best. The color and shape of the lemon add interest, and the juice gives extra flavor and zest to the fish. Garnishes should seem to be natural and most certainly should be simple—never overdone. A touch of green, such as parsley or a small piece of water cress, curly lettuce, or even a sprig of small celery leaves, is good for color contrast and flavor when used to top a piece of meat or chicken or some vegetable. Creamed and mashed potatoes are improved when they are garnished with a little finely chopped parsley, chives, green onions, or green pepper; when chopped sautéed mushrooms are added; when a small amount of deviled ham is mixed with them; or even when the top of the potatoes is sprinkled with so

● Parsley and stuffed olives as a garnish to broiled swordfish add touches of color.

● Even a very simple garnish adds to the attractiveness of a dessert.

simple a garnish as paprika. However, there are some foods, such as vegetables surrounding meat on a platter or a glass of orange juice, that are so attractive by themselves that no garnish is needed.

Leftover vegetables add to the appearance of a casserole dish. A few asparagus spears arranged on the top of a casserole, pieces of pimento, or a few green peas or

● Meals are made more attractive by serving foods together that are different in shape.

beans can be depended on to give an unexpected and interesting color note to a casserole. Some bright quivering jelly, such as cranberry, mint, or currant, on a meat platter; a cheese sauce on cauliflower; tomato sauce on spaghetti; a piece of prune or date in the center of a muffin; a cherry on top of a dish of tapioca pudding; chopped leftover ham or crisp bacon in scrambled eggs or omelet are all simple and easy ways to add color and contrast to foods.

Shapes of Foods

When foods in any one course are varied in shape, the meal is more inviting than when there is a similarity in shape. Repetition of the same shape is monotonous. This would be the effect if round beef patties were accompanied on a plate with pan-browned sliced potatoes and round slices of either beets or carrots. In contrast, a pleasing effect would result if mashed or creamed potatoes and lengthwise slices of the beets or carrots were served with the

● To select just the right flavoring and seasoning is an art. Suitably chosen herbs and spices help to enhance the flavor of food. They may also be used to make food more attractive. The adding of chopped mint to carrots or chopped parsley to creamed potatoes and the sprinkling of paprika on cauliflower are a few examples.

meat patties. Another example of a poor effect in shape would be to plan to have two of the vegetables in a meal prepared by mashing—possibly mashed sweetpotatoes and mashed winter squash. Here there would be monotony in color as well as in the form of preparation.

Flavor and Texture of Foods

The flavor and texture of foods are so closely associated that it is sometimes difficult to know whether it is the flavor or the texture of a food that causes it to be liked or disliked. Flavor is a complex blend of taste and aroma. There are four tastes which can be recognized by the taste buds of the tongue. These four tastes are sweet, salt, sour, and bitter. A few foods have only one of these tastes: sugar is sweet, salt is salt, vinegar is sour, and water cress and spices are bitter. A combination of some or all of these tastes is found in most foods.

To complicate the flavor situation fur-
ther is the fact that foods have many odors which are noted as food is eaten and which are responsible for part of the quality called flavor. The flavor of raspberries, onions, or vanilla, for example, comes mostly from aroma rather than from taste.

Some foods contain only small amounts of the materials that stimulate the taste buds or the sense of smell. Such foods are called "bland" foods. Rice, potatoes, and flour are examples of bland foods. Other foods have unmistakable characteristic flavors which are easily recognized, such as oranges, cherries, peaches, pork, lamb, and fish.

In food preparation it is often desirable to add to, increase, or change the flavor of foods to make them more interesting and more appealing. To do this, flavoring or seasoning ingredients or both are used. The terms "flavoring" and "seasoning" are often used interchangeably, but usually seasoning refers to such ingredients as salt, pepper, spices, and herbs that give piquancy to the food, while flavoring refers to extracts that give flavor.

Some of the desirable qualities that make up food textures are crispness, softness, tenderness, and hardness. When food is very soft, as is a sauce, its texture is called "consistency," and smoothness is desirable. Crispness, softness, tenderness, and hardness are combined in many foods, while other foods have only one kind of texture. For instance, melba toast and many varieties of crackers are both crisp and hard, cakes are soft and tender, but celery and radishes are only crisp. Good-quality meat is tender when properly cooked. Baked custard is soft, but a custard pie is soft and crisp—that is, the custard part is soft while the crust is crisp.

Preparing Foods for Attractiveness

Most foods undergo some changes during preparation, such as changes in shape, color, texture, and flavor. Usually these changes are desired, but how far they are carried has an influence on the appetizing quality of products. When the underlying principles of preparation are followed, the prepared foods will measure up to high standards of attractiveness and they will be appetizing. The principles of preparation for various foods are given in the chapters in Part IV. In addition, a statement concerning the standard of quality for a product is given in many of the recipes in Part V. A few results of preparing foods correctly are mentioned here as examples: Meats will be brown, tender, and juicy; sauces and gravies will be smooth, flavorful, and of the right consistency for the purpose for which they are intended; vegetables will be slightly soft in texture, some-

what like their original shape—unless purposely mashed—and attractive in color and pleasing in flavor.

Serving Foods for Attractiveness

A final step to be considered in attractiveness is the serving of the meal. First of all, there is the table. For it to be attractive, the covers and napkins must be clean; the tableware, chinaware, and glassware sparkling bright and carefully laid; and some kind of decoration placed on the table. All of these contribute to the gratifying quality of the meal you have so carefully planned and prepared.

The food should be neatly arranged on the serving dishes and individual plates to be attractive. When food is served from the table, the responsibility for its attractive arrangement on the individual plates is on the person who does the serving. For example, when meat is carved, as a chicken

● Meals are more interesting when foods with different textures are served together.

Courtesy Chase and Sanborn

or roast, the carver should know how to cut the meat into thin slices and to transfer them to the individual plates, making these plates look tempting and at the same time keeping the platter orderly.

The amount of food placed on the plates can add or detract from the appearance of the meal. An overabundance of food on any plate looks unattractive and may even dull the appetite of a person who needs to be encouraged to eat. It is better for family members to come back for a second helping than to be served overly large portions the first time. It is also better to serve food in small pieces instead of large ones. Large pieces are often overwhelming. Two smaller pieces of food, such as two small potatoes, are usually more inviting than one very large one, even though the actual amount of food may be the same.

The service of meals is discussed in Chapter 7, "Table Setting and Etiquette." If the suggestions given there are followed, you may be sure you have made every effort to have the meals you plan, prepare, and serve for your family as attractive as possible. Then your reward may very well be "Everything looks so good!"

PART I
QUESTIONS FOR SUMMARIZING AND REVIEW

Chapter 1 . . . Planning Meals for Your Family

1. What effect do the attitudes and abilities of the meal planner have on the meals that she serves?
2. What are some reasons for planning meals?
3. What are the advantages of planning meals in advance?
4. What are the two guides to meal planning? How are they helpful?
5. Name the food groups in Canada's Food Guide. Tell the special nutrient contributions made by the foods in each group. Name some foods in each group.
6. Is it possible to plan nutritionally adequate diets using other groupings than in Canada's Food Guide? Explain.
7. Should personal preferences for foods have any influence on family meal plans? What are the results when preferences are taken into consideration and when they are not taken into consideration?
8. What features contribute to a good meal plan?

9. What is the first thing you would do if you were planning a meal for your family?
10. What sources of information are available to the meal planner to help her in planning wise food purchases?
11. How do the newspaper advertisements help the meal planner to save time, work, and money?

Chapter 2 . . . Planning Meals for Health

1. What determines the nutritional status of family members?
2. What knowledge is necessary for the planning of adequately nutritious meals?
3. What are some signs of good health?
4. What is the relationship between body weight and food patterns and eating habits?
5. What are the three functions of food in maintaining good body health?
6. What is a nutrient? Name the nutrients. Give the functions for which each nutrient is responsible.
7. What foods are particularly important as a source of each of the nutrients?

8. What is meant by a complete protein? Which foods are notable for their content of complete proteins?

9. Which of the minerals must be given special consideration to be sure they are included in the diet?

10. Which vitamins must be supplied each day?

11. What influences the amounts and kinds of nutrients needed by individuals?

12. What is meant by "Recommended Nutrient Intakes"?

13. How do food customs, habits, and environmental factors influence a family's way of preparing, serving, and eating food?

14. How should the food intake of the body be divided among the meals of the day?

15. What effect does the number of meals a day have on body comfort and utilization of nutrients?

16. What are some benefits of eating an adequate breakfast?

17. Why is a variety of foods in the diet necessary for good health?

18. What part does hunger play in getting a person to eat?

19. What affects the occurrence of hunger in all individuals?

20. What factors contribute to an individual's acceptance of a wide variety of foods?

21. How might a person's dislike of many foods be a handicap when eating away from home?

Chapter 3 . . . Planning Meals for Variety and Attractiveness

1. Why are the variety and attractiveness of family meals considered to be so important today?

2. What are some ways to get variety in meals? To make meals attractive?

3. How might changing the choice of foods served at a meal influence the eating habits of the family members?

4. What effect might methods used for preparing foods have on an individual's appetite?

5. How might the appearance of the table or the serving of the food influence the appetite? What special consideration should be given when serving food to a child? To a sick person?

EXPERIENCES FOR APPLYING YOUR KNOWLEDGE

1. Discuss the attitudes and/or ability of the meal planner in each of the following meal situations:
a. Breakfast of coffee and doughnuts
b. Lunch of tomato soup, cheese sandwich, milk, apple, and peanut butter cookie
c. Snack of candy served before lunch; after lunch
d. Supper of hot dog on roll, French fried potatoes, coke, chocolate cake
e. Bedtime treat of hot chocolate

2. Observe your mother as she plans, prepares, and serves a meal, and note the kinds of work she does. Then list the several steps involved, for example, deciding what to have, selecting recipes, etc. Check those tasks on the list for which you can take some of the responsibility. Check those tasks which other members of the family might perform satisfactorily.

3. Prepare short histories of family members and their activities to gain an understanding of their food needs and habits. Plan meal patterns and menus to fit their needs. Check the menus to note whether they provide variety as well as good nutrition. Explain briefly how you would serve the foods so that they would be attractive. (See pages 371, 372, 375.) Ask your mother to check whether or not the

menus are practical. If not, adjust them until they are.

4. As you progress in your studies, write complete menus from a series of eight to ten meal patterns carefully selected to provide opportunities to apply your knowledge of how to plan meals for good health, variety, and attractiveness.

5. Contrast menus from various cultures considering foods available in foreign countries. Compute the nutritional adequacy of these menus, using accepted standards. Discuss customs; family life practices; relationship of the nutritional status of the people to the economy of the country. Consider what might be done to make some of the diets of the different countries more nutritious. Have tasting parties of foods common to these cultures.

6. A young married couple have a food budget of $20.00 a week. Both husband and wife work. They seldom eat out but they entertain their parents or friends one night a week for dinner or snacks. While they like all foods, they must limit their caloric intake to keep from gaining weight. They have adequate storage space for all foods, including a combination refrigerator-freezer for perishable items. Working as a class or in small groups:
a. Plan a week's menus for this couple.
b. Prepare a market order for the menus.
c. Compile total costs of all foods needed.
d. Record all decisions made in doing the above.

7. List all the planning steps that are necessary for the preparing and serving of a meal in your own home or in school.

8. Study food and nutrition bulletins, articles, and talks and interpret them in terms of sound, reliable research. Establish criteria for evaluating information. Use these criteria to judge newspaper specials, magazine articles, advertising materials, and information on labels.

9. Use a map of the world and indicate countries where the diet is:
a. Predominantly made up of incomplete protein
b. Predominantly made up of dairy foods
c. Predominantly made up of animal protein foods.
    Tell the effects of each type of diet.

10. Discuss some effects that might result from such situations as these:
a. Eating an inadequate breakfast
b. Going without lunch
c. Lunching on the wrong foods; on too little food; on too much food
d. Eating too many or unsuitable between-meal snacks
e. Not eating the right foods to meet the recommended daily dietary allowances

11. Prepare a colorful poster or use food exhibits to illustrate good sources of each of the following: carbohydrate, fat, protein, calcium, iron, and the different vitamins.

12. Select one of the food nutrients and make the following study:
a. Study the use of this nutrient in the body.
b. Arrange an exhibit or prepare a scrapbook of pictures of foods that are good sources of the nutrient.
c. Plan menus for one day and indicate which foods in the menus are outstanding for their contribution of the nutrient you are studying.

13. Plan menus for one day for a person on a high-calorie diet and for a person on a low-calorie diet. What are the outstanding differences in the choice of foods for the two groups of menus?

CHEESE FONDUE

(Do not write in this book.)

Ingredient	Food Group	Calories	Protein (gm.)	Calcium (mg.)	Iron (mg.)	Vitamin A (I.U.)	Vitamin C (mg.)
Total							
Per serving							

NOTE: For an explanation of abbreviations, see page 18.

14. Select a recipe, such as Cheese Fondue, page 450, or any other recipe of your choice. Then make a chart using the same column headings shown in the chart above. List recipe ingredients in the ingredient column of your chart and fill in the other columns. Consult the table "Nutritive Values of the Edible Part of Foods" on pages 532 to 556 for the amount of each nutrient in each ingredient. Evaluate the recipe as follows:

a. Which groups of Canada's Food Guide are represented?

b. What is the amount of each nutrient in the full recipe, and in each serving?

c. What is your opinion of the value of one serving of the recipe in contributing nutrients to your recommended daily allowance? (See table, "Recommended Nutrient Intakes," on page 18 to help you.)

15. If you were to have the responsibility of packing a lunch for your father or brother, plan what you would include in each of the following situations:

a. If he had a sedentary office position and sat most of the day at a desk

b. If he had an active job, such as some kind of construction work

16. Plan a meal suitable for a family member who is ill. Demonstrate how to set a tray for this meal with a centerpiece or favor added to make the tray more attractive.

17. Plan a menu for one meal that would be suitable for a family with a young child (three years old) and an older member (over sixty-five). Be sure the meal will be liked by the other family members as well.

18. Keep a list of all the foods you eat for three days, including snacks. Be sure these three days are typical of your regular diet. Opposite each food indicate the group or groups of Canada's Food Guide which it represents. Are all of the groups represented each day? If you are not eating foods that you have learned are best for good health, suggest ways to change your diet so that it will be well-balanced.

19. Mary, on a well-planned diet to lose weight, finds that she gets so hungry between meals she can't stay on her diet. Show how a careful distribution of the foods among five small meals instead of the usual three will help her to control her hunger.

20. Many schools are stressing the importance of teaching nutrition to children in the primary grades rather than waiting until they are in high school. Give reasons why this is a

45

better time. Tell how the methods of teaching about foods would need to differ in working with the younger children.

21. It is often desirable to serve one food several times during one week, such as potatoes, apples, ground beef, and cereals, or to serve often, when in season, such fresh foods as asparagus, tomatoes, corn, and strawberries. Make a chart or list to show different ways in which these foods can be prepared to give variety to the meals.

22. With the increase in consumption of refined and sweetened foods, it becomes increasingly difficult to get younger children to like nutritious foods. Plan several menus and methods of preparing and serving foods that will be appealing to this age group. If possible invite some children to a foods class to try these menus. Try similar menus at home for younger brothers and sisters. Ask your mother or father to help you evaluate your meal plans and the results.

23. Many families have a favorite meal, such as spaghetti, that they want served each week. Through a display of the different pasta products available in the markets and a collection of recipes, show how a family can have variety in the spaghetti dinners. Prepare a basic tomato sauce for use by several groups in class or freeze the extra sauce for use later. Use different pasta products and cheeses to prepare a variety of main dishes with the basic sauce.

24. Many individuals neglect to eat breakfast because they aren't hungry, haven't the time, or don't realize the importance of a good breakfast. Plan breakfast menus that are nutritionally satisfying and that will be especially appealing to the following:
a. Child who is late for school and so can't take time to eat
b. Teen-agers who aren't hungry in the morning
c. Child who has to get own breakfast in the morning
d. Person who gets bored of the same old thing

25. Observe the menus for a week served at home, in the school cafeteria, or in a restaurant. Evaluate the appeal of the meals in terms of variety, color, flavor, texture, and temperature. What changes would you make in the menus to have them more appealing?

26. List ways to garnish meat, fish, vegetables, and desserts. Make some of the popular garnishes using fruits and vegetables. (See page 371 for vegetables.)

27. Early explorers left their homes and families to discover the spices that we now have in great quantity and variety in our markets. Arrange a display of seasonings, condiments, herbs, and flavoring extracts. Consult cookbooks for ways in which these ingredients are used. Experiment with recipes using a variety of these seasonings.

28. Prepare an article for a school paper which will show students the value of eating a proper diet and give help in planning and eating such a diet.

4

Managing Meals to Save Time and Effort

■ EVERYTHING you do takes time and effort—that is, it requires you to spend energy. When time and energy can be saved in doing the essential household tasks, there is more time to spend in other activities. And you will get more pleasure from these other activities because you will have more vitality and have the satisfying knowledge that you have not slighted any necessary jobs. Time and energy are like money. You can spend them only once, so it is well for you to learn to spend them wisely.

That part of homemaking that has to do with the preparation of meals for the family is one of the essential daily tasks, and you will have managed well if you learn to be efficient in preparing these daily meals.

A considerable amount of skill is required to prepare a meal so that when served each food will be at its best, be appealing in appearance, and taste good.

Saving Time and Effort by Your Choice of Menus

When planning menus, it is of considerable importance that the amount of time and work required to prepare and serve these meals be given thought. The factors which influence the amount of time and effort needed are (1) the forms of foods selected, (2) the methods of preparation decided upon, and (3) the way in which the meal is served.

In the Forms of Foods Selected

Some foods can be purchased in fresh form only, some are partially prepared, some are ready-to-serve, and some are available in several different forms. It is well to consider not only which of these forms of food will save time and effort, but which are of the desired quality, which are readily accessible, and which come within the food budget.

Fresh foods. This form of food usually requires some kind of preparation before it is cooked, or even eaten raw. The preparation may be a simple treatment like washing, peeling, paring, or cutting up. Or it may require more time and effort, as in shelling peas.

Processed foods. These are the partially or fully prepared products, such as canned and frozen foods, packaged mixes, and ready-to-use and ready-to-eat foods. They are sometimes called "quick-method" or "convenience foods." There are literally thousands on the market and their use is fast becoming a way of life. Because some preliminary preparation has already been given to them, time and work are saved in the kitchen. Many convenience foods have been made possible by the use of so-called "food additives." These are substances which, when incorporated in a food product, exert a beneficial effect on such properties as color, flavor, texture, consistency, and keeping quality. The use of food additives, both in kind and amount, is strictly controlled by regulations of the Food and Drugs Act administered by the Food and Drug Directorate. According to these regulations, any food manufacturer is obligated to establish the safety of the additive substance he intends to incorporate in his food product. For this reason the food industry carries on extensive research before marketing any of the convenience foods and you, as a consumer, can be sure of the purity of all such foods you buy.

Canned foods save time and effort both in preparation and in cooking. Canned foods include fruits, vegetables, meats, soups, and a variety of made dishes, such as corned beef hash, chow mein, chicken à la king, etc. Most of the preparation work has already been done during the canning process. For instance, fruits have been peeled, pitted, sliced, or puréed; vegetables have been pared, cut, removed from the pods, or mashed; meats, poultry, and fish have been cleaned, ground, or cut. Also all canned foods—with a few exceptions, such as vacuum-packed coffee and nuts—are completely cooked and so are ready to serve or heat.

Canned foods are often used as an ingredient in made dishes, saving preparation or cooking time or both. For example, canned fruits are used in pies, puddings, or salads; condensed cream soups, if not fully diluted, are used as quick-and-easy cream sauces for vegetables or leftover meats or casserole dishes. Canned vegetables are also used as an ingredient in casserole-type main dishes.

Frozen foods resemble canned foods, since the preparation preliminary to their use has already been done. In general, there are the following kinds of frozen foods:

1. Fruits and fruit juices, needing only to be defrosted before use (the juice usually must be diluted)
2. Vegetables, most of which need cooking
3. Meats, poultry, and fish, frozen raw— which must be cooked for serving
4. Meats, poultry, and fish, soups, whole dinners, and fruit pies and breads, com-

Courtesy Florida Citrus Commission

● Frozen foods

Courtesy Maxwell House Coffee

● Powdered foods

Courtesy H. J. Heinz Company

● Canned foods

Courtesy Armour and Company

● Ready-to-eat foods

pletely cooked and then frozen—which only need to be heated for serving

The amount of time and effort saved by using frozen food instead of one of the other forms of food will depend on the kind of food used and on the form it replaces. For example, it requires considerable time to prepare orange juice from the fresh fruit, less time to prepare the same amount of juice by mixing frozen concentrate with the proper measure of water, and the least time of all simply to pour the canned or cartoned juice directly from the container into the serving glass.

Whenever a frozen food must be defrosted—for example, fruit for dessert—then the length of time needed for this must be considered. But no time need be wasted waiting for the fruit to defrost if plans are made ahead.

Frozen foods that must be cooked before using may not save many minutes of cooking time when compared to cooking the same product if fresh. Time is saved in preparation, however. It takes longer to cook meat, fish, and poultry from the raw frozen state than it does to cook similar kinds of fresh foods. If these foods are allowed to defrost before cooking is started, time for defrosting must be allowed, but no change need be made in the length of the cooking period over that for the fresh form.

Ready-to-eat and ready-to-use foods as menu items also aid in saving time and effort when preparing meals. Among the ready-to-eat forms of foods are such products as ready-to-serve breakfast cereals, crackers, and melba toast; cold cuts of meat and sliced cheese; and a large assortment of jams, jellies, and relishes. Bakery products, too, from commercial bakeries come ready to eat. Bread, rolls, pies, cakes and cookies, doughnuts, and sometimes desserts like cream puffs, éclairs, and other French pastries may be obtained at local bakeries.

The ready-to-use forms of foods include, in addition to canned and frozen foods, such products as fresh, washed spinach and other greens, and soup vegetables; instant milk, cocoa, coffee, and tea; bouillon cubes; prepared stuffings; and salad dressings. Brown-and-serve rolls and brown-and-

serve sausages, instant mashed potatoes, and chopped meats are other examples of foods that are ready to use. Since all preliminary preparation has been done on foods of this type, only cooking—or in some instances just heating—is required, so they can be ready to serve in a comparatively short time.

Packaged mixes, another type of quick-method foods, are mixtures of some of the ingredients necessary in making batters and doughs, puddings, ice cream, cocoa, and frostings. The use of packaged mixes saves the time of assembling, measuring, and blending ingredients, and washing the measuring utensils.

In the Methods of Preparation

Some methods of cooking take longer than others as, for example, oven cooking as compared with surface cooking of the same food. It takes longer to bake potatoes than to boil them, but there will be less preparation time and less work required than to pare potatoes either before or after boiling. Some foods require more attention than others while they cook. A choice may be made, however, among the foods that take approximately the same amount of preparation time but not the same amount of attention during cooking. For example, it takes about the same amount of time to mix waffles, pancakes, and biscuits. But the biscuits do not require so much attention while baking as waffles or pancakes. Therefore, other things can be attended to while baking biscuits, but not during the baking of waffles or pancakes, which need to be watched quite constantly.

Small pieces of food cook more quickly than large pieces. Quartered potatoes,

Courtesy Oscar Meyer and Company

● Cook the food at the table.

Courtesy Campbell Soup Company

● Have a frozen entree.

Courtesy Reynolds Wrap

● Prepare a broiler meal.

Courtesy Wear-Ever Aluminum, Inc.

● Serve plates from the kitchen.

Courtesy National Presto Industries, Inc.

● Use a pressure saucepan.

sliced or cubed carrots, and cauliflower flowerets will cook to the tender stage more quickly than when these vegetables are cooked whole. Steaks and chops, meat cut for stews, and ground-meat patties will cook more quickly than large pieces of meat, such as roasts.

A salad may be made quickly if wedges are cut from a head of lettuce and served with a prepared dressing. An arranged salad or a tossed salad takes longer to prepare.

In the Serving

By giving thought to meals that can be served easily, you will save yourself both time and effort, especially in trips to the dining table and in the dishwashing that follows the meal. In the following list are some suggestions you might follow for serving foods. You will no doubt think of others.

Serve toast, pancakes, or waffles directly from an electric appliance placed on the dining table.

WAYS TO SAVE TIME IN PLANNING, PREPARING, AND SERVING MEALS

MENUS	PREPARATION AND SERVING
Breakfast	
Orange juice	Use cartoned, canned, or frozen juice instead of fresh.
Cereal	Use ready-to-eat or precooked forms.
Toast	Toast all slices at once in oven, or toast in toaster at table.
Milk	Serve in kitchen or from a pitcher on the table.
Coffee	Use instant coffee instead of brewed.
Lunch	
Cream of tomato soup	Use canned condensed soup instead of home-prepared.
Swiss cheese, lettuce, mayonnaise sandwich	Use packaged sliced cheese and commercial mayonnaise, and serve on plate with soup.
Peaches	Use canned sliced peaches instead of frozen or fresh fruit.
Cookies	Use packaged cookies instead of homemade, and serve on plate with fruit dish.
Milk	Serve in kitchen or from a pitcher on the table.
Dinner	
Baked fish fillets	Bake fish fillets in baking dish, and serve them in the same dish. (Use high-temperature baking method. See Chapter 21, "Fish.")
Baked potatoes	Bake in oven at same time as fish.
Scalloped tomatoes	Use canned tomatoes, and bake in oven at same time as fish.
Cole slaw	Use packaged washed, sliced cabbage instead of whole, and serve in one salad bowl.
Biscuits	Cut in squares instead of round. Bake in oven at same time as fish, potatoes, and tomatoes.
Lemon pudding	Use packaged mix.

Serve salad or soup with a sandwich beside it on the plate.

Serve fruit or ice cream with a cookie or cake at the side of the plate instead of passing a separate dish.

Serve food directly from the cooking dish, if the dish is suitable, instead of arranged in a serving dish.

Serve the vegetables around the meat on a serving platter and not each in a separate serving dish.

Serve all food for one course of a meal on individual plates from the kitchen instead of in separate serving dishes.

The chart at the left also gives some suggestions for saving time in serving meals as well as ways to save time in planning and preparing them.

Saving Time and Effort by Organizing Your Work

Meal preparation is not to be hurried through merely to save time and effort. No sacrifice need be made of those qualities that make for gracious living, since organization of work and also of the time allotted will not hinder but will help to achieve this.

Using good equipment. As you prepare meals with the principles of good management in mind, you will surely notice that the kitchen itself has much to do with the ease or smoothness with which you work. In fact, the kitchen and its equipment have such important effects on the time and energy spent in getting meals that manufacturers of kitchen equipment and architects are devoting a great deal of attention today to kitchens—their design and their equipment. In Chapter 6, "Management in the Kitchen," there is a discussion of kitchen plans, equipment, and utensils.

Making a market order. The first step toward good organization of your work is to make a market order. Take stock of the foods needed to prepare your planned meals, and list all the ingredients required. Check these ingredients to note those already on hand. Then make a list of the ones that must be bought. (See Chapter 5, "Managing Meals to Get Your Money's Worth," page 76.)

Arranging food and equipment. The storage of food and arrangement of equipment at work centers where they will usually be used are other ways that good organization of work can be a timesaver. For example, staples like flour and sugar should be emptied into containers and put with spices, herbs, and extracts in the cabinets near where they are most frequently used. Keep measuring, mixing, and baking equipment at the food-preparation center.

You can also save time in preparing meals if you do such things as wash salad greens and other vegetables and grapefruit and oranges before you store them in the refrigerator.

Preparing a work-and-time schedule. To help in making meal preparation go more smoothly, prepare a work-and-time schedule. Re-examine the menu before you start preparation, and then make your work-and-time schedule. On such a schedule you should list (1) the jobs to be done, (2) the steps to be followed in accomplishing each job, and (3) a rough allotment of the time you believe it will take you to carry out each step. Of course the schedule can be only an estimate, but it ensures you that you will not forget to do some part of the job and that you will have everything ready on time. No work-and-time schedule, even for the same menu, will be the same for everyone. Different persons do not

● Swing out shelves in base cabinets (left) and divided drawers under gas surface burners (right) hold everything needed at the range, and will save countless time and energy in preparing meals.

work at the same rate of speed, and not everyone will do the work in the same order. Differences in individuals, in kitchens, in the kind and arrangement of equipment, in the number of persons who help in the preparation, and in the number who will be served will all affect the work-and-time schedule.

It is a good idea to have a flexible schedule. Some parts of the schedule cannot be changed, but it is well to plan to change or even omit jobs if necessary. If, for example, you plan to serve cocoa at a meal but find that other processes have taken longer than anticipated, you can serve milk instead. Or if you plan to serve creamed cauliflower and the cauliflower has taken longer to cook than you allowed in your schedule, then you can serve the cauliflower buttered.

The use of a schedule has many advantages, particularly when you are first learning to prepare meals:

1. It ensures that you will not forget to do some part of the job.
2. It makes possible having everything ready at the proper time.
3. It helps you to decide on the order of doing each job and how the steps in the several jobs can be fitted together into a sequence that will make the work progress smoothly.
4. It enables you to judge the total amount of time needed to prepare a meal.
5. It helps you to see when or where you can dovetail one task with another—that is, how you can keep two tasks going together at the same time.

To see how a work schedule can be applied, let us take the simple lunch menu given in the chart on page 58. Perhaps you can prepare this meal and serve it to your family on some Saturday.

As you prepare this lunch following the suggested schedule, you might make a mental note of whether you find the order of work and the time allotment right for you. If they are not, jot down adjustments that you feel would let you work more efficiently the next time you decide to follow the same menu or one similar to it.

Saving Time and Effort by Good Work Habits

Time can be measured quite accurately, but except for a feeling of fatigue, there is no way for you to measure effort. In general, time and effort are related, and the shorter the time spent in work the less the effort. This is true to a certain extent only, for even though you can work quickly, you may spend more energy than is necessary unless you develop good work habits.

The best way to form good work habits is to know and follow some important rules that studies show are energy saving. These deal with (1) posture; (2) orderliness in your work; (3) the number and kind of motions made; (4) fitting together various steps, that is, dovetailing jobs and using short-cut methods; and (5) developing safe work habits.

Have Comfortable Working Conditions

Good posture—that is, using your body correctly—reduces strain on your muscles and so delays a feeling of tiredness. To have good posture, your working position should be comfortable when either standing or sit-

● For the least expenditure of energy, the height of the work surface should be such that good posture can be maintained (left). When the surface is too low, the back must be bent (right); when too high, the shoulders must be raised.

HOW TO ORGANIZE YOUR WORK IN PREPARING A MEAL

MENU

Cream of Tomato Soup

Swiss Cheese, Lettuce, and Mayonnaise Sandwich

Peaches Cookies

Milk

Foods Needed	Amounts
Tomato soup (canned condensed)	1 can
Whole-wheat bread (sliced)	8 slices
Butter	⅛ pound
Lettuce	Few leaves
Mayonnaise	¼ cup
Swiss cheese (sliced)	4 slices
Milk	5 cups
Sliced peaches (canned)	14 fl. ounce can
Cookies (packaged)	8 cookies

THINGS TO DO

Set table
Get out dishes
Get out kitchen utensils
Heat and serve soup
Make and serve sandwiches
Serve peaches
Serve cookies
Serve milk
Store remaining bread, cookies, cheese, peaches

THE KITCHEN UTENSILS

Can opener for soup and peach cans
Saucepan for heating soup
Wooden spoon for stirring
Ladle for serving soup into soup cups
Knife for spreading butter and mayonnaise
Knife for cutting sandwiches
Spoon for serving peaches
Bowl and cover for leftover peaches

THE WORK-AND-TIME SCHEDULE

Job	Number of Minutes
About an hour before lunchtime, place can of peaches in refrigerator to chill, and take butter for spreading sandwiches out of refrigerator so it will soften.	2
Set table, get out serving dishes, and warm soup bowls.	5
Get out kitchen utensils and food materials needed.	3
Open can of soup, and pour it into saucepan; stir milk into soup.	2

Job	Number of Minutes
Place soup over low heat, and stir occasionally as you do other work, so soup heats uniformly and does not stick to pan.	1
Place eight slices of bread on working surface at food-preparation center, and spread each slice to the edges evenly with softened butter.	3
Spread four slices of the bread with mayonnaise, and place lettuce and cheese on the other four slices. Put together into sandwiches and cut. Place each sandwich on a plate.	3
Take can of peaches out of refrigerator, open, and put into individual dishes. Place each dish of peaches on a plate with two cookies.	4
Serve soup and milk.	2
Soak saucepan in cold water.	1
Put away any extra food.	1
Carry soup and sandwich plates to table.	2

Approximate total time 29 to 30 minutes

ting. When you are working in the kitchen, you are for the most part standing, but you may sit for tasks like paring apples, cutting beans, or shelling peas. You cannot maintain good posture when standing unless the work height is right for you. The best height is that where you do not have to raise your arms at the shoulders or bend your back to accomplish the task. If your work surface is too high, try a lower one when you can.

Good sitting posture can be maintained when the chair or stool you use is of a height that makes it unnecessary for you to raise your arms and when the seat is wide enough for you to sit in a relaxed position with space beneath the counter or table for your knees. In some kitchens there is no place for knees beneath the counters. In such cases, opening a door in a base cabinet may provide the knee room. Your feet should be provided with a footrest un-

less they can be placed firmly on the floor, and there should be a support for the small of your back.

Keep Work Surfaces Orderly and Clean

Motions are saved when you have a place for everything and keep everything where it belongs. Then you will be able to find and select the right tool for a job without trouble. If you always keep neatness in mind as you work, it will become a habit for you to have your work spaces free from spilled food, your utensils orderly, and your mixing bowls or other utensils rinsed and stacked after use so they are ready for washing—that is, if you cannot wash them right after you use them. A tray is a great help in keeping your work space orderly and clean. You can use it to hold soiled dishes, spoons, and other small utensils as you work. Later the utensils can easily be put into the sink for washing.

● For the least muscular strain while sitting, the body should be erect and the feet flat on the floor (left). Working with the body bent and the feet elevated is tiring (right).

Eliminate Unnecessary Motions

In meal preparation many motions are made, and all of them take a certain amount of effort. You walk, reach, bend or stoop, lift, carry, pull, push, stir, beat, grasp, and hold. There are many examples of each of these motions. You may walk from one work center to another. You reach when you get supplies from a wall cabinet or shelf. You bend or stoop when you place food or equipment on a low shelf or when you place food in some types of ovens. You lift when you put something on a high shelf. You bend and also lift when you take something from a low oven or low refrigerator shelf, or from a low cabinet shelf. You carry supplies from the market, take food from one storage place to another

or to a work center, and take food and dishes to and from the table. You pull when you open a drawer or an oven door and push when you close it. You stir when you make gravy. You beat when you make batters. You grasp and hold when you pour water from a teakettle or pitcher.

You can walk many miles a day and use many of the motions mentioned above during the preparation of meals, but you can save steps and motions when the work centers are in good relation to one another and when tools and food supplies are handy. (See page 98, Chapter 6, "Management in the Kitchen.") Since usually you cannot change the arrangement of work centers in your home or your school kitchens without involving considerable expense, you can try to change your routines so as to save unnecessary effort. One way this can be done is by using a service cart or tray to carry a number of foods in one trip from the refrigerator to the work center where they are to be used and to carry other supplies and utensils from a storage place to a work center or to the dining area. In this way you will avoid repetition of trips. Another way to save steps and motions is to have duplicates of some of the smaller utensils, such as salt and pepper shakers and measuring cups and spoons, so there will be one set at both the mixing and cooking centers. Other ways are to store often-used articles on shelves that are easy to reach and to keep food and equipment at the center where they are first used, such as keeping coffee and coffeepot at the sink if cold water is used or near the range if boiling water is used for coffee making. Another good way to reduce fatigue is to arrange ingredients in a semicircle—all within easy reach—when mixing batters and doughs. There are rotary beaters for beating a small number of eggs, and flour sifters that can be operated with one hand rather than two, as must be done when using the conventional type of rotary beater and flour sifter. A switch on an electric cord prevents having to plug and unplug an electric cord each time on a frequently used electric appliance.

Dovetail Tasks and Take Short Cuts

Dovetailing tasks is very important to economy of time and effort. The chart on page 62 gives some suggestions for dovetailing tasks. No doubt you will find others as you gain experience in meal preparation.

Short cuts as well as dovetailing will aid in saving time and effort. A short cut is a

● Less muscular strain and expenditure of energy are experienced when work surfaces and wall cabinets are at comfortable heights. Work surfaces where preparation processes can be done within comfortable reach (left) and storage cabinets where frequently used items can be reached easily (right) are best.

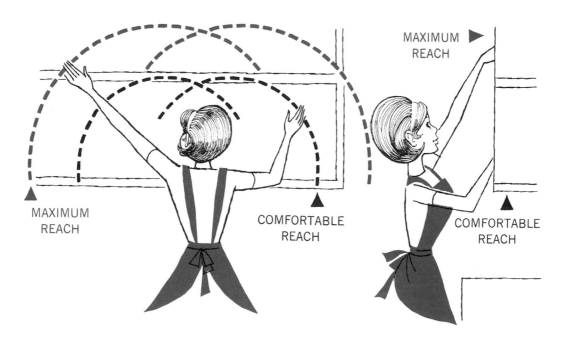

MAXIMUM REACH

MAXIMUM REACH

COMFORTABLE REACH

COMFORTABLE REACH

manner of doing a task which will accomplish the desired result more directly, and therefore more quickly and with less effort than when an unconsidered procedure is used. Many experienced people have learned to save themselves by doing some tasks an easy way, and as a result they do less actual work. There are a number of kinds of short cuts that can be used in meal

preparation, serving, and cleaning up afterward. Some examples of these are given in the chart on pages 63 to 65.

Develop Safe Work Habits

Good work habits are also safe work habits, and safe work habits save time and effort too. The kitchen has been called the most dangerous room in the house because

DOVETAILING TASKS

As breakfast cereal is cooking,	pour milk in glasses. or get bread ready for toasting.
As soup is heating for lunch,	make sandwiches. or arrange salad.
As water is heating to boiling,	pare potatoes. or clean and peel onions.
As meat loaf is baking,	prepare and cook vegetable, and arrange salad.
As roast of meat is cooking,	set table, prepare and cook vegetables, and arrange salad. or whip cream for dessert, which was made earlier in the day.
While clearing up after breakfast or lunch,	bake a pudding. or make a gelatin dessert. or cut and bake cookies from a previously made dough.
While clearing up after dinner,	section grapefruit for breakfast. or squeeze orange juice for breakfast.
While dusting or vacuuming,	bake an already prepared casserole dish for lunch.
While clothes are being washed in automatic washer,	make a cake or pie for dinner dessert.

SHORT CUTS IN PREPARING MEALS

1. Plan ahead how you will proceed so as to use as few cooking utensils as possible.

2. Use only one knife, spoon, or measuring cup for several tasks by rinsing them after each use.

3. Keep tools together that are frequently used together.

4. Keep small utensils at the same place as or near the food with which it is used—that is, keep a paring knife, fruit juicer, and cutting board for preparing fresh juice near the fruit; keep a coffee measure in the coffee container; and keep a scoop in the flour and sugar canisters.

5. Keep pepper, salt, and flour in sifters at the range.

6. To avoid several trips to and from the refrigerator, take from it at one time all the food needed in the preparation of a dish or a meal.

7. Before beginning to prepare a food, assemble all the necessary ingredients and utensils.

8. Use the same measuring cups and spoons for measuring dry and liquid ingredients without washing them in between by measuring dry ingredients first and then liquids or fats.

9. Cook vegetables without paring when possible but brush them well.

10. For easy disposal of waste and to make the cleaning of work surface quicker and easier, pare and peel fruits and vegetables over a paper.

(Continued)

11. For paring carrots and potatoes quickly, use a peeler instead of a knife.

12. To cut celery and snap beans into pieces quickly, hold lengthwise pieces close together on board and cut across with a sharp knife.

13. Scrape the bottom and side of a used mixing bowl with a rubber scraper to make the bowl easier to wash.

14. Use kitchen shears to cut pieces of left-over bacon, parsley, figs, chives, dates, or pimento.

15. Use a slicing board when cutting bread into cubes.

16. To make the cleanup job easier when broiling, line the broiler pan with foil or use a disposable foil broiler pan.

17. To avoid having to reroll and cut the dough from between round biscuits, cut biscuits into squares with a knife.

18. Keep grated cheese on hand in a jar in the refrigerator for ready use.

19. For quicker cooking, bake meat loaf in individual servings or in muffin tins.

20. Cook enough potatoes at one time for two meals.

21. Use wax paper for the flour or crumbs to coat pieces of food for frying. Food that is more substantial, such as meat or chicken, may be shaken with the flour or crumbs in a clean paper bag.

22. To avoid washing the rotary beater more than once when beating egg yolks and whites separately, beat the whites first.

23. Heat milk in the same pan with the cooked potatoes to be mashed instead of using a separate pan.

24. Set the table for breakfast at night. The table may be set for the other meals while food is cooking or chilling.

25. Use a tray when setting the table so as to carry most of the appointments to the table at one time.

26. Prepare one-dish meals.

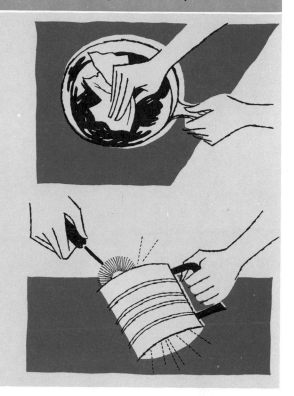

27. To save time in serving and cleaning up, serve meals directly onto individual plates from the kitchen.

28. Put leftover food directly into containers that may be used for reheating the food.

29. Wipe greasy frying pans with paper towels before washing.

30. Clean the flour sifter with a dry vegetable brush.

31. For easier dishwashing, soak syrupy or greasy dishes in hot water and eggy, starchy, or milky dishes in cold water.

about one-fifth of all home accidents occur there. "Safety First" is a good slogan for the kitchen as well as elsewhere. Some ideas for safety in the kitchen are given in the chart on page 66.

Saving Time and Effort in Cleaning Up After Meals

After the meal is over, it will pay you to wash the dishes promptly, since food dries on them if they are allowed to stand, thus making the dishwashing task more difficult. If possible, wash all mixing and cooking utensils as soon as they are empty. The fol-

lowing types of equipment and supplies will help you do an efficient dishwashing job:
1. A sink with space on each side for dishes —soiled dishes on one side and clean on the other
2. A sink large enough to hold a dishpan for washing dishes and a dish drainer in which dishes may be rinsed by pouring scalding water over them, or
3. A double sink, one bowl for washing dishes and the second one for rinsing them
4. A rubber scraper and a dishcloth or composition sponge
5. Absorbent dish towels and a towel rack

6. Hot water and soap or synthetic detergent

7. Scouring pads and scouring powder

8. Paper towels or newspaper for wiping out greasy pans and stiff paper or newspaper for wrapping garbage unless the community requires that garbage and paper be separated when collected

There are a number of satisfactory methods of dishwashing. The method you

(Continued on page 71)

FOR SAFETY IN THE KITCHEN

1. Have a good light at all work centers.

2. Follow directions exactly when using such equipment as ranges, pressure saucepans, pressure canners, or electric mixers.

3. Keep off the floor or out of the way those articles that might cause someone to trip.

4. To avoid slipping or falling, wipe up at once any water or foods spilled on the floor.

5. Keep drawers closed to avoid running into them.

6. Keep cabinet doors closed, unless of sliding type, to avoid bumping your head.

7. Keep work surfaces uncluttered so that sharp knives and other articles that might cause injury can be easily seen.

8. To prevent cuts, wash sharp knives separately.

9. When storing sharp knives, keep them together with the sharp edges all facing one way to lessen the chance of cuts.

10. To avoid burning yourself on the handles of hot pans, use well-padded pot holders. Using long well-padded mitts for oven cooking is also a protection.

11. To avoid the danger of fire, keep paper and cloths away from the range.

12. Keep matches in a safe place, as in a covered tin box or glass jar, to avoid fire.

13. To lessen the danger of falling when you have to reach to a high shelf, use a substantial step stool.

14. To avoid cuts, discard chinaware or glassware that is cracked or chipped.

15. In so far as possible when cutting food, cut away from yourself instead of toward yourself, or use a cutting board.

16. Use a can opener that does not leave rough edges on the can or lid.

17. To avoid having food boil over, use a pan of an adequate size for the amount and kind of food you are cooking.

18. To prevent having saucepans tip over, keep bottoms flat so they will be well balanced on the range.

19. To avoid spilling food in a pan while cooking, keep the handles away from you.

20. When you remove a cover from boiling food, hold it in such a way as to shield your face and hands from steam.

21. Avoid reaching across heated burners or units.

22. When frying and broiling, keep the heat low enough to avoid grease fires.

23. To avoid sputtering or overflowing of grease when deep-fat frying, be sure the food is well drained and lowered carefully into the fat.

24. When broiling, use a pan that allows the fat to drip away from the heat zone. Should a fat fire occur, turn off the heat at once, and smother the fire with a lid, baking soda, or salt, or use a fire extinguisher.

25. Use cooking tongs to remove such foods as corn from hot water, baked potatoes from the oven, or deep-fat-fried foods from hot grease.

SAFETY IN THE KITCHEN

Courtesy National Safety Council

● A cupboard door that has been left open is a menace.

Courtesy National Safety Council

● When the handles of pans protrude, there is always danger of an accident and a burn.

Courtesy Church & Dwight Co., Inc.

● With proper care a grease fire can be avoided, but should one occur, baking soda will quickly put the fire out.

Courtesy National Safety Council

● A sturdy step stool is an asset for reaching articles that are too high to be reached from the floor.

● As soon as the pans and dishes used in food preparation are emptied, fill them with water and add a little detergent. Let them soak.

● Remove the soiled dishes and flatware at the end of each course.

● Rinse the dishes under running water, using a rubber scraper to push any remaining food particles into the garbage drainer.

EASIER DISHWASHING

● Stack to the right of the sink in the order to be washed: glassware, flatware, dinnerware, cooking utensils. Fill the dishpan or sink with hot water and detergent.

● Wash, rinse, and drain the tableware in a right-to-left direction if the arrangement of your kitchen will permit you to do so.

● Rinse the dishes with scalding water, and drain. Allow them to dry in the drainer without wiping, or dry them with a clean, absorbent towel.

All photos courtesy American Cyanamid Company

BASIC RULES FOR WASHING DISHES

1. Scrape the dishes after each meal. For this purpose a rubber scraper or a brush is a good tool. Scrape onto stiff paper, onto several thicknesses of newspaper, or into a garbage bag for good and easy disposal.

2. Rinse dishes with any egg, milk, or starchy food on them in cold water, since hot water tends to cook such foods onto the dishes. Other dishes should be rinsed or soaked in very hot water. It may be necessary to use a scouring pad to remove very resistant foods. Wipe greasy pans with paper towels or newspapers to remove excess grease.

3. Arrange the dishes by putting all those of a similar kind together. This includes stacking plates of one size together. Then the dishes can be washed with a rhythmic motion, using a repetition of the same motion until all of one kind are clean.

4. Place the soiled dishes on the right side of the sink if the sink has a drainboard on both sides. It has been found that when the dishes are washed from right to left fewer motions are required. Because of a particular position in the kitchen, some sinks may have a drainboard on the left side only, in which case an adjustment in the order of washing dishes may be made.

5. Immerse a few dishes at a time in a pan of hot water, using enough soap or other detergent to make the water sudsy. There is less danger of nicking glassware and dishes when only a few pieces are put into the water at one time. The usual order is to wash glassware first, then the tableware, the dinnerware, and last the cooking utensils, unless the cooking utensils have been washed right after they were used. You may prefer to wash the cups before the tableware to perhaps lessen any danger of breaking the handles. If all dishes are rinsed well before they are washed, the order of washing them is not of special importance.

6. Wash the dishes with a dishcloth or a composition sponge, holding each dish in your left hand and the cloth or sponge in your right. Wipe all surfaces of the dish with the sudsy cloth or sponge, being sure that all soil is removed. Scour all pans that are soiled with resistant grease or other hard-to-remove food. If the dishwater becomes greasy, murky, or cold at any time during the dishwashing process, pour it out and get fresh, hot, sudsy water for the remainder of the dishes.

7. Rinse all washed dishes and cooking utensils in very hot, even scalding, water so they will be sanitary as well as sparkling clean. Dishes may be rinsed by dipping them into scalding water, pouring scalding water over them from a pitcher or teakettle, or using a spray attachment on the faucet.

8. Drain the dishes by placing them in an orderly manner in a dish drainer for a few minutes before drying them with a clean dish towel. Dishes may be placed in a dish drainer for rinsing and left to air-dry.

9. Wipe off and dry the table tops and drainboards.

10. Wipe off the range.

11. Take care of all garbage.

12. See that the sink is clean.

13. Wash and rinse thoroughly the dishcloth or sponge and dish towel, and hang to dry.

14. Put lotion on hands to prevent roughness.

[NOTE: In your school kitchen, wash the dishcloth and dish towels in hot water, using plenty of soap or other detergent, and rinse them well. Fold and stretch these cloths over a towel rack to dry so the next class will have clean towels.]

select will depend on the type of equipment available, the arrangement of the sink and working surfaces, and the placement of storage areas for dishes and utensils. Regardless of the method you use, there are some basic rules which may be helpful. (See chart at the left.)

Because of the monotony of dishwashing, some homemakers find a dishwasher a welcome addition to their kitchen equipment. As well as saving effort, such a machine will save time. Dishes are prepared for the dishwasher in the same manner as for hand washing. However, they may be put into the dishwasher as they are brought from the table, after each dish has been scraped or rinsed. Dishes need not be handled twice as in hand washing. Some homemakers wash dishes in the dishwasher only once a day, storing soiled dishes there until ready to wash them or until there is a full load.

There are certain items that should not be put in the dishwasher—for example, hand-painted chinaware may fade after repeated washings, the handles of some

● Any water spilled while washing dishes should be wiped up quickly to prevent slipping or falling.

sterling silver flatware may become loose as a result of the constant application of very hot water, and the finish of bone or wooden handles of steak knives and the appearance of wooden bowls may also be affected by hot water. It is therefore a wise precaution to wash by hand such items as these. In using a dishwasher as in using any other appliance, always read the manufacturer's directions and follow them carefully.

● A built-in under-sink dish washer and food disposer convert waste space into a convenience.

5

Managing Meals to Get Your Money's Worth

■ GETTING the most from the food dollar is a problem that faces every family, no matter what the economic condition of the family is. Since the good health of the family depends on eating nutritious meals, the family's food money must be spent with care so as to get the full value from it. Managing the money expenditures for food will be your responsibility when you have a home of your own. If today you can share this responsibility, you will gain valuable experience for the future.

But before plans are made for spending money for food, the total amount of money in the family income and the other items besides food for which this money is needed have to be considered. The money avail-

able can then be divided or apportioned among all the items. Such an over-all plan of apportioning total money income to all the items of expenditure is called a "financial plan," or as some people like to call , a "budget."

A financial plan does not require a complicated bookkeeping system. Such a plan does, however, involve thinking ahead for spending. When this is done, there is not the danger that too much money will be used for some nonessential purchases, or even that money may run out before all necessary expenditures are met. In this last event the family falls behind financially and goes into debt. If on the other hand, money is spent according to a financial plan, there is greater probability that there will be money for every need.

There are certain expenses that must be taken care of regularly. These are food, shelter (that is, a home and its operating costs like heat, light, and rent or property taxes), and, of course, clothing. In making a budget, money must be set aside first for these necessities. Then there are other expenses—dentist's and doctor's bills, repairs, income taxes, and insurance payments—that are bound to come in every family. And there are additional items, such as recreation, education, church, savings, and investments for which money should be allotted in a family budget. Books dealing with the subject of financial planning usually give a range of percentages for each item within which expenditures should fall for various amounts of income and family conditions. These percentage ranges can serve as guides only, because each family is different from every other family in its amount of income, family make-up, way of living, and, possibly, special needs. You may like to refer to books on the subject for more detailed information on family budgeting. In this text our concern is with managing food expenditures in such a way that full value is received for the money.

The Family Food Budget

Food is one of the essential items in the family budget. Whether the family income is large or small, a fairly large percentage of it must be spent for food. In general, this percentage is around 20 to 21 percent of income before taxes. If the income is small, less money is spent for food than when the income is large, but the percentage of income is greater.

How much money to spend. The amount of money that is needed to buy food for the family is influenced by a number of conditions. Among these is the area in the country where the family lives, since prices for food in the North, South, East, and West may be somewhat different. The location of the home has an effect too. If the family has a home garden or lives near a farm or farmer's market, some foods will probably cost less than if they were purchased in stores. The number in the family and their ages, their sex, and the kind of activity they engage in all affect food expenditures. More food is required and more money is spent in large families than in small ones and in families where there are adolescent girls and boys or more men than women. When family members do manual work or engage in strenuous physical exercise, more food and more money are needed than in families whose members are less active.

How to spend the money. Although some or all of these conditions will affect the total amount of food expenditures in any individual family, the way in which the money is spent determines whether or not full money's worth is obtained. "Full money's worth" means that meals are attractive and well liked by the family. Here the homemaker's interest, imagination, and experience in planning, preparing, and serving meals are all called upon and influence the way she spends the food money. Full money's worth also means spending the food money so intelligently that family meals are nutritious meals. If her funds are ample, her choice of foods is unlimited and her problem should be an easy one. On the other hand, when the homemaker has to make every penny count, she must plan carefully to make the diet for her family an

1. Keep the servings in the Meat and Fish Group to two a day. Use frequently a main dish featuring dry beans or dry peas.

2. Use cheese frequently as a main dish instead of using it to replace part of the milk allowance.

3. Use more than four servings of cereals and bread a day, being sure they are either whole-grain or enriched.

4. Keep the servings of fruits and vegetables to four a day.

5. Follow the recommendations in Canada's Food Guide for the allowance of milk and deep-yellow and dark-green vegetables; also for citrus fruits and other vitamin C–rich fruits and vegetables.

adequate one. The chart above gives some suggestions that she may follow in planning economical menus that still meet the daily allowances stated in Canada's Food Guide. (See pages 10 to 12.)

Adjustments in the servings in Canada's Food Guide suggested in the chart will tend to lower the proportion of the food money that is spent for the more expensive foods and increase the proportion spent for those that are less expensive. As a result, there is not the danger that there will be a sacrifice, because of lack of money, in the allowances for the very important foods—milk, dark-green and deep-yellow vegetables, and the vitamin C–rich foods. Note that it is also possible to make economical choices among individual foods in the groups, as suggested in the Meat and Fish Group in item 1, for the sake of further economy in the food budget.

Buying Food

Before the homemaker is ready to go to the market to buy the food she has planned for her meals, she must decide what foods to buy and list them so that her trip to the stores may be made without taking an undue amount of time. Also, there are the questions of which markets she will patronize and which day of the week she will be likely to find foods most economically priced in them.

The Foods to Buy

Before buying foods, the homemaker must know (1) how many servings she will need, (2) the form she desires, (3) the quality she can use or wants, and (4) the quantity to buy.

The number of servings. In deciding how much of each food she should buy, the homemaker must have some idea of the number of servings she can expect to get from the market units of different foods. For example, how many servings will each one of these make: a pound of onions, one package of frozen broccoli, a 28 fl. oz. can of sliced peaches, a pound of chuck roast of beef, a pound of ground beef?

19 ozs   28 ozs

● Knowing the number of servings in cans of different sizes helps in buying the amount of food you need.

The tables on pages 78–81 and 82 give helpful information of this sort. The "Food Buying Guide" gives the approximate measure of food and the approximate number of servings in a given market unit of many foods. The figures in this table take into consideration the amount of natural waste in foods. Natural waste consists of such things as bone and fat in meats, pods of peas, and unusable outer leaves of lettuce, cauliflower, and broccoli. The second table, "Common Container Sizes," gives the can size and the approximate number of cups of the food contained in the can. It also lists the products usually packed in the cans of each size.

The information in these two tables makes it possible for the homemaker to compare the cost of one serving of several foods of a similar kind. If she knows this, she can decide which food is the most economical one to buy. For example, if she knows the cost of the market unit of a food and the number of servings she can get from this unit, all she needs to do is to divide the cost by the number of servings to find the cost per serving. Comparisons like this are valuable and should be a part of getting ready to market. It is really the cost of each serving that counts in the food bills, and even many half cents saved can mount to quite a sum over a period of time. Costs of servings may be made at home when foods are advertised in the newspapers. Otherwise they must be made quickly in the market.

The forms. There is also a decision to be made in regard to the forms of food to buy. Grocers' shelves are well stocked with many foods in several different forms. In addition to fresh forms, which may be packaged and ready to use or serve, there are frozen foods, canned foods, dried foods, packaged mixes, instant foods, ready-to-eat cereals, and bakery products—all in great variety to make meal preparation easy. The choice of which form to buy will depend on the time available for meal preparation, the family's likes and dislikes, the use to be made of the food, and the cost. Where there is an extra cost, it is for the labor involved in the pre-preparation of the product. The more nearly ready a food is for use, the more it is likely to cost.

The quality. The homemaker must also decide on the quality of food she will buy. It is not always necessary to buy top-quality foods, since there are many uses for which foods of lower quality, and usually lower cost, will serve equally well. For example: The best eggs are fine for breakfast because of their superior size and flavor, but eggs of a lower quality will be satisfactory for use as an ingredient in a recipe. Apples that have a few skin blemishes are just as good as perfect apples for cooking. Canned tomatoes of a lower quality are equally as suitable as tomatoes of a higher grade for making scalloped tomatoes or a tomato sauce. Top-quality tomatoes, however, should be used when they are served plain, since the unbroken, deep-red tomatoes look more attractive than the lighter-colored pieces that are found in canned tomatoes of a lower quality.

The quantity. There are times when it is good marketing practice for the homemaker to buy food in larger quantities than she wants for immediate use. It is necessary that suitable storage space be available and that there be an opportunity to use the food while it is in good condition. Otherwise such a buying practice would result in a waste of food and a loss of money.

● Buy less-tender cuts of meat instead of tender cuts.

● Buy dried or evaporated milk instead of fresh milk.

● Buy lower grades instead of the top grade of some foods.

● Buy the least expensive form—whether fresh, frozen, or canned.

Foods that do not lose quality quickly, such as shortening, flour, and sugar, may be bought in the largest-sized packages that can be stored conveniently and used in a reasonable length of time. A family that does a lot of baking might very well buy flour in 25-pound bags, or even larger quantities, and sugar in 10- or 25-pound bags at one time. But a family that does little or no baking should probably buy only a 2-pound bag. In contrast to these foods, certain other foods cannot be held too long: potatoes may sprout, bread become stale or even moldy, and fresh meats become unfit for use.

The Market Order

A list of foods to be bought when going to market is essential for efficient marketing. This list should have on it the foods that must be bought for preparing meals for several days in advance and any staple foods that are known to be in short supply. It is a good idea to have a pad handy in

THE FOOD DOLLAR

● Buy margarine instead of butter for cooking or as a spread.

● Buy vegetable shortening for cooking and baking.

● Buy the largest quantity you can reasonably use.

● Buy cereals that require cooking instead of the ready-to-eat ones.

the kitchen on which to jot down these staple items as soon as they are noted.

In preparing a market order, the foods should be grouped according to kind. For example, all the dairy products should be listed together, as should all frozen foods, all fruits and vegetables, all meats, and all items for baking. This plan will save shopping time in the market.

In addition to listing foods according to kind, a good market order should have on it the amounts of the various foods that the

homemaker has decided she needs and, when there is a choice, the quality or brand of the product she wants.

With such a carefully prepared list as this, the homemaker can be quite certain that she is managing her food expenditures wisely. However, there are times when she may decide to change her plans. This can happen when she gets to the store and looks over the foods that are on her list. If the quality and cost of any of these foods are not what she expects, she can make another

(Continued on page 81)

FOOD BUYING GUIDE*

For: *Beverages*   *Dairy products*   *Fruits*   *Poultry*
        Cereals   *Fish and shellfish*   *Meats*   *Vegetables*

Group	Item	Market Unit	Approximate Measure as Purchased	Approximate Number of Servings per Market Unit
Beverages	Chocolate	8 ounces	8 squares	30
	Cocoa	8 ounces	2 cups	50
	Coffee	1 pound	5 cups	40–50
	Instant coffee	2 ounces	1 cup	25–30
	Lemonade	1 dozen lemons	2 cups (juice)	16
	Tea	1 pound	6–8 cups	300
Cereals	Bread	1 pound	12–16 slices	
	Corn flakes	18 ounces	16–20 cups	18 (1 cup)
	Corn meal and farina	1 pound	3 cups	25 (⅔ cup)
	Hominy grits	1 pound	2½ cups	15 (⅔ cup)
	Macaroni	1 pound	4–5 cups	14 (⅔ cup)
	Noodles	1 pound	6–8 cups	14 (⅔ cup)
	Rice	1 pound	2⅓–2⅔ cups	12 (⅔ cup)
	Rolled oats	1 pound	5 cups	12 (⅔ cup)
	Spaghetti	1 pound	4–5 cups	15 (⅔ cup)
	Crackers, graham	1 pound	About 66 crackers	15 crackers make 1 cup crumbs
	Crackers, soda	1 pound	About 160 crackers	22 crackers make 1 cup crumbs
Dairy products	Butter	1 pound	2 cups	48 squares (⅓ ounce)
	Cheese, Cheddar	1 pound	4 cups grated	16 (¼ cup)
	Cheese, cottage	1 pound	2 cups	6 (⅓ cup)
	Cream, coffee	1 quart	4 cups (64 tablespoons)	40–50
	Cream, whipping	1 quart	4 cups (7–8 cups whipped)	40–50
	Ice cream	1 quart		6–8
	Milk	1 quart	4 cups	4 (8-ounce) glasses
	Milk, evaporated	1 tall can (16 ounces)	1¾ cups	Equals 3½ cups milk
		1 small can (6 ounces)	⅔ cup	Equals 1⅓ cups milk
	Dry whole milk	1 pound	4¼ cups	Makes 4–4½ quarts milk
	Nonfat dry milk			
	Powder	1 pound	4 cups	Makes 5 quarts milk
	Crystals	1 pound	5⅔ cups	Makes 4¼ quarts milk
	Milk, sweetened, condensed	1 can (15 ounces)	1⅓ cups	Equals 2½ cups milk + 8 tablespoons sugar
Fish and shellfish	Fish, whole	1 pound		1
	Fish, drawn	1 pound		2
	Fish, dressed	1 pound		2
	Fish steaks	1 pound		3
	Fish fillets	1 pound		3
	Fish sticks	1 pound		3
	Clams, live	1 dozen		2
	Clams, shucked	1 pint		3

Group	Item	Market Unit	Approximate Measure as Purchased	Approximate Number of Servings per Market Unit
Fish and shellfish (cont.)	Crab meat	1 pound		6
	Crabs, blue, live	1 dozen		4
	Crabs, Dungeness	1 pound		1
	Crabs, soft-shell	1 pound		2
	Lobster meat	1 pound		6
	Lobster, live	1 pound		1
	Oysters, live	1 dozen		2
	Oysters, shucked	1 pint		3
	Scallops, shucked	1 pound		3
	Shrimp, headless	1 pound		4
	Spiny lobster tails	1 pound		2
Fruit juice, frozen concentrated	Orange, grape, pineapple, pineapple and orange, pineapple and grapefruit	6 fluid ounces		Yields 1½ pints
		12 fluid ounces		Yields 1½ quarts
	Lemonade and limeade	6 fluid ounces		Yields 1 quart
		12 fluid ounces		Yields 2 quarts
Fruits, dried	Apples	1 pound	4 cups	16–20 (½ cup)
	Currants	1 pound	3 cups	
	Dates	1 pound	2½ cups (60)	
	Figs	1 pound	3 cups (44)	10
	Peaches	1 pound	3 cups	12 (½ cup)
	Prunes	1 pound	2½ cups	8
	Raisins	1 pound	3 cups seedless 2½ cups seeded	
Fruits, fresh	Apples	1 pound	3 medium	3
	Apricots	1 pound	8–12	5
	Avocado	1 pound	1	2
	Bananas	1 pound	3	3
	Berries			
	Strawberries	1 quart		4
	Blueberries	1 quart		6
	Cranberries	1 pound	1 quart	16 (⅛ cup)
	Cherries, red	1 quart	2 cups pitted	4 (½ cup)
	Grapefruit	1 pound	1 medium	2
	Grapes			
	Concord	1 pound	1 quart	4
	Tokay	1 pound	2¾ cups seeded	
	Lemons	1 dozen medium	3 pounds	Yields 1 pint juice
	Oranges	1 dozen medium	6 pounds	Yields 1 quart juice, 3 quarts diced
	Peaches	1 pound	4 medium	4
	Pears	1 pound	4 medium	4
	Pineapple	2 pounds	1 medium	6 (½ cup)
	Plums	1 pound	8–20	4
	Rhubarb	1 pound	4–8 stalks	4 (½ cup)
Fruits, frozen		10–16 ounce packages	1–2 cups	2–4

Group	Item	Market Unit	Approximate Measure as Purchased	Approximate Number of Servings per Market Unit
Meats	Boned or ground meat Flank, clod, beef roll, tenderloin, boneless loin, sirloin butt, sirloin strip, heel of round, liver, heart, kidneys, brains, sweetbreads, tongue, sausages, wieners	1 pound		About 4
	Meat with medium amount of bone Steaks, ham slices, rib roasts, chuck, chops, rump roasts, loin roast	1 pound		2–3
	Meat with large amount of bone Shoulder cuts, short ribs, spareribs, neck, breasts, plate, brisket, shank	1 pound		1–2
Poultry[1]	Chicken, ready-to-cook			
	Broiler	1 pound		¼–½ bird per serving
	Fryer	1 pound		2
	Roaster	1 pound		2
	Stewing	1 pound		2
	Duck, ready-to-cook	1 pound		1
	Goose, ready-to-cook	1 pound		1½
	Turkey, ready-to-cook	1 pound		2
Vegetables, dried	Kidney beans	1 pound	2½ cups	9 (¾ cup)
	Lima beans	1 pound	2½ cups	8 (¾ cup)
	Navy beans	1 pound	2⅓ cups	8 (¾ cup)
	Split peas	1 pound	2 cups	7 (¾ cup)
Vegetables, fresh	Asparagus	1 pound	16–20 stalks	4
	Beans, lima, in pod	1 pound	⅔ cup shelled	2 (⅓ cup)
	Beans, lima, shelled	1 pound	2 cups	6 (⅓ cup)
	Beans, snap	1 pound	3 cups, 1 inch	5 (½ cup)
	Beets	1 pound	2 cups diced	4
	Broccoli	1 pound		3
	Brussels sprouts	1 pound	1 quart or less	5
	Cabbage			
	Raw	1 pound	4 cups shredded	7
	Cooked	1 pound		4 (½ cup)
	Carrots	1 pound	2½ cups diced or shredded	5 (½ cup)

The modern supermarket, with its spacious meat, fish, dairy, produce, grocery, and delicatessen departments, offers thousands of different items for the consumers' choice.

● One-dish meals—cooked in the oven or on top of the range—are timesavers because they can be easily prepared and their use eliminates the necessity for extra utensils and serving dishes.

● Fish chowders, with milk and vegetables as part of the ingredients, are rich in nutrients, and with the addition of a salad, they are hearty enough to make a complete main course for a meal.

● An inexpensive and easily prepared meal is a mock porterhouse steak made of ground beef held in shape with strips of bacon. This is broiled on a plank and garnished with mashed potatoes, peas, and carrots to lend variety and interest to the meal.

● Meals prepared with convenience foods can be attractive and nutritious: Canned corned beef hash, corn bread made from a quick mix, sliced melon salad, and a glass of milk are an example of such a meal.

● In a large kitchen such as this, there is adequate space for all work centers and enough space for a desk where menus can be planned, market orders can be made out, and phone calls can be made and received. There is also space for a dining area.

● Small kitchens can be attractive as well as convenient. In this kitchen, with a parallel-wall arrangement, steps are kept to a minimum and work can progress in an orderly fashion from one work center to another because each is near the other.

Courtesy Wood-Mode Kitchens

● Today's kitchens are designed to lighten work, to save steps, and to add extra beauty to the room. In this kitchen, the island cooking unit holds all the utensils and tools needed at the range; a modern refrigerator-freezer, at the left, is concealed by paneled wood doors; and the brick wall double oven has an arched recess for a barbecue pit.

Group	Item	Market Unit	Approximate Measure as Purchased	Approximate Number of Servings per Market Unit
Vegetables, fresh (cont.)	Cauliflower	1 pound	1½ cups	3 (½ cup)
	Celery	1 pound	2 medium bunches or 2 cups diced	4 (½ cup cooked)
	Corn, cut	1 pound		5
	Corn, ears	12 medium	3 cups cut	6
	Eggplant	1 pound	2½ cups diced, 11½-inch slices	5 (½ cup)
	Greens	1 pound		4
	Mushrooms	1 pound	35–45	6
	Onions	1 pound	3 large	4
	Parsnips	1 pound	4 medium	4
	Peas in pod	1 pound	1 cup shelled	2
	Potatoes, sweet	1 pound	3 medium	3
	Potatoes, white	1 pound	3 medium	3
	Rutabaga	1 pound	2½ cups diced	5 (½ cup)
	Squash, Hubbard	1 pound	2⅔ cups diced	4
	Squash, summer	1 pound		2
	Tomatoes	1 pound		3
			4 small	3 (cooked)
			16 slices	4 (raw)
	Turnips	1 pound	3 medium	4 (½ cup)
Vegetables, frozen		9–16 ounce packages	1½–2½ cups	3–6

¹ Yield is 20% less from dressed than from ready-to-cook poultry.

* From *Handbook of Food Preparation*, American Home Economics Association, Washington, D.C., 1959, pp. 7–10.

selection so as to spend the food money to better advantage. Of course this means, in turn, a change in her original menu plans. For example, a cauliflower may prove to be a better buy than the broccoli she had planned to use, or beef for a pot roast may be an exceptionally good buy instead of the chicken. Another time that it is good to keep plans flexible is when some food may be on sale or another one may look especially attractive. Then this food might replace one on the list, or it might be bought for future use if it is a food that will keep in good condition for some time.

Knowing Where and When to Buy

The careful shopper will try to find out not only where but when to buy to best advantage for the best quality of food for the lowest amount of money.

Where to buy. In most communities, there are several stores that sell all kinds of foods and, possibly, several specialty shops that sell only certain kinds. Usually a homemaker has one or two favorite stores.

These may be the ones that are most conveniently located, ones that have a quality of foods that appeal to her, or ones with a friendly atmosphere. But often she can buy to a better advantage in both cost and quality if she spends some time shopping around in other stores before she makes a final purchase. In one of these stores she may find the same quality of meat that she usually buys selling at a lower price, or she may find fruits and vegetables of better quality for the same price in a specialty shop instead of in the supermarket where she customarily trades. Naturally the practice of shopping at several stores takes extra time, but it may pay

COMMON CONTAINER SIZES*

The labels of cans or jars of identical size may show a net weight for one product that differs slightly from the net weight on the label of another product, due to the difference in the density of the food.

Container			Principal Products
Industry Term e.q. 211 = $2\frac{11}{16}$ in.	Consumer Description		
	Approx. Net Weight or Fluid Measure (check label)	Approx. Cups	
202 × 308	5½ oz.	¾	Fruits, vegetables, specialties[1] for small families. 2 servings.
211 × 400	10 oz.	1¼	Mainly condensed soups. Some fruits, vegetables, meat, fish, specialties.[1] 3 servings.
307 × 306	12 oz.	1½	Principally for vacuum pack corn. 3 to 4 servings.
307 × 309	14 oz.	1¾	Pork and beans, baked beans, meat products, cranberry sauce, blueberries, specialties.[1] 3 to 4 servings.
300 × 407	14 oz.	1¾	Principal size for fruits and vegetables. Some meat products, ready-to-serve soups, specialties.[1] 4 servings.
307 × 409	19 oz.	2½	Juices, ready-to-serve soups, some specialties,[1] pineapple, apple slices. No longer in popular use for most fruits and vegetables. 5 servings.
401 × 411	28 oz.	3½	Fruits, some vegetables (pumpkin, sauerkraut, spinach and other greens, tomatoes). 7 servings.
404 × 700	48 oz.	6	"Economy family size" fruit and vegetable juices, pork and beans. Institutional size for condensed soups, some vegetables. 10 to 12 servings.
603 × 700	100 oz.	12½	Institutional size for fruits, vegetables, and some other foods. 25 servings.

Meats, fish, and seafood are almost entirely advertised and sold under weight terminology.

Infant and junior foods come in small cans and jars suitable for the smaller servings used. Content is given on label.

[1] Specialties—Food combinations prepared by special manufacturer's recipe.
* From Canada Agricultural Products Standards Act and Processed Foods and Vegetables Regulations.

CANNED-FOOD BUYING GUIDE

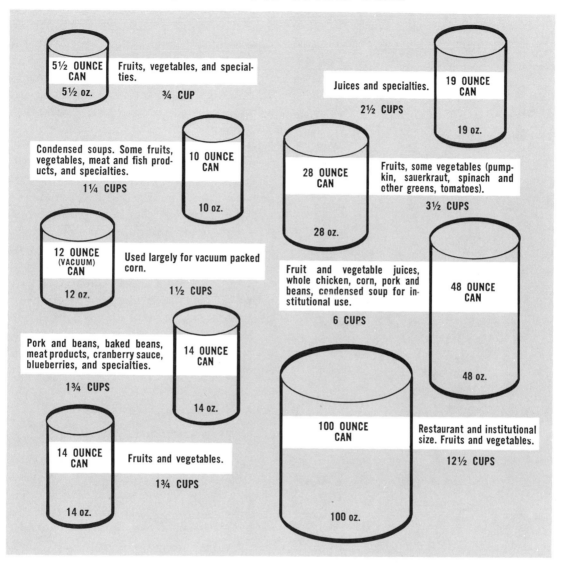

5½ OUNCE CAN — 5½ oz. — Fruits, vegetables, and specialties. ¾ CUP

10 OUNCE CAN — 10 oz. — Condensed soups. Some fruits, vegetables, meat and fish products, and specialties. 1¼ CUPS

12 OUNCE (VACUUM) CAN — 12 oz. — Used largely for vacuum packed corn. 1½ CUPS

14 OUNCE CAN — 14 oz. — Pork and beans, baked beans, meat products, cranberry sauce, blueberries, and specialties. 1¾ CUPS

14 OUNCE CAN — 14 oz. — Fruits and vegetables. 1¾ CUPS

19 OUNCE CAN — 19 oz. — Juices and specialties. 2½ CUPS

28 OUNCE CAN — 28 oz. — Fruits, some vegetables (pumpkin, sauerkraut, spinach and other greens, tomatoes). 3½ CUPS

Fruit and vegetable juices, whole chicken, corn, pork and beans, condensed soup for institutional use. 6 CUPS

48 OUNCE CAN — 48 oz.

100 OUNCE CAN — 100 oz. — Restaurant and institutional size. Fruits and vegetables. 12½ CUPS

● The number of servings for each size of can is given in the last column in the chart on the opposite page.

in the end if getting more value for the money spent is the goal.

In deciding where to buy, a homemaker may be tempted to trade in stores that give trading stamps. The stamps, when accumulated in sufficient numbers, can be used to obtain premiums in household goods. Any store may give trading stamps, but, in general, it is the supermarkets that give them as one means of promoting trade and thus increasing sales. The merchant may or may not raise the price of his merchan-

some later time. It would pay the home-maker to compare the prices of a number of similar foods in a number of markets, including one where stamps are not given, before she decides where to shop.

Discount coupons are another means of sales promotion. Usually these coupons are valid only in a particular market and their value must be applied to definite items, frequently within a definite time period. Some companies insert discount coupons in magazines. The coupons are redeemable in any store in which the goods are sold. Discount coupons can represent a real, though probably small, economy.

When to buy. Some merchants offer weekend specials of some food items. Also newspapers may publish Canada Department of Agriculture lists of plentiful foods. A good manager plans menus to make use of these special offerings. (See Chapter 1, "Planning Meals for the Family," as discussed on page 8.)

Marketing Aids for the Homemaker-Consumer

When the homemaker goes to market, she can have confidence that the food she buys will be wholesome and of specified quality and its package truthfully labeled. This confidence results from laws that regulate the production, processing, packaging, and labeling of the nation's food supply. A buyer should familiarize herself with these laws since they will help her spend food money wisely.

Government Agencies and Food Laws

The primary interest of government agencies in regard to food is to ensure that food is wholesome, and honestly and truthfully packaged and labeled. There are a

● In practically all food markets today—whether large or small—it is the practice for consumers to pay cash for food and carry their purchases home.

dise to cover the cost to him of handling the stamps. If he does increase prices, the consumer does not benefit, since she probably pays in day-to-day spending for the premium goods she gets, supposedly free, at

number of laws in this field but only a few will be mentioned here.

The first law to prevent adulteration of food in Canada was passed in 1875. This law was repealed and replaced by the Food and Drugs Act in 1920. This Act, which is administered by the Food and Drug Directorate of the Department of National Health and Welfare, covers the general principles of food and drug protection while the details are dealt with in the Regulations. A brief outline of some of the Regulations is given in the chart below.

The Meat Inspection Act, incorporating the former Meat and Canned Foods Act, was passed in 1955. It provides that all meat and meat products entering into international and interprovincial trade shall be subject to government inspection and stamped or labelled with the round "Canada Approved" or "Canada" inspection legend indicating that the product is fit for human consumption, but not that the product has been graded for quality.

Quality Grading of Foods

Here again the Federal Government plays a role. The Canada Department of Agriculture has set up quality

PROVISIONS OF THE FOOD AND DRUGS ACT AND REGULATIONS

The Food and Drug Regulations define actual standards of composition or identity. They also state, among other things, what information must appear on the label and where on the label some of this information must appear; what additives may be used in foods, and where, how and in what quantities they may be used. In addition, they establish a list of safe limits for residues of pesticides and weed killers that may appear on foods as a result of farm spraying programs.

Certain information must appear on the main panel of the label.

a. The brand or trade name, if any.
b. The common name; i.e., the name by which the produce is commonly recognized.
c. The net declaration of contents for all packages weighing more than two ounces gross.
d. If composed of more than one ingredient, and if there is no standard for the food in the regulations, a complete listing of ingredients by their common name, in descending order of proportion or by percentage.
e. A declaration of any preservative used.

f. A declaration of any added food color or artificial flavor.
g. In the case of dietetic foods, information considered necessary for the purchaser to know.
h. The name and address of the manufacturer.

Descriptive labelling may be added voluntarily by the manufacturer. For example:

a. Suggested uses for the product.
b. An indication of brand name registration.
c. Recipes.
d. A slogan.

grades for many foods. The use of Federal quality grades is not mandatory. Therefore a food processor may observe them or not as he elects.

As you know, foods of all kinds have characteristics that distinguish them from other foods. It is in terms of these special characteristics that foods are judged and standards of quality set up. Two examples will make this clear. (1) When fresh, the shell of an egg is dull and velvety looking, the white is quite firm, and the yolk round and upstanding. (2) Canned tomatoes are considered of good quality when they are attractive to look at—a bright deep-red color, pieces that are fairly large, and that have no defects.

Information on quality grading and labeling of the various foods appears in Part IV. Foods processed according to Federal specifications for quality grades usually carry labels that denote the grade. (See chart on page 90.)

Labels as Aids in Marketing

A label is considered to be all the written or printed matter that accompanies a food in any way—either tied to it, printed on it, or attached to or contained in the package holding the food. According to the Food and Drugs Act and Regulations, labels must give the information listed in the chart on page 85. But labels usually give more information, designed to help the buyer. The label shown illustrates some types of such additional information.

When manufacturers of foods follow the official government standards and indicate the quality of the product on the label, the buyer knows what to expect in the quality of her purchases. She can then buy for a certain planned use. But some processors

WHAT THE LABEL TELLS YOU

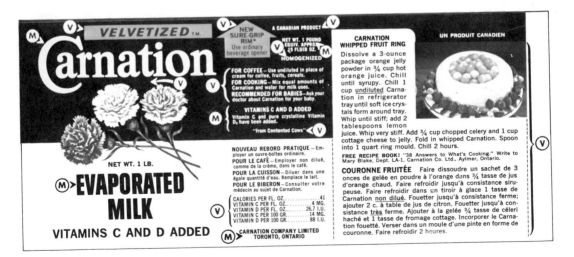

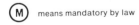 means mandatory by law

(V) means voluntary by canner

● A carefully prepared market list will enable the consumer to buy wisely.

set up their own specifications for quality grades of the foods they manufacture and label the products with what is known as a "brand name." In these cases the buyer must rely on this name. This is quite all right when, through use, she has found brands of the foods she frequently uses that give her satisfaction. There are so many brands of the same kind of food that a real test to determine the best brand for a special use takes time as well as money.

The very large offering of partly and fully prepared foods of all kinds in markets today adds a note of confusion for the homemaker. Many of these foods are not those for which definitions, or standards of identity, have been established by the Food and Drug Directorate, and they do not carry any grade information. Here again the homemaker will need to rely on brand names to guide her in making a selection or base her decision on experience resulting from repeated purchases.

Thrifty Ways with Food

Every homemaker has her own ideas of thrifty ways with food, and most homemakers read articles in magazines and newspapers about stretching the food dollar. The management practices that have been discussed in this chapter are basic ones to follow if the food dollar is to go as far as possible. But managing meals to get one's money's worth involves more than planning what food to buy and buying it. Also important is the way the food is cared for after it is brought home, how it is prepared and served, and what use is made of food that is left over.

Proper Storage of Food

Food should be brought home as soon as possible after it is bought to avoid deterioration. At home the storage conditions for each kind of food must be right so that it will keep its original quality until used. If there is any spoilage, or even a lowering of quality, food as well as money is wasted. Care of food in the home is discussed in the chapters in Part IV. In the chart on pages 88 and 89 there is a summary of proper

(Continued on page 91)

● Grade A eggs are not essential for all purposes. Grade B eggs are suitable for baking as well as for some egg dishes. Eggs of both grades are equally nutritious.

CARE OF FOOD TO RETAIN QUALITY
REFRIGERATOR STORAGE (37°–40° F.)

Food	How Cover	Approximate Time Limit	Comments
Milk, cream	Tightly	3 days	Unpasteurized milk sours and pasteurized milk spoils quickly at room temperature.
Butter, margarine	Tightly	2 weeks	Absorption of unwanted odors and rancidity cause disagreeable flavors.
Eggs	Loosely	3 weeks	Moisture evaporates through the shell if air is dry or warm, and deterioration starts quickly.
Cheese			
Unripened: Soft and semisoft varieties	Loosely	3 days	These cheeses lose quality, and spoilage starts quickly. They should be used promptly.
Ripened: Very hard, hard, and process varieties	Tightly	2–3 weeks	These cheeses keep well when not exposed to the air. Keep in original wrapper; after opening, wrap in foil, wax paper, or plastic wrapping material.
Meats			
Small cuts, organ meats	Loosely	2 days	Original wrapping should be removed. Covering should be loose to permit some evaporation and drying of surface to discourage bacterial growth.
Large cuts beef	Loosely	1 week	
Other meats	Loosely	4 days	
Ground meat	Loosely	1 day	
Fish	Tightly	1–2 days	Better if used promptly because fish spoils quickly.
Poultry	Loosely	1–2 days	Same as fish.
Fresh fruits			
Citrus juice	Tightly	24 hours	Oxygen in air destroys ascorbic acid if held longer.
Berries	Uncovered and spread out	2 days	Subject to rapid deterioration.
Apples	Uncovered	3 weeks (keep dry)	Some varieties of apples may be kept for months.

Food	How Cover	Approximate Time Limit	Comments
Pears	Uncovered	3 weeks	
Peaches	Uncovered	3 weeks	
Citrus fruits	Uncovered	5 weeks (keep in damp air)	
Melons	Uncovered	1 week (keep dry)	
Vegetables, such as lettuce, spinach, cabbage, cauliflower, broccoli, snap beans, celery	Loosely	5 days	Should be protected against loss of moisture to delay wilting and spoilage.
Nut meats	Very tightly	4 months	Rancidity of oil in nuts caused by air and warm atmosphere makes flavor disagreeable.
Salad oils and dressings after opening	Tightly, using original cover	Several months	Rancidity caused by air and too high temperature causes disagreeable flavors. Wiping off of bottle or jar opening a good practice.
Desserts, such as milk puddings, custard pies, éclairs, cream puffs	Loosely	1 day	Desserts made of milk and cream should be eaten very soon, for spoilage is rapid.
Cooked meats	Tightly	2–5 days	

FREEZER STORAGE (0° F. OR LOWER)*

Food	How Cover	Approximate Time Limit	Comments
Fruits	Tightly	1 year	Keep all frozen foods frozen constantly throughout storage time.
Vegetables	Tightly	8 months	
Meats, large cuts			
Beef	Tightly	1 year	Ground meats and cut-up pieces of meat and poultry should not be kept so long as the large cuts.
Lamb	Tightly	1 year	
Veal	Tightly	8 months	
Pork	Tightly	8 months	
Poultry, whole	Tightly	1 year	

*From Consumers All: The Yearbook of Agriculture, U.S. Department of Agriculture, 1965.

CANADA GRADES AT A GLANCE

MEATS

Product	1st Grade	2nd Grade	3rd Grade	4th Grade	5th Grade	6th Grade
Beef	Canada Choice	Canada Good	Canada Standard	Canada Commercial*°	Canada Utility*	
Veal	Canada Choice	Canada Good	Canada Standard	Canada Commercial*°	Canada Utility*	
Lamb	Canada Choice	Canada Good	Canada Standard	Canada Commercial*°	Canada Utility*	
Mutton	Canada Choice	Canada Good	Canada Standard	Canada Commercial*°	Canada Utility*	
Color of Grade Mark	Red	Blue	Brown	Black	Black	

DAIRY PRODUCTS

Product	1st Grade	2nd Grade	3rd Grade	4th Grade	5th Grade	6th Grade
Butter	Canada First Grade	Canada Second Grade*	Canada Third Grade*	Below Canada Third Grade*		
Cheddar Cheese	Canada First Grade	Canada Second Grade*	Canada Third Grade*	Below Canada Third Grade*		
Instant Skim Milk	Canada First Grade					

POULTRY AND EGGS

Product	1st Grade	2nd Grade	3rd Grade	4th Grade	5th Grade	6th Grade
Poultry	Canada Grade Special*	Canada Grade A	Canada Grade B	Canada Grade Utility	Canada Grade C*	Canada Grade D*
Color of Tag	Purple	Red	Blue	Blue	Yellow	Brown
Eggs	Canada Grade A1	Canada Grade A	Canada Grade B	Canada Grade C*	Canada Grade Cracks*	

PROCESSED FRUITS AND VEGETABLES

Canada Fancy   Canada Choice   Canada Standard

* Not usually available in retail stores.
° Canada Commercial is subdivided into three classes—Class 1, Class 2, Class 3.
From Food Grading in Canada—Canada Department of Agriculture—Publication 1283, 1966.

storage conditions for a number of foods. This chart gives the temperatures for storage, how foods should be covered, the approximate length of time usually advised as the storage limit, and some comments of possible changes the foods may undergo if not stored properly.

Careful Preparation of Food

Another way to get full value of the food money is to prepare food carefully. Although it is not possible to improve poor food to any extent in preparing it, it is quite easy to spoil the quality of good food.

WAYS TO USE LEFTOVER FOOD

MEAT AND POULTRY

1. Slice cold and serve with a sauce or relish —chili sauce, catsup, mustard, piccalilli, etc.

2. Reheat in the oven, wrapped in foil to keep the juices in.

3. Slice and reheat in the gravy, adding an herb for different flavor.

4. Slice or chop and use for sandwiches with lettuce and salad dressing.

5. Sliver and mix into a tossed salad.

6. Serve creamed, either plain or as à la king.

7. Make into a stew with leftover gravy and fresh vegetables.

8. Make into a pie with vegetables (also leftovers) and top with pastry, biscuit, or mashed potato.

9. Use as a basis for soup.

10. Make into croquettes or a soufflé.

VEGETABLES

1. Reheat in a saucepan with just enough water to prevent burning. Add butter or margarine, or cover with a cream sauce.

2. Mix with leftover meat or poultry for a stew or pie.

3. Scallop, either plain or with cheese, bits of bacon, or herbs.

4. Purée and use for a soufflé or a cream soup.

5. Make into a salad.

FRUITS

1. Save several kinds and mix together for a fruit cup.

2. Cut and add to a package of prepared gelatin for a molded salad or dessert.

3. Cover with a biscuit dough for a fruit cobbler.

4. Use as a garnish for tapioca cream or Spanish cream.

5. To extra juice add some lemon juice and thicken for a pudding sauce, or use as the liquid for a packaged mix.

BREAD

1. Make into French toast.

2. Cube for scalloped tomatoes, apple brown Betty, or bread pudding.

3. Use as a stuffing for poultry or for pork or veal chops.

4. Make croutons or bread sticks for a soup or salad.

5. Dry to make crumbs for coating foods or for toppings to scalloped dishes.

WAYS TO USE LEFTOVERS

Courtesy Tender Leaf Tea

● Using small amounts of leftover vegetables —raw or cooked—in a salad saves food, adds nutrients, and gives variety to the salad.

Courtesy National Live Stock and Meat Board

● A favorite way to use leftover meat from a roast or steak is to grind it and make it into croquettes.

Courtesy Corning Glass Works

● Another way to extend leftover meat or chicken is to cut it into pieces and add it to a flavorful cream sauce to be served with hot biscuits.

There is danger also of lessening its food value, which is a waste of food and money. When cooking food, or otherwise getting it ready to serve without cooking, such as a salad or fruit cup, the finished product can measure up to a high standard of quality only if the fundamental principles of cookery are followed. In your study of the individual foods (Part IV), you will find that these principles of preparation involve the handling of foods both before and during cooking. These principles also involve cooking temperatures and times and the promptness of serving the foods when they are ready. Foods that are prepared according to basic principles are attractive to look at and so palatable that none is wasted because it is not eaten.

Skillful Use of Leftover Food

When buying food, it is often hard to come out even with the amount needed, and then the task of using that which is left over becomes a problem. The chart on page 91 lists some ways in which extra food may be used.

No matter what it is, the use of a leftover food presents a challenge. There are many ideas in cookbooks and magazines, but you will also want to use your own imagination. In any case, remember that for a dish of leftovers to be appetizing, it is important

● Leftover food will stay fresh longer if wrapped well before refrigeration.

that the food have a good flavor. Here, then, is a place to try seasoning a main dish, vegetable, or salad. Small amounts of highly flavored cheeses, like Blue or Roquefort, add a piquant flavor; chives and garlic are liked by some; and herbs, such as basil, rosemary, marjoram, and oregano, are well worth investigating when the problem is to make a leftover food interesting.

6

Management

in the

Kitchen

■ BESIDES the timesaving and effort-saving ways employed in meal preparation, the kitchen itself and the equipment in it play a large part in efficient meal management. The size and shape of the kitchen, the number of doors and windows in it and where they are placed, and the pieces of equipment and utensils selected and where they are placed influence the amount of time spent each day in the kitchen doing the many tasks connected with the preparation of meals. A well-planned, well-equipped, well-lighted, and well-ventilated kitchen makes it possible to do these tasks in the least time, with a minimum of confusion and fatigue, and with maximum safety.

The kitchen should be a comfortable place in which to work as well as convenient and efficient. To be convenient and efficient, the kitchen need not be new or remodeled, nor need it be equipped with the latest in kitchen equipment. Many a kitchen is both convenient and efficient, even though it is not new. There is a challenge, however, to a homemaker in planning ways to rearrange large pieces of equipment or relocating utensils and appliances in her present kitchen for better working efficiency.

No one kitchen style suits every family equally well because of differences in the way families live. In some homes, in addition to preparing meals, the kitchen is used for other purposes also, but these other activities should not interfere with the kitchen's primary function. Sometimes the kitchen is too small to use for any purpose except meal preparation, while in other situations the kitchen becomes a sort of living center. Some families eat only breakfast in the kitchen, while other families eat all meals there. Or a family may want to eat in a dining area adjacent to the kitchen, although not actually a part of it. A breakfast table in an alcove or, when the kitchen is large enough, at one side of the room, provides an adequate dining area. Some mothers like a spot where young children can be watched at their play while kitchen work is being done. For these mothers a play area and space for toy storage is desirable. Perhaps a breakfast nook can be made to double as a play area. Some families like to have a typewriter or a sewing machine in the kitchen, and some like a center where members of the family can relax or read.

To learn about the factors that make for efficiency and comfort in the kitchen, you will need information about the centers in the kitchen where food is stored, prepared, and served, and where the cleaning up is done; the arrangement of these centers in the room; the lighting and ventilating; and the pieces of equipment needed in each center.

Work Centers

There are three definite types of work connected with meal preparation, and the place where each type of work is done is called a "work center" or "work area." The kitchen is therefore planned around these three work centers. The three types of work done in the kitchen are (1) the preparing of food, (2) the cooking and serving of food, and (3) the cleaning up after the meal has been cooked and eaten. The work center where food is prepared is called a "food storage and preparation center" or merely a "food-preparation center." Here the foods needing preparation for serving are made ready. Most of these foods are kept in a nearby refrigerator or cabinet. The center where food is cooked and served is called a "cooking and serving center," and the center where the cleaning of food and dishes is done is called a "cleaning center" or, sometimes, a "dishwashing center."

When the size of the kitchen permits space for these three necessary work centers with space left over, centers for other activities may be considered. The first of these might be a planning center to facilitate meal planning and preparation. Here cookbooks and recipes can be filed, bills can be taken care of, and menus and grocery lists can be decided upon. A planning desk is a handy place for letter writing and for a telephone. It is a good spot for a TV set or radio, and the surface of a planning desk can double as an extra work counter. When there is no place for a planning desk, the activities just mentioned may be taken care of at one of the regular work surfaces, at a pull-out board, or in the dining area. A drawer can serve as a file for recipes and bills.

The location of each of the work centers depends to a great extent on the size and shape of the kitchen. However, the work centers should be arranged so that there will be little or no traffic through them and so that work can be carried on from one center to another in one direction.

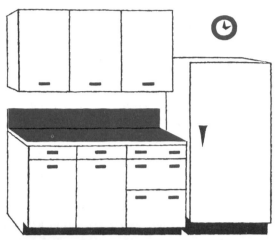

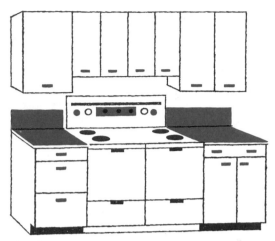

● The food storage and preparation center consists of a refrigerator for perishables, cabinets for staples and for utensils used in mixing and baking, and a work surface.

● The cooking and serving center consists of a range, an adjacent work surface, and storage space for those foods, utensils, and dishes needed in cooking and serving meals.

ARTICLES AT FOOD STORAGE AND PREPARATION CENTER

FOOD SUPPLIES FOR REFRIGERATOR STORAGE

Dairy products	Fruits	Meat	Poultry
Eggs	Vegetables	Fish	Frozen foods

FOOD SUPPLIES FOR CABINET STORAGE

Shortening	Sugar	Prepared mixes	Coconut
Flour	Cornstarch	Spices and herbs	Gelatin
Baking powder	Evaporated milk	Bread crumbs	Syrups and molasses
Soda	Nonfat dry-milk	Canned foods	Vacuum-packed nuts
Salt and pepper	solids	Chocolate	Extracts

UTENSILS FOR CABINET STORAGE

Mixing bowls	Baking pans	Mixing spoons	Graters
Scraper	Bread	Spatula	Cookie sheets
Beater	Cake	Scissors	Cutters
Forks	Pie	Fruit reamer	Biscuit
Knives	Muffin	Strainers	Cookie
Slicing	Casseroles	Pastry blender	Doughnut
Paring	Can and bottle openers	Pastry brush	Flour sifter
Measuring cups	Chopping bowl and knife	Rolling pin	Salad bowl
Measuring spoons	Food grinder		

The Food Storage and Preparation Center

A refrigerator for the storage of perishable foods, cabinets for the storage of staple foods, and utensils used in mixing and baking are needed at the food storage and preparation center. A work surface, such as a table or counter, and possibly small electric appliances, such as an electric mixer and a toaster, are also needed. For convenience, such food supplies and utensils as those given in the chart on the opposite page should be kept at the food storage and preparation center.

The Cooking and Serving Center

Since food is cooked and served at the cooking and serving center, this center needs a range and also a counter or table on which to place food after it has been cooked and to hold serving dishes. Cabinets are needed for the storage of certain foods and for those utensils and dishes used for cooking and serving. For a suggested list of the articles to be kept in the cabinets, see the chart on page 98.

The Cleaning Center

The cleaning center should be located where it is adjacent to or easily accessible to the other two work centers. It is, as a rule, used more than any other kitchen work center because water is necessary for so many of the processes in preparing a meal and cleaning up afterward—for washing such foods as vegetables and fruits before storing, cooking, or serving them; for cooking vegetables and making many soups and hot or cold beverages; for soaking or rinsing soiled mixing utensils and bowls, pots and pans, and dishes after use; and for washing dishes and cooking utensils at the end of the meal. The sink be-

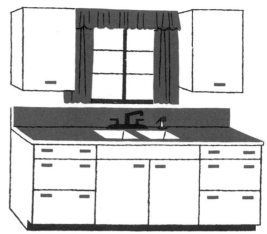

● The cleaning center consists of a sink and base cabinets for storing cleaning supplies and utensils. Certain fruits and vegetables that need no refrigeration may also be stored in these base cabinets provided there are ventilated bins. The wall cabinets above the sink can be used to store the glassware and dishes.

comes, therefore, the main piece of equipment at this center. Facilities for storing dishwashing equipment and cleaning supplies are necessary, and counters on which to place both food and dishes are needed.

Work surfaces are needed on both sides of the sink. One is for stacking soiled dishes, while the work surface or counter on the other side of the sink is needed for the clean, ready-to-dry dishes and the dishes after they have been dried.

Food supplies that do not require refrigeration, such as some fruits and vegetables, can be stored in ventilated bins at or near the cleaning center. Sometimes such bins are part of the cabinets placed at one side of the sink.

Utensils and supplies needed at the cleaning center should be kept at the center or nearby. Base cabinets below and at the side of the sink should provide space for the storage of the dishwashing equipment and

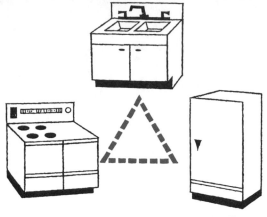

● A kitchen is well designed and efficient when a line drawn to connect one work area with the others forms a triangle.

cleaning supplies. There should also be a rack for dish towels in use and provision for refuse disposers. Drawers in these cabinets should be available for cutlery used at the cleaning center and for the storage of clean towels and aprons. Wall cabinets over the sink or over base cabinets adjacent to the sink are useful for the storage of glassware and dishes. When such space is available for them, these articles can be put away as they are dried. A suggested list of cleaning supplies and utensils to be stored at the cleaning center is given in the chart below.

The Design of the Kitchen

The plan of the kitchen is a factor in determining what equipment can be selected, its size, and the way it is arranged. When the work centers are arranged so that work

ARTICLES AT COOKING AND SERVING CENTER

FOOD SUPPLIES FOR CABINET STORAGE

Salt	Cakes
Pepper	Cookies
To-be-cooked cereals	Jellies
Ready-to-eat cereals	Meat sauces
Bread	Coffee
Crackers	Tea

UTENSILS AND DISHES FOR CABINET STORAGE

Breadbox	Serving dishes
Skillets	Coffee maker
Forks, long handled	Teakettle
Knives	Teapot and strainer
Slicing	Cooling racks
Paring	Ladle
Spoons	Potato masher
Wooden	Roaster
Metal	Tongs
Measuring cups	Chicken fryer
Measuring spoons	Deep-fat kettle
Pancake turner	Griddle
Spatula	Steamer
Covers (lids)	

ARTICLES AT CLEANING CENTER

CLEANING SUPPLIES

Brushes	Silver cleaner
Cleaning powders	Dishcloths
Soaps and detergents	Dish towels
Metal polishes	Paper towels
Scouring pads	Wax paper

UTENSILS

Vegetable cutting board	Shears
Towel rack	Sink strainer
Draining rack	Wastebasket
Dishpan	Colander
Scraper	Double boiler
Garbage container	Strainer
Knives	Vegetable slicer
Saucepans	Apple corer

TYPES OF KITCHENS

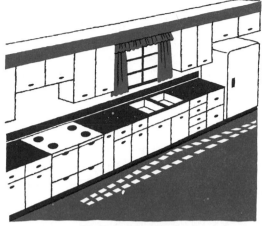

● One-wall kitchen

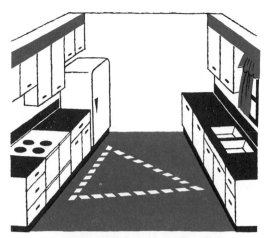

● Parallel-wall kitchen

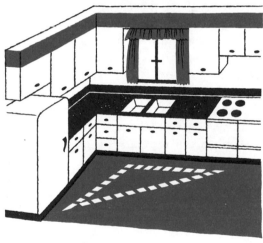

● L-shaped kitchen

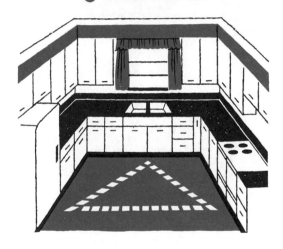

● U-shaped kitchen

● For a description of the four types of kitchen designs, see below.

will proceed from right to left and so that when walking from one center to another the steps, if charted, will form a triangle, the arrangement is efficient. (See drawing on opposite page.)

Usually kitchen designs fall into one of four general types. Which type of kitchen is best depends on the size of the house, the uses to be made of the kitchen, the number in the family, the number of people who will work in the kitchen at one time, and the type of meals usually prepared and served. The four kitchen types (see drawings above) follow:

1. *The one-wall kitchen.* This arrangement is good when all pieces of equipment can be lined up along one wall in a limited area.

Courtesy Westinghouse

● In this modern kitchen there are lights over each work area in addition to the ceiling lights for general room illumination. The dining area within the kitchen, used for serving simple meals, adds to greater efficiency in the use of the kitchen.

2. *The parallel-wall kitchen.* This type of kitchen is economical of space and is suitable for a situation where there is a door at each end of the kitchen area. There are no corners to plan for.
3. *The L-shaped kitchen.* This is a practical arrangement to use, particularly when a dining area can be located at one side or one end of the room.
4. *The U-shaped kitchen.* This type of arrangement has been found to be especially efficient since all work areas are continuous.

Kitchen Floors and Walls

As a sanitary measure as well as to simplify work, all finishes and materials used in kitchen floors and walls should be smooth and easy to clean. Such finishes and materials are available in different colors and in decorative patterns. Thus they add to the room's attractiveness.

Flooring and floor coverings. In addition to being easy to clean, kitchen floors and floor coverings should be comfortable to stand on and durable enough to withstand wear. Wood floors are not so easy to stand on as are some of the floor coverings. Wood floors must be varnished, waxed, or finished in some manner to increase their wearing qualities and to keep them looking attractive. Linoleum is a popular and durable floor covering. It is comfortable to stand on and easily cleaned. Linoleum comes in several qualities and in many colors and designs. The less expensive qualities or grades have a painted surface which wears off somewhat quickly. Since the color goes through to the backing in the better grades, wear is not apparent until the linoleum is worn down. Waxing adds to the life of linoleum and should be restored when it wears off. Otherwise wiping with a dry mop is all that is required except for dirt and grease spots, which can be wiped clean with soap and water.

Rubber tile is relatively expensive, but it is durable and easy to stand on. It may be waxed with a water-emulsion wax to give it a shiny appearance, and it is cleaned just as is linoleum.

Plastic tile or vinyl is durable and easy to stand on. It does not dry out, resists spotting, and is easily cleaned with soap and water. It may be waxed, if desired, to resist scratching.

Walls. Walls and wall coverings in the kitchen should be smooth and easy to clean. Vapors containing grease settle on the walls, making it necessary to wash them occasionally. Kitchen walls are usually finished in one of the following ways: easy-to-wash painted plaster, washable wall paper, linoleum made for the purpose, plastic materials, glass, enameled tile, ceramic tile, and wood. All these are easy to clean with soap and water.

Light and Ventilation in the Kitchen

The tasks that are done in the kitchen require good illumination at all times for the prevention of eye strain and for safety. Preparing food, washing dishes, and reading recipes and package directions all require the right kind and the right amount of light. Accidents often happen when there is not enough light to see clearly, or they may result from eye fatigue caused by too little light or too much glare. The amount of light needed depends on the size of the kitchen; the color of the walls and ceiling, whether light or dark; and the arrangement of the equipment.

Light. Windows may supply enough natural daylight if they are the right size for the kitchen area and are so placed that the light from them falls on the working surfaces without shadows or glare. Should the daylight cause glare on any surface, the use of glass curtains or blinds that can be adjusted to soften the bright light is desirable.

Plenty of daylight is needed over each work center. If the house structure does not permit this, artificial light may be required during the daytime as well as at night. Trees and shrubbery should be kept away from windows that are depended on for daylight.

While some kitchens require artificial light at all times, all kitchens need artificial light for working after dark. A central light may be sufficient to light a small kitchen adequately. A central light is also useful to supply general illumination or over-all light on first entering a dark kitchen if the light is controlled by a light switch at the entrance. When the kitchen is so large that a person at work casts a shadow from a central light, then two lights or, better yet, a light over each work center is needed. Four lights, one in each quarter of the kitchen, will eliminate shadows completely.

Electric lamps are of two general types—the regular or incandescent lamp bulb and the fluorescent tube. Both types will supply adequate light when the fixtures are correctly placed and when bulbs or tubes are of correct wattage. The watt is the unit of measure of electric power, and both incandescent bulbs and fluorescent tubes come in different wattages to provide different

● In many modern homes the oven and surface cooking units are built into the kitchen.

Courtesy Wood-Mode Kitchens

● In the electronic range, cooking is done by microwave energy. The food is heated by absorbing this energy, and cooking times are very short. It takes 8 minutes per pound to roast a ham, 90 seconds to bake cookies, and 90 seconds to fry bacon.

amounts of light. Incandescent bulbs produce a spot of light, while fluorescent tubes give a more diffused illumination, which may be a soft white or a cool white light. Therefore, fluorescent tubes are usually preferred in the kitchen.

Fluorescent tubes, though more efficient than incandescent bulbs, cannot be used directly in a regular light fixture, but require special equipment. This makes the fluorescent light more expensive to put in, but it is less costly to operate.

Ventilation. Ventilating—that is, changing the air in the kitchen—helps to carry away cooking odors, heat, and steam and makes the kitchen a more pleasant room in which to work. The amount of ventilation possible depends on the number of doors which lead to the outside, the number of windows and where they are placed in relation to one another, and the direction and velocity of the air movement outside. Ventilation is better when doors or windows are on opposite sides of the room.

When sufficient ventilation is not possible from doors and windows, a ventilating fan can be used to good advantage.

Equipment for the Kitchen

Kitchen equipment represents a large financial investment, and when thoughtfully selected, used according to manufacturer's directions, and given proper care, it should give years of service. For a kitchen to be efficient and attractive, it need not be equipped with the newest appliances. Many homemakers prepare meals efficiently for years before finding it necessary to purchase new items, but there usually comes a time when equipment and utensils need to be replaced. Most newly married couples also need to buy some equipment even though they may receive many articles as wedding gifts. It will be helpful, then, to consider points on selection, use, and care of the various types of equipment, appliances, and utensils to help you make a wise selection when the time comes.

There are three general categories of kitchen equipment:

1. Large equipment, sometimes called major appliances: The range, refrigerator, freezer, sink, cabinets, garbage disposer, and dishwasher are in this category.
2. Small appliances: The toaster, electric mixer, hand mixer, electric frypan, blender, roaster, waffle baker, sandwich toaster, and portable grill are examples.
3. Food-preparation utensils: Measuring and mixing tools and cooking utensils are included in this group.

Large Equipment

When any one of the large pieces of kitchen equipment is to be selected, the following factors should be carefully considered:

1. Its cost
2. The cost of connecting it to gas lines or water systems or of putting in special electric wiring
3. The size—that is, whether it will go into the space allowed for it and whether it is adequate for the use that is to be made of it
4. Whether any special features that may increase the cost are worth the extra price
5. The ease, convenience, and cost of its operation
6. The amount and kind of care needed and the ease of cleaning

Manufacturers change the features from time to time, so it is well to investigate different makes and models a short time before making a final decision.

Ranges. Many different makes and sizes of ranges are available, and there are many features on them from which to choose. Gas and electric ranges are the two most-used types. Electronic ranges are now made for home use. However, by comparison with other types, they are expensive. Electricity is available to almost every section of the country for electric and electronic ranges, but special wiring is required—that is, a 3-wire 220- to 240-volt service. Gas is readily available in most cities and towns, and liquefied or bottled gas can be delivered to homes where city gas does not reach. Bottled gas is used in the same way as city gas. Electric ranges should be approved by the Canadian Standards Association, and gas ranges should carry the approval of the Canadian Gas Association for safety in operation.

Features on ranges vary with makes and models. There are usually four or more surface units, called "burners" on a gas range and "units" on an electric range. These burners and units are arranged differently on different models; convenience of arrangement should be considered. There will be at least one oven and broiler; there may be two ovens or one extra-size oven to meet different cooking needs. In some models one oven may be placed at eye level above the surface of the range. Sometimes both ovens and surface units are built in as part of the structure of the kitchen in much the same way as the cabinets and sinks are built in. The built-in surface units and oven may or may not be near each other.

Most ranges are equipped with an oven heat regulator and a cooking timer; there may be an automatic oven-clock timer for starting and ending the cooking at preset times, and the clock may also control an outlet to which a small appliance can be connected. Other special features include: a thermostatically controlled griddle; an automatically controlled surface unit; an oven rotisserie; a meat thermometer which registers the temperature of the roasting meat on a control-panel dial; and built-in oven cleaning devices.

Such special features increase the cost of a range. When you are buying a range, such additions should be evaluated in terms of frequency of use and personal satisfaction.

An electronic range uses microwave energy to cook. Microwave energy is similar to the energy that carries radio and television programs but it has a much higher frequency. When these microwaves penetrate and are absorbed by food, the energy of the microwave is converted into heat energy; the food is heated instantaneously through-

● An upright combination refrigerator-freezer keeps the food storage area compact. As in many refrigerators, the interior arrangement provides a place for butter, eggs, and bottles, as well as storage for other kinds of food. Stored and frozen food is easily accessible here because of the separate upright parallel doors to each section.

out its whole mass. In ordinary cooking the surface of the food becomes hot and then the heat is carried into the interior by means of conduction (a relatively slow process). Foods cooked in an electronic range do not reach temperatures much above 212° F. and so they do not become brown and crusty. A special electric unit is added in some of these ranges for browning the top of such foods as biscuits and meats.

The life of a range can be prolonged with good care. Its enameled surface is stain- and acid-resistant. As soon as the range cools, soiled spots should be wiped with a damp soapy cloth, rinsed, and dried. Abrasive cleaners are apt to scratch the enamel. Trays around surface burners and units and drip trays can be removed and washed along with the cooking utensils. There are specially designed, efficient cleaners for cleaning range ovens. Built-in oven cleaning features should be evaluated carefully in terms of convenience as related to the probable added cost.

Refrigerators. All refrigerators are operated mechanically, either by electricity or gas. They provide storage space for perishable foods and keep them in fresh condition for several days, protecting the health of the family and preventing waste of food and money. A good refrigerator should hold temperatures of between 37° and 40° F. Some refrigerators have a built-in freezing compartment. Refrigerator-freezers (appliances which refrigerate food and also freeze food and store frozen food) are also available. The temperature of the freezer part should be maintained at 0° F. The freezer section may be located above or below the refrigerator compartment or upright at its side. Convenience of use should be considered when buying a re-frigerator-freezer.

A gas refrigerator should carry the seal of approval of the Canadian Gas Associa-tion (CGA). This seal is an assurance of safety both in the construction and the per-formance of the equipment. Any gas or electric appliance manufactured in the U.S. for sale in Canada must meet the rigid Canadian, not U.S. standards.

Convenience features for refrigerators in-clude: a storage door; slide-out shelves; re-volving shelves; special compartments for meat, vegetables, butter, and eggs; and ice-cube trays and a storage space for extra ice cubes. Some refrigerators do not accu-mulate any frost, some defrost automati-cally, and some must be defrosted manu-ally. Defrost the latter when the ice coating on the cooling unit is about ¼-inch thick.

Clean the storage compartment of the refrigerator regularly once a week. Of course, any spilled food must be wiped up at once. To keep the refrigerator sweet and clean, wipe it with a warm solution of bak-ing soda (2 or 3 tablespoons of soda to each quart of water).

Home freezers. In homes where much fresh food is available for freezing or where a fairly large stock of food needs to be kept on hand, a home freezer is desirable. A freezer is an aid to meal planning and can reduce time and effort in meal preparation. However, a home freezer is not always a money-saver. Depreciation, cost of repairs, and cost of operation add extra cost to every pound of stored food. To keep this extra cost down, freeze fruits and vege-tables in season when prices are low, take advantage of special sales of meat and poultry, freeze leftover food, and use the freezer to capacity.

Home freezers may be chest (top open-ing) or upright (front opening) in style. The upright freezer is equipped with shelves for easy accessibility of food packages. The chest type contains baskets and space di-viders for this purpose. The operating cost of these two types of freezers is the same. Frost-free upright freezers are also avail-able: the packages of food do not frost over and can be separated easily and there is no accumulation of frost to reduce storage space. A frost-free freezer is more expensive to buy and to operate than other freezers.

The capacity of home freezers is given in cubic feet. The temperatures vary from 0° to −30° F. The lowest temperatures are best for freezing food, but a temperature of 0° F. is satisfactory for storage.

Under ordinary conditions of use, freez-ers need to be defrosted only once a year. Excess frost may be scraped from the inside of the cabinet between defrostings. Use a stiff dull-bladed knife. Home freezers should carry the seal of approval of the Canadian Standards Association to ensure safe performance.

Sinks. Made of enameled iron, steel, or stainless metal, sinks are available either with a single or double bowl and with sin-

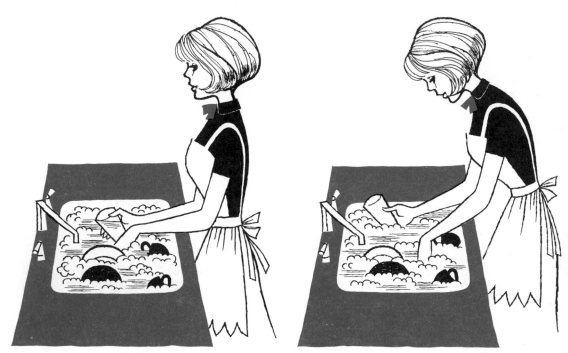

A sink that is of correct height permits a worker to maintain good posture (left). One that is too high or too low for comfortable working tires muscles easily (right).

gle or double drainboards. Instead of drainboards, the sink may be placed next to base-cabinet units, the counters of which are used for stacking soiled dishes and for placing the dishes when dried. Like other pieces of kitchen equipment, sinks vary in size and in features of convenience. When the sink has a single drainboard, it may be on either side of the sink bowl. Drainboards usually slope toward the bowl and are often fluted to let water drain off easily. Sinks are easily kept clean with hot, soapy water and a cloth, plastic sponge, or brush.

A spray attachment, a disposer for garbage, and a mechanical dishwasher as part of the sink are also available for those who will find them useful. (See drawing at the right.)

Electric disposers provide a convenient method of disposing of food waste. There are ordinances in some cities preventing the use of this type of equipment because it is believed that the existing sewage systems are not adequate to handle it should a large percentage of homes dispose of their

A spray attachment built into the sink is a helpful addition for rinsing dishes.

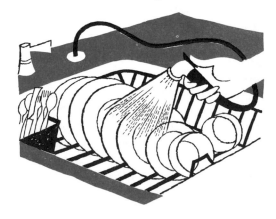

waste by such means. Electric disposers should be operated and cared for as manufacturers direct.

Dishwashers are sometimes connected as part of the sink. They may be an entirely separate unit but connected permanently to the plumbing, or they may be a movable unit that can be used at the sink and then stored in a convenient place in the kitchen. Some automatic dishwashers are filled from the top and some from the front. Dishes that have been washed automatically are very sanitary because the water used in dishwashers is much hotter than the hands can stand.

Dishes, scraped and rinsed as for hand dishwashing, may be put into the dish-

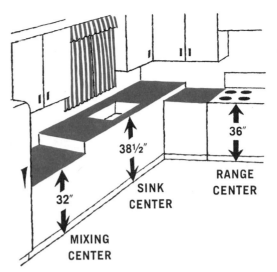

● These heights for cabinets, sink, and range have been generally found to be the most efficient for the different processes at the centers.

washer as they are brought from the table. Soiled dishes may be kept in the dishwasher until there are enough for a load, and they may be left there after they are washed until a convenient time is found to put them away. Dishwashers should be given the care that is recommended by the manufacturer. Special dishwasher detergents which do not suds are advised for use in a dishwasher because suds interfere with the washing action.

Storage cabinets. There are two general types of storage cabinets: floor, or base, cabinets and wall cabinets. They may be custom-made or factory-built and made of wood or metal. To prevent warping, wood cabinets should be made of well-seasoned wood and metal cabinets of rigid steel. All metal parts should be rustproof. Cabinet doors and the fronts of cabinet drawers on metal cabinets should be insulated to reduce noise as doors and drawers are opened and closed.

● A dishwasher is like a pair of extra hands, whether it is built into the kitchen or is a portable one. Hotter water can be used for washing dishes mechanically than when they are hand-washed, and this assures a greater degree of sanitation.

Courtesy General Electric Company

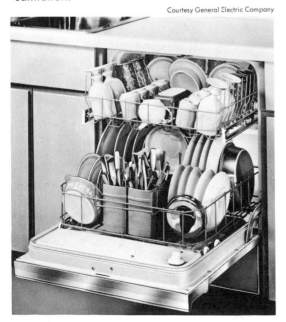

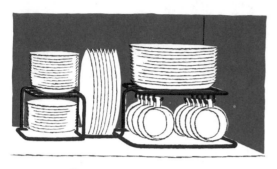

Storage rack for dishes

Storage cabinet for mixer

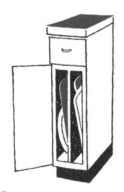

Vertical file for trays

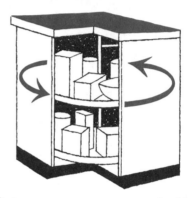

Base corner merry-go-round cabinet

Tops of base cabinets are used as work surfaces and are made of materials that should be easy to keep clean. They should also be stain-resistant and waterproof, and they should resist any scorching from hot pans that may be placed on them. Such materials as linoleums, made especially for the purpose; plastic and vinyl materials, which are available under a number of trade names; stainless metals; ceramic tile; and hard woods are all suitable.

The height of base cabinets is fairly standard—36 inches high. Widths of cabinets vary and will depend on the space a cabinet is to occupy.

Wall cabinets are made in the same widths as are base cabinets. There should be at least 16 inches between the top of the work counter and the bottom of the wall cabinet. This will give enough room for an electric mixer to be kept beneath the wall cabinet. Wall cabinets are usually put over base cabinets and sometimes over the sink. When they are over the sink, there should be 30 inches between the sink and wall cabinet. The top shelf of a wall cabinet should be no higher than 6 feet from the floor for a person of average height to reach. Wall cabinets sometimes extend to the ceiling.

Large drawers in base cabinets may be used for the storage of pots and pans. Revolving shelves, either in base or wall cabinets, but especially in corner cabinets, utilize lower spaces efficiently and make the articles stored on these shelves very accessible.

Shelves in wall cabinets may be adjusted to the right distance between them for the articles to be stored there, and in this way waste space between shelves will be avoided.

A vertical file construction provides a special place for trays, baking sheets, pan covers, racks, and large platters.

Step shelves in wall cabinets at the food-preparation center are also spacesavers. Small canisters or small packages of spices, dessert mixes, extracts, measuring cups, and other small articles are easily located when stored on step shelves.

There are ventilated cakeboxes and breadboxes built into some cabinet drawers. Pull-out boards for rolling, cutting, or chopping and slide-out racks or boards on which to hang such kitchen tools as ladles and spoons are available.

A swing-out shelf for an electric mixer built over the work surface at the back of the food-preparation center is another convenience. When not in use, the mixer on its shelf can be pushed out of the way. There are also base cabinets made especially for the storage of an electric mixer.

Cabinet care is an easy matter. Wiping the shelves with warm, soapy water and rinsing with clear water is usually all that is required. Or a wax polish may be used for cleaning. The frequency of cleaning depends on the amount of use and on the amount of greasy dirt that settles on shelves. Crumbs can fall into partly opened

● A pull-out shelf in a base cabinet provides extra work space and allows some processes to be carried on in greater comfort than on a standard-height counter. The rolling of doughs and the mixing of batters are examples.

drawers; hence drawers should be cleaned at frequent intervals. Drawers lined with washable or renewable liners are easily and quickly cleaned. A vacuum-cleaner crevice tool is good for cleaning cabinet drawers. All spilled food should be cleaned up at once and filmy dust removed from the outside of wall and base cabinets.

Small Electric Appliances

A wide variety of small electric appliances is offered for home use. Among those that have been found to be helpful as time-savers and energy-savers are toasters, griddles, waffle bakers, coffee makers, knife sharpeners, can openers, carving knives, hand mixers, blenders, frypans, broiler-rotisseries, and ovens that bake, broil, and toast.

When deciding to buy any of these small appliances, it is well to balance the amount of time and energy it will save and the general satisfaction it will give you against the cost, the space required to store it, the care it will need, and the amount of use it will

Courtesy General Electric Company

● Dutch skillet

Courtesy Westinghouse

● Non-stick broiler frypan

Courtesy Westinghouse

● Toaster

Courtesy Sunbeam Corporation

● Blender

Courtesy Westinghouse

● Non-stick electric griddle

Courtesy General Electric Company

● Rotisserie-broiler-baker

APPLIANCES

Courtesy Sunbeam Corporation

● Automatic percolator

Courtesy Dominion Electric Corporation

● Electric knife

Courtesy Sunbeam Corporation

● Standard mixer

Courtesy Hamilton Beach

● Hand mixer

Courtesy General Electric Company

● Waffle baker

Courtesy Sunbeam Corporation

● Can opener-knife sharpener

be given. Any appliance that is worth the investment in it deserves to be used as directed and to be given the care suggested by the manufacturer.

Most small appliances can be moved easily. Some can be used for cooking informal meals right at the table. In fact, it is possible to plan menus which can be prepared using only wisely chosen small appliances. Such temporary use of small appliances is helpful to the small apartment dweller, the bride setting up housekeeping, and the family moving into a new home.

No special wiring is required to operate these appliances, but sufficient electric wiring is necessary to ensure enough current for all the electric equipment and small appliances in use in homes today. It is possible to overload an electric circuit when too many appliances are used at one time. It is important to locate the circuits for convenient use. Information about electric circuits should come from an expert. The homemaker should know how many circuits there are in the kitchen and what electric equipment can be used on each one. It is well to have the refrigerator connected to a separate individual circuit. The electric range requires special wiring, as it will not operate on the voltage of the regular house current.

Food-preparation Utensils

There is such a wide assortment of utensils for food preparation that deciding which to buy can be confusing. All of these utensils are made in a variety of sizes and shapes. Some have only one use, while others have several uses. Also food preparation utensils are made of different materials, and they are available in a wide range of costs. Because of differences in cost, the features of food preparation utensils should be evaluated so that the greatest return for the money spent for them may be obtained.

In regard to size, it is well to think of family size and the kind of meals usually prepared. Then the capacity of the utensil bought will be satisfactory. The shape influences the balance in the hand and thus the ease in handling the utensil. In a cooking utensil the bottom surface must be flat to ensure good contact with the heating unit whether on the top of the range or in the oven. This makes for economy in fuel consumption.

Versatility in use is another good feature, for it means that one utensil will do the work of two or even more.

The material used in top-of-range cooking utensils is usually aluminum, stainless steel, cast iron, or porcelain enamel. Each material has its advantages and disadvantages. Aluminum has superior heating properties and distributes heat evenly over the bottom surface of a utensil. However, aluminum needs special care to keep it bright and shiny. Stainless steel conducts heat well but distributes it unevenly; therefore, stainless steel utensils are usually clad on the bottom surface with either copper or aluminum, or they may have a core of carbon steel or copper. Stainless steel utensils are durable and require little extra care to keep them in good condition. But if there is a copper surface, special cleaning preparations must be used. Cast iron conducts heat well and evenly. If the utensil is large, it is heavy. Cast iron is durable, although it rusts unless carefully dried after each use. Porcelain enamel is glass, fused on a metal base. It has good heat conduction properties and is relatively light in weight. The glass coating is apt to chip, and it stains easily.

All types of cooking utensils are available with a special interior finish to which food does not stick. The nonstick finish is applied to various base materials in different ways according to the manufacturer. It is important to follow his directions in using the equipment. The nonstick coated utensils cost more than the similar uncoated type, so it is well to consider their use before spending the extra money.

Where skillet cooking or roasting of meat is called for, you may find the special finish quite useful. Since food does not stick to it, cleaning is easy. However, thorough cleansing with a good detergent is necessary to avoid build up of a greasy film. On the other hand, a nonstick finish would not be of value in saucepans used for boiling food where sticking is not a problem. And it would be of doubtful value in baking pans where greasing is needed for easy removal of the baked product.

Courtesy Committee of Aluminum Producers, The Aluminum Association

● The basic utensils shown above are as follows (from top left to right): liquid measuring cup, large strainer, sifter, mixing bowls, coffee maker, piepan, double boiler, custard cups, small strainer, meat thermometer, cookie sheet, rubber scrapers, measuring spoons, funnel, cake pans, 2-quart saucepan, slotted spoon, jar opener, rotary beater, kitchen shears, measuring cups, square cake pan, covered skillet, cooking spoon, ladle, can opener, cake rack, rolling pin, 8-inch skillet, spatula, utility knife, paring knife, carver, slicer, two-tined fork, wooden spoons, 1-quart saucepan.

113

PART II
QUESTIONS FOR SUMMARIZING AND REVIEW

Chapter 4 ... *Managing Meals to Save Time and Effort*

1. What are the advantages to the homemaker who is skillful in her use of time and energy in meal preparation?
2. In what three ways may time and effort be saved in meal preparation? Give some suggestions for each way.
3. When might the methods of preparing and serving foods be the deciding factors in the choice of menu used for a family meal?
4. What information should be included in a work-and-time schedule for meal preparation?
5. How does the arrangement of the kitchen and its equipment and the work habits of the homemaker influence the amount of time and energy used in preparing family meals?
6. Why is proper posture so important whether you stand or sit at your food-preparation tasks?
7. What is meant by ·short cuts? By dovetailing?
8. What are some suggestions for safe work habits in the kitchen?
9. How can you keep to a minimum the work of cleaning up at the end of a meal?

Chapter 5 ... *Managing Meals to Get Your Money's Worth*

1. What is the relationship between consumer choices and marketing practices?
2. How do government agencies serve the consumer of food?
3. What factors should determine how the food budget is spent?
4. How can a nutritious diet be obtained when the amount of money available for food is limited?
5. What are the questions considered in advance by the careful food shopper?
6. What is an efficient way to organize a market order?
7. What are some important government laws in regard to foods?
8. What are the Federal grades for meat? For eggs? For butter?
9. What are food additives? What purposes do they serve?
10. What is the role of the Federal Government in regard to food additives?
11. What are the advantages of reading labels?
12. How would marketing habits be affected by the storage space available for the different types of food?
13. What are some ways you can suggest to avoid waste of food and, as a result, of money?
14. What challenges does leftover food present to the meal planner?

Chapter 6 ... *Management in the Kitchen*

1. What is the relationship of equipment and its installation and storage to meal management tasks?

2. What effect does the knowledge and skill of the homemaker have on her choice of equipment for the kitchen?

3. What influences the kitchen plans and equipment acquired by an individual family?

4. Upon what are efficiency and comfort in the kitchen dependent?

5. What is a good arrangement for the work centers in the kitchen in relation to one another?

6. What features should be considered in the selection of equipment for the kitchen?

7. Of what value are the seals of approval on electrical and gas equipment?

8. What knowledge is needed for the safe use of electrical equipment?

9. What is the function of small appliances in meal management?

10. How can food preparation tasks be simplified through the proper use of appropriate tools?

EXPERIENCES FOR APPLYING YOUR KNOWLEDGE

1. Study the food products available in the market. List as many types of timesaving and effort-saving foods as you can find. Discuss ways in which the use of these foods will save you time and effort. Plan and prepare meals using these foods. Evaluate the results.

2. Invite a home economist from your local utility company to demonstrate in your class some timesaving and worksaving methods of food preparation.

3. Set the table for dinner, using a tray to carry table appointments to the table. Compare the amount of time this takes with the amount of time taken when no tray is used. Repeat the procedure to compare the amount of time needed to carry food to the table for dinner.

4. Plan a simple menu to serve guests which can be prepared in advance, leaving a minimum of last-minute preparations after the guests have arrived, thus freeing the homemaker to visit with her guests.

5. Plan several breakfast and dinner menus suitable for a family with a mother who works outside the home. Show how, by good management practices, attractive and nourishing meals can be served without the homemaker

having to spend an undue amount of time in the kitchen. Tell the form of food selected for each menu item when there is a choice of several forms. Prepare one of the meals, carrying out timesaving and effort-saving steps. Evaluate the meal as to its appetite appeal and the quality of food prepared.

6. Plan two menus for dinner at home and include in them the same kinds of food. Prepare menu 1 on one Saturday and menu 2 on another Saturday as follows:

a. In menu 1 plan to prepare all foods from the individual ingredients—possibly in the menu have a meat or fish; two vegetables; a green salad; a cake, pudding, or gelatin dessert; and coffee. In menu 2 use foods similar to those in menu 1 but which are partly or fully prepared products—that is, frozen, canned, or a packaged mix.

b. Follow the same organization procedures for each of the two meals.

c. Keep a record of the time it takes you to prepare each meal, noting the time when you start and the time when you have it ready to serve.

d. Keep a record, in the same manner, of the time needed to clear away each meal. (The serving time should be the same for both meals.)

e. Determine the cost of each meal.

f. Evaluate each meal for quality. Possibly ask your family for their opinion.

g. Draw conclusions concerning the two meals in regard to time and effort, to cost, and to quality. Keep in mind that your findings apply to these two meals only. However, your findings may be an indication of a general relationship in these three aspects of meal preparation.

7. Conduct a time-and-motion study in your kitchen at home or in the foods laboratory to demonstrate the relationship of kitchen arrangement and storage facilities to time and energy used in meal preparation. Keep a record of the number and kinds of motions and the time used in preparing a simple meal. Discuss the ways in which the kitchen arrangement and storage facilities affected the use of time and energy. Suggest ways for changing the storage in each work center to make for more efficient meal preparation.

8. Bring to class newspaper clippings about accidents in the kitchen. Analyze causes of these accidents and suggest means of preventing them. Prepare a list of safety hazards found in the foods laboratory or in your kitchen at home. Discuss procedures which may be used to prevent accidents or to handle accidents resulting from the hazards.

9. Demonstrate food preparation during which errors in safety and sanitary practices are deliberately made. As the list of demonstration errors is discussed, have the students demonstrate the correct procedure and show why it is a better one.

10. Compare the following food preparation techniques, and report on the differences in time and effort needed for each technique. Which way is your preference?
a. Using a flour sifter that requires the use of two hands or one that can be operated by one hand

b. Scraping carrots with a sharp knife or with a floating-blade peeler

c. Beating egg whites with a hand beater or with an electric egg beater

d. Using a separate measuring cup and mixing bowl for making an instant pudding or a large measuring cup for both measuring and mixing the pudding

11. Make a study of the time spent in cleaning up after a meal. Suggest ways to save time in carrying out this task.

12. Plan nutritious and appetizing meals for three days for a young couple using a limited money allotment. Prepare the meals for one day and submit for class evaluation.

13. Select low-cost foods and use them to prepare some basic meals. Compare costs involved and the savings when using some items which are considered leftovers.

14. Shopping for food is much easier if you use a grocery list. As you prepare the list, group the foods according to their location in the store where you usually shop. Test your grouping when you visit the store to help your parents with the family marketing.

15. Cooperate with your mother in preparing a shopping list for the week. Be sure to consider family preferences, special sales, home storage space, and time available for food preparation.

16. Choose a food, such as a peach. Taste it as the raw fresh fruit and then in the canned, frozen, and dried forms. Try to describe the differences in color, flavor, and texture. Compare the prices of one serving of the fruit in each form and decide the unique value of each one.

17. Arrange a field trip to a food market. Ask the manager to discuss some of the factors that are involved in the cost of food. Study ways to reduce some of the costs due to poor consumer practices.

18. Keep a record of the cost of foods in season in your locality and compare with the cost of the same foods bought out of season, that is, when shipped in from distant growing areas (for example, asparagus, tomatoes, corn, and strawberries). You will have to extend this activity over a period of time to be able to compare these prices. What conclusions do you draw from this study?

19. Compare the cost per 1-cup serving of a number of different ready-to-eat and to-be-cooked cereals. Compare the nutritional value of each serving and determine the greatest nutritional value for the money spent.

20. Study the federal and provincial laws that protect our food. Look up local laws that have to do with controlling the sanitary conditions of the food supply. Discuss in class the effectiveness of both federal and local laws in your community.

21. Study how the Federal Government controls the chemicals that may be added to food. Look at the labels on processed foods to determine what chemical additives might be present. What additives are used to preserve color, flavor, texture, and quality? Are additives used for any other purpose than those just given?

22. Make a study of package labels, product information, and other sources of consumer information. What help is available in evaluating this information? What information is required by law and what is supplied by food processors?

23. Make the following observations in a large market and report your findings to the class.

a. Are any fresh fruits and fresh vegetables grade-labeled? If so, which ones?

b. How are fresh fruits and fresh vegetables packaged? What are the advantages and disadvantages of the different methods of packaging?

c. Look at the shelves where canned and packaged foods are displayed. List the brands and note how they are labeled as to quality (e.g. with descriptive words or letters) and other information.

d. Tell how you can use your findings when you shop for food.

24. Examine labels on several brands of such staple products as baking powder or margarine. Note whether or not the ingredients listed on the labels of the different brands are alike. Using comparable weights, calculate the cost of each brand.

25. Find a canned fruit and a canned vegetable that are available in a 14-ounce can (four servings) and also in a 28-ounce can (seven servings). Find the cost per can, and compute the cost per serving of the fruit and the vegetable from the two sizes of cans. Note the advantages of buying either size.

26. Discuss in class the uses for different grades of such canned foods as tomatoes and peaches. When possible, use different grades of canned foods in the learning experiences done in the foods laboratory. Evaluate the results.

27. Study the use of leftover foods by dividing the class into three groups. Have one group take meats, another vegetables, and another cereals. To prepare for the group discussion, bring to class suggestions from mothers, or from cookbooks, magazines, and newspapers for interesting ways to use these foods when some are left over from a meal. These suggestions can be compiled in a booklet to be used at home.

28. Make a study of the effects of advertising on young people.

29. Study the arrangement of your kitchen at home. Show by drawing on graph paper where the large equipment is placed. Estimate the number of trips from the kitchen to the dining area in serving dinner. Can you suggest any changes that might save steps?

30. Analyze the advantages of (a) a U-shaped kitchen, (b) an L-shaped kitchen, (c) a parallel-wall kitchen, and (d) a one-wall kitchen.

31. Decide whether the work surfaces in your kitchen at school and at home are the best height for you to work comfortably, and whether they are large enough for you to do easily the tasks that are required. Study ways to adapt the work surfaces to satisfy your requirements where necessary.

32. Locate the labels on the small electrical equipment in your school or home kitchen. What do the labels tell about (a) wattage, (b) seals of approval, (c) manufacture? Summarize the information found on all the equipment examined. Which information is required by law and which information is supplied by the manufacturer?

33. Take advantage of the opportunity to use as many of the various pieces of equipment in your school kitchen as possible. Be sure to read all the directions and understand how each is operated.

34. Look over the various pieces of small kitchen equipment in your home. Are there any that seem to be especially helpful as timesavers? Are there any that are seldom used or that seem to be useless? Tell in class why you approve of some and do not think others are helpful.

35. Decide what large equipment, small appliances, and food-preparation utensils you feel would be helpful when you start a home of your own. Check the items as follows:
a. For those that are absolutely necessary, use one check mark.
b. For those that would make food preparation easier but are not absolutely necessary, use two check marks.

36. Demonstrate the use of small electrical appliances, such as mixer, frypan, blender. Point out the timesaving and effort-saving features. Tell how some of these appliances might be used for outdoor cooking or in place of some of the large appliances. Plan and prepare a meal using the small appliances entirely.

37. Arrange an exhibit of cooking utensils made of different materials, such as aluminum, stainless steel, enamelware, and glass. If you have used such utensils, what can you say about them from the point of view of use, ease of cleaning, and appearance?

38. Visit the utensil department of a store. Study the different labor-saving devices, sometimes called "gadgets." Discuss in class their relative merits. Make an exhibit of the gadgets which you feel aren't worth having, and label each one as to its poor features. If possible, borrow these gadgets from the foods laboratory, the school cafeteria, or a homemaker rather than buying them.

39. How many different food-preparation jobs can each of the following small tools selected from your school or home kitchen perform? Explain.

Spatula	Slotted spoon
Rotary beater	Meat grinder
Pastry blender	Square grater
Vegetable parer	Strainer

7

Table Setting

and

Etiquette

■ MEALTIME can provide opportunities for the family to enjoy one another's company. Away from the rush of other affairs, it is possible to create a leisurely atmosphere which will give pleasure to all. It is especially pleasant for the family to sit down to a healthful, appetizing meal served on a table set in good taste and in harmony with their manner of living. And mealtime is more enjoyable when everyone is mannerly and considerate of the others.

As you gain experience in planning and preparing meals, you should learn about the different kinds of table appointments and the different ways to serve meals. You should also know how to conduct yourself at the table. The basic rules of table setting and service are simple and flexible. (See diagrams on pages 124 and 125.) The rules of table conduct are more definite. Because the dining space in many homes is an extension of the living room or a special place in the kitchen, the trend is toward informality in table setting and service.

Table Appointments

Selection of table appointments—table coverings, tableware, glassware, and dinnerware—depends on their suitability to the types of meals customarily served and on the manner of serving the meals. Many girls, looking forward to the day when they will have use for them, collect tableware and table coverings, and sometimes glassware and chinaware, ahead of time. If you would like to do this, beauty, durability, and cost, as well as the amount of care that will be needed, are all points you should consider carefully. What you select will influence the attractiveness of your dining table. Thus, to make an intelligent selection of table equipment, you will need to have information about the different kinds available to guide you in choosing those that are suitable and practical.

Table Covers

Table covers may be made of any of a number of different fabrics, including linen, cotton, rayon, nylon, or combinations of these. They may also be made of such materials as cellophane, plastic, raffia, bamboo, cork, or paper. The napkins used with table covers are usually made of fabric or paper.

Tablecloths and napkins. The tablecloth may be one which covers the entire table and hangs over the edges 8 or 10 inches, as a dinner cloth. Or it may be a cloth that partly covers the table, as a lunch or breakfast cloth. Tablecloths come ready-made in a variety of sizes, colors, and designs, as well as in different materials, or they may be bought by the yard. Napkins vary in size, and those used at dinner are usually larger than those used at breakfast and lunch. Tablecloths and napkins should harmonize in fabrics and color.

Place mats or individual mats. Setting the table with place mats instead of a tablecloth has become very popular. One mat is used at each place, leaving part of the table bare. Place mats are easily laundered because a spot on one requires the laundering of only a small piece while a spot on a tablecloth may necessitate the laundering of the entire cloth.

COVERS FOR THE DAY'S MEALS

● Breakfast

● Lunch

● Dinner

All photos courtesy Oneida, Ltd., Libby, and "What's New in Home Economics"

Protective pads or silence cloths. Used beneath a tablecloth, a pad or silence cloth reduces clatter and protects the table's finish from the heat of hot dishes. Special pads and cloths are available for such a purpose, but outing flannel, cut to fit either the table or each place mat, is effective and inexpensive.

Tableware

Eating and serving utensils and a few decorative pieces are called "tableware." There are two types of tableware: (1) flatware, consisting of such pieces as the knives, forks, and spoons used by each person and the serving pieces; and (2) holloware, consisting of pieces like cream pitchers and sugar bowls, serving dishes, teapots and coffeepots, candlesticks, trays, and vases. Both flatware and holloware are made of sterling or solid silver, plated silver, and stainless metal. Some holloware pieces are made also of pewter.

Flatware may be purchased in place settings of any number. A place setting consists of the pieces needed for one place at the table, such as a knife, a fork, a teaspoon, a salad fork, and, possibly, a larger spoon for soup, cereal, or dessert. Sometimes a butter spreader is included. Also, the individual pieces may be purchased separately for any number of people. The choice of which way to purchase flatware is a matter of personal preference.

Sterling silver. According to law, sterling silver is made of 925 parts of pure silver and 75 parts of an alloy. It is made in four different weights. The heavier the weight, the more expensive the silver. Sterling silver lasts for years and improves with use. It is often handed down from generation to generation in a family.

Plated silver. Tableware made of a base metal other than silver over which a coating of silver is applied is called "plated silver." The more silver used for coating, the better the quality. Some silver plate is designated by such terms as "double plate" or "triple plate." These terms refer not to the number of coats of silver applied, but to the amount of silver used. For example, in triple plating, 6 ounces of silver are used for each gross of teaspoons. The weight of silver used for coating other pieces is in the same proportion to their weight. Good plated silver comes in many attractive patterns, and with care it will last a lifetime.

Stainless steel. Tableware made of a special steel alloy is called "stainless steel." It is formed from solid pieces of metal without the addition of any coating. Stainless steel tableware is popular, and many beautiful designs are available in it. It is, like the others, of lifetime durability.

Care of tableware. If it is to look its best, tableware should be washed in hot, sudsy water as soon as possible after use, rinsed, and towel-dried immediately to prevent water-spotting. Since tableware is easily scratched, it is best to wash it separately from other table appointments. Tarnish should be removed from both sterling and plated ware by rubbing the pieces with a soft cloth moistened with a cleaner especially made for silver. Then the pieces should be rubbed with a clean cloth to polish them and washed in the usual way. Since stainless metal does not tarnish, it requires no cleaning or polishing other than careful washing after each use.

Glassware

The usual pieces of table glassware are drinking glasses, juice glasses, sherbet glasses, sauce dishes, and salad and dessert plates. Drinking and juice glasses come in several sizes, depending on the number of fluid ounces they will hold. Shapes as well as sizes vary. Quite often pieces of glassware come in matching patterns and colors, and an entire set of dishes may be made of glass. There are also miscellaneous pieces, such as cream and sugar sets, cups and saucers, dishes for relishes and jellies, and candlesticks.

The method of making glassware, along with the materials used in its manufacture, is responsible for producing glassware with different characteristics and of different colors. Glassware depends for its beauty on its shape, its sparkle, its color, its design, or on a combination of these characteristics. Cost depends on the ingredients used in making the glass and on the labor involved in forming the various items and in achieving the decorative effects. The two general types of glassware that are most commonly used for the table are blown glass and pressed glass.

Blown glass. Made by highly skilled workmen, blown glass objects are shaped by blowing air into molten glass. One piece is formed at a time. If there is a design in the piece, it is cut or etched into the glass by hand. Because of the unique skill necessary in its making, blown glass is quite expensive.

Pressed glass. When liquid glass is pressed or blown into molds, it is called "pressed glass." Designs, if used, may be right in the molds. The process of making pressed glass can be carried on comparatively quickly, and less skill is needed than to make blown glassware. So by comparison pressed glassware usually costs less than blown glass.

Care of glassware. Because it is easily chipped, cracked, or broken, glassware must be handled carefully. It should be washed in hot, clean, sudsy water; rinsed in hot, but not boiling water; and towel-dried to polish it and to prevent its water-spotting. If glassware is permitted to drain dry, it may become water-spotted.

Dinnerware

The term "dinnerware" refers to dishes for table use. The dishes may be china, semiporcelain, pottery, glass, or plastic. Of whatever material they are made, there is a wide choice of shapes, colors, and decorations.

Dinnerware, like tableware, may be purchased in sets—that is, the pieces usually needed for each cover for a given number of people, as four, six, eight, or twelve. There may or may not be serving pieces available to match, as platters and vegetable dishes. Sometimes dishes are available in open stock, which means that it is possible to buy as many pieces of one kind as is desired. One piece may be bought at a time to add to the supply already on hand or as a replacement should a dish be broken. Open-stock dishes may be discontinued at any time by the manufacturer, however.

China, semiporcelain, and pottery. The materials used and the treatment given in the manufacture of china, semiporcelain, and pottery are different, but all of them are made from clays to which other materials have been added.

In the process of manufacture, china, semiporcelain, and pottery dishes are all dipped into a protective coating called a "glaze." These coated dishes are heated, and when cooled, this glaze hardens to pre-

SETTING A BASIC COVER

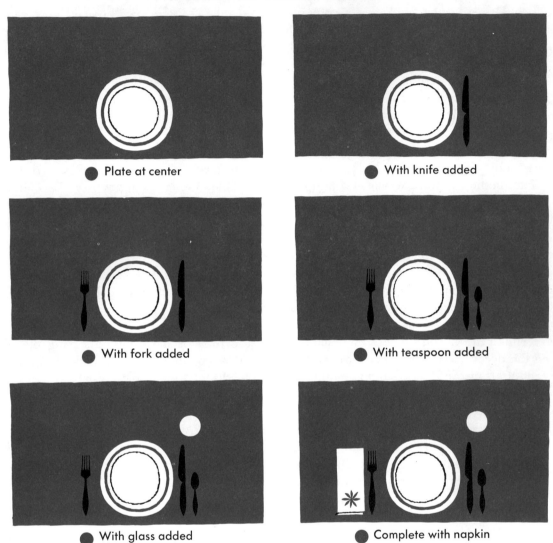

● Plate at center

● With knife added

● With fork added

● With teaspoon added

● With glass added

● Complete with napkin

● When the cover is complete, the appointments should be lined up evenly and about an inch from the edge of the table.

vent the absorption of moisture by the body of the dish. Glazes vary in hardness, glossiness, transparency, and color. In the firing of china, the glaze becomes indistinguishable from the body of the dish and will not chip off. Semiporcelain is not fired at such a high temperature as china, and the glaze is distinguishable from the body of the dish. This glaze may chip if the dish is accidentally knocked. The glaze on pottery, which is fired at an even lower temperature than semiporcelain, cracks, or crazes, easily.

Designs on dishes may be placed on the body of the dishes before they are dipped

SETTING ADDITIONAL APPOINTMENTS

● With cup and saucer

● With second glass

● With soup spoon

● With salad fork

● With salad plate

● With bread-and-butter plate

● Additional appointments are determined by the menu, but regardless of the number of appointments placed at a cover, those at the edge of the table should line up evenly.

into the glaze. Dishes decorated in this way are referred to as "underglaze." When the design is applied to dishes after the glaze has been fired on, it is called "overglaze." Overglaze decoration is not so durable as underglaze, but it may be more colorful, since in underglaze decoration the colors are likely to be changed by the heat when the dishes are fired in the process of manufacture.

Melamine. The hardest of all plastics is melamine. It is molded into dinnerware under a number of brand names, and is available in several hundred attractive patterns and colors. This dinnerware is virtually unbreakable and may be washed safely in any dishwasher. It should not be used for any cooking purposes.

Glass. Glass dinnerware is also available today. Some of this glass is transparent; other kinds look like china. Glass dinnerware is heat-resistant to hot water. Certain kinds of glass are sufficiently heat-resistant to be used for both cooking and serving; in other kinds of glass, food may be frozen, then cooked, and finally served in the same dish.

Care of dinnerware. Use mild soap or other detergent for washing dinnerware, as strong washing compounds will remove some decorations, particularly the overglaze type. Store fine dinnerware in racks especially made to prevent scratching the dishes (see drawing on page 108) or stack plates and saucers with soft cloth or paper between each dish.

Table Setting

Rules for setting the table are based on convenience. When you learn the basic rules for table setting, you can adjust them, with little difficulty, to the menu, the table appointments available, and the comfort of the family. As you read the following directions for setting the table, refer to the drawings on pages 124 and 125. Carefully placed table coverings, whether a cloth or mats, form the background for the napkin, tableware, glassware, and dinnerware used at the meal. The space used by one person at the table is referred to as a "cover." A width of at least 20 inches should be allowed for each cover, and an even greater width is desirable if the table is large enough. A simple decoration will help to make the table attractive.

How to place the table covering. If you are using a tablecloth, place it over a silence cloth or pad, and center the cloth evenly on the table. If you prefer to use place mats, put one at each cover so that each mat is straight along the edge of the table and about ½ to 1 inch from the edge. Napkins go to the extreme left of the cover, with the open edge of the napkin either to the right or to the left and about ½ to 1 inch from the table's edge. When there is not room for the napkin at the left, it may be placed in the center of the cover.

How to place the tableware. Flatware is placed at each cover in the order in which it is to be used, from the outside in, and about 1 inch from the edge of the table. Place the forks, with the tines up, at the left of the cover, and place the knife, with the cutting edge toward the inside, at the right of the cover. Then put the spoons, with the bowls up, at the right of the knife. If no knife is required at the meal, as for example when a salad is served with a prepared sandwich for the main course, the salad fork is placed at the right of the cover instead of at the left. Butter spreaders are placed across a bread-and-butter plate, if one is used, either parallel with the edge of the table or parallel with the rest of the silver.

When the meal is to be served at the table—that is, family-style service—the serving pieces should be placed conveniently near the person who is to serve. Place the carving knife and fork and serving spoons at the right of the cover of this person, putting the carving knife at the right of the serving fork and the serving spoons at the right of the knife. Or if the table is a small one, place the carving knife at the right of the serving platter with the serving spoons beside it, and the serving fork at the

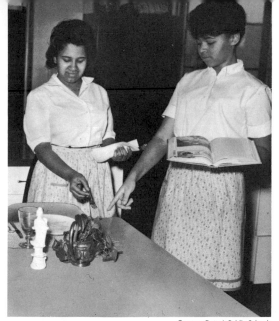

Courtesy Detroit Public Schools

● Each piece of tableware is held by its handle as it is put in its proper place at the cover. Knife blades, fork tines, and bowls of spoons are never touched with the hands.

left of the platter. The serving platter will be at the top of the server's cover.

How to place the glassware. Tumblers or goblets are placed just above the knife, either directly in line with it or slightly at the right of the tip of the knife. If two glasses are needed, as when water and milk or water and an iced beverage are served at the same meal, place the second glass at the right of the water glass. Glasses of very cold beverages may deposit moisture on the table covering, so put a coaster or a small plate beneath them. For iced beverages, the coaster or underplate should be large enough to hold a spoon for stirring or at least to support the tip of the spoon. If a juice or cocktail is served as an appetizer, put the filled juice or sherbet glass on a plate in the center of each cover. At breakfast, place the juice glass at the right of the water glass or at the center above the cover.

How to place the dinnerware. If bread-and-butter plates arc used, they are placed at the tip of the fork. When the food is to be served from the table, place the plates for each course before the person who will serve. If the food is to be passed so each person may help himself, then put a plate at each cover.

If a hot beverage is to be served at the table, place the cups and saucers before the person who will pour the beverage, either at the right or left according to the amount of space. Each cup should be on its own saucer with the handle of the cup at the right. When there are more cups and saucers than can be arranged this way, one cup may rest inside another with the two saucers under them, but no more than two cups should be stacked together.

Put the salad plates next to the salad bowl if the salad is to be served from the bowl. Or put an individual salad plate that has been served in the kitchen at the left of each cover. When the table is small, it is permissible to place the salad plate at the top left, or even at the right, should that be more convenient.

How to place the accessories. Put salt and pepper shakers at the top of each cover or one pair between but above each two covers. Dishes containing relishes, condiments, jams or jellies, and bread or rolls should be placed within easy reach and in a manner to make the table look somewhat symmetrical. Put the silver that is needed for serving these foods at the right of each dish.

How to place the table decorations. Flowers of some kind are quite commonly selected for a table decoration. A small plant, an ornamental piece of pottery, a china or glass figure, fruit, or candles in candlesticks are also used sometimes.

127

VARIETY IN TABLE DECORATION

Courtesy Syracuse China Corporation

● Candles and pine cones

Courtesy Steuben Glass

● Bowl of tea roses

Courtesy Syracuse China Corporation

● Tall candles and low flowers

Courtesy Lenox, Incorporated

● Bowl of fruit

Courtesy Syracuse China Corporation

● Lilies and candles

Courtesy Dennison Manufacturing Company

● Homemade ornaments

Whatever the decoration you select, it should be in good taste and be artistically arranged. Its colors should harmonize with the room, the dishes, and the food that is served. It should be either low enough or high enough so those at the table can see one another over or under it.

Usually the table decoration is placed in the center of the table because there is no other place for it when the entire table is set. However, if there are no covers at one end or along one side of the table, the decoration may be placed "off center" on either the vacant end or side.

How to set a tray for tray meals. It is sometimes convenient to serve food on a tray when a person eats alone, when a meal is served buffet style, or when dessert is served before a television set. Sometimes trays are also convenient when meals are served on the patio or at a barbecue. Tray service is usually necessary for the invalid or convalescent.

The same care is needed in setting a tray as in setting a table. The table appointments are placed in the same manner on a tray as they are at a cover on a table. An attractive tray cloth or a place mat with a matching napkin is used. A tumbler is better than a goblet for tray service because the tumbler is less likely to tip over.

Table Service

There are three general styles of table service—informal, formal, and compromise. The degree of informality and formality varies, depending on the standards maintained and on the family situation.

Informal service. For informal table service the members of the family perform the duties connected with serving the

● In informal table service the food may be served in the kitchen on individual plates which are then placed before each family member. Some foods, such as bread, butter, celery, and olives, are passed at the table so that each person may help himself.

meals. There are three ways to serve meals informally:

1. Food is brought to the table in serving dishes and served by the host or hostess. Then the served plates are passed around the table to each family member. This is referred to as "family service."
2. Food is brought to the table in serving dishes, and these dishes are passed around the table so each member of the family can help himself.
3. Food is served in the kitchen onto individual plates, and a served plate is placed before each family member.

In some families the service is a combination of these ways.

Coffee, tea, or milk may be poured either at the table or in the kitchen, as desired. For ways of applying family service to

● Practicing good table conduct in your group at school will help you to form correct habits. Sit erect, enter into cheerful conversation, and eat slowly.

meals, see Chapter 9, "Preparing and Serving Breakfast," Chapter 10, "Preparing and Serving Lunch or Supper," and Chapter 11, "Preparing and Serving Dinner."

Formal service. In one type of formal service, food is served from the table. But, unlike the informal family service, a waitress is required. The waitress carries the plates, after they have been served by the host or hostess, to each person at the table, serving one at a time. She passes foods, such as bread or rolls or relishes, for each one to serve himself, she keeps the water glasses filled, and she removes the soiled dishes at the end of each course. This service is sometimes called "English service." Except for the waitress, it resembles family service. (See No. 1 on page 129.)

In another type of formal service, no food is served from the table. It is arranged on serving dishes and passed by the waitress or butler, who serves a portion to each person or allows each person to help himself. Sometimes in formal service each course is arranged on an individual plate and placed before the person. Since this style of service requires one or more waitresses or butlers, depending on the number to be served, it is not much used in the home, and it is not considered especially hospitable for home use. You may, however, encounter it in hotels, in exclusive restaurants, and in modified form at banquets.

Compromise service. There is yet another type of table service which is about as formal as is practical for present-day living. The name "compromise" is sometimes used for this service because it uses features of both types of formal service. Some of the food, arranged in the kitchen, is served in individual servings or passed in serving dishes, and part of the food is served from the table. The decision as to which food or course is to be served each way is optional and is usually decided on by the hostess. The service of a maid is desirable, although it is possible for one member of the family to act as a waitress. (See Chapter 11, "Preparing and Serving Dinner.")

Table Etiquette

Good table manners, like other conventional rules of conduct, should be so natural that no one thinks of them as manners. Those who know and practice good manners are poised and at ease and usually have the reputation of being well bred. Good manners at the table make meals more pleasant for others. Although we may

GOOD TABLE CONDUCT

1. Be well groomed when you come to the table. It is unpleasant for others to see uncombed hair, an unclean face, or dirty hands, fingernails, and clothing.

2. Come to the table promptly when called. It is discourteous to make others wait for you, and it is thoughtless of the person who prepared the meal.

3. Wait for others instead of rushing to the table ahead of them. When there are older or more important persons, permit them to precede you to the table.

4. Be seated only after all have assembled at the table, and then sit down from the left side of your chair. In this way there is no confusion, as is the case if some sit down from one side and some from the other side of the chairs.

5. If you are a man or a boy, help the women and girls to be seated. This is done by gently pushing the chair as the lady on your right sits down.

6. If it is the family custom to say grace at the table, sit or stand quietly while it is being said.

7. Wait to eat until all have been served.

8. Sit erect and do not slump or loll on the table, lean against it with your arm, or rest your elbow on the table. Your left hand should rest in your lap when not in use.

9. Keep your elbows close to your sides as you eat so as not to interfere with someone next to you. Even when there is ample room, it looks better to keep your elbows close to your side rather than spreading them out like wings.

10. Be observant of the needs of others. See that food is passed to them. Do not serve yourself first, unless the hostess asks you to do so, because it is selfish and indicates that you feel more important than the others. When food is passed to you, accept it and serve yourself in turn.

11. Apologize in the event of an accident, and then try to forget your disaster. Such an occurrence is likely to happen to anyone, and excessive talk about it cannot change the situation and only emphasizes it more.

12. Use a handkerchief only when absolutely necessary, and then do so as unobtrusively as possible.

13. Keep your hands away from your face and hair.

14. Do not argue or quarrel. Serenity when eating contributes to good digestion. Listen to others when they are talking, but make some contribution to the conversation yourself.

USING THE KNIFE, FORK, AND SPOON

● Cutting food

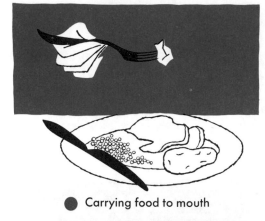

● Carrying food to mouth

● Placing knife and fork when not using

● Using soup spoon

not be aware of it ourselves, others quickly detect a lack of good manners. There is a little four-verse poem by an unknown author called "You Tell on Yourself," and one verse goes like this:

"You tell on yourself by the way you walk
  By the things of which you delight to talk
  By the manner in which you bear defeat
  By so simple a thing as how you eat."

You will want your table manners to be such that even so simple a thing as "how you eat" will prove that you are well bred and not self-centered, as is the person who is indifferent to the effect he has on others.

When you have good table manners, there are quite a number of things you will be sure to do and some that you will be sure not to do. If, at each meal, you practice correct behavior, your actions will soon become automatic and natural.

There are three general rules that govern acceptable conduct at the table:

1. Be thoughtful and considerate of others.
2. Handle your table equipment correctly.
3. Eat quietly, without attracting attention, and without being offensive to others.

Each of these three rules is made up of a number of other and more specific rules.

132

You may be familiar with most of them, but in your study of table etiquette you will want to review them.

The first sign of good table conduct is your thoughtfulness of others in the family or of anyone who may be at the table wherever you are eating. Suggestions for good table conduct are given on page 131.

Another indication of good table conduct is the way you handle your table equipment. The rules for handling and using table equipment are given in the chart below.

Even when table manners are flawless, the process of eating is not an especially pretty sight. So it becomes especially important to see that you eat as quietly and as inconspicuously as possible. The object in mannerly eating is not to see how quickly you can finish your meal but to eat so you and those who eat with you get pleasure and satisfaction from eating together. For comfortable, pleasant eating habits, see the suggestions in the chart on pages 134 and 135.

When You Eat Out

USE PREVENTATIVES

The rules of etiquette when eating out are essentially the same as those when eating in your own home or when you are a guest in someone's home. However, there

---

HANDLING TABLE EQUIPMENT

1. Place the napkin in your lap.

2. Use the napkin, as needed, to touch your mouth lightly with a blotting motion.

3. When cutting food, hold the knife and fork as shown in the drawing on page 132.

4. When carrying food to your mouth, hold the fork as shown in the drawing on the opposite page.

5. When not in use, keep the knife across the plate as shown in the drawing on page 132.

6. Use a teaspoon for soft foods, holding it in the same manner as you do the fork.

7. Cut salad foods with the fork whenever possible. Use a knife only when the food is difficult to cut with a fork.

8. Place the soup spoon, beverage spoon, and dessert spoon as shown in the drawings on pages 134 and 136.

9. Use the service tableware when you serve yourself from a serving dish—never use your own tableware.

10. Pass food that is in a serving dish with a handle so that the handle is toward the person to whom the dish is passed.

11. Never play with the tableware.

12. When lifting a goblet, hold it at the base of the bowl.

13. Lift a beverage cup by its handle with one hand. Never hold it in two hands when drinking.

14. When passing plates, be careful not to put your thumb on the inside of the plate or to touch any of the food on the plate.

15. Leave used dishes in place at the end of the meal. Do not push them away from you, and do not stack them.

16. When you are through eating, place the knife and fork in the center of the plate as shown in the drawing on page 134.

17. At the end of the meal, lay the napkin on the table at the left of your plate, folded if at home, and unfolded neatly if you are a guest.

WHEN FINISHED EATING

● When soup is served in a soup plate, leave the spoon in the soup plate (left). When soup is served in a cup or bowl, leave the spoon on the saucer (right).

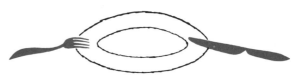

● Place the knife and fork firmly in the center of the plate (left). Never rest the handle of the knife or fork on the table (right).

GOOD EATING HABITS

1. Take small bites and eat slowly. Fast eating often results in a mouth crammed full of food, which is unpleasant to see.

2. Chew with your mouth closed, and do not talk until your mouth is empty.

3. When eating food, cut off each bite as you eat it. It is permissible for adults to cut an entire serving for young children all at one time, but not for themselves.

4. Lift food to your mouth when you eat; do not lower your head to the food.

5. Eat all the food taken on a fork or spoon at one time; never withdraw some of it. For example, when eating ice cream, eat all you put on the spoon; do not remove the spoon from your mouth with some uneaten ice cream on it. It is better to take less on the spoon in the first place.

6. Have your mouth empty when you drink water or beverages.

7. Sip beverages; do not gulp them.

8. When a food, such as potatoes, soup, or a beverage, is too hot to eat, wait until it cools. Do not blow on it or wave something in the air to cool it.

9. Dip a soup spoon into the soup away from you and never fill the spoon completely. This will prevent the soup from dribbling out and over the spoon. Sip soup noiselessly from the side of the spoon—not from the tip—and do not put the entire spoon in your mouth. A cream soup is never sipped from the soup cup, but it is permissible to drink a clear, thin soup, such as bouillon or consommé, from the cup.

are a few special points that are well to know so that you will be at ease when eating in a public place.

Eating out may mean eating most informally at a soda fountain, in your school cafeteria, in a tearoom or restaurant, or in a hotel dining room. You may be eating with your parents, with a group of girls, with a mixed group of both boys and girls, or with only one other person. When a boy invites a girl to eat out with him, he should play the role of host.

When you are an invited guest, your host or hostess decides on the place to eat. When you are assigned to a table in the restaurant, you precede your host or hostess as

GOOD EATING HABITS (Continued)

10. Break—do not cut—bread or rolls into small pieces before buttering. Butter each small piece just before it is eaten. A whole or even a half slice of bread should never be buttered at one time, nor should a piece of bread be laid on the table while it is being buttered. A hot biscuit or roll may be buttered at one time, however, by breaking it apart and buttering it while it is still hot.

11. Put butter, jelly, or marmalade on bread or toast with a bread-and-butter knife, if one is provided. Otherwise use a regular knife.

12. Keep the table as free from crumbs as possible. Food such as bread, cookies, and cake belong on a plate, not on the table cover. Greasy crumbs look untidy on the table and soil the linen.

13. When there is a bread-and-butter plate, use it also for relishes, celery, olives, and pickles, and for jam or jelly for your bread. Otherwise place these foods on your plate. When jelly is served as an accompaniment to the meat, such as mint jelly with lamb, the jelly goes on your plate beside the meat. Condiments that are to be used with meat, fish, or poultry are also placed on your plate with the food they are to accompany.

14. Do not touch foods with your hands except for certain so-called "finger foods," such as olives, celery, carrot sticks, and potato chips; bread, rolls, and most sandwiches; some kinds of cake; and corn on the cob. With these exceptions, the hands should not be used to touch food—that is, food should not be pushed onto a fork or spoon or otherwise manipulated with the fingers. Eating chicken by holding a piece in the fingers is permissible only at pickup suppers, picnics, and other very informal occasions at home if it is a family custom. When you are out, it is not good table conduct to eat chicken with the fingers unless your hostess suggests it.

15. Eat cake that is covered with a sticky frosting or whipped cream with a fork. You may eat unfrosted cake or cake with a hard frosting with your fingers.

16. Keep each food separate on your plate as you eat. It is not pleasant to see an untidy plate. Also, it is a bad practice to mop up gravy and sauce with a piece of bread or potato. This does not mean that gravy and sauce should not be eaten, but it is unattractive to see a person wipe his plate clean in this fashion.

17. Remove fruit pits from the mouth with a spoon, or better yet, cut the flesh of the fruit from the pit before eating the fruit. A fish bone is removed from the mouth as inconspicuously as possible with the fingers and placed on the side of the plate. A napkin may be used to screen the removal of objects from the mouth.

18. Never use your fingers to dislodge particles of food that cling to your teeth and make you uncomfortable. Nor should you roll your tongue around in your mouth to dislodge food. A toothpick should not be used for any purposes except in private.

WHAT TO DO WITH THE SPOON

● When finished eating from a saucedish, place the spoon either in the dish (above) or on the plate (below).

● The spoon should be left on the plate beside the sherbert dish or on the saucer of the beverage cup (above), never in the dish or cup (below).

you go to it if a waiter leads you to the table. Otherwise, the host leads the way. When you have looked at the menu and decided what you would like to eat—most likely after some suggestions from your host —you tell him your choice and he does the ordering for you. When it seems more con-

venient to do so, it is all right for a girl to give her order directly to the waiter.

Menus in restaurants usually offer food either à la carte or table d'hôte. When a meal is served à la carte, the price is given for each dish ordered; and when a meal is served table d'hôte, the entire meal is served at a fixed price. If there is something you would like during the meal, you tell your host what it is. He attracts the attention of the waiter and makes the request for you.

It is in poor taste to be conspicuous in any way when you are in a public place, and loud talk and laughter should be avoided. It is not necessary to be unmannerly to have a good time.

8

Preparing Meals

■ YOU have learned that there are many advantages when the homemaker uses good management in planning meals for her family. Good management is also valuable in preparing meals. Here it means organizing meal-preparation procedures and following recipes correctly so good meals may be assured. Good management also means paying attention to suitable grooming and to personal habits while at work in the kitchen.

Organizing Meal-preparation Procedures

When you are learning how to prepare meals, it will help you if you think through all the things you have to do and jot them down. Then you can arrange the tasks in the order that you plan to do them. Of course when you become experienced in meal preparation, you can keep an organization plan such as this in mind without writing it down.

Although your organization plans will be different for different meals and for different situations, such as times when you may have someone to help you, they are similar in general outline and include the steps listed in the chart on page 139. In the next three chapters the steps in this plan are followed in carrying out the actual preparation and serving of the three meals of the day—a breakfast, a lunch, and a dinner.

Following Recipes

As you use recipes, three things are necessary if you are to get good results in the products you make:

1. You must know how to measure the ingredients accurately.
2. You must be familiar with the terms you find in the recipes.
3. You should understand the reasons for the methods given in the directions.

Measuring Ingredients

The three kinds of measures used in recipes are described in the chart below.

Whatever the kind of measure used, it is essential that ingredients be measured accurately. Too much or too little of even one ingredient may throw off balance the right proportion of the ingredients to one another. To help you in making your measurements accurate, see directions and drawing on pages 427 to 429.

● Before beginning meal preparation, consult the recipe or directions for preparing the food you plan to use to be sure that you have all the ingredients and the necessary equipment on hand.

MEASURES USED IN RECIPES

Volume measures: These measure amounts of food in terms of volume—that is, gallon, quart, pint, cup, or fraction of a cup. Volume measures are used for measuring dry ingredients like flour and sugar, liquid ingredients like milk and molasses, and solid ingredients like butter and margarine. Volume measures are used also for measuring such foods as grated cheese, small berries, and chopped nuts.

Weight measures: These measure amounts of food in terms of weight—that is, pound or fraction of a pound and ounce or fraction of an ounce. Weight measures are used less frequently in food preparation than are volume measures. Meat, fish, cheese, butter, and chocolate are some foods for which a weight measure may be listed in recipes. Weight measures are often used for the fruit and sugar in making jams and jellies.

Unit measures: These measure amounts of food in terms of number—that is, one or some other specified number of a food. Unit measures are used for such foods as eggs, many fresh fruits like apples and oranges, and pieces of canned fruits.

Knowing Food-preparation Terms

The terms used in recipe directions have definite meanings, and many of them may be new to you. So that you may become familiar with recipe terms, there is a list of the terms that are frequently used, with their definitions, on pages 143 to 148. For example, you will learn what to do if told to "cut in" the fat with the flour when making pastry; to "fold" the beaten egg white into a pudding; to "beat" the batter when making a cake; or to "stir" in the milk when making a white sauce. And you will find what the difference is between such terms as "chopping" and "dicing." In following the direction "separate the egg" or "egg, separated," see the drawing on page 240.

Understanding Recipe Directions

Practically all types of foods undergo some kind of treatment in their preparation, even if it is so simple a procedure as washing, paring, or cutting, as in prepar-

STEPS IN PREPARING A MEAL

Step 1. Review the menu and get out the recipes.

Step 2. Make a list of the supplies and equipment needed for the meal as follows:
  a. List the foods called for, including all ingredients in all recipes.
  b. List the cooking equipment.
  c. List the table and serving appointments.

Step 3. Make a market order.

Step 4. Make a work-and-time schedule as follows:
  a. Refer to the recipes and note the time that each recipe must be started, taking into consideration the time the meal is to be served.
  b. Note which tasks may be dovetailed with others and what short cuts, if any, may be taken. (See Chapter 4, "Managing Meals to Save Time and Effort.")

Step 5. Add to the schedule, if you are working in a group, the assignment of tasks as follows:
  a. Who is to make each dish.
  b. Who is to act as hostess at the table.
  c. Who is to be responsible for serving the food (the "waitress").
  d. Who is to be responsible for each of the clearing-away tasks—dishwashing, dish drying, putting away the dishes and utensils.

Step 6. Prepare the meal by following these steps:
  a. Put on your apron and wash your hands.
  b. Refer to the schedule and, if a member of a group, note your special task.
  c. Assemble ingredients, cooking equipment, and table and serving appointments from the list made in Step 2.
  d. Prepare the dish or carry out what other tasks have been assigned to you.

Step 7. Serve the meal.

Step 8. Clear away the meal, wash the dishes, and put everything away, by following assigned tasks.

Step 9. Evaluate the meal.

METHODS OF PREPARATION

Courtesy General Electric Company

1. Applying heat to food

Courtesy Reynolds Wrap

2. Keeping moisture in food

Courtesy Westinghouse

3. Removing moisture from food

Courtesy Frigidaire

4. Removing heat from food

Courtesy Poultry and Egg National Board

5. Adding air to food

ing raw fruits and vegetables. But recipe directions usually call for preparation processes that are more complicated than this, involving one or more of the following treatments:

1. Applying heat to food, as in boiling, baking, broiling, roasting, and frying
2. Keeping moisture in food, as in the storing and preparation of salad greens, fruits, and vegetables
3. Removing moisture from food, as in toasting and baking
4. Removing heat from food, as in chilling and freezing
5. Adding air (or other gas) to food, as in beating eggs and cream, and in leavening batters and doughs

Some of these processes leave food relatively unchanged, while others modify the food in appearance, texture, consistency, and flavor. Some of these processes may even alter the original food value of the food.

The detailed method or procedure followed in preparing a product is based on a rule, or, as it is called, a "principle of cookery." A principle depends on the ingredients in the recipe, and, in some cases, even on the nutrients that are in one of the ingredients. For example, custards are cooked at a low temperature because of the proteins in the egg ingredient of the custard recipe. At a high temperature the egg proteins would toughen and the custard would be curdled. (See recipe for Soft Custard on page 457.) You will find a discussion of the principles of preparation for different foods in Part IV. The methods of preparing foods based on the principles are applied in the recipes in Part V.

When you prepare foods by following principles of cookery, you are applying

● Being clean, neat, and attractive is important when working in the kitchen. A simple apron will protect your dress and add a touch of color to your outfit.

science to food preparation. It is only in this way that your product can measure up to a high standard of quality.

But food preparation involves art as well as science. Color, flavor, and texture combinations, as well as arrangement for serving, must all be considered if you want to present your masterpieces artistically and to best advantage. In Chapter 3, "Planning Meals for Variety and Attractiveness," you will find a discussion of ways to make your meals attractive.

At Work in the Kitchen

In addition to knowing how to organize procedures and to follow recipes when preparing meals, there are other things for you to think about. What will you wear in the

● Students at work in the school kitchen are clean and neatly dressed. Work surfaces are uncluttered. The table is properly set. Each one is carrying out the task required, and there is no confusion.

kitchen? Will you look clean, neat, and attractive when you work there? And will your habits of work be sanitary and above reproach?

Your Grooming

Tennis players, airplane pilots and stewardesses, nurses, and many other people wear clothes which are appropriately designed for the kind of work they do. As you work in the kitchen, you, too, will want to wear clothes that are suitable. You will not need a uniform, but you will need clothes that make it possible for you to work with ease and safety. The work of food preparation includes many motions, and your clothes should be loose enough so as not to restrict these motions and thereby cause discomfort. Plain, washable dresses are appropriate because they are easily cleaned. If, in some situations, it is not convenient to wear a washable dress, a simple apron or a smock will protect your dress and, at the

same time, add a touch of color to your outfit. Boys working in the kitchen will want to wear tailored aprons of a heavy material rather than something that looks feminine. At all costs, avoid wearing any dress, apron, or smock that might cause an accident. Sleeves, pockets, and loops may catch onto pan handles, causing hot foods to spill; or they may catch onto knobs of ranges, doors, or cabinets. You will not tire so easily if your shoes are comfortable and have fairly low heels. Shoes with high heels are tiring and a hazard.

Neatness and cleanliness in the kitchen are *musts*. Soiled clothing is neither neat nor sanitary. It keeps you from looking your best and encourages sloppiness in work habits. When you work with food, always have your hair neatly arranged. A band of some kind helps to hold back loose ends and keeps your hair out of the way so you do not have to bother with it while you are working. Clean hands and well-cared-for nails are another *must* when working with food. Be particularly careful of nail polish that is chipping.

Your Personal Habits

Sanitary habits in the kitchen are essential because the person who prepares meals has a duty to see that everything is done to safeguard the family's health. Also, it is pleasanter for those who eat the food if they are certain that it has been handled in a sanitary manner. This is one of the reasons that many people prefer to eat at home—because they know the conditions under which the food has been prepared.

Here are some of the practices to follow to ensure good personal habits in the preparation of meals:

1. Always wash your hands before you handle food. Wash your hands again if you touch anything unrelated to food preparation, especially something that might carry germs, such as a handkerchief.
2. Keep your hands away from your hair and face.
3. Always use a separate spoon for tasting —never the stirring spoon.

Courtesy Lincoln High School, Philadelphia

● It is well to decide how satisfactory each food is by evaluating the meal with the teacher. If any food is not up to standard, now is the time to learn how to improve it.

4. If a utensil should fall on the floor, wash it before using it again.
5. Keep the dish towel and dishcloth, when not in use, on a rack or in some other clean place, and do not use them again if they should fall on the floor.

TERMS USED IN FOOD PREPARATION

bake: To cook by dry heat in an oven or oven-type appliance in either covered or uncovered containers. When applied to meats in uncovered containers, the term "roast" is generally used.

barbecue: To cook meat or poultry slowly on a revolving grid or spit over coals or under an open flame or electric unit, usually basting it with a highly seasoned sauce.

baste: To moisten meat or other foods with a liquid, while cooking, to add flavor and to prevent the surface from drying. Usually melted fat, meat drippings, fruit juice, or a sauce is used for the liquid.

beat: To make a mixture smooth or to introduce air by using a brisk over-and-over motion with a spoon or a wire whisk. (See drawing on page 144.) A rotary

TECHNIQUES IN FOOD PREPARATION

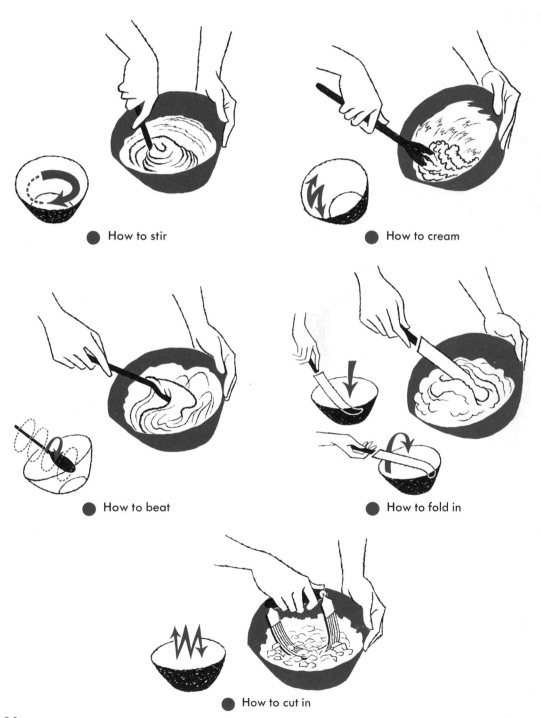

How to stir

How to cream

How to beat

How to fold in

How to cut in

Robert E. Coates

● Colorful table appointments, colorful foods, and a festive informality are the keynotes of a meal served in the patio.

● Outdoor foods served indoors for a teen-age party. Here each guest helps himself to hamburger or wiener from the grill and makes his own sandwich to his liking. Punch is available on the sideboard whenever desired, and cake will be cut when the guests are ready for dessert.

● Foods for camping out must be hearty, easy to prepare in large quantities, and of a type that can be served and eaten easily. Note how well the foods in this meal contrast in color, flavor, and texture. Other appropriate foods are kabobs, broiled steaks, and chicken.

FRESH-COCONUT PATTIES

CANDIED GRAPEFRUIT PEEL

NUT BRITTLE
COCONUT DREAM ROLL
FONDANT-STUFFED DATES
ALMOND NOUGAT

PASTEL POPCORN BALLS

WALNUT CREAMS
VANILLA AND CHOCOLATE CARAMELS
BONBONS

CARAMEL PECAN SLICES

FRENCH CHOCOLATE BALLS
FONDANT-DIPPED ALMONDS

Robert E. Coates

● Numerous varieties of candy can be made at home with little effort and with much satisfaction. When you understand the principles of making crystalline and noncrystalline candies (see Chapter 33), you can proceed with confidence to make any of the candies shown here stored in these beautiful containers.

● Cookies can be international too: From top to bottom: Macaroons (Italy); Mincemeat Turnovers and Drop Cookies (England); Spritz Cookies and Fattigsmanskakor—fried cookies—(Scandinavia); Chocolate-dipped Sugar Cookies, Frosted Christmas Cookies, Chocolate Crunch Cookies, and Brownies (America); and Lace Cookies and Meringuettes (France).

● A cheerful setting is particularly important for breakfast. Colorful, gay table settings do not have to be costly nor fancy—a small centerpiece of gay flowers, a bright-colored tablecloth, or colored dishes are often all that is necessary to create a cheerful atmosphere.

● The setting for dinner is often much more elaborate than the simple, gay setting for breakfast —fine-quality linen, sterling silver, quality china, and glassware can be used for dinner, the largest and most leisurely meal of the day.

● Informal service is popular in today's busy world. This buffet meal—whether for family or guests —involves all the principles of good meal planning and preparation. The tempting casserole dish, the toasted bread, the crisp salad greens, and the mixed fruits make an adequate, satisfying meal. The serving dishes are appropriate and interesting and the table setting in the background is attractive but not expensive.

beater or an electric mixer may also be used for beating.

blanch: To allow a food to stand in boiling water or steam for several minutes. Usually this term applies to loosening the skins of fruits and nuts or to inactivating enzymes and shrinking food for freezing.

blend: To mix two or more ingredients until all are thoroughly combined.

boil: To cook in water, or a liquid that is mostly water, in which bubbles rise continually and break on the surface. The boiling temperature of water at sea level is 212° F.

braise: To cook meat or poultry slowly in a covered utensil in a small amount of liquid or in steam, either in an oven or on a surface unit. The food may or may not have been browned in fat.

bread: (1) To coat with fine, dry bread or cracker crumbs; or (2) to coat with crumbs, then with milk or diluted slightly beaten egg, and again with crumbs. See **coat.**

broil: To cook by direct heat over coals or under an open gas flame or electric unit in a broiler.

brown: To make the surface of a food brown in color by frying, toasting, baking, or broiling.

brush: To cover lightly with another food, such as fat or egg white, usually with a pastry brush.

candy: (1) When applied to fruit, fruit peel, or ginger—to cook in a heavy sirup until plump and transparent; then drain and dry. (2) When applied to partially cooked sweetpotatoes or carrots—to cook in sugar or syrup until glazed.

caramelize: To heat sugar or foods containing a large amount of sugar slowly until a brown color and characteristic caramel flavor develop.

chill: To place in a refrigerator or other cold place until cold but not frozen.

chop: To cut with an up-and-down motion into small pieces, using a sharp knife and wooden board or a chopper and wooden bowl. (See drawing on page 147.)

coat: (1) To cover a food with another ingredient, usually flour, corn meal, dry bread crumbs, or sugar, by dipping or rolling the food in the other ingredient until all sides are covered or by putting the food with the other ingredient in a paper bag and shaking the bag. (See drawing on page 147.) (2) To form a film on a surface, as on a spoon.

cookery: The complete process of food preparation.

cooking: The application of heat to food.

core: To remove the core, or central portion, from fruits such as apples and from vegetables such as lettuce.

cream: To work one or more foods until soft and creamy by rubbing with the back of a spoon or other utensil against the side of a bowl (see drawing on page 144) or by beating with an electric mixer. This term is applied to the mixing of fat and sugar in place of "blend."

cube: To cut into ½-inch solid pieces with six equal sides.

cut: To divide foods into smaller pieces with a knife or with scissors.

cut and fold: Same as **fold.**

cut in: To distribute solid fat in small pieces evenly through dry ingredients, using two knives, a fork, or a pastry blender in a cutting motion. (See drawing on page 144.)

deep-fat-fry: To cook food in a kettle containing enough hot fat to cover the food until a brown crust forms and the center is done.

devil: To make a food "hot" by adding spices or condiments.

dice: To cut into very small cubes (about ¼ inch). (See drawing on page 147.)

dip: To cover a food with a dry substance such as sugar or a moist substance such as beaten egg.

dissolve: To make a dry substance pass into solution.

dot: To scatter small bits of one ingredient, such as butter, margarine, or cheese, over the surface of a food.

drain: To pour off a liquid from a food.

dredge: To sprinkle or coat with flour or fine crumbs.

dust: To sprinkle lightly, usually with flour or sugar.

flake: To break a food lightly into small pieces with a fork.

flour: To dust the surface of a food lightly with flour.

flute: To decorate an edge, such as of pastry, with a scalloplike design.

fold: To blend ingredients by repeatedly cutting vertically down through the mixture with the edge of a spoon or a rubber spatula, sliding the spoon or spatula across the bottom of the bowl, and then turning the mixture over. (See drawing on page 144.)

freeze: To lower the temperature of a food to its freezing point or below.

fricassee: To cook by braising—usually applied to fowl, veal, or rabbit cut into pieces. See **braise.** The term also describes the food so cooked, as fricasseed chicken.

frost: To decorate the surface of a food, usually cake or cookies, with icing or frosting.

fry: To cook in hot fat. See **pan-fry** and **deep-fat-fry.**

garnish: To add a small amount of one food to another food for the purpose of decorating it.

glaze: To coat with a thin sugar syrup, thus giving a food a shiny surface.

grate: To obtain fine particles of a food by rubbing it over a rough surface, such as a grater.

grease: To rub lightly with a fat, such as butter, margarine, salad oil, or shortening.

grill: Same as **broil.**

grind: To cut or crush food by putting it through a food chopper or meat grinder.

heat: To raise the temperature of a food.

knead: To work dough with the hands, using a pressing motion accompanied by folding and stretching. (See illustration on page 322.)

marinate: To let stand in a mixture, usually French dressing, for a specified length of time to add flavor.

mash: To make a food soft and smooth by crushing or beating.

melt: To change a solid to a liquid by means of heat.

mince: To cut or chop into very small pieces with a sharp knife or chopper.

mix: To combine two or more ingredients in any manner that effects a distribution.

mold: (1) To shape a food in the hands; or (2) to pour a liquid food into a mold and allow it to become firm, as gelatin.

pan: To cook a vegetable in a tightly covered skillet, using a small amount of butter, margarine, or bacon drippings. No water is added.

pan-broil: To cook uncovered on an ungreased or lightly greased hot surface, usually a skillet, pouring off excess fat as it accumulates.

COMMON PROCESSES USED IN FOOD PREPARATION

● Dicing

● Chopping

● Coating

pan-fry: To brown or cook uncovered in a small amount of fat in a skillet.

parboil: To boil in water until partially cooked before completing the cooking by another method.

pare: To cut off the outside covering, as of a potato or an apple.

pasteurize: To preserve liquids, such as milk and fruit juices, by heating sufficiently to destroy certain microorganisms and to arrest fermentation. The temperature used varies with the food but commonly ranges from 140° to 180° F.

peel: To strip off the outside covering, as of a banana or an orange.

poach: To cook gently in a hot liquid below the boiling point, using care to retain shape.

preheat: To heat an oven or a broiler to the desired cooking temperature before putting in food.

purée: To force cooked food through a sieve or strainer to make a pulp.

quarter: To cut into four pieces.

render: To remove fat from the connective tissue of meat by heating the meat slowly at low heat until the fat melts and can be drained off.

roast: To cook, uncovered, by dry heat, usually in an oven. See **bake.**

roll: (1) To move a piece of food by turning it over and over, usually to cover it with a substance such as sugar, flour, or crumbs. (2) To make smooth or flat with a rolling pin or the hands, such as dough for pastry or for baking powder biscuits.

sauté: To brown or cook uncovered in a small amount of fat, turning frequently.

scald: To heat a liquid to just below the simmering point.

scallop: To bake a food, usually cut into pieces, with a sauce or other liquid in a baking dish, such as scalloped potatoes.

score: To cut a surface lightly by marking with lines.

scrape: To remove the outside skin by rubbing the surface with a knife.

scrub: To clean thoroughly with a brush.

sear: To brown the surface of meat quickly with high heat.

season: To add seasonings, such as salt, pepper, herbs, or spices, to a food to improve the flavor.

section: To separate the flesh from the membrane and skin, as in removing the flesh of grapefruit.

shape: To make into the desired form.

shell: To remove the outer covering, such as pods of peas and shells of nuts and shrimp.

shred: To cut or tear into thin strips or pieces with a knife or shredder.

sift: To put dry ingredients through a flour sifter or fine sieve.

simmer: To cook in a liquid just below the boiling point (185° to 210° F. at sea level) on a surface unit. At simmering temperature, bubbles form slowly and collapse below the surface.

singe: To hold over a flame to burn off hairs, as on poultry.

skim: To remove a film from the surface of a liquid, such as the fat from soup, the foam from syrup for jelly, or the cream from the top of milk.

slice: To cut into thin, flat pieces, as a slice of bread.

sprinkle: To shake a fine ingredient, such as flour or sugar, chopped parsley, or crumbs, over the surface of a food.

steam: To cook in the steam which arises from boiling water with or without pressure.

steep: To let stand in hot liquid below the boiling point in order to extract flavor, color, or other qualities.

sterilize: To destroy microorganisms in or on a food by using steam or by boiling in water for a specified length of time.

stir: To mix ingredients, using a circular motion with a spoon, for the purpose of blending or securing a uniform consistency. (See drawing on page 144.)

strain: To separate a liquid from a food by means of a sieve or strainer.

toast: To brown a food by direct heat or in an oven.

unmold: To loosen and remove a food from a mold in which it has been placed to give it a special shape.

whip: To beat rapidly, usually with a rotary beater, a whisk, or an electric mixer, to increase volume by incorporating air, as in egg whites, whipping cream, and gelatin dishes.

9
Preparing and Serving Breakfast

■ BREAKFAST is often a hurriedly eaten meal because some members of the family are rushing to get to work or to school. Consequently, the meal is likely to be slighted. Since breakfast is too important to the health of everyone for this to happen, you will need to learn to be efficient in preparing this meal and to know how to serve it. Then when you have the responsibility of preparing and serving breakfast at home, the meal can be enjoyed in a leisurely manner.

At school you will prepare and serve a breakfast in cooperation with others in your class group, but your time may be limited, possibly, to a single and rather short class period. If you do have only one single period, even though there are several of you working together, you should select a menu that may be prepared and served without hurry in the time allowed. The menu on page 150 is a good choice.

In the preparation of this breakfast, you will want to organize your preparation procedures and include in them your plan for serving the meal. Since you are working in a group, these plans will be made cooperatively and, when time is short, will have to be done beforehand. In Chapter 8 on page 139 you will find a list of the steps that should be followed in the preparation of any meal.

In carrying out the following plan for preparing and serving breakfast, it is as-

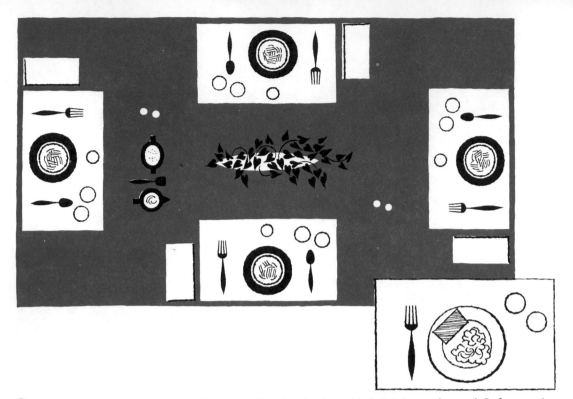

● This table is appropriately set for a breakfast beginning with fruit juice and cereal. Before setting a table, always check the menu to see what table appointments are needed. Then select tablecloth or place mats, centerpiece, tableware, chinaware, and glassware that will be suitable. At the start of a second course consisting of scrambled eggs and toast, each table cover should look like the insert at the bottom. Juice glasses and cereal bowls have been removed.

sumed that four members of your class working together constitute a family and that you have a single period in which to prepare and serve the breakfast.

Step 1 in the plan for preparing a meal is to review the menu and the recipes used in it.

The Menu
Grapefruit Juice
Ready-to-Eat Cereal
Sugar Milk
Scrambled Eggs
Cinnamon Toast Milk

The Recipes
Scrambled Eggs (page 464)
Cinnamon Toast (page 483)

Step 2 is to make a list of the supplies and equipment needed for preparing and serving the meal. (See chart at the right.)

Step 3 is to make a market order.

The Market Order
(*To be checked with your teacher*)

Grapefruit juice	1 19-ounce can
Ready-to-eat cereal	3 cups
Milk	5¼ cups
Sugar	⅓ cup
Eggs	4
Salt	½ teaspoon
Pepper	⅛ teaspoon
Butter or margarine	¼ cup
Parsley	⅛ bunch
Bread	4 slices
Cinnamon	¾ teaspoon

150

Step 4 is to make a work-and-time schedule, and Step 5 is to assign the tasks when working in a group. (See schedule on page 152.) Since you are preparing and serving this breakfast with three others in your group, all four of you will carry out the tasks simultaneously. You have three to five minutes in which to make personal preparation for work, fifteen minutes for each preparation assignment, fifteen minutes for serving and eating the meal, and ten to twelve minutes in which to clear it away and put the kitchen in order. This is a total of forty-five minutes. The evaluation of your meal will have to be made at some other convenient time. If there are more than four in your group, or possibly only three, you will need to make adjustments in this work-and-time schedule. It is possible that your class period is longer than forty-five minutes, and then either the preparation and serving plans or the evalu-

THE SUPPLIES, EQUIPMENT, AND TABLE APPOINTMENTS NEEDED[1]

SUPPLIES		EQUIPMENT	
Grapefruit juice	1 19-ounce can	Juice glasses	4
Cold cereal	3 cups	Cereal bowls	4
Milk	2 cups	Plates	4
Sugar	2 tablespoons	Milk pitcher	1
		Sugar bowl	1
Eggs	4	Skillet	1
Milk	¼ cup	Bowl	1
Salt	½ teaspoon	Rotary beater or electric mixer	1
Pepper	⅛ teaspoon	Measuring spoons	1 set
Butter or margarine	1 tablespoon	Stirring spoon or spatula	1
Parsley	⅛ bunch	Plates	4
Bread	4 slices	Small bowl	1
Sugar	3 tablespoons	Measuring spoons	1 set
Cinnamon	¾ teaspoon	Board	1
Butter or margarine	3 tablespoons	Spatula	1
		Sharp knife	1
		Baking sheet	1
		Broiler	1
		Serving plate	1
Milk	3 cups	Glasses	4

Additional Table Appointments

Centerpiece	1	Forks	4
Place mats	4	Teaspoons	4
Napkins	4	Sugar spoon	1
Water glasses	4	Salt and pepper sets	2

[1] Supplies and equipment are listed for the preparation of each product.

ation of the meal might be included in this longer period.

Step 6 is to prepare the meal:

a. Put on your apron, and wash your hands.

b. Refer to the work-and-time schedule below, and note what your tasks are.

c. Assemble the ingredients, equipment, or table appointments needed for your special tasks.

d. Prepare the food or carry out other tasks assigned to you. Where you use a recipe, follow the measurements and the method of preparing it carefully. You will add to your interest in following any recipe if you understand the reason for its method of preparation. You can learn about the principles of cooking the product you are preparing by reading its principles of preparation in Part IV.

THE WORK-AND-TIME SCHEDULE FOR PREPARING BREAKFAST

Group Member	Job Assignment	Time
All	Get ready to work.	10:00–10:05
Girl No. 1	Set table. Fill water glasses, milk glasses, and fruit-juice glasses. Place all on table at individual covers. (Juice should have been chilled by placing can in refrigerator early in morning.)	10:05–10:20
Girl No. 2	Fill cereal bowls, place on plates, take to table, and place in center of individual covers. Fill sugar bowl and milk pitcher for cereal, and take to table. Consult with group member who is setting the table as to where sugar bowl and milk pitcher should be placed. Close cereal package and return to storage shelf.	10:05–10:20
Girl No. 3	Make cinnamon toast. Arrange on serving plate, and put where toast will keep warm.	10:05–10:20
Girl No. 4	Wash and freshen parsley garnish, and place on paper ready for garnishing when eggs are served. Scramble eggs. Serve on warmed, individual plates. Put where eggs will keep warm. Rinse rotary beater in cold water. Put bowl in which eggs were beaten and skillet to soak in cold water.	10:05–10:20
All	Eat breakfast.	
Girl No. 1	Act as hostess.	10:20–10:35
Girl No. 4	Act as waitress.	
Girls No. 1 and 4	Clear table at end of meal.	
Girls No. 2 and 3	Wash and dry dishes.	10:35–10:45
Girls No. 1 and 4	Put dishes and other appointments and equipment away.	

● Allocate the work of getting and serving the breakfast among the group members. For this breakfast, Girl No. 1 sets the table; Girl No. 2 gets the cereal, milk, and sugar ready and places them on the table; Girl No. 3 makes the toast; and Girl No. 4 prepares the scrambled eggs and acts as waitress.

Thus for this breakfast you would read about egg cookery in Chapter 16, "Eggs." If your particular assignment is to set the table, however, read Chapter 7, "Table Setting and Etiquette," for general directions for setting the table. Then for details for setting the table for this breakfast, check with the drawings on page 150 and . . .

. . . lay a place mat at each cover.

. . . place a centerpiece, either a bowl of flowers or a plant, in the center of the table. It may rest directly on the table or, if you like, a place mat may be laid under it.

. . . lay a napkin beside the mat at the left.

. . . place on the mat a fork at the left and a teaspoon at the right.

. . . place three glasses: the water tumbler on the place mat near the upper right-hand corner, the glass for milk to the right of the water glass and slightly nearer the edge of the table, and the juice glass at the center but above the place where the cereal service will be placed. It will save steps and time for you if you assemble all these glasses on a tray, fill each in the kitchen, and then place them at the covers directly from the tray.

. . . place each salt and pepper set in a convenient place between two covers a little nearer the center of the table than the top of the place mats.

. . . let the member of the group who is responsible for the cereal know that you are ready to place it on the table, and working with her, place a cereal service—the filled bowl resting on a plate—in the center of each cover. Check to see that the plate rests at the same distance from the edge of the table as the fork and spoon. Then set the sugar bowl and milk pitcher on the table with the pitcher at the right of the sugar bowl. Put the sugar spoon on the table between the two pieces.

. . . tell the group that breakfast is ready to serve.

Step 7 is to serve the meal. The group assembles at the table, sits down from the left of the chairs, and unfolds their napkins, placing them in their laps.

The hostess, decided on by the group, indicates that it is time to eat by starting to drink the grapefruit juice. When everyone has finished drinking the juice, each glass is returned to its place above the cover. The milk and sugar for the cereal are then passed around the table with the handles of the milk pitcher and sugar bowl toward the person to whom they are offered.

When all at the table have eaten their cereal, the fruit juice and cereal services are removed by the member of the group who has been delegated to act as waitress. If this is your task, you will . . .

. . . lay your napkin beside your cover.

. . . go to the left of the hostess and, with your left hand, pick up the plate and cereal bowl. Transfer these to your right hand and then, with your left hand, pick up the fruit-juice glass.

. . . carry these to a tray on a serving table, or to a teacart if one is available.

. . . then continue around the table, going preferably to the right—that is, counterclockwise—until all the cereal dishes and juice glasses have been removed.

. . . carry the tray with the soiled dishes to the kitchen.

(Continued on page 158)

● All four girls should be ready to enjoy the meal at the same time.

● Again the work for cleaning up is divided among the group with Girls No. 2 and 3 washing and drying the dishes and Girls No. 1 and 4 putting them away.

● In the fruit: Use fresh fruit in season or stewed fruits.

● In the cereal: Use different kinds and vary the toppings.

BREAKFAST MENUS

● In the main dish: Have your eggs and toast together as French toast.

● In the bread: Have a sweet bread now and then.

It is now time to serve the scrambled eggs and cinnamon toast. If you are acting as waitress, you will...

...remove the plates of egg from the warm oven, and garnish each with a sprig of parsley.

...carry two plates to the table, go to the left of the hostess, and place the plate in your left hand in the center of her cover. Transfer the second plate to your left hand, and place it in front of the person at the right of the hostess, also from her left side.

...serve the two remaining plates of egg in the same manner.

...get the plate of toast, and place it on the table.

...take your seat, and ask someone to help herself to toast and to pass the plate.

Step 8 is to clear the table after the meal, wash the dishes, and put them away. (See drawings on page 155.) After the meal is over, there will be only a short time in which to wash the dishes and to put the kitchen in order. When two of the girls have cleared the table, the other two girls will wash the dishes. To do so, they will...

...pile the cooking utensils on one drainboard of the sink.

...scrape, rinse, and stack the soiled dishes, silver, and glasses as they are brought to the kitchen. The plates should be rinsed and stacked in piles, with those of like size together, and the silver and glasses should be rinsed.

...wash in hot, soapy water.

...rinse in very hot, clean water, and place to drain; then towel-dry.

...dry the drainboards, and wash the sink.

...wash the dish towel and dishcloth, and stretch them over a towel rack to dry.

Now the two girls who cleaned the table will put away the dishes, equipment, and table appointments.

Step 9 is evaluating the meal. We all learn by experience, and any experience is made more meaningful if we review it on its completion. Therefore, an evaluation of your work is important while you are learning to prepare meals. Then you can see the good points and profit by them. You can see the bad points also, and think of ways to avoid making them another time. In evaluating the breakfast, you might discuss with your group and your teacher questions such as those in the chart below. This step can be done later if there is not enough time during the class period.

EVALUATION OF THE BREAKFAST

Did we work together as a team?
Did each of us assume her individual responsibility?
Did our kitchen look neat and orderly as we worked?
Was the fruit juice chilled?
Were the scrambled eggs attractive to look at, well flavored, hot, and tender?
Was the toast crisp and well flavored?
Was the milk cold?

Was the table correctly laid and did it look attractive?
Was the meal served on time?
Was the meal served correctly?
Was the clearing away done well and efficiently?
As a result of this evaluation, what suggestions can we as a group make to improve our whole procedure when we prepare and serve another breakfast?

10

Preparing and Serving Lunch or Supper

■ ONE of your problems in meal preparation is to learn how to prepare and serve lunches. Lunch is usually the noonday meal, but it may not be eaten by the whole family together. You have a responsibility, therefore, to gain experience in preparing and serving several kinds of lunches. There is the lunch suitable for a homemaker alone, which she might like to have on a tray while she rests and listens to the radio or watches television. Other lunches include the lunch suitable for the homemaker and young children or older people; the lunch suitable for carrying in a lunch box; and the lunch suitable for Saturday noon, which should be moderately hearty if all the family are together. The moderately hearty lunch is also suit-

able for the usual evening meal or supper in families that have their hearty meal at noon.

Meals where young children and older people are part of the group and the carried lunch are discussed in Chapter 2, "Planning Meals for Health." In this chapter we shall consider the preparation and serving of a moderately hearty lunch both at school and at home, and of a very simple lunch suitable for serving on a tray.

Preparing and Serving Lunch or Supper at School

For this lunch you might select the menu on page 160. This menu has been planned for a meal that may be prepared and

● Whether lunch is eaten in a cafeteria or restaurant or is carried from home, the food selected should represent about one-third of the daily food requirements.

served quite easily in a double class period by a group of four working together. If the time available is only a single period, adjustments in the working plans will have to be made. In this case, the lunch might be prepared and served in a period preceding the school lunchtime or, possibly, two periods could be devoted to it. But whatever the situation, the preparation plans, the recipes, and the supplies and equipment for both kitchen and dining room are the same. Only the work-and-time schedules and job assignments would be different. In the charts on pages 163 to 165, schedules are suggested for each of the two situations.

According to the plan for preparing any meal (page 139), Step 1 is to review the menu and get out the recipes.

THE MENU

Waldorf Salad
Quick Cinnamon Rolls   Tea
Chocolate Cornstarch Pudding
with Coconut Topping

THE RECIPES

Waldorf Salad (page 503)
French Dressing (page 504)
Quick Cinnamon Rolls (page 495)
Tea (page 434)
Chocolate Cornstarch Pudding (page 456)

Step 2 is to make a list of the supplies and equipment needed for the meal. (See chart at the right.)

160

THE SUPPLIES, EQUIPMENT, AND TABLE APPOINTMENTS NEEDED[1]

SUPPLIES		EQUIPMENT	
Lettuce	¼ head (about 8 leaves)	Sharp knife	1
Apples (small)	2	Measuring cup	1
Celery	1 stalk	Measuring spoons	1 set
Salt	¼ teaspoon	Mixing bowl	1
English walnuts (shelled)	3 tablespoons	Tablespoon	1
Mayonnaise (optional)	2 tablespoons	Fork	1
		Serving plates	4
Sugar	¼ teaspoon	Measuring cup	1
Dry mustard	½ teaspoon	Measuring spoons	1 set
Paprika	½ teaspoon	Jar with tight cover	1
Salt	¾ teaspoon		
Pepper	¼ teaspoon		
Salad oil	⅞ cup		
Vinegar	¼ cup		
Flour	2¼ cups	Flour sifter	1
Baking powder	3 teaspoons	Spoon	1
Salt	1 teaspoon	Measuring cup	1
Shortening	¼ cup	Measuring spoons	1 set
Milk	¾ cup	Mixing bowl (medium size)	1
Butter or margarine	3 tablespoons	Mixing bowl (small size)	1
Brown sugar	½ cup	Board	1
Cinnamon	½ teaspoon	Pastry blender	1
		Rolling pin	1
		Spatula	1
		Sharp knife	1
		Cake pan	1
		Serving plate	1
Butter or margarine	3 tablespoons	Serving plate	1
Tea	4 teaspoons	Teakettle or saucepan	1
Lemon	6 slices	Measuring spoons	1 set
Sugar		Measuring cup	1
		Teapot	1
		Plate for lemon	1
		Sugar bowl	1
Sugar	¼ cup	Double boiler	1
Cornstarch	2¼ tablespoons	Spoon	1
Salt	¼ teaspoon	Measuring spoons	1 set
Cocoa	¼ cup	Measuring cup	1
Milk	2 cups	Individual molds	4
Vanilla	½ teaspoon	Serving dishes	4
Flaked coconut	2 tablespoons	Serving plates	4

[1] Supplies and equipment are listed for the preparation of each product.

(Continued)

● This well-set luncheon table is both attractive and suitable for the suggested lunch menu. See the chart on page 161 and below for the table appointments used.

Step 3 is to make a market order.

The Market Order
(Assuming staple foods on hand)

Lettuce	8 leaves
Apples (small)	2
Celery	1 stalk
English walnuts	3 tablespoons
Salad oil	⅞ cup
Vinegar	¼ cup
Milk	2¾ cups
Butter or margarine	6 tablespoons
Shortening	¼ cup
Tea	4 teaspoons
Lemon	1
Flaked coconut	2 tablespoons

THE SUPPLIES, EQUIPMENT, AND TABLE APPOINTMENTS NEEDED (Continued)

Additional Table Appointments

Centerpiece	1	Butter spreaders	4
Place mats	4	Butter serving knife	1
Napkins	4	Lemon fork	1
Water glasses	4	Sugar spoon	1
Bread-and-butter plates	4	Salt and pepper sets	2
Cups and saucers	4	Tile for teapot	1
Forks	4	Plate and napkin for	1
Teaspoons	8	crumbing	

Step 4 is to make a work-and-time schedule, and Step 5 is to assign the tasks for each member of the group.

The schedule shown below is based on the assumption that a group of four work cooperatively as a family; that they will have a double class period for preparing, serving, and clearing away the meal and for evaluating their work; and that the organizational planning will have been done in a preceding period or as an out-of-class assignment.

The schedule on pages 164 and 165 is arranged for a group of four working together and making some preparation in a period preceding the one in which the lunch is prepared, served, and cleared away. The evaluation of the project will need to be made at a later time.

Step 6 is to prepare the meal. Although the work-and-time schedules for preparing the lunch are different in the two situations, the steps you will follow in the preparation procedure in each case are the same:

a. Put on your apron, and wash your hands.

b. Refer to the work-and-time schedule, and note your special tasks.

THE WORK-AND-TIME SCHEDULE FOR PREPARING LUNCH IN A DOUBLE CLASS PERIOD

Group Member	Job Assignment	Time
All	Get ready to work.	10:00–10:05
Girls No. 1 and 2	Prepare chocolate cornstarch pudding, mold, and set in refrigerator. Measure coconut garnish. Set table, and fill water glasses. At 10:45 unmold pudding into serving dishes, and garnish. Place dishes on serving plates.	10:05–10:50
Girl No. 3	Prepare and bake cinnamon rolls. Make tea. Fill sugar bowl, slice lemon and put on serving plate. At 10:45 put butter and rolls on serving plates. Place all on table.	10:05–10:50
Girl No. 4	Make salad in this order: Wash lettuce, pat leaves dry, and crisp it in refrigerator. Make dressing. Prepare celery, nuts, and apples. Mix ingredients as in recipe. Arrange salads on individual plates and place on table in center of each cover. Store extra dressing in refrigerator.	10:05–10:50
All	Serve and eat the lunch. (Group selects hostess and waitress.)	10:50–11:10
All	Clear away the lunch. (Group decides who will wash dishes and who will dry them and put them away.)	11:10–11:20
All	Evaluate the meal: Planning, preparation of the food, serving of the meal, and clearing it away.	11:20–11:30

c. Assemble the ingredients, equipment, or table appointments needed for your special tasks.

d. Prepare the food or carry out other tasks assigned to you. Before preparing the recipes for this meal, read Chapter 31, "Salads and Salad Dressings," pages 379 to 388; Chapter 23, "Quick Breads," pages 308 to 316; and in Chapter 32, "Desserts," page 392.

Be ready to take your place at the table at the appointed time, and assume any special tasks which have been assigned to you.

If you are the member who is to be responsible for setting the table, refer to Chapter 7, "Table Setting and Etiquette," for the basic rules. The table will be set, of course, in the same way regardless of the length of the period, and the serving of the meal will be the same also. (Refer to the diagram on page 162 for details for setting the table.)

Step 7 is to serve the meal. At the appointed time the girls will take their places at the table, sit down from the left of the chair, and unfold their napkins in their laps. Assuming that your duty is to act as hostess, you will now ask someone to help herself to the rolls and butter and to pass these plates. You will then pour the tea and

THE WORK-AND-TIME SCHEDULE FOR THE FIRST OF TWO PERIODS IN PREPARING LUNCH

Group Member	Job Assignment	Time
All	Get ready to work.	10:00–10:05
Girl No. 1	Wash lettuce, put in moisture-resistant bag, and place in refrigerator to crisp. Make French dressing. Use jar for mixing and for storing dressing until needed. (Calculate cost of 1 cupful of the dressing. Compare this with cost of ready-made French dressing and report to class at time problem is evaluated.) Wash, dry, and put away cooking equipment. Wash dish towel and dishcloth.	10:05–10:35
Girl No. 2	Prepare quick cinnamon rolls. Place in pan, cover, and put in refrigerator. Wash, dry, and put away equipment. Wash dish towel and dishcloth.	10:05–10:35
Girls No. 3 and 4	Make chocolate cornstarch pudding. Pour into individual molds, and place in refrigerator. Wash, dry, and put away equipment. Wash dish towel and dishcloth.	10:05–10:35
All	Consider the preparation of the salad by discussing with your teacher and group members the characteristics of a good salad. Compare your ideas with pictures of salads which you have found in magazines at home and brought to school. Draw conclusions as to the characteristics of a nicely prepared and arranged salad.	10:35–10:45

● The waitress brings the salads on a tray to a side table and serves them individually to each person, beginning with the hostess.

hand the cups and saucers to the person next to you who will pass them around the table. You will also see that the sugar and lemon are passed.

After the salad is eaten and the dishes are to be removed, the waitress will . . .

. . . take the cinnamon-roll plate and the butter plate to the kitchen.

THE WORK-AND-TIME SCHEDULE FOR THE SECOND OF TWO PERIODS IN PREPARING LUNCH

Group Member	Job Assignment	Time
All	Get ready to work.	10:00–10:05
Girls No. 1 and 3	Finish salads, arrange on plates, and place on table.	10:05–10:20
Girl No. 2	Bake rolls. Make tea. Slice lemon, and put on plate. Fill sugar bowl. Put butter and rolls on serving plates. Place all on table.	10:05–10:20
Girl No. 4	Set table, and fill water glasses. Unmold puddings, place in serving dishes, and garnish. Place serving dishes on serving plates.	10:05–10:20
All	Serve and eat the lunch. (Group selects hostess and waitress.)	10:20–10:35
All	Clear away the lunch. (Group decides who will wash dishes and who will dry them and put them away.)	10:35–10:45

The hostess pours the tea and passes each cup to the girl at her right.

...carry a tray to the dining room, and put it on the side table.

...go to the left of the hostess, pick up her soiled salad plate with the left hand, transfer it to the right hand, and then pick up the bread-and-butter plate. Place these dishes on the tray, with the smaller plate on top of the salad plate.

...go to the person at the right of the hostess and, from the left side, remove her salad plate and bread-and-butter plate. Place these on the tray, then remove the remaining plates from the table.

...remove salt and pepper sets, picking up each piece separately, and placing it on a small tray or clean plate.

...brush away any crumbs on the table using a napkin and plate that are on the side table for that purpose.

...carry the tray with the soiled dishes to the kitchen.

Now the waitress is ready to place the dessert. To do so she will . . .

...carry a tray with dessert services to the dining room and place it on the side table.

...pick up two dessert services, go to the left of the hostess, and lay the service in the left hand in the center of the hostess's cover.

...transfer the other dessert service to the left hand, and place it, from the left, before the person seated to the right of the hostess.

...serve the other dessert services in the same manner.

...take her seat.

At this time the hostess asks if anyone would like tea. If so, the cup and saucer, with the spoon resting on the saucer, are passed to the hostess, who fills the cup.

NOTE: If preferred, the teacups may be filled before the waitress takes her seat. Then she will carry the cup and saucer to the hostess. Since the cup and saucer are at the right of each person, the waitress will go to the right side and pick them up with her right hand. She will, of course, go to the left

166

side of the hostess as this will be more convenient.

Step 8, clearing away after the lunch, is done in the same way as you cleared away after breakfast. (See page 158.) You may want to read again the discussion of dishwashing in Chapter 4, "Managing Meals to Save Time and Effort," pages 65 to 71.

In Step 9 you will evaluate, or review, the lunch with your group and consider whether everything was done as well as you would have liked. (See chart at the left.)

As you discuss these questions, have some member of the group act as secretary to jot down any constructive ideas that will help you in doing another similar project more efficiently.

For an alternate and more formal service

EVALUATION OF THE LUNCH

Did all in the group work together congenially to prepare, serve, and clear away the meal?

Was the work-and-time schedule satisfactory?

Were the task assignments about equal in the amount of work involved?

Did everyone accomplish her task independently?

How did the kitchen look during the lesson and when it was time to leave?

Was the salad attractive in appearance and well seasoned?

Did the cinnamon rolls meet a standard of quality that satisfied you?

Was the chocolate cornstarch pudding smooth and firm?

Was the lunch served on time?

Was the table correctly and attractively laid?

Was the service carried out as well as you expected?

Was the conversation interesting to everyone?

of the first course, the salad, rolls, and tea are served after the guests are seated. Then a waitress is needed. She will . . .

. . . carry a tray with four salad plates to the dining room and place it on the side table.

. . . place the salad plates on the table in the same manner as described on page 166, for placing the dessert services.

. . . go to the side table, pick up the tray and carry it to the kitchen.

. . . place the teapot on the tile at the hostess's right, using her right hand.

. . . place the plate of cinnamon rolls on the table, be seated, and then pass the rolls to the person next to her. She waits to help herself to a roll until the plate gets back to her.

The hostess now asks someone to help herself to butter and to pass the plate. Then the hostess pours the tea, passes the cups and saucers to the person beside her, and asks her to pass them around the table.

Preparing and Serving Lunch or Supper at Home

If you prepare and serve the same meal for lunch or supper at home, it will help you to gain experience. Since you will have other activities on that day, you might want to use some of the convenience foods as a way of saving time and effort. It will give you experience in management. Of course the use of such foods will not give you as much practice in the actual preparation of food, but they will not change the way of serving the meal. You could use a packaged mix for the dough for the cinnamon rolls. Here one measurement takes the place of those that would be needed for the flour, salt, baking powder, and fat if you

Courtesy Campbell Soup Company

Courtesy Sealtest

● In the preparing and serving: Though simple, luncheon dishes can be prepared and served so that they are appetizing.

Courtesy United Fresh Fruit and Vegetable Association

● In the use of colorful foods: Red, green, yellow, and white vegetables make a colorful picture for a luncheon dish.

168

LUNCHEON ATTRACTIVE

Courtesy California Prune Advisory Board

● In unusual dishes: Rolled meat with a gelatin salad makes an interesting texture contrast as well as being flavorful.

Courtesy Sealtest

Courtesy National Association of Margarine Manufacturers

● In dressing up desserts: Plain ice cream or bakery cake can be made more attractive and appetizing with a little imagination.

mixed the dough from the ingredients. Also, the first step in the mixing is already accomplished for you. A chocolate pudding mix is a timesaver in making the pudding because, again, there are fewer measurements to make. You may save still more time if, instead of chilling the pudding in molds, you pour it directly into the individual dishes in which you intend to serve it. Then all that you need to do at the last minute is to add the coconut. Finally, you can save time and work if you use a ready-made salad dressing instead of preparing one.

For Step 1, review the menu and get out the recipes (page 139).

Then do Step 2 by listing the supplies you will need, check them with those already in the kitchen, and make a market order (Step 3). Since you will be using some packaged mixes, as you buy them read the directions on the package labels and add to your list any necessary ingredients called for. This is assuming that you will go to the store yourself to buy the food.

In Step 4 you will think through the equipment you will need for cooking and serving, and then make a work-and-time schedule. The schedule shown below is given as a guide. It may not be right for you, but it can be adjusted to the speed with which you work and the arrangement of your kitchen.

Step 5 will be omitted because it refers to work in a class group.

For Steps 6, 7, and 8 see the "Guide for Work-and-Time Schedule in Preparing Lunch at Home" given below.

GUIDE FOR WORK-AND-TIME SCHEDULE IN PREPARING LUNCH AT HOME

Time	Order of Work
After breakfast	Make pudding, pour into serving dishes, and place in refrigerator to chill. Wash, dry, and put away cooking utensils.
11:10–11:20	Prepare celery, nuts, and apples for Waldorf salad. Marinate and place in refrigerator.
11:20–11:30	Set table, including cutting lemon, putting butter on plate, and filling sugar bowl.
11:30–11:55	Prepare cinnamon rolls, and put in oven. Measure water for tea, and put on to boil. Arrange salad on plates for serving. The lettuce should have been washed and stored in a moisture-resistant bag when it was brought home.
11:55–12:00	Take pudding from refrigerator, garnish with coconut, and place sauce dishes on plates ready to take into the dining room at the right time. Make tea. Take cinnamon rolls from oven, and arrange on serving plate. Fill water glasses.
12:00–12:30	Serve lunch by following same procedure used in class. (See pages 164 to 167.)
12:30–1:00	Clear away lunch, and put kitchen in order.

For Step 9 you might take a few minutes as soon as lunch is over and the kitchen is in order to go over in your mind the lunch you have prepared and served to your family by asking yourself such questions as these:

What feeling of satisfaction did I get from my accomplishment?

How did my family react to my lunch?

Did my schedule give me time to work without a feeling of hurry? Or did I allow too much time for some of the steps?

What changes would I make in my menu or in the way I organized my work?

Did I work neatly?

Was the salad attractive?

How did the cinnamon rolls and the pudding compare in appearance and flavor with these products made from the ingredients at school? Were they good enough to warrant the time I saved by using the two mixes?

The Tray Lunch

In these days of interesting TV programs, the meal arranged on a tray gives the person who is at home alone an opportunity to take advantage of such programs while eating. A tray lunch may be carried conveniently to the living room or to any other place that is desired. When there is something of interest to occupy one's attention, lunch is less likely to be eaten hurriedly. Sometimes it is the daily paper or a book or magazine. Sometimes it is mail or advertising booklets.

There are other situations when a tray meal may be desired or perhaps even necessary. If there is an invalid in the family, service of all meals on a tray may be necessary. In summer the family may like to carry a tray to the porch or garden. Or a Sunday-evening supper might be served to guests on a tray.

Just as much thought should be given to a meal to be served on a tray and just as much care paid to the preparation of the food and organization of the work as are given to a meal served on the table. If a tray meal is to fulfill its main purpose of contributing to convenience, then the whole meal must be on the tray at the same time. It takes a fairly large tray to hold one plate of fair size, a bread-and-butter plate or salad plate, a cup and saucer, a water tumbler, and a small dessert dish. These, with the appropriate appointments, fill the limited space. If a teapot or coffeepot is on the tray, it may be necessary to omit the bread-and-butter plate or the salad plate.

Steps 1 to 6, the organization and the preparation procedures, are the same as those in preparing meals for service at the table.

Step 7, serving the meal, differs because it involves only the setting of the tray and arranging in a balanced manner the dishes containing the food. The tray represents an individual cover, and it is set in accordance with the same rules as though it were at the table. A simple linen or other fabric place mat is good, or one of the smooth plastic types might be used. You will need a napkin, and if you select a paper one, be certain it is large and made of strong paper. In addition, you will need a water tumbler and salt and pepper shakers. The other appointments will depend on the menu.

The arrangement of the pieces on the tray is the usual one for an individual cover. However, balance of weight has to be considered. For example, when a pot full of tea or coffee is at the right of the tray,

● Tray meals are more and more popular for people viewing television as they eat. The tray should be set up the same as the cover for a meal at the table in so far as space allows.

the rest of the appointments may have to be shifted slightly to the left in order to balance the extra weight of the filled pot.

Step 8, clearing away after the meal, is fairly easy because all the soiled dishes are on the tray and can be carried to the kitchen in one trip. When in the kitchen, the clearing-away procedure follows the same steps as for a meal that is served in the conventional manner.

It is probable that, right now, your interest in tray meals is in their use for entertaining. If you wish to gain experience in using them for this purpose, why not undertake a class project in which you imagine that you are having a Sunday-evening supper party for a group of three friends (your class group)? You might plan your own menu or, instead, choose one of the lunch menus given on page 9 in Chapter 1, as these are equally suitable for Sunday-evening suppers.

To proceed with this "party," refer to the steps given in the first part of this chapter and follow them as you make your plans. Since you are carrying out the project in class, why not make the plans cooperatively with your group (in this case, your guests). When your plans are complete, consult your teacher so that all will be in readiness for the period in which you expect to have the party.

11

Preparing and Serving Dinner

■ DINNER, whether served at noon or at night, is the largest meal of the day, and more different foods are included in it than usually make up either breakfast or lunch. But with your experience in preparing and serving these two meals, you are ready now to undertake the dinner with confidence.

Preparing and Serving an Informal Dinner

Today the many partially prepared foods and those that are completely ready for serving make it possible to reduce the time and work required to prepare a meal. The cost of meals in which these foods are used will depend upon just what foods are selected. The attractiveness of meals, too, will depend on the special foods selected and upon the skill of the cook in using them. In a class problem of preparing and serving dinner, it might add interest and broaden your experience if you and your group would plan to use some of the partly prepared and fully prepared foods in the meal.

In preparation for such a problem, a good first step would be to visit a local supermarket or grocery store. There you could look over the offering of partly prepared and fully prepared foods and decide which ones you would like to use. But before you decide definitely on the menu, further study is needed, and this might very well cover several class lessons. After such a study, you would be able to plan your menu more intelligently. For instance, suppose you are thinking of fried chicken as a

The group members are discussing the menu for an informal dinner. One girl is taking notes while two girls are looking at different packages of food and another is studying a cookbook.

main dish. You should spend time to determine whether the raw parts, the frozen breaded parts, or the frozen breaded-and-cooked parts will give the best results in time of preparation, in the quality of the fried chicken, and in its cost.

Then there are different forms of vegetables. For example, you will find frozen French-fried potatoes and potato chips that are completely cooked and need only to be browned or heated for serving. Also, there are several kinds of partially prepared potatoes which require little further preparation. Among these are instant mashed potatoes, scalloped potatoes, and potatoes au gratin. And before deciding which other vegetables to include in your dinner menu, you may want to compare the fresh vegetables that are in season with similar vegetables that are frozen or canned.

For a dessert, you might like to compare the different forms of apple pie. Here again, it would be profitable to spend one class period comparing a bakery pie and a frozen pie with an apple pie that you make with the basic ingredients—flour, salt, shortening, water, apples, and seasonings.

There are also packaged mixes for the pastry of the pie which you could test as well in making such a comparison.

These are only a few suggestions, and you will, most certainly, find many more in your visits to the market.

In further preparation for your dinner, you should keep a record of your opinions of the relative quality of the forms of the foods you are comparing and the time you take to prepare each one. It would be of interest also to determine the cost of each dish. For this last, you may need to consult your teacher in order to get the prices of some of the individual ingredients you have used. Suppose you decide on this menu:

THE MENU

Fried Chicken

Mashed Potatoes   Buttered Peas

Bread and Butter[1]

Celery, Carrot Sticks, Olives

Apple Pie

Coffee   Cream and Sugar[1]

[1] These foods need not be included in writing a menu, but it is helpful, until you are experienced in meal preparation, to have the entire meal written down for you to refer to.

Then, based on the results of your study, the following time-and-effort-saving items might be decided on:

Fried chicken —Frozen breaded-and-cooked chicken parts
Mashed potatoes—Instant mashed potatoes
Buttered peas —Canned peas
Apple pie —Bakery pie
Coffee —Instant coffee

Now your group is ready to organize plans for preparing and serving this dinner with special emphasis on saving time and effort. You will need time to make these plans, perhaps in class, or as an out-of-class cooperative project for the group. To do this, follow the same plan that you used for breakfast and lunch:

Step 1: Review the menu and get out any recipes that you may need. (In the dinner you are preparing, the recipes or directions will be on the package or can.)

Step 2: List ingredients, equipment, and table appointments.

Step 3: Make a market order.

Steps 4 and 5: Prepare a work-and-time schedule, listing assignments for each girl.

To help you in this, the schedule given below is suggested for a group of four, working together, with a double class period in which to complete the entire problem exclusive of the evaluation. This last will have to be made at a later time.

THE WORK-AND-TIME SCHEDULE FOR PREPARING DINNER

Group Member	Job Assignment	Time
All	Get ready to work.	10:00–10:05
Girl No. 1	Prepare chicken, arrange on platter, and put in warm oven. Just before serving time, garnish with sprig of parsley. Put four plates in oven to warm. Prepare celery and carrot sticks, and arrange these with olives in one serving dish.	10:05–10:35
Girl No. 2	Prepare potatoes. Prepare peas. Place vegetables in serving dishes, and put where they will keep warm. Put bread and butter or margarine on serving plates.	10:05–10:35
Girl No. 3	Heat apple pie, if desired. Make coffee. Fill cream pitcher and sugar bowl. Cut pie, and arrange pieces on individual plates for serving.	10:05–10:35
Girl No. 4	Set table, and fill water glasses.	10:05–10:35
All	Serve and eat the dinner. (Special duties of hostess and waitress are described in Step 7, pages 176 to 178.)	10:35–11:05
All	Clear away the dinner, and put kitchen in order. (Group decides who will wash dishes and who will dry them and put them away.)	11:05–11:20
All	Assemble data on cost of all food in preparation for discussion in evaluation session.	11:20–11:30

When it is time to prepare the dinner, the group proceeds in the usual manner (Step 6)—that is, each member carries out the assignment as listed in the organization schedule. As each of you works, decide whether the time allotted in the schedule is sufficient or, on the contrary, whether it is too generous.

If setting the table is your special assignment, you will find directions for placing the table appointments below. You can also check with the diagram on page 177. Set the table as follows, and as you do it, be very careful that you keep in mind the details of placing each appointment. (See Chapter 7, "Table Setting and Etiquette.")

At each cover, place a place mat and napkin; a knife, two forks, and one teaspoon; a bread-and-butter plate with butter spreader on it; and a glass for water.

On the table, place centerpiece; two salt and pepper sets, between and above two covers; and, when ready, the dish of relishes, the plate of bread, and the butter or margarine, with a serving knife on the table at the right of the butter plate.

At the hostess's cover, place serving fork and spoon, to the left and right respectively of the space above the cover where the platter of chicken will be placed; a protective pad on which to place the platter of hot chicken to protect the table from the heat; two serving spoons for the vegetables at the right and in line with the teaspoon; and two protective pads on which to place the hot vegetable dishes, one at the left and the other at the right of the cover.

On a side table, place pitcher of cold water (fill glasses at table just before the meal is served); a tile for the coffee maker; four cups and saucers, stacked by twos if necessary; a filled cream pitcher and sugar bowl with sugar spoon beside sugar bowl; and a small plate and napkin for crumbing the table.

At the appointed time for serving the dinner (Step 7), all the group, except the one who has been delegated to act as waitress, take their places at the table and unfold their napkins. Let us assume that you are the waitress. To place the first course, you will . . .

. . . carry the warm plates to the table, and place them before the hostess from her left side. You will need to use both hands for this.

. . . return to the kitchen, carry in the platter of chicken, and place it, from the left, in the space provided for it above the hostess's cover.

. . . get the two vegetable dishes, carrying them on a tray if it is easier for you than in your hands. Put one dish on the side table in the dining room, and place the other one on one of the pads beside the hostess's cover. Then place the other vegetable dish on the other pad. In placing these dishes, go to the side of the hostess on which the pad rests and, unless you need both hands, use the hand farthest from the hostess.

. . . take your seat.

[NOTE: The order of placing a course should be as follows: plates, meat, vegetables.]

Now the hostess serves the first course by filling each plate with the chicken and vegetables. She hands the filled plate to the person at her right, who, in turn, passes it to the next person, who keeps it. This person is opposite the hostess, since there are only four at the table. The hostess hands the second filled plate to the person at her

● This dinner table is ready for the hostess to serve the first course. See page 176 for a description of the setting.

right and the third one to the person at her left. She then serves herself.

While the hostess is busy serving, you (as waitress) might take the responsibility of seeing that the bread, butter, and relishes are passed. In doing this, try to avoid interfering with the passing of the main-dish plates. It may be necessary to wait to pass these last foods until the chicken and vegetables have been served.

When everyone has finished eating the first course and the dishes are ready to be removed, you will...

...lay your napkin beside your plate, and leave your chair. Then go to the left of the hostess, pick up the platter, and carry it to the kitchen.

...remove the two vegetable dishes, in each case from the side of the hostess on which it is placed, and carry them to the kitchen.

...pick up the bread plate and the butter plate, and carry them to the kitchen. Remove the relish dish. If you have a tray on the side table, all three of these dishes may be taken to the kitchen at the same time.

...go to the left of the hostess, pick up her plate with your left hand, transfer the plate to your right hand, and then take the bread-and-butter plate with your left hand. At the side table put the small plate on top of the larger one, and leave them both on the side table while clearing the second cover. Take these soiled plates to the kitchen, and clear the remaining covers in the same way. If you have a tray on the side table, the

177

● In clearing the table after the first course, the waitress removes the vegetable dishes from the side of the hostess at which they were placed.

● The salt and pepper sets are the last to be removed before the dessert is served. Placed, one at a time, on a small tray or plate, they are taken to the side table or buffet.

soiled plates from the first two covers may be placed on it while you are removing the last two covers, and all four may then be carried to the kitchen at one time.

. . . take a small tray to the table, and remove the salt and pepper sets. In doing this, pick up each piece individually.

. . . brush the crumbs from the covers, going to the left of each person.

. . . fill the water glasses if necessary.

The table is now clear, except for the centerpiece, the water glasses, and a fork and teaspoon at each cover. So you are ready to place the dessert. To do so, you will . . .

. . . place the coffee cups and saucers at the right of the hostess's cover, and place the tile also at her right in a position convenient for her to pour the coffee. Place the cream, sugar, and sugar spoon where she can reach them easily. Place

the coffee maker on the tile. The hostess now pours the coffee.

. . . return to the kitchen, and carry in two plates of dessert. Place the one in your left hand before the person at the right of the hostess from her left side. Transfer the second dessert plate to your left hand, and place it before the next person at the right. Continue in this manner around the table with the two remaining dessert plates.

. . . take your seat.

[NOTE: By serving the hostess last with dessert, she will not be interrupted while she is pouring the coffee. As she fills each cup, adding cream and sugar according to each one's preference, she passes the coffee around the table in the same way as she passed the main-course plates.]

When the group starts Step 8—clearing away the meal and washing the dishes—

● After the table has been cleared, the coffee cups and saucers are placed at the right of the hostess's cover with the tile for the hot coffeepot also at her right. The sugar bowl, cream pitcher, and sugar spoon are put within easy reach, and the coffeepot is placed on the tile.

they should find the cooking utensils soaking in warm water. The members of the group whose duty it is to wash and dry the dishes will rinse the soiled dishes, first scraping any that need it, and stack them in piles according to size. Then, as two of the group are busy washing and drying the dishes, the other two girls can put all articles away as they are ready and put the kitchen in order. Finally, the dishcloth and towels are washed and stretched on a rack to dry so they are ready for another class.

For Step 9, there are a number of points that might be considered in reviewing this meal—first, your opinions regarding the meal itself and its preparation, and second, how you feel about the use of convenience foods in a meal. (See chart below.)

Discuss among yourselves and with your teacher ways in which you might improve your practice another time in carrying out

EVALUATION OF THE INFORMAL DINNER

THE MEAL AND ITS PREPARATION

Did the general appearance of the meal please you?
What were some good or bad texture and color features?
Were the various dishes appetizing in flavor?
Was the meal ready on time?
Was the time schedule satisfactory, or was too much or too little time allotted for the preparation of some foods?
Did the service of the dinner run as smoothly as you expected?
Did the group work well together, with each member assuming full responsibility for the task assigned to her?

THE USE OF CONVENIENCE FOODS

Do we believe that the dinner would have been more attractive and appetizing had we not relied on the convenience foods? In what instances might another form have been better?
What was the cost of the dinner, as it was prepared, in comparison with the cost of the meal had these foods been prepared from the ingredients? (These costs should have been figured as part of each preparatory lesson.)
Approximately how much time was saved in preparing the meal by using the convenience foods? To determine this accurately, you would have to have a situation in which a second meal would be prepared using similar foods prepared from the several ingredients.

● The group may wish to evaluate their work over a cup of tea. A critical look at each task—planning, scheduling, preparing, and serving—will show where or if improvement is needed.

a similar problem, and discuss the value of using convenience foods in your meals. Keep in mind, however, that your judgments are based on the results of one meal only.

Preparing and Serving a More Formal Dinner

Perhaps you will want to entertain a group of your friends at dinner at home in a more formal way than is usual for your immediate family. Or your class at school might be responsible for a dinner for the principal and some of the teachers, members of the Board of Education, or possibly a group from the Parent-Teachers Association. To make such occasions somewhat festive, a more elaborate meal than is normal might be prepared and a more formal way of serving it might be followed than the informal family style.

To serve a meal in such situations, the compromise service would be in order. (See page 130.) At home a member of the family can act in the capacity of a waitress, while at school one or two members of the class can be chosen for this responsibility. Compromise service calls for some differences from family service in both table setting and in the details of serving. To illustrate the way a dinner at school would be served using compromise service, the following menu has been selected:

THE MENU

Half Grapefruit
Baked Ham
Candied Sweetpotatoes   Buttered Peas
Rolls
Tossed Salad
Chocolate Cream Pie
Coffee

Plans for preparing the meal are carried out in the usual manner. The specific details of any plan will depend on the decision of the class regarding the forms of the various foods to use. In the interest of saving time, canned ham, canned sweetpotatoes, and frozen peas might be selected. The pastry for the pie could be made from a pie-crust mix, and the filling from a prepared pudding mix. Or a regular ham, fresh sweetpotatoes, and fresh peas may be the choice, and the dessert might be made from basic ingredients. When a meal is prepared from foods in these more basic forms, it will be well to review the chapters in Part IV on the foods included—that is, Chapter 19, "Meats," pages 261 to 278; Chapter 22, "Vegetables," pages 298 to 307; Chapter 31, "Salads and Salad Dressings," pages 379 to 388; and Chapter 27, "Pastries," pages 349 to 356.

Details are given here for setting the table and serving the dinner in the compromise-service style.

According to Step 2, a list will have been made of all of the appointments necessary for setting the table. If you are the waitress, refer to this list and proceed as described below. Assume that there will be six people at the table—the principal, who will act as the host, a teacher appointed to be the hostess, and four others.

On the table, place a tablecloth; a centerpiece; and three salt and pepper sets, above and between two covers.

At each cover, place a knife, two forks, and one teaspoon; a bread-and-butter plate with butter spreader on it; a goblet; and a napkin.

Ewing Galloway

● This table has been set for a more formal dinner. In what way does it differ from a dinner table set for an informal meal?

● For a dinner salad, wedges of lettuce are quickly prepared.

Courtesy Western Growers Association

181

Courtesy Wheat Flour Institute

● Dinner breads may consist of several types of yeast rolls.

Courtesy Ac'cent International

● Vegetables do not have to be dull. There are many varieties and ways to prepare them. (See recipes in Part V.)

On a side table, place forks for dessert and a knife for cutting and serving the pie (these are put on a small doily-covered tray or plate); a filled cream pitcher and sugar bowl, with spoon or tongs for the sugar; a filled water pitcher; extra butter with butter server; and a plate and napkin for crumbing.

Just before the dinner is ready, pour the water, put a serving of butter on each bread-and-butter plate, place the fruit service at each cover, and announce to the hostess that "dinner is served."

The hostess will lead the way to the table and assign the guests to their places, or they will find their places by means of place cards. It is customary to seat the man and woman guests of honor at the right of the hostess and host, respectively.

The hostess picks up her spoon as a signal that all may start eating. When the grapefruit has been eaten, the main course is served (Step 7). To serve the main course, you will...

...bring two warm dinner plates from the kitchen, and place one on the side table. Then with the other in the left hand, go to the left of the hostess, pick up the fruit service with the right hand, and place the dinner plate before her. [NOTE: Unless otherwise directed, all serving is done to the left of the guests.]

...then exchange the soiled fruit plate for a second dinner plate at the side table, go to the person at the right of the hostess, and exchange the service at that cover.

...go to the side table, pick up the first soiled fruit plate, and take both to the kitchen. Bring in two more warm dinner plates.

...continue to exchange the fruit plates for the dinner plates in the same way. [NOTE: While you are busy removing the first course, another member of the class in the kitchen is carving, arranging, and garnishing the meat on a hot platter and putting the vegetables in hot serving dishes. If this were a home dinner, this could have been done before the meal was announced and the

SIMPLE, INEXPENSIVE
MAIN DISHES FOR
DINNER

Courtesy Quaker Oats Company

● Meat loaf, which is relatively inexpensive, makes a simple main dish for dinner.

Courtesy National Fisheries Institute

● Halibut is but one of many kinds of fish that can be served for dinner. There are many ways to prepare fish for this meal. (See recipes in Part V.)

Courtesy Lowry's Foods, Inc.

● Spaghetti with sauce is a flavorful, popular, and inexpensive main dish for dinner. With cheese in the sauce, it is a meat alternate.

● A fancy cake with a beverage makes a festive dessert for dinner.

foods placed where they would keep hot.]

...place the serving silver on the platter and in the vegetable dishes in positions convenient for each person to use as he helps himself to the food.

...carry the meat to the table, go to the left of the hostess, and hold the platter low so she may help herself easily. Continue around the table to the right until all are served. Take the platter to the kitchen.

...serve the vegetables in the same way.

...pass the rolls.

When the guests have finished eating the main course, you will...

...exchange the main-course plates for the plates of salad in the same manner as the soiled fruit plates and hot dinner plates were exchanged.

...fill the goblets with water if necessary, and pass the rolls and serve the butter as needed.

When the salad has been eaten, you will...

...remove the salad plates and the bread-and-butter plates. To do this, take the salad plate from the left, using the left hand; change it to the right hand; and then remove the bread-and-butter plate with the left hand. Carry these two plates to the side table, and lay the smaller plate on the salad plate.

...continue to remove the soiled plates in this manner, going to the kitchen with the soiled dishes after each two covers have been cleared.

...take a tray to the table, and remove the salt and pepper sets. If there should be unused silver at any cover, remove it

● At a more formal dinner the food is often passed by the waitress. The dish should be held low enough and near enough so that each person can help himself comfortably.

184

also. Place the salt and pepper sets and unused silver on the side table.

...crumb the table.

You are now ready to place the dessert course and coffee. To do so, you will...

...take the tray or plate of dessert silver from the side table, and place a dessert fork at the right of each cover, using the right hand, and the serving knife for the pie at the right of the hostess's cover.

...put the dessert plates in the center of the hostess's cover.

...bring the pie from the kitchen, and place it above her cover.

...stand to the left of the hostess, and as she serves each piece of pie, pick up a filled plate with the left hand and, going to the left of each person in order around the table, place the pie before each of the guests and the host.

...place the coffee at the right of each person, using the right hand and starting with the hostess.

[NOTE: A teaspoon is on each saucer, and the cups are filled in the kitchen.]

...place the cream and sugar with sugar spoon or tongs on a tray, and pass to each person.

...fill goblets if necessary.

Dessert tableware is brought from a side table on a tray or plate for more formal table service. Here the waitress places a fork at the right of each cover and a serving knife at the right of the hostess's cover.

For Step 8, clearing away and cleaning up after the meal, the usual procedure is followed as for an informal dinner or any other meal. (See pages 178 and 179.)

Make your evaluation (Step 9) of the formal dinner and its service by carrying on a class discussion in which such questions as those in the chart below are used.

EVALUATION OF THE FORMAL DINNER

Were the organization plans for preparing the meal such that the work moved along smoothly? If not, make some specific suggestions which you believe would result in an improvement and explain why you think so.

Was the food well prepared, attractive, and flavorful? Would you suggest any changes in either the menu, the method of preparation, or the form of food used? Give reasons for any changes you believe to be desirable.

In serving by compromise style, part of the meal may be served from the table and part from the kitchen as is decided by the hostess. Do you think the service would have been quicker, smoother, and just as satisfactory if the main course had been served at the table and the dessert served from the kitchen? Discuss this point in class.

12

Entertaining

■ THE CHIEF aim when entertaining friends is to make them feel sincerely welcome and to see that they enjoy themselves. You should also find real pleasure yourself in helping others to have a good time. There are a number of ways in which you can offer hospitality to your friends: You can give a party or a tea; you can entertain at one of the regular meals of the day; you can have a buffet supper; or when the weather permits, you can have a party or serve a meal out of doors. To share with others the companionship of your family at one of the daily meals can be a happy experience for you, for your family, and for your friends.

Some of your entertaining may be formal, and some of it may be informal.

Sometimes you may ask only a few guests, and sometimes you may invite many. No matter how you entertain or how many you have, advance planning is needed, just as it is for family meals, except perhaps when you entertain in a very impromptu manner—and even then you will need to do some quick mental planning.

When you plan, you give your guests the impression that entertaining is easy for you and a pleasure. If you do your best and then do not worry about the things you cannot help, you will avoid tension. A nervous hostess is not a gracious hostess, nor can she make her guests feel at ease. The food you plan, the number of people you will serve, and even, perhaps, the manner in which you serve will depend on the type of entertaining you have in mind. The steps you go through in making your plans and organizing your work to save time and effort and the principles used in preparing the food are just the same as for planning and preparing family meals.

The difference in the several ways to entertain is in the selection of the refreshments or menus and in the manner in which the food is served. For some kinds of entertaining you may want to use the family's best china and silver, but elaborate table appointments are not necessary for the success of the occasion. Even such simple appointments as paper plates and napkins can be attractive when the table is neatly set and the food is appealing.

In order to enjoy entertaining, try to have as much of the work done as possible before your guests arrive, and know exactly what you are going to do after they come. Otherwise you are likely to have to work all the time the guests are present and not have time to enjoy your own party.

Until you feel that you are experienced in party-giving, keep the refreshments or meals simple. It is also good judgment to serve foods you know you can prepare and serve successfully. If you want to use a new or elaborate recipe, try it first on the family before attempting to serve it to guests.

Ideas are given in this chapter to help you in entertaining guests at home. For any kind of entertaining, however, preliminary steps are necessary. (See drawings on page 188.)

Perhaps you have a well-earned reputation for, or can become expert in, one kind of entertaining—serving buffet suppers, giving picnics or barbecues—or for preparing a special dish, such as pizza, chili con carne, heavenly hamburgers, a casserole dish, or some fancy dessert. If so, you may want to repeat this same type of entertaining or the same special dish now and then, perhaps with minor changes to give a different slant to the party yet keep your reputation as a hostess intact.

For your table decorations you may wish to carry out a theme that is appropriate to a special day, a season of the year, or a special event, such as Halloween, Valentine's Day, an engagement shower, a football game, etc.

Whenever you entertain, you should circulate among your guests rather than devote an excessive amount of time to only one or two. Discuss topics in which each is interested, and try not to let one guest take the limelight.

If you are serving snacks to your friends, you may let them help with the clearing-up work as part of the fun, but for all other kinds of entertaining, you should wait until your guests have gone before clearing up and washing the dishes.

Entertaining at Parties

Parties are of many kinds, ranging from small to large, from simple to very elaborate, and from the casual or impromptu gathering to events that are planned well in advance. The party may be one in which one person entertains and supplies all the refreshments, or it may be a cooperative one in which several or all contribute some food, as at a picnic, a potluck supper, or a barbecue.

When planning the refreshments for a party, you will need to take into account the time of the year as well as the time of day they are to be served. Suppose you have planned refreshments for an after-

WHAT TO DECIDE IN HAVING A PARTY

● Whom to invite

● Kind of party

● Date and time

● How to invite guests

● What to serve

● What to do and buy

Courtesy American Institute of Baking

● Doughnuts with cider or fruit juice are easy to prepare, simple to serve, and yet festive.

Courtesy Armour and Company

● When the guests make their own sandwiches, they can select their own fillings.

skating party in the winter when your guests will be both cold and hungry. Then you will undoubtedly serve hot food and perhaps a hot beverage. If, on the other hand, you have asked friends to your home on a warm afternoon, you will want to serve a light refreshment and a cooling beverage.

Impromptu Kitchen or Snack Parties

There are probably many times when impromptu, or spur-of-the-minute, entertaining is an ideal way for you to extend hospitality to your friends, such as those times when they want some place to go after school or after a game.

When you have an impromptu party, though, you should be sure it does not conflict with the activities of other family members. Then you must plan for the food you will serve, be it ever so simple, and make some mental notes of the way you will organize the working out of your plans. Are you going to ask everyone to help? If so,

you will assign the jobs so everything will move along smoothly instead of all trying to do one job at the same time.

You cannot decide ahead of time what the refreshments will be for spur-of-the-moment entertaining, so you will have to depend on the food available. Suppose you

● A kitchen party may be a sit-down meal or a serve-yourself and stand-up-to-eat affair, but either way all the guests contribute to the preparation of the meal.

Arthur Schatz from Black Star

know there is enough milk on hand to serve milk shakes. Then you can have each guest make his own to his liking. Or if you decide to have sandwiches, each may make his own, selecting his favorites from the fillings you provide. But if you want to have toasted cheese sandwiches and a soft drink, you might appoint one of the group to oversee the toasting, another to fill the glasses with ice for the drinks, and someone else to pass the napkins (paper, of course).

More Formal Parties

For a more formal party you must make your plans well ahead of the date you set for the party so you can invite your guests and give them time to reply to your invitation. Then when you know how many are coming, you can complete your party plans.

The table setting will vary with your menu and serving plans, but of course the table should be carefully and attractively set. For a dessert party, small tables or individual trays may be used, following the rules for table setting as they apply to this one course.

At the bottom of the page are some ideas for party menus which might be used as patterns or from which an appropriate selection might be made for the kind of party you are planning. (The recipes for many of the foods in these menus are given in Part V.)

Entertaining at Teas

Serving tea in the late afternoon is a pleasant custom that provides a time for relaxation and companionship. An afternoon tea may be very informal or very formal, as you wish. Informal teas are usually served for just a few friends, while a more formal tea or a reception is given when you want to invite a larger number. Of course, if you choose, you may serve coffee or cocoa instead of tea, and in the summer you may serve an iced beverage.

SUGGESTED PARTY MENUS

I
Barbecued Hamburgers on Buns
Whole Fresh Fruit
Beverage

II
Toasted Cheese Sandwiches
Celery   Olives   Carrot Strips
Baked Apples
Lemonade

III
Assorted Cold Cuts   Sliced Cheese
Potato Chips
Pineapple Upside-down Cake
Beverage

IV
Pizza   Celery
Fresh Fruit
Beverage

V
Strawberry Shortcake   Whipped Cream
Mints   Nuts
Hot Beverage

VI
Vanilla Ice Cream   Chocolate Sauce
Butterscotch Cookies
Tea

● For a formal tea the table as well as the food should contribute to the total effect of beauty.

Informal Teas

When friends arrive unexpectedly during the afternoon, you will have to make some quick plans for refreshments. For simple refreshments, such as would be served at a "drop-in" tea, you will have no big problem. Because tea is a staple, you will no doubt have some on hand. A cup of tea and a dainty sandwich or a cookie or two are refreshments enough for unexpected guests. But cinnamon toast, or toasted muffins or biscuits with jelly or preserves—homemade when available—make good accompaniments to tea if you do not have time or materials to make sandwiches. Of course when you invite a few friends to come in during the afternoon for tea, you will have an opportunity to prepare some delicacies in advance.

Formal Teas

For a formal tea, you invite people a week or ten days ahead of time, letting them know the hours during which you will expect them. You will have ample time to make your plans in detail. You may want to ask one or two good friends to help you pour and serve. If you are serving a formal tea at school, one of your group will be selected to pour the tea and another the coffee, if both beverages are to be served. Another member can be responsible for setting the table, and it should be the job of one member to see that the serving dishes are replenished from time to time. Another member will be appointed to take the responsibility of keeping the soiled dishes removed.

To serve a formal tea, set the table with

191

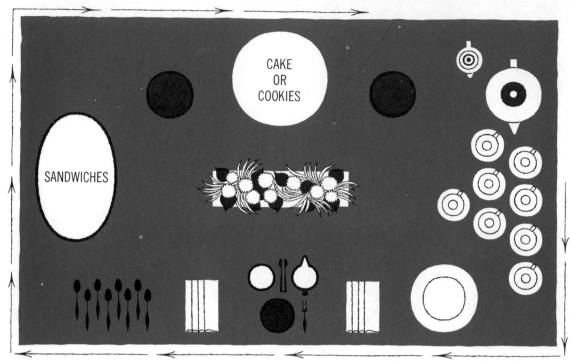

CAKE
OR
COOKIES

SANDWICHES

● Whatever is served at a tea, the food should be arranged for easy access of the guests and in logical progression, beginning at the right where the cups have been placed and moving in one direction around the table, as shown by the arrows. If both coffee and tea are served, the tea is served at one end of the table and the coffee at the other end.

a dainty cloth, and place a tea service at one end of the table as shown in diagram above. When coffee also is served, place the coffee service at the other end of the table. Cups, saucers, and plates are arranged near the beverages for convenience. When a saucer is placed beneath the beverage cup, the plate under it must be of a size that will accommodate the cup and saucer as well as hold the refreshments. There is less chance that the cup will slide on the plate when it is on its saucer, but you may prefer to put the cup directly on the plate so there will be more room for the refreshments.

Make your tea table attractive by using some particularly interesting and appro-

priate decoration. The decoration does not have to be elaborate because the tea and coffee services, the dishes, napkins, and silver, as well as the plates of tempting food, all help to make the table attractive. Because your guests may serve themselves directly from the table, it is easier to take care of a larger number if the table is placed in the center of the room so that guests can serve themselves from both sides. Then the decoration looks best in the center of the table. When the table is along a wall so that guests serve themselves from one side only, the decoration will look well if placed an equal distance from the ends but toward the wall rather than in the center of the table. When candles are used, they are also a part of the decoration, but they should not be used at a tea unless they are needed for light.

The same type of refreshments are served at a formal tea as at an informal tea, except that at a formal tea there may be a greater variety of refreshments. Small cakes, nuts, and candies, in addition to fancy sandwiches and cookies, add to the interest of the occasion. Since all the guests are unlikely to arrive at the same hour, each one is served as she comes. When a guest has been served, she may find a chair and sit as she eats, or she may eat while standing as she talks with other guests.

Receptions

A reception is similar to a formal tea, but the refreshments are more elaborate. Because they are more elaborate, assistance is needed for serving. Let us assume that you are entertaining friends at a reception and that your refreshments include tea and coffee, chicken salad, buttered rolls, orange sherbet, tiny cupcakes, cookies, nuts, and mints. To serve this graciously, you would need to ask two friends to pour the beverages. You would need other friends, or perhaps special waitresses, to take care of serving the plates containing the salad and rolls and later to take the soiled plates from the guests and serve them the dessert. The guests go to the table for the beverage and to help themselves to the nuts and mints.

Entertaining at Buffet Meals

When you want to entertain more guests than can be accommodated comfortably at the dining-room table, serving the meals buffet style is convenient. In buffet service each guest serves himself directly from a table on which the food has been arranged. (See diagram on page 194.)

When you plan a menu for a buffet meal, you will have to take into consideration the situation in which the food is eaten. For example, if the guests eat from a plate while standing, it is obviously impossible for them to use a knife for cutting food. But if the guests are to sit at previously set small tables, you may plan to have foods that require the use of a knife. Plan to serve food that will look well on the table—that is, be a picture in itself—since the food will be on the table when the guests arrive. Also, plan to have foods that will still look appetizing after several servings have been taken. Food, as a rule, looks neater throughout the serving period when it is arranged in individual portions. For example, a gelatin salad made into individual molds and placed in individual lettuce cups is better

● The buffet meal is a convenient and casual way of serving a large number of guests.

Darrow M. Watt

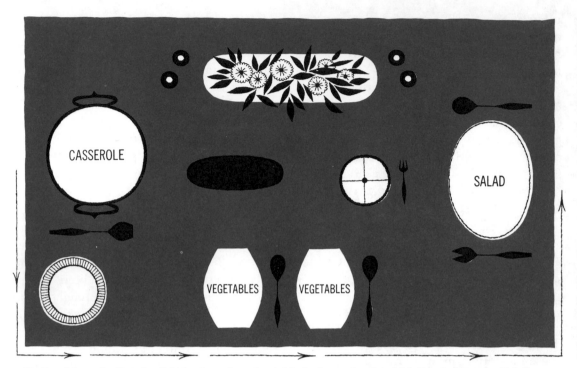

● Food for a buffet should be placed on the table in the order in which it is to be selected. For example: The main dish should be near the plates (as shown at the left). The vegetables should be placed next (center) with bread and relishes above them, and the salad should be placed last (see right). Here the guests serve themselves as they progress in one direction around the table, as shown by the arrows.

● Card tables might be set up with individual covers for the convenience of the guests (left), and the beverage might be placed on a side table so the guests may help themselves (right).

than a large mold of gelatin salad which will become unattractive after several servings have been removed. If you decide to serve a hot food, find a way to keep it hot. This can be done by replenishing the food frequently or, if it is a casserole type of dish, by keeping it in a chafing dish over an electric warmer or by using an electric casserole. Some menu suggestions are given in the chart at the right for simple buffet meals which you might prepare yourself and serve to friends for a weekend meal. The recipes for all the foods in these menus will be found in Part V.

The same care and thought should be used in setting the table for a buffet meal as for any other meal. The table appointments you need will depend on the menu. Use a simple table decoration, and plan foods that will help to make the table look attractive. To facilitate serving, place the food for each course near each other, and have the appointments for them conveniently and systematically placed on the table. The dessert may be placed on a nearby table or brought in after the main course is finished. If necessary, the beverage service may be placed on another table in the room.

There are several ways in which the service of a buffet can be carried out. The simplest and most informal way is for each guest to help himself to tableware and food from the buffet table and then to stand while eating, with freedom to move about and talk with other guests. But while this is the simplest way for the hostess, it is difficult for the guests to hold a plate and eat while standing. Also, some provision must be made for taking care of the soiled dishes from the main course before the guests help themselves to dessert.

Another and more convenient way to serve a buffet meal is by providing each guest with a previously set tray on which to place the food as it is served to him by someone else. It is necessary to have someone serve, as it would be difficult to balance a tray and help oneself to food at the same time. The guests then find convenient places to sit and each uses the tray as a sort of lap table. When the main course is finished and the soiled plates removed, the guests carry their trays to the table where they help themselves or are helped to dessert and more beverage if desired.

Probably the most comfortable way of serving a buffet meal is to have small tables laid with the necessary table appointments. (See diagram on page 194.) After the guests have helped themselves to the various foods at the buffet table, they go to the small

SUGGESTED BUFFET MENUS

I

Wieners	Potato Salad
Cole Slaw	Deviled Eggs
Olives	Pickles

Hot Biscuits
Chocolate Cake
Beverage

II

Meat Loaf   Frozen French-fried Potatoes
Stuffed Tomato Salad
Corn Muffins
Orange Cream Sherbet   Cookies
Beverage

III

Chicken à la King in Toast Cups
Refrigerator Rolls
Peas   Celery
Cherry Turnovers
Beverage

● The principles of food preparation remain the same whether the meal is cooked out of doors or in, and the same care should be given to the arrangement and appearance of the table appointments no matter what they are made of.

● Certain foods lend themselves better than others for outdoor cooking, serving, and eating.

tables so that they may be seated while eating. When the main course has been finished, the soiled dishes are removed by the person who is assisting the hostess. The guests either return to the buffet table for dessert and more beverage or are served the dessert and beverage at the tables from a side table or from the kitchen.

Entertaining at Regular Meals

When people entertain at mealtime, it is usually for lunch or dinner, but sometimes people entertain for breakfast—especially when they are planning an occasion for the weekend or over a long holiday period. When having guests for a meal, you may make a different selection of foods than you would for the family, or you can prepare and serve the meal in a somewhat different manner than you would ordinarily do. But essentially, planning a meal for guests means putting into practice what you have learned about planning, preparing, and serving meals for the family.

Out-of-Door Meals

Out-of-door eating is so well liked today that such affairs as clam bakes, corn roasts, barbecues, or ox roasts are annual events in some localities. Many families like to entertain by serving refreshments or whole meals on the porch, in the patio, or in the back yard when the climate and weather make it comfortable to be outside. Usually, part of the food is cooked over an out-of-door fireplace or on a portable grill. When the out-of-door fireplace or grill is used, cooking becomes part of the entertainment and often the son or the father assumes the role of chef.

Whether the food is cooked indoors or outdoors, the principles of preparation remain the same. Cooking space is often limited for out-of-door cooking, and this fact must be considered when plans are made.

If food is prepared in the kitchen and served on the porch or patio, hot foods can often be kept at serving temperature in the oven. Foods such as baked beans, scalloped potatoes, or chili con carne are quite easily kept warm in the casseroles in which they have been cooked.

If food is prepared at home and carried some distance to a picnic spot, special care is needed to see that all foods are at their very best. Sandwiches should be wrapped in moistureproof wrappings to keep them fresh. If sandwiches are to be made on the spot, the fillings should be carefully packed. Lettuce, sliced tomatoes, chopped eggs and olives, and cold cuts, prepared ahead of time, should be wrapped separately so as to carry well. Small glass jars and plastic or wax-coated containers make good carriers for such foods. Deviled eggs, potato salad, chicken salad, or seafood salads can be covered in tightly closed glass jars. Foods that are to be served hot can sometimes be kept warm in a covered casserole or in a covered utility dish or pan by wrapping the dish in newspapers. Vacuum jugs are useful to keep either hot beverages hot or cold ones cold.

Foods such as wieners, steaks, hamburgers, chicken parts, kabobs, or coffee can be cooked at the last minute on a grid, an electric grill, or over an open fire. Foil-wrapped food may be prepared ahead of time, ready to cook at the proper moment.

At outdoor meals, usually everyone is hungry, and food that can be cooked

197

Peter Buckley

● Picnicking away from home requires careful planning so nothing is forgotten.

quickly is welcome. Foods that require long cooking, such as barbecued meat or chicken or corn roasted in the husks, should be started early enough so that they will be done at serving time. When you know the preferences of your guests for out-of-door foods, by all means plan to serve such foods.

Guests can eat a grilled hamburger sandwich or barbecued chicken as they gather round the out-of-door grill or fireplace, but it is better to have a picnic table from which to serve the meal. The food may be arranged on the picnic table so that each person can serve himself buffet style, or various plates of food can be passed for each one to help himself. If your guests sit down to eat, even though you use table appointments suitable for out-of-door eating, such as stainless steel tableware or plastic or paper plates, forks, and spoons, you will want to set each cover as for a meal indoors. Be sure that the table is neat and orderly and that the food is appealing and attractive!

PART III
QUESTIONS FOR SUMMARIZING AND REVIEW

Chapter 7 . . . Table Setting and Etiquette

1. How is an individual's personality reflected in her table-setting practices and her table etiquette?
2. What are the important features in creating an attractive atmosphere for eating?
3. What factors must be considered by the homemaker if the family mealtime is to be a pleasant experience?
4. What determines the mealtime patterns followed by different families?
5. Explain how basic principles of serving meals can be adapted to any changes that might arise in equipment and modes of living.

6. What is the relationship between the manner of meal service, knowledge of table equipment and design principles, and selection of table appointments?
7. What determines why some homemakers prefer one type of table appointment over another?
8. Why are the basic rules of table setting and service likely to be simple and flexible while the rules of table conduct are more definite?
9. What are the advantages of having the rules for table conduct essentially the same?

10. What are some social blunders in table etiquette that you should avoid when (a) sitting at the table, (b) using a napkin, (c) using a knife, (d) using a fork, (e) eating soup?
11. What are some of the objectionable table habits of others you have noticed when you have eaten in a restaurant?

Chapter 8 . . . Preparing Meals

1. What determines success in meal preparation?
2. How have technological changes in food processing affected food products in regard to types, uses, and care?
3. What is involved in good management in meal preparation?
4. What are some advantages of making a work-and-time schedule in meal preparation?
5. What four things are necessary to have success in the use of recipes and in creativity in food preparation?
6. Name the five basic methods of food preparation. Give examples of changes in foods resulting from their use.
7. What is meant by a "principle of cookery"? How is it determined?
8. How do the principles of cookery influence the methods of preparing the following foods: (a) meat, (b) eggs, (c) vegetables, (d) muffins, (e) yeast breads?
9. Would more nutrients be retained by baking potatoes or by boiling them in their skins? Explain.

10. How are science and art used in cooking to ensure food products of high standards of quality?

Chapters 9, 10, 11, . . . Preparing and Serving Breakfast, Lunch, Supper, Dinner

1. What determines the meal patterns, table-setting practices, and types of services used by families?
2. How can efficiency in meal preparation influence eating habits of family members?
3. Why is the breakfast meal considered to be so important for all people?
4. How might changing the choice of foods served at the different meals influence the eating habits of family members?
5. What factors are necessary for successful group work?
6. How might evaluation of present work habits result in more successful food-preparation experiences in the future?
7. What effect does the use of convenience foods have on meal-management practices?
8. What factors affect the expenditure of resources and the attractiveness of meals?

Chapter 12 . . . Entertaining

1. Name four uses of food in addition to its use as a source of nutrients.
2. What are some of the steps necessary to give a successful party?
3. What are your responsibilities as a hostess when you entertain your friends?
4. What is the difference between a formal tea and an informal tea?

EXPERIENCES FOR APPLYING YOUR KNOWLEDGE

1. Divide the class into groups to discuss the following questions. Then develop a bulletin board display of pictures to represent the ideas presented:
a. What is the meaning of mealtime?
b. What equipment is essential for everyday meals? Why?

c. What makes a meal a "company meal"?
d. How are family traditions sometimes expressed by means of meal service and table settings?

2. Make a study of the different kinds of tableware, glassware, chinaware, and table

coverings available in the stores (or shown in newspapers or magazines). Arrange displays of the different types of place settings and tell about materials used for making, costs, variety of uses, care needed, and good design features.

3. Through pictures or actual table settings, show the different types of table settings and meal service suitable for the following family situations:
a. A family of four who like to watch television on Sunday while eating dinner
b. A family of six whose relatives join them for large holiday meals. (Gathering of ten adults and eight teen-agers. The dining room can accommodate six people at the table).
c. The family of five who like to sleep late on Saturday mornings
d. A family with small children
e. A family who eat outdoors often
f. A young married couple who entertain often

4. Practice using readily available materials for simple, attractive centerpieces for different occasions and for large and small tables. Emphasize variety in content, size, color, and season application. Display these arrangements in different focal points (e.g. principal's office) throughout the school building.

5. Hold a contest in your class on arranging complete table settings. Select some special occasion for your meal. Plan to have some members of the Parent Teachers Association act as judges.

6. Using one of the menus for dinner on page 9, point out the differences in setting the table for this meal when served family style and when served compromise style. Explain the main differences in the details of serving.

7. Draw diagrams of one cover set for a lunch menu on page 9, showing how the cover would look before each course.

8. Demonstrate and practice the correct way to handle the various pieces of tableware, glassware, and chinaware at the table.

9. Role play or prepare skits showing:
a. Good and bad table manners
b. Procedure a young couple should follow when dining at a large restaurant

10. Observe in a school cafeteria or in a restaurant examples of poor table manners. Explain why these practices are objectionable and how they affect others.

11. Plan a "Good Table Manners Week" in the school. Enlist the aid of the faculty, student council, cafeteria personnel, and students in an effort to improve the table manners in school. Place posters in the cafeteria promoting socially acceptable manners.

12. Discuss in class personal cleanliness as it relates to the handling of food. Name important good-health practices which can be followed in the school kitchen as well as at home.

13. Become aware of the local health requirements for all people working in jobs concerned with the handling of food.

14. Pre-plan steps in meal preparation by using simple job charts.

15. Look at recipes in cookbooks and notice the different ways recipes are written. Tell which manner of writing you prefer and why. Select a recipe that is not written according to your preference and rewrite it in the way you prefer. Be sure that each ingredient is included and each step is clearly stated.

16. Arrange to experiment in class with recipes chosen by you and your mother. Invite mothers to class to share in this experience.

17. Make a collection of cookbooks. Ask the school librarian to lend you some for display.

Summarize the types of cookbooks available and the qualifications of the people writing them. Give reasons why you think the public has become so interested in cooking and in collecting cookbooks.

18. Conduct a class quiz or contest on terms used in cookery. (Demonstrations and the use of pictures and transparencies add to the effectiveness of the definitions.)

19. Demonstrate the preparation of a simple recipe (biscuits, page 494), using different methods of mixing. Judge the finished product, using the standards (page 494) for appearance, flavor, and texture. Determine the reasons for the differences noted as they relate to the methods used.

20. Tell how many different ways various spoons could be used. Repeat for other table equipment.

21. Conduct a foods-laboratory contest to see which group of students can prepare a simple meal using the least number of special pieces of equipment.

22. Display kitchen equipment that does a specific thing, such as measuring. Demonstrate the variety of uses and the proper technique to be used for each.

23. Prepare a display of kitchen appliances and utensils. Do the following for each item:
a. Tell for what food preparation it is used.
b. Note the safety precautions.
c. Describe or demonstrate a variety of ways it may be used.

24. Demonstrate how to measure the following, using the most efficient method:
a. 1 cup flour
b. ¾ cup sugar
c. ¼ cup milk
d. 1 tsp salt
e. 3 tsp baking power
f. ½ cup butter
g. ⅛ cup fat
h. ½ egg

25. Working cooperatively with your class group, plan menus for the three meals in one day in which you use any of the suggested patterns given on page 4. Then do the following:
a. Look up the recipes needed to prepare the meals.
b. Discuss the problems involved in following each recipe in order to obtain an excellent product.
c. Make a work schedule and market order for one of the meals.
d. Make a list of the cookery methods to be used and the principles involved.
e. Prepare the meal; serve the meal.
f. Evaluate the meal.

26. Gain experience in food preparation by carrying out at home as many of the following food-preparation processes as possible. Review the principles and methods of preparation that apply to these foods. Make all your plans, do the marketing if needed, and use good work habits. Ask your family to evaluate the results of your work and you yourself decide whether or not you feel a definite satisfaction in your accomplishment. Select from the following list those products your family will like or make your own selection. (Recipes for these products can be found in Part V.)

Applesauce	Quick cinnamon rolls
Buttered spinach	Yeast rolls
Potato salad	Chocolate cake
Cream soup	Drop cookies
Cooked cereal	Fruit gelatin dessert
Baked ham slice	Refrigerator ice cream
Fried chicken	Fudge

27. Give a demonstration before the class on food preparation, selecting a dish of your own choosing. Include in the demonstration an explanation of the principles of preparation involved, the place of the food in a meal, and ways in which it might be served.

28. Give a demonstration before the class on the making of sandwiches, both the regular type to be used for lunch and the dainty type to be used at a tea. (See Chapter 24, pages 324 to 332.) If there is a freezer available, wrap the finished sandwiches and freeze them for use at some later time, perhaps when demonstrating a carried lunch and the setting of a tea table. (See Chapter 2, page 29, for information about the carried lunch and Chapter 34, page 420, for information about freezing sandwiches.)

29. Hold a baking contest in the class. Let each student prepare the same product. Appoint judges from another home economics class to evaluate the results.

30. Make a display of attractive salads, showing different food combinations and arrangements. Include a display of the different salad greens available in your market. Tell the costs of the different greens. Explain how salads can be used to avoid waste of food. (See Chapter 31, page 379, for information on salads.)

31. Hold a food sale to raise money for a special school event. Groups of students should be responsible for the preparation of the products, the sale, and the bookkeeping involved. A sale held at a holiday season, such as Thanksgiving, could provide an opportunity to include other items, such as centerpieces, favors, and placemats.

32. Prepare a gift basket of food for a new family moving into the neighborhood. Such foods as candy, jelly, cookies, or a hot casserole dish make welcome gifts. A complete holiday meal planned around Canada's Food Guide and including foods appropriate to the season is especially good for a family with a sick mother.

33. Cooperate with a science class in demonstrating the use of science in food preparation.

34. Read page 302 on the rules for boiling vegetables. Consult the Table on Nutritive Values of Foods in Part VI. Make a chart showing the relative retention of thiamine and ascorbic acid in 1 cup of the cooked vegetable when green snap-beans and when cabbage are boiled in a small amount of water for a short time and in a large amount of water for a long time. Explain.

35. Plan some menus you might use for breakfasts for people who don't like to eat breakfast or who don't take the time to eat. Take into account the season of the year and the availability of fresh fruits. Suggest different ways to serve fruits, cereals, breads, and beverages, as well as different meal patterns to make a variation. Prepare one or more of these breakfasts for your family. Ask your mother and father to help you evaluate your project.

36. Keep a class account of violations of laboratory safety code and a merit list of outstanding performances. Determine what can be done to reduce the number of violations of the safety code.

37. Keep a laboratory record of the food-preparation principles emphasized in each learning experience. Summarize the different ways these principles are used. Evalute the results of your experiences, and determine new approaches to using these principles for more experience.

38. Prepare, serve, and clear away one meal —either a breakfast, a lunch, or a dinner—at home over a weekend. Follow the procedures that you have learned for preparing meals in general (Chapter 8) and for the preparation and serving of the individual meal (breakfast, Chapter 9; lunch, Chapter 10; or dinner, Chapter 11). Evaluate your activity by checking with the evaluation charts on the following pages: for breakfast, page 158; for lunch, page 167; for dinner, page 179. If your answer to any of these questions is negative, tell how you could improve your methods when you prepare your next meal.

39. Select a menu suitable for dinner which can be made with both convenience foods and standard recipes. Choose recipes that are similar in quantity, choice of ingredients, and nutritive value. Have the class prepare both meals: one with the convenience foods, and one following the standard recipes. Record costs of ingredients and preparation time (include shopping, preparation, and cooking time) needed for each meal. Compare the palatability of the two meals, their cost, and the time required for preparation. Decide which of the convenience foods is a saving in time, energy, and/or money.

40. Use a set of menus for a week's meals. Develop family situations, such as a working mother, a family of eight on a limited budget, an elderly couple, and decide which of the items on the menus should be made from convenience foods. Tell why this decision is the best use of family resources.

41. As hostess of your class group, tell the one who is to act as waitress in detail how to serve a lunch, beginning with the appointments and the foods to place on the table. Suggest to her how each item should be brought to the table or removed and where it should be placed. Base your instructions on this menu:

Bouillon   Wafers
Cheese Fondue
Fruit Salad
Cocoa

42. Prepare a formal Christmas tea for your mothers or faculty members. Select committees to act as hostesses, to prepare the food, to prepare the table decorations, and to set the table and serve. Each student should outline the duties connected with the assignment, cooperating with others to be sure all tasks will be taken care of properly.

43. Make a diagram of a tea table as it would look if you were going to serve an informal tea. If possible, prepare and serve the tea. A similar plan might be carried out at home to entertain a few friends.

44. Make complete plans for entertaining friends at a buffet supper. Organize the work, starting with the planning of the menu and including all the steps through the final check-up.

45. List all the food supplies, cooking equipment, utensils, and table equipment needed for a cookout, using a menu of your own choosing. Explain the method you would use in the preparation of each food. Select recipes and tell how the method of preparation is related to the principles of preparation. (See chapters in Part IV for information.) If possible, plan, prepare, and serve the cookout for members of your family and a few guests.

PART IV . . .

The Foods

for

Your

Meals

● *The physical and chemical properties of foods influence the foods' appearance, texture, and flavor, and determine how the food is handled, classified, processed, and prepared for serving.*

13

Fruits

■ FRUIT ranks high as one of the most abundant, attractive, and appealing of all foods. The fruits used today do not differ in kind from the wild fruits found by the early settlers of our country, but much has been done to improve them. Present-day knowledge of production, transportation, and ways to keep them makes possible a wide choice of fruits for practically all families. In addition to being well liked, fruits are an important source of several vital nutrients.

Forms of Fruits

Fruits are obtainable in fresh, canned, frozen, and dried forms. Canned, frozen, and dried fruits are called "processed" fruits because they have undergone some treatment, or process, to make them keep longer. The pro-

duction of most fruits is seasonal, and processed forms are available when fresh fruits are unobtainable.

Fresh Fruits

Most of the fruit consumed in Canada is bought and eaten in its fresh form. Except for apples, blueberries and strawberries, however, we do not produce enough of any variety of fruit to supply all the demands of the Canadian consumer. Some fruits, such as the citrus fruits, bananas and pineapples must be imported as they cannot be grown in this country. Other fruits are imported because the growing season in Canada is so short. Today, however, the country where a fruit is grown and the season of production have less to do with the availability than formerly. Because of improved methods of refrigeration in storage and transportation, most of the following fresh fruits can be purchased in most sections of Canada at some time during the year:

Apples	Grapes	Peaches
Apricots	Lemons	Pears
Bananas	Melons	Pineapples
Berries	Nectarines	Plums
Cherries	Oranges	Rhubarb
Grapefruit		

Processed Fruits

Processed fruits include canned, frozen, and dried fruits. In these forms, fruits are obtainable at all seasons of the year and in all parts of the country. Processed fruits keep well and require little or no preparation for serving. For these reasons they are a convenience in saving time and effort in meal preparation.

Although the methods of processing fruits differ, the basic purpose in all methods is to control the action of microorganisms and enzymes so that the fruits are no longer liable to spoil.

Canned fruits. Most common fruits are found in the canned form. Some of them are canned whole; some are halved, sliced, or cubed. Apples are canned as sauce and as baked apples. The juice of many fruits is canned either as juice, nectar, or as a concentrate. Nectars are fruit juices to which some of the fruit pulp and the cooking water have been added. The concentrated juices are diluted before using.

Frozen fruits. The freezing of fruits is done quickly at very low temperatures. Some fruits are frozen without sugar, but usually they are sweetened before freezing. Fruit juices, too, are frozen. They come as single-strength and double-strength juices and as concentrates.

Dried fruits. Dried fruits are different in type according to the kind of fruit and to the way in which water is evaporated from it. For sun-dried fruits, such as raisins and currants, water is evaporated in the open air. Artificially dried fruits, such as prunes and dates, are dried by means of controlled heat and air flow. Other methods for drying fruits are being developed. A film or a foam of the fruit, in a concentrated form, is dried and then crushed to make a powdery product. This is easily reconstituted by mixing with cold water. Examples here are apple flakes for making applesauce and grapefruit and orange crystals for reconstituting into juice. The flavor and color of such products are comparable to the fresh product. In freeze drying, the fruit is first frozen, then placed in a chamber under reduced pressure and slightly elevated temperature so that the frozen water of the fruit passes directly into vapor. You may find fruits of this kind in some ready-to-eat cereals and in cake and pudding mixes.

Food Value of Fruits

Each kind of fruit has a characteristic taste and aroma that distinguishes it from other kinds. Some fruits are tart, some sweet, and some are bitter; yet all provide enjoyment in eating, stimulate the appetite, and contribute importantly to the food value of the diet.

Vitamins. Whether fresh, canned, frozen, or dried, practically all fruits contain vitamins in generous amounts. But the vitamins are present in different amounts in different kinds of fruits. The citrus fruits, cantaloupes, and strawberries are unique for their vitamin C content. Watermelon and such yellow-fleshed fruits as apricots, peaches, and cantaloupe are special sources of vitamin A. Most fruits contain the B vitamins, but they are not as important a source of these vitamins as are some other foods.

Minerals. Fruits also contain generous amounts of minerals. Oranges, blackberries, loganberries, strawberries, blueberries, and cantaloupe rank high in importance for the

● Fresh

Harold M. Lambert

● Canned

Courtesy National Canners Association

● Frozen

Courtesy Birds Eye Frozen Foods

● Dried

Courtesy National Canners Association

minerals calcium and iron. Oranges are unique for their richness in calcium.

Dried fruits make significant contributions of minerals because the evaporation of water from the fruits leaves the minerals—and other nutrients as well—in more concentrated amounts. Figs, raisins, dates, apricots, peaches, and prunes all have a high content of calcium, phosphorus, and iron.

Carbohydrates. Sugar, cellulose, and pectin are present in all fruits. Except for dried

fruits, the sugar content in fruits is not large, and so fruits with a low sugar content are relatively low in calories. This fact, together with their high mineral and vitamin content, makes such fruits a good choice for a light dessert or a between-meal snack when the meals have already satisfied the energy requirement for the day. (See Chapter 2, "Planning Meals for Health.")

Cellulose and pectin are in the cell walls of fruits. Cellulose is not digested, but it serves the unique purpose of supplying bulk to the food, thus helping to stimulate the digestive process. Pectin is not digested either. Its value lies in its property of causing jelly to form when an acid fruit is cooked with sugar. (See Chapter 34, "Food Preservation," page 422.)

Proteins and fats. There are such small amounts of proteins and fats in fruits that the contribution of these two nutrients is of minor importance.

Ways to Use and Serve Fruits

The many kinds and forms of fruits, the many ways to use and serve them, and, above all, their excellent food value make fruits an invaluable part of daily meals.

At breakfast. It has become a generally accepted custom to serve fruit at breakfast because of its appetite-stimulating quality as well as its good food value. A bowl of attractively arranged fresh fruits placed on the breakfast table allows each member of the family to select a fruit according to his taste. Or one kind of fruit may be served to all.

Some examples of the many ways that fruit can be served at breakfast are given in the chart below.

At other meals. To get the amount needed each day, fruit should be served at other meals as well as at breakfast. Some suggestions for using fruits at other meals than breakfast are given in the chart on page 211.

Principles of Preparation of Fruits

There are three principles to keep in mind when preparing fruit. These have to do with (1) the retention of food value, (2) the prevention of darkening of the surface of cut fruit, and (3) the effect of cooking on the shape of the cooked fruit.

Retention of Food Value

The preservation of vitamin C is of most concern in preparing fruit. This vitamin is easily destroyed by air. Therefore, in any method of preparation, unnecessary exposure of the fruit to air should be avoided. If the fruit is to be served raw, it should be prepared shortly before it is to be used. If this is not possible, it should be held in the refrigerator.

WAYS TO SERVE FRUIT AT BREAKFAST

Oranges and grapefruit: As juice; halved; sectioned; sliced

Bananas: Cut lengthwise and sprinkled with powdered sugar and lemon juice; sliced crosswise and served with milk or cream; sliced crosswise and served on cereal

Berries: Served on cereal; served alone with cream or milk; served whole with hulls on (strawberries) and arranged around a mound of powdered sugar—to be eaten with the fingers

Peaches: Served whole and unpeeled; sliced and sweetened; sliced and served on cereal

Melons: Cut in half, if small; cut in wedges, if large; scooped out and served as balls

Dried fruits: Stewed and served with some of the liquid; several kinds mixed together and served as compote; stewed and cut into small pieces and served over cereal

Frozen fruits: Defrosted and served with some of the liquid or over cereal

Canned fruits: Served with some of the liquid or over cereal

● Citrus fruit is of great value in supplying vitamin C, which is needed in the diet every day.

When fruit is cooked, the heat increases the destructive action of air on vitamin C. As a result, the cooking time should be short. A cover on the pan may be of some help in excluding air. When fruit is canned, air is shut out very largely during the heating process, so canned fruit retains most of its vitamin C. However, when a can of fruit has been opened, the vitamin needs to be protected by storing any unused portion in a tightly covered container in the refrigerator.

Another point to keep in mind is that vitamin C is not uniformly distributed in fruit, but a relatively large portion of it is near the skin. Because of this, apples or other fruits should be pared as thin as possible.

In preparing fruit juice—for example, orange or lemon juice—it is best not to strain the juice, as this brings it into contact with air and causes unnecessary destruction of vitamin C. Also, the metals in some strainers hasten the destruction of this vitamin. There is waste, too, if the pulp is not used, since the pulp contains a good proportion of the vitamin C of the fruit. Juices should be kept in the refrigerator tightly covered, and it is best if they are used within twenty-four hours.

Prevention of Darkening of Cut Surfaces

The flesh of certain fresh fruits darkens on exposure to air. Bananas, apples, peaches, and pears are familiar examples. These fruits should be prepared immediately before serving to prevent darkening. However, if they must be held, a little lemon juice or other acid fruit juice sprinkled over them aids in keeping their original color. Chilling also helps in preventing the darkening of fruit.

Effect of Cooking on the Shape of Fruits

When fresh fruits are cooked in water, the cellulose in the cell walls is softened, so that the fruits lose their shape and, with sufficient cooking, fall apart. This is the method used for making sauces, such as apple and cranberry sauces. If fresh fruits are cooked in a sugar syrup, the cellulose is not softened and the fruits retain their shape but become somewhat transparent. This is the method used for making stewed fruits, such as stewed apples, and peaches. In stewing dried fruits, water is used, which makes the fruit plump up.

Buying Fruits

The buying of fruits presents some problems. When buying fresh fruits, it is necessary to know how they are sold and how to judge their quality by looking at them. When buying processed fruits, the information given on the container's label must be understood. (See chart on page 213.)

Buying fresh fruits. There is no uniform measure of quantity by which the different kinds of fresh fruits are sold. They may be sold by the unit, as are avocados and melons; by the pound, as are apples, peaches, and winter grapes; or by the pint or quart, as are berries. All fresh fruits are perishable, and it is therefore particularly necessary to be able to recognize the signs of good quality when buying them. Quality grades for a number of fresh fruits packed in consumer-sized packages have been established by the Canada Department of Agriculture, but they are not widely used in the retail stores. In general, good-quality fruits look fresh and bright in color. They are of good size for the particular kind; they are free from blemishes; they are not underripe; and they have no signs of overripeness.

Buying canned fruits. Canned fruits are packed in cans or jars of several sizes, and usually there is information on the label of the container to tell the quality of the contents. In the table "Common Container Sizes" on page 82, you will find information about the sizes of containers in which fruits are packed and on the measure of fruit in them. The selection of the right size of container for the particular use of a fruit is important to avoid waste. And selection from among several quality grades of canned fruits is also a good practice, since those of a lower grade cost less and are often equally as satisfactory as are canned fruits of a higher grade for use in pies, cobblers, and other made dishes where shape and size of pieces are unimportant.

In Chapter 5 on page 85 there is a description of the requirements under the Food and Drugs Act and Regulations for the labeling of food products. In accordance with these regulations, the label on a can of peaches, for example, will state the name of the fruit; the form in which it is packed, either whole, halves, or sliced; the kind of liquid in the can, whether heavy, medium, or light syrup, or water; the net weight of contents; and the name and address of the packer or distributor. If the number of servings is stated, the amount considered a serving is also given.

This information is important, but it does not tell you anything about the quality of the fruit. To learn about this, you must examine

WAYS TO SERVE FRUIT AT LUNCH OR DINNER

As an appetizer: As juice; several fruits, fresh or canned, combined in a fruit cup; melon balls or wedges; half a grapefruit

In a salad: One or more fruits arranged with a salad green; one or more fruits in a molded gelatin or frozen salad; peaches, pears, or pineapple with cream or cottage cheese

As a garnish or accompaniment to the meat course: Broiled fruits; sauces; pickled or preserved fruits

As a dessert: One kind of fruit served alone, either fresh, frozen, canned, or stewed dried; several kinds of fruits combined in a fruit cup or compote; one kind, made into a sauce, baked, or broiled; used as an ingredient in a cooked dessert, as in pie, shortcake, pudding, dumplings, etc.; in a molded gelatin dessert

In the carried lunch: Fresh fruits; uncooked dried fruits; cooked fruits and canned or frozen fruits, if suitably packed for carrying

As a between-meal snack: Fresh fruits; uncooked dried fruits

FRUIT FOR THE DAY'S MEALS

Courtesy Cereal Institute, Inc.

● For breakfast, seasonal fruit may be served with cereal in addition to the fruit of another kind or form served as a starter.

Courtesy United Fruit Company

● For luncheon, fruit salads are refreshing either as a main course or as an accompaniment.

Courtesy Florida Citrus Commission

● For dinner, broiled grapefruit may be served as a starter or as a dessert.

the label further. You will find the quality indicated in one of the three ways described in the chart below.

Buying frozen fruits. The kinds of frozen fruits on the market are constantly increasing. The Federal government has established quality standards for a number of these frozen fruits, and the letters and words describing them are the same as for canned fruits. However, these seldom appear on the label, and you will need to rely on brand names in making your selection.

Buying dried fruits. Dried fruits are sold in boxes or in transparent moisture-resistant bags. Some fruits are packaged according to the size of the fruit—that is, the number of pieces in a pound. Some fruits are packaged whole, and some are in pieces. When the word "tenderized" is on the package, it means that the process of drying has been carried far enough to cook the fruit partially. Such fruit contains more moisture than other dried fruits, and it does not need to be soaked before cooking. Federal standards have been set up for dried fruits, but it is not customary to find

Courtesy National Cranberry Association

● For a sauce or a jelly, fruit is cooked in water. For a stewed fruit which is to hold its shape, fruit is cooked in syrup.

these on consumer-sized packages. It is necessary to rely on brands that you have found satisfactory to give the quality you like.

Care of Fruits in the Home

Since the joy of serving and eating fruits is in their color, taste, and aroma, all fruits—whether fresh or processed—should not only

QUALITY GRADING ON CANNED FRUIT

Most processed fruits are sold by grade in Canada. About 95 percent of the production in every province is from plants registered for federal inspection and grading. Only products from federally registered plants are eligible for interprovincial and export trade.

Graded fruit is designated by the descriptive words: Fancy, Choice, or Standard, and if federally graded, "Canada" is a part of the grade name.

Non-registered plants may not use a "Canada" grade name on their products. Sale of such products must be confined to the province in which they were produced. Only Quebec has provincial regulations covering the grading of fruit processed in non-registered plants.

Imported fruits for which grades are established must carry a grade mark, and must meet the federal grade standard for that grade. Imported fruit products cannot have "Canada" as part of their grade name when sold in original containers.

Courtesy Armour and Company

● Apples combined with a tender, flaky crust—whether latticed, one-crust, or two-crust —make apple pie Canada's favorite dessert.

be selected with care but properly stored after they are bought.

Care of fresh fruits. Because of their perishable nature, fresh fruits should be used soon after they are purchased. From the time fruits are brought into the home until they are used, they require cool, dry storage. For the best storage conditions for some fruits, see the chart "Care of Food to Retain Quality" on pages 88 and 89.

Fresh fruits should be washed before using to remove any dirt that may cling to them during their passage from grower to consumer. Washing fresh fruits will also remove the residue left on them from the pesticides used to kill crop pests. Safe amounts of tolerance for the quantity of these pesticides that may remain in or on food have been set by the Food and Drug Directorate, but careful washing is needed if the fruits are to be clean. Special attention should be given to cleaning the stem and blossom ends of such fruits as apples because grit lodges there.

Care of canned fruits. When stored in a cool, dry place, canned fruits, including fruit juices, will keep indefinitely without spoilage. However, even under these conditions, the quality deteriorates slowly, impairing the color and flavor of the fruits and even their food value. Canned fruits become perishable after the cans are opened, and should be treated accordingly.

Care of frozen fruits. The freezer or the freezing compartment of a refrigerator is the only place to keep frozen fruits and frozen juices until ready for use. When defrosted, these products must be used promptly.

Care of dried fruits. If they are tightly covered and stored in a cool, dry, dark place, dried fruits keep well for several months. After they are cooked, they are perishable and refrigeration is necessary.

14

Grains and Their Products

■ GRAINS is the name given to the seeds of certain grasses that are used as food. These seeds are processed, or milled, in many different ways and give such products as flour, meal, and breakfast cereals. Their use as a cereal is so common that the grains are often called "cereal grains." Some kind of grain is grown in practically every country in the world, and the grain itself and the products made from it are staple foods of all peoples.

The Cereal Grains

Wheat, corn, rice and oats are the most widely used of the cereal grains. Rye, barley and buckwheat have their uses but take a less important place as food.

Wheat. Wheat is the bread grain of the world because most of the bread used in all countries is made from wheat flour. Wheat is grown in all parts of the world, but Canada is one of the countries that produces a great deal more than she needs and is able to export it in large quantities. The three Prairie provinces produce approximately 95 percent of Canada's wheat with Saskatchewan harvesting about 50 percent of this. Most of the remainder is grown in Ontario. There are many varieties of wheat but all can be grouped into three classes: (1) the hard wheats, (2) the soft wheats, and (3) the durum wheats. The hard wheats differ from the soft wheats in that they have a higher protein content. The flour made from the hard wheats is especially suited for making yeast breads. The durum wheats are used for milling a flour called durum or semolina, which is suitable for making macaroni, spaghetti, and other macaroni products.

THE PARTS OF ALL GRAINS

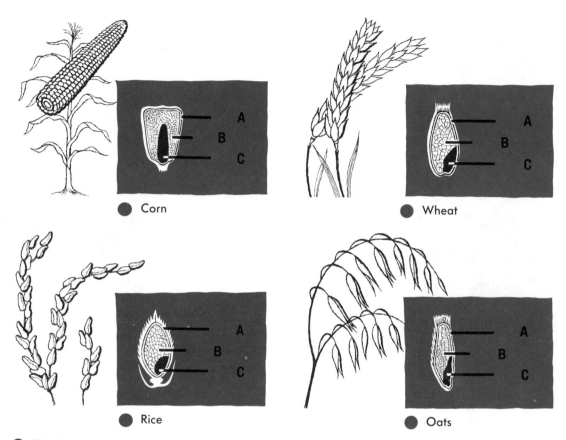

Corn

Wheat

Rice

Oats

● The three parts of seed kernels and nutrients in each part: (A) bran, or outer covering, rich in minerals, vitamins, cellulose; (B) endosperm, or largest part of kernel, rich in starch, protein; (C) germ, at one end under bran covering, rich in protein, fat, minerals, vitamins.

Corn. Although corn is the largest of all agricultural crops grown in the United States, in Canada it is grown in much smaller amounts as soil and climate conditions are not as favorable as the North Central states. The chief growing area is in Ontario which produces over 90 percent of Canadian corn, but since not enough is grown to supply our needs some is imported. As a cereal, corn is used as corn meal and breakfast cereals. In addition, other important food products that are made from corn are cornstarch, corn syrup, and corn oil.

Rice. Rice is grown in great abundance in the Asiatic countries and in India, where soil conditions are especially suited to its cultivation but are not favorable for raising wheat and corn. Rice is, therefore, the staple cereal grain of the people in these parts of the world. In the United States rice is grown in several of the Southern states with Louisiana, Texas, Arkansas, Mississippi, and southern California leading in its production. Rice is used to make breakfast cereals and desserts. Also, it is sometimes used as a starchy vegetable to replace potatoes in a meal.

Oats. Oats is used chiefly as a breakfast cereal and as an ingredient in breads, cookies and desserts.

Rye, barley, and buckwheat. These three grains take a minor place among grain crops in this country. Rye is used in the form of flour which is mixed with wheat flour to make rye bread. Barley is not used extensively, but small amounts of it are made into pearl barley which is used in some soups to give flavor, added food value, and a slightly thick consistency. Buckwheat is, strictly speaking, not a cereal grain, but its dry seeds have similar uses to the seeds of the true grains. It is popular among the people of northern Europe, but in this country it is only the flour made from it that is used. Buckwheat pancakes prepared with a mixture of buckwheat and wheat flour are a favorite breakfast bread.

Some Grain Products

Modern industry has invented so many ways of milling grains that grains are available to us in many forms. This is possible because the seed kernels of all grains are composed of three distinct parts: (1) the bran, which is the outside covering and consists of several layers; (2) the germ, which is at one end of the kernel, just underneath the bran; and (3) the endosperm, which makes up the remaining and largest part of the kernel.

In the milling of some grain products, the kernels are left more or less whole, although they may be greatly changed in shape. Brown rice, rolled oats, and puffed breakfast cereals are examples of such products.

In the more usual method of milling grains, the kernels are finely ground so that the bran, germ, and endosperm parts can be separated from each other. After they are separated, the three parts may be blended together again or only the endosperm may be used. When only the endosperm is used, the grain product is said to be "refined." White flour and farina breakfast cereal are examples.

In contrast, a product in which all parts of the kernel are blended is a whole-grain product and is called "unrefined." Whole-wheat flour, also called "graham flour," and the brown granular breakfast cereals are examples.

Rice. Unrefined rice is a whole-kernel rice. It is brown in color due to pigments in the bran. White, or polished, rice is refined rice made by removing the bran and germ and then passing the kernels through a machine to give them a polished surface.

Corn meal. Corn meal is a grain product in which the kernels are ground fairly fine. New-process corn meal is the refined type, since the germ and most of the bran are discarded in milling it. Old-process corn meal is unrefined because it retains most of the bran and germ. Both types of corn meal are available as white and yellow meals with the color depending on that of the corn kernels from which the meal is made.

Flour. Flour is a powdery grain product, made either from the ground endosperm only or by reblending all or almost all of the three ground parts of the kernel. Since wheat flour is the most important of all flours, the term "flour" means wheat flour. A flour from another grain is designated by the name of the grain.

There are three types of refined flours—all-purpose, cake and pastry, and cake. All-purpose flour is milled from a mixture of hard and soft wheats. It has a high-protein content. This flour is suitable for making yeast breads, quick breads, cakes, cookies, and pastries. Instantized, instant-blending, or quick-mixing flour is a special kind of all-purpose flour. The milling technique produces a granular flour instead of one with the usual powdery character. This granular flour is easily blended with cold liquids without any tendency to form lumps. It does not pack and so may be poured directly into a cup on measuring without the usual preliminary sifting recommended when making flour mixtures. However, it is well to use two tablespoons less of this flour for each

217

Courtesy Standard Brands

● Bread is called "the staff of life" because it is so rich in nutrients.

cup in recipes calling for sifted flour. Cake and pastry flour is a soft-wheat flour. It has less gluten than all-purpose flour and the granules are finer. It is used for making all kinds of flour mixtures other than yeast breads. Cake flour is made from soft-wheat varieties and thus contains less protein than the all-purpose flours. Also it is ground extremely fine. Its chief use is for making cakes.

Breakfast cereals. In making breakfast cereals, different kinds of grains are used, and they are processed in different ways to make many different cereals. Cereals that are completely cooked in processing are called "ready-to-eat cereals." Among these are both unrefined and refined cereals. Then there are both unrefined and refined kinds that must be cooked. Many of the cereals requiring cooking are in a form for quick cooking. In making these, the kernels are extensively ground, cut, or flattened, and are given special steam cooking. In some cases the chemical disodium phosphate has been added. These treatments make it possible to cook quick-cooking cereals in a much shorter time than is required for the regular kind of

uncooked cereals. There is also a form of uncooked cereal that requires only stirring into hot milk for preparation before serving.

Macaroni products. The macaroni products, which include macaroni, spaghetti, vermicelli, and noodles, are made from a paste of semolina flour mixed with boiling water. Because semolina flour is milled from the endosperm of the durum wheat kernels, it is very high in protein content. Macaroni products are made in many different shapes and sizes. However, there are four general forms. They are (1) tubes, such as macaroni; (2) solid rods, such as spaghetti and the tiny rods or threads of vermicelli; (3) ribbonlike strips, such as noodles; and (4) fancy shapes, such as sea shells and letters of the alphabet. In addition to plain noodles, there are egg noodles. Egg noodles differ from other macaroni products in that they contain, on a dry weight basis, not less than 4 percent egg yolk solids.

Food Value of Grain Products

The seed kernels that are the source of all grain products contain carbohydrates—cellulose and starch—fats, proteins, minerals, and vitamins. These nutrients are distributed among the bran, germ, and endosperm parts that are shown in the drawings on page 216.

Unrefined grain products. Since unrefined grain products contain all the parts of the kernel and therefore all the nutrients, they have the highest food value of all grain products. They supply calories in generous amounts, and proteins, minerals (especially phosphorus and iron), and the vitamins thiamine, riboflavin, and niacin. In addition, they contribute cellulose. Some of the proteins in grains lack certain of the essential amino acids. (See Chapter 2, "Planning Meals for Health," page 16.) Other proteins contain all the essential amino acids but only in small amounts. As a result, the proteins in grains rank below the proteins in animal foods. In spite of this, the proteins in cereals do make a valuable

CEREALS AND GRAINS IN OUR DAILY MEALS

Courtesy Quaker Oats Company

● For breakfast, a hot or cold cereal and/or a bread helps in providing the daily requirements for the Bread and Cereals group in Canada's Food Guide.

Courtesy Quaker Oats Company

● For lunch, a hot quick bread adds interest and contrast to the meal.

Courtesy Processed Apples Institute, Inc.

● For dinner, grains such as rice are often used instead of potatoes.

Courtesy Mueller's Macaroni Products

● Macaroni and spaghetti can be used as a main dish occasionally in place of meat, provided they are supplemented with a food that has a complete protein, such as a meat or cheese.

contribution to the total amount of this nutrient needed in the diet.

Refined grain products. Because most of the bran and the germ of the kernel is lost in the milling of refined grain products and they contain, chiefly, only the endosperm, their food value is limited largely to calories and proteins. With removal of the bran and the germ, the cellulose and fat have been removed as well as a large share of the phosphorus, iron, thiamine, riboflavin, and niacin.

Enriched grain products. Since all grain products are important in meals, all should make a generous contribution to daily diets. To ensure this, present practice is to put back into the refined products the nutrients—iron, thiamine, riboflavin, and niacin—that they have lost in the refining process. Such products are called "enriched." Although enrichment is optional in Canada, most flour and consequently bread is "enriched" with amounts specified by Food and Drugs regulations. Some breakfast cereals are enriched with these three vitamins and iron, while others may be fortified with only one. Read the labels on the cereal packages to know which nutrients have been added.

In the United States restored breakfast cereals are available. In these the amounts of the nutrients put back are about equal to the levels in the whole kernel. In the enriched products the levels of the nutrients returned are not necessarily those of the whole kernel. Rice that is treated in a way to retain the nutrients of the bran and germ is called "converted" rice.

Uses of Grain Products

Breakfast cereals, flours, and macaroni products are the forms of grain products that are used most widely in food preparation.

The to-be-cooked kind of breakfast cereal is a basic hot dish for breakfast. There are many different kinds available, and it is easy to add interest to breakfast if different hot cereals are served on different days. The ready-to-eat cereals may be served for the sake of further variety. These are particularly good for breakfast when it is necessary to save time. The use of cereals for breakfast is a good practice, since the nutritive value of the cereal itself is supplemented with the vitamins, minerals, and excellent proteins of the milk that usually accompanies it.

Another use for breakfast cereals is as an ingredient in recipes. The to-be-cooked cereals can replace some of the flour. For example, a mixture of rolled oats and flour is used for making oatmeal bread or oatmeal cookies. These cereals may also be used in making meat loaves. Among the ready-to-eat cereals, the flaked kinds make a good variation from the more usual buttered bread crumbs as a topping for a baked casserole dish. Some cookie recipes call for ready-to-eat cereals, and some candies include these cereals.

The uses of flours will not be given here, since more complete discussions of their uses are given in the several chapters on flour mixtures (Chapters 23 to 27).

Macaroni products come in so many sizes and shapes that they provide an excellent means of getting variety into meals. They can be used in soups, in salads, as an accompaniment to the main dish, or as the main dish itself. Noodles and alphabet pieces increase the calorie value of soups. A hearty salad made of macaroni with some flavorful food, such as pieces of cooked ham, makes a satisfying lunch. Noodles buttered and sprinkled with poppy seeds, or spaghetti with a tangy tomato sauce can be served as an accompaniment to the main dish. And any of the macaroni products can be used as the chief ingredient of a main dish when a complete protein food is included as another ingredient —for example, macaroni and cheese. In addition, all macaroni products are relatively inexpensive.

Principles of Preparation of Grain Products

Since grain products come in such a variety of forms and have so many different uses, there are several principles involved in the cooking of flours and cereals.

Flour Used as a Thickening Agent

Flour is used to thicken sauces, gravies, and puddings because of the starch that it contains. When a starchy ingredient, in this case flour, is heated in water or another liquid, such as milk, the little granules of starch in it absorb hot water and swell. As a result, the swollen starch particles take up more space in the liquid, crowd against each other, and make the whole product thicker. Just how thick a mixture will become depends on the proportion of the flour, which contains the starch, to the liquid. This is taken into consideration when the recipe is made. If the flour is added directly to a hot liquid, it tends to stick together and form lumps. To prevent this, one of three methods is used: (1) The flour may be mixed with a small amount of melted or liquid fat before the main liquid is added, (2) the flour may be mixed with sugar, or (3) the flour may be first mixed with a small amount of the cold liquid ingredient of the recipe before it is added to all the liquid. Which method is chosen will depend, of course, on the recipe. After this initial step in preparation, the flour mixture is blended with the liquid, either cold or hot, and cooked, with constant stirring, until the starch is completely cooked and the right thickness obtained. See recipes in Part V.

PRINCIPLES OF STARCH COOKERY

● The principle of using cornstarch or flour in thickening liquid is illustrated in the making of a pudding:

1. Mix cornstarch and sugar to separate starch granules. (In a white sauce mix flour with melted fat or oil.)

2. Stir in milk to make a smooth paste, and place over heat.
3. Keep stirring as mixture cooks and thickens.

4. When mixture reaches the desired consistency, remove from heat and pour into a mold or pastry crust.

All photos courtesy Corn Products Company

Flour Used in Making Flour Mixtures

When flour is used in making flour mixtures, an entirely different principle is involved than the one in which flour is used as a thickening agent. Here it is the proteins that are important. This principle is discussed in Chapter 23, "Quick Breads."

Cooking Breakfast Cereals

Breakfast cereals of the to-be-cooked kind are cooked in water. It is the starch in them that influences the cooking procedure, for the little granules of starch must be made to swell and so thicken the cereal. For good flavor and ease of digestion, the cereal must be completely cooked. All this is achieved by letting the cereal cook at the boiling temperature for several minutes over direct heat, or by letting the cereal reach the boiling temperature over direct heat and then placing it over boiling water and covering it. To prevent the cereal from sticking together as it cooks and thus forming lumps, the pieces are kept separate by stirring them slowly into rapidly boiling water and continuing the stirring until the water boils again.

If the cereal is one of the whole-grain types, the cellulose which it contains will need to be softened. This, however, is not a problem, since the length of time required to cook the starch will be sufficiently long to have a softening effect on the cellulose. If a greater softening is desired, all that is needed is to extend the cooking time several minutes.

Use of Cornstarch in Cookery

Cornstarch, which is almost entirely starch, is also used in cookery to thicken liquids. The principle involved in the use of cornstarch as a thickening agent is the same as has been described for the use of flour as a thickening agent. Because cornstarch contains more starch than does flour, a smaller proportion of cornstarch to liquid is needed for the same degree of thickening.

Buying Grain Products

Grain products are staple foods, and market shelves are stocked with a great variety of them. This is especially true of breakfast cereals. Among the kinds that must be cooked at home are the flaky-type cereals, like oat flakes and wheat flakes, and granular types, like farina. Among the ready-to-eat cereals are flaked corn, rice, and wheat. There are ready-to-eat cereals that contain various dried fruits that freshen when milk is added in the cereal bowl. Breakfast cereals of both kinds are available in packages of several sizes. And there are single-serving sizes of one or more varieties of the ready-to-eat cereals packaged together. As to cost, it is wise to buy the largest size package that may be used conveniently. In general, the to-be-cooked cereals cost less per serving than the ready-to-eat kinds, and the latter packaged in the single-serving packages are the most expensive of all.

All-purpose flour is packaged in 2-pound, 5-pound, 10-pound, or even larger bags. No more should be bought than can be used in a reasonable length of time because the keeping quality of flour must be taken into consideration.

Cake and pastry flour is packaged in 3½-pound, 7-pound and 10-pound bags.

Cake flour is packaged in boxes that are usually 2 pounds in weight. As a rule, cake flour is more expensive than the all-purpose type. Since the use of cake flour is more or less limited to the making of cake, thought should be given to whether the other types of flour will not be as satisfactory. (See page 217.)

Rice is marketed as short grain, medium grain, and long grain. These kinds of rice have similar uses, and appearance is the only important difference among them. When cooked, the long-grain rice is fluffier than the others. It is usually the most expensive.

In buying grain products of any form, there are many manufacturers' brands from which

Courtesy Cereal Institute, Inc.

● Cold cereal is just as nutritious as hot and a refreshing breakfast for hot days.

to make a choice. All are good, and personal experience gained through using different brands from time to time is the best guide when marketing for these staples. A more important consideration is to note whether or not the product is a whole-grain one or, if refined, one that is enriched.

According to law, when any food product is enriched or fortified, the fact must be stated on the label of the package. In addition, the label must carry a list of the nutrients added, and their amounts. Since many of the grain products are enriched and because this enrichment affects the nutritive value of meals, it is important to examine the label on the package to be sure of getting full value for money spent.

Care of Grain Products in the Home

All grain products should be stored in the home in closed containers in a cool, dry place. The cartons in which breakfast cereals, rice, and meals are purchased are suitable for storage if the design is such that the package can be closed fairly tightly again after it is once opened. A covered can is a convenient storage receptacle for flour. It can be closed more easily than the bag in which the flour is bought, and it has the advantage over the bag in that the flour can be measured out more easily for use in cooking. If these precautions are followed, grain products will have excellent keeping qualities with the one exception of the unrefined kind. This kind contains the fat-rich germ of the kernel, and if the product is held too long, the fat is apt to become rancid.

Sometimes in warm weather, flour and other cereal products may become infested with weevils or grain moths. Like those that are rancid, these products are unfit for use and should be discarded.

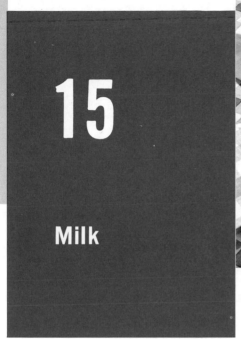

15

Milk

■ YOU probably have some milk every day in one way or another. You may drink a glass of milk at each meal and sometimes between meals. Or you might have milk on your cereal in the morning, in a cream soup or sauce at noon, and in a dessert at night. Besides these sources, you get milk in small amounts in bread, biscuits, or cake.

Regardless of the way in which you obtain milk, it always provides you with valuable nutrients. In fact, milk is more nearly perfect in nutrient quality than any other food. For this reason, milk and the products that are made from it are of great value and importance in the diet all through life.

Forms of Milk

Most of the milk produced and sold in this country receives some kind of special handling before it is sold. This handling includes the processing of milk to make it safe and sanitary, the processing of milk to produce a variety of milk products, and the processing of milk to put it into forms that will keep over relatively long periods of time. The several forms of milk that result from these different processing methods are described in the chart on page 226, and they are available in most stores in our country.

Food Value of Milk

The reason that milk can be called "the most nearly perfect food" is because it contains some of all the nutrients—that is, proteins, carbohydrates, fats, minerals, vitamins, and water.

Proteins. The proteins in milk, casein and lactalbumin, are complete proteins which contain all of the essential amino acids and therefore have excellent nutritive value.

225

FORMS OF MILK

Raw milk: Milk as it has been taken from the cow without any treatment other than cooling the milk.

Pasteurized milk: Raw milk that has been heated to destroy disease-causing bacteria. (145° F. for 30 minutes or 161° F. for 15 seconds)

Homogenized milk: Pasteurized milk that has been forced through fine openings to break large fat globules in the milk into small ones that remain distributed throughout the milk.

Vitamin D milk: Milk fortified with vitamin D to the extent of 300 to 400 I.U. per 30 ounces. Usually pasteurized and homogenized.

Partially skimmed milk: Milk from which part of the milk fat has been removed. The most common type is 2% but 1% is available. May be fortified with vitamins A and D.

Skim milk: Milk from which practically all the fat has been removed. May be fortified with vitamins A and D, and with milk solids-not-fat.

Concentrated milks: Milks from which all or much of the water has been removed. Includes the following types:

    Dried whole milk: Powdered milk made by evaporating practically all of the water from pasteurized whole milk.

    Dried skim milk: Powdered milk made by evaporating practically all of the water from pasteurized skim milk. Also called "nonfat dry milk" and "nonfat-dry-milk solids."

    Evaporated milk: Whole milk from which about 60% of the water has been removed. The milk is then sealed in cans and sterilized. Usually contains 300 to 400 I.U. per reconstituted 30 ounces and 40 mg vitamin C per reconstituted pint.

    Condensed milk: Pasteurized milk from which about 60% of the water has been removed. Sugar is then added to the milk, which is then sealed in cans.

    Concentrated fresh milk: Milk made by removing two-thirds of the water from pasteurized, homogenized whole milk. The milk is then rehomogenized, repasteurized, and packaged. Must be stored near freezing temperatures.

    Concentrated frozen milk: Fresh concentrated milk frozen and held at 10° to 20° F. Must be used soon after defrosting.

Fermented milks: Milks with an acid taste and a slightly thickened body. They are made by treating pasteurized whole, skim, or partially skimmed milk with various acid-forming bacteria. Examples are cultured buttermilk, acidophilus milk, and yoghurt.

Chocolate milk: Whole milk, pasteurized and homogenized, and flavored with chocolate syrup or cocoa and sugar. It contains not less than 3% milk fat.

Chocolate drink (dairy drink): Skim milk, pasteurized and flavored with chocolate syrup or cocoa and sugar as for chocolate milk. It contains not less than 2% milk fat.

Cream: The fat-rich portion of milk. Cream is classified according to fat content as follows:

    Light or coffee cream: Cream with a fat content of between 18 and 30%.

    Medium or light whipping cream: Cream with a fat content of between 30 and 36%.

    Heavy or heavy whipping cream: Cream with a fat content of over 36%.

Sour cream: Cream of about 18% fat, homogenized, and then soured with acid-forming bacteria.

Half-and-half: Very light cream, containing not less than 11.5% fat. Half-and-half usually has been homogenized.

Carbohydrate. Lactose, the carbohydrate in milk, is a sugar and adds calorie value to milk.

Fat. The fat in milk, called "milk fat" or "butter fat," also contributes to the calorie value of milk. The fat of milk, however, contains important amounts of vitamin A and small amounts of vitamin D. Because of their extremely low fat content, skim milk and non-fat dry milk are used instead of whole milk by people who are trying to cut down on their calorie intake.

Minerals. The most important minerals in milk are calcium, phosphorus, and iron. Milk is the best source of calcium of any individual food. In fact, milk is so rich in calcium that 1 quart supplies more than the recommended allowance for adults and young children and about four-fifths of the allowance for adolescents. See the table "Recommended Daily Nutrient Intakes" on page 18. Milk is also a very valuable source of phosphorus. The iron in milk, although present in only small amounts, is in a specially usable form.

Vitamins. Milk is a very important source of riboflavin and it would be difficult to obtain the recommended amount of this vitamin without the use of milk in the diet. It is also an important source of niacin and provides some thiamine. Vitamin A is present only in the fat of milk, so that there is practically no vitamin A in skim milk unless it has been added. In the summer, the milk fat also contains small amounts of vitamin D which is essential for the normal development of bones and teeth of infants and children, but unless this vitamin is added to the milk it cannot be considered a good source. Vitamin D is added to evaporated milk in amounts which supply 300-400 I.U. per reconstituted 30 ounces. This ensures that babies taking evaporated milk formulae receive the recommended amount of vitamin D. Although milk contains a small amount of vitamin C, most evaporated milks contain added ascorbic acid in amounts of approximately 4 mg per ounce.

NUTRIENTS SUPPLIED BY MILK

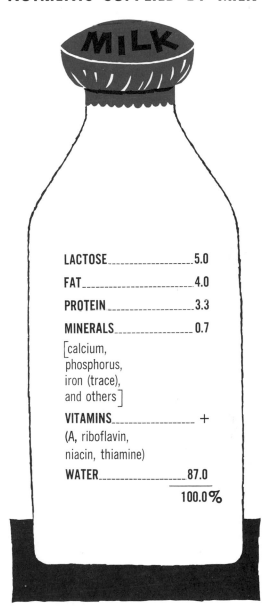

LACTOSE _____ 5.0
FAT _____ 4.0
PROTEIN _____ 3.3
MINERALS _____ 0.7
[calcium, phosphorus, iron (trace), and others]
VITAMINS _____ +
(A, riboflavin, niacin, thiamine)
WATER _____ 87.0
                          100.0%

● Although the proportion of water in milk is high, the nutrients in the solids make outstanding contributions to the diet. Milk contains the greatest number of nutrients of the highest quality of any single food. Its body-building-and-repairing proteins and its growth-promoting-and-body-functioning minerals and vitamins are unique contributors to health.

Courtesy Cereal Institute, Inc.

● For breakfast: over cereals

Courtesy Cereal Institute, Inc.

● For lunch: in a creamed dish

Courtesy The Borden Company

● For between-meal snacks: in milk drinks

Courtesy Junket Brand Foods

● For dinner: in puddings and other desserts

Uses of Milk

Milk can be used as a beverage, either alone or in a variety of combinations, and in many ways as an ingredient in recipes. Because of this and the fact that it has such excellent food value, milk is one of the most indispensable of all foods. Since milk may be obtained in so many forms, there is no excuse for not getting some milk into the daily diet.

As a beverage. A glass of good, cold milk is refreshing, not only to drink at mealtime, but also for a between-meal snack. Some people prefer flavored milk, such as cocoa, hot and cold chocolate drinks, milk shakes of various flavors, and café au lait (half milk and half coffee).

As an ingredient in recipes. Milk is used as an ingredient in many recipes, contributing to the flavor, texture, and consistency of the product, and, of course, at the same time adding greatly to its food value. Milk is used as the base for several types of milk soups, among the most common of which are oyster stew, fish and vegetable chowders, and cream of chicken, tomato, pea, or mushroom soups. Milk sauces are used as a gravy over meats, fish, poultry, and vegetables and, when sweetened, over various desserts. A very thick milk sauce is also used as the foundation for croquettes and soufflés. Milk is the basic ingredient in such desserts as rice pudding, baked Indian pudding, rennet pudding, some gelatin desserts, and fruit milk sherbets. Finally, milk is the liquid ingredient used most frequently in making batters and doughs for baked products.

When canned or dried. When condensed milk is used in food preparation, special recipes are needed because of the extra sugar that the milk contains. Special recipes are needed also when evaporated and dried milks are used just as they come from the can or package. However, when evaporated and dried milks are reconstituted by the addition of water, they may be used in food preparation in practically the same measurements as whole milk, provided they are reconstituted according to the directions that are given in the chart below.

Principles of Preparing Foods with Milk

There are a few simple principles that will help you understand what happens when you prepare dishes that contain milk. These principles are concerned with the effects of heat, acid, rennin, and tannins on the nutrients of milk.

Effect of Heat

You may have noticed that sometimes a film forms on the surface of milk as it is being heated. This film is composed of some of the proteins, minerals, and fat of milk. It can be avoided if the milk is covered during the heating period, since evaporation at the surface of the milk encourages its formation. Another way to prevent the film from forming is to make a froth of bubbles on the surface by beating the milk with a rotary beater. The bubbles lessen the evaporation. This principle is applied to the making of cocoa and chocolate in which the last step in preparation is a thorough beating.

Effect of Acid

When milk comes into contact with an acid, the protein casein in the milk coagulates—that is, comes out of solution—and makes the milk curdle. When the coagulated casein settles out in a large, smooth clot, it is called "clabber," and when it separates into small particles, the particles are called "curds." The liquid which is left after the coagulated casein separates from the rest of the milk is called

---

TABLE OF EQUIVALENTS FOR USE OF EVAPORATED AND DRIED MILKS

EVAPORATED MILK

A 6-ounce can (2/3 cup) with 2/3 cup of water yields 1 1/3 cups of whole milk.

A 1-pound can (1 2/3 cups) with 1 2/3 cups of water yields 3 1/3 cups of whole milk.

DRIED WHOLE MILK

3/4 to 1 cup of dried whole-milk powder with 4 cups of water yields 4 cups of whole milk.

NONFAT DRY MILK

1 1/3 cups of nonfat dry-milk powder with 4 cups of water yields 4 cups of skim milk.

PRINCIPLES OF MILK COOKERY

Courtesy Idaho Potato and Onion Commission

● The use of thickened milk when preparing scalloped potatoes lessens the likelihood of action by the tannin in the potatoes. Otherwise the tannin may coagulate the proteins of the milk, thus giving a curdled appearance.

Courtesy Junket Brand Foods

● In making a rennet pudding, heat the milk to lukewarm, add the rennin, and pour immediately into serving dishes. Let stand undisturbed so that the milk will coagulate in a large, smooth clot.

"whey." Whey has a greenish-white color and contains all the nutrients of milk except casein. The color is given to the whey by the vitamin riboflavin.

This effect of acid on casein is encountered when an acid food like tomato purée is mixed with milk, as in the making of cream of tomato soup. Curdling is likely to occur, but it can be avoided if these special precautions are taken:

1. Thicken either the milk or the tomato purée before the two are blended.
2. Stir the tomato purée slowly into the milk so that only small amounts of acid are brought into contact with the milk at one time.
3. Mix the heated tomato purée with the heated milk just before the soup is to be served.

When mixing an acid food or juice with milk in the preparation of a dish that is not to be cooked, as in making lemon milk sherbet, the acid food or juice should be stirred slowly into the milk, and the mixture should be frozen immediately.

Effect of Rennin

Rennin, an enzyme used by the body in the digestion of milk, causes the protein casein of milk to coagulate. Rennin is available in both tablet and powdered form and may be added to milk to make rennet pudding. After the rennin is added, the milk should not be stirred, since rennin coagulates casein almost immediately, forming a smooth clot all through the milk. Stirring would break the clot and cause the pudding to whey. Rennin should be added to milk heated only to body temperature—that is, lukewarm—since that is the temperature at which the enzyme acts best. Temperatures much above body temperature will destroy the enzyme. Rennin does not coagulate the casein in evaporated milk and makes too soft a clot in reconstituted dried milks. This is probably due to some slight change in the casein during processing.

Effect of Tannins

Some vegetables—potatoes, for example—contain substances called "tannins." When potatoes and milk are heated together, the tannins are likely to coagulate the milk proteins. The coagulation sometimes occurs in scalloped potatoes and accounts for their curdled appearance. This tendency to curdle can be lessened if the milk is made into a thickened sauce before being added to the potatoes and if the cooking temperature is kept moderate.

Marketing Milk

Milk is a highly perishable food, and therefore special attention is given to the sanitary conditions under which it is produced and handled on its way to the consumer.

All forms of milk other than canned and dried are "bottled" in wax-paper or plastic cartons or in scrubbed and sterilized bottles. In sanitary dairies these containers are filled and capped automatically and kept in refrigerated rooms until time for delivery in refrigerated trucks. The size of the container may be a gallon, a half gallon, a quart, a pint, or a half pint.

Evaporated milk is available in 6- and 16-ounce cans. Condensed milk is obtainable in 14- and 15-ounce cans.

Dried whole milk is packaged in tin cans that vary in size from 1 to 50 pounds. After the milk is placed in the can, the air is removed and an inert gas is introduced. Then the can is tightly sealed. This way of packaging is necessary because of the tendency of the fat in dried whole milk to become rancid if it is in contact with air.

Nonfat dry milk is packaged in glass jars, lined paper containers, or cardboard cans, which vary in size from 6.4 ounces to 5 pounds. The nonfat dry milk may be packed loose or in separate envelopes, each containing enough to make 1 quart of skim milk when water has been added.

In modern sanitary dairies, cartons of milk are quickly filled and sealed by machine.

Courtesy National Dairy Council

The advantage of canned and dried forms of milk is that they have been treated in such a way that their keeping qualities are improved. For this reason, canned and dried milks are a convenience to have on the kitchen shelf at all times. Another advantage of canned and dried milks is that they cost less than fresh milk, and this lower cost makes it possible for families of even low income to have milk readily available.

Grading and Inspection of Milk

Fluid milk for retail sale is not graded in Canada and there are no uniform federal standards for the production and handling of milk among the different provinces. Raw milk and cream for use in manufactured products, such as skim milk powder, is graded by federal dairy products inspectors and the maximum number of bacteria is specified by the Food and Drug Directorate.

Provincial legislation defines standards for the handling of milk in the different provinces. These standards are controlled by the provincial and municipal health departments and provide for the sanitary inspections of farms and dairies. These are carried out by local health inspectors. The standards describe conditions that must be met regarding the health of the cows and the men handling them as well as the sanitary conditions of the dairy barns and the dairies bottling the milk. The standards also state the number of bacteria that can be present in the milk. Pasteurization is compulsory in many, but not all, provinces and communities in Canada, although pasteurized milk only is sold in the larger communities.

The level of fat in milk, which must be milk fat only, is controlled by the Food and Drug Directorate and both upper and lower limits are specified according to the form of milk described on the label. The different forms of milk are described on page 226.

 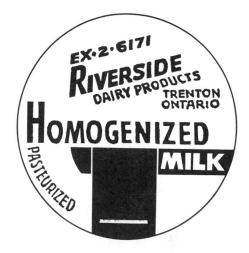

● These bottle caps indicate that the milk is homogenized and pasteurized.

Care of Milk in the Home

Since modern methods of producing and handling milk have made it possible to obtain clean, safe milk, it is our responsibility to see that milk is kept in this condition by giving the milk proper care in the home.

Care of bottled and cartoned milk. Whether milk is delivered to the home or brought from the store, the container—either glass or carton—should be rinsed under running water, wiped with a clean cloth, and put into the refrigerator. Modern refrigerators have a special shelf designed to hold milk bottles or cartons where a suitable holding temperature is maintained. The temperature considered best for milk is 40° F. (degrees Fahrenheit). At this low temperature any acid-forming bacteria that survive pasteurization develop slowly, and the milk will keep in good condition for three days.

Milk in clear bottles should never be allowed to stand in a strong light. Light destroys riboflavin, and milk is one of the most important sources of this vitamin. When using milk, the amount needed should be poured out from the container and the rest of the milk returned to the refrigerator immediately. This should be done not only to avoid exposing the milk to light, but also to prevent it from becoming warm. Milk containers should always be kept covered to protect the milk from absorbing flavors of other foods in the refrigerator.

Care of canned milk. Both evaporated and condensed milk keep very well, provided the cans are stored in a cool, dry place. Storing in a warm place will cause canned milks to darken.

After a can of milk has been opened, any unused portion should be kept in the refrigerator and given the same care as fresh milk. It may be kept in the can or poured into a clean jar and tightly covered. Canned milk will retain good quality for several days.

Care of dried milk. Both forms of dried milk can be stored in their original containers. The containers must be tightly closed after each use. The cans of dried whole milk should be kept in the refrigerator, but a cool, dry place is best for the storage of nonfat dry milk.

16

Eggs

■ EGGS make a valuable contribution to family meals. They can be used in a variety of ways—either served alone or combined with other foods—and of great importance is the fact that eggs are high in nutritive value.

The term "fresh eggs" does not necessarily mean eggs that have been laid recently, since the date on which eggs are laid may have little to do with their freshness. Instead, freshness is determined by the care, or refrigeration, given to them beginning immediately after they are laid. In other words, eggs that have been under refrigeration for some time may be fresher than those that have been laid more recently but not refrigerated. Therefore, the term "fresh" refers to the quality of eggs rather than to their age.

It is not difficult to determine the quality of an egg when broken out of the shell. A fresh egg has a thick, firm white that stands up well over the yolk and holds the yolk closely within it. The white does not spread out around the yolk as does the thinner white of an egg of poor quality. The yolk of a fresh egg is firm and stands high, rather than flat as in an egg that is not so fresh.

To determine the freshness of an egg in the shell is not quite so easy. Candling is a commercial method used for this purpose. In the candling process an egg is held before a strong beam of light which shines through the egg and shows the air space at one end. In a fresh egg the size of the air space is small. It increases as the egg decreases in quality. The light also shows the position of the yolk which, in a fresh egg, is held firmly in the center of the white with its outline barely showing through the shell. In an egg of poor quality, the yolk is not held firmly and, as the egg is moved in front of the beam of light, the yolk will throw a shadow that can be seen through the shell. Experts can tell by the size of the air space and by the yolk's shadow the measure of an egg's freshness or the quality of an egg. It is by this means of candling that eggs are graded.

The color of the shell and the yolk does not affect the quality, flavor, or nutritive value of an egg. And, once the egg is out of the shell, no one can tell whether its shell color was brown or white. The color of the shell depends upon the breed of the hen, while the color of the yolk depends on the food given to the hen.

Food Value of Eggs

Eggs are very high in nutritive value. They are eaten just as eggs or as part of many made dishes where they have the same food value as if they were eaten alone. However, when eggs are a part of a made dish, such as a custard, soufflé, or cake, the amount in each serving determines the amount of nutrients contributed.

USES OF EGGS IN FOOD PREPARATION

1. To thicken liquids, as in the making of custards and certain sauces

2. As a coating for some foods that are to be fried

3. To bind several ingredients together, as in vegetable and meat loaves and croquettes

4. In varying amounts in most batters and doughs to add color, flavor, and structure to the product

5. As a means of introducing the leavening agent air into food mixtures like soufflés and some kinds of batters—especially egg whites beaten to a foam

6. In the making of meringues, emulsions, fruit whips, and eggnogs

Proteins. The proteins in eggs are of great value, since they are complete proteins. In this respect they resemble the proteins of milk. They are present in eggs in relatively large amounts as compared to many other foods.

Fat. The fat of eggs is in the yolk only. It is responsible in large measure for the calorie value of eggs. The color pigments of the yolk are dissolved in the fat, as are the vitamins A and D.

Minerals. Iron and phosphorus are the most important minerals in eggs, and they are present only in the yolk.

Vitamins. The vitamins for which eggs are of greatest value are vitamin A, riboflavin, and vitamin D. Vitamin D is of special importance, since it is not widely distributed among foods. Eggs contain only a fair amount of thiamine.

Uses of Eggs

There are many ways to prepare eggs when they are cooked alone: They may be cooked in the shell, either soft or hard; poached; fried; baked or shirred; scrambled; or made into an omelet. When combined with other ingredients, eggs are used in the preparation of a wide variety of dishes, since they blend with practically all other foods. (See chart at the left.)

Principles of Preparing Foods with Eggs

Since eggs have so many uses in food preparation, it is impossible to give just one principle of cooking that applies to all of them. Therefore, in the discussion that follows, the principle involved in each use will be explained separately.

When Eggs Are Cooked Alone

When eggs are cooked, the proteins in them become coagulated—that is, clotted—with the result that the egg becomes firmer. If the temperature used is relatively low, the cooked egg,

EGGS IN THE DAY'S MEALS

USDA Photo

● Breakfast: Prepared in many ways as the main dish of the meal.

Courtesy American Institute of Baking

● Lunch: Made into a salad for a sandwich filling.

Courtesy Corn Products Company

● Dinner: Used as an ingredient in cake or other desserts.

although firm, has a desirable tender texture. On the other hand, if the temperature of cooking is high, the coagulation of the proteins is carried too far and the egg becomes tough, and even rubbery. Prolonging the time of cooking eggs, even at low temperatures, tends also to have a toughening effect. Therefore, when cooking eggs alone, it is necessary to consider (1) the temperature, which should be kept relatively low; and (2) the cooking period, which should be no longer than is needed to give the degree of doneness that is desired.

These principles are illustrated in the following brief description of ways of handling eggs when cooked alone. You will find detailed procedures in the recipes in Part V.

To cook eggs in the shell. When eggs are soft-cooked or hard-cooked, the water surrounding them must be held at the simmering temperature—that is, below boiling—to make the cooked egg tender. The length of time eggs are cooked in the shell will determine their firmness. If they are to be hard-cooked, eggs are held in the simmering water for a longer time than if they are to be soft-cooked. The temperature of the eggs when they are put into the simmering water will affect the time needed for them to become either soft- or hard-cooked. Obviously, the colder they are, the longer the cooking time required. If you do not have a thermometer to guide you, perhaps you can recognize simmering and boiling from the description of one observant person who has said, "When the water smiles it is simmering, and when it laughs it is boiling."

To poach eggs. A poached egg is one that has been dropped into water, milk, or broth. The temperature of these liquids must be below the boiling point to carry out the principles of low-temperature cooking of eggs. The length of cooking time is regulated to give the desired firmness to the poached egg.

To fry eggs. When eggs are cooked in a small amount of fat, they are fried. The pan is held over very low heat and the time of fry-

ing kept to a minimum to give just the desired firmness. To hasten the cooking of the tops of the eggs, the pan may be covered or the eggs may be basted with some of the hot fat.

To bake or shirr eggs. An egg that is placed in a buttered ramekin and cooked in the oven at moderate heat until firm is called a "baked egg" or a "shirred egg."

To scramble eggs. There are several ways to scramble eggs, but usually the eggs are slightly beaten, a small amount of milk is added, and then they are cooked in a pan containing some melted fat. The pan is kept over low heat, and the eggs are stirred slowly as they cook. In this way the proteins will coagulate evenly and in large masses, and the whole will be tender.

To make omelets. There are two types of omelets: plain (French) or puffy. For a plain omelet, the whole egg is beaten together. For a puffy omelet, the whites and yolks are separated, beaten separately, and then blended. Both types of omelets are cooked over low heat in a skillet containing some melted fat and, as in all other ways of cooking eggs, only long enough to give the preferred firmness. The puffy omelet is then placed in an oven at 350° F. until the top is dry.

When Eggs Are Used to Thicken Liquids

When eggs are used to thicken liquids, as in custard, they are beaten slightly so they can be easily blended with the liquid. Then heat is applied. As the egg proteins become coagulated, the clot forms evenly all through the liquid. When this happens, the clot entraps the liquid and all the other ingredients of the mixture to make a smooth and velvety thickened product. As in the cooking of eggs alone, the temperature must be relatively low and the length of cooking time carefully regulated so that it is not extended beyond the time when the desirable thickness is obtained. If the temperature of cooking is too high or the time too long, the coagulated protein mass becomes rubbery, squeezes out some of the

237

● Fried eggs

Courtesy Poultry and Egg National Board

● Poached eggs

Courtesy Poultry and Egg National Board

● Omelet

Courtesy "Better Homes and Gardens"

● In shell

Courtesy Poultry and Egg National Board

● For methods of preparing these common egg dishes, see page 237, and for recipes, see pages 463 to 465.

liquid, and gives the product a rough texture. The dish is said to be "curdled" and, of course, it is of inferior quality.

In custards. There are two types of custards: baked custards and soft, or stirred, custards. In both custards the ingredients and their proportions are the same, but they are cooked in different ways except that the temperatures used during cooking are relatively low for both.

For a baked custard, the raw mixture is poured into a baking dish or individual cups.

MAKING CUSTARDS

● For a soft custard: Stir scalded milk slowly into beaten eggs and sugar (left). Return to double boiler, and cook over water that is just below simmering, stirring constantly until custard coats a spoon (right).

All photos courtesy "Better Homes and Gardens"

● For a baked custard: Bake in individual cups surrounded by hot water (left) or in a large casserole placed in a pan of hot water. The custard is done when a knife inserted into it comes out clean (right).

The baking dish or cups are placed in a pan and surrounded with hot water to the depth of the custard. Then the pan is put in an oven at about 350° F. The moderate heat of the oven and the hot water surrounding the baking dish or cups give just the right degree of heat to coagulate the egg proteins and cause the whole mixture, which is undisturbed as it cooks, to set in a thick, smooth, velvety mass.

For a soft, or stirred, custard the mixture is cooked in the top of a double boiler with the water in the bottom part held below boiling.

● Eggs are an ingredient in muffins, cakes, cookies and many other baked products.

The mixture is stirred constantly as it cooks in order to keep the egg evenly distributed throughout the mixture and to keep the heat evenly applied to it. The finished custard is soft, compared to the baked custard, but it is thick, smooth, and velvety. Cooking of both custards must be stopped when just the right

● To separate an egg, first crack it, holding it over a small dish; then break the shell apart and let the white drain into the dish, keeping the yolk in the lower half of the shell. Transfer the yolk to the other part of the shell and drain remaining white into the dish. Put yolk and white into separate bowls.

amount of firmness or thickness is reached. Otherwise an undesirable curdled condition will result. There are tests to tell you when this stage is reached. You will find these in the recipes for custards in Part V. You may sometimes find other directions for cooking custards without the hot water surrounding them, but better results are assured when the water is used. Custard mixtures are strained in order to remove the cordlike pieces—chalazae—that hold the yolk of an egg in place. A baked custard is strained before cooking, and a soft custard either before or after cooking as desired.

In sauces. As in making a soft custard, sauces thickened by eggs require careful attention to temperature and time of cooking. The liquid in such sauces may be a fruit or vegetable juice, fish or meat stock, or a white sauce. A precaution must be observed when following a recipe for a sauce if the recipe calls for the use of hot liquid—juice, stock, or white sauce. In this case, if the beaten egg is poured directly into the hot liquid, the egg proteins will coagulate as they come in contact with the liquid, and the coagulated particles will give the sauce a curdled character. To prevent this from happening, a small portion of the hot liquid is stirred slowly into the beaten egg to dilute it, and then this egg- and liquid-mixture is stirred into the rest of the hot liquid.

When Eggs Are Used for Coating and Binding

Raw eggs have an adhesive quality which makes them useful for coating the outside of croquettes and pieces of food before they are fried. The food is dipped into slightly beaten egg to coat it, and then it is dipped into crumbs, corn meal, or flour, which adheres to the egg. When the food is fried, the egg proteins in the coating become coagulated and so prevent the food from absorbing too much fat. Also, the coating makes a crisp outer surface and contributes some flavor to the product.

● A delicately browned meringue makes an attractive topping for a one-crust pie. To make the meringue, beat the egg whites until they are foamy. Then beat in the sugar gradually, and continue beating until the meringue stands in peaks.

Another use for eggs based on their adhesive property is for binding several ingredients together, as in making meat and vegetable loaves and croquettes. In this use of eggs and when they are used for coating, the amount of egg is so small that it is not necessary to observe the rule of low-temperature cooking.

When Eggs Are Used as an Ingredient in Baked Products

Eggs are used in baked products to contribute to their framework. The proteins of the eggs, when coagulated, along with the coagulated gluten of the flour, give structure to such foods. Popovers, muffins, and angel food cake are three examples. Eggs also add color and flavor to baked products. The way eggs are incorporated into these foods and the baking temperatures employed vary according to the product being made. You will find detailed directions in the recipes in Part V.

When Eggs Are Used to Introduce Air into Food Mixtures

When air is beaten into raw egg whites, a foam is formed. The air bubbles in the foam are surrounded by films of egg white, and the proteins in the egg white make the bubble films strong and somewhat elastic. For this reason, a large amount of air can be incorporated and held in the foam. With continued beating, the air bubbles become very fine, and the egg-white foam will still hold its shape when the beater is withdrawn slowly from it. When an egg-white foam is used as a recipe ingredient, the air captured in it expands if

● The soufflé is light and fluffy because of the air in the beaten egg whites.

the mixture is heated. This causes the batter or other product, such as a soufflé or omelet, to increase in volume until the heat makes the bubble walls firm by coagulating the proteins in them. The low-temperature principle for cooking eggs permits considerable expansion of the air before the bubble walls are made too rigid to expand. In this way beaten egg whites serve to introduce the leavening agent air into food mixtures.

If sugar is added while egg whites are being beaten, a meringue is made. Uncooked meringue is used as a garnish for desserts. If preferred, small mounds of it may be cooked slightly by holding them for a few minutes on top of hot water. Also a meringue may be baked at 325° F. until it is a delicate brown on top and somewhat firm throughout. A cooked meringue like this last makes a final touch to a lemon meringue pie. Fruit pulp, when blended with a meringue, makes a fruit whip which is served either uncooked or baked as desired.

A very sweet egg-white foam is used in making meringue shells. The meringue shells are baked at very low temperatures—250° to 300° F.—until they are thoroughly cooked throughout and slightly brown on the surface. The baked shells may be filled with whipped cream, ice cream, or fruit for party desserts.

The whites of very cold eggs cannot be beaten to a foam as quickly or as well as those at room temperature. Therefore, it is best to remove eggs from the refrigerator fifteen to twenty minutes before they are to be beaten. Another precaution to observe is to beat egg whites only a short while before they are to be used for, on standing, some of the white drips or leaks from them, and the volume decreases. Even if such a foam is beaten again, the quality is never quite so good as it was originally.

Egg yolks and whole eggs do not hold so much air as do the whites and so do not make such a good foam. The fat in the yolk interferes with the ability of either the yolk or the whole egg to retain air. Beaten yolks or beaten whole eggs may help to leaven batters and doughs that include other leavening agents besides air, such as butter cakes or muffins and other quick breads. In the case of egg whites, enough air can be incorporated so that it gives almost all the leavening action needed. Examples of this use of egg-white foam are the cakes of the sponge family, foamy omelets, and soufflés.

When Eggs Are Used to Stabilize Emulsions

The making of emulsions is another use for raw eggs. An emulsion is made by beating oil and another liquid, usually vinegar or lemon juice, together so thoroughly that the oil is distributed as tiny drops all through the other liquid.

Temporary emulsions. This type of emulsion will separate on standing, and the oil will rise to the top and stay there until the mixture is beaten again. French dressing is an example of a temporary emulsion.

Permanent emulsions. This type of emulsion will not separate on standing. It is made when either egg yolk or whole egg is used with the two liquids. Then on beating, the egg surrounds the drops of oil somewhat in the same manner as it surrounds the air bubbles in an egg-white foam. The egg thus holds the oil drops evenly distributed throughout the emulsion so they do not rise to the top as the mixture stands. Mayonnaise dressing is an example of a permanent emulsion.

Buying Eggs

The peak of egg production is in the months from early spring until the end of May. After this the production falls off, and it is lowest in the fall and winter. When the supply is largest, eggs are put into cold storage and held there, at temperatures just above freezing, for marketing in the months of lowest production. This practice of cold storage of eggs helps to keep a fairly uniform supply of eggs in the markets throughout the year.

CANADA GRADES OF EGGS BY SIZE (WEIGHT)

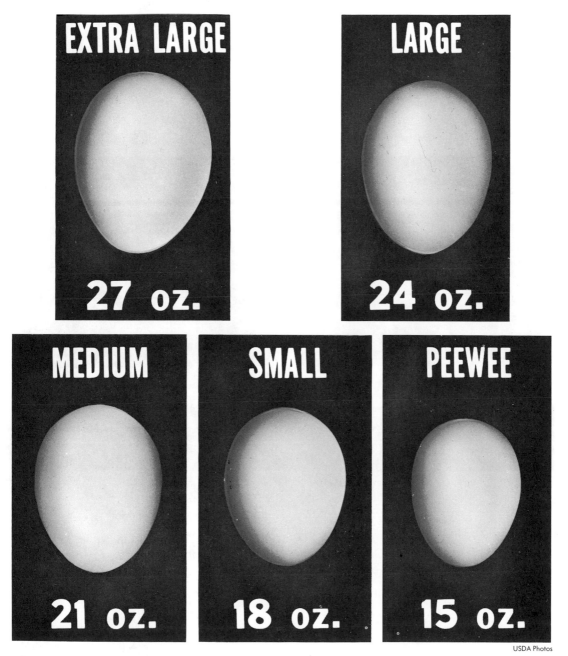

EXTRA LARGE — 27 oz.

LARGE — 24 oz.

MEDIUM — 21 oz.

SMALL — 18 oz.

PEEWEE — 15 oz.

USDA Photos

● Egg sizes are based on weight. These are the five weight classes—Extra Large, Large, etc.—with the minimum weight for each in ounces per dozen. The size has nothing to do with the quality of the egg.

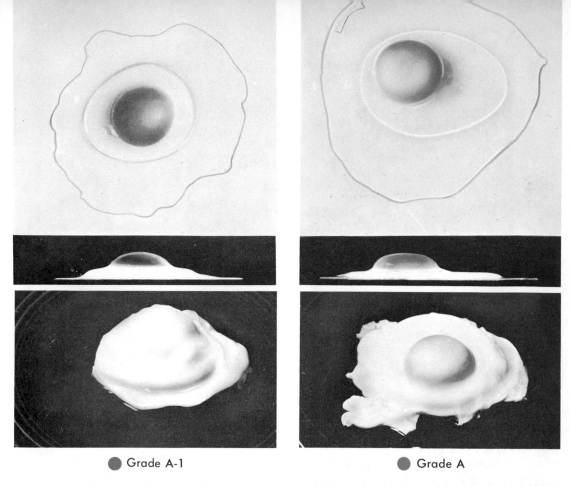

Grade A-1   Grade A

SUMMARY OF CANADIAN STANDARDS*

QUALITY FACTOR	A-1 QUALITY	A QUALITY
Shell	Clean Unbroken Practically normal	Clean Unbroken Practically normal
Air cell	⅛ inch or less in depth Immobile	³⁄₁₆ inch or less in depth Not floating
White	Clear Firm	Clear May be reasonably firm
Yolk	Well centered Indistinct yolk shadow Free from defects	May be fairly well centered An indistinct yolk outline Free from defects

* Eggs—The production identification and retention of quality in eggs, Canada Department of Agriculture, 1961.

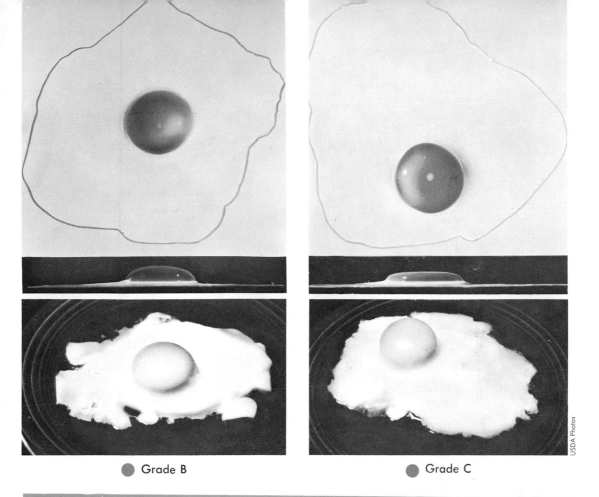

● Grade B   ● Grade C

FOR GRADES OF EGGS BY QUALITY

B QUALITY	C QUALITY
Clean to very slightly stained Unbroken May be slightly abnormal	Clean to moderately stained Unbroken May be abnormal
⅜ inch or less in depth	May be over ⅜ inch in depth
Clear May be slightly weak	May be weak and watery Small blood clots or spots may be present
May be off center but floats freely Outline may be well defined May be slightly enlarged and flattened Absence of meat or blood spots	May be off center but does not adhere to shell membrane Outline may be plainly visible May be enlarged and flattened May show clearly visible germ development but no blood spots in excess of ⅛ inch diameter

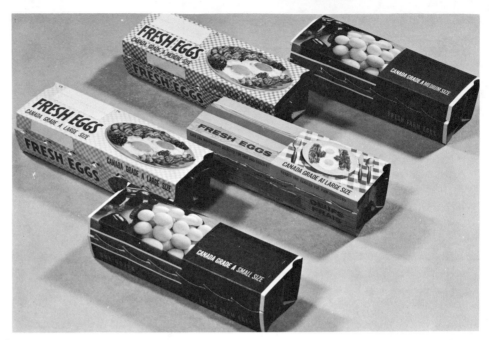

● The label on the egg carton states the official grade ("Canada Grade A") and size ("Large") of the eggs in the carton.

Eggs are sold by grade in all provinces. Grade marks (including sizes for Canada Grades A-1 and A eggs) must be shown on cartons and bulk displays of eggs in retail stores. All grades must be free from discolored yolks and blood spots. Canada Grade A is the grade most usually available in retail stores. The grades are: Canada Grade A-1, Canada Grade A, Canada Grade B, Canada Grade C, and Canada Grade Cracks.

The advantage of knowing about quality grades of eggs is that there are good uses for eggs of all grades. There is no need to pay for top-quality eggs if eggs of lower grades will be satisfactory. The best eggs are appreciated for their delicate flavor, so Grades A-1 and A eggs are especially good for cooking in the shell, poaching, frying, scrambling, and making omelets. But when they are to be combined with other ingredients—as in baked foods and custards—Grade B eggs are suitable. In some cases, even Grade C eggs may be used in baking.

When buying eggs, it is advisable to consider size and weight as well as quality. Eggs of different sizes are available in many markets. The smaller eggs weigh less than the larger ones and cost less. (See page 243.)

Care of Eggs in the Home

Eggs are kept under refrigeration in the markets in order to maintain their good quality. They should be placed in the refrigerator as soon as they are brought into the home. It is better if eggs are kept in the closed carton in which they were bought or in a covered bowl to prevent odors from penetrating the porous shells and to avoid evaporation of moisture from the interior of the eggs. If it is necessary to wash an egg, this should be done when it is to be used—never before. Another precaution that should be observed in keeping egg quality is to return the carton or bowl to the refrigerator as soon as the eggs that are needed are taken from it. (See chart, "Care of Food to Retain Quality," on pages 88 and 89.)

17

Cheese

■THROUGHOUT centuries cheese has been a valued food for man. Today cheese still ranks high among foods in importance and popularity. There are many different varieties of cheese, and each one has its own special flavor. In addition to the flavor that cheese provides, it has excellent food value. Some kinds of cheese keep so well that they can be kept on hand in the refrigerator for a long time. With such qualities as these, it is apparent why cheese is used frequently in the planning of flavorful and nutritious meals.

Kinds of Cheese

All cheese is made from milk. Most of it is made from cow's milk, but some varieties are made from the milk of sheep or goats. The manner in which cheese is made, or manufactured, differs according to the variety of the cheese. In general, though, the process starts with the coagulation of the milk protein casein to form the curd. The curd, which is the part used to make the cheese, is then separated from the liquid whey, pressed, salted, and finally "ripened." It is the manner in which each of these steps is done, particularly the ripening step, that gives a cheese its appearance, consistency, texture, and flavor.

One of the outstanding differences among cheeses, which is brought about during their manufacture, is the variation in their consistency, or hardness. This characteristic is a convenient one to use in classifying them. Some cheeses are very hard, and some are soft. Others are neither very hard nor soft. Those that are neither very hard nor soft are classed as hard cheeses and semisoft cheeses. Another class of cheese includes the process varieties. Process cheeses are made from a number of different cheeses which are ground and mixed together. An emulsifying agent is

247

There are hundreds of varieties of cheeses, each with a distinct flavor, but all may be classified within five groups—very hard, hard, semisoft, soft, and process.

CLASSIFICATION OF CHEESES

CLASS AND VARIETY	DESCRIPTION	USES
Very hard cheeses		
Parmesan	Pale yellow; crumbly	Grated, as a flavoring for soups and other made dishes
Pineapple	Deep yellow; shaped like a pineapple; shiny corrugated surface	Dessert
Sapsago	Green; flavored with clover leaves and clover	Grated, as a flavoring
Hard cheeses		
Cheddar[1]	Almost white to deep yellow	Dessert; sandwich fillings; as an ingredient in made dishes; canapés
Edam	Creamy yellow; shaped like a ball; covered with deep-red waxy material	Dessert; cheese tray
Swiss	White to pale yellow; large holes, or eyes, distributed throughout	Dessert; sandwich fillings; cheese tray
Gruyère	Pale yellow; small holes, or eyes, distributed throughout	Dessert; sandwich fillings; cheese tray
Semisoft cheeses		
Roquefort	Made with sheep's milk; a greenish marbled effect with molds; wrapped in foil (made only in France)	Dessert; canapés
Blue	Similar to Roquefort, but made with cow's milk	Dessert; canapés

added, and then they are heated until a smooth, waxy mass is formed. Because of the heating which these cheeses undergo, they are sometimes called "pasteurized process cheeses." A few representative varieties of each class of cheese and some special uses are described in the chart below.

Food Value of Cheese

Since cheese is made from milk, it contains many of the nutrients that are present in milk. However, these nutrients are found in very different proportions from those in the original milk. Cheese has no carbohydrate, but it contains more protein and fat than milk does.

Protein. Cheese has a high protein content, ranging from about one-fifth to one-third of the cheese. The protein is largely casein.

Fat. Cheese made from whole milk is rich in fat. Some cheeses have a fat content as much as one-third of their weight. Cheddar cheese and cream cheese are examples of such fat-rich varieties. On the other hand, cottage cheese that is made from skim milk contains less than 1 percent fat.

CLASSIFICATION OF CHEESES (Continued)

CLASS AND VARIETY	DESCRIPTION	USES
Semisoft cheeses (continued)		
Brick	Red-brown waxy surface; brick-shaped; small holes, or eyes, distributed throughout	Dessert; sandwich fillings; cheese tray
Soft cheeses		
Cottage	White, with curds of various sizes; an unripened cheese	Salads; sandwich fillings
Cream	White to cream-colored; smooth; an unripened cheese	Salads; sandwich fillings
Camembert	Yellow; very soft and creamy; covered with grayish rind; wrapped in foil	Dessert; canapés
Process cheeses		
Process	White to deep yellow	Dessert; cheese tray; sandwich fillings; as an ingredient in made dishes
Process cheese food	Similar to process cheese, but with added cream, skim milk, or whey; sometimes flavored with fruits, vegetables, or meats	Dessert; sandwich fillings; as an ingredient in made dishes
Process cheese spread	Similar to process cheese food, but contains more moisture for spreading consistency; sometimes flavored with fruits, vegetables, or meats	Dessert; sandwich fillings; as an ingredient in made dishes

[1]Canadian cheese is a domestic Cheddar cheese.

● Cheese is an excellent food for use in a main dish, such as a cheese soufflé, as an alternate for meat because of its high content of complete proteins.

Minerals. The minerals in cheese resemble those in milk, so cheese, like milk, is an outstanding source of calcium and phosphorus.

Vitamins. Besides being rich in fat, cheese made from whole milk has excellent vitamin A value. In contrast to milk, cheese is only a fair source of riboflavin, since most of the whey in which this vitamin is dissolved is pressed out of the curd during manufacture.

Uses of Cheese

Cheese is truly a many-use food. It is nutritious and flavorful, and it goes well with many other foods when it is used as an ingredient. Practically all varieties of cheese are suitable for serving plain, either as an accompaniment to another food such as crackers, bread, or pie, or as an appetizer. Almost all varieties make a satisfying ending to a meal. Although some varieties are considered better than others for certain uses, just which ones are selected for each use is a matter of personal choice. Only by personally experimenting with the different kinds of cheese that you find in your local markets can you decide. In contrast, when cheese is to be used as an ingredient in a made dish, the choice of variety is not so great. For this purpose an aged Cheddar cheese or process cheese will give the best results.

When served plain. Since there are so many varieties, serving cheese plain need never become monotonous. Crackers spread with cheese may be served with soup or salad, or as canapés—a type of appetizer. Cheese sandwiches always make a good addition to the lunch or picnic box and, either plain or toasted, are appropriate for lunch, for supper, or for between-meal snacks. A cheese tray on which slices of several varieties of cheese are arranged in an orderly pattern makes an interesting and rather unusual type of dessert. A cheese tray of this sort is usually served with crackers and often with fresh fruit. It should not, of course, follow a hearty meal. A piece of cheese is a favorite accompaniment to fruit pies in many parts of the country.

As an ingredient in recipes. In some recipes, cheese is the chief ingredient. Cheese soufflé and Welsh rarebit are two examples. Because of its richness in protein, cheese dishes of this kind may be used occasionally for the main dish in a meal instead of meat, fish, or poultry. In other recipes, smaller portions of cheese are used chiefly to contribute flavor to the product being made, such as cheese sauces, cheese dressings, cheese omelets, or in scalloped vegetable casseroles.

Principles of Preparing Foods with Cheese

When a dish containing cheese as an ingredient is cooked, the heat should be moderate because of the richness of protein in cheese. You will recall from your study of eggs

● In a salad

● For plain or toasted sandwiches

● As an ingredient

● As a topping

(page 235) that the rule for cooking foods high in protein is to apply low or moderate heat in order that the protein will not become tough. If the protein of the cheese is toughened by too high a cooking temperature, the cheese may take on a rubbery consistency that is objectionable. But if the heat is moderate, the protein is not toughened, and the cheese will remain soft and tender. High temperatures tend also to make the fat seep out of cheese, while lower temperatures do not have this unwanted effect. When directions call for heating cheese alone, a low temperature is obtained by heating it over simmering water.

Buying Cheese

The most important consideration in buying cheese is the use for which it is intended. If the cheese is to be used without cooking—

Courtesy R. T. French Company

● Because of the high content of protein in cheese, it should be cooked at a moderate temperature as are meat, eggs, milk, and other foods high in protein.

as a sandwich filling, on a cheese tray, or as an accompaniment to another food in the menu—the greatest factor in buying should be that of the consistency and flavor of the cheese. If, on the other hand, the cheese is to be used for cooking, consideration should be given to its character when heated. That is, the cheese should be a variety that will melt to a soft, smooth, tender mass. A well-ripened Cheddar cheese has this characteristic and is among the best of all cheeses for cooking. In fact, Cheddar cheese is a good all-round cheese.

Packages of Cheddar cheese are labeled according to age—"old," "medium," or "mild"—and show the net weight.

The official grades are:
Canada First Grade
Canada Second Grade
Canada Third Grade
Below Canada Third Grade

Grade names for Cheddar cheese are the same as for butter. Practically all Cheddar cheese sold is Canada First Grade quality, but it is not usually marked as such in retail stores. Grades differ in flavor, texture, and color.

Keeping quality is another point to think about when buying cheese. In general, the process cheeses rank first in this respect, with the very hard and the hard varieties of cheese having only slightly less good keeping qualities.

The size of the package or the quantity to buy at one time should also be of concern. Usually there will be some advantages in cost if larger amounts are purchased, but buying a large quantity is not a saving unless the cheese can be used within a reasonable time. This is especially true of the soft varieties. Small pieces of some varieties of hard and semisoft cheeses, if about one inch in size, can be frozen and stored as long as six months. As with all frozen foods, careful wrapping is necessary. The defrosting of the frozen cheese should be done in the refrigerator.

Care of Cheese in the Home

All cheese is perishable. All varieties should be covered and stored in a cold place, preferably in the refrigerator. If the cheese is packaged in some kind of wrapping material, this may serve as the covering, but the wrapper should be closed carefully over the cheese after the package has been opened. If the cheese is in a glass or jar, the lid should be replaced tightly after each use. Some cheeses have an outer coating which serves as a protective cover. If mold growth starts on the surface of a cheese, it should be cut off before it penetrates into the cheese.

18

Fats and

Oils

■ FAT may make up 100 percent of a given food as it does in lard and olive oil, or it may be present along with other nutrients in various proportions. There are large amounts of fat in butter and margarine, smaller amounts in plant seeds, and exceedingly small amounts in most vegetables. The term "fat" is applied to a fat that is solid at room temperature and "oil" to one that is liquid at room temperature. It is correct, however, to use the term "fat" for either solid or liquid form. In general, food fats come from animal sources and food oils from plant sources.

Food Value of Fats and Oils

Fat is one of the six nutrients, and its most important role in our diets is to supply energy. About 40 percent of the total calories of the daily diet may well come from fats. The calorie value of fats is about 2¼ times greater than the calorie value of either carbohydrates or proteins. From this comparison it can be seen that pure fats like lard, oils, and hydrogenated vegetable shortenings, and foods rich in fat like butter, margarine, pastry, and salad dressings, are all foods that are rich in calories.

Fats are not given as a separate group in Canada's Food Guide, since an adequate amount of fat will be provided when foods from the five groups are included in the day's meals. Also, fats of all kinds are used as ingredients in many prepared dishes. Thus there is little danger that a diet will be deficient in this nutrient.

Some fats are carriers of vitamins A and D. Butter and fortified margarine are examples.

WAYS OF USING FATS AND OILS

Courtesy National Association of Margarine Manufacturers

● About one-third of the total calories of the diet may come from fats and oils.

Courtesy Ann Pillsbury's Home Service Center

● As a shortening in pastry

Courtesy Best Foods, Inc.

● In dressings for salads

There are fats from plant sources that contain some vitamin E. Another nutritive contribution of fats is their supply of the necessary fatty acids. When fats are made ready in the digestive tract for use by the body, the simpler substances formed are glycerin and fatty acids. Among the fatty acids are some that are required for best bodily health. Recently attention has been focused on certain of the oils because of their possible beneficial effect on the circulatory system. These oils are designated as "polyunsaturated oils."

Buying Fats and Oils

The purpose for which you expect to use a fat will influence the kind you buy. Since the various fats have special uses, these uses will be considered as each kind of fat is discussed later in the chapter. But in making a selection among the many different brands of each kind of fat that you will find on the market, experience must be your guide. An exception, however, is in the selection of butter, for official federal quality grades for butter have been established.

When several different kinds of fats will serve the same purpose, you should consider cost. In general, among the solid fats, lard and the hydrogenated vegetable shortenings cost less per pound than margarine, and margarine costs less per pound than butter. Among the oils, olive oil is usually the most expensive. For some fats and oils, you may save on cost by buying larger units. However, the amount of use should be large enough to warrant such a purchase.

Definitions of the different kinds of fats and oils and labeling requirements for them have been set up by the Food and Drugs Act and Regulations. These regulations make it possible for the consumer to know the ingredients that are present in the fat she is buying. Some information in regard to labeling requirements will be found in later sections of this chapter.

Care of Fats and Oils in the Home

Fats and oils should be kept tightly covered during storage, since exposure to air causes them to deteriorate and develop a rancid flavor. Lard, butter, and margarine should be kept at refrigerator temperature, but the vegetable shortenings and oils keep satisfactorily at room temperature. (See chart, "Care of Food to Retain Quality," on pages 88 and 89.)

Butter

Butter is an important milk product. Unlike other milk products, such as evaporated and dried milks, butter is composed largely of the fat of milk with only small amounts of the other milk nutrients. In fact, the Food and Drugs Act and Regulations for butter require that it contain at least 80 percent milk fat. Butter for interprovincial trade must be graded.

Food value of butter. Butter is so rich in fat that it has a high calorie value, with 1 tablespoon supplying approximately 100 calories. The other nutrient of importance in butter is vitamin A. Butter is one of the most concentrated sources of this vitamin.

Uses of butter. Butter is the table fat preferred by many people. It is used for spreading on breads and for adding flavor to hot vegetables. For many years butter was used in baked products to contribute flavor and tenderness to them. Although many people still like to use butter for these purposes, other fats, less expensive in cost, are available, so that these uses of butter are not so important as formerly. The same is true in the use of butter for frying foods.

Buying butter. The characteristics of good-quality butter are that (1) it has a pleasing fresh odor and taste; (2) it has salt uniformly distributed throughout, unless it is the unsalted or so-called "sweet butter" variety; (3) it has a smooth, somewhat waxy texture; and (4) when spread, it covers a surface evenly and shows no tendency to crumble.

● Most butter manufacturers grade their butter according to the Canadian government standards, even though government grading of butter is optional unless the butter is to be shipped from one province to another.

There are butter grades to guide you in buying butter. These grades have been established by the federal government, and although their use is optional, they are followed quite generally by butter manufacturers. All creamery butter must be graded and marked accordingly. The grade mark must be shown on the main panel of the wrapper and carton in which the butter is sold. Cut and wrapped creamery butter must be sold in net weights of ¼ pound, ½ pound, 1 pound, or multiples of 1 pound.

In establishing grades for butter, the characteristics of quality that were described above are considered. The grade is designated according to the degree of excellence of the butter in each characteristic. (See chart below.)

Whipped butter is butter into which air or an inert gas has been introduced. The butter has a softer consistency and so spreads easily.

Margarine

Compared to butter, margarine is a fat of much more recent times. It was made first in France and introduced into the U.S.A. about 1875; however, it did not become legal for sale in Canada until 1949. Instead of using just cream, as in buttermaking, margarine is manufactured by churning various kinds of oils with milk in such a way that the resulting product resembles butter in consistency. Originally animal fats, called "oleo oils," were used and, for this reason, "oleomargarine" was the name first applied to the new fat. Today oils from vegetable sources such as corn, cottonseed, and soybeans, have almost entirely replaced the oleo oils, and therefore the name "margarine" is preferred as being more correct than oleomargarine. Before churning, some of the oils are partially

QUALITY GRADES FOR BUTTER

Canada First Grade: Highest quality. Excellent flavor, well made, smooth, waxy texture, uniform in color.

Canada Second Grade: Slightly lower in quality and is generally used for cooking.

Canada Third Grade and Below Canada Third Grade: Rarely found on the retail market.

hardened to a soft-solid consistency by a process called "hydrogenation."

Food value of margarine. Like butter, the unique contribution of margarine to the diet is its high-energy value, with 1 tablespoon supplying about 100 calories. Almost all margarine is fortified with vitamin A. Fortified margarine is considered the equivalent of butter in food value and can be used when desired as an alternate to butter. In addition to having vitamin A added, some margarines also have vitamin D added.

Uses of margarine. Among all the different kinds of fats, margarine is the one that most nearly resembles butter in nutritive value and in flavor. For these reasons margarine may be used interchangeably with butter as a spread for bread and for flavoring hot vegetables. Margarine also serves as a shortening ingredient in baked products and for frying foods.

Buying margarine. There are many different brands of margarine, and the one selected is a matter of personal preference. In making a choice, you should consider flavor and the ease of spreading the margarine on breads. Whipped margarine and the very soft kind that is packaged in two containers to the pound have excellent spreading qualities.

You should be interested, too, in reading the package label to note the information given there. The manufacture and sale of margarine are under the jurisdiction of the provinces, subject, however, to the general provisions of the Food and Drugs Act and Regulations. You will find a statement of the vitamin content on the label and also the kind of oil used in the margarine. In addition, you may find a statement of the percentage by weight of saturated fatty acid content and the percentage by weight of the polyunsaturated fatty acid content, on a total fat basis. However, these statements will only appear on the label if the proportions meet the Food and Drug Directorate requirements. These regulations help the consumer distinguish margarines with a high content of polyunsaturates and low content of saturates.

The package label must give information about any ingredients used for coloring and flavoring purposes, as well as any preservative that is added. Also, the label bears the name and address of the manufacturer and the weight of the contents of the package.

Lard

Lard is the soft, bland fat that is separated from the fat-rich tissues of the hog by a process called "rendering." The location on the animal from which the tissue is taken has much to do with the quality of the lard. The best quality comes from the so-called "leaf fat" that lines the abdominal cavity.

Uses of lard. Lard has such excellent shortening properties that it is the fat preferred by many for making pastry where shortness is an important characteristic. Lard makes a good frying fat. It can be used in quick breads, yeast breads, and pastry to contribute to their tenderness. Those lards that are manufactured by the improved methods of rendering and refining are better suited for making batters and doughs than are the less highly refined lards. However, special techniques must be used when lard is the shortening chosen for making cakes.

Buying lard. As a rule, lard is sold under a brand name. Because it is an animal product, all lard that is shipped from one province to another comes under the jurisdiction of the federal Meat Inspection Act and must be manufactured in plants that are inspected by federal inspectors. The label on the package gives the name and address of the manufacturer or distributor of the lard and carries the round inspection legend "Canada Approved" or "Canada."

USES OF FATS AND OILS IN COOKING

Courtesy Committee of Aluminum Producers, The Aluminum Association

● In pan-frying, a thin layer of heated fat or oil is used to prevent the food from sticking to the pan.

● In deep-fat frying, a sufficient amount of heated oil or fat is used to completely immerse the food to be cooked, although the fat does not penetrate the food.

Courtesy "The American Home." Photo by F. M. Demarest

● Fat or oil is used in pastry to make the mixture "short" and in other flour mixtures for tenderness.

Shortenings

Shortenings are bland, unsalted fats of soft consistency that are made from fats and oils by the process of hydrogenation. There are some shortenings of this type in which both animal and vegetable fats are blended.

The process of treating oils with hydrogen has the effect of raising the melting point of the oil and thus converting it into a fat with the desired soft-solid consistency. In addition to the hydrogenation of the oil, different manufacturers employ special treatments that are peculiar to the shortening they are manufacturing. In general, these treatments are used for the purpose of making a shortening that will blend easily with the several ingredients used in making cakes and the more simple baked products. The manufacturers give their own brand names to these shortenings.

Uses of shortenings. Shortenings are used for all kinds of frying. They may be used interchangeably with lard for making pastry, as they have excellent shortening properties.

● Doughnuts when properly fried in deep fat will have a crisp brown surface and no evidence of fat having soaked to the inside.

Courtesy Wheat Flour Institute

These fats also contribute to the tenderness of baked products of all kinds. In addition, many recipes for cakes call for shortening instead of butter or margarine.

Buying shortenings. Modern shortenings make a relatively inexpensive fat for general cooking purposes. When expense is a factor, they are a wise choice. The large 3-pound can is a more economical buy than the 1-pound package. If the label on the can or package does not say that the product is 100 percent vegetable shortening, you can assume that, in all probability, there is some animal fat present in the shortening.

Vegetable Oils

Vegetable oils, often called "salad oils," are pressed out from those seeds and nuts that have a relatively high fat content. These include the olive, rapeseed, corn, and soybean, all of which, with the exception of the olive, are Canadian crops. Some olives are grown in the United States, but the bulk of the olive oil on the market is imported from countries of southern Europe, such as Spain and Italy, where olive trees are grown extensively. Sunflower is another plant grown in Canada and is the source of sunflower seed oil.

Uses of vegetable oils. All the vegetable oils can be used for frying. They can replace solid fats in sauces, such as a white sauce, and in some quick breads, such as muffins. There are also recipes for pastry that call for an oil instead of the more solid fats—butter, margarine, or vegetable shortening. In the making of cakes with fat, special recipes are needed when oil is used instead of solid fat. Certain cake recipes, such as Chiffon Cake (page 440), have been developed in which oils are used rather than solid fats.

However, the unique use of oils is for making salad dressings, such as French dressing

259

and mayonnaise. This, no doubt, accounts for the name "salad oils" so frequently applied to them. The oil you select for making a salad dressing will depend upon the flavor you like and on the cost of the oil. Olive oil gives the most flavor, but as has been pointed out earlier, it is apt to be the most expensive of the salad oils. When you use a flavorless oil, you will need to give greater attention to the seasoning ingredients in the salad dressing.

Buying vegetable oils. Vegetable oils are packaged in tin cans or glass bottles. The bottles are often made of dark-colored glass in order to protect the oil from light, since light as well as air increases the tendency of the oil to become rancid. According to the Food and Drugs Act and Regulations of the Department of National Health and Welfare, labels on the containers must state what the oil is, the kind of oil, and its weight and volume. When the product is one containing several kinds of oils, these are named in the order of the decreasing amounts by weight of each oil.

Deep-fat Frying

Deep-fat frying is a process of cooking in which a food is completely immersed in hot fat. This method of frying is used for the preparation of such foods as doughnuts, French fried potatoes, fruit fritters, etc. It can also be used as a method to fry chicken, fish, croquettes, and certain vegetables. For deep-fat frying, special deep kettles with baskets are available, as well as electric fryers equipped with thermostatic temperature controls. Additional information on deep-fat frying is given in the chart below.

DIRECTIONS FOR DEEP-FAT FRYING

1. Use hydrogenated shortenings, good-quality lards, or any salad oil except olive oil for the fat.

2. Use enough fat in the kettle so that the food can be surrounded by hot fat, with room at the top for the fat to bubble over the food as it fries.

3. Unless the temperature of the fat is thermostatically controlled, it is advisable to use a deep-fat-frying thermometer. Clip the thermometer to the side of the kettle with the bulb submerged in the hot fat.

4. Lower the food gently in a basket into the hot fat, since the moisture in the food will cause the fat to sputter, and if violent, the fat may overrun the kettle and catch fire.

5. Be careful to keep the heat at the right temperature if the heat is regulated by hand. Cold food placed in hot fat will lower the temperature of the fat.

6. Do not overheat fat because it will break down chemically if overheated and cause a disagreeable taste in the food. Yet if the fat is not hot enough, the food will absorb the fat, becoming fat-soaked and unpalatable.

7. When the fried food is done, remove it from the fat and place it on absorbent paper to take up surface fat.

19

Meats

■ MEAT is one of the most popular of all foods. It is flavorful, and when cooked correctly, it is attractive. Meat may be prepared in so many ways that it lends variety and interest to any meal in which it is served. And it has a high nutritive value. Our meat supply comes from hogs, from which we get pork; cattle, from which we get beef and veal; and sheep, from which we get lamb and mutton. In some parts of the country, venison will be found during the deer-hunting season.

Cuts of Meat

When an animal carcass is divided into portions, each portion is called a "cut" of meat. These may be the large wholesale cuts or the smaller retail cuts. In some markets, there are wholesale cuts from which the meat dealer takes the smaller retail cuts at the time the meat is bought by the consumer. In other markets, the retail cuts have already been made. These are wrapped in transparent moisture-resistant paper and displayed in refrigerated cases ready for purchase.

All cuts of meat contain lean, which is the muscle tissue of the animal; connective tissue; and fat. Some cuts contain bone as well. The relative amounts of muscle tissue, connective tissue, and fat making up a cut are important, for they have an influence on the tenderness of the meat. In general, those cuts in which there is the smallest proportion of connective tissue are the most tender. The fat, if distributed in small deposits throughout the muscle, also contributes to tenderness. Such fat is called "marbling fat" in contrast to the large deposits of fat that lie between the various

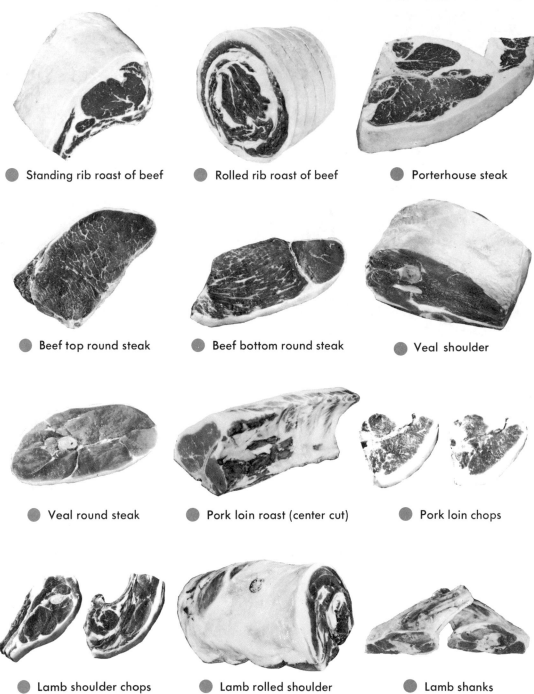

Standing rib roast of beef

Rolled rib roast of beef

Porterhouse steak

Beef top round steak

Beef bottom round steak

Veal shoulder

Veal round steak

Pork loin roast (center cut)

Pork loin chops

Lamb shoulder chops

Lamb rolled shoulder

Lamb shanks

VEAL, PORK, AND LAMB

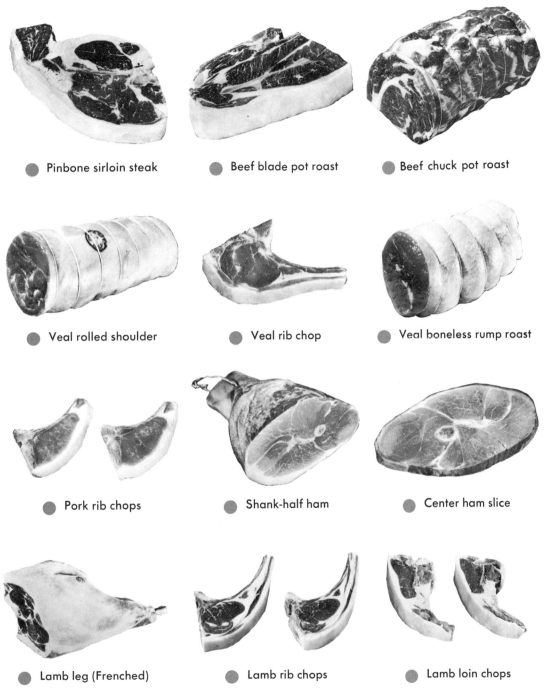

Pinbone sirloin steak

Beef blade pot roast

Beef chuck pot roast

Veal rolled shoulder

Veal rib chop

Veal boneless rump roast

Pork rib chops

Shank-half ham

Center ham slice

Lamb leg (Frenched)

Lamb rib chops

Lamb loin chops

All photos courtesy National Live Stock and Meat Board

muscles and the connective tissue. On this basis, it is possible to divide cuts of all kinds of meats into tender cuts and less-tender cuts. These with certain of the internal organs of the animal give three groups of meat cuts. Some examples of cuts of meats in the three groups follow:

1. Tender cuts: The loin and ribs of beef, veal, lamb, and pork; the leg of veal, lamb, and pork
2. Less-tender cuts: The round, rump, flank, and chuck of beef; the shoulder and breast of veal and lamb; the shoulder of pork
3. Variety meats: The liver, kidney, heart, tongue, and brains of beef, veal, lamb, and pork; the sweetbreads of beef, veal, and lamb

Tenderness of meat when cooked is a desirable characteristic, and cooking methods are used that will enhance this quality. For example, moisture is used for cooking the less-tender cuts to bring about a softening, hence tendering, of the connective tissue. (See "Moist-heat Methods" on page 267.)

However, the relative tenderness in meat cuts is becoming a less significant factor in choice among them because today meat can be tenderized. So-called "meat tenderizers" containing protein-reacting enzymes are available which can be sprinkled over the surface of the meat prior to cooking to cause a tendering action to take place. This tendering action is largely localized in the outer parts of the meat. Also, there is a commercial process in which protein-reacting enzymes are introduced into the circulatory system of the animal before it is slaughtered. These enzymes supplement those naturally occurring in the tissues and bring about uniform tendering action throughout all cuts during the cooking process. The advantage of this process is to increase the number of cuts that are tender and therefore suitable for cooking by dry-heat methods. (See "Dry-heat Methods" on page 267.) You may find these cuts sold under special brand names in your markets.

Forms of Meat

Meat is available in several forms—fresh, cured, canned, and frozen. These different forms, in addition to the three different kinds of animals and the various kinds of cuts, provide an ample selection of meat from which to choose when planning family meals.

Fresh meat. Meat that is sold just as it comes from the animal without any special treatment is considered fresh meat. It probably has hung in the cooling rooms of the packing house for several days or even as long as five weeks. During this holding time, called "aging," the natural enzymes in the tissues bring about desirable changes that contribute to the flavor and tenderness of the meat.

Cured meat. In contrast to fresh meat, cured meat has been treated with such materials as sugar, salt, spices, certain chemicals, and often, wood smoke. These materials have a preservative action, so that cured meat keeps longer than fresh meat. Examples of cured pork are ham and bacon, and of cured beef are dried beef and corned beef. Sausages are made from pork, beef, or veal. Some cured meats are completely cooked in processing.

Canned meat. Canned meat is generally meat that has been fully cooked. Among canned meats there are hams, corned beef, dried beef, hash, and wieners. Another canned meat, generally called "luncheon meat," may be made of just one kind of meat or of several kinds ground together. Also, stews and other dishes containing meat are canned. These cooked canned meats are a great help in saving time and effort in preparing a meal.

Frozen meat. Frozen meat may be either uncooked or cooked. Large cuts like roasts are usually uncooked. Smaller cuts, including chops, cutlets, and small steaks, may be either uncooked or cooked. There are also many frozen made dishes in which meat is the chief ingredient. As a rule, these require only heating to defrost and then bring to serving temperature. Meat pies and the so-called "TV

● Meats are excellent protein food whether they are tender cuts (such as a roast), less-tender cuts (such as chuck or round steak ground), or variety meats (such as liver). Variety meats, in addition, rate high for their minerals and vitamins.

dinners" are examples of these frozen products. Besides the meat, they usually include one or two vegetables. All frozen meats are held for purchase in freezing chests in the markets. Frozen meats, like canned meats, are a convenience food and are popular when the time for preparing a meal is limited. The package labels carry cooking directions and should be carefully followed.

Food Value of Meat

It is fortunate indeed that meat, which plays such an important role in meals from aesthetic and flavor viewpoints, is a highly nutritious food.

Calories. All meat furnishes calories, but the number varies with the fat content of the meat and increases with the amount of this fat eaten.

Proteins. Meat supplies larger amounts of proteins than it does of any other nutrient. Meat proteins have excellent nutritional value, since they are complete proteins and so provide all of the essential amino acids.

Minerals. Lean meat supplies an abundant amount of phosphorus and iron, and liver and kidney provide even larger amounts of these two minerals. Pork liver ranks first in iron content, followed by the livers of lamb, calf,

and beef. Beef, lamb, and pork kidneys supply about equal amounts of iron and rank ahead of calf kidney. Heart muscle is rich in iron.

Vitamins. All lean meat contains riboflavin and niacin in important amounts, and some thiamine. Pork muscle is unique for its richness in thiamine. Liver and kidney contain more riboflavin, niacin, and thiamine than muscle meats do, with the exception of the thiamine in pork muscle. Liver and kidney also supply Vitamin A in liberal amounts.

Uses of Meat

Meat is used chiefly at dinner as the main dish or special feature. The accompanying vegetables and salad are selected with the idea of blending with the meat in flavor and contrasting with it in color.

Meat as one of the ingredients of a made dish, such as a meat loaf or stew, makes a main dish that is attractive for a simple dinner, lunch, or supper. Leftover meat may be used in this way as an ingredient, it may be sliced and served cold, or it may be used as part of a substantial salad. Meat can be used in making hearty sandwiches for lunch at home or to be carried to school or work.

Cuts of meat that contain much bone are a basic ingredient in making soup stock. The

MEAT COOKERY

Moist-heat Methods

H. Armstrong Roberts

● Braising

Courtesy Aluminum Cooking Utensil Company, Inc.

● Cooking in liquid

Dry-heat Methods

Courtesy National Live Stock and Meat Board

● Roasting

Courtesy Reynolds Wrap

● Broiling

● Keep heat moderate for all meat cookery. For directions on cooking by each of the above and other moist-heat and dry-heat methods, see pages 471 to 481 in the recipes.

stock is rich in flavor and may be served alone or made into a variety of soups, depending on the ingredients added to it.

Principles of Cooking Meat

The reason for cooking meat is to make it palatable. To be palatable, meat should be attractive in appearance, tender, juicy, and well flavored. For pork, cooking is needed not only to make it palatable but also to destroy a parasite, called "trichina," which may infect it and make the meat unsafe to eat.

When meat is cooked, the proteins in it are coagulated and the connective tissue is softened. Low temperatures are used, since they cause the proteins to coagulate without becoming too hard. This avoids any toughening effect. Another advantage of using low temperatures is that the cooking time must of necessity be relatively long. Thus there is ample opportunity for the connective tissue to be made softer and for the meat to become more tender. Also, there is less loss of moisture and fat when meat is cooked at low temperatures. As a result, the meat is more juicy and has a better flavor.

The low-temperature principle is applied in the three methods of meat cookery: (1) dry heat, (2) moist heat, (3) cooking in fat.

Dry-heat Methods

Broiling, pan-broiling, and roasting are the dry-heat methods of cooking meat. No water is used, and the meat is left uncovered. Any juice that comes from the meat during cooking is made up largely of fat that melts and seeps out. Dry-heat methods are used for cooking the tender cuts of meat which contain little connective tissue and do not need the tenderizing effect that comes from cooking in liquid. These methods are also applicable to the cuts of meat taken from animals that have undergone the commercial tenderizing process and which would fall otherwise into the less-tender group of cuts.

Broiling. Meat is broiled by subjecting it to direct heat from hot coals, a gas flame, or a glowing electric element. The meat is kept at a moderate temperature by regulating the distance of the meat from the source of heat. A distance of about three or four inches is good. When one side is cooked, the meat is turned and the broiling continued until the meat is cooked on the other side.

Pan-broiling. Meat is pan-broiled by placing it in a hot skillet without added fat. As the fat cooks out of the meat, the fat is poured off, with only enough left in the pan to prevent the meat from sticking. Because of the low-temperature cooking requirement, the pan should not be heated so hot that the fat smokes. The meat should be turned once or twice during broiling to ensure even cooking throughout.

Roasting. Large tender cuts of meat, such as ribs of beef, legs of lamb, loins of pork, and hams, are cooked by roasting. An open pan is used, and the meat is placed in the pan with the fat side up. The fat melts and drips over the sides of the roast, basting it as it cooks. Low oven temperatures of 300° to 350° F. are used for whatever length of time is needed to give the desired degree of "doneness'—rare, medium, or well done. At this low-to-moderate oven temperature, the proteins are not hardened and the cooked meat is tender, juicy, and well flavored. The "Timetable for Roasting Meats" on page 472 gives the approximate number of hours required to cook roasts of different kinds of meat to each degree of doneness. The times are only approximate. For greater accuracy, a meat thermometer can be inserted into the center of the piece of meat. The meat is then cooked until the center reaches the temperature required to give the degree of doneness preferred. See the table on page 472 for these temperatures.

Moist-heat Methods

Braising and cooking in liquid are the moist-heat methods of cooking meat. They are

267

● To pan-broil bacon, place slices in cold skillet and heat slowly. Turn bacon when it is half-cooked, and drain off the fat as it accumulates.

used for cooking less-tender cuts of meat with relatively large amounts of connective tissue in them. When moisture is present during the cooking process, there is a considerable softening of this tissue.

Braising. In braising, meat may be browned. Then it is covered tightly and placed over very low heat, or in an oven at about 300° to 350° F. As the meat cooks, juices come from it to make the liquid, or a small amount of water, stock, or vegetable juice may be poured around the meat.

Cooking in liquid. Large pieces of meat may be entirely covered with water and cooked at the simmering temperature. "Boiled beef" and corned beef are examples of meats cooked by this method. In contrast, small pieces of meat may be barely covered with water and then simmered. This method is used in making stews. Stews contain vegetables which are added toward the end of the cooking time.

Cooking in Fat

Pan-frying and deep-fat frying are the two methods used for cooking meat in fat. Frying is best suited to cooking small, thin pieces

of meat or croquettes made of leftover meat where a crisp brown surface is desired. Frequently, the meat pieces are dipped into seasoned flour or dried crumbs before they are fried. This coating lessens fat absorption in both frying methods, contributes some flavor, and gives an attractive brown surface to each piece of meat.

Pan-frying. Meat is pan-fried when it is cooked in a small amount of hot fat. Unlike pan-broiling, the fat is not poured off as it accumulates. The fat should not be allowed to smoke, for this indicates that the temperature is so high as to cause the fat to break down chemically. When this happens, products are formed that have irritating fumes and a disagreeable taste.

Deep-fat frying. For deep-fat frying, enough fat is used to cover the meat pieces or croquettes. Since the temperatures used for deep-fat frying are higher than those used for pan-frying, the fats that are suitable are those with a relatively high smoking temperature. These are vegetable shortenings, oils, except olive oil, and lard.

Inspection and Quality Grading of Meat

Meat is a very perishable food and one in which there is a wide range of quality from the best to the poorest. Because of these facts, the federal government and the individual provinces carry on an inspection service to control the sanitary conditions in the meat processing industry. In addition, the federal government has set up standards of quality for meat. These government services assure the consumer of getting wholesome meat, and make it possible to select meat from among several quality grades.

Meat Inspection

The Government of Lower Canada, in 1805, instituted "An Act to Regulate the Curing, Packing and Inspection of Beef and Pork."

HOW TO MAKE GRAVY

(See recipe on page 471.)

● 1. Drain drippings from pan in which meat has been cooked.

● 2. Return desired amount of fat to pan, add flour, and blend thoroughly.

● 3. Slowly stir in liquid, bring to boil, and let boil for 2 or 3 minutes.

● 4. Pour smooth, hot gravy into a hot serving dish.

CANADA GRADES OF MEAT

CANADA CHOICE (Red Brand)

From young steers and heifers with a high proportion of meat to bone. Has a good covering of fat, and light tracings of fat in the lean (called marbling).

CANADA GOOD (Blue Brand)

From young steers and heifers. Has a slightly lower proportion of meat to bone and usually less fat than Canada Choice.

CANADA STANDARD (Brown Brand)

From young steers and heifers. Has a lower proportion of fat to lean meat than Canada Good.

CANADA COMMERCIAL (Black Brand)

Class 1: from young steers and heifers less fleshy than Canada Standard but having maturity and fat similar to Canada Choice. *Class 2:* from young cows and heifers older than those for Class 1 but with the same maximum fat covering. *Class 3:* from steers, heifers and young cows of same maturity as those for Class 2 but overfat and wasty.

CANADA UTILITY (Black Brand)

Class 1: from steers, heifers and young cows of poor quality with a slight fat covering. *Class 2:* from mature cows and oxen of medium or better formation and quality with a moderate fat covering. *Class 3:* quality and finish are lower than Class 2.

Photo courtesy Canada Department of Agriculture

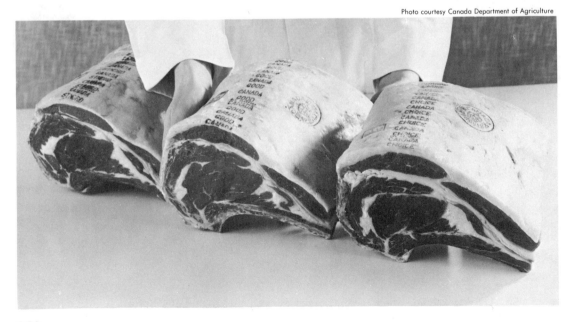

A round "Canada Approved" or "Canada" inspection stamp is applied to carcasses that have been health inspected by federal government veterinarians. This stamp—not to be mistaken for a grade mark—is the consumer's assurance that the meat is wholesome and has been dressed under sanitary conditions. Edible dyes are used for stamps and grade marks.

Federal inspection for wholesomeness covers all meat to be shipped from a packing house located in one province to another for sale.

The law that now applies is the Meat and Canned Foods Act of 1907. According to its provisions, all meat and poultry entering foreign trade must be inspected by government veterinarians. The inspection makes certain that the animals are healthy, the conditions of the packing house sanitary, and that the health of the operators is satisfactory.

Meat that passes inspection is marked with a round stamp. Meat which does not pass inspection is condemned and cannot be used for food. The mark appears on all large wholesale meat cuts but does not appear on the smaller retail cuts sold in pre-packaged form.

The Meat Inspection Act of 1959 applies to the sanitary condition of meat that is processed and sold interprovincially.

In addition to covering fresh meat, the two laws just described apply to processed meats like sausage, canned and frozen meats, and meat dishes. The containers for these products bear an inspection stamp similar to the stamp on fresh meat. All ingredients in the processed meats must be wholesome, and the products must not be adulterated. The label must carry the name of the product, a list of the ingredients in it, the net weight, and the name and address of the manufacturer.

By far the largest amount of meat and meat products in Canada is federally inspected. However, some meat is produced and sold within the borders of a single province and does not come under the supervision of the federal law. For a guarantee of the wholesomeness of such meat, reliance must be placed on provincial health regulations.

Quality of Meat and Meat Grades

Unlike the federal inspection for wholesomeness just described, the federal grading service for quality of meat is not required by law. However, most meat packers believe the grading of meats for quality to be so useful to the consumer when buying meat that they make use of the service and undertake the relatively small fee charged by the federal government to cover the cost involved. There is no charge for the inspection of meat for wholesomeness, since this inspection is mandatory.

The quality of meat depends on the animal from which it comes. In making his judgment, the grader takes into consideration the shape of the animal before it is slaughtered; and after it is slaughtered, he takes into consideration the amount and distribution of fat on the meat and surrounding the internal organs. Finally, he considers the character of the lean meat, the fat, and the bone. When he has decided on the quality, the grader stamps the meat with a roller that goes the entire length of the carcass so that each retail cut shows the assigned quality grade. (See chart on page 276.)

In general, meat that falls in the top quality grades (Prime and Choice) is the most attractive in appearance. The individual cuts are compact in shape and have a high proportion

Standing Rib Roast

Both photos Stern from Monkmeyer

● Left: With the guard up, insert the fork firmly between the two top ribs. From the far outside edge, slice across the grain toward the ribs. Make the slices an eighth to three-eighths of an inch thick. Right: Release each slice by cutting close along the rib with the knife tip. After each cut, lift the slice on the blade of the knife to the side of the platter.

of meat to bone. There is a good covering of fat on them which in beef and lamb is white and hard and in pork white and somewhat soft. In beef there is good marbling. The color of the flesh of beef is bright red. Young veal is grayish-pink and older veal dark pink. The flesh of lamb is light red and of mutton dark red. The flesh of pork is grayish-pink. The bone ends of all young animals are pink-to-red and porous-looking. When cooked, high-quality meat is tender, juicy, and flavorful.

Buying Meat

In the usual markets only one or two grades of meat are sold, and they will depend on the preference of the majority of the customers. In the case of beef, there is more Choice-grade meat produced than any other quality and

it is the highest grade available. There is only about half as much Good grade beef available in the stores as Choice grade.

When the meat is cut from the large whole-sale piece, the quality grade mark can be seen. With the prepackaged meats, however, the buyer must, as a rule, rely on her own ability to judge quality. If she keeps in mind the characteristics of quality for each kind of meat discussed at the left, she will soon become able to select fresh meat with confidence. In addition to considering quality, the buyer should take note of the general sanitary condition of the market counter and the cleanliness habits of the personnel.

In buying cured meats, there are several things besides quality to be considered. Hams are available that have been made in three different ways. There are the regular hams

(*Continued on page 276*)

MEAT: I

Rolled Rib Roast

● Left: With the guard up, push the fork firmly into the roast on the left side an inch or two from the top. Slice across the grain toward the fork from the far right side. Uniform slices of an eighth to three-eighths of an inch thick make desirable servings. Right: As each slice is carved, lift it to the side of the platter.

Porterhouse Steak

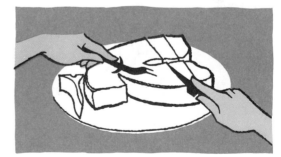

● Left: Holding the steak with the fork inserted at the left, cut close around the bone. Right: Then lift the bone to the side of the platter where it will not interfere with carving, and cut across the full width of the steak. Make wedge-shaped portions, widest at the far side. Each serving will be a piece of the tenderloin and a piece of the large muscle.

Baked Whole Ham

● Left: Insert the fork and cut several slices parallel to the length of the ham. Right: Turn the ham so that it rests on the surface just cut. Hold the ham firmly with the fork, and cut a small wedge from the shank end. Keep the fork in place to steady the ham, and cut thin slices down to the leg bone.

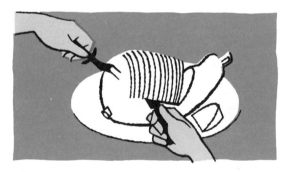 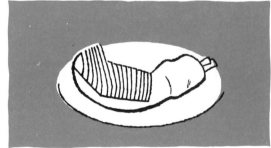

● Left: Release slices by cutting along the bone at right angles to slices. Right: For more servings, turn the ham back to its original position and slice at right angles to the bone.

Pork Loin Roast

 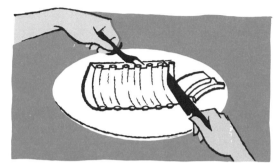

⬤ Left: Before the roast is brought to the table, remove the backbone by cutting between it and the rib ends. Right: Insert the fork firmly in the top of the roast. Cut close against both sides of each rib. In a small loin each slice may contain a rib; if the loin is large, it is possible to cut two boneless slices between ribs.

Roast Leg of Lamb

 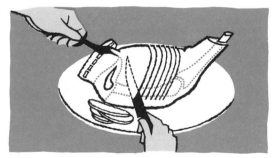

⬤ Left: Insert the fork firmly in the large end of the leg, and carve two or three lengthwise slices from the near thin side. Right: Turn the roast so that it rests on the surface just cut. The shank bone now points up from the platter. Insert the fork in the left of the roast. Starting at the shank end, slice down to the leg bone. Parallel slices may be made until the aitch bone is reached. One-quarter to three-eighths of an inch is a desirable thickness. With the fork still in place, run the knife along the leg bone, releasing all the slices.

which have been heated in the smoking step to an internal temperature of 142° F. Because slight cooking has occurred at this temperature, some manufacturers call these hams "tendered." They require further cooking before they can be eaten. There are ready-to-eat hams which during the smoking process reach an internal temperature of 155° F. These hams are completely cooked, but if cooked a little more before they are eaten, they are more palatable. Finally, there are the fully cooked hams which are completely cooked but not smoked. These are usually large hams that have been cured and boned, and then pressed into heavy molds and completely cooked. This kind of ham is frequently used in the market for slicing. The label on ham tells the type of ham, whether it is a regular ham or one of the ready-to-eat kind, and often will give cooking directions. It is very important to read these labels since ham, like fresh pork, must be thoroughly cooked to make it safe to eat because of possible infection from the trichina organism.

Bacon, another cured meat, may be sliced from the whole piece by the butcher, or it may already be sliced and wrapped in either half-pound or pound packages. The number of slices in a package differs according to the width and thickness of each strip. In the pound package the average number is around 18 to 22 slices. Best-quality bacon has a strip of lean along one side which is about one-half as wide as the fat portion. But there is good bacon with less lean than this, and personal preference as to the amount of lean versus fat varies. Back bacon is made from the pork loin after the bone has been removed. It is cured and smoked in the same way as regular bacon, but it is almost all lean. Back bacon may be sliced and used like regular bacon, or it may be left in a large piece and roasted for use as the main dish in a meal.

Fresh and cured meat, even that which is prepackaged, is sold by the pound. Before buying meat by the pound, it is necessary to know how many pounds are needed to serve a given number of persons. With chops or slices of meat, it is only necessary to count the number of pieces needed. If a piece of meat is larger than those of individual-serving size, the decision is not so easily reached. An amount of meat that weighs 4 ounces is considered an average-sized serving, so that 1 pound of meat which is all lean will serve four people. In the table "Food Buying Guide" on pages 78 to 81 there is a list of meats grouped

QUALITY GRADES OF MEAT

BEEF	LAMB AND YOUNG MUTTON	MUTTON	VEAL	PORK[1]
Canada Choice	Canada Choice	Canada Choice	Canada Choice	Canada A
Canada Good	Canada Good	Canada Good	Canada Good	Canada B
Canada Standard	Canada Commercial	Canada Commercial	Canada Commercial	Canada C
Canada Commercial	Canada Utility	Canada Utility	Canada Utility	
Canada Utility				

[1] These federal grades for pork are not marked on the large wholesale cuts as are those for the other kinds of meat.

according to the amount of bone they contain. The table also gives the approximate number of servings that may be counted on from the meats in each group.

The brand name of cured, canned, and frozen meats is no doubt the best guide in buying them. By experimenting with a number of different brands, you should be able to find one that is satisfactory in quality and cost. The net weight of the contents that is stated on the label will enable you to make an estimate of the number of servings of meat available in the can or package.

Care of Meat in the Home

Meat, like milk, is a food that deteriorates very quickly unless it is given suitable care. Because meat is expensive compared to many other foods, any spoilage is a waste not only of food but also of money. And if spoilage has started in meat, even though it has not reached the point of being detectable by odor and appearance, the meat is a hazard to health.

Care of fresh and variety meats. Fresh and variety meats should be wiped with a damp cloth, placed on a dish, covered lightly with wax paper or aluminum foil, and stored in a very cold part of the refrigerator. Such care of meat is essential, since bacteria can easily grow on its moist surface. The cold temperature and the slightly dry surface that forms when only a loose covering is used are conditions that discourage bacterial growth. After meat has been cooked, any unused portion should be stored in a very cold part of the refrigerator. The meat should be covered so that the surface, made dry by cooking, will not dry further and become unpalatable. (See chart, "Care of Food to Retain Quality," on pages 88 and 89.)

Care of cured, canned, and frozen meats. Most cured meats that are made by modern processes require refrigeration. In the case of canned meats, a cool, dry storage place is satisfactory for all kinds except canned hams weighing over 1½ pounds. Because larger-sized canned hams have not been completely sterilized in processing, they are a perishable product and need to be stored in the refrigerator. Frozen meats, like all other frozen foods, are stored in the freezing compartment of the refrigerator or in a home freezer to keep them solidly frozen until they are to be prepared for cooking.

Gelatin

Gelatin is an important product which is manufactured by the meat industry because it is made from the bones and certain connective tissues of animals. These tissues contain a protein substance called "collagen" which can be changed into gelatin. Gelatin may be made in the form of thin sheets or broken into pieces. For use in cookery, it is sold in a finely granulated form.

Food value of gelatin. Gelatin is an incomplete protein, and therefore it cannot be relied upon as the only protein in the diet. Gelatin may, however, make a contribution to the daily protein allowance if complete proteins are supplied by other foods.

Uses of gelatin. The chief use of gelatin in food preparation is as a carrier of other foods. It provides a means of making many attractive salads and desserts. Gelatin in solution, provided it is in sufficient concentration, solidifies into a jellylike mass. Hot milk or vegetable or fruit juices can be used to dissolve the gelatin and thus make the bulk of the jellied mass in salads and desserts.

Principles of preparation of gelatin. The first step in preparing gelatin is to allow it to stand for several minutes in a small amount of cold water. During this time the gelatin absorbs water and becomes a soft translucent mass. It is now hydrated gelatin and can be dissolved in a hot liquid. In recipes which call

277

Both photos courtesy Knox Gelatine

● To make a gelatin mold: Sprinkle granulated gelatin on a small amount of cold water to soften, and then dissolve in hot liquid. Either fruit or vegetable juice or hot water may be used for the hot liquid (left). Arrange cut fruit or pieces of vegetable in the bottom of a mold and add just enough slightly chilled gelatin mixture to cover them (right). Chill until the gelatin sets, and repeat until the mold is complete.

● To unmold gelatin: Dip mold into hot water or cover outside with a hot, damp cloth.

Courtesy West Bend Aluminum Company

for at least 1 tablespoon of sugar, dry granular gelatin may be mixed with the sugar, instead of standing in cold water, and then added directly to the hot liquid. The hot gelatin mixture is poured into a mold and allowed to chill until firm and jellylike. Several hours are required for this "setting," with the exact time depending upon the degree of cold. The usual concentration of gelatin to liquid for a jellylike product is 1 tablespoon of gelatin to 1 pint of liquid, including that amount of cold water that is used to hydrate the gelatin. In some brands one envelope contains an amount of gelatin that will solidify 1 pint of liquid. The amount may be more or less than 1 tablespoon, depending on the so-called "strength" of the gelatin.

20

Poultry

■ THE SEVERAL kinds of domesticated poultry commonly used—chickens, turkeys, ducks, geese, guineas, squabs, and Rock Cornish game hens—have much in common. They all have delicately flavored meat, although that of ducks and geese is most flavorful. They also furnish complete proteins. All kinds of poultry find a welcome spot on the menu because of their own goodness and because they increase the number of choices for the main course. Another advantage of poultry is the relatively low cost of some kinds—especially chicken or turkey.

Of all the kinds of poultry, chickens are the most abundant and are most frequently used. Turkeys are now popular as a year-round bird, since smaller turkeys are being raised for smaller families. Ducklings, or young ducks, and geese are also popular, as are Rock Cornish game hens, the use of which is increasing.

Game birds are favored by many people, although they are not generally available unless there is a hunter in the family. There are a few farms, however, where wild turkeys, pheasants, and some quail are raised for the game-bird enthusiast, and there are some specialty farms where guineas and squabs are raised.

Forms of Poultry

Live poultry is offered for sale in some localities, but the usual forms found on the market are fresh poultry, such as dressed and ready-to-cook; frozen poultry; and canned poultry.

Fresh poultry. Fresh poultry comes liveweight, dressed, or ready-to-cook. Liveweight poultry has the feathers, head, and feet left on, and the insides have not been removed.

279

Photos courtesy Canada Department of Agriculture.

● Poultry today is available frozen, fresh, and canned.

Dressed poultry has only the feathers removed. Ready-to-cook birds have had the feathers, head, and feet removed. They have been drawn —that is, the inner parts have been removed. The liver, gizzard, and heart, called the "giblets," and the neck have been washed, wrapped, and placed inside the body cavity. Ready-to-cook poultry is sold as the whole bird or in smaller parts. In many localities barbecued chickens and ducks are available and roasted chickens and turkeys can be ordered.

Frozen poultry. A great deal of poultry is frozen at packing plants for convenience and for safety in transportation. Most of this frozen poultry is in the ready-to-cook form. Chickens and turkeys are frozen whole or as parts. There are also boneless turkey roasts in rolled shape. These are made of all white meat, all dark meat, or of a combination of both kinds. They are packaged raw, fully cooked, or smoked. Turkeys and Rock Cornish hens that are stuffed and then frozen are other kinds of frozen poultry. Frozen poultry is convenient to use in meal preparation since it need only be cooked to be ready for serving.

Canned poultry. Chicken is canned in several different forms. The whole bird may be canned, the bird may be cut into pieces, or only the meat may be canned. Turkey meat is obtainable in canned form. Chicken and tur-

key pastes, suitable for use in canapés or as sandwich fillings, are also available in cans. And there are such specialties as chicken and turkey á la king in cans.

Food Value of Poultry

Poultry of all kinds contains proteins, fats, minerals, and vitamins. The proteins are complete proteins and therefore have the same high nutritive quality as those of meat and fish. Some kinds of poultry are richer in fat content than others. Geese have the highest percentage of this nutrient. Iron and phosphorus are two important minerals found in poultry. Niacin, thiamine, and riboflavin are three vitamins for which poultry is valuable.

Uses of Poultry

Poultry is such a versatile form of meat that it can be prepared in ways appropriate for any meal. It can be used as a main-course dish, whether the meal is a formal or informal dinner, a lunch or supper, or even a breakfast or combination late breakfast and early lunch. There are also many ways in which, once cooked, the poultry meat may be used. Among these uses are for salads; as a filling for sandwiches, either sliced alone or cut up and mixed

(Continued on page 284)

● Poultry is a nutritious food because it contains complete proteins as well as important minerals and three of the B vitamins.

TO FRY CHICKEN

(See recipe on page 492.)

● 1. Coat the chicken pieces with seasoned flour.

● 2. Brown the coated pieces in shallow fat, and cover the pan.

● 3. Chicken is done if the meat is soft when tested with a fork.

OTHER WAYS TO COOK POULTRY

(See recipes on pages 491 and 492.)

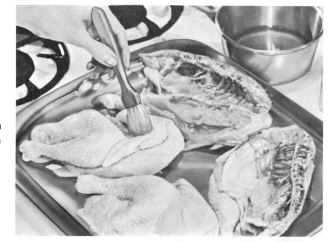

● To broil: Brush poultry parts with melted fat or oil, season, and broil on each side until tender and browned.

● To bake: Brush poultry parts with melted fat or oil, season, and bake uncovered until tender and brown, basting occasionally.

Both photos courtesy Poultry and Egg National Board

● To simmer: Place poultry parts in seasoned water, bring to boil, reduce heat, cover, and simmer until tender.

Courtesy General Electric Company

with some kind of salad green; and as an ingredient in various made dishes, such as croquettes, casseroles, and creamed chicken. The liquid in which chicken is stewed can be used as a base for soups.

Principles of Preparation of Poultry

Because poultry contains a large amount of protein, the rule for protein cookery applies to poultry also. This rule, you will remember, is to use moderate temperatures for cooking. High temperatures harden the protein, producing a toughening effect, while lower temperatures keep the poultry meat as tender as possible. For broiling, roasting, or frying, the use of moderate heat has an added advantage: There is less evaporation of moisture and less loss of fat and juice. As a consequence, the meat remains juicy. When moist heat is used in cooking poultry, moderate temperatures are obtained by letting the liquid in which the meat is cooked simmer rather than boil.

For a timetable on roasting different kinds of poultry and recipes for cooking poultry, see Part V.

Buying Poultry

The best practice in buying poultry is to look for the inspection and grade marks. (See chart below.) However, since all poultry is not inspected and graded, you should learn to recognize the characteristics of good quality that are given in the chart below. In determining quality, it is also helpful for you to know the brand name of the packer. If you like the brand that you purchase, you may want to select the same brand another time. On the other hand, if the bird is not up to your standard, you will probably avoid this brand the next time you shop for poultry.

Poultry should be bought for a definite cooking purpose. The dry-heat methods of broiling, roasting, and frying do not increase tenderness, so only young, tender poultry

FEDERAL POULTRY INSPECTION

Health inspection is the responsibility of federal veterinarians stationed in eviscerating plants approved and registered by the Health of Animals Branch, Canada Department of Agriculture. Poultry found wholesome in plants operating under federal government inspection has the "Canada Approved" or "Canada" inspection legend on the tag, bag or insert.

Grading of poultry is compulsory for wholesale trade and sale in retail stores in most major cities. The grade mark is printed on a metal breast tag, transparent bag or label insert. All poultry for interprovincial or export trade must be graded, and eviscerated poultry must also be health inspected. Imported dressed and eviscerated poultry must conform to Canadian grade standards although the word "Canada" does not appear in the grade mark.

Poultry is graded on conformation: Presence of deformities that affect appearance or normal distribution of flesh, for example, a crooked keel bone.
Flesh: Distribution and amount on the carcass.
Fat covering: Distribution and amounts in specific areas.
Dressing: Presence of defects such as discoloration, tears, pinfeathers, bruises or other blemishes.

Poultry grades are: Canada Grade Special*, Canada Grade A, Canada Grade B, Canada Grade Utility, Canada Grade C*, Canada Grade D*.

*Not usually available in retail stores.

CHICKEN
CANADA **A** GRADE

YOUNG TURKEY
CANADA **A** GRADE

● Poultry in interprovincial commerce must have the federal label showing that it has been inspected for wholesomeness. As with meat, inspected poultry may also be graded for quality—Grade A being the best, as shown below.

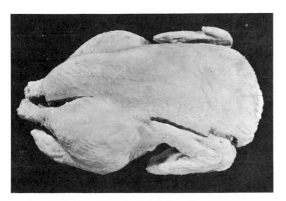

● Canada Grade A boiling fowl

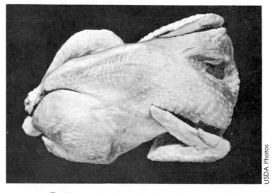

USDA Photos

● Canada Grade B boiling fowl

should be selected for cooking by these methods. More mature birds are suitable for cooking by the moist-heat methods of braising and simmering. When cooked in liquid the connective tissue is softened and the flesh becomes tender.

Buying chickens. Broiling and frying chickens are nine weeks old and have a ready-to-cook weight ranging from 2 to 3 pounds. The smaller birds are best for broiling and the larger ones for frying. Roasting chickens are older, about twelve weeks of age, and they weigh, when ready to cook, from 3 to 5 pounds. More mature chickens are about one and one-

half years old and weigh from 4 to 6 pounds dressed weight. They are less tender than the roasting chickens but are satisfactory for cooking in liquid, such as in making fricasseed chicken. Chickens that are cut up are sold as halves, or quarters, or in smaller pieces.

Buying turkeys. Turkeys are different in size, depending on the breed rather than on the age. Some breeds are about the size of fairly large chickens. Ready-to-cook turkeys of some breeds vary in weight from 4 to 8 pounds, while others may weigh from 10 to 14 pounds for hens, and from 17 to 24 pounds for toms. Half turkeys and turkey parts are

TO STUFF AND ROAST POULTRY

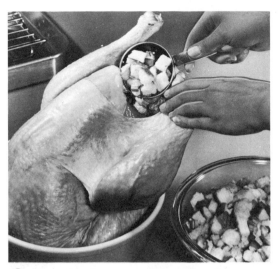 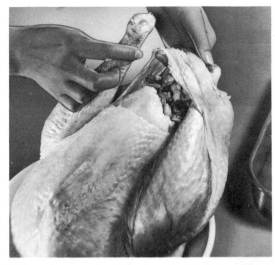

● To stuff and roast poultry, follow these steps: (1) Place prepared stuffing into body cavity, but do not press it in (left). (2) Hold the legs firm by putting them inside the skin at the base of the body cavity (right).

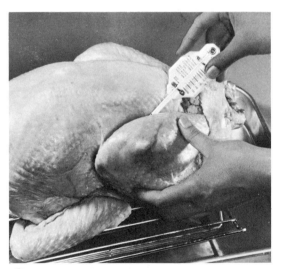 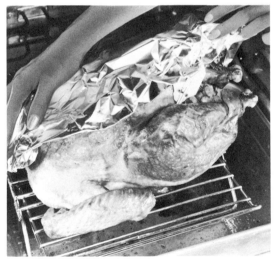

● (3) Insert meat thermometer between thigh and body (left). (4) Brush with melted butter or margarine, and put on a rack in an uncovered roasting pan. Baste occasionally during roasting. If necessary, cover with foil to avoid over-browning (right).

All Photos Courtesy Poultry and Egg National Board

sometimes available for those who do not wish to buy a whole bird.

Buying ducklings. Ducklings are young ducks, and they make up the major part of this kind of poultry that is sold. The Pekin type of duckling constitutes about 80 percent of all ducklings sold in Canada. They are carefully fed because the food they eat affects the flavor of the meat. Ducklings are marketed both dressed and ready-to-cook. Ready-to-cook ducklings are marketed when young, between nine and twelve weeks of age, and weigh from 3½ to 5 pounds. Older ducks, which are seldom seen on the market now, weigh more, but the additional weight is mostly fat. As a rule, there is less meat on duckling, weight for weight, than there is on other kinds of poultry.

Buying Rock Cornish game hens and guinea hens. Rock Cornish game hens weigh about 1 pound. They are usually sold frozen and ready-to-cook and are packaged in moistureproof bags. Guinea hens are also sold frozen and ready-to-cook. One guinea hen will make two or three servings. Like ducklings, these birds are more or less of a delicacy.

Care of Poultry in the Home

Poultry, like meat, is perishable and requires suitable care in the home. Otherwise undesirable changes take place which make the poultry unpalatable and may even cause a serious illness to occur. (See chart, "Care of Food to Retain Quality," on pages 88 and 89.)

Care of fresh poultry. Fresh poultry of all kinds should be stored in the refrigerator. If it is the packaged type, either the wrapped parts or a ready-to-cook bird, the wrapping material should be removed and replaced loosely, or a new covering should be put over it. If the bird is the dressed type that has been freshly cleaned in the market, it needs a thorough washing inside and out before it is placed, loosely covered, in the refrigerator.

Care of frozen poultry. Frozen poultry should be kept frozen until time to defrost it for cooking. Although it is not necessary to defrost a frozen bird, thawing will make the cooking more uniform throughout. It will also shorten the cooking time and make it easier to judge the time needed. The exception as to whether or not to thaw frozen poultry is the frozen stuffed bird. Cooking of this should start while it is still frozen since, during the long thawing period, any harmful organisms in the dressing will develop and cause spoilage. To defrost frozen poultry, place it, in its original wrapper, on a tray in the refrigerator. If it is not wrapped, cover it with wax paper or a plastic material. If necessary to defrost poultry more quickly than in the refrigerator, place it in the original wrapper, or other water-tight covering, under running cool water, or immerse it in water at about room temperature. Change the water as it chills. Defrosted poultry should be cooked immediately. The following table may be used as a guide for defrosting poultry in the refrigerator:

Chickens:	Approximate time
4 pounds or over	1 to 1½ days
Less than 4 pounds	12 to 16 hours
Ducks, 3 to 5 pounds:	1 to 1½ days
Turkeys:	
18 pounds or over	2 to 3 days
Less than 18 pounds	1 to 2 days
Pieces of large turkey (half, quarter, half breast)	1 to 2 days
Cut-up pieces	3 to 9 hours
Boneless roasts	12 to 18 hours

Care of stuffing for poultry. The stuffing should be made and put into a bird just before time to roast it. Stuffing is subject to spoilage if allowed to stand at room temperature for any length of time. If it must be prepared ahead, store it in the refrigerator and put it into the bird just before roasting time. Stuffing a turkey the day before it is to be cooked is unwise for, even in the refrigerator,

HOW TO CARVE POULTRY

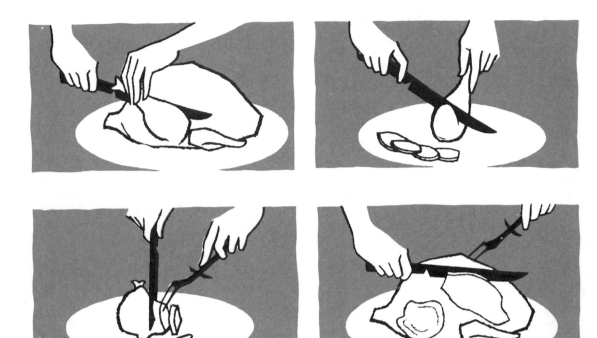

● (1) To remove leg (thigh or second joint and drumstick), hold the drumstick firmly with the fingers, pulling gently away from the body of the bird. At the same time cut through the skin between leg and body (first drawing). Continue as follows: (2) Press leg away from body with flat side of knife. Then cut through joint joining leg to backbone and skin on back. (3) Slice drumstick meat holding drumstick upright at a convenient angle to plate, and cut down, turning drumstick to get uniform slices (second drawing). (4) Slice thigh meat, holding thigh firmly on plate with a fork and cutting slices of meat parallel to the bone (third drawing). (5) To remove wing, cut deep into the breast to the body frame parallel to and as close to the wing as possible. Cut through joint attaching it to frame. (6) Slice white meat. Beginning at front, starting halfway up the breast, cut thin slices of white meat down to the cut made parallel to the wing (fourth drawing). The slices will fall away from the body as they are cut to this line. Continue carving until enough meat has been carved for first servings.

the large amount of stuffing packed into the body cavity is an ideal place for the growth of spoilage organisms that might be in the stuffing. Even when the turkey has been sufficiently roasted, the very cold stuffing may not have reached the temperature during roasting that is required to destroy these organisms, thus making the stuffing unsafe to eat.

Care of leftover poultry. If any poultry is left after a meal, it should be covered lightly and placed immediately in the refrigerator. Leftover poultry should be used within two days. It is considered good practice to remove any of the stuffing that is unused and to refrigerate it separately from the bird, especially when the bird is very large.

21

Fish

THE WATERS bordering the long coast lines of Canada and the many inland lakes and rivers abound in fish of many different kinds. Getting these fish out of the waters and distributing them fresh to the markets or processing them into one form or another is a large and profitable industry. Since there are so many different kinds of fish, it is convenient to group them into two classes: finfish and shellfish. These classes, a brief description of each class, and some examples of each class are given in the chart on page 291.

Forms of Fish

Although the actual catching of fish is limited in area, the fact that fish may be frozen, cured, or canned makes it a food that is available throughout the year in all parts of the country.

Fresh Fish. The supply of fresh fish varies with location and season. In the waters of the Atlantic, haddock, flounder, mackerel, cod, and lobster are abundant. Clams and oysters are harvested on both Atlantic and Pacific coasts, while the bulk of Canadian crab comes from British Columbia, as well as some shrimp. The Bay of Fundy, N.S., is the center of the Canadian sardine industry. The waters of the Pacific Coast and the rivers flowing into them are noted for salmon. The inland lakes and rivers have such fish as trout, pickerel, and perch. In any location the different kinds of fish found there are limited to certain seasons of the year. For example, shad is plentiful in the late spring, haddock and halibut in the summer, and salmon in the summer and fall months.

Frozen fish. Frozen fish is packaged as steaks, fillets, and small whole fish. It is frozen

CLASSES OF FISH

● Finfish

● Shellfish

in a form for easy shipping and storing and thus provides a supply of fish in all parts of the country at all times of the year. Frozen fish is ready for cooking, since all waste parts have been removed. Some frozen fish is cooked before it is frozen, so that it needs only to be heated for serving.

The plants where fish are frozen are located, as a rule, at the fishing ports so that the time between catching the fish and freezing it can be short. This practice makes the frozen product, when cooked, practically equal to cooked fresh fish in appearance and flavor.

Cured fish. Salted, smoked, and pickled fish are the three kinds of cured fish.

Salted fish is salted in either dry salt or brine. Then it is dried to make a dry product, such as dry salt codfish, or it may be held in the brine to make a brine-packed salt fish, such as salmon and mackerel.

Smoked fish is made from a mildly salted fish by a smoking treatment. Usually in the modern method of smoking fish, the smoking period is of short duration and the fire is not very hot. Finnan haddie (haddock), kippers (large herring split in half), salmon, whitefish, eel, and sturgeon are examples of fish cured in this way. Small fish of the herring family are

Courtesy National Fisheries Institute

● The protein content of fish is high, and the proteins are the valuable complete proteins. One of the important food values of salt-water fish is its iodine content.

packed in oil after they have been salted and smoked. These include sardines, pilchards, and anchovies.

Pickled fish is cured in a brine that contains vinegar and sometimes spices. After the process is completed, the pieces are packed in jars for further keeping. Herring is the most important kind of pickled fish, although other

CLASSIFICATION OF FISH		
CLASS	**DESCRIPTION**	**EXAMPLES**
Finfish	With fins and a backbone	
	May be fresh-water fish living in rivers or lakes	White fish; brook trout; pickerel; yellow perch
	or	
	salt-water fish living in the ocean	Haddock; cod; bluefish; salmon
Shellfish	Without fins and a backbone	
	May be mollusks, having two enclosing shells	Clams; oysters; scallops; mussels
	or	
	crustaceans, having a hard upper shell and a soft under shell	Shrimp; lobster; crab; prawns

● Seafood may be served in many tempting ways: as the basis for a spread, for a salad, as a creamed dish, or for before-dinner cocktails.

kinds like haddock, mackerel, and trout are sometimes pickled.

Canned fish. Many different kinds of fish are available in the canned form. The most popular among them are salmon, tuna, sardines, and the flaked meat of large fish, such as cod and haddock. The various kinds of shellfish, when canned, are delicacies. They can be served cold as they come from the can, they can be heated, or they can be used as an ingredient in the preparation of some dish. Since canned fish keeps well, a supply of different kinds is convenient to have on hand in the kitchen.

Food Value of Fish

Fish, if included frequently in menus, not only brings variety to meals but makes a valuable contribution to the diet, since all the nutrients except carbohydrate are represented. These nutrients occur in varying amounts according to the kind of fish.

Proteins. The protein content of fish is high, and the proteins are the valuable complete proteins. (See page 16.) In this respect, fish resembles meat and poultry in its nutrient value.

Fats. The fat content of fish is low except in such kinds as salmon, pompano, shad, tuna, mackerel, herring, and brook and lake trout.

Minerals. Fish is important for the mineral phosphorus, and it is fairly rich in calcium. It is not such a good source of iron as is meat. One of the unique values of fish is the iodine content of the salt-water varieties.

Vitamins. Vitamins of the B group are found in fair amounts in fish. Vitamins A and D are present in the fat or oil, especially the oil of the fish liver. Some of the fish-liver oils

292

are so rich in these two vitamins that they provide a supply of vitamins A and D which are used as dietary supplements. The liver oils of the cod and halibut are the ones most commonly used for this purpose. Vitamins A and D are also present in the body parts of those fish in which the oil is distributed throughout the fish.

Uses of Fish

Since so many kinds and forms of fish are available, there are ways of using fish in all the daily meals.

As an appetizer. Pickled and smoked fish are often used as part of an appetizer course, for their distinctive flavor stimulates the appetite. Crab, shrimp, and lobster, either fresh, frozen, or canned, may be served as a shellfish cocktail for the beginning course at lunch or dinner. For those who enjoy raw oysters and clams, these shellfish make a popular intro duction to a dinner.

As a soup. A favorite way to use fish is in chowder. Chowder is such a hearty soup that it may be used as the main dish at lunch or supper. Other hearty soups are oyster and lobster stews in which whole oysters are included in the former and pieces of lobster in the latter. There are also cream soups made of fish. In these, if the fish is a shellfish, the cream soup is called a "bisque." All these soups may be made from the ingredients or, where more convenient, they can be found in the canned or frozen forms.

As a main dish. Fresh or frozen fish, prepared in any one of a number of ways, makes an attractive main dish. For dinner, a whole fish of medium size, such as haddock, weakfish, or bluefish, is suitable for stuffing and baking, while fillets, steaks, and small fish, either whole or split in half, are good for broiling and frying. For lunch, leftover cooked fish or canned fish can be used for salads, soufflés, or creamed dishes. For breakfast, one of the cured fishes makes an appetizing and hearty·

TO BROIL FISH

● Top: Place the fish on a heated, greased, heat-proof platter or broiler pan (do not use rack). Brush with melted butter or margarine, and put in heated broiler compartment about 3 inches from the heat. If the pieces are thick, turn them when they are half-cooked. Bottom: Garnish the fish with lemon wedges. The shape and color of the lemon have eye appeal, and the lemon juice adds a zesty flavor.

Photos courtesy National Fisheries Institute

Photos courtesy U.S. Bureau of Commercial Fisheries

● First roll the fish in crumbs. Then place the fish in heated shallow fat in a skillet. Turn carefully as the fish browns.

dish. Broiled salt mackerel, creamed finnan haddie, and fish cakes are examples of main dishes suitable for breakfast.

Principles of Preparation of Fish

Fish is rich in protein. Therefore, it needs to be cooked at moderate temperatures to prevent the protein, when it is coagulated, from becoming hardened. Because the connective tissue of fish is delicate and easily softened, the cooking time is usually short. If cooked too long, the flesh of the fish is apt to fall apart. In general, the methods for cooking fish are the same as those for cooking meat and poultry. (See chart on opposite page.)

Buying Fish

People who live in different parts of the country soon become familiar with the kinds of fish that are typical of their locality and know the season when they are most abun-

dant. It is at the peak of the season that such fish are most reasonable in price and best in quality.

What to Look For in Buying Fish

Since fish is an exceedingly perishable food, it is essential to know the characteristics that indicate its freshness.

Finfish. There are several characteristics of freshness in finfish that you can readily notice by looking at it. The eyes are full—not sunken into the sockets—and they are bright and clear-looking; the gills are bright red; the scales cling tightly to the skin. On closer examination, the fins feel stiff, and the flesh firm and elastic to the touch. Finally, the flesh has a fresh fishlike odor without any suggestion of an odor of decomposition.

Shellfish. Shellfish are sold in the shell; shucked—that is, removed from the shell; and as cooked fish. All forms are quickly perishable, and care is needed in selecting them. When buying clams and oysters in the shell, select only those that have the two shells tightly clamped together. In buying clams of the soft-shell variety, the two shells may be slightly apart, but when touched the shells should draw together.

Scallops are always shucked for sale, since the only part of the scallop that is eaten is the muscle that holds the two shells together and controls their movement. If the scallop is large, possibly about 1 or 2 inches in diameter, it is the deep-sea, or ocean, variety. If it is smaller than this, it is the cape or bay scallop. This variety is sweeter than the deep-sea scallop and is considered a greater delicacy. The flesh of the deep-sea scallop is white and of the bay scallop creamy white or pinkish in color.

Lobsters and crabs should be alive when you buy them, and they must be kept alive until the time of cooking. Lobsters caught in Southern waters of both hemispheres are called "rock" or "spiny" lobsters. These are really crayfish, not true lobsters. Unlike lobsters that are found off the Atlantic Coast, the rock lobster does not have the large claw. Only the meat in the tail part is used. The tail meat, still enclosed in the shell, can be purchased frozen. It is often labeled "African lobster." Soft-shelled crabs are the same variety of crab

WAYS TO COOK FISH

Baking: Large whole fish and thick fillets and slices of fish are suitable for baking. Whole fish are sometimes stuffed. Oven temperatures of 350° F. are recommended, with the length of time depending on the size and thickness of the fish. Sometimes higher temperatures (around 500° F.) are suggested for baking small fish or fillets and steaks, but at these temperatures the baking time must be very short. Otherwise, the protein will be hardened and the connective tissue softened too much.

Broiling: A good method for cooking small thin fish, larger fish that have been split and laid open, and shellfish like lobster and scallops is broiling. A moderate temperature is achieved by keeping the surface of the fish several inches from the source of heat.

Cooking in water: Pieces of large fish and some shellfish, such as lobster and shrimp, may be cooked in water. The water surrounding the fish is held at simmering temperature in order to carry out the moderate-temperature rule of cooking foods high in protein content.

Cooking in steam: The same type of fish that is cooked in water may be steamed. In this method the fish is placed on a perforated plate over boiling water and is surrounded with steam. The pan holding the fish must be tightly covered. This method of cooking fish is often called "poaching."

Pan-frying: A suitable method for cooking small whole fish and fillets and steaks of larger fish is pan-frying. Frequently, the fish is coated with flour or corn meal or with milk or egg and fine bread crumbs so that the surface will become crisp and brown. The fat must not be heated so hot that it smokes.

Deep-fat frying: Small and fairly thin pieces of fish and scallops, clams, oysters, and shrimp may be deep-fat-fried. The fish should first be coated with egg and fine crumbs. This coating makes the outside crisp and attractively brown in color and also helps to prevent the absorption of fat by the pieces of fish. The temperature of the fat for deep-fat frying is in the moderate range of from 350° to 375° F., according to the sizes of the pieces. In general, the larger pieces are fried at the lower temperature.

● Fish is easily available to many people, and the good flavor of really fresh fish is ensured when you catch your own supply.

as the hard-shelled, Atlantic-coast blue crabs, but they are young crabs caught just after one hard shell has been shed in the growing process and before the new and larger shell has had time to harden. The shell, as well as the meat of these soft-shelled crabs, is eaten.

Unlike lobsters and crabs, shrimp, before they are sold, usually have the head removed, after which they curl up. When fresh, the thin shells covering the body of the shrimp are firmly attached and there is no odor of decomposition where the head has been removed. Prawns are shrimplike crustaceans. They are larger in size than shrimp but are used in the same manner in preparing various dishes.

Amount of Fish to Buy

The amount of fish that you will need to buy for serving depends upon the way you find it prepared in the market and whether or not you need to consider waste. Frozen fish has been prepared ready for cooking and there is no waste. This is true also of canned fish, some kinds of cured fish, and the meat of shrimp, crab, and lobster that has been removed

from the shell after being cooked. If you buy any of these shellfish alive, you will need to make allowances for the shell, which is waste. In the case of finfish, there may be considerable waste. For example, there is a large amount of waste in the whole or round fish— that is, the fish just as it comes from the water —and also in the drawn fish from which the entrails only have been removed. There is less waste in the dressed fish, which is the fish from which entrails, head, tail, fins, and scales have been removed, and only a little waste in steaks from large fish. There is no waste at all in the fillets of finfish. In the table "Food Buying Guide" on pages 78 to 81 there is information on the number of servings you may expect to get from 1 pound of fish of different kinds when prepared for sale in the ways described. You will find that the number of servings ranges from one serving from 1 pound of whole, round finfish to six servings from 1 pound of cooked crab and lobster meat.

Inspection of Fish

Before the Department of Fisheries will inspect any fresh or frozen fish product, the processing plant itself must meet specific requirements as they pertain to construction, sanitation, operation and equipment. Once the plant has been approved by the Department under established standards, any of its fish products, including round and dressed fish, fillets, steaks, fish sticks and similar portions will be eligible for inspection.

Frozen Fish Products

If a frozen fish product complies with clearly defined quality, processing and packaging specifications, the packer may identify his product with the designation "Canada Inspected" within a line drawing of a maple leaf marked on the wrappers, labels, containers, or, where practicable, on the whole fish.

Fresh Fish Products

Inspected fish, which is to be marketed in the fresh state as whole fish, fillets or steaks, may be identified by having the words "Processed Under Government Inspection" within a line drawing of a maple leaf marked on the wrappers, labels or containers.
102

Care of Fish in the Home

The form in which fish is bought determines how it should be cared for. It is important that you follow the practices that are recommended.

Care of fresh fish. In order to be sure of having a good fresh quality of this form of fish, you should buy it in a market where it is kept well refrigerated, either resting on cracked ice or imbedded in ice. Then you should take it home as soon as possible, cover it tightly, and place it in a very cold part of the refrigerator. The tight cover is desirable, since even the freshest of fish has an odor which might affect the odor and taste of other foods. It is best not to hold fresh fish longer than 24 to 48 hours. The same care given to fresh raw fish should be given to leftover cooked fish, and to the meat of shrimp, crab, and lobster that may have been purchased already cooked.

Care of frozen fish. Frozen fish is not perishable as long as it is kept frozen. The fish should be held in the freezing unit of the refrigerator or in the freezer until time to prepare it for cooking. It is best to start cooking frozen fish while it is still frozen, or at least only slightly defrosted. If, for any reason, the fish becomes thawed, it must be cooked immediately.

Care of cured fish. If the cured fish is one of the salted types, it must be kept well covered and in a cool place. All other kinds of cured fish should be stored in the refrigerator. Since the curing process provides some preservative action, cured fish can be held for a longer time than fresh uncooked fish.

Care of canned fish. Canned fish has excellent keeping qualities and therefore does not need refrigeration. It may be stored in any convenient storage place in the kitchen. Once opened, canned fish must be used promptly. If it is prepared ahead of time for serving, as in being marinated for a salad, it should be placed in the refrigerator.

22

Vegetables

VEGETABLES play an important role in our daily meals. They are bright in color and have many different textures, thus adding to the attractiveness of our meals. They are varied in flavor, with each vegetable having its own distinctive characteristic in this respect. Vegetables are helpful to the menu planner in getting variety into her meals because there are so many and because each one can be prepared in so many ways. Vegetables contribute several important nutrients to our diet.

Classification of Vegetables

Since there are so many kinds of vegetables, it is customary to group or classify them according to some common characteristic. Such classifications based on part of plant, color, and flavor are given in the chart at the right. This chart is useful in menu planning for several reasons: (1) It is considered better to serve in the same meal vegetables that come from different parts of plants rather than from the same part. For example, one would not serve peas and beans, both seeds, or parsnips and beets, both roots, in the same meal. An exception might be the serving of lettuce and another leaf vegetable at the same meal, such as one as a salad or part of a salad and one as a vegetable. (2) Having vegetables of different but harmonious colors in the same meal lends interest and variety to the meal. Also, it is less monotonous. For example, peas served with sweetpotatoes make a more appealing color effect than would peas and spinach. (3) A meal is more appetizing if only one strong-flavored vegetable is used. Cauliflower and yellow turnip would not be a good combination in flavor. Carrots, which are mild in flavor, would be more suitable with the cauliflower.

Forms of Vegetables

Like fruits, vegetables are seasonal foods, and many of them can be grown plentifully and economically only in certain localities of the country. Modern methods of refrigerated storage and transportation help in distributing fresh vegetables from the growing areas to all parts of the country. Methods of processing vegetables make them available in frozen, canned, and dried forms at all times of the year, even in the out-of-season months, and in all parts of the country.

Fresh vegetables. Vegetables brought to the kitchen from the garden, a nearby farm, or a market where they are kept moist and crisp have the best quality and flavor. For example, sweet corn and peas are thought by many to have a better flavor if cooked and eaten soon after they are harvested. But often vegetables are not available from such sources. However, present-day marketing methods are very efficient and, in many stores, the fresh vegetables are surrounded with cracked ice, which aids in keeping their original fresh quality. Some fresh vegetables, such as spinach, kale, and other greens, are cleaned and packaged for sale. These vegetables are practically ready for cooking. It is wise, however, to look them over and wash them, since there may be some wilted leaves and coarse stems that need to be removed and some sand still clinging to the leaves.

CLASSIFICATION OF VEGETABLES

CHARACTERISTIC	EXAMPLES
Part of plant	
Root	Parsnip; beet
Tuber (thickened underground stem)	Potato
Bulb	Onion
Stem	Asparagus; celery
Leaf	Spinach; kale; water cress; chard; lettuce
Flower	Cauliflower; broccoli
Seeds	Peas; beans
Fruit	Tomato; eggplant; squash
Color	
Green	Escarole; Brussels sprouts; peas; broccoli; many leaf vegetables
Yellow	Squash; carrot; sweetpotato; yellow turnip (rutabaga)
Red	Radish; beet; red cabbage; red onion
White	Cauliflower; white turnip; white onion; parsnip
Flavor	
Strong-flavored	Yellow and white turnip; onion; cauliflower
Mild-flavored	Corn; squash; carrot; peas; beans

WAYS TO SERVE VEGETABLES

Courtesy American Can Company

● As a juice: Vegetable juices, garnished and flavored with a lemon peel, are a popular appetizer for any meal.

Courtesy United Fresh Fruit and Vegetable Association

Courtesy American Dairy Association

● Cooked: Numerous varieties of fresh, frozen, or canned vegetables contribute to the healthfulness and appeal of any lunch or dinner.

● Raw: Fresh vegetables are particularly valuable when served raw because they retain most of their original food value.

Frozen vegetables. Frozen vegetables are similar to fresh vegetables in color and flavor. All steps preliminary to cooking have been taken care of in the processing. All that is needed is to cook and season them. Consequently, time and effort are saved in preparing meals. (See Chapter 4, "Managing Meals to Save Time and Effort.") A supply of frozen vegetables can be kept on hand in the home freezer or freezing compartment of the refrigerator. One kind of vegetable may be frozen alone or several mixed together. Some are frozen in a flavorful sauce, and there are frozen dishes in which vegetables are combined with other foods to make a simple main dish.

Canned vegetables. Like frozen vegetables, canned vegetables can be stored conveniently and prepared quickly. Sometimes canned vegetables cost less than the fresh or frozen forms and then they make a contribution to thrifty meals. Because of the high heat used in processing, the flavor of canned vegetables is changed from that of cooked fresh vegetables.

Dried vegetables. Some vegetables are dried—that is, most of the water is evaporated from them. Today most dried vegetables are commercially prepared. During the drying process, their character is changed, so that they no longer resemble fresh vegetables. Dried vegetables such as peas, a variety of beans, lentils, and many herbs are well known.

Recent methods of commercial dehydration of vegetables permit some dried vegetables to take their place among convenience foods in the market. Among these more recent products are the various dehydrated potato products which include instant mashed potatoes, potato flakes for frying, and potatoes in a form for scalloping. Dehydrated vegetables for soups are also popular.

Food Value of Vegetables

Vitamins and minerals are the two nutrients for which vegetables are so greatly valued. Although many of the vitamins and minerals are widely distributed among all vegetables, certain vegetables are outstanding in the amounts they contain of these nutrients. For example, the following vegetables are especially notable for vitamin C: broccoli, green peppers, leafy green vegetables, tomatoes, raw cabbage, cauliflower, and asparagus. Dark-green and deep-yellow vegetables are excellent sources of vitamin A and the mineral iron. (See Canada's Food Guide on pages 10 to 12.)

In addition to vitamins and minerals, other nutrients are found in vegetables. All vegetables contain some proteins even though the amounts may be small, but the proteins are not complete proteins since they do not contain all the essential amino acids. Dry peas and dry beans contribute substantial amounts of proteins. Among the dry beans the soybean is unique because it contains a complete protein.

Young succulent vegetables like sweet corn and peas are fairly rich in sugar. The white potato is among our best sources of starch. This vegetable, although not particularly rich in either iron or vitamin C, nevertheless makes a valuable contribution to the daily quota of these nutrients because it is used so commonly in our meals.

Besides sugar and starch, two other carbohydrates, cellulose and pectin, are found in all vegetables. They give bulk to the diet, but they have no food value.

Uses of Vegetables

Breakfast is the only meal of the day at which vegetables are not served. Potatoes and vegetable juices may be exceptions to this. Vegetables are chiefly used as part of the main course at lunch or dinner, where potatoes are often served together with one or two other vegetables. However, such dishes as vegetable casseroles or soufflés and loaves which have vegetables as their chief ingredient may be used as the main dish for one of these meals. A main dish of dry beans or peas, because of their high protein content, serves occasionally as an alternate for meat instead of being used as an accompaniment to it. A beverage of milk or cocoa could supply the complete protein. Also, vegetables can be used as the entire main course. As an example, a vegetable plate, with four or five different vegetables attractively arranged and supplemented with egg or cheese, is a delicious main course for a light meal.

One of the most popular uses of vegetables is in salads. Both raw and cooked vegetables can be used. Vegetable salads range all the way from those using only salad greens, such as escarole, chicory, water cress, or lettuce, to hearty salads, such as potato salad or one containing several different vegetables. Vegetables are also used, but in lesser amounts, in soups and as appetizers and garnishes.

Principles of Preparation of Vegetables

There are several principles on which the cooking of vegetables is based so as to retain a maximum amount of their original food value and be pleasing in color, texture, and flavor. These principles are applied whether the vegetables are fresh, frozen, canned, or dried.

Fresh Vegetables

In the cooking of fresh vegetables, the starch and protein in them are cooked and the cellulose framework is softened. As a result of these changes, flavors are modified and the vegetables become less crisp. It is very important to cook vegetables correctly so that they will retain a large amount of their nutritive value. They will also look attractive, taste good, and keep some of their original texture when they are cooked correctly.

Retaining nutritive value. Some minerals and the vitamins thiamine and vitamin C dissolve readily in water. Heat also is destructive of these two vitamins. Because of these facts, there are two rules or principles to follow in cooking vegetables to avoid any great losses of these nutrients: (1) Cook vegetables without water or in as small an amount of water as possible. (2) Cook vegetables for as short a time as possible.

Baking vegetables in their skins prevents loss of water-soluble nutrients. Prepare potatoes, sweetpotatoes, and winter squashes this way.

Panning vegetables also reduces losses of soluble nutrients. In panning, the cut-up vegetable is stirred into a little melted butter or margarine, or in oil in a skillet. When it is coated with the fat, a very small amount of water is added, the skillet tightly covered, and the vegetable cooked over low heat until it is tender.

In boiling vegetables, follow the rules given in the chart above to keep down the loss of minerals, vitamin C, and thiamine.

RULES FOR BOILING VEGETABLES

1. Do not presoak the vegetable.

2. Use only a small amount of water.

3. Add the vegetable to boiling salted water, or add boiling water and salt to the vegetable.

4. Cover.

5. Bring the water back to boiling quickly after adding the vegetable.

6. Lower the heat but keep the water boiling.

7. Cook the vegetable only long enough to give it the desired amount of tenderness.

8. Serve the vegetable immediately after it is cooked.

9. Reserve any remaining cooking liquid for use in soups or sauces.

Retaining natural colors. During cooking, green vegetables may become slightly brownish in color because of changes which take place in the chlorophyll—the green color substance in vegetables. The more quickly green vegetables are cooked, the less chance there is for this color change to occur. Occasionally white vegetables, like cauliflower and onions, become yellowish in color, and red vegetables, like red cabbage and beets, turn slightly purplish in color. For the white and red vegetables, a small amount of vinegar or lemon juice added to the cooking water will help to prevent these color changes. A short cooking time also is of advantage.

Obtaining excellent flavors. The freshness of vegetables has much to do with their fine flavor when cooked. As vegetables, with the exception of potatoes, lose their freshness, some of the sugar turns to starch, and they lose their sweetness.

Some of the compounds in vegetables that give them their flavor are volatile—that is,

WAYS TO PREPARE VEGETABLES

Courtesy National Association of Margarine Manufacturers

● Buttered

Courtesy Idaho Potato and Onion Commission

● Baked

Courtesy National Canners Association

● Creamed

Courtesy National Canners Association

● Scalloped

they escape in the steam during boiling. If the cooking time is kept short and the saucepan in which vegetables are cooked is kept covered, there is less flavor loss. With those vegetables that belong to the cabbage family, for example, broccoli, Brussels sprouts, and cauliflower, prolonged cooking causes a strong, unpleasant flavor to develop. It is because of this strong flavor that these vegetables are frequently called "strong-flavored" vegetables. Actually they are mild in flavor unless over-

cooked, for when the cooking time is short, there is not time for the unpleasant flavor to develop.

Keeping pleasing textures. The crisp texture so desirable for vegetables when served raw is fairly easily obtained by proper care and refrigeration. Opinions differ in respect to what is considered a desirable texture for cooked vegetables. Present-day standards call for vegetables that still retain a slightly crisp texture. However, for those to whom this

Courtesy National Canners Association

● Dry peas and dry beans make a main dish that may be used occasionally instead of meat, provided their incomplete proteins are supplemented by a food that contains a complete protein, such as milk.

crispness is distasteful, a softer texture can be obtained if the cooking period is lengthened slightly. In any case, vegetables should never be cooked until they are mushy.

Frozen Vegetables

Commercially packed frozen vegetables should be cooked according to the directions on the package. Boiling is the best method to use, and the same rules apply to the cooking of frozen vegetables as to fresh ones. They are placed, preferably while still frozen, in a saucepan containing a small amount of boiling water, and the saucepan is then covered. After the water again comes to the boiling point, a frozen vegetable requires a slightly shorter cooking time than does the same kind of fresh vegetable, since, in processing, the frozen vegetable has already been scalded or steamed. The vegetable will cook more uniformly if the pieces are separated with a fork as soon as possible after cooking starts.

Canned Vegetables

Canned vegetables are completely cooked in the canning process and therefore need only to be reheated in meal preparation. As some of the soluble nutrients have dissolved out of the vegetables into the liquid in the can, the vegetables should be reheated in this liquid. It may be drained from the vegetable, boiled until some water is evaporated, and then the vegetable added and heated in the more concentrated liquid. In this way all the liquid may be served with the vegetable. Or any liquid left over after heating the vegetable can be used in soups or sauces or blended with tomato or other vegetable juices for a vegetable cocktail.

Dried Vegetables

Dried vegetables, such as peas and beans, require a soaking period in water before they are cooked. This soaking may be done in cold water for a long period of time, such as overnight, or it can be done in hot water in less time. Beans or peas should be boiled in the soaking water to avoid any loss of thiamine which may have dissolved in it. Thiamine is the vitamin for which dry beans and dry peas are especially valuable. The cooking time of these dried vegetables may be greatly shortened by adding a small amount of baking soda to the cooking water (⅛ teaspoon of baking soda to 1 cup of dry beans and 2½ cups of water). When baking soda is added, great care must be taken not to overcook the peas or beans.

Buying Vegetables

Whether you buy the fresh, canned, frozen, or dried forms of vegetables, you should know what qualities to look for in making your selection.

Buying fresh vegetables. Fresh vegetables may be sold by the pound, by the volume measure, or by the individual unit or piece. For example, you might buy peas, lima beans, and onions by the pound; Brussels sprouts by the quart; beets and carrots by the bunch; and cauliflower, lettuce, and squash by a single unit. There is a trend, however, toward selling all kinds of vegetables by weight, even such vegetables as cucumbers, cabbage, and cauliflower. This is good practice, since it ensures getting better value for your money than buying by the individual unit.

In general, fresh vegetables of good quality have a bright, fresh appearance and good shape, they are not underripe or overripe, and they are reasonably free from surface blemishes. Some vegetables have, in addition, special characteristics that denote quality: The compactness of heads of cabbage and of flower clusters in broccoli and cauliflower; good weight in relation to size as in squash, cucumbers, and tomatoes; and brittleness of stems in asparagus and celery and of pods in snap and wax beans are all special characteristics that should be considered in buying these vegetables.

Buying canned vegetables. The Food and Drugs Act and Regulations has established definitions and standards of identity for many canned vegetables. They have also established labeling requirements and these are described in Chapter 5, page 85. The label on each can must state the common name of the vegetable and its form, for example, diced beets; the net contents of the can; the name and address of the canner. The size of the cans used for vegetables and the measure of volume found in the cans are given in the table "Common Container Sizes" on page 82.

The manufacturer may, if he likes, print additional information on the label. This information is different with different manufacturers and with the kind of vegetable, but it usually indicates quality, the maturity of the vegetable and its size, the style of the pack, and the number of cupfuls of the product in the can. Sometimes even a recipe and suggestions for using the vegetable are given on the label. (See illustration on page 86.)

QUALITY GRADES OF CANNED VEGETABLES

(According to the Canada Department of Agriculture)

If the vegetable has been canned according to Canada Department of Agriculture standards, the label will carry a grade name, such as Canada Fancy, Canada Choice or Canada Standard. If a product fails to meet the lowest prescribed grade for it, yet is sound, wholesome and fit to eat, it must be marked "Sub Standard." Products so labeled are not commonly found in stores.

Most canned vegetables are sold by grade in Canada. About 95 percent of the production of every province is from plants registered for interprovincial and export trade.

Non-registered plants may not use a "Canada" grade name on their products. Sale of such products must be confined to the province in which they are produced. Only Quebec has provincial regulations covering the grading of vegetables canned in plants not registered with the Canada Department of Agriculture.

Imported canned vegetables for which grades are established must carry a grade mark and must meet the federal grade standard for that grade. Imported canned vegetables cannot have "Canada" as part of their grade name when sold in original containers.

Courtesy Westinghouse

● To keep vegetables crisp and fresh, it is important to store them properly in a hydrator. A convenient kind is one that is separate from the rest of the refrigerator.

Canned vegetables, like canned fruits, are packed in several quality grades. Standards for these grades have been set by the Canada Department of Agriculture and are considered official standards. However, if a packer does not grade his product according to these standards, he may not use a "Canada" grade name on his products and sale must be confined to the province in which they were produced. When a manufacturer follows official standards, he labels his products according to government designations of grades. Sometimes a manufacturer will use several brand names. In these cases the brand name as well as the

"Canada" grade will indicate quality. For this reason it is often impossible to find different quality vegetables with the same brand name.

Occasionally imperfect cans containing vegetables, and other foods as well, may be found in the markets. Some cans are dented. The food in dented cans is just as good as food in perfect cans and may be bought with confidence. In fact, some markets sell dented cans of food at lower prices and it is good economy to buy them. On the other hand, if the can is bulged, the food in it has probably spoiled because of bacterial action that causes the formation of a gas. Such cans should not be purchased. In most markets bulging cans are removed from the shelves as soon as discovered and so are not available to the consumer. Some cans of acid vegetables and fruits may have bulged ends because of the presence of hydrogen gas. This is not dangerous. Hydrogen gas is formed through the reaction of the food acids with the iron that is exposed on the can. Since it is not possible to distinguish the kind of gas that has formed, no bulged cans should be bought.

Buying frozen vegetables. Frozen vegetables are stored in retail markets in chests at such low temperatures that the vegetables are kept in the same solidly frozen state as they were when delivered to the store. Some frozen vegetables can now be obtained in two qualities. The best quality is labeled "Canada Fancy"; the lower quality is labeled "Canada Choice." The vegetables used for Canada Choice are somewhat inferior in original quality to those used for the rest of the frozen pack, but the same care is used by the industry in freezing them. If the letters "Canada" precede the grade designation, the vegetables have been processed under the continuous inspection of an official of the Canada Department of Agriculture.

Buying dried vegetables. Dried vegetables are usually sold in cardboard packages or in bags made of cellophane or a similar moisture-resistant material. Although dried vegetables have good keeping qualities, they should be bought in amounts that can be used within about three to four months. If kept too long, they may become infested with insects.

Care of Vegetables in the Home

The manner in which you care for vegetables in the home will, of course, depend on whether they are fresh, canned, frozen, or dried.

Care of fresh vegetables. There are a few fresh vegetables which need to be stored in a cool, dry place. Among these are sweetpotatoes, onions, and some of the late fall crops like pumpkins and winter squashes. Turnips and parsnips are late vegetables that require cool, but slightly moist, storage to keep in good condition.

White potatoes require special care in storage if they are to retain good quality. They should be stored in a dark place to prevent them from turning green on the surface so that they are unfit for use. The temperature should be well below room temperature, but above 40° F., to prevent some of the starch from being converted to sugar and thus giving potatoes an undesirable sweet taste. The cool temperature will also lessen sprouting.

For almost all other vegetables the best storage condition is in the hydrator of the refrigerator, where the temperature is cold and the surroundings are moist. Before placing vegetables in the hydrator, it is well to look them over, remove any imperfect parts, and wash them thoroughly. As is true of fruits, careful washing of fresh vegetables is necessary to make certain that grit and spray residue are removed. The various salad greens will keep crisp for several days if they are inspected and carefully washed before they are placed in the hydrator. A covered bowl or plastic bag can be used as a substitute for the hydrator if necessary.

Care of canned vegetables. Canned vegetables should be stored in a cool, dry place. Although canned vegetables will keep for many months, it is best to use one season's supply before the next year's crop comes on the market. There is some loss of original quality and nutritive value with prolonged storage even under the best conditions.

Care of frozen vegetables. The packages of frozen vegetables should be put immediately in the freezing compartment of a refrigerator or in a freezer and held there until it is time to cook them. Frozen vegetables can be kept for long periods, even months, if they are not allowed to defrost. In case a vegetable does thaw, it should be used immediately, since if it remains long in the thawed condition, it is likely to spoil.

Care of dried vegetables. Dried vegetables keep well if they are stored in tightly covered containers in a cool, dry place. Because small insects sometimes get into packages of dried vegetables and cause spoilage, it is a good idea to examine the vegetables frequently.

23

Quick Breads

■ FLOUR MIXTURES is the name of a group of baked foods having flour as the basic ingredient. They include quick breads, yeast breads, cakes, cookies, and pastries.

Quick breads are a very important kind of flour mixture because these breads can be made quickly and because there is such a wide variety of them. Even though they differ widely in appearance and flavor, they all have the common characteristic of rising quickly to become porous and light—that is, to become leavened. It is because they are leavened quickly that they are called quick breads as contrasted to yeast breads, which are leavened slowly. Quick breads are not so sweet as cakes and cookies as a rule, and they are not so high in fat as pastries.

Types of Quick Breads

Since there are such differences among the quick breads, it is customary to group them according to the consistency of the unbaked mixtures. The consistency depends on the proportion of liquid and flour in a mixture. On this basis there are three types of quick breads. (See chart on page 311.)

Ingredients in Quick Breads

Flour, liquid, salt, and a leavening agent are always used in making quick breads. In addition, sugar, fat, and eggs are often included as ingredients. It is the ingredients used, the manner of mixing them together,

BATTERS AND DOUGHS FOR QUICK BREADS

● Popovers, pancakes, and waffles are made with a pour batter.

● Loaf breads, muffins, corn bread, and some coffeecakes are made with a drop batter.

● Biscuits and doughnuts are made with a soft dough.

STEPS IN MAKING MUFFINS

(See recipe on on page 496.)

1. Measure and sift together flour, sugar, baking powder, and salt into bowl.

2. Stir milk into well-beaten egg, and add melted shortening.

3. Pour into dry ingredients, and stir until ingredients are just blended and batter is still rough-looking.

4. Fill well-greased muffin pans two-thirds full. Bake for 25 minutes, or until golden brown.

HOW A GOOD MUFFIN SHOULD LOOK

● The outside of a good muffin is uniform in shape with a slightly rounded top. The inside has an even grain and is without tunnels.

and the way they are cooked that make possible the large variety of quick breads.

Flour. All-purpose flour is the kind most generally used. Whole-wheat flour may be used for variation, for many people like its flavor. Some quick breads are made with corn meal instead of flour, or with a mixture of flour and either corn meal or rye flour.

Liquid. The liquid in quick breads is usually sweet milk, although some recipes call for sour milk or cream. Either evaporated or dried milk can be used in place of regular sweet milk. Molasses, water, and sour milk are used as the liquid in gingerbreads and some kinds of quick-bread loaves.

Salt. Salt is the common seasoning. In addition, it has a beneficial effect on the quality of the baked product.

Leavening agents. A leavening agent is the material used in quick breads to leaven them

TYPES OF QUICK BREADS

Pour batters: These batters are so thin in consistency that they can be poured from the mixing bowl. They contain about 1 part of liquid to 1 or 1½ parts of flour. Examples are popovers, pancakes, and waffles.

Drop batters: Since drop batters have a consistency too thick to be poured, they must be lifted from the mixing bowl with a spoon and dropped into the baking pan. They contain about 1 part of liquid to 2 parts of flour. Examples are muffins and some kinds of coffee-cakes.

Soft doughs: Soft doughs are so stiff in consistency that they can be molded on a floured board. They contain about 1 part of liquid to 3 parts of flour. Examples are biscuits and doughnuts.

Courtesy H. J. Heinz Company

Courtesy Church & Dwight Co., Inc.

● Left: Waffles may be served plain, as a base for a creamed dish, or when especially sweet, as a dessert. Right: Quick loaf breads are good for sandwiches with or without a filling.

Courtesy Betty Crocker of General Mills

Courtesy Birds Eye Frozen Foods

● Left: Biscuit dough is a good topping for meat pies and is extra attractive when made into pin-wheels. Right: A rich biscuit dough, with sugar and egg added if desired, is perfect for a shortcake with fresh fruit in season.

—that is, to make them rise during baking to produce products that will be porous and therefore delicate and tender in texture. Baking powder, which supplies the leavening gas carbon dioxide, is the most generally used leavening agent.

There are three types of baking powders: (1) tartrate baking powders, (2) phosphate baking powders, and (3) sulphate-phosphate baking powders, sometimes called double-acting baking powders. All three types contain baking soda as a common ingredient. The other compound or compounds mixed with the baking soda give the baking powder its name. In all three types the fundamental reaction is the same—that is, the baking soda reacts with the other compound or compounds to form carbon dioxide. Instead of baking powder, baking soda in combination with some acid, such as the acid in molasses, buttermilk, sour milk, sour cream, or vinegar, can be used to provide the leavening agent carbon dioxide.

Beaten eggs will introduce air, which has leavening action, and some air is always introduced by the mixing techniques used. Finally the liquid in quick breads gives some leavening action when it is turned into steam during cooking.

Sugar. Granulated sugar is the sweetener generally used in quick breads. If the more distinctive flavor of brown sugar is desired, the recipe will list it as the type of sugar to be used.

Fat. Butter and margarine are used for their pleasing flavors, but when it is not important for a fat to contribute flavor, a bland type like one of the vegetable shortenings is satisfactory. Lard, too, may be used, as well as bacon drippings and chicken fat, provided the flavors will blend with the flavors of the other ingredients.

Eggs. Eggs of medium size are suitable for making quick breads. For most quick breads, Grade B eggs are equally as satisfactory as those of Grade A quality.

Food Value of Quick Breads

Quick breads have good food value, but the particular value of each kind will be influenced by the ingredients used. Flour, milk, eggs, sugar, and fat contribute calories. Milk and eggs are especially important, for they contribute complete proteins and some minerals and vitamins. If enriched flour or whole-wheat flour is used, the iron and the three B vitamins which these flours contain give additional food value.

Uses of Quick Breads

Quick breads of one kind or another may be used for each meal of the day and for between-meal snacks as well. The less-sweet kinds, such as muffins, biscuits, griddlecakes, and waffles, are suitable for breakfast. They go well with cereal and with bacon and eggs or any other main dish. Biscuits and muffins are also good luncheon breads. Sometimes waffles served with a creamed food like mushrooms or chicken make a main dish for lunch or Sunday-night supper.

The sweeter kinds of quick breads, for example, gingerbreads, sweet waffles, and fruit pancakes, may be used as desserts. A sweetened biscuit dough that is baked and then covered with fresh fruits, such as shortcake, and uncooked dough that is placed on top of fruit and then baked, such as fruit cobbler, are two other desserts.

Principles of Preparation of Quick Breads

The principles involved in the preparation of quick breads are (1) the formation and role of gluten and (2) the way in which gluten is modified by the leavening gases—air, carbon dioxide, and steam—to give the open, porous, or leavened character to the finished product.

Flour contains two proteins called "gliadin" and "glutenin." When flour is mixed with

313

STEPS IN MAKING BISCUITS

(See recipe on page 494.)

1. Cut the fat into dry ingredients until mixture is as fine as corn meal.

2. Add the milk all at once, and stir to make a soft dough.

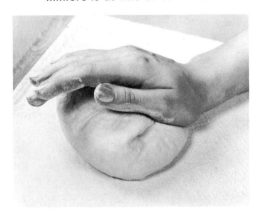

3. Knead the dough gently eight to ten times.

4. Roll the dough or pat with hands until it is of desired thickness.

5. Cut into round biscuits with cookie cutter or square biscuits with knife.

6. Place on ungreased baking sheet, and bake for 12 to 15 minutes.

HOW A GOOD BISCUIT SHOULD LOOK

● The outside of a good biscuit is uniform in shape with a flat top. The inside has a flaky, even quality, and it is not too dry or too moist.

liquid, these two proteins unite to form gluten throughout the batter or dough. As gluten is formed, it becomes meshlike in structure because it entraps leavening gases. These gases consist of air stirred in or introduced by beaten eggs, and of carbon dioxide from baking powder or from baking soda and an acid ingredient. During baking, more carbon dioxide is made, and this gas and the air expand. In addition, the liquid in the hot mixture changes to steam and expands. Because gluten has an elastic quality, it stretches and holds these expanding gases within its meshes. But soon the heat of cooking coagulates the gluten proteins, and the gluten becomes more or less rigid and resists further stretching. When the leavening gases have reached the right point of expansion needed to give the characteristic inside structure for each kind of quick bread, the heat used in cooking makes the gluten meshwork firm.

In addition to the leavening action, other changes occur in cooking. Such changes include the development of flavor and the browning of the surfaces to an attractive golden color.

Some quick breads, like griddlecakes, are baked on a hot griddle instead of in an oven. Others, like doughnuts, are fried in deep hot fat, or, like waffles, are baked in a special waffle iron. The same principles apply in cooking these quick breads that apply to those baked in the oven.

Buying Ingredients for Quick Breads

If you include many quick breads in your meal planning, you should have an ample supply of staple ingredients on hand. Packaged mixes and ready-baked quick breads as well as ready-to-be-baked quick breads are also available.

Buying the ingredients. One of the ingredients in making quick breads is enriched all-purpose flour, available in 2-, 5-, 7- or 10-pound packages, or larger ones. Sugar is another staple ingredient, and the usual market units are either 1- or 2-pound boxes or 5- or 10 pound bags. Salt, baking powder, and baking soda are available in packages of several convenient sizes. The quantity of fats that you can keep on hand will depend on your storage facilities because cool temperatures are needed for storing them. The hydrogenated

315

● Muffins made of bran flakes with raisins and served with cottage cheese and fruit salad make a satisfying lunch for the Lenten season.

vegetable fats, called "shortenings," are satisfactory fats to use in quick breads. Eggs and milk are day-to-day supplies and, of course, require refrigeration. If you use Grade B eggs and the evaporated or dried forms of milk, you will find a considerable saving in the cost of the quick breads.

Buying mixes and bakery products. There are often times when you will need to prepare

a meal in a hurry. Then the packaged quick-bread mixes are convenient. Some of these require only the addition of milk; others call for milk and eggs, and sometimes melted fat as well. A variety of ready-to-be-baked quick breads will be found in the refrigerator case in many stores. It is good practice to keep a supply of several kinds on hand.

Ready-baked quick breads are ready to serve almost immediately. A loaf of quick bread need only be sliced, while such products as muffins and biscuits require only warming. Frozen waffles are among the ready-made quick breads that are ready to eat as soon as they have been warmed.

Care of Quick Breads in the Home

All types of quick breads, whether made at home or bought in the store, should be kept in a cabinet or box that can be tightly closed. Quick breads lose moisture quickly and become dry, so they do not store well. Flavor, too, is less pleasing if the storage period is extended longer than two or three days, even under the most favorable conditions.

● Hot corn bread served with sautéed ham, sausage, or bacon adds to the enjoyment of a winter meal.

24

Yeast

Breads

■ LIKE quick breads, there are many different yeast breads—ranging all the way from the plain loaf of bread to the elaborate sweet coffee or tea ring filled with fruits, nuts, and spices. Yeast breads are alike in that the carbon dioxide used to leaven them is produced by yeast.

Types of Yeast Breads

There are three types of yeast breads, namely, plain and fancy breads, plain and fancy rolls, and yeast-raised doughnuts.

Breads. Plain breads are the simplest of all yeast products. They are white, whole wheat, or rye, or a variation of them.

Fancy breads are found in great variety. They include raisin breads, coffeecakes, tea rings, cinnamon buns, and crumb cakes. These may be filled and frosted to make them very fancy.

Rolls. Plain rolls are similar to plain bread, but they may be slightly sweeter. Some have eggs in them and special flavoring. They are often shaped in a variety of ways.

Fancy rolls are made from a sweet yeast dough and may be variously flavored. They may be frosted or filled with raisins, candied cherries, coconut, nuts, and other flavorful ingredients, as desired. Fancy rolls may be shaped in a number of different ways.

Doughnuts. Yeast-raised doughnuts are fried in deep hot fat, whereas the other yeast-raised products are baked.

Ingredients in Yeast Breads

The essential ingredients needed for making all kinds of yeast breads are flour, liquid —either milk or water—salt, and yeast. Usually sugar and fat are used, and for the fancier types of breads, eggs, fruits, nuts, and other

317

VARIETIES OF YEAST BREADS

Courtesy Standard Brands

● Most of what we call "bread" is yeast bread—whether white, whole wheat, rye, or variations.

Courtesy Wheat Flour Institute

● Yeast rolls, either plain or fancy, are most flavorful when served hot—that is, when freshly baked or when reheated.

Courtesy Wheat Flour Institute

● Yeast breads that are sweet contain more sugar, fat, and eggs but are made in the same way as plain breads.

flavorings are included. Flour, milk, fat, eggs, and fruits are discussed in the chapters dealing with these foods.

Yeast, the other essential ingredient used in yeast breads, is a tiny plant. When it is placed in warm surroundings and finds suitable food, it will carry on its life processes. During these processes carbon dioxide is formed. The warm temperature and the suitable food are found in bread dough. As a result, tiny bubbles of carbon dioxide are formed all through the dough because the yeast is well distributed during the mixing of the dough. As the bubbles of gas expand, the dough increases in bulk, or is said to be "raised" by yeast. This means of leavening is called "fermentation" and takes a longer time than it does to leaven doughs by means of baking powder, or soda and an acid ingredient.

Food Value of Yeast Breads

Although yeast breads are largely energy-giving foods, they can supply the diet with other nutrients as well. Iron, thiamine, riboflavin, and niacin are present in good amounts when enriched flour is used in making bread. If whole-wheat flour is used, these same nutrients will be present as well as the valuable proteins of the whole-wheat kernel. The use of milk, instead of water, for the liquid provides an excellent source of protein. Milk supplies calcium and riboflavin in outstanding amounts also. If the milk is whole milk, vitamin A is added. In fact, the contribution of milk to the nutritive quality of breads can be so great that in some breads extra milk in the form of dried milk powder is used in addition to fluid milk. Yeast breads that contain eggs will also have the same nutrients as eggs.

Uses of Yeast Breads

Bread is a staple food in daily meals. It is a healthful food, and its somewhat bland flavor blends well with other foods. For these reasons, it is customary to serve one form of bread or another at all meals.

Buttered toast, toast and marmalade, hot rolls, and coffeecake are all favorite yeast breads to serve at breakfast as accompaniments to the other foods.

At lunch, hot, freshly baked rolls add to the enjoyment of a salad. Sandwiches with a bowl of hearty soup make a good cold-weather lunch. In addition, sandwiches are a standard part of the carried lunch—either to school or to work. Sandwiches are discussed more fully later in the chapter.

At dinner, plain bread is always acceptable. Rolls made with a rich dough are delicious as a special treat for the family and always add a festive note to a company meal.

Yeast breads have many special uses also. Bread in milk is a good afterschool or before-bed snack. Dainty bread sandwiches are used as refreshments at afternoon teas. Toast is served as an accompaniment for many creamed foods. Fancy rolls and tea rings are often used as desserts at a simple lunch or supper.

Principles of Preparation of Yeast Breads

The leavening of dough by means of carbon dioxide produced by yeast and the strengthening of the gluten framework by kneading are the principles on which the making of yeast breads are based. These principles can be understood most easily by following the breadmaking process step by step. The steps are similar for all yeast breads.

Mixing. The first step is the mixing of the ingredients flour, liquid, water or milk, sugar, salt, fat, and yeast. When the flour becomes wet, gluten is formed from the flour proteins, gliadin and glutenin. Sugar supplies food for the yeast and gives flavor to the bread. Salt also gives flavor and has a firming effect on the gluten. Fat makes the bread tender. Yeast, as it grows, supplies the carbon dioxide for leavening.

Kneading. The soft dough which results from mixing the ingredients is turned out on

WAYS TO USE LEFTOVER BREAD

● For croutons or soft bread crumbs

● For stuffings, for toppings for casseroles, or as extenders for other foods

● For toast and toast cups

a floured board and kneaded. Kneading is a process in which the dough is worked with the hands on a board until it looks smooth and satiny and has little bubbles of carbon dioxide showing under the surface. Kneading of the dough gives the yeast a better opportunity to start growing and make carbon dioxide than does the mixing process. Kneading also makes the gluten become firmer and more elastic so that it will withstand the considerable stretching it must undergo and still hold the gas that is formed slowly during the fermentation step.

Fermenting. Following the kneading process, the dough is held in a warm place for a while, possibly about an hour, until it is a little larger than double its original bulk. This is the fermentation step.

Although the yeast plants begin to grow while the dough is being kneaded, or even as the ingredients are being mixed, it is during the fermentation step that they have the greatest opportunity to be active and produce carbon dioxide in largest amounts. The temperature is warm, and there are food materials in the dough, such as sugar, minerals, and vitamins, that the yeast plants like. It is from sugar that yeast makes carbon dioxide.

With these favorable conditions, more and more carbon dioxide is produced as the fermentation step is continued. Eventually the dough about doubles in volume. By this time the gluten has lost some of its elasticity, and the dough mass is ready for the next step.

Shaping. The dough is again kneaded to break up the gas bubbles and distribute them evenly throughout the dough. Then it is molded into loaves, rolls, or other shapes as desired, and placed in suitable baking pans. After another short period of fermentation in the pans to allow for some increase in size of the shaped dough, it is ready for baking.

Baking. During baking, the yeast plants are killed. The gluten proteins are coagulated so that the framework is made somewhat rigid in its porous structure. The flavor is developed, and the loaf becomes brown and crusty.

Cooling. After the baked bread is taken from the oven, it is removed from the baking pan and placed on a rack. The bread is left uncovered until it is cool and ready for storing. Of course, if the bread is to be served hot, it needs to be cooled only long enough to be handled comfortably.

Buying Ingredients for Yeast Breads

When you buy yeast breads, you will find many different kinds from which to choose. If you are planning, however, to make the bread or rolls at home, selection of the ingredients will be important.

Buying the Ingredients

You will want to be sure to buy or have on hand such ingredients as fat, sugar, salt, and if needed, eggs. You will probably decide to use milk for the liquid because of its contribution to the nutritive value of the bread. You can use fluid milk. Or you can use evaporated or dried milk instead if these forms are more convenient or if you wish to take advantage of their lower cost. Flour and yeast are the other two ingredients that you will need to buy. These are discussed below.

Flour. All-purpose flour is the kind of flour sold in most parts of the country for use in making yeast breads. It is possible that in your particular locality a flour called "bread flour" is sold, and this, of course, is very well suited for making all yeast-leavened products. Another fact to keep in mind is the importance of selecting enriched flour.

Yeast. Yeast is sold in a dry granular form or in moist cakes called "compressed yeast." The dry form of yeast is packaged in small envelopes, each of which is stamped with a date that gives the time after which the yeast will begin to lose its full strength. When you buy dry yeast, it is well to note the date in case you do not expect to use it immediately. Compressed yeast must be kept refrigerated and used within several days after it is bought.

321

● (1) Scald milk, and stir in shortening, sugar, and salt. (2) Sprinkle yeast over lukewarm water in large mixing bowl. (3) Cool milk mixture to lukewarm, and stir into softened yeast.

● (4) Add about one-third of the flour and beat until smooth, and then stir in the remaining flour to make a soft dough. (5) Turn the dough onto a floured board. (6) Knead the dough until smooth.

YEAST BREAD OR ROLLS
on pages 527 and 528.)

● (7) Place the dough into a slightly greased mixing bowl and cover. (8) Let the dough rise until approximately double in bulk.

Courtesy Wheat Flour Institute

● (9) Shape the dough into loaves or rolls, and allow it to rise again until almost double in bulk. Then bake. Bread should be uniformly shaped, have a thin brown crust, and be even in grain (right).

Buying Partially Prepared Yeast Breads and Bakery Products

Sometimes you may not find it convenient to make yeast bread by starting with the separate ingredients. Then a packaged yeast-bread mix may be your choice. Such a mix usually contains all the ingredients for bread or rolls except the liquid. Stirring in the liquid and finishing the process takes little time.

Brown-and-serve bread and rolls are convenient to use when the saving of time and effort in preparing a meal is important. These breads have been partly baked by a baking company and only need to be heated for a short time to finish the baking process and to brown them.

Completely finished yeast-bread products are available in all bakery stores and in many other kinds of stores as well. Packaged yeast-bread mixes and frozen yeast breads are to be found in frozen food or refrigerator cases. There are so many varieties of these products that a wide choice is possible.

Care of Yeast Breads in the Home

All kinds of yeast breads and rolls when stored in the home should be placed in a tightly covered box or cabinet with small perforations in it. The covered box keeps out dust and moisture and prevents the products from drying. The tiny holes allow ventilation, which is necessary to keep the original fresh flavor of the yeast products. Many people think that storing bread in a refrigerator will keep it fresh. This is a mistaken idea, for although mold growth is delayed, the staling action is actually hastened by refrigerator storage. However, when it is desirable to have an extra supply on hand, bread may be stored in a freezer.

Sandwiches

Sandwiches range all the way from the hearty type to those that are so dainty they make only one or two bites. Many sandwiches are so substantial that they are served as the major part of a meal—at home, at school, or at work. If the sandwiches are a little less hearty, they can be served as an accompaniment to other foods in a meal, such as a soup or salad. Dainty sandwiches are suitable for part of the refreshments at a party. Sandwiches made with only one slice of bread—that is, not covered with another slice—are open-faced sandwiches. If an open-faced sandwich is very small, it is called a "canapé." Canapés are also served as an appetizer at the beginning of a meal.

All kinds of breads, including white, whole wheat, cracked wheat, and rye, are used for sandwiches. Split rolls, too, are used. For hearty sandwiches, the thicker slices of bread are best, and, as a rule, the crusts are not removed. For dainty sandwiches, thin slices of bread are used. To make them even daintier, the crusts are usually cut off after the sandwiches are made.

In all kinds of sandwiches the bread or split rolls are spread with softened butter or margarine, or sometimes as a variation, with mayonnaise or salad dressing. Whichever is used, it should be spread to the edge of each slice of bread or split roll.

The ingredients for sandwich fillings are many and varied. When several different ingredients are used, the proportions need not be exact. The list of ingredients in a filling recipe serves as a guide, and slight changes in the amount of one or more of them will not spoil the filling. In fact, such changes may add interest to an otherwise familiar sandwich. Many fillings are suitable for both hearty and dainty sandwiches, but the amounts may vary. Usually the filling is spread more liberally on the bread or roll for a hearty sandwich and less liberally for a small sandwich.

The illustrations on pages 325 to 332 show an efficient way to make sandwiches and how to wrap them. These illustrations also give some ideas for making fancy sandwiches.

Some suggestions for fillings for different kinds of sandwiches will be found in the recipes in Part V on pages 505 to 509.

MAKING SANDWICHES

● Sandwiches, like bread, may be plain or fancy. The procedures for making the following kinds of sandwiches are illustrated on the next seven pages:

Making Plain Sandwiches, page 326
Wrapping Sandwiches, page 327
Making Cheese Angles, page 328
Making Rolled Sandwiches, page 329
Making Open-faced Sandwiches, pages 330–331
Making Sandwich Variations, page 332

For further ideas on kinds of sandwiches and suggestions for
fillings, see the recipes on pages 505 to 509 in Part V.

MAKING PLAIN SANDWICHES

1. Lay out slices of bread in rows, and spread with butter or margarine to the edge.

2. Scoop fillings onto the bread in the two center rows, using a measure to be sure the amount is the same on all.

3. Spread fillings to the edge, and cover each with a slice of bread from the outer row.

All photos courtesy American Institute of Baking

WRAPPING SANDWICHES

1. Place an oblong piece of wax or moistureproof paper with the short sides parallel to the counter top. Center the sandwich so that the top and bottom crusts are parallel to the long sides of the paper.

2. Bring ends of paper together, forming a stay-in edge, which will keep out air.

3. Fold in the bottom of the paper to form a neat, secure package.

Moistureproof paper bags are available for quick packaging of sandwiches.

All photos courtesy American Institute of Baking

MAKING CHEESE ANGLES

Photos courtesy American Institute of Baking

● Trim the crusts from a loaf of both wholewheat and white bread of uniform size. Cut each loaf diagonally lengthwise to make two triangles. Place the widest side of each triangle flat on the board and cut in half, making eight triangles altogether. Spread one side of each triangle with a cheese filling. Reassemble the triangles into two loaves by alternating the triangles of each kind of bread (top). Wrap each loaf in moistureproof paper, and chill. To serve, unwrap each loaf, cut into slices, and then cut each slice in half (left).

MAKING ROLLED SANDWICHES

Photos courtesy American Institute of Baking

● Slice a loaf of bread lengthwise, and trim the crusts from the slices. Spread each slice with a cream cheese-olive filling, and cut in half crosswise. Press stuffed olives firmly together across the narrow end of each slice. Roll the slices as for a jelly roll, starting at the end with the olives (top). Wrap each roll tightly in moistureproof paper, and chill thoroughly. When ready to serve, unwrap and cut each roll into slices (right).

For plain open-faced sandwiches or canapés, spread thin slices of small loaves of rye bread with a well-seasoned filling. Garnish with water cress and thin slices of stuffed olives.

For fancy open-faced sandwiches or canapés, cut bread into small fancy shapes and spread with a favorite filling. Top with cucumber slices or bits of jelly, whichever is appropriate for the filling used.

FACED SANDWICHES

● Make sandwiches filled with peanut butter, jelly, or sharp cheese. Spread softened cream cheese on top of each sandwich, and remove crusts. Cut each in half and each half into three oblong sections.

● Dip the cream-cheese-covered side of the oblong sections into flaked coconut or chopped nuts for further decoration.

MAKING SANDWICH VARIATIONS

● Cut the ends from wiener or finger rolls, and remove the center of each roll with an apple corer. Stuff with a chicken—egg salad filling by forcing the mixture into the roll, working it in from each end. Wrap in moistureproof paper, and chill. To serve, unwrap each roll and slice into rings.

Photos courtesy American Institute of Baking

● Spread a thin slice of white bread with a filling, cover with a slice of whole-wheat bread, spread this slice with a filling, and cover with another slice of white bread. Press slices together, wrap in moistureproof paper, and chill. To serve, unwrap, trim off crusts, and slice into thin sandwches. Repeat to make the desired number of rainbow bars.

25

Cakes

and

Frostings

■ CAKES are another type of flour mixture. They resemble the quick breads in that they are leavened quickly, but they differ from quick breads in that they have a sweeter taste. All cakes have flour as the basic ingredient; all contain a relatively large proportion of sugar, some eggs, and usually a liquid; and all are leavened quickly. But some cakes contain fat and some do not. This difference in fat content is used to group cakes into two separate classes: (1) cakes with fat, or butter cakes; and (2) cakes without fat, or sponge cakes.

Classes of Cakes

Whether or not cakes contain fat has such an effect on them that the cakes in the two classes differ from each other in appearance,

texture, and flavor. These classes, together with examples of cakes in each class, are described in the chart on page 335.

Food Value of Cakes

The food value of cakes will vary according to the ingredients in them. For instance, vegetable shortenings supply calories, but if either butter or margarine is the fat used, the cakes will have vitamin A value in addition. Milk and eggs will supply valuable proteins, some vitamins, and some minerals. If enriched all-purpose flour is used, its vitamin and mineral contents will further increase the food value. The special cake flours are not usually enriched. However, despite the presence of the nutrients mentioned above, cakes, in the

333

CLASSES OF CAKES

Courtesy Swans Down Cake Flour

● There are two general classes of cakes: those made with fat, called "butter cakes" (above), and those made without fat, called "sponge cakes" (below).

Courtesy Stokely-Van Camp, Inc.

quantities eaten, can be depended upon only for calories.

Forms of Cakes and Their Uses

There are many uses for cakes, and it is the meal planner who decides how they will fit into the daily meal patterns. The form in which a cake is baked also has some influence on the way it will fit into the menu.

Layer cakes. These are large cakes made by placing two or more shallow layers of baked cake, usually the cake-with-fat type, one on top of another, and spreading a filling between them. Frequently the top layer is covered with a sugar frosting. Layer cakes are cut into individual servings and, among all cakes, are best suited for serving alone as a dessert.

Loaf cakes. Loaf cakes are large also, but they are plainer in appearance than layer cakes. Loaf cakes may be frosted or not, as desired. Cakes of this type are sliced and served alone for dessert, or better, are served as an accompaniment to ice cream or fruit. Slices of loaf cake are especially good to serve with afternoon tea, since they can be handled easily with the fingers. A slice of loaf cake is a convenient and appetizing addition to the carried lunch.

Cupcakes. These are small cakes—each one a single serving—that may be used in the same way as loaf cakes. Cupcakes may be frosted, but before frosting them, the way they are to be served should be considered so that ease of handling them will not be sacrificed to decoration. Cupcakes may be made of batter from either of the two classes of cakes.

CLASSIFICATION OF CAKES

CLASS	DESCRIPTION
Cakes with fat	Contain fat—butter, margarine, or vegetable shortening; delicate and tender in texture; different in flavor according to particular flavoring used
Plain and rich cakes	Plain cakes contain less fat, sugar, and egg than rich cakes; texture slightly less delicate and tender
Gold and white cakes	Gold cakes contain only yolk of egg instead of whole egg; white cakes contain only egg white
Chocolate, fudge, and devil's food cakes	All flavored with chocolate; fudge and devil's food cakes most richly flavored with chocolate, darker in color, and more tender in texture
Cakes without fat	Do not contain fat; have a larger proportion of egg than cakes with fat; texture is spongelike; flavor depends on whether egg yolk or egg white is used and on particular flavoring used
Sponge cakes	Contain both egg yolk and egg white; yellow in color
Angel food cakes	Contain the white of egg only; white in color
Chiffon cakes	Not a true example of a cake without fat; resembles the sponge cake in egg content but contains a liquid fat as one ingredient; also resembles sponge cakes in appearance and texture.

FORMS OF CAKES

● Cupcakes may be either butter cake or sponge cake, of any type of flavor, and they may have a variety of decorations.

● Sheet cakes are easy to make and convenient to serve and to store.

● A layer cake not only is an accomplishment, but when artistically frosted it is an object of beauty.

STEPS IN MAKING CAKE (CONVENTIONAL METHOD)

(See recipes on page 437.)

●Left: Sift flour, measure, and add other dry ingredients except sugar. Right: Cream shortening and sugar together until well blended.

●Left: Beat egg into the shortening and sugar mixture. Right: Stir in the dry ingredients which have been sifted together, alternating with the milk.

All photos courtesy Wesson Oil Company and Snowdrift

Sheet cakes. This form of cake is made by baking the cake batter, either a cake with fat or a cake without fat, in a large shallow pan. After the cake has been baked, it can be cut into individual pieces and frosted, if desired. Pieces of sheet cake are good to serve with ice cream or cut-up fruit. A very thin kind of sponge sheet cake may be spread with jelly and then rolled to make a jelly roll. When sliced thin for serving, it makes a flavorful dessert.

Upside-down cakes. As the name indicates, upside-down cakes are served bottom side up. In making such a cake, a fruit mixture or separate pieces of fruit are placed in a greased pan and the cake batter is then poured into the pan on top of the fruit. When the cake is baked, it is turned out onto a plate with the top side down and the fruit on top. This gives the upside-down effect. Such cakes make attractive desserts, especially when topped with whipped cream.

Principles of Preparation of Cakes

The formation of gluten from flour, and the way the other ingredients in the mixture and the baking conditions affect the gluten, are the principles involved in cakemaking. These principles differ slightly according to whether the cake is one with fat or one without fat.

Cakes with Fat

The principles of preparation as they apply to cakes with fat are as follows:

Flour. The flour used in making these cakes plays the same role that it does in making quick breads and yeast breads. It supplies the gluten which entraps bubbles of the leavening gases—air, steam, and carbon dioxide—to make the porous framework of the cake. Cake flour supplies a smaller amount of gluten than all-purpose flour does, and the gluten is more delicate in structure. These characteristics, together with the extremely fine granulation of cake flour, give cakes a delicate, tender texture. For these reasons some people prefer cake flour instead of all-purpose flour for cakemaking, and many recipes specify this kind. However, excellent cakes are made from both flours. If desired, all-purpose flour may be used in a cake recipe calling for cake flour by substituting ⅞ cup of all-purpose flour for each cup of the cake flour.

Leavening agents. The leavening of cakes with fat is obtained in the same way as in quick breads. (See pages 313 and 315.) This is in contrast to the slow leavening of yeast breads. Baking powder, or baking soda with sour milk, buttermilk, or molasses, is a source of carbon dioxide. The liquid, usually milk, is changed to steam throughout the cake batter as it bakes, and the steam contributes leavening action. Another leavening agent is air that is introduced into the batter during the mixing process. When a cake recipe calls for the separation of the whites and yolks of the egg and the whites are beaten to a foam before they are added to the batter, a further source of air is supplied to serve as a leavening agent.

Other ingredients. Fat, sugar, eggs, and liquid are other ingredients used in making cakes with fat. They affect the flour gluten, and, in addition, each one makes a special contribution to the cake.

Fat and sugar have a weakening effect on the gluten framework and tend to make the texture of the cake tender and delicate. When either butter or margarine is used, the fat adds flavor. Sugar contributes the sweetness characteristic of cakes and aids in giving a golden-brown color to the crust of light-colored cakes.

Eggs, because of their proteins, strengthen the gluten framework and give some flavor and color to the cake. Milk, or some other liquid ingredient, makes gluten from the flour proteins and causes the baking powder to act and provide carbon dioxide. Milk also gives the desired consistency to the uncooked mixture, which is either a pour batter or a drop batter depending on the recipe and method of making the cake.

Baking. Cakes with fat are baked at moderate temperatures of, usually, between 350° and 375° F. In this temperature range the rate of expansion of the leavening gases, entrapped in the gluten framework, and the rate of coagulation of the gluten proteins are such that the porous structure of the cake formed during mixing and baking becomes more or less rigid. Toward the end of the baking time, which is determined by the size of the cake, the sugar on the surface caramelizes and gives a golden-brown color to the crust.

Cakes Without Fat

The principles of making cakes without fat are slightly different from those of making cakes with fat.

Eggs. In this class of cakes, eggs are used in such a large proportion that their proteins contribute largely to the framework. Of course some of the framework is supplied by the gluten from the flour. The eggs are the sole source of liquid in cakes without fat. They are always beaten to a foam—the yolks and whites

STEPS IN MAKING CAKE (QUICK METHOD)

(See recipe on page 438.)

● Left: Sift dry ingredients into a mixing bowl. Right: Add the shortening and part of the milk.

● Left: Beat thoroughly. Right: Add the remainder of the milk, the eggs, and the flavoring, and beat again about 3 minutes, or until batter is smooth.

All photos courtesy Wesson Oil Company and Snowdrift

separately for a sponge cake and just the whites for an angel food cake. In this way, enough air is incorporated into the mixture and held in the gluten-and-egg protein framework to act as the chief leavening gas. Steam from the liquid of the eggs is the only other leavening material.

Other ingredients. The other ingredients of this class of cakes are flour, sugar, and flavoring. These are used for the same purposes as in the making of cakes with fat. In angel food cakes a small amount of cream of tartar is added to the egg whites before they are beaten so they will beat to a more stable foam.

Baking. For baking this type of cake, temperatures of 350° F. or less are usually used. The reason for the low temperature is that much of the batter framework consists of eggs which, because of their proteins, require a low cooking temperature. Higher temperatures

STEPS IN MAKING CHIFFON CAKE

(See recipe on page 440.)

● Left: Pour the oil into a well made in the center of the sifted dry ingredients, add the unbeaten egg yolks, water, and flavoring, and set aside. Right: Beat the egg whites until foamy, add cream of tartar, and beat in the sugar to make a stiff meringue.

● Left: After beating flour–oil–egg-yolk mixture until smooth, fold it into the meringue. Bake in an ungreased tube pan. Right: Invert the pan to cool the cake before removing it.

than 350° F. are sometimes used, but then the length of baking period must be shortened. The changes that occur in the batter during baking are similar to those that occur in the baking of cakes with fat—that is, the leavening gases expand and become entrapped in the egg and gluten framework, which is coagulated by heat and becomes more or less rigid.

Care of Cakes After Baking

Cakes with fat are allowed to cool slightly in the pans for several minutes on a cake rack —10 minutes if time permits. During this time the porous structure becomes rigid enough so that the cakes are not damaged while they are being removed from the pans. After they are removed from the pans, the cakes are placed on racks for further cooling.

Cakes without fat and chiffon cakes are left in the baking pans, which are inverted, until they are entirely cold. The porous structure of sponge, angel food, and chiffon cakes is so delicate that these cakes may collapse unless the pans remain inverted until the cakes become cold and fairly rigid.

Buying Ingredients for Cakes

You will find many ingredients available on the market for making cakes. If you decide to use a cake mix or a bakery cake instead, you will also find a wide selection available.

Buying the ingredients. The ingredients used in making cakes are the same as those used in making quick breads. You may want to keep on hand a number of special flavorings, such as vanilla, lemon, and orange extracts, and such ingredients as chocolate, coconut, and a variety of spices. Also, you may prefer to use cake flour instead of all-purpose flour, and if so, there are several different brands available. Cake flours are usually packaged in 2-pound cartons. They are likely to be more expensive than all-purpose flour. For the fat you may select butter, but either margarine or one of the vegetable shortenings

Courtesy Corn Products Company

● A good chiffon cake is spongelike in texture, has a fine, even grain, and a flavor that is characteristic of flavoring used.

is very satisfactory. As in the making of quick breads, Grade B eggs are quite as good to use as Grade A eggs in making cakes—both those with fat and those without fat.

Buying mixes and bakery cakes. When you want to serve a cake at some special occasion and your time is limited, you may find it convenient to use a packaged cake mix. In the cake-with-fat class, there are many kinds, including plain and chocolate mixes, as well as spice and other flavors. In the cake-without-fat class, mixes for angel food, sponge cake, and chiffon cake are available. Since the packaged mixes for cake contain most of the ingredients, you will only need to add water or milk. Some require the addition of an egg or two.

Perhaps you will want a different kind of cake from those you are used to making at home, or a cake that is specially decorated. Then a bakery cake may be the one you will select. The baker, through training and experience, is equipped to make fillings and frostings that are more elaborate than most home bakers can attempt. However, as a cre-

● The use of a cake mix saves time in assembling the ingredients, measuring, and mixing, although the baking time is the same as for a cake made from basic ingredients.

ative outlet, some girls and homemakers enjoy learning how to decorate cakes.

Evaluating mixes versus ingredients. With such a variety of cake mixes on the market and such an array of bakery cakes easily obtainable, you may perhaps be puzzled as to whether or not it is worthwhile to take the time to make a cake starting with the individual ingredients. This same thought applies to the making of quick breads, yeast breads, cookies, and pastries.

There are several points to think about in making your decision. Of course you save time when you use the mixes or bakery products, and many times such a saving is necessary. But cost and quality of the product are other considerations. It is impossible to make a gen-

eral comparison in regard to either factor. Which is the least expensive—the homemade one, the one made from the mix, or the one bought in the bakery—will depend on the individual product, the particular brand of mix you use, or the bakery. On the other hand, your skill in baking will have a great deal to do with the quality factor. Very often the homemade cake or biscuits or rolls are far superior to the "bought" product or to one made from a mix.

Another point that you should always consider, but one that is hard to measure exactly, is the sense of accomplishment and personal satisfaction that you can derive from having made a delicious home-baked cake or a pan of hot rolls, starting with the basic ingredients.

STEPS IN FROSTING A CAKE

1. Brush off the excess crumbs from the sides of the layers.

2. Frost the top of the lower layer, and put the next layer over it. Then frost the sides of both layers.

3. Frost the top, swirling with a spatula in a "carefully careless" manner.

All photos courtesy Wesson Oil Company

Care of Cakes in the Home

Cakes should be stored in tightly covered but well-ventilated containers. In this way, cakes will keep their original moist condition for several days and, because of the ventilation, they will also retain their fresh flavor longer.

Cake Frostings

Frostings are sugar-rich coverings that may be used on all kinds of cakes. In layer cakes the frosting can be spread between the layers as well as on the top unless a special filling is made. Sometimes frostings are referred to as "icings."

There are two general types of frostings: (1) those which are made by blending ingredients together until they are creamy but which do not require cooking and (2) those which are cooked.

Uncooked Frostings

Icing sugar is the most suitable kind of sugar to use for making uncooked frostings, since its fine grain gives a frosting which is smooth and velvety. The liquid that is mixed with the sugar provides the flavor in uncooked frostings. It may be fruit juice, egg white, a mixture of coffee beverage and melted chocolate, or just melted chocolate and a small amount of milk or cream. Sometimes softened butter is blended into the frosting. In an uncooked frosting, the spreading consistency is obtained by adjusting the proportions of sugar and liquid. Beating the frosting vigorously will give it a creamy, almost fluffy texture. Uncooked frostings that contain some fat, either butter or the fat that is in cream or chocolate, remain soft and creamy longer than the very simple type made merely by mixing icing sugar with fruit juices or egg white. This simple type of uncooked frosting without fat tends to dry out more quickly and to become hard.

Cooked Frostings

These frostings are a little more elaborate than the uncooked frostings. One of the cooked frostings is like fudge. In order to get a consistency for spreading, the mixture is not cooked quite as long as for candy. Another kind of cooked frosting is made by boiling a sugar syrup until it makes a firm ball in cold water or reaches the correct temperature on a candy thermometer; then the syrup is beaten into stiffly beaten egg whites. (See chart, "Temperatures and Tests for Syrup and Candies," on page 402.) A third kind of cooked frosting is similar to this except that the sugar, water, and unbeaten egg whites are mixed together in a pan and placed over boiling water. The frosting mixture is beaten steadily as it cooks until it stands up in peaks. It is then of the right consistency for spreading on the cake.

The extent of cooking the syrup for a cooked frosting and the amount of stirring required to make the frosting the right thickness for spreading are techniques that require care. If the frosting is too thin to spread by the time it has cooled, the syrup has not been cooked enough—that is, either the firmness of the ball formed in cold water or the temperature reading on the candy thermometer was not judged accurately. This condition can be remedied by placing the bowl of frosting in a pan of boiling water and stirring the frosting for a few minutes so that it will cook sufficiently. Then when it is removed from the boiling water and stirred, it will thicken to spreading consistency. If the frosting becomes too thick to spread easily, either it has been stirred too long or the syrup may have been overcooked. In either case a small amount of warm water, perhaps only part of a teaspoon, can be stirred into the frosting cautiously until the frosting will spread easily.

In all three kinds of cooked frostings, very fine sugar crystals are desired in order that the frostings will have a creamy texture. (See Chapter 33, page 404.)

26

Cookies

■COOKIES are really little cakes. They are sweet and have flavors similar to the flavors of cakes. However, cookie recipes call for little or no liquid, so the unbaked mixture is thicker than a cake batter. Cookie dough is either soft or stiff. Cookies are flatter than cakes, and they are made in a variety of shapes—round, oblong, and square. Sometimes, for special holidays and for children, they are made into fancy shapes, such as animals, stars, and Christmas trees.

Types of Cookies

There are drop cookies, rolled cookies, refrigerator cookies, molded cookies, pressed cookies, and bar cookies. The chief differences among these six types of cookies are in the stiffness of the dough and the way the dough is handled in shaping the cookies. The different types of cookies are described in the chart on page 347.

Food Value of Cookies

The food value of cookies is similar to that of plain unfrosted cakes, with calories their chief contribution. Like cakes, whatever other food value they have depends upon the ingredients in them.

Uses of Cookies

Cookies are used in much the same way as cakes. They are not, however, quite so suitable for serving alone for dessert, since most kinds of cookies are not frosted and not as sweet as cakes. Cookies with a crisp texture

TYPES OF COOKIES

● Drop cookies

● Rolled and cut cookies

● Refrigerator cookies

● Molded cookies

● Pressed cookies

● Bar cookies

make a pleasing accompaniment to a dessert of cut fruit, fruit sauces, or ice cream. When cookies are cut into dainty shapes, they are convenient and attractive to serve with tea or coffee at an afternoon tea or reception. When served with an ice or ice cream, they make a tempting refreshment for an afternoon or evening party. For these purposes cookies have an advantage over cake because they are easier to handle. Among the favorite ways to use cookies are in the carried lunch or as a between-meal or a before-bedtime snack.

Principles of Preparation of Cookies

The ingredients used in making most cookies are the same as those used for cakes with fat. These ingredients are flour, sugar, salt, fat, eggs, milk, leavening agents, and flavorings, and each has the same role to play that it has in making cakes. All-purpose flour is used rather than cake flour, which may be preferred in making cakes. Brown sugar is sometimes used for its special flavor. In some cookie recipes, molasses or honey may replace some of the sugar and milk. In other recipes, sour milk or sweet or sour cream may take the place of sweet milk. If cream is used, it adds fat, and such a recipe will call for a relatively small amount of other fat. Chocolate, spices, nuts, and dried or candied fruits are often used in cookies for flavor.

Buying Ingredients for Cookies

Before making cookies, you will need to buy whatever ingredients or flavorings you do not have on hand, or you may wish to buy a cookie mix or packaged cookie dough.

Buying the ingredients. When you make cookies, you will use about the same ingredients as you do for cake. But you will need to have all-purpose flour, since cookie recipes seldom call for cake flour. If you make cookies often, you will find it convenient to have a good supply of flavorings on hand.

CLASSIFICATION OF COOKIES

TYPE	DESCRIPTION
Drop cookies	Made from a soft dough which is pushed from a spoon onto a baking sheet in the size desired; less evenly shaped than rolled cookies
Rolled cookies	Cut from a thin sheet of a stiff dough with cutters of various shapes; evenly shaped and usually thin
Refrigerator cookies	Cut from a roll of a dough which has been chilled until very stiff; less evenly shaped than rolled cookies and thick or thin, as desired
Molded cookies	Made from small portions of a stiff dough which are shaped or molded with the hands; may be left in shape of balls or slightly flattened
Pressed cookies	Made from a stiff rich dough which is forced through a cookie press to make cookies of various shapes
Bar cookies	A soft dough baked in a shallow pan; when cool, the baked sheet is cut into oblong or square shapes, as desired

● Use your imagination in decorating cookies. Uncooked frosting and small dragees or candies, candied cherries or other candied fruits, nuts, dates, and coconut make attractive decorations.

Buying mixes and bakery cookies. There are a number of special mixes on the market for making cookies. There are also many kinds of packaged cookie doughs in the refrigerator case. These doughs are ready to slice or cut, and some of them are ready to spread in a pan for making bar cookies. They have an advantage in times of emergency when there is not an opportunity to make cookies from basic ingredients.

In bakeries, cookies are often arranged on large trays and sold by the pound. In some bakeries, cookies are wrapped in dozen lots in transparent moisture-resistant paper. In stores other than bakeries, cookies are generally sold in cardboard packages, sometimes with cello-phane on one side so that you can see what they look like.

Care of Cookies in the Home

All types of cookies should be stored in tightly covered containers to keep them fresh. A slice of bread in the container helps to keep soft cookies soft. An earthenware cookie jar or a tin box with a tight-fitting cover are often used. The package in which commercial cookies are sold is usually lined with moisture-resistant paper. After a package has been opened, the paper should be folded around the remaining cookies and the package closed as tightly as possible.

27

Pastries

■ THE PASTRY DOUGH used for making pies is a stiff dough in contrast to the softer dough of yeast breads and biscuits. The ingredients in pastry dough are all-purpose flour, salt, fat, and water. The fat may be a soft, solid fat, such as one of the vegetable shortenings, or it may be an oil.

Flakiness and tenderness are the chief characteristics of pastry. Soft, solid fat gives a more flaky quality to the baked pastry than oil does. Hot water is used sometimes in making pastry dough, but it produces a crumbly rather than a flaky pastry.

Kinds of Pastries

After a pastry dough has been prepared, it can be shaped in various ways to make several kinds of pastries. Among these are pies, tarts,

and turnovers. A description of these pastries with some examples of each kind follows:

One-crust pies. For these pies a piepan is lined with a thin layer of dough. Sometimes this layer of dough is first baked and then a cooked filling is added to the baked pie shell. The filling can be topped with meringue or whipped cream, if desired. Lemon meringue and chocolate cream pies are two examples. For such one-crust pies as custard and pumpkin, the uncooked filling is poured into an unbaked pie shell and the dough and filling are then baked at the same time.

Instead of lining a piepan with dough, a layer of unbaked dough may be placed over cooked or uncooked fruit, vegetables, meat, poultry, or fish in a deep dish and all baked together. Deep-dish chicken, apple, peach, and berry pies are examples.

HOW PASTRY IS USED

● For a one-crust pie

● For a two-crust pie

● For tarts

● For turnovers

Two-crust pies. Pies made by lining a pie-pan with a thin layer of dough, adding a filling, and then covering the filling with a thin layer of dough are called "two-crust pies." The dough and filling are baked at the same time. Apple, blueberry, cherry, and rhubarb are examples of the many kinds of two-crust pies.

Tarts. Tarts are the same as one-crust and two-crust pies except that each tart is an individual serving. When a top crust is used, it may be cut out in fancy designs or shapes. Cherry, lemon meringue, and custard tarts are but a few of the many kinds.

Turnovers. Two-crust pies just large enough for individual servings are called "turnovers." To make them, an uncooked filling is placed on one-half of a thin layer of dough, and the other half of the dough is folded over it. Then the edges of the dough are pinched together to seal the turnovers, and they are baked. Turnovers can be made with any kind of filling—apple, tuna fish, raspberry jam, and mincemeat being examples.

Food Value of Pastries

Pastry doughs contain a relatively large amount of fat, and many of the fillings contain a fair amount of sugar. For these reasons, all pastries have a high calorie value. Fruit pies and those with a custard filling contribute some minerals, vitamins, and proteins. These nutrients will be found also in the deep-dish pies containing mixtures of vegetables with meat, poultry, or fish.

Uses of Pastries

Pastries are used chiefly as desserts. However, meat or fish pies are used for main dishes, and sometimes pastry is used as an accompaniment for soups and salads.

As a dessert. There are so many different kinds of pastries from which to choose a dessert that variety is easily achieved. Fruit, custard, and lemon chiffon pies, as well as tarts

and turnovers with different fillings, are only a few of the many kinds.

As a main dish. Deep-dish pies made of meat, fish, or poultry are attractive and appetizing main dishes for a family or party meal and are a way of using leftovers. Deep-dish pies are also a different way of serving canned varieties of meat, fish, or poultry. In addition to the gravy or sauce, a few vegetables may be added to the filling. The filling is then covered with a delicate pastry dough and baked.

As an accompaniment. Cheese or cinnamon sticks are simple kinds of pastry accompaniments to serve with soups and salads. A pastry dough may be made especially for these, or bits of dough left over from making a pie may be used.

Principles of Preparation of Pastries

The ingredients used, their proportions, the procedures followed in mixing the ingredients together, and the baking of the finished doughs all have a bearing on the principles of pastry making.

All-purpose flour is used. A vegetable oil can be used for shortening, but a soft, solid fat like lard, a vegetable shortening, or butter or margarine will give a more flaky pastry. For each cup of flour, ¼ or ⅓ cup of fat is required. The smaller amount is better if either an oil or lard is used; otherwise ⅓ cup is more satisfactory. Also, for each cup of flour, ½ teaspoon of salt is required unless the fat is salted. Then a little less salt is better. Butter and margarine are examples of salted fat. From 2 to 2½ tablespoons of water are used with each cup of flour.

The first step in making pastry dough is to sift the salt with the flour. Then cut the fat into the salt-flour mixture until it is finely divided and evenly distributed among the flour particles. Next add water. As the water is stirred into the flour-salt-fat mixture, it comes in contact with the flour particles that

STEPS IN MAKING PLAIN PASTRY

Courtesy Betty Crocker of General Mills

● Left: Cut the shortening into the flour until the pieces are about the size of peas. Right: Sprinkle water over the flour-shortening mixture, and cut it in to make a stiff dough.

Courtesy Betty Crocker of General Mills

Courtesy "The American Home." Photo by F. M. Demarest

● Left: Form the dough into a ball. Right: Roll the dough on a floured board until it is about 1 inch greater in diameter than the top of the piepan. Then place the dough in the pan.

lie between the pieces of fat and makes many short pieces, or strands, of gluten. The fact that gluten has been formed in short pieces is what gives the baked pastry its tender and flaky qualities. An oil, in contrast to a solid fat, mixes so closely with the flour that the gluten strands are extremely short. Thus an oil pastry, although tender, is crumbly rather than flaky.

The next step in making pastry is to roll out the dough to a thin layer so that it can be shaped. In addition to shaping, rolling of the dough serves two other purposes: (1) It flattens into layers the short strands of gluten and the tiny pieces of fat that are between them. (2) It seals in between these layers more or less of the air which was entrapped during the mixing step. As a result, the rolled-out, moist dough consists of layers of gluten, fat, and air. It is necessary to have air in the dough, since

SHAPING DOUGH FOR A PIE SHELL

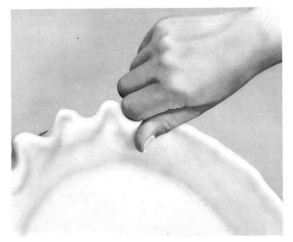

1. After trimming the dough so it is even, fold the edge under, and flute with the fingers. Then chill.

2. Prick the dough in many places with a fork, and bake.

3. Cool the pie shell before pouring in the cooked pie filling.

All photos courtesy Betty Crocker of General Mills

air and the steam from the water used are the leavening gases in plain pastry. During the baking, the water is changed to steam and the air expands. Thus the layers are pushed apart and tiny spaces are left between them. This effect gives the delicate, tender, and flaky quality characteristic of a good pastry.

Pastry dough is baked at a high temperature of around 400° to 425° F. so that the steam and expanding air will push the layers of gluten and fat apart quickly before the gluten proteins become coagulated and make the dough rigid. However, the type of pie influences the baking temperature in some cases. If it is a two-crust pie, a one-crust pie shell, or a pastry topping for a deep-dish pie, the oven is held at the high temperature for the entire baking period. If it is a one-crust pie with a custard filling, the temperature is lowered to 350° F. after 15 to 20 minutes in order to cook the custard filling at low heat.

Buying Ingredients for Pastries

The ingredients needed for making pastry dough for pies, tarts, and turnovers are among the usual staple foods found in the home. Some ingredients also are usually available for the filling. However, there are a few points to keep in mind if you are making special plans to buy the ingredients.

Buying the ingredients. In buying ingredients for making pastry dough, select all-purpose flour, and either oil, lard, a vegetable shortening, or butter or margarine for the fat. Since the fruit used in pies will be cooked, it need not be as perfect as fruit that is served alone for dessert or for eating out of hand. Canned fruits are good for making fruit-filled pies, and they need not be of the highest quality.

Buying mixes and bakery pastries. There are a number of prepared pastry mixes on the market to which only water needs to be added to make the dough. Some of these mixes include the filling in the package. Excellent pas-

tries can be made from most of the packaged mixes and, no doubt, time can be saved in meal preparation by using them. But the finished product may not give the same sense of satisfaction that is present when the basic ingredients are used to make a beautiful pie for the family.

Bakery pies save time and often they are very good. But as with the use of the pastry mixes, serving a bought pie may not give the sense of personal satisfaction or the family's taste satisfaction obtained from a homemade pie. Frozen pies also are available in the markets—meat, fish, and poultry pies for the main course of a meal as well as pies for dessert.

Other Pastries

There are other pastries more elaborate than the kinds described so far in this chapter. These are often called "French pastries." Among them are cream puffs and éclairs. Cream puffs and éclairs are individual pufflike pastry shells made from a soft dough containing eggs in addition to flour, salt, fat, and water. The dough expands greatly during baking so that the centers become almost hollow, making a shell. This shell is round for cream puffs and oblong for éclairs. The baked shells are filled with a custard filling, whipped cream, or sometimes ice cream. Cream puffs are frequently served with a sweet sauce and are not frosted. Éclairs are always frosted.

Serving of cream puffs and éclairs. These pastries are particularly popular and attractive for dessert. Very tiny cream puffs and éclairs—just big enough for one or two bites— make a delicious and unusual refreshment for an afternoon tea. Arranged alternately with little cakes on a serving plate, they add a festive note to such a party.

Principles of preparation of cream puffs and éclairs. To make cream puffs and éclairs, the fat is melted in hot water. The flour is beaten into this liquid, and then the eggs are added and beaten in. By this procedure the

SHAPING DOUGH FOR A TWO-CRUST PIE

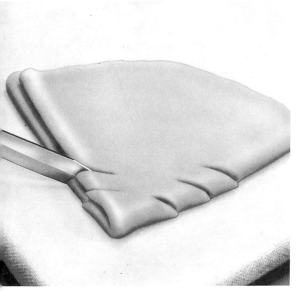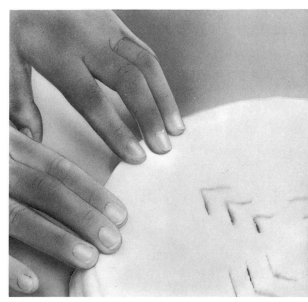

● Left: Fold rolled-out dough for the top crust into quarters and cut several gashes in it. Right: Lay the gashed dough over a pie filling in a pastry-lined piepan.

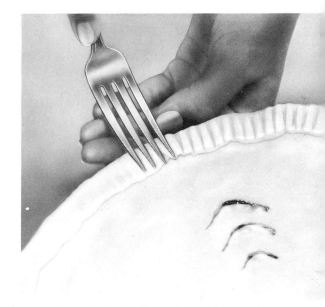

● Left: Fold the extended edges of the dough over the top of the pie. Right: Press the two layers of dough together. Pressing with the tines of a fork is easy and makes a pretty edge.

● Éclairs and other French pastries are not made from a plain pastry dough. (See page 354 and below.)

fat and the eggs are thoroughly blended with the flour, and air is incorporated into the dough. The dough is fairly soft, yet firm enough to hold a high shape when pushed from a spoon onto a greased sheet for baking. The dough should not flatten out.

Cream puffs and éclairs are baked at high temperatures of 425° to 450° F. so that the steam and air will expand quickly and make a puffed-up, shell-like pastry with walls of coagulated egg proteins and flour gluten sur-

rounding a hollow space. It is customary to lower the oven temperature to 350° F. when the pastry shells become brown. After this point there will not be any further expansion, and the lower heat will allow the centers to dry a little without overbrowning the surface.

The pastry shells must be cooled before they are filled.

Care of Pastries in the Home

All pies are best when served the day they are made. But if it is convenient to make several fruit pies at one time, these may be kept for one day quite satisfactorily. On the other hand, if the pie fillings contain milk or eggs, or meat, fish, or poultry, there is danger of spoilage. If, for any reason, it is necessary to keep them for a day or two, they should be held in the refrigerator.

Baked pie shells made of plain pastry dough and unfilled cream puffs and éclairs can be kept satisfactorily for several days if more are made than are needed for immediate use. They should be kept in a covered, ventilated box in a cool place. If they are heated for a few minutes before they are filled for serving, they will regain their freshness. Filled cream puffs and éclairs should always be used within several hours of being made; otherwise the filling will soak into the pastry shell.

When a home freezer is available, extra pies and even filled cream puffs and éclairs can be wrapped carefully in freezer paper and frozen for future use.

28

Beverages

■ MILK, cocoa and chocolate, coffee and tea, and fruit and vegetable juices are beverages used at meals or in-between meals. Milk has so many uses in food preparation in addition to its use as a beverage that an entire chapter is devoted to its study. (See Chapter 15, "Milk.") A hot beverage is relished by many people as a meal accompaniment. But whatever beverage is chosen, whether hot or cold, it helps to supply the body with some of the liquid needed each day.

Food Value of Beverages

The food value of beverages ranks from a high value for milk, cocoa, and chocolate to none whatever for coffee and tea. The food value of fruit and vegetable juices depends on the kind of juice and its concentration.

Milk. The superiority of milk as a beverage is unquestioned. Its use in this way in the diet is important for people of all ages but especially so for young people who have not as yet attained full growth. The amounts recommended for daily consumption are given in the Milk Group of Canada's Food Guide. (See page 10.) Drinking milk as a beverage either at meals or between meals is one way of ensuring that you will obtain the amount considered best for you. Teen-agers, you will note, require four or more 8-ounce cups each day.

Cocoa and chocolate. Cocoa and chocolate contain starch, protein, fat, and some minerals. According to law, chocolate must contain at least 50 percent fat, whereas cocoa can vary from 10 to 22 percent fat. When cocoa and chocolate are made into beverages, the usual liquid is milk. These beverages are

Courtesy Kellogg Company

● Milk is the best all-round beverage for teen-agers—either for a snack or at meals.

Courtesy Florida Citrus Commission

● Whenever you drink orange juice, you are getting a good share of the necessary vitamin C for the day.

Courtesy National Canners Association

● Tomato juice also supplies vitamin C but in smaller amounts.

BEVERAGES

● Icy cold fruit ades are a tempting and refreshing beverage on a hot day.

● Iced tea is a favorite beverage for meals during hot weather.

● Coffee, too, may be served as an iced beverage.

high in food value because of their own nutrients as well as those nutrients supplied by the milk. The sugar used to make both cocoa and chocolate also adds to their calorie value.

Coffee and tea. Although coffee and tea do not have any food value, their appeal is due to their pleasant flavor and the refreshing effect of the caffeine that they contain. However, some people like to add sugar and either cream or milk to coffee, and sugar and lemon, cream, or milk to tea. These additions will give the beverages some food value, but even so, coffee and tea should never replace milk in the diet.

Fruit and vegetable juices. The high vitamin C content of orange juice makes this juice outstanding among fruit juices. A large proportion of the original food value of fruits and vegetables is obtained in the juice when these are pressed out for beverage purposes. (See Chapter 13, "Fruits," page 210, and Chapter 22, "Vegetables," page 301.) If fruit juices are diluted, as in making lemonade, orangeade, or punch, the concentration of the nutrients is greatly reduced and consequently the food value of the beverage is limited. Usually some sugar is added to fruit ades and punch, but even with this addition, these beverages are valued chiefly for their refreshing qualities rather than for their nutrients.

Soft drinks. Soft drinks are used widely as refreshing beverages, since they taste sweet and have well-liked flavors. The sugar, which is the only nutrient in these drinks, supplies energy; otherwise soft drinks are completely lacking in food value. The too frequent use of soft drinks can increase the calorie intake more than may be desirable and, at the same time, crowd out beverages which are nutritious, such as milk and orange juice.

Uses of Beverages

A beverage is usually served at every meal, and milk is the most important one of all. For special occasions a fruit beverage, like orange juice, lemonade, or a punch made of several fruit juices mixed together may be part of the refreshments. Chocolate, cocoa, coffee, and fruit juices are frequently used as flavoring ingredients also.

At meals. Although family custom is the usual guide in selecting the beverage served at meals, a common Canadian practice among adults is to start the day with coffee at breakfast. Of course, some adults like tea instead, and the young members may prefer a choice of milk, cocoa, or chocolate. The milk in cocoa and chocolate will help to supply the daily allowance of this food. Frequently, the breakfast fruit is a juice.

When entertaining. Entertaining one's friends around the tea table or at a porch party on a hot summer's day may be very pleasant. On these occasions, as at meals, there is a choice of beverage. Hot tea, coffee, chocolate, or cocoa are always acceptable. But if the day is hot, a cold beverage may be preferred for its refreshing effect. Iced coffee or tea, one of the cold fruit beverages, such as lemonade, or a punch of several juices mixed together are all good choices. Punch is always suitable for one of the beverages at a formal tea or reception. For a snack, at any time, milk shakes can be enjoyed as an impromptu refreshment. But at a dinner that is a little more elaborate than the regular family meal, coffee is the usual beverage. It may be served with the dinner, to accompany the dessert, or in the living room at the end of the meal.

As a flavoring ingredient. Chocolate or cocoa is a popular flavoring for cakes and cookies, puddings of many kinds, soufflés, ice creams, and a large array of candies. Coffee also is a good flavoring ingredient. Coffee ice cream, coffee gelatin, and coffee candies are popular.

Tea is not used as a flavoring ingredient except in iced beverages. In such beverages it frequently gives the basic flavor with which other flavors are blended by the addition of different kinds of fruit juices.

HOT BEVERAGES

Courtesy Baker's Chocolate

●Hot chocolate is a welcome beverage for a meal or a snack on a cold day.

Courtesy Tender Leaf Tea

●Hot tea is a refreshing and relaxing beverage in midafternoon.

Harold M. Lambert from Frederic Lewis

●Hot coffee is preferred by most adults for a breakfast beverage.

Courtesy Birds Eye Frozen Foods

● Ice-cold punch and little cakes are suitable refreshments for a crowd.

Fruit juices are used to flavor puddings, cookies, cakes, and pie fillings.

Principles of Preparation of Beverages

The principles of preparing the different kinds of beverages vary as described in the following sections.

Cocoa and Chocolate

In making cocoa and chocolate, the starch in the cocoa or chocolate needs to be given special attention. Thus the principle of starch cookery is followed. (See page 221.) This principle is applied in the following steps for preparing these beverages:

1. In cocoa, the cocoa and sugar are mixed together, and then cold water is stirred in.

This separates the tiny starch particles of the cocoa. If chocolate is used, the starch particles are already separated in the cake of chocolate. Therefore, less care is needed in mixing the pieces of chocolate with the sugar before stirring in the cold water.

2. The cocoa or chocolate mixture is boiled until it is syrupy. This causes the starch particles to swell and thicken the water. Also, boiling cooks the starch thoroughly.

3. Milk is stirred into the cocoa or chocolate sirup. The whole mixture is then heated. This allows the flavors to blend as the beverage becomes hot.

Coffee

Before considering the preparation of coffee, it is necessary to know something about the coffee bean itself. The coffee bean contains caffeine, which gives the stimulating effect to the beverage. There are several fatlike compounds in the coffee bean that give the beverage desirable flavors. There are also tannins which, if dissolved into the beverage, will give it a bitter taste.

The making of coffee is called "brewing." It is generally agreed that the beverage should be refreshing and have a pleasing flavor without any suggestion of bitterness. The principle of brewing which is applied to obtain these qualities is as follows:

1. Ground coffee is brought into contact with water that is just below boiling temperature. Water of this temperature dissolves the caffeine into the beverage, but it does not dissolve the tannins. There is also less escape of steam than from boiling water, which would carry away the desirable flavor-giving compounds with it. As a further assurance of retaining these flavor-giving compounds, the beverage should be served as soon as it has finished brewing.
2. The length of time for brewing depends on the coffee maker used.

A coffeepot, or even an ordinary saucepan with a tight-fitting cover, is a simple coffee maker and makes the so-called "steeped" or "boiled" coffee. If the principle of brewing is carefully followed, the temperature of the water surrounding the ground coffee will be brought to boiling and *immediately* lowered to a temperature just below this. The coffee is allowed to steep for about three to five minutes. Then the brew is strained from the coffee grounds.

There are several more elaborate kinds of coffee makers. In the vacuum type, the coffee and water are held together at the right temperature and for the right length of time for steeping. In contrast, in the drip and percolator types of coffee makers the water, at the right temperature, passes through the ground coffee, once in the drip coffee maker and repeatedly in the percolator. Both the vacuum and percolator types of coffee makers are

● A chocolate float is a good make-your-own party snack for after school.

available equipped with automatic devices that control the temperature and time of brewing automatically.

Tea

Like coffee, tea leaves contain caffeine, tannins, and certain materials that give tea its characteristic delicate flavor. As in coffee, the object in brewing tea is to dissolve the caffeine, keep the flavor in the beverage, and yet avoid dissolving the tannins, which would make the beverage bitter. The principle of brewing is as follows:

1. Tea leaves are placed in a scalded teapot, and boiling water is poured over them. In the interval of pouring, the temperature of the water drops to just below boiling. The pot is scalded so as not to cool the water further.
2. The brewing is continued for about three to five minutes, with the pot placed where the tea will keep hot. The tea is poured, without the leaves, into another hot teapot; or if a tea bag is used, it is removed.

● Beverages that come in powdered form for instant use are so simple to prepare that even a child can use them.

Fruit and Vegetable Beverages

Fruit and vegetable juices should be refrigerated as soon as they are prepared to retain their fresh flavor and to have the greatest food value.

Buying Beverages

Cocoa, chocolate, coffee, and tea are all available in a number of different types, and each type is available in a number of different brands. The particular selection of type and brand is entirely a matter of individual preference. The care required when buying milk has been discussed in Chapter 15, pages 231 and 232, and will not be considered here.

Buying cocoa. One of the differences among types of cocoa is in the amount of fat they contain. Breakfast cocoa is the most usual type, and it must, by law, contain at least 22 percent fat. If breakfast cocoa is very dark in color, it has been manufactured by the "Dutch Process" in which the cocoa is treated with an alkali that causes the pigments in it to darken. There is little difference in the flavor of the beverages made from regular breakfast cocoa and Dutch Process breakfast cocoa. There are other cocoas on the market that contain less fat than the breakfast type, but none of them makes the quality of beverage that breakfast cocoa makes.

Instant cocoa is another type of cocoa. It is a mixture of cocoa, sugar, and milk solids. All that is required to make a beverage is to stir the instant cocoa into hot water. Such a ready-to-serve cocoa is convenient to have on hand for making a snack after school or to use when a meal must be prepared in a hurry.

Buying chocolate. There are a number of different types of chocolate: bitter chocolate, to which no sugar has been added in its manufacture, semi-sweet and sweet chocolates, both of which contain sugar, and milk chocolate, which is sweet chocolate with milk solids added. Most chocolates are available in cakes, bars, wafers, or as small pieces. There is also a semi-liquid, or pre-melted, type of chocolate packaged in foil or plastic envelopes. This is unsweetened cocoa combined with a vegetable oil.

Buying coffee. There are many brands of coffee. Before deciding which one will suit the family best it is a good idea to experiment with several different ones. Brands differ in respect to the varieties of coffee beans used and on the extent to which the beans are roasted. Both factors influence the flavor of the coffee beverage.

Practically all brands of coffees are packaged already ground to different degrees of fineness, or they may be ground to the desired fineness at the time of purchase. The most coarsely ground coffee is called "regular" or "percolator grind," next in fineness is "drip grind," and the most finely ground is "fine"

● Frozen orange juice is one of the most popular of all frozen foods.

or "pulverized grind." The kind of grind used depends on the coffee maker. For a coffeepot or a percolator, the regular grind of coffee is most suitable. For the drip coffee maker, the drip or a fine grind is best. For the vacuum-type coffee maker, a very fine grind is recommended.

In order to be sure that the ground coffee is fresh, it is best to select that which is packed in vacuum cans or to have it ground for you. Ground coffee in such vacuum containers keeps fresh almost indefinitely until the can is opened. If a store sells large quantities of coffee, already ground coffee, packaged in bags or cartons, should also be very fresh.

Instant coffee, a powdered or granular form of coffee, is quickly dissolved in water. Like the ready-to-serve cocoa, instant coffee is convenient to have on hand.

Decaffeinated coffee is a special type of coffee from which 95 to 97 percent of the caffeine of the coffee beans has been removed before roasting. Such coffee is preferred to the usual type by people who do not care for the stimulating effect of the caffeine.

Buying tea. In buying tea, the first decision to be made is whether to choose black, green, or oolong tea. These are general types of teas. Their difference depends upon the manner in which the tea leaves of the plant are dried. Unless a family has a strong liking for one tea over another, a pleasing variety can be had by using all three types at different times.

The terms "orange pekoe" and "pekoe" often found on packages of black or fermented tea are not the names of types of tea but refer to the size and tenderness of the leaves used. Orange pekoe tea has no flavor of orange. However, some teas are flavored or scented and then are so marked. Jasmine tea is an example.

As with coffee, there is a choice to be made among the many brands of tea. Tea may be sold in bulk, but more often it is found in packages of different weights or in tea bags, which hold enough tea for making one or

● Beverages for a packed lunch may be kept either hot or cold in a thermos bottle.

more cups of beverage. There is an instant tea which dissolves in water and has no leaves to be disposed of. And there is an instant tea packaged with sugar and lemon flavoring that provides a quick and easy way of making the iced beverage.

Buying fruits and vegetables for beverages. The buying of fruits and vegetables has been discussed in Chapters 13 and 22. However, the special point to remember here is that in selecting fruits and vegetables for juice, smaller, less perfect products are satisfactory.

Buying fruit and vegetable juices. There is a wide choice of commercially prepared fruit and vegetable juices. These juices may be fresh, canned, or frozen. They include the juice of a single fruit or vegetable—for example, orange, prune, or tomato juice—or blends of two or more kinds—for example, pineapple-grapefruit juice or a mixture of vegetable juices. Not all juices are available in each form. As a rule the fresh and canned juices are ready to use as they come from the container, while the frozen products are concentrated and require some dilution after defrosting.

Care of Beverages in the Home

Milk, as you know, must be kept under refrigeration at all times as a precaution against spoilage. Also, its refreshing quality as a beverage is best when it is thoroughly chilled.

Fruit and vegetable juices, whether fresh, frozen, or canned, should be placed in the refrigerator if it is necessary to hold them after they are prepared for serving. This is important from a flavor viewpoint and because the juices retain vitamin C better when they are cold.

Cocoa, chocolate, coffee, and tea are all valued for their flavor, and this is best when the beverage is made from a product that retains all its original fine flavor. Since some of the materials contributing flavor can escape into the air, the containers holding these products should be kept tightly closed. Another precaution to take with coffee is that, unless it is vacuum-packed, it should be bought in small enough amounts to be used fairly soon. The day-to-day opening of a coffee container permits the escape of some of the flavor.

29

Appetizers

■APPETIZERS are flavorful, attractive, and often dainty foods. They are served either just before a luncheon or dinner or as a first course to stimulate the appetite for the meal which is to follow. Care must be taken in the selection of food for the appetizers, both in kind and amount, so they will sharpen, not dull, the appetite. Otherwise the purpose of appetizers is defeated.

Appetizers have other functions besides stimulating the appetite. They add a festive note to an occasion and help to create an atmosphere of leisure and relaxation for the rest of the meal. Small amounts of certain kinds of leftover foods may be used for appetizers, provided they are served in ways that are colorful and flavorful.

Types of Appetizers

Appetizers may be grouped into seven types: (1) fruits, (2) juices, (3) cocktails, (4) canapés, (5) spreads and dips, (6) hors d'oeuvres, and (7) relishes. As you learn more about each type, you will see what a large assortment of food there is from which to prepare these appetite teasers. (See chart on page 370.)

Food Value of Appetizers

Since there is some food value in all foods, appetizers naturally provide some nutrients. Protein, fat, carbohydrate, minerals, and vitamins are supplied in so far as these nutrients

●Hors d'oeuvres

●Spreads

●Dips

●An appetizer may be served in the living room before the meal.

● Fruit or vegetable juice

● Fruit or seafood cocktail

● An appetizer may be served as the first course of the meal.

● Relish tray

● Finger foods

● A tray of relishes or finger foods may be passed for appetizers with the meal.

are contained in the foods used for the appetizers. Foods that are low in energy value are best to use for appetizers, since too much energy-giving food served before a meal may destroy rather than enhance the appetite.

It is difficult to appraise appetite appeal. Yet we know that food which looks good, smells good, and tastes good, eaten in an atmosphere of leisure and freedom from tension, appeals to the appetite. On the other hand, it

IDEAS FOR APPETIZERS

Fruits: Grapefruit halves, either plain and served chilled or broiled and served hot, are easily prepared. Melon segments, balls, or rings, garnished with lemon or lime wedges for added tartness, are also easily prepared.

Juices: Fruit juices alone or blended and vegetable juices alone or blended give a variety of colors and flavors.

Cocktails: Mixed fresh fruits, cut in bite-sized pieces, make a cocktail that is tart in flavor and crisp in texture. Canned fruit cocktail requires no preparation but is somewhat sweet for an appetizer.

Seafoods like shrimp, crab meat, or lobster, covered with a piquant sauce, make more elaborate cocktails. Clams and oysters, served on the half shell and accompanied with a spicy sauce, are more simple.

Canapés: Canapés, or small open-faced sandwiches, made with a well-seasoned piquant spread are attractive appetizers. Canapés may be made of different bases, such as bread, toast, crackers, or pastry; cut in different shapes; and spread with different foods. A tray with several kinds of canapés passed as an accompaniment to a juice appetizer adds interest to the start of a meal.

Spreads and dips: Spreads are made of well-seasoned food mixtures similar in consistency to sandwich fillings. A spread placed in a dish surrounded by crisp crackers, melba toast, bread sticks, or tiny biscuit halves supplies the "makings" for do-it-yourself canapés. A small spreading knife accompanies the spread.

Dips are very soft spreads into which the accompanying cracker, melba toast, potato chip, or bread stick is dipped.

Hors d'oeuvres: Hors d'oeuvres are colorful, highly seasoned portions of food that are small enough to be eaten from the fingers or with a small pick. They often accompany a juice appetizer. Among popular hors d'oeuvres are buttered popcorn or puffed cereals, pieces of sharp cheese or cream cheese balls dipped in chopped chives or nuts, olives rolled in bacon, tiny highly seasoned meat balls, little sausages or pieces of wieners, quarters of deviled eggs, smoked oysters, and shrimp with a suitable dressing. Tiny cream puffs and bite-sized biscuits filled with a delicately seasoned seafood, such as crab meat or shrimp, are also served as hors d'oeuvres.

Relishes: Olives, pickles, and crisp raw vegetables, such as radishes, celery, green onions, cauliflowerets, and carrot or cucumber strips, are simple but flavorful appetizers. They may be served with a juice or be used as a garnish for a tray of canapés or hors d'oeuvres. Small salads made of crisp greens and a tart dressing are refreshing as an appetizer for a summertime meal.

PREPARING RAW VEGETABLES ATTRACTIVELY

● To make carrot curls, remove the skin and cut carrots into paper-thin strips with a rotary blade peeler. Then roll up each strip, fasten with a toothpick, and chill in a bowl of ice water.

● Before slicing a cucumber, score it lengthwise all around with a fork. Cut the slices thin and chill.

● Radishes can be cut into attractive shapes. In making radish roses, remove the root end but leave a little of the stem. Place cut radishes in ice water to open.

All photos courtesy Wesson Oil Company

is known that food eaten under tension or in a hurry and food that looks dull, uninteresting, and unattractive can often destroy even a keen appetite.

Ways to Serve Appetizers

The success or failure of food appeal may depend on the way the food is served. It is best to keep appetizers simple in content and form, but make them as attractive and interesting as possible. They may be served either in the living room or at the table.

In the living room. Serving appetizers in the living room before a meal is a pleasant custom. Whatever is chosen must be of a sort that is easy to serve and to eat away from the table, such as fruit and vegetable juices with a suitable accompaniment. When guests are present, the serving of appetizers in the living room gives the hostess a chance to slip away to add any final touches either in the dining room or kitchen. Perhaps this interlude will give her enough time to get the main course on the table so that all will be at its very best when family and guests assemble.

The custom of serving appetizers in the living room has other advantages also. It brings the family members together for a bit of leisure and creates a festive mood. If there are guests, the before-meal period helps to make the guests feel at home.

At the table. Appetizers may be served at the table as a first course at either lunch or dinner. For example, several small hors d'oeuvres, pieces of smoked fish, a sardine, and a deviled egg with a relish of sliced pickled beets may be served together on a plate. Oysters or clams on the half shell are usually served on a bed of cracked ice, with a cocktail sauce in a small container in the center of the plate. Fruit cocktail or seafood cocktail in a sherbet glass is also suitable. A salad, too, may be served as a first course, and relishes, served along with the soup course, can be enjoyed right through the main course of the meal.

Garnishes

Both garnishes and appetizers should be colorful. Appetizers are served separately, while garnishes are served with a food for appearance only, but they may be eaten if desired. In addition to being colorful and edible, garnishes add flavor and texture contrast. They may be as simple as a sprinkling of chopped chives on cottage cheese or a sprig of parsley added to a small ball of cream cheese. Bits of colorful pimiento can easily be added to decorate a cracker which has been spread with a drab-colored fish paste. A few leaves of mint on a fruit cup or a green or red maraschino cherry on half a grapefruit adds both color and flavor. Softened cream cheese or fish pastes "piped" around open-faced sandwiches, or canapés, give a fancy touch. Cucumbers may be sliced with the well-washed skin left on for color harmony, and before slicing, they may be fluted with a fork.

30

Soups

■ SOUP MAKING should not be considered a simple procedure. To make soup with just the right flavor and other quality characteristics takes skill. Soup is served in two ways at meals. It may be served in place of or in addition to an appetizer to introduce the meal, or it may be served as the main course or part of the main course.

Types of Soups

There are two general types of soups: (1) soup made with a stock base of meat, chicken, or fish; and (2) soup made with a milk base. When a milk-base soup contains finely strained, puréed vegetables or certain types of puréed fish, it is a cream soup. When it contains, instead, pieces of vegetable or fish, it is a chowder or stew.

Fruit soups are an exception to these two general types. They are made of one kind of fruit or of several kinds of fruit purées mixed together, usually thickened and served cold.

Stock-base Soups

These soups are made by simmering the meat, bones, and trimmings of beef, veal, chicken, or fish in water for several hours. The resulting liquid is meat or fish stock. When made from beef, the stock is rich brown in color, and when made from veal, chicken, or fish, the stock is light in color.

Clear soups are usually made from a stock that has been clarified, or cleared, after it is strained away from the solid ingredients. Such soups are called either "bouillon" or "consommé." These clear soups are sometimes served with a few finely diced vegetables, a few fine noodles, or a little rice, barley, or alphabet macaroni in them.

Soups are of two general types—stock-base soups and milk-base soups. Chicken noodle soup (left) and jellied consommé (right) are stock soups. The other two soups at the right are milk-base, or cream, soups.

Jellied soups are made from a concentrated beef, veal, or chicken stock which has been clarified and then chilled until it becomes quite firm and jellylike. The stock is made concentrated by prolonging the cooking in the preparation of the stock so as to extract as much gelatin as possible from the bones and trimmings. Commercial jellied soups, as a rule, contain added gelatin.

Broth is also made from a stock, and although it has been strained, it has not been clarified, as are bouillon and consommé. Broths are either plain—that is, just the stock as strained from the meat, bones, and trimmings—or they may contain small pieces of meat or some kind of cereal, added after straining. Barley, rice, noodles, alphabets, or vermicelli are the cereals commonly used.

Milk-base Soups

These soups include cream soups (cream of tomato soup), chowders (clam or vegetable chowder), and stews (oyster stew).

Cream soups. In cream soups the milk is usually made into a cream sauce. The vegetables or fish for the soup are puréed—that is, the cooked vegetables or fish are put through a sieve. For this reason, cream soups are sometimes referred to as "purées." The term is adapted from the French.

Some cream soups are called "bisques." This term once meant a special type of soup made of shellfish, but it is now used for any kind of rich cream soup.

Chowders and stews. In contrast to cream soups, the milk in chowders and stews is not usually thickened, and the vegetables and fish are in small pieces. Corn, potato, and fish chowders are familiar examples. Fish chowders always contain small pieces of several different vegetables as well as fish. As in other instances, there are exceptions to the rules. There are two entirely different kinds of clam chowder with enthusiasts for each: Boston clam chowder, which is made with the usual milk base, and Manhattan clam chowder, which is made with water instead of milk and has tomatoes as an important ingredient.

A stew is similar to a chowder, but it has fewer ingredients in the milk—usually only oysters, clams, shrimp, or lobster.

Fruit Soups

Fruit soups are not as familiar to people in Canada as are the kinds of soups discussed above, but it is worthwhile to become acquainted with them for they are appetizing and flavorful. Fruit soups may be made from one or more kinds of fruit—fresh, canned, or dried. The fruit may be whole or puréed, depending on the country in which the soup had its origin. Most fruit soups are served cold, although some are served hot.

Food Value of Soups

The food value of soups depends on the type and the individual foods that are used in making them. Clear soups and broths cannot be counted on for many or any of the nutrients. They supply liquid and are served mainly for their appetite-contributing qualities. Cream soups are often served as a prelude to a light meal. They can be counted on for part of the day's total milk requirement. For anyone in the family who is reluctant to drink milk, a cream soup can be one source for the daily milk requirement. Cream soups are the most nutritious of all soups except the hearty chowders. The quantity of vegetable or fish purée that is used in cream soups is usually about equal to the milk and therefore contributes to the nutritive value.

Soups that are used as the main course or as part of it should make a significant contribution to the day's diet. The various kinds of milk-base soups, if served in generous portions, will meet this requirement. This is true also of chicken broth with noodles, Scotch broth with small pieces of meat and rich with barley, and vegetable soup made with a broth and thick with many kinds of vegetables.

Ways to Serve Soups

Part of the stimulating quality of hot soups lies in their warmth as well as in their flavor. Soups that are intended to be served hot should be very hot, and serving them in heated soup dishes will help to keep them hot. On the other hand, soups that are to be served jellied or cold are unappetizing unless they are well chilled.

With garnishes. A small amount of garnish adds to the attractiveness or eye appeal of soups. Even such a simple garnish as a thin slice of lemon on a clear stock-base soup adds both color and flavor. A sprinkling of chopped chives, parsley, water cress, or other crispy greens on the top of soups is both pretty and flavorful. A few croutons give a texture contrast. On a cream soup a small amount of whipped cream makes the soup more attractive and, on such a soup as cream of tomato, it provides a color contrast.

There are other kinds of foods that, added to soups as a garnish, contribute also to their heartiness. Noodles, slices of wieners, or grated cheese may be a garnish, or they may change a light soup to a hearty one. Dumplings, when tiny, can be considered a garnish. If large, the dumplings become part of a soup to be served as the main course or part of it.

With accompaniments. It is customary to serve a first-course soup with an accompaniment. Like garnishes, accompaniments should have eye appeal, and many of them will be liked for their texture contrast. Croutons can be served as an accompaniment instead of as a garnish. Plain or buttered crackers that have been sprinkled with paprika and toasted or melba toast may be served with soups.

Principles of Preparation of Soups

Since soups are relished for their flavor, the foods used in making them should be treated in such a way that their flavor-giving substances go into the liquid. At the same time,

⬤ The basic ingredient for a stock soup is meat, poultry, or fish (left). The basic ingredient for a cream soup is milk (right).

the nutrients in the foods will dissolve into the soups. The principles of soup making, therefore, are just the opposite of those used in the preparation of the same foods where flavor and nutritive values should be left in the food.

Stock-base Soups

In making soups of this type, the largest amount of flavoring and nutritive substances will be extracted if the water comes into contact with many surfaces of the food. For this reason, any bones used must be cracked in several places. Meat, poultry, or fish and any vegetables need to be cut into small pieces. As a further aid to dissolving substances from all the ingredients, cold water must be used. The cold water with the ingredients is brought very slowly to the simmering point and simmered for several hours. Meat is sometimes browned in hot fat to develop greater flavor before it is covered with the water.

After the simmering is finished, the liquid is strained from the solid material to make a broth. If, instead, it is to be served as a clear

soup, the broth must be clarified. To accomplish this, a slightly beaten egg white and the shell are added to the cooled broth and brought slowly to the boiling point with constant stirring. As the egg protein coagulates, the solid particles become entangled in it and can be removed by straining. Sometimes sufficient gelatin dissolves from the meat bones so the clear broth solidifies when chilled to make a jellied soup.

Milk-base Soups

There are two principles to be kept in mind when making a cream soup. One of these is the principle of starch cookery, since the flour used in thickening the soup has a high starch content. (See page 221 for the principle of starch cookery.) The second principle involves vegetable cookery, because puréed vegetables are used in some cream soups. The vegetables should be cooked in such a way as to retain their flavor and nutritive value. (See page 302 for the principles of vegetable cookery.) Then these vegetables, when puréed and added to the cream-sauce base, will carry their own good flavor and nutrients into the soup.

In making a chowder, the vegetables or pieces of fish are usually cooked in the milk and, therefore, all the nutrients and flavoring materials are kept in the soup. In many chowders increased flavor is obtained by browning some of the cut-up vegetables.

Buying Soups

Homemade soups are well worth making, even though there are a number of ingredients to prepare and a knowledge of seasonings is needed. Good homemade soups are really simple to make, but they require either a fairly long period of time or constant attention, depending on the type. In contrast, there are commercial soups in several forms and of many varieties that require a minimum of preparation: Canned soups, frozen soups, meat extracts, and dehydrated soups are all available.

Buying ingredients for home-prepared soups. When buying the ingredients for a meat stock, a soup bone with some meat on it is the best choice. If the meat dealer cracks the bone in several places, more flavor can be extracted. It is a good plan to ask for the bones and trimmings from steaks and from beef and veal roasts when buying these cuts because they can be used for making a meat stock. For making a chicken stock, a mature chicken will give a more flavorful stock than a younger chicken.

As a soup-making aid, several kinds of dried vegetables or ready-cleaned fresh vegetables, packaged together in a cellophane bag, are available in stores. Their use eliminates the need to buy the many different vegetables needed in making soups and saves time in preparation.

Buying canned soups. Ready-to-serve and condensed canned soups are available in both stock and cream-soup varieties. Ready-to-serve canned soups are heated as they come

Courtesy Kellogg Company

● Concentrated cream soups are useful for creamed dishes (above) and as sauces (below).

Courtesy Campbell Soup Company

377

At formal dinners, a clear soup is frequently served as a first course. Clear soups served in cups with handles, such as these, may be sipped from the cup.

from the can. These full-strength canned soups contain a high percentage of water. In the case of condensed soups, however, some of the water has been removed in processing. Therefore, some liquid must be added before heating them.

When you buy canned soups, you should read the labels to learn whether the soups are the ready-to-serve or the condensed kind. Since you will have to add a liquid to a condensed soup, you will get more servings from a can of condensed soup than from a can of the same size of the ready-to-serve type.

When you buy a jellied soup, you should look at the label to be sure gelatin is listed as an ingredient.

Another point to keep in mind when buying canned soups is that the condensed kinds are convenient for using in sauces, gravies, and casserole dishes right from the can, with the appropriate amount of liquid added to give a suitable consistency. The ready-to-serve soups cannot be used in these ways.

Buying frozen soups. Also available are frozen condensed soups in cans which must be kept frozen until ready to use. Since these are condensed soups, they are prepared in the same way as the unfrozen condensed soups.

Buying meat extracts and dehydrated soups. Meat extracts are designed primarily for making soups when time is limited, for a cup of broth or consommé may be made merely by dissolving the cube of extract in boiling water. They have excellent keeping qualities and are convenient for emergency use. In addition to their use for making soups, they may be used to add flavor to casserole dishes, gravies, and sauces, as well as to other soups.

Like canned soups, dehydrated soups of both stock base and milk base are available. They require the addition of water or water and milk and a short cooking period. These soups have good keeping quality, and having a supply of them on hand adds variety to the choice of easily prepared soups.

31

Salads and Salad Dressings

IT IS difficult if not almost impossible to define a salad because there are exceptions to every definition. There are different types of salads and different kinds of each type. The purpose of serving salads in meals is to bring zest to meals by contributing variety and flavor and by giving contrasts in color and texture. Salads also contribute to the nutritive value of meals.

Types of Salads

There are several types of salads. Those made only of greens are called "green salads." In some salads, the salad greens form a background for other foods. These salads are usually designated according to the food used in them. Fruits, vegetables, meat, poultry, fish, or eggs, used alone or mixed with such other foods as celery, are examples. Also, there are gelatin salads, sometimes called "molded salads," frozen salads, and hot salads.

Green salads. Lettuce of various kinds, endive, water cress, escarole, and celery cabbage are commonly called salad greens. Although all of them are called "greens," they vary in shade from yellowish-green to dark green. When several of these salad greens are used together in one salad, the various shades are attractive. Several different greens are frequently torn apart, mixed in a large bowl, and tossed gently with a flavorful dressing until the leaves are coated with it. This makes a tossed salad. Sometimes small strips of cooked

379

TYPES OF SALADS

● Tossed green salad

● Mixed fruit salad

● Molded gelatin salad

● Main-dish chicken salad

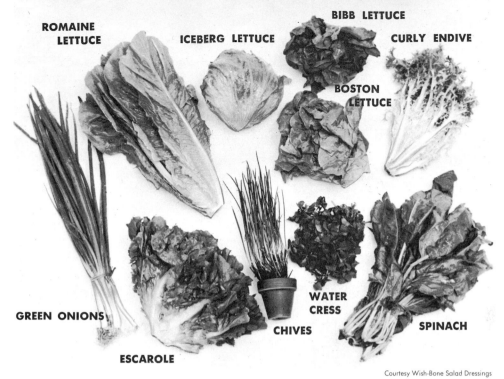

ROMAINE LETTUCE

ICEBERG LETTUCE

BIBB LETTUCE

CURLY ENDIVE

BOSTON LETTUCE

GREEN ONIONS

ESCAROLE

CHIVES

WATER CRESS

SPINACH

● Any of the leafy greens may be used alone or mixed with several others in a salad. Green onions and chives provide added flavor.

meat, poultry, bits of crisp bacon, or cheese are added to make a more substantial salad than one of all greens.

Fruit salads. Either one particular kind of fruit or a number of kinds arranged on salad greens makes a popular and eye-appealing salad. Fruit salads may be made of fresh, frozen, canned, or dried fruits. Only fruits that do not become soft or mushy should be used. Such small fruits as berries or sweet pitted cherries may be used whole, while large fruits such as peaches and pears are often cut into halves or sliced. Apples and bananas are sliced, and grapefruit and oranges are cut into slices or sections. Sometimes large fruit is cut into small pieces, especially if several kinds are to be mixed together in one salad.

Vegetable salads. A wide variety of vegetable choices is available to give not only flavor and texture differences to vegetable salads but many color combinations as well.

Sometimes raw vegetables are used and sometimes cooked vegetables, or both raw and cooked vegetables may be used together. In addition to salad greens, raw tomatoes, cabbage, cucumbers, green peppers, radishes, and celery are frequently used. There are other raw vegetables, used less often perhaps, that are equally good, such as pieces of cauliflower, white turnip, red cabbage, and carrot. When green cabbage is used alone with a cream dressing, it is called "cole slaw" and is usually served without a salad green as a background.

Meat, fish, poultry, and egg salads. When meat, fish, poultry, or hard-cooked eggs are arranged on greens, the salad is of the hearty type. Cut celery is often mixed with pieces of these foods for crispness. Pieces of a cooked vegetable may also be included in the salad for color and flavor. Sliced hard-cooked eggs are sometimes used alone on salad greens or diced and mixed with vegetables. When pieces

381

of meat, fish, or poultry are used in salads, the pieces should be large enough to be identified.

Gelatin salads. Fruit and vegetable juices make attractive gelatin or molded salads. Pieces of different foods—for example, fruits, vegetables, or meats—can be folded into the gelatin liquid as it begins to thicken. This makes it possible to have a great variety of molded gelatin salads.

Frozen salads. Frozen salads may be made with a base of whipped cream and mayonnaise into which cut fruits, vegetables, or meats are added. Or the base may be of gelatin into which any one of these ingredients, together with mayonnaise, whipped cream, or cream cheese, is stirred. Frozen salads, usually richer than other types of salads, are limited in use.

Hot salads. Wilted lettuce, hot cole slaw, and hot potato salad are less popular than cold, crisp salads because of their lack of texture contrast with other foods in the meal, but they are served for variety in flavor and in certain combinations with other foods in the menu.

Food Value of Salads

The food value of salads depends on the foods in them and on the type and amount of salad dressing served with them. However, the practice of including fresh raw fruit and vegetable salads almost every day in one or two meals helps to ensure a liberal supply of vitamins and minerals in the diet.

Salad greens. Salad greens are low in calories but rich in vitamins and minerals. In general, the very deep-green leaves, such as escarole, water cress, and green lettuce, are of great value for their contribution of vitamin A, riboflavin, and iron to the diet. Another dietary asset of salad greens is that they are made up of comparatively large amounts of cellulose, which aids digestion.

Other ingredients. Below are three examples of the ways in which ingredients, other than salad greens, affect the food value of salads: (1) A salad using meat, fish, poultry, or eggs will supply some protein; (2) one of tomatoes, green pepper, raw cabbage, or cauliflower will add vitamin C; and (3) a dressing on a salad will increase the energy value in proportion to the amount of oil used in making the dressing and the amount used on the salad. You will find additional information on the food value of the different foods used in salads in the chapters in Part IV that deal with each type of food.

Uses of Salads

The place of salads at lunch, supper, or dinner varies. Salads may be served as an appetizer course at the start of the meal, as a main course, as an accompaniment to the main course, after the main course, or as a dessert. There are many kinds of salads suitable for serving at any of these times. Salads may be served at the table from a large bowl or platter, or each salad may be arranged on an individual plate. The manner chosen for serving them will depend on the menu, the time available for preparation, and individual preference.

As an appetizer. It is a custom in some families and in many restaurants to serve a light salad with a tangy dressing at the beginning of a meal to stimulate the appetite. A tossed green salad with a spicy French dressing is especially good for this purpose. Care should be taken so that neither the amount served nor the ingredients selected for making it are appetite-satisfying.

As a main course. Hearty and substantial salads are appropriate for the main course at lunch or supper. Those made of meat, fish, poultry, or hard-cooked eggs are examples of hearty salads. Less hearty, but also appropriate, are salads made of several kinds of fruits or vegetables. The addition of nuts or cheese helps to make such salads more satisfying for a main course. The portions of a main-

Courtesy Best Foods, Inc.

● Cole slaw, which consists of shredded cabbage and a cream dressing, is a somewhat different version of a salad. It is particularly valuable because raw cabbage has such a high content of vitamin C.

course salad are usually larger than the portions of a salad that is used as an appetizer or as an accompaniment to the main course.

As an accompaniment. Any type except a very hearty salad is suitable to serve as an accompaniment to a main course. The type will depend on the menu, but unless the meal is light, the portions should be relatively small. Often a tossed salad or one made of either raw or cooked vegetables may take the place of one of the vegetables in the meal.

As a separate course. The same type of salad that is used as an accompaniment to the main course of a meal is suitable for serving as a separate course following the main course. A cracker, a piece of melba toast, or cheese

straws make a pleasing accompaniment to the salad served this way.

As a dessert. Salads containing fruit are the most appropriate ones for dessert. Fruit salads may be made of one kind of fruit only, as half a pear, or they may be made by arranging several kinds of fruit on a plate. Fruit molded in gelatin and frozen fruit salads with a whipped cream base are the most elaborate of the dessert salads.

Principles of Preparation of Salads

There are three important principles to remember in salad making: A salad should be artistic both in color and in arrangement, it should be crisp in texture, and it should be so fresh that the original food value of all ingredients is retained.

Color and arrangement of salads are important from an aesthetic viewpoint. Fresh, crisp greens give the brightest colors. Other colors depend on the ingredients used, and here reliance rests on the salad maker. Whatever the selection, the colors should give a harmonious appearance.

Arrangement, like color, is a matter of individual preference. In general, a simple arrangement is best, and good taste dictates that salads should look like food rather than be designed as something fancy or inedible. When the ingredients in salads are arranged to give height, the effect is usually more pleasing than when the ingredients are arranged flat on the plates. Also, the ingredients should not extend onto the rims of the plates.

Texture contrast—that is, crispness and hardness as contrasted to the softness of other foods—depends, like their food value, on the freshness of the salad materials. This is especially true of salad greens and of raw vegetables and fruits, for it is only when these ingredients are fresh that they will be crisp and firm.

Just as freshness is important to the color and to the texture of a salad, freshness is neces-

383

Courtesy Wesson Oil Company

● To loosen the skin of a tomato so that it can be peeled easily for a salad, rotate the tomato slowly over heat.

sary if the salad is to have good food value. Freshness is indicated by a crisp texture and a bright color. Wilted greens are likely to have lost a large amount of their original vitamin A. All raw vegetables as well as the greens used in a salad should be fresh, and fruits must not be overripe.

Buying Salad Greens

There are three types of head lettuce commonly found in markets: (1) iceberg lettuce, a crisp head type that is large in size, compact, and firm, with leaves ranging from pale green to white in color; (2) Boston lettuce and bibb lettuce, which are also lettuce of the head type but smaller and less firm than iceberg, with leaves that are smoother, greener, and more tender; and (3) romaine or cos lettuce, a very loose, elongated head, with rather coarse leaves, shading from dark-green outer leaves to light-green inner leaves.

In buying lettuce, select heads that have a crisp, fresh appearance. Do not select lettuce that shows any signs of rust or decay. However, outside leaves can be broken, bruised, or

slightly wilted without lowering the quality of the head, but too many such leaves are wasteful. The heads of iceberg lettuce should be very compact and those of Boston and bibb lettuce fairly firm. The leaves in heads of romaine are folded only loosely so that even the inner part of the heads may be examined for defects.

Other greens include chard, chicory, spinach, water cress, dandelions, endive, and escarole. These greens are best when the plants are young. At that time the leaves will have a fresh appearance and a bright-green color.

Care of Salad Greens in the Home

Salad greens are high on the list of perishable foods. In the interval between the time these foods are bought and used, they require special care if they are to maintain their original good quality. Some of the soil in which the greens are grown clings to the leaves and stalks and may be found in the wrinkles of curled leaves and in the ridges of celery stalks. Greens must therefore be thoroughly washed to remove all dirt and grit. If celery is difficult to clean, a stiff brush will help. Washed greens may be placed in a refrigerator hydrator or wrapped in some kind of moisture-resistant material and refrigerated.

Salad Dressings

Most salads are prepared with a salad dressing, although sometimes a fruit salad, especially when it is an arranged fruit plate, is served without one. Tomatoes and cucumbers may be "dressed" with vinegar rather than with a salad dressing. Wilted lettuce is made with seasoned hot vinegar and bacon fat—a modified type of dressing. Whatever the dressing, it should give an added zest to the salad.

There are three basic types of salad dressings—French, mayonnaise, and cooked-base dressings. With these basic types and the many variations of seasonings for each, a

PREPARING TOMATOES FOR STUFFING

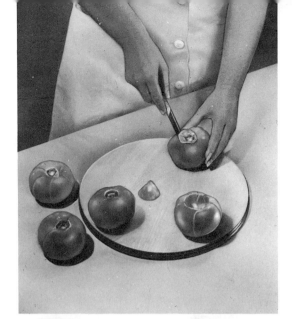

● 1. Cut around the stem of each tomato, and remove the stem.

● 2. Slice the tomato into sections, but leave the sections joined at the bottom.

● 3. Loosen the sections, and place a suitable filling in the cavity.

All photos courtesy Wesson Oil Company

CARE OF SALAD GREENS

● Left: Wash greens under cold running water. Center: Dry them carefully with a towel. Right: Store in a plastic bag in the refrigerator.

● Left: Remove the core from head lettuce. Center: Wash the lettuce under cold running water. Right: Store in the hydrator of the refrigerator.

● Left: Wash stalks of celery under cold running water. Center: Dry the celery with a clean towel. Right: Store in the hydrator of the refrigerator.

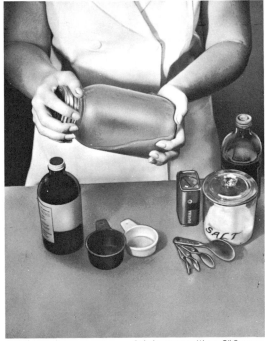

● To make a French dressing, put all the ingredients in a bowl and beat (left) or put in a jar and shake (right). (See recipe on page 504.)

dressing is always available to suit the salad. There is a Spanish proverb which states that the best recipe for a salad dressing calls for a quartet to compose it—"a spendthrift for oil; a miser for vinegar; a counsellor for salt; and a mad-man for mixing." Seasonings such as cayenne and garlic can ruin the flavor of a salad when overused.

French dressing. A typical French dressing is an emulsion of salad oil, vinegar or lemon juice, and seasonings. (See page 40.) The oil and acid separate on standing. Therefore, it is convenient to make this type of dressing in a jar with a tight-fitting cover so that it can be shaken to re-form the emulsion before it is used.

There are commercial French dressings available on the market in many varieties of flavor. According to law, these dressings must contain at least 35 percent oil. Like the French dressings made at home, some of the commercial dressings separate on standing. There are others, however, that do not have this tendency because they contain an ingredient called an "emulsifying agent." This ingredient keeps the oil and vinegar or lemon juice permanently mixed. When such an ingredient is present, it is stated on the jar label.

Mayonnaise dressing. As for a French dressing, a salad oil, vinegar or lemon juice, and seasonings are used to make mayonnaise dressing; but the ingredients are beaten slowly and alternately into egg yolk to form a permanent emulsion—that is, one which does not separate. The addition of various ingredients and seasonings are used to make many favorite dressings with mayonnaise as a base. For example, Russian dressing is made by the addition of chili sauce, chopped onion, and chopped green pepper to mayonnaise, while

387

● Mayonnaise is more difficult to make than French dressing (see recipe on page 503), but it is preferred by many for chicken salad, fruit salad, or gelatin salads.

Thousand Island dressing is made by the addition of chili sauce, sweet pickle relish, and chopped hard-cooked eggs. For a fruit salad, whipped cream is a good addition to mayonnaise dressing.

If you do not care to make mayonnaise dressing yourself, you will find many brands on the market. However, you should read the labels very carefully. A real mayonnaise dressing will be labeled "mayonnaise" and will have, according to law, at least 65 percent oil in it. In contrast to this, there is a type of dressing containing less oil that is called "salad dressing." Such a dressing is good to use occasionally and will cost less than a true mayonnaise dressing.

Cooked-base dressing. Vinegar, thickened with flour or cornstarch, and sometimes with egg yolk as well, is used to make a cooked-base salad dressing. Seasonings are added to the thickened base and, if desired, whipped cream, sour cream, or salad oil may also be added. Cooked dressings provide variety and are less rich than French and mayonnaise dressings. There are a number of brands of cooked dressings on the market from which to make a selection for those who do not wish to make a dressing from the basic ingredients.

32

Desserts

■ DESSERTS are sweet foods that are appropriate for serving at the end of lunch or dinner. Although desserts are not essential, they have a definite place in meal patterns, since a sweet food at the end of a meal gives a sense of satisfaction—a sense of being well fed. Sweetness is the only common characteristic of all desserts. In other respects, desserts are different because of differences in the ingredients used in them and in the methods of preparing them. Besides sugar, however, some one ingredient is common to a number of different desserts. This fact makes it possible to group desserts into five types or classes as follows: fruit desserts; milk desserts; gelatin desserts; biscuit, cake, and pastry desserts; and frozen desserts. Such a grouping is convenient, since a class to which a dessert belongs indi-

cates the principle on which its preparation is based. Another advantage of this grouping is in meal planning, since the dessert should be selected in relation to the other foods in the meal. When the main course is rich or hearty, a simple light dessert is a welcome climax. When, instead, the main course is light, a more elaborate and filling dessert is appropriate. For example, you may prefer a fruit, a gelatin, or a frozen dessert after a hearty dinner. Also, you will find a fruit dessert more appropriate than a milk dessert such as a milk-rich custard or rice pudding if the meal begins with a cream soup or has creamed chicken as the main course. On the other hand, the custard or rice pudding is an appropriate dessert to end a meal featuring a salad or a broiled meat.

● A cheese tray with fresh fruit at the end of a meal not only is satisfying but has excellent food value.

Fruit Desserts

Fruit desserts are among the most simple of all desserts to serve, and they are easy to prepare. They are a good choice for a summertime meal or for a meal that is rich and hearty. Fresh fruits, either raw or cooked, are always acceptable, but canned and frozen fruits and cooked dried fruits are equally good.

Fresh fruits. A juicy raw fruit, well chilled, is refreshing and appetizing and has a natural sweet flavor. Oranges, grapefruit, apples, peaches, pears, grapes, berries of all kinds, and melons of many varieties are easily obtainable in most parts of the country when they are in season. Some people consider that the natural sweetness of fruit is most appealing, while others like to add sugar. For variety, several different fruits, cut in small pieces, may be mixed together to make a fruit cup.

To give further variety in using fresh fruit, the fruit may be cooked. Then appearance,

flavor, and texture are all changed. A pan full of apples or pears can be baked to make dessert for several meals. Fruit sauces are convenient too, and for these apples are a favorite fruit. A dish of applesauce accompanied by molasses cookies or spice cookies makes a good dessert. Stewing is another way of cooking apples, peaches, plums, pears, and cherries. In making a sauce, the fruit is completely mashed, while in stewing, each piece of fruit retains almost its original shape. A bit of spice or small pieces of crystallized ginger added to stewed fruit will give a subtle flavor. Some fruits may be broiled and used as dessert, but except for grapefruit, broiled fruit is more often used as an accompaniment to the main course of a meal. You will find the principles of cooking fruit in Chapter 13, "Fruits," pages 209 and 210.

Canned and frozen fruits. These are forms of fruits that may be served at any time, but they are especially handy when fresh fruits are out of season or for the emergency shelf. With a supply of several varieties of each form on hand, attractive desserts may be prepared quickly and with little effort. Some canned and frozen fruits are unsweetened, but for dessert, those that are packed in sugar syrup are more suitable. Canned fruits are refreshing if they are well chilled before they are served.

Frozen fruits must be defrosted, either completely or with some bits of ice still remaining, as desired. If they are defrosted in the refrigerator, the thawing is more even throughout the whole mass of fruit. It is important to serve frozen fruits as soon as they are defrosted, for they tend to darken on standing.

Dried fruits. Dried fruits are more concentrated in flavor than fresh fruits because they contain so little water. This pronounced flavor makes many kinds of dried fruits desirable for dessert, either when served alone or used as an ingredient in a recipe. Several kinds of cooked dried fruits mixed together and served as a dessert is known as a "compote."

FRUIT DESSERTS

Courtesy Florida Citrus Commission

A. Devaney, Inc.

● Whether raw or cooked, fruit desserts can be served plain or arranged more elaborately and served with a sauce or whipped cream.

Milk Desserts

Desserts are among the many kinds of dishes in which milk is an important ingredient. In fact, milk desserts provide a way to help you meet the total amount of milk recommended for your daily diet. (See Chapter 2, "Planning Meals for Health," page 32.) Milk desserts, as a rule, have a thick consistency. The ingredient used to make the milk thick is a basis for classifying the different kinds of milk desserts. Very often milk desserts are called "puddings."

Rennet pudding. This is a very simple milk dessert in which the enzyme rennin in tablet form is used to make milk—which has been sweetened, flavored, and warmed—thicken or clot into a smooth, velvety mass. (See Chapter 15, "Milk," pages 230 and 231.) Rennet

● Milk desserts are thickened with either cornstarch, rennin, eggs, or cereal.

Courtesy Corn Products Company

MILK DESSERTS

pudding is an easily prepared dessert and has a mild flavor. The flavor can be varied by using different flavorings, such as vanilla, grated orange and lemon rind, or some spice. Rennet pudding mixes are available. These contain powdered rennin, sugar, and flavoring and need only to be stirred into warm milk for easy preparation.

Milk and cereal desserts. Cornstarch and flour as well as cereal products like rice, farina, and corn meal contain a fairly large proportion of starch. The starch is the ingredient responsible for the thick and creamy consistency of the milk-cereal desserts. The principle of using starch as a thickening material is described in Chapter 14, "Grains and Their Products," pages 221 to 223.

Rice, farina, and corn-meal puddings may be plain, or they can be dressed up with raisins, dates, or some other dried fruit to make even more delicious and nutritious desserts. Johnny Cake, an Eastern Canadian dessert, is made from corn meal, and usually served with maple syrup.

Cornstarch puddings are usually made with cornstarch, but flour can be used instead to thicken the milk. Vanilla, chocolate, caramel, and maple are popular flavorings for these puddings.

Milk and egg desserts. These desserts, in which the milk is thickened with egg, are called "custards." The principle involved here is described in the discussion of egg cookery in Chapter 16, "Eggs," pages 237 to 240. To provide variety, each kind of custard may be flavored differently and served in different ways. For example, one kind of soft custard that can be made is floating island. For this, only the egg yolks are used in the custard. The egg whites are used in the meringue, which is dotted over the custard in small mounds or "islands." The contrast in color of the white meringue and the yellow, chocolate, or caramel color of the custard adds to the attractiveness of the dessert.

For variety in baked custards, a baked fruit custard can be made by pouring an uncooked custard mixture over fruit in the bottom of a baking dish. Placing a little caramel syrup in the bottom of an individual baking dish before pouring in the custard mixture gives another variation. After the custard has been baked and chilled, it can be turned out from the baking dish. The caramel syrup will then flow over it as a sauce.

Milk, cereal, and egg desserts. In these milk desserts both a cereal product and eggs are used to provide their thick consistency. Since the cereal takes the place of some of the eggs used, these desserts are considered modified custards. Bread pudding, which resembles a baked custard, and tapioca cream pudding, which is like a soft custard, are examples of this kind of dessert.

In bread pudding the soft bread crumbs absorb the milk and therefore give some thickening effect in addition to that caused by the eggs. Because of the bread crumbs, a bread pudding is not quite so smooth and velvety in consistency as a baked custard.

In making tapioca pudding, two principles are involved—starch cookery and egg cookery. Tapioca contains starch and, like all starchy foods, needs a fairly high temperature to make the starch particles swell. To accomplish this, tapioca is cooked with milk until the tapioca is clear. When the tapioca is clear, the starch is cooked. Then the slightly thickened tapioca-milk mixture is blended slowly with the eggs and the sugar, which have been beaten together; and the cooking is continued over hot, but not boiling, water, so that as the egg protein coagulates, the thickening action is completed.

Gelatin Desserts

Gelatin desserts are many and varied. They range from a simple fruit gelatin to an elaborate jelly filled with beaten egg whites and whipped cream. As a rule, gelatin desserts are molded in a fancy dish or mold, and they should be firm enough to hold the shape of the dish if turned from it for serving.

The thickening of liquids by means of gelatin is the principle followed in making all gelatin desserts. This principle has been explained in Chapter 19, "Meats," page 277. In general, the principle first involves the hydrating of the dry gelatin—that is, the combining of the dry gelatin with a small amount of cold water. The hydrated gelatin is then dissolved in a hot liquid, and the hot liquid gelatin is chilled. As it chills, it becomes firm.

The wide variety in gelatin desserts is obtained by the use of different liquids to dissolve the hydrated gelatin, by the different ways of treating the liquid gelatin as it cools, and by the addition of different ingredients to the liquid gelatin. These variations are described here.

Plain gelatin desserts. These are usually made with a fruit juice, which if strained, will make the finished jelly clear and sparkling. As a variation, a plain gelatin jelly may have pieces of fruit in it. The fruit is added to the liquid gelatin when the gelatin becomes slightly thick and just before it is poured into the dish for molding.

Whips. Whips are plain gelatin desserts that are fluffy in appearance. They are made by beating the liquid gelatin when it becomes slightly thick with a rotary beater so that air is held in the gelatin.

Sponges or snows. This type of gelatin dessert has a spongelike quality. Unbeaten egg white is added to the slightly thickened liquid gelatin, and this is beaten with a rotary beater until the mixture holds its shape when it is poured into the mold or serving dish.

Custard-base gelatin desserts. These gelatin desserts are similar to the snows, but they have a smoother and more compact texture. Either hot milk or hot soft custard is used to dissolve the hydrated gelatin. When this mixture becomes slightly thickened, it is blended with beaten egg white or a meringue.

Whipped-cream gelatin desserts. These are the most elaborate of all gelatin desserts. They are spongelike and velvety in texture. In making them, either whipped cream and beaten egg white or whipped cream alone is folded into a slightly thickened plain or custard gelatin.

Packaged gelatin desserts. All the gelatin desserts just described can be made from packaged mixes which contain the basic ingredients—that is, gelatin, sugar, and flavoring. All that is required is to add water.

GELATIN DESSERTS

Courtesy National Canners Association

Biscuit, Cake, and Pastry Desserts

The desserts that have been described so far in this chapter may be considered fairly simple. They are suitable for serving at the end of hearty meals. Desserts of the biscuit, cake, and pastry type, on the contrary, are richer in

● Gelatin desserts can be plain, whips, or sponges, or they can be served in combination with a sherbet or ice cream.

393

BISCUIT, CAKE, AND PASTRY DESSERTS

● Desserts made of a biscuit dough, such as a fruit cobbler, of a cake batter, such as an upside-down cake, or of a pastry dough, such as tarts, are all appropriate for a light meal.

Biscuit desserts. A soft dough such as is used for making biscuits is the basis for these desserts. (See Chapter 23, "Quick Breads," page 314.) Most of the ingredients are the same as those commonly used for biscuits—flour, salt, baking powder, fat, and milk. In addition, sugar is always added to provide the sweetness needed for desserts. Sometimes eggs too are included to give greater richness. Instead of making biscuit doughs from the basic ingredients, a prepared biscuit mix may be used.

A dough like this is used for a shortcake. After it is baked, it is split across through the center and a sweetened fruit, such as strawberries or peaches, is spread over the bottom half. Then the fruit is covered with the top half, and more fruit is poured over it all.

quality. For this reason, they are good for serving with light meals because their filling quality will give a feeling of satisfaction when the meal is finished. The principles on which the preparation of these desserts is based have been explained in the chapters on quick breads, cakes, and pastries. These chapters should be referred to in connection with the study of these products as they are used in making desserts.

Whipped cream as a garnish turns a shortcake into a festive dessert. For variation, the biscuit dough may be baked in individual portions instead of in one large piece.

A cobbler is another dessert made from a rich biscuit dough. For this, canned or frozen fruit, or sweetened fresh fruit, is placed in a shallow baking dish and heated in the oven until it is very hot. Then the dough is spread over it and the baking finished. Cobblers are served either hot or cold, with plain or whipped cream or a fruit or custard sauce.

Still another use for a biscuit dough is in making fruit dumplings. For these, the dough is rolled out thin and cut into squares. An apple, which has been peeled and cored, is placed in the center of each square and sweetened and flavored. Then the points of the dough square are brought up over the apple and pressed together. Sometimes half of a fresh peach is used instead of an apple. Dumplings are served either hot or cold, with plain or whipped cream, a fruit sauce, or a hard sauce.

Cakes. Frosted layer cakes and cupcakes are the most suitable cakes for serving alone as dessert. Plain cakes, such as an unfrosted cupcake or a slice of loaf cake, sponge cake, or angel food cake, make excellent accompaniments for fruit or frozen desserts. If served alone, however, such unfrosted cakes may be too plain. Cakes are discussed in Chapter 25.

Pastries. Pastry, whether it is a pie, tarts, or turnovers, is even more popular for dessert than cake. Pastry is rich and makes a hearty dessert. When pastry is planned for dessert, the other foods in the meal should be light enough so that there will still be an appetite for the pastry. Pastries are described in Chapter 27.

Frozen Desserts

Frozen desserts are especially appealing for meals during the summer, but many people like them just as well during the colder months

FROZEN DESSERTS

Courtesy Sealtest

● Baked Alaska—ice cream covered with a meringue and browned in the oven—is supreme among frozen desserts. (See recipe on page 462.)

of the year. Frozen desserts are appropriate for serving at lunch or dinner no matter what the menu, since they can be light or hearty according to the kind selected.

Kinds of Frozen Desserts

The different kinds of frozen desserts can be classified on the basis of whether or not they are stirred during the freezing process. Another way of classifying them is to group them according to the ingredients they contain. Based on this latter grouping, there are the following kinds of frozen desserts: ices and frappés, sherbets, ice cream, mousses, and parfaits.

Ices and frappés. These are frozen desserts made of a sugar syrup that is flavored with fruit juice. A frappé is less solidly frozen than an ice and therefore has a somewhat mushy consistency. Both ices and frappés are light and refreshing. Either makes a welcome dessert on a very hot day.

Sherbets. There are two kinds of sherbets: (1) milk sherbet in which the fruit juice is sweetened and then blended with milk instead of a sugar syrup and (2) sherbet that contains some gelatin or beaten egg white. Because of these added ingredients, both kinds of sherbets are slightly firmer in consistency and finer in texture than ices.

Ice cream. These frozen desserts contain cream as one of the ingredients. A Philadelphia ice cream contains only sweetened and flavored cream. Crushed fruit or chocolate, caramel, or maple are examples of flavorings that can be used in the cream. Another kind of ice cream has a custard base to which the cream and a flavoring are added. A very rich custard type of ice cream is called "French ice cream."

Mousses. These are very rich frozen desserts that are firmer and more compact than ice creams. They are usually made of only sweetened and flavored whipped cream, but some mousses contain a small amount of gelatin to increase their firmness. A mousse is never stirred as it is being frozen, in contrast to ice cream which is usually stirred during the freezing process.

Parfaits. Parfaits resemble mousses in richness. A sugar syrup is poured over either beaten egg yolks or egg whites, and then whipped cream and a flavoring are stirred into the mixture. A parfait is frozen without stirring. If egg yolks are used, the parfait is a golden parfait. If egg whites are used, it is an angel parfait.

Ways to Serve Frozen Desserts

All kinds of frozen desserts may be served plain or, very often, with cake or a cookie as an accompaniment. Ice cream can be made more elaborate by covering it with a sauce— and sometimes whipped cream, marshmallow, cherries, or nuts. Crushed fruit, chocolate, butterscotch, and maple sauces are favorite toppings for vanilla ice cream. Occasionally an ice, frappé, or sherbet is served as an accompaniment with the main course of a dinner.

Principles of Preparation of Frozen Desserts

With the exception of frappés, which are soft in consistency and coarse in texture, all frozen desserts should have a firm, but not hard consistency and a fine, smooth texture. A firm frozen dessert will not melt on the plate too quickly. One with a fine texture will have such tiny ice crystals in it that they will hardly be detected by the tongue, and the sensation will be one of smoothness. These two characteristics—(1) firm, but not hard, consistency and (2) fine, smooth texture—together with a desirable flavor are the qualities of a good frozen dessert.

The flavor of frozen desserts is of course influenced by the ingredients used in them. The qualities of consistency and texture also are influenced by the ingredients. In addition, these two qualities are affected very importantly by the conditions of freezing the dessert.

Freezing and frozen desserts. In your science class you have learned that water freezes to ice at 32° F. and that, as this change occurs, heat is given up to the surrounding atmosphere and to objects in contact with the water. As long as the temperature stays at 32° F., or even drops to a lower temperature, the ice remains frozen. But if the temperature increases, even a minute amount above 32° F., the ice will melt and change to water. In this melting of ice, heat is absorbed from the surrounding atmosphere and from objects in contact with the ice.

Another fact that you have learned in your science class is that when a substance—for example, sugar or salt—is dissolved in water, the freezing of water to ice and the melting of ice to water takes place at a temperature lower than 32° F. Just what the lower temperature of freezing and melting is depends upon how much of the substance is dissolved in the water. The greater the amount of the substance dissolved, the lower the temperature will be.

In making frozen desserts, we apply these facts. The mixture that we are freezing always contains water, either added as such or as part of the milk or cream. The mixture also contains sugar and usually salt. Our object is to change the water to ice. Since sugar and salt are dissolved in it, the temperature must be lowered to below 32° F. in order that this change can take place. There are two ways to accomplish this condition.

One way is to pour the mixture to be frozen into a refrigerator tray and place it in the freezing compartment of an automatic refrigerator. The cold control must be set at the coldest position, which will be well below 32° F. In this very cold environment, heat passes from the relatively warm dessert mixture to the air, and the mixture becomes steadily colder until at some point below 32° F. the water in it begins to freeze to ice. The additional heat liberated from it during this freezing of water to ice also passes into the surrounding air. Since water is distributed all through the dessert mixture, it will freeze in the form of crystals of ice. If the change from water to ice takes place fast enough, the crystals will be tiny and the texture of the frozen dessert will be fine and smooth. Beating the mixture once or twice during the freezing also helps to keep the crystals small. After the mixture has frozen, the temperature of the freezing compartment should be raised slightly above that at which freezing occurred and the frozen dessert held at this temperature until time for serving. This will give the dessert the right consistency for serving—that is, firm but not hard.

The other way of freezing desserts is by means of an ice-cream freezer. The distinguishing feature between these two ways of freezing desserts is in the stirring of the mixture. In the ice-cream freezer, continuous stirring beats the mixture as it freezes and thus incorporates bubbles of air into the mixture.

Courtesy "Better Homes and Gardens"

● Ice cream made in a freezer is continuously churned as it freezes.

The films around the air bubbles are thin, and the water in these films will freeze into tiny ice crystals. Desserts that are frozen in an automatic refrigerator can be stirred with a rotary beater at intervals during freezing. This has a beneficial effect on the consistency and texture of the product, although it is not as effective as the continuous stirring done in the ice-cream freezer. Many recipes designed for freezing desserts in the refrigerator give the direction to whip the cream or even to incorporate some beaten egg whites as well. The air bubbles introduced by these means improve the consistency and texture of the dessert when it is frozen in this way.

Ingredients and frozen desserts. One example has just been given of how ingredients influence the consistency and texture of frozen desserts. Also, you will recall that the firmer consistency and finer texture of sherbets as

397

● When ice cream is made in a refrigerator tray, it is only beaten once or twice during the freezing process.

compared to ices are the result of either the use of milk instead of water or the addition of beaten egg white or gelatin to the mixture.

Good consistency and fine texture are obtained in ice cream if the unfrozen mixture is thick enough to retain the air bubbles that are beaten into it. In Philadelphia ice cream, the cream provides satisfactory thickness. In the custard type of ice cream, the custard contributes the thickness. If desired, an even thicker custard can be made by (1) using un-diluted evaporated milk for part of the milk in the recipe, (2) using some flour or corn-starch in addition to the eggs in making the custard, or (3) adding a small amount of gelatin to the hot custard. Very frequently recipes designed for freezing mixtures in the refrigerator will list these ingredients. They, together with whipped cream instead of plain cream, or beaten egg white, make very thick mixtures suitable for freezing in this way. The thickest of all desserts in the unfrozen state are the mousses and parfaits, both of which contain a large proportion of whipped cream.

Food Value of Desserts

Desserts of all kinds, with the possible exception of simple fruit desserts, are high in calorie value. Sugar, which gives desserts their sweet quality, is the ingredient that is largely responsible for the high calories. Just what additional nutritive value desserts will have depends on the other ingredients in them besides sugar. Fruit desserts or desserts of other kinds containing fruit—for example, fruit ices and ice creams and fruit-rich gelatin desserts —will provide some vitamins and minerals. Desserts that are rich in milk, such as all the milk desserts and some of the gelatin and frozen desserts, play an important role in contributing milk to the daily diet and thus provide excellent protein, some minerals, and some vitamins. Some desserts of the flour-mixture type contain fairly large amounts of fruit, such as fruit pies, or of milk, such as custard pies. In general, however, desserts typical of this group make their chief contribution to the calorie needs of the diet.

33

Candies

■ MAKING CANDY is fun. It can be a project to help you raise money for some special occasion. Or you may entertain friends, while away an afternoon, or perhaps entertain your younger brothers or sisters on a rainy day by making candy. Whatever the purpose, candymaking gives you an opportunity to use your imagination, and, best of all, to practice your skill in cooking techniques. Only by using the right techniques can perfect candies be achieved.

Classes of Candies

There are many kinds of candies, and many ingredients are used in them to provide a wide variety of flavors. Fundamentally, however, candies are classified as either crystalline or noncrystalline in character.

Crystalline Candies

Fondant, fudge, and penuchi are popular crystalline candies—that is, they contain many tiny sugar crystals. They are easily made at home.

Uncooked fondant. The most simple of all the marvellous candies to make are the uncooked ones. One of these, uncooked fondant, is made by blending icing sugar and flavoring into condensed milk, or by stirring icing sugar, evaporated milk or cream, and flavoring into slightly beaten egg white. Among the flavorings used in these fondants are vanilla, chocolate, coconut, chopped nuts, and candied or dried fruits.

Cooked fondant. This is a soft, fine crystalline candy that has many uses. Candy patties are made of flavored fondant that has been melted and then dropped from a spoon

CLASSES OF CANDIES

● Crystalline candies, such as peanut-butter fudge, contain tiny sugar crystals.

● Noncrystalline candies, such as peanut brittle, do not contain sugar crystals.

Photos courtesy Western Beet Sugar Producers, Inc.

into flat, round shapes and allowed to harden. They may be dipped into chocolate to make chocolate-covered patties, but this requires more expert handling than can be done easily at home. Fondant of various flavors may also be molded into different shapes, and if desired, dipped into chocolate.

Fudge. This is another soft, fine crystalline candy. It is often flavored with chocolate. Fudge may be poured into a square pan and, when firm, cut into squares; or it can be molded by the hands into balls.

Penuchi. This candy is similar to fudge in texture and softness. However, it does not contain chocolate, and it is made with brown sugar instead of the white granulated sugar that is used for fondant, and as a rule, for fudge.

Noncrystalline Candies

Caramels, nougats, divinity, taffies, and brittles are noncrystalline candies and do not contain any sugar crystals. In general, they are a little more difficult to make than are the crystalline candies.

Caramels. Caramels are waxy in texture and firm, yet not hard, in consistency. Caramels are made with a number of different flavorings, such as vanilla, chocolate, honey, and maple. For variety, caramels may be coated with chocolate.

Nougats. These are a more elaborate kind of noncrystalline candy than caramels although they resemble them in consistency. To make nougats, a sugar syrup is poured over stiffly beaten egg whites. For this reason, nougats are more porous in texture than caramels. As a rule, nougats contain honey as an ingredient and, in addition, almonds and pistachio nuts.

Divinity. This is a modification of nougat. It, too, is made by pouring a sugar syrup over stiffly beaten egg whites, but it has a much more porous texture than nougat candy. Divinity does not contain honey, but nuts and candied fruit are often added.

Taffies. Taffies are pulled candies that can be made in many twisted shapes. Some taffies include molasses as well as sugar. Others contain honey, corn syrup, or even chocolate. Whatever the flavor, the cooked syrupy mass is cooled until it just begins to thicken and can be handled. Then it is taken in the hands and pulled until it is cold and so firm that, when twisted and cut into pieces, these pieces will hold their shape.

Brittles. These are candies that are made by letting a cooked syrup spread out into a thin layer to cool and harden. When the syrup is hard, it is so brittle that it can easily be broken into pieces. Nuts of different kinds are frequently stirred into the syrup just before it is poured. Peanut brittle is a favorite brittle.

Ingredients in Candies

If a list were made of all the ingredients used in making candies, it would be very long indeed. Therefore only a few of those ingredients most frequently used in homemade candies are considered here.

Sugar. The basic ingredient in all kinds of candies is sugar. This may be granulated sugar or one of the several brown sugars—yellow, light brown, or dark brown. Some recipes call for both granulated and brown sugar. If the recipe does not state which kind of brown sugar is meant, it is a good plan to use either the yellow or light-brown sugar. The more decided flavor of dark-brown sugar is likely to mask other flavors in the candy. For uncooked candies, icing sugar is used. This is so finely powdered that it gives firmness to the candy and a smooth, rich, creamy texture.

Syrup. Molasses, honey, and maple syrup are rich in sugar and are sometimes used along with granulated sugar in making candy. In addition to contributing sugar, each syrup gives a characteristic flavor. Light corn syrup is another syrup frequently used. However, it is used not so much for its sweetness or flavor as for the creamy texture it gives the candy. Dark corn syrup, which may be used in dark-colored candies, not only influences texture but gives flavor as well.

Liquid. The liquid ingredient in a candy depends on the kind of candy being made. Usually this liquid ingredient is water or milk. In some candies, cream or evaporated milk is used. Syrups, if used, provide some liquid, so that recipes calling for a syrup include less milk or water. In uncooked candies, condensed or evaporated milk and egg white contribute the liquid.

Eggs. Egg whites are listed in some candy recipes and, if so, they are usually used in the stiffly beaten form. In this form, they contribute to the special kind of texture that is characteristic of the candy. Egg white in uncooked candies is only slightly beaten, since its purpose is to provide liquid.

TEMPERATURES AND TESTS FOR SYRUP AND CANDIES *

PRODUCT	TEMPERATURE At sea level (degrees F.)	TEST	DESCRIPTION OF TEST
Syrup	230–234	Thread	Syrup spins a 2-inch thread when dropped from fork or spoon.
Fondant Fudge Penuchi	234–240	Soft ball	Syrup, when dropped into very cold water, forms a soft ball which flattens on removal from water.
Caramels	244–248	Firm ball	Syrup, when dropped into very cold water, forms a firm ball which does not flatten on removal from water.
Divinity Marshmallows Popcorn balls	250–266	Hard ball	Syrup, when dropped into very cold water, forms a ball which is hard enough to hold its shape, yet plastic.
Butterscotch Taffies	270–290	Soft crack	Syrup, when dropped into very cold water, separates into threads which are hard but not brittle.
Brittle Glacé	300–310	Hard crack	Syrup, when dropped into very cold water, separates into threads which are hard and brittle.
Barley sugar	320	Clear liquid	The sugar liquefies.
Caramel	338	Brown liquid	The liquid becomes brown.

* From *Handbook of Food Preparation*, American Home Economics Association, Washington, D.C., 1964, p. 30.

Flavoring ingredients. Many different kinds of flavoring ingredients are used in making candies. Probably vanilla and chocolate are the favorites, but mint, wintergreen, orange, lemon, or coffee are used occasionally. Coconut and all kinds of nuts and dried fruits add interest to candy. Butter or margarine contributes flavor and richness to some candies. All these flavoring ingredients increase the attractiveness of candy and modify its sweet taste.

Food Value of Candies

The chief nutrient in candy is the carbohydrate sugar. This, as you know, contributes only calories to the diet. There are other nutrients in the various ingredients used in candies, but since these ingredients are usually present in small amounts, candy cannot be relied upon as a source of any one of these nutrients. Good nutrition practice tells us that foods which supply calories should contribute, as well, some other nutrient or nutrients, in fair amounts at least. Since this is not true of candies, their value as a source of calories should only be supplementary to the calories contributed by other foods.

Principles of Preparation of Candies

In making candy, the ingredients of the recipe, the extent of cooking, and the techniques of handling the syrup after cooking all have an influence on the results obtained.

Crystalline Candies

When a mixture of sugar and liquid, either alone or with other ingredients, is put over heat, it will begin to boil at about the temperature of boiling water. With continued boiling three things happen:
1. Some water evaporates.
2. The mixture becomes more and more syrupy because the sugar becomes more and more concentrated.

Courtesy Western Beet Sugar Producers, Inc.

● Using a candy thermometer is the best way to determine when candy is done. For other tests, see the chart on the opposite page.

3. Because the sugar becomes concentrated, the temperature of the boiling syrup rises.

This increase in temperature can be observed by the use of a candy thermometer. Since different candies need to have just the right concentration of sugar, recipes will usually state the temperature to which the syrup should be cooked to give that concentration.

Everyone does not have a candy thermometer available. However, there is another way of judging when the candy mixture has been cooked to the right temperature to give the right sugar concentration. This other way is the so-called "ball test." To make this test, about 1 teaspoon of the boiling syrup is dropped into cold water and held there about 1 minute. As the syrup cools, it hardens and forms a ball. At first, when the sugar syrup is not very concentrated, the ball will be soft when pressed between the fingers. Later, with further boiling and increasing concentration, the ball will be hard, and eventually it will be so hard that it will be brittle and crack. The

403

● Everyone likes fudge—provided it is not too soft or too sugary. To achieve a creamy texture, the sugar crystals must be very tiny. To keep the sugar crystals tiny in fudge and other crystalline candies, beat the syrup vigorously after it has been cooked and properly cooled.

chart "Temperatures and Tests for Syrup and Candies" on page 402 gives the temperature of the syrup and the character of the ball formed in cold water for various candies.

When the boiling of the candy syrup is completed, the syrup is removed from the heat. The technique of handling it at this point is very important in order that the sugar will crystallize into very tiny crystals. These tiny sugar crystals are responsible for the creamy texture that is characteristic of a good fondant, fudge, or penuchi. To accomplish this, the hot candy syrup must be allowed to cool to lukewarm without agitation. Then it is stirred or beaten. By following this technique, many tiny sugar crystals will form, and with continued beating, each crystal will be kept separate from the others. There will soon be so many tiny crystals that the mass becomes almost firm and is difficult to stir. It is then ready for pouring into a pan or for shaping.

As further assurance that the sugar crystals will be tiny, a small amount of corn syrup is often used as one of the ingredients. Corn syrup has the property of interfering with the formation of sugar crystals in such a way that the crystals remain small.

Noncrystalline Candies

For caramels, nougats, and other noncrystalline candies, the ingredients used in the recipes are relied upon to prevent sugar crystals from forming and thus give each kind of candy its characteristic texture. Among these ingredients are corn syrup, honey, evaporated milk, and cream. To prevent crystallization, they must be present in fairly large proportions. Either a candy thermometer or the ball test can be used to judge when the syrup for these candies has been cooked to the right concentration. These candies are poured into pans as soon as cooking is finished.

404

34

Food

Preservation

■ FOOD PRESERVATION means the caring for food in such a way that it will keep in good condition for a long period of time. In rural areas there are farms where fruits, vegetables, and poultry will be found in abundance. There may even be supplies of meat. In addition, many families have gardens of their own, and they may raise more fruits and vegetables than they can use at harvest time.

If you know about ways to preserve such products for out-of-season use, you can have a stock of foods on hand which will help you in planning and preparing meals. By preserving foods, you will not need to make such frequent shopping trips. You can save time and effort in the preparation of meals and often save money in the food budget as well.

Why Foods Spoil

All fruits and vegetables and all meats will spoil unless some means are taken to prevent their spoilage. Enzymes, bacteria, yeasts, and molds are the agents responsible for the spoilage of these foods.

Enzymes. In fruits and vegetables there are substances called enzymes that are responsible for the ripening process. Enzymes do not stop their activity after fruits and vegetables are harvested but continue to act until finally the products become overripe so that they spoil and are unfit for use. The situation is the same in animal products. The enzymes that carry on life processes in animals continue their action in meats as well and will cause them to spoil.

WAYS TO PRESERVE FOOD

● By canning

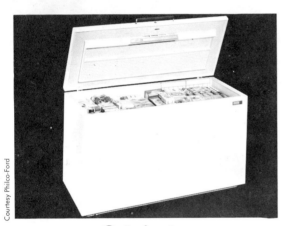

● By freezing

● By making jelly

Bacteria, yeasts, and molds. Bacteria, yeasts, and molds are tiny organisms. They are so tiny in fact that they can only be seen with a microscope and therefore are given the name of "microorganisms." When these microorganisms lodge on food, either fruits and vegetables or animal products, they grow and bring about changes in the food which make it unpalatable or, in some cases, even unsafe.

Ways of Preserving Foods

Canning, freezing, and jelly making are the common ways of preserving foods that will be discussed in this chapter. For other methods of food preservation, such as making fruit preserves and jams and the dehydration and pickling of fruits and vegetables, specific directions may be found in cookbooks or bulletins of your state agricultural experiment station.

Buying Foods to Preserve

The choice of foods for preservation is important. The time, effort, and cost involved in preserving foods are such that only good-quality, strictly fresh foods should be used. Preserving foods does not improve their quality. Freshness and good quality are found most frequently in home-grown fruits and vegetables and in home-killed meats and poultry. Failing such a source, foods should be purchased from a nearby farm or a high-quality market. Variety as well as freshness must be considered because some varieties of fruits and vegetables are better adapted to freezing than others. Books and pamphlets which give directions for freezing will give such information.

Canning Foods

Canning is the preservation of food by sealing it in airtight containers and applying heat. Home canning is a very old but still a good way of preserving food. It can be used for fruits of all kinds, for many vegetables, and for meats and poultry.

Principle of Canning

The principle on which the canning method of food preservation is based is that heat, if sufficiently high and if applied for a sufficient length of time, will destroy all spoilage agents. Since enzymes cannot withstand high temperatures, they are destroyed by the heat and therefore their action in foods stops. The other spoilage agents—bacteria, yeasts, and molds—cannot live in very hot surroundings. All that are in the food are thus killed by the application of sufficient heat. The airtight sealing of the food in containers prevents any new bacteria, yeasts, and molds from reaching the food. Properly canned foods will keep more or less indefinitely.

Methods of Canning Foods

Two methods are used for canning foods. In both methods the food is given preliminary preparation, according to its kind, and then it is packed into clean containers. The containers are closed, and the food and containers are heated, or "processed" as it is called, at the same time. In one method the processing is done in a boiling-water bath at 212° F. In the other method the processing is done in a pressure canner at 240° F.

Processing in the boiling-water bath. In this method of canning, the containers, having been filled with food and closed, are put into a deep kettle containing hot or boiling water. Hot water is used for raw-pack canning—that is, the packing of containers with raw, prepared food—whereas boiling water is used for hot-pack canning. In the latter case, the food is precooked for a short time before it is put into the containers. The water in the kettle should extend about 2 inches above the containers. It is then brought to a rolling, steady boil so that the temperature surrounding the containers will be 212° F., the temperature of boiling water. The length of time that the processing is continued depends on the food.

Processing in the steam-pressure canner. In this method of processing, the filled and closed containers are heated in a pressure canner in which they are surrounded by steam at temperatures above 212° F. Although the temperature may be higher, 240° F. is the temperature most often used. The length of processing time is adjusted to the food being canned.

Selection of Method for Canning Foods

According to their acidity, foods fall into two groups: those that are relatively high in acid and those that are relatively low in acid. It is their acid content that determines whether they should be canned by being processed in the boiling-water bath at 212° F. or in the pressure canner at a higher temperature.

Foods high in acid. When foods have a high-acid content, the bacteria, which are most difficult of all of the spoilage agents to destroy, are killed at temperatures of 212° F., or even lower if the foods are held at these temperatures for an adequate length of time. Thus the highly acid foods, such as tomatoes and all fruits, may be canned by the boiling-water-bath method.

Foods low in acid. In contrast to the highly acid foods, those that are low in acid require more heat, since the bacteria in low-acid foods can withstand higher temperatures and still live to cause spoilage. All vegetables, except tomatoes, and all meats and poultry are low-acid foods. Canning by the pressure-canner method at a temperature of 240° F. is recommended for them. It is possible to process these foods at 212° F., but at this temperature, heating would have to be continued for so long a time to kill the bacteria that the appearance, texture, and flavor of the foods would be impaired.

Containers for Canning Foods

Containers for canning foods are made of glass or tin in several sizes. The lids of tin containers are sealed tightly onto the cans with a special sealing device before the processing

(Continued on page 414)

407

● Only highly acid foods, such as tomatoes and fruits, are canned in a water-bath canner at 212° F. Preliminary treatment of such acid foods to be canned by this method depends on the kind—whether it is to be packed into jars cold or hot, and whether or not fruit is to be sweetened.[1] Specific directions

● 1. Select fresh, firm, unblemished tomatoes of uniform size and ripeness. Those with decayed spots and cracks are unfit for canning. Wash only enough at one time for a canner load.

● 2. Put the washed tomatoes into a kettle of boiling water for about ½ minute to loosen the skins, and then quickly dip the tomatoes into cold water. Drain.

[1] To make a syrup for sweetening fruit, boil sugar and water or fruit juice together for 5 minutes. To make a thin, medium, or heavy syrup, use for each quart of water or juice, 2, 3, or 4¾ cups sugar, respectively. Select the syrup that is best suited to fruit and taste. Cover the prepared fruit in jars with the boiling syrup. To sweeten very juicy fruits, add ½ cup sugar to each quart of raw prepared fruit. Then heat the sweetened fruit to simmer-

WATER-BATH CANNER (212° F.)

must be followed exactly for each food that is processed. Such directions are given here showing step-by-step procedures for the raw-pack canning of tomatoes in a water-bath canner. Follow authoritative directions for canning other acid foods.

● 3. Remove the stem ends and peel the tomatoes; then cut them into quarters or leave whole, as desired. Have the jars and closures clean, ready to pack the tomatoes into them.

● 4. Tomatoes may be packed into jars either raw or boiling hot (hot-pack), as desired. For raw pack, put the tomatoes (whole or in pieces) into the hot, clean jars. Press the tomatoes until jar spaces fill with juice, or cover with hot tomato juice to within ½ inch of the top of the jars. (For hot-pack tomatoes, bring quartered tomatoes to boiling before filling the jars, and pack loosely. Work knife blade down side of jars to remove air bubbles.) *(Continued)*

ing before packing. The darkening of such fruits as peaches or pears during preparation may be prevented by dropping the pieces of fruit into water containing 2 teaspoons each of salt and vinegar to each gallon. Fruit should be well drained before it is heated or packed.

5. Add 1 teaspoon salt to each quart of tomatoes. Wipe top and threads of jars with a clean, damp cloth, and adjust the closures.

6. As each jar is filled, put it on the rack in the canner of hot (not boiling) water. Add boiling water to bring the water level to 1 or 2 inches over jar tops. There should be a little space at the top of the canner to allow the water to boil. (For hot-pack canning, the water in the canner should be boiling when jars are put in.)

WATER-BATH CANNER (212° F.) (Continued)

● 7. Cover canner and bring the water to a boil. Start to count processing time when water boils. At altitudes less than 1,000 feet above sea level, process pint jars 35 minutes, quart jars 45 minutes. Remove cover far side up so that steam escapes away from you. (For hot-pack tomatoes, process both quart and pint jars 10 minutes.)

● 8. Remove jars from canner at once at end of processing period. Adjust lids according to directions of jar manufacturer. Cool jars quickly on rack in upright position away from drafts. When cold, test jars for perfect seal by turning them partly over in your hand and observing if any liquid seeps out. If any jar is not sealed, use the food promptly or repack into another jar and reprocess. Label jars and store in a cool, dry place.

Courtesy Ball Brothers Company

Courtesy Ball Brothers Company

Courtesy Ball Brothers Company

● All vegetables except tomatoes and pickled vegetables are canned in a steam-pressure canner at 240° F. The preliminary treatment of the food differs somewhat, depending on the kind of vegetable and whether it is packed into jars raw or boiling hot. The jars must be clean and the closures should be in perfect condition.

The pressure canner must be kept clean and in good operating condition. The pet cock and safety valve openings must be unclogged. The dial gauge indicating pounds of pressure and temperature in the canner should be checked occasionally for accuracy. (Ask your local appliance dealer for advice about this.) Follow manufacturer's directions for use of the steam-pressure canner.

Specific directions are given below for the hot-pack canning of snap beans in a steam-pressure canner, and they must be followed exactly. Directions are given in parentheses for raw-pack canning when they differ.

1. Select only fresh, firm, young, and tender snap beans. Wash the beans well through several changes of water, lifting them out of the water each time so that the dirt will not drain back over them. Trim and cut the beans into pieces of desired size (top), preparing only enough at one time for a canner load.

2. Get jars ready by heating in water. Follow manufacturer's directions for each type of jar and closure. When using jars requiring rubber rings, always use new rings of correct size for the jar. Then place the beans in a saucepan, cover with boiling water, and boil for 5 minutes (center).

3. Pack boiling-hot beans loosely into clean, hot jars to within ½ inch of the top. Add ½ teaspoon salt to each pint, and cover beans with hot cooking liquid, leaving a ½-inch space at the top of the jar (bottom). Boiling water may be used instead of cook-

STEAM-PRESSURE CANNER (240° F.)

ing liquid if the liquid is dark, gritty, or strong-flavored. Work a knife blade down the sides of the jars to remove air bubbles. (For raw-pack beans, put prepared raw beans into jars, add salt, and cover with boiling water.) Wipe the rims of the jars, and adjust the closures according to the type of jar used.

4. Set the filled jars on a rack in the pressure canner so that the steam can flow around each jar (top). Have 2 or 3 inches of boiling water in canner. Close canner following manufacturer's directions. Begin to count processing time when the pressure reaches 10 pounds (240° F.) at sea level.[1] Hold the pressure steady by regulating the heat beneath the canner. Process pint jars 20 minutes, quart jars 25 minutes, for both hot and raw pack.

5. At the end of the processing period, remove the canner from the heat and let the pressure fall to zero. Then slowly open the vent in the cover. Remove the cover, tilting the far side up so that the steam escapes away from you (center). Remove the jars from the canner at once, and if required, complete the seal. Some jars are self-sealing, so manufacturer's directions should be followed.

6. Cool the jars on a rack in an upright position away from drafts. When cold, test for perfect seal by following manufacturer's directions (bottom). Observe if any liquid seeps out. If not sealed, use food right away or empty jars and repack and reprocess, proceeding as for fresh food. Label jars and store in a cool, dry place.

[1]At altitudes of 2,000 feet or more an adjustment must be made in the number of pounds of pressure required to give a temperature of 240° F. Consult your provincial Department of Food and Agriculture Extension Service home economist for correct processing pressure for your altitude.

Courtesy Ball Brothers Company

Courtesy Ball Brothers Company

Courtesy Ball Brothers Company

step in the canning procedure. Glass jars are fitted with a number of types of lids. These are adjusted in different ways, and the manufacturer's directions that accompany them should be followed carefully.

Directions for Canning Foods

In canning, a definite length of time is recommended for processing each food. Specific directions for canning may be found in bulletins published by the Consumer Section, Canada Department of Agriculture. Bulletins are also available across the country from the departments of agriculture in each province. Directions for canning tomatoes and snap beans will be found on pages 408 to 413.

Food Value of Canned Foods

When fruits and vegetables are canned, there is always liquid surrounding the pieces. Since some vitamins and minerals are soluble in water, some of these nutrients in the food will have been dissolved. Because of this, it is important, from a food-value standpoint, to use the liquid. The syrup around canned fruit can be served with the fruit or used in beverages or in some desserts. The liquid in canned vegetables may be served with the vegetables, but if preferred, it can be used in soups, sauces, and stews.

Vitamin C and thiamine are two vitamins that undergo some destruction when foods are heated to high temperatures. Therefore, canned vegetables probably will contain smaller amounts of these two vitamins than the cooked fresh vegetables. A further loss of these same vitamins, especially vitamin C, will take place when canned foods are stored for several months unless the storage temperature is below room temperature.

Use of Canned Foods

In general, canned fruits, vegetables, meats, and poultry may be used in the same ways as the fresh products. The serving of fruits and vegetables raw and the cooking of meats and poultry as roasts are, of course, exceptions.

Before using any canned food, whether home-canned or commercial, it should be examined for signs of spoilage. If bacteria should survive the processing conditions and remain in the food, they are liable to develop further during storage, especially if the storage temperature is not sufficiently cool. One sign of spoilage is the presence of gas. This is evident by a little spurt of the gas when the container is opened, or it may have caused the jar closure to loosen. In a commercial can the gas causes the ends of the can to bulge. Another sign of spoilage is an acid taste but no formation of gas. This condition is called "flat sour." Although the presence of gas or flat-sour spoilage may not cause the food to be harmful, it is a wise precaution to discard such food.

In some cases of home canning, spoilage occurs through the improper sealing of the jar closure. Then air can enter and carry with it bacteria, yeasts, and molds, which grow and make the food unfit for use.

There is one special kind of spoilage possible in home-canned food that is dangerous. Such spoilage is caused by a microorganism called *"Clostridium botulinum"* that is extremely difficult to destroy in a low-acid food. This microorganism causes the condition known as "botulism." If, for any reason, in home canning the time and temperature conditions are not adequately controlled, the microorganism may survive, grow in the food, and produce poisonous substances called "toxins." These toxins may be present even though the food shows no visible signs of spoilage. Thus as a safeguard, it is recommended that all home-canned low-acid foods be boiled for several minutes before they are tasted or served. This will destroy both the growing microorganism and the poisonous toxins. In commercial canning the processing conditions of time and temperature are so rigidly controlled that there is practically no danger of a canned food being spoiled because of this microorganism.

414

● A well-stocked food freezer can be a great convenience.

Storage of Canned Foods

A place which is cool, dry, and dark is best for storing canned foods. In some homes a cabinet in the basement is satisfactory, provided the basement is not damp. When the kitchen cabinet must be used for storage, it is well to reserve the coolest location on the shelves. Although canned foods can be kept for several years, their quality will not be so good after the first year. It is wise to can only the amount of food that will be used before the next season's supply is available.

Freezing Foods

Freezing is a method of preservation in which food is placed in such cold surroundings that it becomes frozen very quickly. For good-quality frozen foods, temperatures of 0° F. or lower are necessary. Many homes have freezers or a special freezing compart-

ment in the refrigerator as part of their equipment; others make use of nearby commercial freezer-locker plants for freezing and storing foods. Some home refrigerators have a storage compartment for holding food that has already been frozen. Its temperature is not low enough to freeze foods as quickly as is desirable; therefore, a storage compartment should not be confused with a freezing compartment.

Principle of Freezing

The principle of the preservation of food by freezing is based on the fact that enzymes act very, very slowly, and microorganisms do not thrive at the low temperatures of around 0° F. Therefore, in the frozen state food keeps its original character. But since the spoilage agents are not destroyed, their activity begins again as soon as the food becomes warmer. For this reason frozen food should be used as soon as possible after it has been defrosted.

415

STEPS IN FREEZING STRAWBERRIES

1. Wash, hull, and cut the strawberries. Sprinkle sugar over them, using ¾ cup sugar to each quart of berries. Turn the berries over and over until the sugar dissolves and juice forms.

2. Pack the berries into containers suitable for freezing, leaving a ½-inch space at the top. Place a piece of crumpled parchment paper on the top of the berries, and press them down into the juice.

3. Seal the containers tightly, and place them in the freezer.

USDA Photos

Methods of Freezing Foods

In general, the procedure followed in freezing foods starts with the preparation of the food according to its kind. Next, it is carefully packed into suitable containers or wrapped with a special type of moisture-vapor-resistant packaging material. After excluding as much air as possible from around the food, the package is sealed tightly. Then it is placed without delay into the freezer.

Fruits. All fruits are washed. Berries are left whole or sliced, and larger fruits are peeled and cut into pieces, as desired. Then the prepared fruit is packed into containers for freezing in one of three ways: (1) packed plain without any sweetening, (2) mixed with dry sugar before being packed, or (3) put into the containers and covered with a sugar syrup. The containers are then sealed and placed in the freezer immediately. It is important that the whole process be carried out in as short a time as possible so that the highest quality of frozen fruit may be obtained. Some of the light-colored fruits, like peaches, apples, and apricots, tend to darken during freezing and freezer storage. To avoid this, ascorbic acid may be added.

Vegetables. After being prepared in the usual manner as for cooking, vegetables to be frozen must be heated for several minutes before they are packed into the containers. This preheating is called "blanching" or "scalding" and is used to destroy enzymes. If any enzymes should remain in the vegetables, their action, even though very slow because of the intense cold, would cause the vegetables to lose color and flavor during the freezer-storage period.

Vegetables are blanched usually in boiling water. The vegetables, either in a covered wire basket or tied loosely in cheesecloth, are lowered into the boiling water and the kettle is covered. Blanching is continued for the length of time stated in the directions for freezing a particular vegetable. Another method of blanching is in steam. In this method the basket or cheesecloth holding the vegetables is placed on a rack over boiling water in a tightly covered kettle. In this way steam instead of boiling water surrounds the vegetables. Following the blanching step, the vegetables are cooled very thoroughly in cold water and then drained and packed into containers. As soon as a few containers are sealed, they are placed into the freezer.

Meats and poultry. It is considered wise to freeze meats and poultry only if they are of excellent quality, plentiful, and relatively inexpensive. Meats should be packaged in the quantities that can be used at one time, and poultry should be cut as it is to be used in cooking. Unlike fruits and vegetables, these foods are not, as a rule, packed in containers but are wrapped in the moisture-vapor-resistant kinds of wrappings that are made especially for the purpose. Wrapping must be done so carefully that air will be squeezed out from around the food, thus letting the paper fit closely and tightly around it. As soon as possible after the meats and poultry are wrapped, the packages should be placed into the freezer.

Baked products. Yeast rolls and bread, biscuits, muffins, pies, cakes, and cookies are among the baked products that can be frozen. They will provide a means of saving time and effort in preparing meals on particularly busy days. Rolls and bread should be baked before they are frozen, but unbaked biscuits and muffins freeze satisfactorily. One biscuit can be separated from another by placing double pieces of wax paper, cellophane, or other freezer wrapping between them. Muffin batter should be frozen in paper baking cups.

So far as quality is concerned, most pies, cakes, and cookies may be frozen either before or after they are baked. If you have a home freezer, you may like to experiment and decide for yourself which way you prefer. When it is a question of saving time in preparing a meal on some later day, then freezing the baked pie, cake, or cookies would certainly be the better plan. If a sponge cake or angel food

STEPS IN FREEZING PEACHES

● (1) Wash, pit, and peel the peaches. Put about ½ cup cold syrup into each pint container. (A syrup made with 3 cups sugar to each quart water is frequently used. For a less-sweet syrup, the proportion is 2 cups sugar to each quart water, and for a sweeter syrup, equal parts of sugar and water are used.) Slice the peaches directly into the syrup (left). (2) Add more syrup to cover the peaches, but leave a ½-inch space at the top of the container (right).

● (3) Put a piece of crumpled parchment paper on top of peaches, and press them down into the syrup (left). (4) Wipe all sealing edges clean, and cover container tightly (right). Place in freezer.

418

STEPS IN FREEZING SNAP BEANS

● (1) Wash, trim, and cut the snap beans. Blanch by placing them in boiling water for 3 minutes (left), using a gallon of water for each pound of beans. (2) Remove the beans from the blanching water, and plunge into cold water (right). When the beans are cold, drain them.

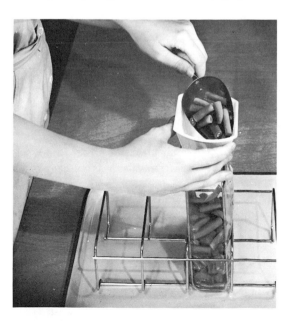 

● (3) Pack the beans into containers, leaving ½-inch head space (left), or pack in plastic bags. (4) Close the containers or plastic bags (right), and place in the freezer.

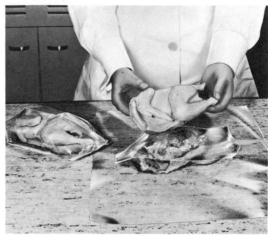

Photos courtesy Frigidaire

● Separate pieces of meat and poultry with a double layer of wrapping material before packaging them for freezing.

cake is put into the freezer, however, it should be baked first because only the baked cake will freeze satisfactorily.

Freezer wrappings, rather than rigid containers, are better suited for packaging most kinds of baked goods. The baked goods must be wrapped and sealed carefully in order to avoid damaging the product and yet to be sure that all air is excluded and the wrapping paper sealed tightly. If pies and baked cakes are frozen before they are wrapped, they can be more easily handled.

A cake batter may be frozen in waxed cartons and later thawed and transferred to pans for baking, or the batter may be frozen in the pan in which it will be baked. Of course if you choose the latter method, you will need to own several baking pans.

Sandwiches. Since sandwiches will keep in frozen storage for several weeks, they can be made in advance. When packed in a lunch box, they will thaw during the morning and be just right for eating at lunchtime. It is a good idea to spread both slices of bread with butter or margarine and to be sure that the filling is made of foods that freeze well. Raw

vegetables that lose crispness, hard-cooked egg whites that become rubbery, mayonnaise which separates, and jams and jellies that tend to soak into the bread are not recommended.

Packaging Materials for Freezing Foods

Packaging materials used for quick freezing include wrapping papers, freezer foil, several kinds of bags, and rigid containers of cardboard, glass, plastic, and metal. The material must have two qualities: (1) It must resist loss of moisture from the food and (2) it must prevent air from passing through it and reaching the food. Loss of moisture causes drying of all foods and discoloration of meats and poultry. Contact with air will cause meat and poultry fats to become rancid and fruits to darken. In addition to resistance to passage of moisture and air, packaging materials should be clean, strong at very low temperatures, odorless, and easy to use.

Directions for Freezing Foods

The Canada Department of Agriculture has published pamphlets in which directions are given for freezing many individual kinds of foods. In addition, the departments of agriculture of the various provinces supply bulletins which give valuable information on this subject. Directions for freezing strawberries, peaches, and snap beans will be found on pages 416, 418, and 419.

Food Value of Frozen Foods

The food value of frozen fruits is about equal to that of fresh fruits. In frozen vegetables there is some loss of water-soluble minerals and vitamins in the blanching and subsequent cooling, but the extent of this loss is not great. In addition, there may be a slight loss of vitamin C and thiamine during freezer storage. Other than this, any change in the food value of frozen vegetables when they are cooked for serving is comparable to any such change that occurs in the cooking of the corresponding fresh vegetables.

When meats and poultry thaw, juice flows from them. This juice is called "drip." Since some nutrients have dissolved in it, it is important to use the drip along with the meats and poultry in the cooking process whenever possible. The extent of loss of juices can be reduced if the defrosting time is not unnecessarily prolonged.

Use of Frozen Foods

Frozen fruits can be used in practically all of the ways in which fresh fruits are used in meals except for eating out of hand. It is important to observe caution in defrosting frozen fruits, for they are at their best when still very cold. In fact, many people prefer the fruit to have some ice crystals still remaining in the pieces. The time required for defrosting frozen fruit will be shorter if done at room temperature rather than in the refrigerator. However, if the fruit is defrosted in the refrigerator, the thawing will be more even throughout the whole mass.

Frozen vegetables also serve the same purpose in meals as do the fresh vegetables. The rule for cooking them is to place them in a small amount of boiling water while they are still solidly frozen and to cover the saucepan. In general, the cooking time, after the water comes back to the boiling point again, is somewhat shorter for the frozen vegetable than for the corresponding fresh vegetable.

When the frozen product is either meat or poultry, the usual practice is to defrost it before starting to cook it. It is possible to begin the cooking while the food is still frozen, but then the cooking time must be lengthened.

Products like bread, pies, cakes, and cookies that are frozen after they are baked may be defrosted by holding them in their sealed wrappings at room temperature. The time required will depend on the size of the individual piece. Another way to defrost frozen baked products is to place them, still in their sealed wrappings, in a warm oven at about 250° to 300° F. This method of defrosting seems to give the product more nearly its freshly baked character than does thawing at room temperature.

Pies that are frozen unbaked may be baked without defrosting, or they may be thawed first and then baked. In both cases, the wrapping is removed.

● Mold the wrapping material closely to pies, cakes, or other irregularly shaped products to exclude the air.

Courtesy Reynolds Wrap

Cake batters that are frozen in the cartons will need to be defrosted so that the batter can be poured into the pans for baking. If, instead, the batter is frozen in the pan, it may be baked from the frozen state. Or the batter in the pan may first be defrosted and then baked. Either one of these procedures is satisfactory.

If cookie dough is frozen, it needs to be defrosted only to a point that will make it soft enough to handle—to slice, to drop, or to roll for cutting.

Storage of Frozen Foods

When the home freezer is held at 0° F. or lower, the storage conditions are considered adequate for all kinds of frozen foods. It is wise to follow the manufacturer's directions as to the amount of unfrozen foods that can be placed in the freezer at one time. When food is removed from the freezer, the lid or door should not be held open any longer than is necessary. These precautions are followed to keep the temperature of the freezer as nearly uniform at 0° F. as possible. Where there are uneven temperature conditions, there is apt to be some lessening of the quality of the frozen food.

The length of the storage period also needs to be considered. Fruits and vegetables will remain in good condition for long periods of time—certainly until the next crop is available. For meats and poultry, shorter storage times are advisable. These are given in the chart "Care of Food to Retain Quality" on pages 88 and 89.

Jelly Making

Fruit jelly is made by cooking fruit juice with sugar until it is of such a consistency that it will become firm when cooled. Like canning, the making of fruit jellies, jams, and preserves is a very old way of preserving fruits. However, pieces of fruit are used in making jams and preserves.

Principles of Jelly Making

There are two principles involved in jelly making. One has to do with its keeping quality and the second with the reason jelly is formed.

Keeping quality. One of the early steps in making jelly is the boiling of the fruit until it is so soft that the juice can be strained away from it, leaving only the pulp. During this boiling process, enzymes and also the microorganisms that are originally present in the fruit are destroyed. But as the jelly-making procedure continues, there is a chance that other bacteria, yeasts, and molds from the air may enter the juice, or later even lodge on the surface of the finished jelly. If this happens, the bacteria will not thrive because jelly contains a quantity of sugar, and bacteria do not like sugar. But it is different with yeasts and molds. These microorganisms *do* like sugar and will grow and cause the jelly to spoil. To prevent this, the top of the jelly in the glass is covered with a thin layer of paraffin and, for further protection, a metal lid.

Jelly formation. Besides the fact that it must have good keeping quality, good jelly must retain the shape of the mold when it is turned out onto a dish. This jellying property is due to the pectin found in many fruit juices. When sugar is dissolved in the juice and the whole boiled for a short time, water evaporates and the sweetened juice becomes thicker. Finally, it becomes so thick that, when a small amount of it is turned from the side of a spoon, two thick drops form, cling side by side to the edge, and drop off as a sheet of jelly. This is a sign that the juice and sugar have been cooked together long enough to give the right consistency. It is now time for the next step in the jelly-making process—that of pouring the hot mass into jelly glasses for cooling. As it cools, the jelly will become clear, firm, and jellylike.

Methods of Making Jelly

The selection of fruit is the first thing to consider in making jelly. It should be a fruit

DIRECTIONS FOR MAKING JELLY

Courtesy Kerr Glass Manufacturing Corporation

● Jelly should be firm but not stiff, and when cut, the edges should retain sharp angles. To make a good jelly, follow these directions:

1. Wash all fruit thoroughly, handling carefully. If berries are used, lift from water.
2. Cut large fruit into small pieces of fairly uniform size. Remove the caps and stems from berries, and leave whole.
3. Boil the fruit in water according to the amount given in the chart on page 424.
4. Drip the hot, cooked fruit through a jelly bag into a bowl. Press the bag to get all the juice possible, and re-strain juice.
5. Wash the jelly glasses. Sterilize the glasses by placing them on a rack in a pan of hot water. Boil 10 to 15 minutes.
6. Add sugar to the juice according to the amount stated in the chart on page 424. Heat together the fruit juice and correct amount of sugar to the boiling point, stirring only until the sugar is dissolved. Boil rapidly until two distinct drops of syrup are formed on the side of a spoon and run together into a "sheet." Remove from heat and let stand.
7. Drain the hot jelly glasses, and place them on a tray.
8. Remove any scum that may have formed on the hot jelly. Pour the hot jelly at once into the glasses to within ¼ inch of the top. Cover with a towel, and let stand undisturbed until the jelly is firm.
9. Pour hot melted paraffin over the entire surface of the jelly to make a good seal. Cover with a clean, dry lid. Label, and store in a cool, dry place.

that has a good content of pectin and preferably some acid as well. Acid helps the pectin to make firm jelly. Some fruits that contain both pectin and acid are currants, tart apples, crab apples, blackberries, cranberries, and some varieties of grapes. Since the acid content decreases during ripening, the fruit should be just barely ripe. Another advantage of such fruit is that the pectin in it has better jellying ability than it has after the fruit has become overripe or even very ripe. Directions for making fruit jelly will be found in the charts on pages 423 and 424.

Food Value of Jelly

Jellies of all kinds contain a large amount of sugar with very little of any other nutrient. For these reasons the chief contribution of jellies to the diet is energy.

Uses of Jelly

Jelly served with meats provides a flavor contrast that is appetizing. Jelly also provides a color contrast to many foods and thus adds interest to meals. Another favorite use of jelly is for a quick dessert at the end of a meal. Served with cream cheese or cottage cheese for spreading on crackers, the dessert takes only a minute to prepare. Jelly also adds a note of color when used to top such puddings as rice and tapioca.

Bread and jelly sandwiches are popular. A simple lunch or supper can be planned around them. They are always acceptable in the packed lunch for school, for work, or for a picnic. And when jelly sandwiches are small and cut in fancy shapes, they make a dainty refreshment that can be served with afternoon tea.

PROPORTION AND TIME CHART FOR MAKING JELLY

FRUIT	WATER Quantity needed for each pound of fruit (cups)	BOILING TIME To extract juice from fruit (minutes)	SUGAR Amount needed for each cup of juice[1] (cups)
Apples	1	20–25	¾
Crab apples	1	20–25	1
Blackberries			
Firm fruit	¼	5–10	¾–1
Very soft fruit	None	5–10	¾–1
Cranberries	3	5–10	¾
Currants	¼ or none	5–10	1
Grapes such as Concord	¼ or none	5–10	¾–1
Plums, Wild Goose type	½	15–20	¾
Quinces	2	20–25	¾

[1] Never use more than 6 cups of juice for a batch.

PART V . . .

The Recipes

for Your

Meals

Introduction to Recipes

It is a satisfaction as well as a great help to own a file of favorite recipes. In building such a file, you should be discriminating and start with basic recipes from which you can make many variations. For example, you can follow a basic recipe for biscuits, muffins, or a gelatin mixture and, by using your imagination but without disturbing the correct proportion of basic ingredients, make several similar although different products. With basic recipes as a beginning, you can add other recipes from time to time until you have a worthwhile file of your own.

It is important to select tested recipes—that is, recipes in which the proportions of ingredients have been adjusted accurately and the method of making has been worked out in de-

tail so as to give the best results. In tested recipes that include a baking step, the size of the baking utensil and the right temperature and time of baking are stated. Many tested recipes also give the number of servings that each will make. You will find tested recipes in most cookbooks, in some newspapers, in many magazines, and in the publications of the provincial departments of agriculture as well as the Canada Department of Agriculture. In addition, manufacturers of food products have developed recipes featuring their individual foods.

Tested recipes that give excellent results at sea level and altitudes up to about 2,500 feet may not be usable at higher altitudes. This difficulty is caused by the difference in atmos-

STEPS IN FOLLOWING A RECIPE

1. Read the recipe through thoughtfully.

2. Be sure you have all the ingredients listed.

3. Assemble all ingredients and equipment, and arrange them in a convenient and orderly manner at your work space.

4. Use mixing and cooking utensils suitable for the size of the product you are making.

5. Take care of any preliminary steps in the procedure, such as:
   a. Heating water, scalding milk, or melting chocolate
   b. Chopping or mincing such ingredients as nut meats or onions
   c. Removing eggs from the refrigerator if they are to be beaten
   d. Greasing baking utensils
   e. Turning on the oven so that it can be heating to the temperature called for

6. Be familiar with all the terms in the recipe. (See pages 143 to 148.)

7. If necessary, look up the principles on which the steps in the recipe are based. (See chapters in Part IV, "The Foods for Your Meals.")

8. Always measure accurately by using accepted techniques.

STANDARD MEASURING CUPS AND SPOONS

● From left to right: (1) Cup for measuring dry ingredients with graduation marks indicating ¼-cup divisions. (2) Four nested cups with measuring capacities of ¼, ⅓, ½, and 1 cup. (3) Cup for measuring liquids with space above full-cup mark for easier measuring and lip for pouring. (4) Set of spoons with measuring capacities of ¼, ½, and 1 teaspoon and 1 tablespoon.

pheric pressure at different elevations. If you live at the higher altitudes, it would be well for you to select recipes that have been developed for use at your particular altitude. In Canada, only those areas in the high Rockies may be confronted with this problem. Some manufacturers of ready-to-bake mixes give instructions for high altitude baking.

As you use your recipes, you may want to make them even more valuable by inserting marginal notes for future reference. For example, you might note the preparation time, a special brand of one of the ingredients, or some suggestions for garnishing or serving.

The recipes in this book are tested recipes. They have been selected to illustrate the many principles of preparation that you will study in the chapters in Part IV, "The Foods for Your Meals." In writing these recipes, the following style was chosen from the several styles that are in common use:

1. The ingredients are listed in the order of use.
2. The method or procedure of making is given in numbered steps.
3. Suggestions are made about the size of cooking utensils to use wherever necessary.

4. When needed, the temperature and time of cooking are stated.
5. Tests to determine when some products are sufficiently cooked are included.
6. The expected number of average-sized servings is given. This is approximate, since opinions differ and individual servings may be smaller or larger than the amount usually considered average.
7. As an aid in evaluating products, many recipes include a statement of a standard describing the characteristics necessary for a good-quality product.

How to Follow Recipes

In Chapter 8, "Preparing Meals," there are some general directions for using recipes. In the chart on the opposite page are some specific steps to follow.

Measuring Techniques

The accuracy with which you measure the ingredients in almost all recipes is of the utmost importance to your success in meal preparation.

To help you make accurate measurements, the measuring techniques for the ingredients

Flour

● (1) Before measuring, sift the approximate amount of flour needed onto clean paper or into a bowl. (2) Spoon the sifted flour lightly into a measuring cup of the correct size until the cup is overfull. Do not shake the cup as the flour will pack in it. Run a spatula or knife through the flour to remove any air pockets. (3) Level off the extra flour with the broad blade of a spatula or knife so that the measured flour is just level with the top of the cup.

Sugar

● (1) Spoon the sugar lightly into a measuring cup of the correct size until the cup is overfull. Do not shake the cup as the sugar will pack in it. (2) Level off the extra sugar with the broad blade of a spatula or knife so that the measured sugar is just level with the top of the cup.

Baking Powder, Baking Soda, Salt, and Other Spices

● (1) Fill a measuring spoon of the correct size overfull with the dry ingredients. (2) Level off the extra amount with a spatula or knife.

Brown Sugar

● Unlike other dry ingredients, brown sugar should be packed into a measuring cup of the correct size before leveling it off.

COMMON INGREDIENTS

Measuring Shortening by
the Water-displacement Method

● (1) Fill a measuring cup with the amount of water equal to the difference between the measure of fat desired and the full cup. (For ½ cup shortening, use ½ cup water.) (2) Put shortening in cup until the level of the water is just even with the one-cup line. (3) Drain off the water.

Liquids and Syrups

● To measure liquids: (1) Pour the liquid into a glass measuring cup, filling it to the mark desired. (2) Judge the level of the liquid in the cup by holding the measuring line at eye level.

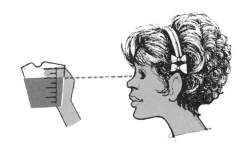

● To measure syrup: (1) Oil the measuring utensil lightly before pouring in the syrup. (2) Judge the level of the syrup by holding the cup with measuring line at eye level. (3) Scrape syrup out with rubber spatula.

commonly used are given on pages 428 and 429.

Further Helps for Using Recipes

Following are a few general suggestions which have been found necessary or helpful in using recipes:

1. When beating eggs separately, beat the egg whites first, and do not wash the beater before beating the egg yolks. Follow this method when beating both egg whites and cream.
2. When using a thermometer for judging the temperature of boiling candy syrup or a fat for deep-fat frying, be sure that your eyes are level with the top of the mercury column as you read the temperature.
3. For ease of incorporating liquid into a flour-shortening mixture, put the liquid in a depression, or "well," made in the mixture.
4. In making batters and doughs where the step calls for adding dry and liquid ingredients alternately, add each in three installments, starting with the dry ingredients. This prevents the mixture from becoming either too stiff or too thin.
5. When baking foods, use either an oil or a softened solid fat for greasing the baking utensils. A light coating of flour on the

greased surface may be used for cakes, or the pan may be lined with wax paper which has been greased.

6. When removing a gelatin dish from the mold, loosen the gelatin around the top with the tip of a paring knife and dip the mold into hot water for several seconds. Then carefully let the gelatin slide onto a serving dish.
7. Before serving such foods as sauces, gravies, or vegetables, taste them whenever possible, and, if necessary, add more butter or margarine, salt, pepper, or other seasoning. Always use a separate spoon for tasting.

TERMS COMMONLY USED TO DESCRIBE OVEN TEMPERATURES *

TEMPERATURE (degrees F.)	TERM
250 and 275	Very slow
300 and 325	Slow
350 and 375	Moderate
400 and 425	Hot
450 and 475	Very hot
500 and 525	Extremely hot

*From *Handbook of Food Preparation*, American Home Economics Association, Washington, D.C., 1964, p. 29

COMMON EQUIVALENT MEASUREMENTS FOR FOOD

DRY AND LIQUID MEASUREMENTS

16 tablespoons	=	1 cup
12 tablespoons	=	¾ cup
10⅔ tablespoons	=	⅔ cup
8 tablespoons	=	½ cup
5⅓ tablespoons	=	⅓ cup
4 tablespoons	=	¼ cup
2 tablespoons	=	⅛ cup or 1 liquid ounce
1 tablespoon	=	3 teaspoons
Few grains	=	less than ⅛ teaspoon

LIQUID MEASUREMENTS

2 cups	=	1 pint (U.S.)
4 cups	=	1 quart (U.S.)
4 quarts	=	1 gallon

DRY MEASUREMENTS

8 quarts	=	1 peck
4 pecks	=	1 bushel
16 ounces	=	1 pound

Table of Contents for Recipes

BEVERAGES

COCOA

4 servings

3 tablespoons sugar
¼ cup cocoa
⅛ teaspoon salt
1 cup water
3 cups milk

1. Put sugar, cocoa, and salt in saucepan, and mix thoroughly.
2. Stir in water gradually.
3. Cook over low heat, stirring occasionally, for about 5 minutes, or until mixture is thick and syrupy.
4. Stir in milk, and heat, stirring occasionally, until cocoa begins to simmer.
5. Remove from heat.
6. Beat with rotary beater until frothy to prevent skin from forming on surface.
7. Serve in cups, and garnish with marshmallow or whipped cream, if desired.

STANDARD: Creamy brown in color; slightly thicker in consistency than milk; free from sediment or film on surface; a moderately strong flavor of chocolate.

HOT CHOCOLATE

Follow recipe for Cocoa except use 1½ to 2 squares unsweetened chocolate, cut into several pieces, instead of ¼ cup cocoa.

STANDARD: Darker in color and a stronger flavor of chocolate than Cocoa.

TEA

5 servings

4 teaspoons tea
or
4 tea bags
4 cups freshly boiling water

1. Pour boiling water into teapot, cover, let stand for several minutes to heat pot, and drain.
2. Put tea or tea bags in hot teapot.
3. Pour freshly boiling water over tea, and cover teapot.
4. Let stand for 3 to 5 minutes, depending on strength desired, and then stir.
5. Strain tea into another hot teapot or remove tea bags before serving.
6. Serve with sugar and milk or lemon, as desired.

STANDARD: Sparkling clear without any sediment; color depending on kind of tea used in making beverage—black tea: light to medium amber in color, green tea: yellow-green in color; flavor distinctive of kind of tea used.

ICED TEA

Follow recipe for Tea except for these differences:
1. Use twice the amount of tea.
2. Pour hot tea over ice cubes in tall glasses.
3. Garnish with mint, if desired.
4. Serve with sugar and lemon slices or wedges.

COFFEE

4 servings

6 tablespoons coffee
or
3 coffee measures
3 cups water (cold or hot, according
to kind of coffee maker used)

Steeping Method

1. Put regular grind of coffee and cold water in coffee maker, mix, and cover.
2. Bring to a boil, and immediately reduce heat.
3. Leave over heat (steep) for 3 to 5 minutes.
4. Strain coffee from grounds before serving.
5. Serve with cream and sugar, as desired.

NOTE: Mixing a crushed egg shell with ground coffee and cold water helps to make steeped coffee clearer.

Vacuum Method

1. Put cold water in lower part of coffee maker.
2. Put drip grind of coffee in upper part, insert in lower part, and cover.
3. Heat water until most of it has risen into upper part, and for about 3 minutes longer.
4. Turn off heat, and allow to stand until coffee drains to lower part.
5. Remove upper part, and cover coffee.
6. Serve with cream and sugar, as desired.

Percolator Method

1. Put water in percolator, using cold or hot water according to manufacturer's directions.
2. Put regular grind of coffee in coffee basket, insert in percolator, and cover.
3. Heat until water starts to percolate.
4. Allow to percolate for 6 to 8 minutes after water in the percolator tube starts to change color, depending on strength of coffee desired.
5. Remove basket, and cover coffee.
6. Serve with cream and sugar, as desired.

Drip Method

1. Put drip grind of coffee in coffee basket, and insert in lower part of coffee maker.
2. Pour boiling water over ground coffee, and cover.
3. Keep coffee maker over low heat as water drips through ground coffee.
4. Remove basket, stir coffee, and cover.
5. Serve with cream and sugar, as desired.

STANDARD: Dark amber in color; sparkling clear without any sediment; a marked coffee aroma and pungent but not bitter taste; a distinct yellow tinge when cream is added.

ICED COFFEE

Follow recipe for Coffee except for these differences:
1. Use twice the amount of coffee.
2. Pour hot coffee over ice cubes in tall glasses.
3. Serve with cream and sugar, as desired.

CHOCOLATE MILK SHAKE

2 servings

¼ cup Chocolate Sauce (page 513)
or
¼ cup chocolate syrup
2 cups milk
½ cup vanilla or chocolate ice cream

1. Blend chocolate sauce or syrup and milk in electric blender or by shaking in jar with tightly fitting cover.
2. Divide ice cream between two tall glasses.
3. Pour chocolate-milk mixture over ice cream.
4. Serve immediately.

VARIATIONS: Use Butterscotch Sauce (page 513), instead of chocolate sauce, with vanilla ice cream.

Use ½ cup frozen fruit, partly defrosted, instead of chocolate sauce, with vanilla ice cream.

Blend ice cream in blender with milk and flavoring.

435

EGGNOG

1 serving

1 tablespoon sugar
Few grains salt
1 cup milk
¼ teaspoon vanilla
1 egg, slightly beaten
Few grains nutmeg (optional)

1. Put sugar, salt, milk, vanilla, and egg in mixing bowl.
2. Beat with rotary beater until frothy.
3. Strain into pitcher.
4. Pour into glasses, and sprinkle with nutmeg, if used.

NOTE: The egg may be separated, and the white beaten until stiff, and folded in last.

VARIATIONS: Add 1 tablespoon malted milk, and beat with ingredients in step 2.

Add 2 tablespoons chocolate syrup, and beat with ingredients in step 2.

● Iced drinks should always be served on a coaster so that moisture accumulating on the outside of the glass does not dampen the linen or mar the table.

LEMONADE

3 servings

½ to ¾ cup sugar
½ cup lemon juice
3 cups water

1. Put sugar, lemon juice, and water in pitcher.
2. Stir until sugar is dissolved.
3. Put ice cubes in tall glasses.
4. Pour lemonade over ice cubes, and let stand for several minutes to chill.
5. Garnish with cherry, mint, or lemon slice, as desired.

STRAWBERRY PUNCH

About 25 half-cup servings

1 10-ounce box frozen sliced strawberries, defrosted
1 6-ounce can frozen orange juice, undiluted
1 6-ounce can frozen lemonade, undiluted
1½ quarts water
1 pint ginger ale

1. Crush defrosted strawberries.
2. Mix undiluted fruit juices and water, and chill.
3. Add ginger ale and crushed strawberries just before serving.
4. Pour over ice cubes in punch bowl or large pitcher.

Courtesy Best Foods, Inc.

CAKES AND FROSTINGS

Cakes

PLAIN LAYER CAKE
Two 9-inch round layers

2 cups sifted cake flour
or
1⅞ cups sifted all-purpose flour
2½ teaspoons baking powder
½ teaspoon salt
½ cup shortening
1 cup sugar
2 eggs, unbeaten
¾ cup milk
1 teaspoon vanilla

Oven Temperature: 375° F.

1. Sift together flour, baking powder, and salt onto wax paper.
2. Put shortening and sugar in mixing bowl, and cream until well blended.
3. Stir in unbeaten eggs, one at a time, and then beat until light and fluffy.
4. Stir in sifted dry ingredients alternately with milk to make a batter, and stir until batter is well blended. (See page 430.)
5. Stir in vanilla.
6. Pour batter evenly into greased layer-cake pans.
7. Bake at 375° F. for 25 to 30 minutes, or until cake springs back when touched lightly with finger.
8. Place pans on wire rack for 5 to 10 minutes.
9. Remove cake from pans, and place on wire rack to cool.
10. Frost when cold.

NOTE: Two 8-inch pans may be used for thicker layers or three 8-inch pans for thinner layers, as desired.

STANDARD: Layers symmetrical in shape with slightly rounded tops; crust thin and golden brown; crumb even and fine in grain, moist and tender in texture; well flavored with vanilla.

PLAIN CUPCAKES
Twelve 2¾-inch cupcakes

1¾ cups sifted cake flour
1½ teaspoons baking powder
¼ teaspoon salt
½ cup shortening
1 cup sugar
2 eggs, well beaten
⅔ cup milk
1 teaspoon vanilla

Oven Temperature: 375° F.

1. Sift together flour, baking powder, and salt onto wax paper.
2. Put shortening and sugar in mixing bowl, and cream until well blended. *(Continued)*

3. Add well-beaten eggs slowly, and beat until light and fluffy.
4. Stir in sifted dry ingredients alternately with milk to make a batter, and stir until batter is well blended. (See page 430.)
5. Stir in vanilla.
6. Pour batter into greased muffin pans, filling them one-half to two-thirds full.
7. Bake at 375° F. for 20 to 25 minutes, or until cupcakes spring back when touched lightly with finger.
8. Place pans on wire rack for 3 minutes.
9. Remove cupcakes from pans, and place on wire rack to cool.

NUT CUPCAKES

Follow recipe for Plain Cupcakes except stir ¾ cup finely chopped nuts into finished batter.

QUICK-METHOD CAKE
(One-bowl)
Three 8-inch round layers

2¼ cups sifted cake flour
3 teaspoons baking powder
1 teaspoon salt
1½ cups sugar
½ cup shortening, at room temperature
1 cup milk
2 eggs, unbeaten
1½ teaspoons vanilla

Oven Temperature: 375° F.

1. Sift together first four ingredients into bowl of electric mixer.
2. Add shortening and about ⅔ cup of the milk.
3. Beat at medium speed for 2½ minutes.
4. Add the rest of the milk, unbeaten eggs, and vanilla.
5. Beat at medium speed for 3 minutes.
6. Pour batter evenly into greased layer-cake pans which have been lined with wax paper that has also been greased.
7. Bake at 375° F. for 25 to 30 minutes, or until cake springs back when touched lightly with finger.

8. Place pans on wire rack for 5 to 10 minutes.
9. Remove cake from pans, and place on wire rack to cool.
10. Frost when cold.

> STANDARD: Layers symmetrical in shape with slightly rounded tops; crust thin and golden brown; crumb even and slightly open in grain, delicate in texture; well flavored with vanilla.

CHOCOLATE CAKE
Two 9-inch round layers

2 cups sifted all-purpose flour
2½ teaspoons baking powder
¼ teaspoon baking soda
½ teaspoon salt
3 squares unsweetened chocolate
½ cup water
½ cup shortening
1⅔ cups sugar
3 eggs, unbeaten
1 teaspoon vanilla
1 cup buttermilk

Oven Temperature: 365° F.

1. Sift together *twice* flour, baking powder, baking soda, and salt onto wax paper.
2. Cut unsweetened chocolate into several pieces, add water, and cook over low heat, stirring constantly, until a thick paste is formed.
3. Cool.
4. Put shortening and sugar in mixing bowl, and cream until well blended.
5. Stir in unbeaten eggs, one at a time, and then beat until light and fluffy.
6. Add chocolate paste and vanilla, and beat well.
7. Stir in sifted dry ingredients alternately with buttermilk, stirring after each addition until batter is smooth. (See page 430.)
8. Pour batter evenly into greased layer-cake pans.
9. Bake at 365° F. for 35 minutes, or until cake springs back when touched lightly with finger.

10. Place pans on wire rack for 5 to 10 minutes.
11. Remove cake from pans, and place on wire rack to cool.
12. Frost when cold.

STANDARD: Layers symmetrical in shape with slightly rounded tops; crust and crumb medium-dark chocolate in color; crumb even and fine in grain, velvety and tender in texture; delicately flavored with chocolate.

SPICE CAKE
Two 9-inch round layers

2 cups sifted cake flour
2½ teaspoons baking powder
¼ teaspoon salt
½ teaspoon cinnamon
½ teaspoon cloves
½ teaspoon ginger
½ cup shortening
1 cup sugar
2 eggs, unbeaten
¾ cup milk

Oven Temperature: 375° F.

1. Sift together *twice* flour, baking powder, salt, and spices onto wax paper.
2. Put shortening and sugar in mixing bowl, and cream until well blended.
3. Stir in unbeaten eggs, one at a time, and then beat until light and fluffy.
4. Stir in sifted dry ingredients alternately with milk to make a batter, and stir until batter is well blended. (See page 430.)
5. Pour batter evenly into greased layer-cake pans.
6. Bake at 375° F. for 25 to 30 minutes, or until cake springs back when touched lightly with finger.
7. Place pans on wire rack for 5 to 10 minutes.
8. Remove cake from pans, and place on wire rack to cool.
9. Frost when cold.

NOTE: Two 8-inch pans may be used for thicker layers or three 8-inch pans for thinner layers, as desired.

STANDARD: Layers symmetrical in shape with slightly rounded tops; crust thin and brown; crumb even and fine in grain, moist and tender in texture; rich, spicy flavor.

SPONGE CAKE
One 10-inch cake in tube pan

6 eggs, separated
1 cup sugar
Grated rind of 1 lemon
2 tablespoons lemon juice
½ teaspoon salt
1 cup sifted cake flour

Oven Temperature: 325° F.

1. Put egg yolks in mixing bowl, and beat, with rotary beater or electric mixer at high speed, until thick and lemon-colored.
2. Add sugar gradually with continued beating.
3. Add grated lemon rind and lemon juice, and beat well.
4. Add salt to egg whites, and beat, with clean rotary beater or electric mixer at high speed, until stiff but not dry.
5. Cut and fold one-half of the stiffly beaten egg whites into egg-yolk–sugar mixture.
6. Sift in flour, about ¼ cup at a time, and blend after each addition by cutting and folding.
7. Cut and fold in the rest of the stiffly beaten egg whites.
8. Pour batter into ungreased tube pan, and draw a spatula through it to remove entrapped large air bubbles.
9. Bake at 325° F. for 1 hour, or until cake springs back when touched lightly with finger.
10. Invert pan over inverted funnel or neck of bottle, and allow cake to become cold before removing. (About 1 hour.)

STANDARD: Symmetrical in shape with slightly rounded top; crust light brown in color; crumb golden yellow, even and fairly fine in grain, tender and somewhat sponge-like in texture; pleasing lemon flavor.

ANGEL FOOD CAKE
One 10-inch cake in tube pan

1 cup sifted cake flour
1¼ cups sifted sugar
½ teaspoon salt
1¼ cups (10 to 12) egg whites, at room temperature
1 teaspoon cream of tartar
1 teaspoon vanilla
1 teaspoon almond extract

Oven Temperature: 325° F.

1. Sift together *twice* flour and sugar onto wax paper.
2. Add salt to egg whites, and beat, with rotary beater or electric mixer at high speed, until foamy.
3. Sprinkle cream of tartar over foamy egg whites, add vanilla and almond extract, and beat until stiff but not dry.
4. Sift flour-sugar mixture, a little at a time, onto stiffly beaten egg whites, cutting and folding gently after each addition until well blended.
5. Pour batter into ungreased tube pan, and draw a spatula through it to remove entrapped large air bubbles.
6. Bake at 325° F. for 1 hour, or until cake springs back when touched lightly with finger.
7. Invert pan over inverted funnel or neck of bottle, and allow cake to become cold before removing. (About 1 hour.)
8. Dust cake with icing sugar, or frost with uncooked frosting.

STANDARD: Symmetrical in shape; crust very light brown and somewhat moist; interior white, even and fine in grain, moist and velvety in texture; delicately flavored with almond.

● Angel food cake is sometimes served with fresh fruit and whipped cream similar to a shortcake.

440

CHIFFON CAKE
One 9-inch cake in tube pan

1⅛ cups sifted cake flour
¾ cup sugar
1½ teaspoons baking powder
½ teaspoon salt
¼ cup oil
2 egg yolks, unbeaten
¼ cup water
1 teaspoon vanilla
½ cup (about 4) egg whites
¼ teaspoon cream of tartar

Oven Temperature: 350° F.

1. Sift together flour, ½ cup of the sugar, baking powder, and salt into mixing bowl.
2. Make a depression in center of ingredients, and add oil, unbeaten egg yolks, water, and vanilla, but do not beat.
3. Beat egg whites until foamy, sprinkle cream of tartar over them, and add the rest of the sugar, beating it in gradually with rotary beater or electric mixer at high speed to make a stiff meringue.
4. Beat flour–oil–egg-yolk mixture until smooth.
5. Pour over meringue, and cut and fold gently until color is uniform.
6. Pour batter into ungreased tube pan.
7. Bake at 350° F. for 35 to 40 minutes, or until cake springs back when touched lightly with finger.
8. Invert pan over inverted funnel or neck of bottle, and allow cake to become cold before removing. (About 1 hour.)

Courtesy Stokely-Van Camp, Inc.

ORANGE CHIFFON CAKE

Follow recipe for Chiffon Cake except for these differences:
1. Use 2 tablespoons orange juice and 2 tablespoons water instead of ¼ cup water.
2. Use grated rind of ½ orange instead of vanilla.

GINGERBREAD

One 12x8x2-inch sheet

2½ cups sifted all-purpose flour
1½ teaspoons baking powder
½ teaspoon baking soda
½ teaspoon salt
1 teaspoon ginger
1 teaspoon cinnamon
1 teaspoon cloves
½ cup shortening
½ cup sugar
2 eggs, well beaten
1 cup molasses
1 cup boiling water

Oven Temperature: 350° F.

1. Sift together *twice* flour, baking powder, baking soda, salt, and spices onto wax paper.
2. Put shortening, sugar, well-beaten eggs, and molasses in mixing bowl, and beat until well blended.
3. Stir in sifted dry ingredients alternately with boiling water, and stir only enough to just blend ingredients. (See page 430.)
4. Pour batter into greased pan which has been lightly floured.
5. Bake at 350° F. for 40 to 45 minutes, or until gingerbread springs back when touched lightly with finger.
6. Place pan on wire rack to cool for 5 to 10 minutes.
7. Cut into squares while still in pan.
8. Serve warm as a dessert with applesauce or whipped cream, or serve as a hot bread with butter or margarine.

PINEAPPLE UPSIDE-DOWN CAKE

One 8x8-inch cake

1 tablespoon butter or margarine
⅓ cup light-brown sugar, firmly packed
6 slices canned pineapple
8 candied cherries
1¼ cups sifted cake flour
1½ teaspoons baking powder
½ teaspoon salt
¼ cup shortening
¾ cup sugar
1 egg, well beaten
½ cup milk
1 teaspoon vanilla

Oven Temperature: 350° F.

1. Melt butter or margarine in baking pan, and sprinkle light-brown sugar over it.
2. Arrange pineapple slices and candied cherries attractively over light-brown sugar and butter or margarine.
3. Sift together flour, baking powder, and salt onto wax paper.
4. Put shortening and sugar in mixing bowl, and cream until well blended.
5. Add well-beaten egg, and beat until light and fluffy.
6. Stir in sifted dry ingredients alternately with milk to make a batter, and stir until batter is well blended. (See page 430.)
7. Stir in vanilla.
8. Pour batter over fruit in baking pan.
9. Bake at 350° F. for 40 minutes, or until cake springs back when touched lightly with finger.
10. Place pan on wire rack to cool for 5 to 10 minutes.
11. Loosen cake around edges, and invert onto serving plate.
12. Serve with whipped cream, if desired.

Frostings

BUTTER-CREAM FROSTING
For two 8-inch or 9-inch round layers

2 tablespoons butter or margarine,
  softened
3 cups icing sugar
3 tablespoons milk
Few grains salt
1 teaspoon vanilla

1. Put softened butter or margarine and 1 cup of the icing sugar in mixing bowl, and cream until blended.
2. Add milk, salt, vanilla, and 1 cup of the icing sugar, and blend well.
3. Add the rest of the icing sugar, a little at a time, stirring and creaming until frosting is smooth and of a consistency suitable for spreading.

> STANDARD: A soft, creamy frosting; sweet in taste and mildly flavored with vanilla.

VARIATIONS: Use cold strong coffee, frozen concentrated orange juice, or apricot nectar instead of milk, and omit vanilla.

CHOCOLATE-CREAM FROSTING
For three 8-inch or two 9-inch round layers

⅓ cup butter or margarine
2½ squares unsweetened chocolate
3 cups icing sugar
¼ cup light cream or milk
Few grains salt
1 teaspoon vanilla

1. Put butter or margarine and unsweetened chocolate, cut into several pieces, in mixing bowl.
2. Place mixing bowl in hot water, and melt butter or margarine and chocolate.

3. Remove from hot water, add 1 cup of the icing sugar, and cream it until it is well blended.
4. Add the rest of the icing sugar alternately with light cream or milk, creaming after each addition.
5. Add salt and vanilla, and cream until frosting is smooth and of a consistency for spreading.

> STANDARD: A soft, creamy, chocolate-flavored frosting.

DOUBLE-BOILER FROSTING
For two 8-inch or 9-inch round layers

1½ cups sugar
⅓ cup water
2 egg whites
1 tablespoon light corn syrup
Few grains salt
½ teaspoon vanilla

1. Mix all ingredients, except vanilla, in top of double boiler.
2. Place over boiling water in bottom of double boiler, being sure water is boiling.
3. Cook for 1 minute, stirring constantly, and then for 2 more minutes without stirring.
4. Remove from heat.
5. Beat over hot water, with rotary beater or electric mixer at high speed, until mixture forms peaks.
6. Add vanilla, and beat for 1 minute longer.
7. Frost cake immediately.

> STANDARD: A snowy-white, fluffy frosting; very sweet in taste and pleasingly flavored with vanilla.

SEAFOAM FROSTING

For two 8-inch or 9-inch round layers

1¼ cups sugar
1¼ cups light-brown sugar, firmly packed
½ cup water
⅛ teaspoon salt
2 egg whites
1 teaspoon vanilla

1. Put sugar, light-brown sugar, and water in medium-sized saucepan, and heat, stirring until sugar is dissolved.
2. Cook, without stirring, until syrup reaches beginning of hard-ball stage (250° F.).
3. Cool undisturbed.
4. Add salt to egg whites, and beat, with rotary beater or electric mixer at high speed, until very stiff.
5. Pour syrup, about one-third at a time, into stiffly beaten egg whites, and beat, with rotary beater or electric mixer at medium speed, after each addition only enough to incorporate syrup.
6. Remove beater after last portion of syrup is beaten into egg whites, add vanilla, and continue beating with a tablespoon until frosting is of a consistency for spreading.
7. Frost cake immediately.

PRECAUTION: When pouring syrup into stiffly beaten egg whites, be careful not to move saucepan any more than is necessary, and do not scrape syrup from sides of pan. Otherwise the frosting will not be creamy in texture.

STANDARD: Similar to Double-boiler Frosting except light tan in color and flavored with brown sugar.

DARK CHOCOLATE FROSTING

For two 8-inch or 9-inch round layers

1½ cups sugar
½ cup milk
1 tablespoon butter or margarine
⅛ teaspoon salt
2 egg yolks, beaten until thick
4 squares unsweetened chocolate, melted
1 teaspoon vanilla

1. Put sugar, milk, butter or margarine, and salt in saucepan and heat, stirring until sugar is dissolved.
2. Cook, without stirring, until syrup reaches soft-ball stage (236° F.).
3. Pour syrup slowly over beaten egg yolks, and beat, with rotary beater or electric mixer at medium speed, while adding.
4. Add melted unsweetened chocolate and vanilla, and beat until frosting is of a consistency for spreading.
5. Frost cake immediately.

NOTE: If frosting becomes too stiff to spread easily, stir in a few drops of warm water.

STANDARD: A rich chocolate frosting, somewhat like fudge in texture.

● A dark chocolate frosting is particularly appealing on a pure white cake, such as this angel food cake.

CANDIES

POPCORN BALLS
About ten 2½-inch balls

¼ cup butter or margarine
1 cup popcorn
½ teaspoon salt
½ cup molasses
½ cup dark or light corn syrup
½ tablespoon vinegar
1½ tablespoons butter or margarine

1. Melt butter or margarine in large skillet.
2. Add popcorn, and spread evenly on bottom.
3. Cover tightly, and shake skillet over heat until corn is popped.
4. Put popped corn in mixing bowl, sprinkle with salt, and mix gently.
5. Put molasses, corn syrup, and vinegar in large saucepan, and mix.
6. Boil, stirring occasionally, until syrup reaches soft-ball stage (240° F.). (See page 402.)
7. Continue to boil, stirring constantly, until syrup reaches soft-crack stage (270° F.). (See page 402.)
8. Add butter or margarine, and stir in until just melted.
9. Pour syrup over popped corn, stirring gently to mix thoroughly.
10. Shape with hands, when cool enough to handle, into balls about 2½ inches in diameter.
11. Place on wax paper to harden.

NOTES: A corn popper may be used instead of a covered skillet.

In forming balls, use as little pressure as possible so that popped corn will not be broken and balls will not be too tightly packed.

A little butter or margarine on hands before shaping balls helps to keep candy from sticking to hands.

VARIATION: Use any type of puffed breakfast cereal instead of popcorn.

FONDANT
About 1 pound

2 cups sugar
2 tablespoons light corn syrup
1¼ cups water

1. Put sugar, light corn syrup, and water in saucepan, and heat, stirring until sugar is dissolved.
2. Cover saucepan when syrup begins to boil, and cook for 3 minutes.
3. Remove cover, and boil, without stirring, until syrup reaches soft-ball stage (238° F.). (See page 402.) Occasionally wipe off any sugar crystals which may be on sides of saucepan above boiling syrup, using a fork

with a piece of wet cheesecloth wrapped around the tines.

4. Pour on cold, wet platter, and cool to lukewarm. *Do not scrape saucepan.*
5. Beat with a spatula until mixture is white and creamy, and then knead in hands until smooth and satiny.
6. Store fondant in tightly closed container until ready to use.

STANDARD: Very white; smooth and creamy in texture; very sweet in taste.

PEPPERMINT PATTIES

1 cup Fondant
2 to 3 drops oil of peppermint

1. Put fondant in top of double boiler, and place over simmering water in lower part.
2. Let melt, stirring only enough to blend.
3. Stir in oil of peppermint.
4. Drop mixture from tip of teaspoon onto wax paper or lightly oiled baking sheet, making patties about 1 or 1½ inches in diameter.
5. Lift patties loose carefully from wax paper or baking sheet as soon as cool.

NOTE: If fondant begins to harden before all of it is made into patties, replace top of double boiler over hot water to remelt.

VARIATIONS: Use other flavoring oils, and add a few drops of appropriate color.

CHOCOLATE FUDGE
About 1¼ pounds

2 squares unsweetened chocolate
2 cups sugar
⅔ cup milk
1 tablespoon light corn syrup
2 tablespoons butter or margarine
1 teaspoon vanilla

1. Cut unsweetened chocolate into several pieces, put in saucepan with sugar, milk, and light corn syrup, and heat, stirring until sugar is dissolved.
2. Boil, stirring often, until syrup reaches soft-ball stage (236° F.). (See page 402.)
3. Remove from heat, add butter or margarine, but do not stir, and set aside to cool to lukewarm (110° F.).
4. Add vanilla, and beat until mixture loses its shiny appearance and a small amount holds its shape when dropped from a spoon.
5. Pour into lightly greased 9x5x3-inch pan.
6. Cut into 1-inch squares when cold.

STANDARD: A crystalline candy with crystals so fine that texture is creamy; surface glossy; dark rich brown in color; flavor of chocolate. The pieces should be evenly cut and uniform in size.

PENUCHI
About 1¼ pounds

2 cups light-brown sugar
⅔ cup milk
1 tablespoon butter or margarine
1 teaspoon vanilla
1 cup chopped nuts

1. Put light-brown sugar and milk in saucepan, and boil, stirring constantly, until syrup reaches soft-ball stage (236° F.). (See page 402.)
2. Remove from heat, add butter or margarine, but do not stir, and set aside to cool to lukewarm (110° F.).
3. Add vanilla, and beat until mixture is thick and creamy.
4. Stir in chopped nuts.
5. Pour into lightly greased 9x5x3-inch pan.
6. Cut into 1-inch squares when cold.

STANDARD: A crystalline candy with crystals so fine that texture is creamy; surface somewhat dull; light gray-brown in color; flavor of brown sugar and nuts. The pieces should be evenly cut and uniform in size.

DIVINITY

About 1¼ pounds

2⅓ cups sugar
⅔ cup light corn syrup
½ cup water
¼ teaspoon salt
2 egg whites, stiffly beaten
½ teaspoon vanilla
1 cup chopped English walnuts

1. Put sugar, light corn syrup, water, and salt in saucepan, and heat, stirring until sugar is dissolved.
2. Boil, without stirring, until syrup reaches hard-ball stage (265° F.). (See page 402.)
3. Remove from heat.
4. Pour syrup gradually into stiffly beaten egg whites, beating constantly with rotary beater or electric mixer at medium speed.
5. Continue to beat until mixture holds its shape when dropped from a spoon.
6. Add vanilla and chopped English walnuts, and mix thoroughly.
7. Put in lightly greased 9-inch square pan.
8. Cut into 1-inch squares.

NOTE: If preferred, divinity may be dropped from a spoon onto wax paper.

STANDARD: A noncrystalline candy with a soft, slightly porous texture; less sweet in taste than Fondant.

PEANUT BRITTLE

About 1 pound

1 cup sugar
¼ cup molasses
¼ cup water
2½ tablespoons butter or margarine
½ teaspoon baking soda
1 cup chopped peanuts

1. Put sugar, molasses, and water in saucepan, and heat, stirring until sugar is dissolved.
2. Boil, without stirring, until syrup reaches hard-crack stage (300° F.). (See page 402.)

3. Remove from heat, add butter or margarine and baking soda, and stir just enough to mix well.
4. Stir in chopped peanuts.
5. Pour onto well-greased baking sheet, and smooth out with a spatula.
6. Pull out with hands to make a thin sheet of candy as soon as cool enough to handle.
7. Break into irregular-shaped pieces when cold and firm.

PRECAUTIONS: Before pouring the candy from the saucepan, wipe off any sugar crystals that may be on the sides of the pan near the pouring lip, using a fork with a piece of wet cheesecloth wrapped around the tines. Also, do not scrape the saucepan after pouring the hot candy from it. If crystals drop into the candy, they may cause the brittle to crystallize.

STANDARD: A noncrystalline candy with a brittle, slightly porous texture; surface golden brown and glossy; nuts evenly distributed; flavor of molasses.

MAPLE TAFFY

About ½ pound

⅓ cup sugar
½ cup light corn syrup
½ cup maple syrup
¼ cup water
1 tablespoon butter or margarine
1/16 teaspoon baking soda

1. Put sugar, light corn syrup, maple syrup, and water in saucepan, and heat, stirring until sugar is dissolved.
2. Boil, stirring occasionally, until syrup reaches soft-crack stage (275° F.). (See page 402.)
3. Remove from heat, add butter or margarine and baking soda, and stir just enough to mix well.
4. Turn into greased pan, and let stand until cool enough to handle.
5. Scrape up mixture, and shape into one large ball with hands.

446

6. Pull, and when light in color and rather firm, stretch out into a long twisted rope, and cut into 1- to 2-inch pieces with scissors.
7. Wrap each piece in wax paper.

NOTES: If the taffy cools too much before it is pulled, it will be hard to work. If this happens, the taffy may be softened by placing it in a warm oven for a few minutes.

A little cornstarch on the fingers helps to keep the taffy from sticking to them.

> STANDARD: A noncrystalline candy with a slightly chewy texture; surface glossy; creamy white in color; flavor of maple sirup. The pieces should be uniform in size.

STUFFED DATES

Dates
Fondant (page 444)
Sugar

Optional
English walnuts, cut in quarters
or
Pecans, cut in halves

1. Wash dates, and dry on paper towel.
2. Cut each date lengthwise and remove pit.
3. Work fondant in hands until soft.
4. Fill center of each date, allowing some fondant to extend from open side.
5. Roll in sugar, and press a piece of nut, if used, into fondant.

CANDIED ORANGE PEEL

About ¼ pound

Peel of 4 medium oranges
2 cups sugar
1 cup water in which orange peel is cooked
Sugar

1. Wash oranges thoroughly, and dry.
2. Cut through skin with a sharp knife, and remove peel in four sections.
3. Cover peel with cold water, bring to a boil, and cook slowly until soft.
4. Drain, saving water for making the syrup
5. Scrape out white inner part of skin with a teaspoon, and cut peel into thin strips with scissors.
6. Put the 2 cups of sugar in saucepan, add water, and boil, without stirring, until syrup reaches soft-ball stage (238° F.). (See page 402.)
7. Add orange peel, and cook slowly for about 10 minutes, or until most of the water has evaporated.
8. Drain in strainer.
9. Drop pieces of peel, a few at a time, in sugar on wax paper, using a fork to separate pieces.
10. Shake off excess sugar, cool, and store in covered container.

CANDIED GRAPEFRUIT PEEL

Follow recipe for Candied Orange Peel except for these differences:
1. Use peel of 2 small grapefruit.
2. Cut through skin with a sharp knife, and remove peel in six sections.
3. Use fresh water for making the syrup rather than the water in which peel is cooked.

CEREALS

BREAKFAST CEREALS

4 servings

2 cups water
½ teaspoon salt

Cereal
Coarse granular, ½ to ⅔ cup
Fine granular, ⅓ to ½ cup
Rolled, ⅔ to 1 cup

Method 1 (*For regular-type cereals only*)

1. Put water and salt in top of double boiler, place over direct heat, and bring water to a boil.
2. Sprinkle cereal in slowly, stirring constantly.
3. Reduce heat.
4. Boil cereal gently, stirring occasionally, for 3 minutes.
5. Place over boiling water in bottom of double boiler.
6. Cover, and cook, stirring once, for 30 to 40 minutes.
7. Serve hot with sugar and milk or light cream.

Method 2 (*For regular-type and quick-cooking-type cereals*)

1. Put water and salt in saucepan, and bring water to a boil.
2. Sprinkle cereal in slowly, stirring constantly.
3. Reduce heat.
4. Boil cereal gently, stirring occasionally, for 15 to 20 minutes if regular-type cereal, or for 1 to 5 minutes if quick-cooking-type.
5. Serve hot with sugar and milk or light cream.

NOTES: Some of the coarse granular cereals require longer cooking than 20 minutes. Consult the package label.

Quick-cooking cereals differ in character among the different brands. Therefore, the directions on the package label should be consulted for specific proportions of cereal, water, and salt, and for length of cooking time.

STANDARD: A consistency just thick enough for cereal to hold its shape when poured into cereal bowl; free from lumps and with cellulose softened; flavor characteristic of the cereal with no suggestion of uncooked starch taste.

FRIED CORN-MEAL MUSH

6 servings

2 cups water
½ teaspoon salt
½ cup corn meal
Flour

1. Cook corn meal as directed in Breakfast Cereals, Method 1.
2. Pour into lightly greased 7x3½x2½-inch loaf pan.
3. Cool.
4. Cover, and chill in refrigerator until firm.
5. Turn out of loaf pan, and cut in slices ½ inch thick.
6. Coat each slice with flour.
7. Fry in well-greased skillet until brown on one side, and then turn and brown on other side.
8. Serve with maple syrup or Brown-sugar Syrup (page 514).

BOILED RICE

6 servings

1 cup rice
2 cups water
1 teaspoon salt

1. Put rice, water, and salt in 3-quart sauce-pan.
2. Cover tightly, and bring water to a boil, stirring once or twice.
3. Reduce heat, replace cover, and simmer, without stirring, for 14 minutes.
4. Test rice at end of 14 minutes. If not soft when a grain is pressed between fingers, add about 2 tablespoons water if necessary, replace cover, and simmer for 2 to 6 minutes longer.
5. Remove from heat, fluff rice lightly with a fork, and let stand in covered saucepan for 5 to 10 minutes to steam-dry.
6. Serve as accompaniment to meat.

STANDARD: Snowy white; moist, tender, and fluffy; every grain distinct; pleasing in flavor.

SPAGHETTI WITH TOMATO-MEAT SAUCE

6 servings

3 tablespoons shortening or salad oil
1 onion, finely chopped
½ clove garlic, minced
½ pound ground beef
1½ cups canned tomatoes
½ cup tomato paste
1½ teaspoons salt
⅛ teaspoon pepper
2 quarts water
2 teaspoons salt
8 ounces spaghetti
¼ cup Parmesan cheese

1. Heat shortening or salad oil in large skillet.
2. Add finely chopped onion and minced garlic, and cook until onion is light brown.
3. Add ground beef, and cook until brown.
4. Add canned tomatoes, tomato paste, the 1½ teaspoons salt, and pepper, and simmer, stirring occasionally, for 1 hour.
5. Bring water to a boil in medium-sized kettle, and add the 2 teaspoons salt.

6. Add spaghetti, and boil for 10 minutes, or until spaghetti is soft when pressed between fingers.
7. Drain.
8. Put on hot platter, cover with hot sauce, and sprinkle with Parmesan cheese.

NOTE: If desired, ground beef may be made into balls as follows:
1. Omit step 3.
2. Mix ground beef with ½ teaspoon salt, and shape into six balls.
3. Roll balls in flour, and brown in 1 table-spoon shortening or salad oil in small skillet.
4. Put browned balls in the tomato sauce 15 minutes before sauce is done (step 4 above).

SPANISH RICE

4 servings

3 tablespoons butter, margarine, or salad oil
⅓ cup chopped onion
⅓ cup chopped green pepper
1 cup packaged precooked rice
1 cup water
1 cup canned tomatoes
2 teaspoons sugar
1 teaspoon salt
⅛ teaspoon pepper
1 bay leaf
3 tablespoons grated Cheddar or Parmesan cheese (optional)

1. Heat butter, margarine, or salad oil in skillet.
2. Add chopped onion and chopped green pepper, and cook until onion is yellow.
3. Add precooked rice, water, canned tomatoes, sugar, salt, pepper, and bay leaf, and bring to a boil.
4. Cover, and simmer for 10 to 15 minutes, or until rice is tender when pressed between fingers.
5. Remove bay leaf.
6. Serve hot, sprinkled with grated cheese, if used.

VARIATION: Put Spanish rice mixture in casserole, sprinkle top with the grated cheese, and bake at 400° F. for about 15 minutes, or until cheese is melted.

449

CHEESE

CHEESE SOUFFLÉ

4 servings

3 tablespoons butter or margarine
3 tablespoons flour
½ teaspoon salt
Few grains cayenne
1 cup milk
1⅓ cups grated sharp Cheddar cheese
4 eggs, separated

Oven Temperature: 300° F.

1. Make White Sauce (page 510) with first five ingredients.
2. Remove from heat, add grated cheese, and stir until melted.
3. Cool slightly.
4. Beat egg whites, with rotary beater or electric mixer at high speed, until stiff but not dry.
5. Beat egg yolks with same rotary beater or electric mixer at high speed.
6. Stir beaten egg yolks into cheese sauce.
7. Cut and fold sauce gently into stiffly beaten egg whites.
8. Pour into ungreased 1½ quart casserole.
9. Bake at 300° F. for 1¼ hours.
10. Serve immediately.

STANDARD: An unevenly shaped surface, part golden brown and part yellow; uniformly light and porous throughout; a distinct flavor of cheese.

CHEESE FONDUE

4 servings

1 cup soft bread crumbs
1 cup grated sharp Cheddar cheese
1 tablespoon butter or margarine
½ teaspoon salt
⅛ teaspoon paprika
1 cup milk, scalded
3 eggs, separated

Oven Temperature: 325° F.

1. Put soft bread crumbs, grated cheese, butter or margarine, salt, and paprika in scalded milk in top of double boiler, and place over hot water in bottom part.
2. Stir until cheese is melted.
3. Remove from heat.
4. Beat egg whites, with rotary beater or electric mixer at high speed, until stiff but not dry.
5. Beat egg yolks slightly with same beater.
6. Add beaten egg yolks to first mixture, and stir to blend thoroughly.
7. Fold into the stiffly beaten egg whites.
8. Pour into ungreased 1½-quart casserole.
9. Bake at 325° F. for about 45 minutes, or until top feels firm when touched lightly with finger.
10. Serve immediately.

WELSH RAREBIT ON TOAST

4 servings

2 tablespoons butter or margarine
2 tablespoons flour
½ teaspoon salt
¼ teaspoon dry mustard
1 cup milk
1 cup grated Cheddar or process cheese
1 egg, slightly beaten
4 slices thin toast

1. Make White Sauce (page 510) with first five ingredients in top of double boiler over direct heat.
2. Remove from heat, add grated cheese, and stir until melted.
3. Cool slightly.
4. Stir in slightly beaten egg.
5. Place over hot water in bottom of double boiler, and cook, stirring constantly, until egg is cooked and the mixture smooth.
6. Pour immediately over thin toast, and garnish with paprika or parsley.

CHEESE CUSTARD

4 servings

1 cup soft bread cubes
1 cup grated Cheddar or process cheese
1 cup milk
1 egg, slightly beaten
¼ teaspoon salt
Few grains pepper

Oven Temperature: 350° F.

1. Put soft bread cubes and grated cheese in layers in greased 1-quart casserole.
2. Put milk, slightly beaten egg, salt, and pepper in mixing bowl, and mix thoroughly.
3. Pour over bread cubes and cheese.
4. Place casserole in baking pan, pour hot water into pan to a depth of the cheese mixture, and put in oven.
5. Bake at 350° F. for about 45 minutes, or until a knife inserted into center of custard comes out clean.
6. Serve in casserole.

BAKED MACARONI AND CHEESE

5 servings

1½ quarts water
1½ teaspoons salt
⅔ cup broken macaroni
1½ tablespoons butter or margarine
1½ tablespoons flour
½ teaspoon salt
⅛ teaspoon pepper
1¼ cups milk
1 cup grated Cheddar or process cheese
½ cup Buttered Soft Bread Crumbs
(page 482)

Oven Temperature: 400° F.

1. Bring water to a boil in medium-sized kettle, and add the 1½ teaspoons salt.
2. Add broken macaroni, and boil for 10 minutes, or until slightly soft.
3. Make White Sauce (page 510) with butter or margarine, flour, the ½ teaspoon salt, pepper, and milk while macaroni is boiling.
4. Remove sauce from heat, add grated cheese, and stir until melted.
5. Drain water from cooked macaroni, and stir macaroni into cheese sauce.
6. Pour into greased 1-quart casserole, and sprinkle evenly with buttered soft bread crumbs.
7. Bake at 400° F. for 15 minutes.
8. Serve in casserole.

NOTES: Some brands of macaroni swell more than others in cooking, with the result that the baked macaroni and cheese will differ in thickness according to the brand used.

A little butter or margarine in the water when macaroni is boiling helps to keep the water from boiling over.

451

COOKIES

OATMEAL COOKIES
(Drop)

About 6 dozen 2½-inch cookies

1 cup sifted all-purpose flour
½ teaspoon baking soda
1½ teaspoons salt
1 cup shortening
½ cup sugar
1 cup light-brown sugar, firmly packed
1 egg, well beaten
¼ cup warm water
1½ teaspoons vanilla
3 cups uncooked quick-cooking rolled oats
½ cup chopped nuts
or
½ cup seedless raisins, cut in half

Oven Temperature: 350° F.

1. Sift together flour, baking soda, and salt onto wax paper.
2. Put shortening, sugar, and light-brown sugar in mixing bowl, and cream until well blended.
3. Add well-beaten egg, warm water, and vanilla, and beat until light and fluffy.
4. Stir in sifted dry ingredients.
5. Add uncooked rolled oats and chopped nuts or cut raisins, and blend thoroughly to make a soft dough.
6. Drop onto greased baking sheet, about 2 inches apart, using 1 rounded teaspoon of dough for each cookie.
7. Bake at 350° F. for 12 to 14 minutes.
8. Remove cookies immediately from baking sheet to wire rack to cool.

STANDARD: Medium-brown cookies with a rough surface; slightly short in texture; sweet in taste with a nutlike flavor.

BROWNIES
(Bar)

Sixteen 2-inch squares

⅓ cup butter or margarine
2 squares unsweetened chocolate
2 eggs, well beaten
1 cup sugar
1 teaspoon vanilla
¾ cup sifted all-purpose flour
½ teaspoon salt
½ teaspoon baking powder
1 cup chopped nuts

Oven Temperature: 350° F.

1. Put butter or margarine and chocolate in top of double boiler over hot water, and heat, stirring occasionally to make a smooth paste.
2. Cool slightly.
3. Stir in well-beaten eggs.
4. Add sugar and vanilla, and mix well.
5. Sift together flour, salt, and baking powder onto wax paper.
6. Stir into chocolate mixture.
7. Add chopped nuts, and mix well.
8. Pour into well-greased 8-inch square pan, and spread evenly.
9. Bake at 350° F. for 30 minutes.
10. Cool in pan placed on wire rack.
11. Turn onto board, and cut into squares.

STANDARD: Dark chocolate-brown squares; soft and slightly chewy in texture; sweet in taste with a strong flavor of chocolate.

PECAN BARS
(Bar)
Sixteen 1x4-inch bars

2 eggs, unbeaten
1 cup light-brown sugar, firmly packed
⅓ cup shortening, melted
½ cup sifted all-purpose flour
½ cup chopped pecans
1 teaspoon vanilla

Oven Temperature: 350° F.

1. Beat eggs, with rotary beater or electric mixer at high speed, until light and frothy.
2. Stir in light-brown sugar.
3. Add melted shortening, flour, chopped pecans, and vanilla, and blend thoroughly.
4. Pour into well-greased 8-inch square pan.
5. Bake at 350° F. for 25 minutes.
6. Cool in pan placed on wire rack.
7. Turn onto board, and cut into squares.
8. Sprinkle with icing sugar, if desired.

STANDARD: Golden-brown bars; soft and slightly chewy in texture; not very sweet in taste but with a flavor of pecans.

NUT BALLS
(Molded)
About 4 dozen balls

1 cup butter or margarine
½ cup icing sugar
2 cups sifted all-purpose flour
¼ teaspoon salt
1½ teaspoons vanilla
¾ cup pecans, finely chopped

Oven Temperature: 400° F.

1. Put butter or margarine and icing sugar into a mixing bowl, and cream until light and fluffy.
2. Stir in flour and salt.
3. Stir in vanilla and finely chopped pecans.
4. Shape dough into balls with hands, using about 1 teaspoon of dough for each ball, and place directly on greased baking sheet.
5. Bake at 400° F. for 10 to 12 minutes.

6. Remove balls immediately from baking sheet to wire rack to cool.
7. Roll in icing sugar while still warm, if desired.

STANDARD: Light-tan balls; tender and slightly crumbly in texture; not very sweet in taste but with a distinct flavor of pecans.

PEANUT-BUTTER COOKIES
(Molded)
About 4 dozen 2-inch cookies

1½ cups sifted all-purpose flour
1 teaspoon baking soda
½ teaspoon salt
½ cup shortening
⅓ cup peanut butter
½ cup sugar
½ cup light-brown sugar, firmly packed
1 egg, unbeaten
½ teaspoon vanilla

Oven Temperature: 350° F.

1. Sift together flour, baking soda, and salt onto wax paper.
2. Put shortening, peanut butter, sugar, and light-brown sugar in mixing bowl, and cream until well blended.
3. Add unbeaten egg and vanilla, and beat until light and fluffy.
4. Stir in sifted dry ingredients, and blend thoroughly to make a stiff dough.
5. Shape dough into balls with hands, using about 1 tablespoon of dough for each ball, and place directly on greased baking sheet.
6. Flatten each ball with a fork.
7. Bake at 350° F. for 12 minutes.
8. Remove cookies immediately from baking sheet to wire rack to cool.

STANDARD: Medium-brown cookies; crisp in texture; sweet in taste with a pronounced flavor of peanuts.

BUTTERSCOTCH COOKIES
(Refrigerator)
About 4 dozen 2-inch cookies

1½ cups sifted all-purpose flour
1 teaspoon baking powder
½ teaspoon salt
½ cup shortening
1 cup light-brown sugar, firmly packed
1 egg, unbeaten
½ teaspoon vanilla
½ cup finely chopped nuts

Oven Temperature: 375° F.

1. Sift together flour, baking powder, and salt onto wax paper.
2. Put shortening and light-brown sugar in mixing bowl, and cream until well blended.
3. Add unbeaten egg, vanilla, and finely chopped nuts, and beat until light and fluffy.
4. Stir in sifted dry ingredients, and blend thoroughly to make a stiff dough.
5. Shape dough into roll with hands, wrap in wax paper, and chill in refrigerator several hours or overnight.
6. Remove wax paper, cut dough into slices about ⅛ inch thick, and place directly on greased baking sheet.
7. Bake at 375° F. for 8 to 10 minutes.
8. Remove cookies immediately from baking sheet to wire rack to cool.

STANDARD: Medium-brown cookies; very tender and short in texture; flavor of brown sugar and nuts.

SPRITZ
(Pressed)
About 6 dozen cookies

2¼ cups sifted all-purpose flour
½ teaspoon baking powder
¼ teaspoon salt
1 cup butter or margarine
¾ cup sugar
1 egg, unbeaten
1 teaspoon lemon extract

Oven Temperature: 400° F.

1. Sift together flour, baking powder, and salt onto wax paper.
2. Put butter or margarine and sugar in mixing bowl, and cream until well blended.
3. Add unbeaten egg and lemon extract, and beat until light and fluffy.
4. Stir in sifted dry ingredients, and blend thoroughly to make a fairly stiff dough.
5. Put dough in cookie press, and make desired shapes on ungreased baking sheet.
6. Bake at 400° F. for 8 to 10 minutes.
7. Remove cookies immediately from baking sheet to wire rack to cool.

NOTE: These cookies may be decorated with colored sugar, finely chopped nuts, thin strips of preserved ginger or angelica, or tiny hard candies (nonpareils). The decoration should be sprinkled on the cookie before baking.

STANDARD: Rich light-brown cookies; very tender in texture; sweet in taste with a flavor of lemon.

VANILLA COOKIES
(Rolled)
About 7 dozen 2-inch cookies

2½ cups sifted all-purpose flour
1 teaspoon baking powder
½ teaspoon salt
1 cup butter or margarine
1 cup sugar
2 eggs, well beaten
2 teaspoons vanilla

Oven Temperature: 350° F.

1. Sift together flour, baking powder, and salt onto wax paper.
2. Put butter or margarine and sugar in mixing bowl, and cream until well blended.
3. Add well-beaten eggs gradually, and beat until light and fluffy.
4. Stir in vanilla.
5. Stir in sifted dry ingredients, and blend thoroughly to make a stiff dough.
6. Chill dough until firm, and then roll, with floured rolling pin on lightly floured board, until dough is ⅛ inch thick.

7. Cut cookies with floured cookie cutter.
8. Lift cookies with a spatula, and place on ungreased baking sheet.
9. Bake at 350° F. for 12 to 14 minutes.
10. Remove cookies immediately from baking sheet to wire rack to cool.

STANDARD: Rich cookies, light brown in center, shading to darker brown on edges; slightly crisp in texture; sweet in taste with a flavor of vanilla.

CHOCOLATE-COCONUT DROPS
(Drop)
About 3 dozen 1½-inch drops

2 ounces chocolate
1 can sweetened condensed milk
½ pound dried coconut

Oven Temperature: 325° F.

1. Melt chocolate over hot water.
2. Add sweetened condensed milk and dried coconut gradually, and mix well.
3. Drop onto slightly greased baking sheet about ¾ inch apart, using about 1 teaspoon of dough for each drop.
4. Bake at 325° F. for 12 to 15 minutes.
5. Remove drops immediately from baking sheet to wire rack to cool.

CEREAL-FLAKE MACAROONS
(Drop)
About 3 dozen 1½-inch macaroons

½ cup sugar
¼ teaspoon salt
2 egg whites, stiffly beaten
2 cups cereal flakes
½ cup dried coconut

Oven Temperature: 325° F.

1. Beat sugar and salt gradually into stiffly beaten egg whites.
2. Fold in cereal flakes and dried coconut.
3. Drop onto greased baking sheet, about 2 inches apart, using 1 teaspoon of dough for each macaroon.
4. Bake at 325° F. for 15 to 20 minutes, or until light brown.
5. Remove macaroons immediately from baking sheet to wire rack to cool.

TEA COOKIES
(Drop)
About 5 dozen 2-inch cookies

1 cup butter or margarine
⅔ cup sugar
2 eggs, well beaten
1 teaspoon vanilla
1½ cups sifted all-purpose flour

Oven Temperature: 375° F.

1. Put butter or margarine and sugar in mixing bowl, and cream until light and fluffy.
2. Add well-beaten eggs and vanilla.
3. Stir in sifted flour, and blend thoroughly.
4. Drop onto greased baking sheet, about 2 inches apart, using 1 teaspoon of dough for each cookie.
5. Spread thinly with a knife or a spatula dipped in cold water.
6. Bake at 375° F. for 8 minutes, or until edges are browned.
7. Remove cookies immediately from baking sheet to wire rack to cool.

STANDARD: Rich wafer cookies, crisp, delicate texture; light-brown center, thin edge of brown; flavor of vanilla.

DESSERTS

VANILLA CORNSTARCH PUDDING
(Blanc Mange)
4 servings

¼ cup sugar
3 tablespoons cornstarch
¼ teaspoon salt
2 cups milk
½ teaspoon vanilla
2 egg whites, stiffly beaten (optional)

1. Put sugar, cornstarch, and salt in top of double boiler, and mix thoroughly.
2. Stir in milk.
3. Cook over direct heat, stirring constantly, until mixture boils.
4. Place over boiling water in bottom of double boiler.
5. Cover, and cook, stirring once, for 10 minutes.
6. Stir in vanilla and stiffly beaten egg whites, if used.
7. Pour into small molds that have been wet with cold water and drained but not dried.
8. Cool to about room temperature, and place in refrigerator to chill and become firm.
9. Turn out onto individual dishes for serving.
10. Serve with Chocolate Sauce (page 513), sweetened crushed fruit, or defrosted frozen fruit.

STANDARD: Velvety smooth throughout; delicate, yet firm enough to hold shape of mold when turned from it; a mild flavor of vanilla.

CHOCOLATE CORNSTARCH PUDDING
4 servings

¼ cup sugar
2 tablespoons cornstarch
¼ teaspoon salt
1½ squares unsweetened chocolate
2 cups milk
½ teaspoon vanilla

1. Put sugar, cornstarch, and salt in top of double boiler, and mix thoroughly.
2. Add unsweetened chocolate cut into several pieces.
3. Stir in milk.
4. Cook over direct heat, stirring constantly, until mixture boils.
5. Place over boiling water in bottom of double boiler.
6. Cover, and cook, stirring once, for 10 minutes.
7. Stir in vanilla.
8. Pour into small molds that have been wet with cold water and drained but not dried.
9. Cool to about room temperature, and place in refrigerator to chill and become firm.
10. Turn out onto individual dishes for serving.
11. Serve with cream and a sprinkling of sugar, or garnish with sweetened whipped cream or flaked coconut.

VARIATION: Use ¼ cup cocoa instead of chocolate, and mix it with the sugar, cornstarch, and salt (step 1).

SOFT CUSTARD

4 to 5 servings

3 eggs, unbeaten
¼ cup sugar
¼ teaspoon salt
2 cups milk, scalded
½ teaspoon vanilla

1. Put unbeaten eggs in mixing bowl, and beat until thoroughly blended but not foamy.
2. Stir in sugar, salt, and scalded milk.
3. Pour into top of double boiler, and place over boiling water in bottom part.
4. Reduce heat immediately, and keep water just below simmering.
5. Cook, stirring constantly, until mixture thickens and coats the stirring spoon.
6. Place top of double boiler immediately in cold water, and continue to stir custard until it cools slightly.
7. Stir in vanilla.
8. Strain into serving dish, and chill.

STANDARD: Smooth and velvety with consistency of heavy cream; yellow in color with shade depending upon color of egg yolks; mild in flavor.

VARIATIONS: Flavor with grated nutmeg instead of vanilla.

Serve custard over cooked dried fruit, drained canned fruit, sliced bananas, or orange sections.

BAKED CUSTARD

4 to 5 servings

3 eggs, unbeaten
¼ cup sugar
¼ teaspoon salt
2 cups milk, scalded
½ teaspoon vanilla

Oven Temperature: 350° F.

1. Put unbeaten eggs in mixing bowl, and beat until thoroughly blended but not foamy.
2. Stir in sugar, salt, scalded milk, and vanilla.
3. Strain into custard cups, filling each to about ½ inch from top.
4. Place in baking pan, pour hot water into pan to about ¾ inch from top of cups, and put in oven.
5. Bake at 350° F. for 40 to 45 minutes, or until a knife inserted into center of custard comes out clean.
6. Remove cups immediately from hot water, and let custard cool.
7. Turn out onto individual dishes for serving.

STANDARD: Very lightly browned on top; velvety and firm throughout, but only firm enough to hold its shape when turned from custard cup; mild in flavor.

RENNET PUDDING

4 servings

1 tablespoon water
1 rennet tablet
2 cups milk
3 tablespoons sugar
1 teaspoon vanilla

1. Put water in small dish, add rennet tablet, crush, and mix until dissolved.
2. Heat milk until lukewarm (about 100° F.).
3. Add sugar and vanilla to lukewarm milk, and stir until sugar is dissolved.
4. Stir dissolved rennet into warm mixture.
5. Pour *immediately* into individual serving dishes, and chill.
6. Garnish with a sprinkling of nutmeg, grated orange rind, crushed fruit, or a bit of soft jelly, as desired.

CARAMEL FLOATING ISLAND

4 to 5 servings

⅔ cup sugar
½ cup water
1½ cups milk
2 egg yolks, unbeaten (reserve whites)
2 eggs, unbeaten
⅛ teaspoon salt

Meringue
2 egg whites, unbeaten
⅓ cup sugar

1. Put the ⅔ cup sugar in skillet, and place over low heat.
2. Stir gently until sugar melts and forms a medium-brown syrup.
3. Add water slowly, and cook until syrup, which solidifies when water is added, is dissolved. There should be about ½ cup of caramel syrup.
4. Stir caramel syrup into milk, and add more milk if needed to make 2 cups of the caramel-milk mixture.
5. Put unbeaten egg yolks and unbeaten eggs in mixing bowl, and beat until thoroughly blended but not foamy.
6. Stir in caramel-milk mixture and salt.
7. Pour into top of double boiler, and place over boiling water in bottom part.
8. Reduce heat immediately, and keep water just below simmering.
9. Cook, stirring constantly, until mixture thickens and coats the stirring spoon.
10. Place top of double boiler immediately in cold water, and continue to stir custard until it cools slightly.
11. Strain into serving dish, and chill.
12. Dot with mounds (islands) of Meringue (page 488) made with the 2 unbeaten egg whites and ⅓ cup sugar.

TAPIOCA CREAM

5 servings

2 cups milk
2 tablespoons quick-cooking tapioca
¼ cup sugar
⅛ teaspoon salt
2 eggs, separated
½ teaspoon vanilla

1. Put milk, quick-cooking tapioca, sugar, and salt in top of double boiler, and place over boiling water in bottom part.
2. Cover, and cook, stirring occasionally, for 15 minutes.
3. Beat egg whites, with rotary beater or electric mixer at high speed, until stiff but not dry.
4. Beat egg yolks with same rotary beater or electric mixer.
5. Stir a small amount of the hot tapioca-milk mixture into beaten egg yolks, and then stir this into the rest of the tapioca-milk mixture.
6. Place over simmering water in bottom of double boiler, and cook, stirring constantly, until mixture thickens and coats the stirring spoon.
7. Stir in vanilla.
8. Place top of double boiler immediately in cold water, and continue to stir tapioca cream until it cools slightly.
9. Fold in stiffly beaten egg whites, leaving some of it in large masses to make dessert look attractive.
10. Pour into serving dish.
11. Garnish with grated nutmeg, bits of dark-colored jelly, or maraschino cherry.

> STANDARD: Similar to Soft Custard (page 457), but because of the tapioca in it, thicker in consistency than custard and somewhat rough; delicate in flavor.

ORANGE GELATIN

4 to 5 servings

½ cup cold water
1 envelope unflavored gelatin
½ cup boiling water
½ cup sugar
⅞ cup strained orange juice
⅛ cup strained lemon juice

1. Put cold water in mixing bowl large enough to hold all ingredients, sprinkle gelatin over water, and let stand to soften.
2. Add boiling water, and stir until gelatin is dissolved.

3. Add sugar, and stir until it is dissolved.
4. Stir in strained orange and lemon juices.
5. Pour into small molds.
6. Chill in refrigerator until firm.
7. Unmold (see page 430) onto individual dishes for serving.
8. Garnish with whipped cream, or surround with Soft Custard (page 457).

> STANDARD: A sparkling clear jelly; firm enough to hold shape of mold when turned from it, but not so firm as to be tough; a pronounced flavor of orange.

ORANGE GELATIN WHIP

Chill Orange Gelatin mixture to a consistency slightly thicker than raw egg white. Beat, with rotary beater or electric mixer at high speed, until it is light and fluffy. Chill until firm. Unmold and serve as orange gelatin.

LIME or LEMON SNOW
6 servings

½ cup cold water
1 envelope unflavored gelatin
¾ cup boiling water
¾ cup sugar
1 teaspoon grated lime or lemon rind
¼ cup strained lime or lemon juice
⅛ teaspoon salt
2 egg whites, unbeaten

1. Put cold water in mixing bowl large enough to hold all ingredients, sprinkle gelatin over water, and let stand to soften.
2. Add boiling water, and stir until gelatin is dissolved.
3. Add sugar, and stir until it is dissolved.
4. Stir in grated lime or lemon rind, strained lime or lemon juice, and salt.
5. Cool to about room temperature, place in refrigerator, and chill until consistency of raw egg white.
6. Add unbeaten egg whites, and beat, with rotary beater or electric mixer at high speed, until mixture will hold its shape.

7. Pour into mold that has been wet with cold water and drained but not dried.
8. Chill in refrigerator until firm.
9. Unmold (see page 430) onto serving dish, and surround with Soft Custard (page 457).

SPANISH CREAM
6 servings

¼ cup cold water
1 envelope unflavored gelatin
2 egg yolks, unbeaten
2 tablespoons sugar
¼ teaspoon salt
1¾ cups milk, scalded
1 teaspoon vanilla

Meringue
2 egg whites, unbeaten
⅓ cup sugar

1. Put cold water in small bowl, sprinkle gelatin over it, and let stand to soften while making custard.
2. Make Soft Custard (page 457, steps 1 to 5) with unbeaten egg yolks, the 2 tablespoons sugar, salt, and scalded milk.
3. Add softened gelatin and vanilla while custard is still hot, and stir until gelatin is dissolved.
4. Cool while making Meringue (page 488) of unbeaten egg whites and the ⅓ cup sugar.
5. Add meringue to custard-gelatin mixture, and beat, with rotary beater or electric mixer at medium speed, until well blended.
6. Pour into small molds that have been wet with cold water and drained but not dried.
7. Chill in refrigerator until firm.
8. Unmold (see page 430) onto individual dishes for serving.
9. Garnish with pieces of canned fruit or defrosted frozen fruit, if desired.

NOTE: Canned apricot halves or frozen strawberries or raspberries give attractive color and flavor contrasts to Spanish cream.

> STANDARD: A spongelike dessert, soft and tender, yet firm enough to hold shape of mold when turned from it; sweet but bland in flavor.

PRUNE WHIP

4 servings

⅔ cup prune pulp (about ½ pound prunes)
⅓ cup sugar
⅛ teaspoon salt
½ teaspoon grated lemon rind
1 teaspoon lemon juice
3 egg whites, stiffly beaten

1. Prepare prune pulp by removing pits from cooked prunes (see recipe for Stewed Dried Fruit on page 469) and forcing the prunes through a sieve.
2. Add sugar, salt, grated lemon rind, and lemon juice, and stir until sugar is dissolved.
3. Fold in stiffly beaten egg whites.
4. Pour into top of double boiler, 1½- or 2-quart size.
5. Cover, and cook over boiling water in bottom of double boiler for 45 minutes.
6. Place in warm serving dish.
7. Garnish with whipped cream.

APRICOT WHIP

Use ⅔ cup apricot pulp instead of prune pulp, and follow directions for Prune Whip.

APPLE BROWN BETTY

4 servings

¼ cup butter or margarine, melted
2 cups small, soft bread cubes
½ cup sugar
¼ teaspoon salt
½ teaspoon cinnamon
2 medium apples
⅓ cup water

Oven Temperature: 375° F.

1. Mix melted butter or margarine with bread cubes.
2. Put sugar, salt, and cinnamon in small bowl, and mix.
3. Wash, quarter, core, and pare apples, and cut in about ½-inch slices.
4. Arrange alternate layers of buttered bread cubes and apple slices in 1-quart casserole, starting and ending with bread cubes, and sprinkle each layer of apple slices with some of the sugar mixture.
5. Add water.
6. Bake at 375° F. for about 45 minutes, or until the top bread cubes are brown.

VARIATIONS: Use brown sugar instead of granulated sugar.

Mix 2 tablespoons raisins with sugar, salt, and cinnamon (step 2).

Mix 1 tablespoon grated lemon rind with sugar, salt, and cinnamon (step 2).

BLUEBERRY COBBLER

6 to 8 servings

½ cup sugar
2 tablespoons cornstarch
⅛ teaspoon salt
1 19-ounce can (2½ cups) blueberries and juice
1 teaspoon lemon juice
½ recipe Rich Biscuits (page 495)
1 tablespoon milk

Oven Temperature: 400° F.

1. Put sugar, cornstarch, and salt in saucepan, and mix thoroughly.
2. Add canned blueberries and juice and lemon juice.
3. Cook, stirring constantly, until mixture boils for ½ minute.
4. Pour into 1½-quart casserole.
5. Make rich biscuit dough, using 1 tablespoon more milk than in recipe.
6. Drop by tablespoonfuls onto hot blueberries.
7. Bake at 400° F. for 25 to 30 minutes.
8. Serve warm with cream or Hard Sauce (page 513).

VARIATIONS: Use canned cherries or canned peaches instead of blueberries.

PHILADELPHIA ICE CREAM
(Ice-cream Freezer)
6 to 8 servings

1 quart light cream
¾ cup sugar
1½ teaspoons vanilla
Few grains salt

1. Put light cream, sugar, vanilla, and salt in mixing bowl, and stir until sugar is dissolved.
2. Pour into freezer can of crank-type ice-cream freezer, and freeze as follows:

Freezing Directions for Crank-type Freezer

1. Assemble freezer according to manufacturer's directions.
2. Use 1 part coarse salt to 8 parts crushed ice in outer tub of freezer.
3. Turn freezer crank until it begins to turn hard and for about 1 minute longer.
4. Drain off water accumulated from melting ice.
5. Wipe top and upper sides of freezer can, and remove lid.
6. Remove dasher, scrape ice cream from it and from sides of can, and pack ice cream down in can.
7. Put cork in hole in lid, and replace lid.
8. Pack outer tub with 1 part coarse salt to 4 parts crushed ice.
9. Insulate by covering freezer with heavy cloth.
10. Let stand several hours before serving.

STANDARD: A very smooth-textured frozen dessert; firm, yet not too firm in consistency; a pronounced flavor of vanilla.

VANILLA ICE CREAM
(Ice-cream Freezer)
8 to 10 servings

¾ cup sugar
2 tablespoons flour
⅛ teaspoon salt
1½ cups milk
2 eggs, slightly beaten
1½ cups heavy cream
1½ teaspoons vanilla

1. Put sugar, flour, and salt in top of double boiler, and mix thoroughly.
2. Add milk, and cook over direct heat, stirring constantly, until mixture boils for about 1 minute.
3. Stir a small amount of the hot mixture into slightly beaten eggs, and then stir this into the rest of the hot mixture.
4. Place over simmering water in bottom of double boiler, and cook, stirring constantly, for about 2 minutes.
5. Cool, and stir in heavy cream and vanilla.
6. Pour into freezer can of crank-type ice-cream freezer, and freeze as directed in recipe for Philadelphia Ice Cream.

STANDARD: A very smooth-textured frozen dessert; firmer in consistency than Philadelphia Ice Cream; a delicate flavor of vanilla.

CHOCOLATE ICE CREAM

Add 2 squares unsweetened chocolate, cut into several pieces, to sugar, flour, salt, and milk, and cook as in step 2 of Vanilla Ice Cream.

PINEAPPLE ICE
(Ice-cream Freezer)
6 to 8 servings

2 cups water
½ cup sugar
Few grains salt
1 19-ounce can (2½ cups) pineapple juice
⅓ cup lemon juice

1. Put water, sugar, and salt in saucepan, and boil gently for 5 minutes.
2. Add pineapple juice and lemon juice.
3. Pour into freezer can of crank-type ice-cream freezer, and freeze as directed in recipe for Philadelphia Ice Cream.

QUICK CHOCOLATE ICE CREAM
(Refrigerator)
6 to 8 servings

2 egg whites, stiffly beaten
1 cup heavy cream, whipped
1 5½-ounce can chocolate syrup

1. Stir stiffly beaten egg whites into whipped cream.
2. Stir in chocolate syrup.
3. Pour into ice-cube tray, and place in freezing compartment of refrigerator or in home freezer. If in freezing compartment, set temperature control at coldest point.
4. Freeze.

ORANGE CREAM SHERBET
(Refrigerator)
4 to 5 servings

½ cup milk
½ cup sugar
1 cup strained orange juice
2 tablespoons lemon juice
½ tablespoon grated orange rind
1 egg white
2 tablespoons sugar
½ cup heavy cream, whipped

1. Put milk and the ½ cup sugar in mixing bowl, and mix.
2. Add strained orange juice, lemon juice, and grated orange rind, and stir until sugar is dissolved.
3. Pour into ice-cube tray, and place in freezing compartment of refrigerator or in home freezer. If placed in freezing compartment, set temperature control at coldest point.
4. Chill until slightly frozen.
5. Beat egg white, with rotary beater or electric mixer at high speed, until foam is fine, and then beat in the 2 tablespoons sugar.

6. Fold beaten egg whites and whipped cream into slightly frozen fruit-sugar mixture, blending well.
7. Return to refrigerator or freezer, and finish freezing.

NOTE: When the fruit juices are added to the milk-sugar mixture, the milk may curdle. If this happens, proceed with the preparation of the sherbet, for it will be all right when it freezes.

BAKED ALASKA
8 servings

1 oblong layer of sponge or pound cake about 1″ thick
5 egg whites
¾ cup sugar
1 teaspoon vanilla
1 quart brick ice cream

Oven Temperature 450° F.

1. Cut layer about 1 inch larger all around than the brick of ice cream.
2. Place on wooden board, and set aside.
3. Beat egg whites, with rotary beater or electric mixer at high speed, until foam is fine, and add sugar gradually, beating after each addition, until the meringue stands in peaks.
4. Beat in vanilla.
5. Place brick of ice cream on top of cake layer on wooden board, and spread meringue over top and down the sides of ice cream, sealing carefully to the board.
6. Bake on board at 450° F. for 5 minutes, or until meringue is light brown.
7. Serve immediately.

NOTE: The secret of preventing the ice cream from melting in the hot oven is the insulation provided by the wooden board, the cake, and the meringue.

EGGS

SOFT-COOKED EGGS
4 servings

4 eggs, at room temperature
1 quart cold water

Cold-water Method

1. Put eggs in saucepan, and cover with cold water.
2. Bring water quickly to a boil, and remove saucepan from heat.
3. Cover, and let stand for 3 to 5 minutes, depending on degree of doneness preferred.
4. Remove eggs from water, and serve immediately.

Boiling-water Method

1. Put cold water in saucepan, and bring to a boil.
2. Put eggs into boiling water, and remove from heat.
3. Cover, and let stand for 6 to 8 minutes, depending on degree of doneness preferred.
4. Remove eggs from water, and serve immediately.

HARD-COOKED EGGS
4 servings

4 eggs, at room temperature
1 quart cold water

Cold-water Method

1. Follow directions for Soft-cooked Eggs, Cold-water Method, but let eggs stand for 20 minutes.
2. Cool eggs immediately in cold water to reduce possible darkening on surface of yolks and to make it easier to remove the shells.

Boiling-water Method

1. Follow directions for Soft-cooked Eggs, Boiling-water Method, but reduce heat to keep water just below simmering, and hold for 25 minutes.
2. Cool eggs immediately in cold water to reduce possible darkening on surface of yolks and to make it easier to remove the shells.

> STANDARD: A smooth, shiny surface; evenly tender throughout; a dry, crumbly yolk.

FRIED EGGS
4 servings

2 tablespoons butter, margarine, or
  bacon drippings
4 eggs
Salt
Pepper

1. Heat butter, margarine, or bacon drippings in skillet until hot enough to make a drop of water sprinkled on fat break into small bubbles and sputter.
2. Break eggs, one at a time, into cup or saucedish, slip each egg into heated fat, and reduce heat.
3. Cook slowly for 3 to 4 minutes, or to desired doneness. Top of eggs may be cooked by basting with the hot fat or by covering skillet.
4. Sprinkle with salt and pepper.
5. Serve immediately on hot platter, and garnish as desired.

> STANDARD: A uniformly cooked surface; yolk unbroken and near center with a thin film of cooked white over it; pleasingly flavored with salt and pepper.

SCRAMBLED EGGS
4 servings

4 eggs
¼ cup milk
½ teaspoon salt
⅛ teaspoon pepper
1 tablespoon butter, margarine, or
   bacon drippings

1. Put eggs, milk, salt, and pepper in mixing bowl, and beat, with rotary beater or electric mixer at low speed, until whites and yolks are well blended.
2. Heat butter, margarine, or bacon drippings in skillet until somewhat bubbly.
3. Pour in egg mixture, and reduce heat.
4. Cook slowly, lifting egg mixture from bottom and sides of skillet with a spatula as it begins to thicken. Do not stir, but let mixture thicken in large masses.
5. Serve immediately on hot platter, and garnish with parsley, if desired.

NOTE: Eggs may be scrambled in the top of a double boiler, over simmering water in the bottom, with occasional stirring with a spoon.

STANDARD: Uniformly yellow in color throughout; large tender masses of cooked egg; a well-seasoned flavor.

VARIATIONS: Add 2 tablespoons chopped cooked bacon or ham or 1 tablespoon chopped chives or parsley to egg mixture before cooking.

PLAIN or FRENCH OMELET
4 servings

5 eggs
⅓ cup milk
½ teaspoon salt
⅛ teaspoon pepper
2 tablespoons butter, margarine, or
   bacon drippings

1. Put eggs, milk, salt, and pepper in mixing bowl, and beat with a fork until well blended.
2. Heat butter, margarine, or bacon drippings in skillet until hot enough to make a

drop of water sprinkled on fat break into small bubbles and sputter.
3. Pour in egg mixture, and when it begins to thicken around the edges, reduce heat.
4. Lift edges, as mixture cooks, with a spatula or fork, and tilt pan slightly to allow uncooked portion to run underneath.
5. Increase heat to brown bottom when egg mixture is almost set.
6. Loosen all edges carefully, fold omelet in half, and roll it out of skillet onto hot platter.
7. Serve immediately.

STANDARD: Uniformly medium brown in color; delicate and tender in texture throughout; pleasing in flavor.

VARIATIONS: Add a flavorful food, such as chopped parsley or chives, mixed herbs, bits of crisp bacon, grated cheese, or tart jelly, to omelet before folding (step 6).

PUFFY OMELET
4 servings

5 eggs, separated
⅓ cup water
½ teaspoon salt
⅛ teaspoon pepper
2 tablespoons butter, margarine, or
   bacon drippings

Oven Temperature: 350° F.

1. Beat egg whites, with rotary beater or electric mixer at high speed, until stiff but not dry.
2. Add water, salt, and pepper to egg yolks, and beat with same beater until thick and lemon-colored.
3. Fold into stiffly beaten egg whites, being careful not to overmix.
4. Heat butter, margarine, or bacon drippings in large skillet (about 10 inches in diameter) until hot enough to make a drop of water sprinkled on fat break into small bubbles and sputter.
5. Pour in egg mixture, and reduce heat.
6. Cook slowly for 8 to 10 minutes, or until puffy and lightly browned on bottom.

7. Place in oven at 350° F., and bake until top feels dry when touched lightly with finger.
8. Make a ½-inch deep cut across omelet slightly to right of center, turn larger half over smaller half, and roll omelet from pan onto hot platter.
9. Serve immediately.

> STANDARD: Uniformly medium brown in color; light, fluffy, and tender in texture throughout; pleasing in flavor.

POACHED EGGS ON TOAST
4 servings

4 eggs
4 slices buttered toast

1. Fill skillet with water to depth of 2 inches, and put over heat to boil.
2. Break eggs, one at a time, into cup or saucedish, and slip into boiling water.
3. Cover, and turn off heat immediately.
4. Allow eggs to remain in hot water for 3 to 5 minutes, or until whites are firm and a film covers yolks.
5. Place buttered toast on hot platter, and lift each egg from skillet with a skimmer or slotted spoon, drain, and place on a slice of toast.
6. Serve immediately.

> STANDARD: Oval in shape; the yolk covered with a thin film of cooked white; uniformly cooked throughout; delicate in flavor.

CREAMED HARD-COOKED EGGS ON TOAST
4 servings

1½ teaspoons prepared mustard
¼ cup grated cheese
1½ cups hot Medium White Sauce (page 510)
4 hard-cooked eggs
4 slices crisp toast

1. Add prepared mustard and grated cheese to hot medium white sauce, and stir until cheese is melted.
2. Cut hard-cooked eggs into quarters or slices, as desired.

3. Place a slice of crisp toast on each individual plate.
4. Arrange one egg on each slice of toast.
5. Pour sauce over eggs and toast.
6. Serve immediately.

DEVILED EGGS
4 servings

4 hard-cooked eggs
2 teaspoons prepared mustard
1 teaspoon lemon juice
⅛ teaspoon salt
Few grains pepper
Mayonnaise

1. Cut hard-cooked eggs in half lengthwise.
2. Remove yolks, and mash with fork.
3. Add prepared mustard, lemon juice, salt, and pepper.
4. Blend in enough mayonnaise to make mixture smooth and fluffy.
5. Fill egg whites with this mixture, making a rough surface.
6. Garnish with finely chopped chives or parsley, if desired.

FRENCH TOAST
3 servings

1 cup milk
¼ teaspoon salt
2 eggs, slightly beaten
6 slices bread
3 tablespoons butter, margarine, or shortening

1. Add milk and salt to slightly beaten eggs in mixing bowl.
2. Dip slices of bread into mixture.
3. Heat butter, margarine, or shortening in skillet until hot enough to make a drop of water sprinkled on fat break into small bubbles and sputter.
4. Brown slices of bread on one side, and then turn and brown on other side.
5. Serve immediately on hot plates with syrup or jelly.

> STANDARD: Uniformly brown in color with slightly crisp crust; tender and moist but not soggy; pleasing in flavor.

FISH

BAKED FISH
4 servings

1½ pounds fish fillets or steaks
¾ teaspoon salt
⅛ teaspoon pepper
1½ tablespoons lemon juice
1 teaspoon grated onion
3 tablespoons butter, margarine, or
   other fat, melted
Paprika

Oven Temperature: 350° F.

1. Wipe fish with damp cloth, and cut into serving-sized pieces.
2. Sprinkle both sides with salt and pepper.
3. Mix together lemon juice, grated onion, and melted butter, margarine, or other fat in shallow dish.
4. Dip each piece of fish into the lemon-juice mixture, place in greased baking dish, and pour the rest of the mixture over fish.
5. Bake at 350° F. for 25 to 30 minutes, or until fish flakes easily when tested with a fork.
6. Place fish on hot platter, pour cooking juices over it, and sprinkle generously with paprika. Add other garnish as desired.

NOTE: If frozen fish is used, defrost it before cooking, or bake as it comes from the package, allowing more baking time.

PAN-FRIED FISH
4 servings

1½ pounds fillets, steaks, or small pan-
   dressed fish
½ teaspoon salt
⅛ teaspoon pepper
1 egg, slightly beaten
1 tablespoon water
¾ cup dry bread crumbs, corn meal, or
   flour
¼ to ⅓ cup butter, margarine, shortening,
   or bacon drippings

1. Wipe fish with damp cloth, and cut into serving-sized pieces.
2. Sprinkle both sides with salt and pepper.
3. Mix slightly beaten egg and water in shallow dish.
4. Put dry bread crumbs, corn meal, or flour in another shallow dish.
5. Heat butter, margarine, shortening, or bacon drippings in skillet. Fat should be ⅛ inch deep in skillet.
6. Dip fish in egg-water mixture, and then coat in dry bread crumbs, corn meal, or flour.
7. Place in hot fat, keeping heat low enough so fat does not smoke.
8. Cook fish on one side for about 5 minutes, or until brown, and then turn carefully and cook on other side until brown and until fish flakes easily when tested with a fork.

9. Place fish on hot platter, and garnish with parsley or thinly sliced cucumbers which have been marinated in French Dressing (page 504).
10. Accompany the fish with Tartar Sauce (page 512) or Hollandaise Sauce (page 511).

NOTE: If frozen fish is used, defrost it before cooking.

BROILED FISH
4 servings

1½ pounds fish fillets or steaks
3 tablespoons butter, margarine, or other fat, melted
½ teaspoon salt
⅛ teaspoon pepper

1. Wipe fish with damp cloth, and cut into serving-sized pieces.
2. Place fish on greased broiler pan, brush with melted butter, margarine, or other fat, and sprinkle with salt and pepper.
3. Put broiler pan in preheated broiler so fish is 3 inches from heat.
4. Broil thin fillets for 5 minutes, and do not turn.
5. Broil thick fillets for 5 minutes on one side, turn and brush second side with melted fat, and sprinkle with salt and pepper.
6. Broil all fillets until fish flakes easily when tested with a fork.
7. Place fish on hot platter, and spread with Lemon-butter Sauce (page 512).

NOTE: If frozen fish is used, defrost it before cooking.

SALMON TIMBALES
4 servings

1 7¾-ounce can (1 cup) salmon
¾ cup milk
1 egg, slightly beaten
1 cup soft bread crumbs
1 tablespoon minced onion
½ teaspoon salt
Few grains pepper
1 tablespoon chopped parsley

Oven Temperature: 375° F.

1. Drain oil from salmon, put in mixing bowl, remove bones and skin, and flake into small pieces.
2. Add milk to slightly beaten egg.
3. Stir in flaked salmon and all remaining ingredients.
4. Pour into four well-greased custard cups.
5. Place in baking pan, pour hot water into pan to depth of the fish mixture in cups, and put in oven.
6. Bake at 375° F. for 45 minutes, or until a knife inserted into center of custard comes out clean.
7. Turn out onto hot platter, and surround with Mock Hollandaise Sauce (page 511), Pea Sauce (page 511), or Cream of Mushroom Sauce (page 512).

NOTE: The mixture may be baked in a well-greased loaf pan instead of in custard cups.

CODFISH CAKES
8 servings

1 quart water
1 cup shredded salt codfish
2 cups diced potatoes
1 egg, slightly beaten
1 tablespoon butter or margarine
Few grains pepper
Salt (optional)
2 tablespoons shortening

1. Put water in saucepan, and bring to a boil.
2. Add shredded salt codfish and diced potatoes, and cook until potatoes are tender when tested with a fork.
3. Drain thoroughly, and dry by placing saucepan over heat for a few seconds.
4. Mash thoroughly.
5. Add slightly beaten egg, butter or margarine, and pepper, and beat with a spoon or wire whisk until light and fluffy.
6. Taste, and add salt, if necessary.
7. Flour hands, and shape mixture into round, flat cakes 1 inch thick.
8. Heat shortening in skillet, and brown codfish cakes on both sides.
9. Serve on hot platter accompanied with chili sauce or catsup.

TUNA FISH CROQUETTES

4 servings

1 7-ounce can (1 cup) tuna fish
1 tablespoon minced onion
1 tablespoon lemon juice
¼ cup butter or margarine
¼ cup flour
½ teaspoon salt
1 cup milk
Fine dry bread crumbs
1 egg, slightly beaten
2 tablespoons water

1. Drain oil from tuna fish, put in mixing bowl, and flake into small pieces.
2. Stir in minced onion and lemon juice.
3. Make White Sauce (page 510) of butter or margarine, flour, salt, and milk.
4. Add to seasoned tuna fish, and blend thoroughly.
5. Chill in refrigerator for 2 hours or longer.
6. Sprinkle a generous layer of fine dry bread crumbs on wax paper.
7. Mix slightly beaten egg and water in shallow dish.
8. Divide chilled fish mixture into eight portions.
9. Shape each into ball, drop into crumbs, and roll into cylinder.
10. Coat all sides with egg-water mixture.
11. Roll again in crumbs, and place on pan.
12. Chill in refrigerator for about 30 minutes.
13. Pan-fry in hot fat ¼ inch deep for about 10 minutes, turning to brown on all sides.
14. Drain on absorbent paper.
15. Serve on hot platter surrounded with Pea Sauce (page 511) or accompanied with Tartar Sauce (page 512).

CREAMED SHRIMP

6 servings

1½ pounds shrimp
2 cups Medium White Sauce
   (page 510)
½ teaspoon onion juice
½ teaspoon celery salt
1 tablespoon minced pimento
1 small can sliced mushrooms
6 Toast Cups (page 482)
2 tablespoons chopped parsley

1. Cook, shell, and clean shrimp.
2. Make medium white sauce, and add onion juice and celery salt.
3. Add shrimp, minced pimento, and sliced mushrooms, and bring to a boil.
4. Serve in toast cups, and sprinkle with chopped parsley.

To Cook, Shell, and Clean Shrimp

1½ pounds shrimp
1½ quarts water
¼ cup vinegar
1½ teaspoons salt
1 bay leaf
6 peppercorns

1. Wash shrimp.
2. Put all remaining ingredients in saucepan, and bring water to a boil.
3. Add shrimp, bring water to simmering, and simmer for 10 minutes.
4. Drain, and cool shrimp under cold water.
5. Remove tiny legs, and peel off shell.
6. Cut shrimp on curved side, and remove dark vein.

DEVILED CRAB MEAT

4 servings

2 tablespoons butter or margarine
1 tablespoon flour
1½ tablespoons minced parsley
2 teaspoons lemon juice
¾ teaspoon horseradish
½ teaspoon salt
½ cup milk
1 7-ounce can (1 cup) crab meat
2 hard-cooked eggs, chopped
⅓ cup Buttered Soft Bread Crumbs
   (page 482)

Oven Temperature: 400° F.

1. Melt butter or margarine over low heat.
2. Stir in flour, minced parsley, lemon juice, horseradish, salt, and milk.
3. Cook, stirring constantly, until thick.
4. Flake crab meat, and remove any shells.
5. Add chopped hard-cooked eggs and flaked crab meat to sauce, and mix.
6. Put in four greased custard cups, and sprinkle with buttered soft bread crumbs.
7. Bake at 400° F. for 10 minutes, or until bread crumbs are brown.

FRUITS

BAKED APPLES
4 servings

4 baking apples
¼ cup sugar
½ teaspoon cinnamon
¼ teaspoon salt
1 teaspoon butter or margarine
⅓ cup water

Oven Temperature: 400° F.

1. Remove stems, wash and core apples, and pare a strip about 2 inches wide around stem ends.
2. Place, with pared ends up, close together in baking dish.
3. Mix together sugar, cinnamon, and salt, and place a tablespoonful in cavity of each apple.
4. Put ¼ teaspoon butter or margarine on top of each apple.
5. Pour water into baking dish.
6. Bake at 400° F. for 40 to 45 minutes, or until apples are soft when tested with a fork. Baste apples occasionally as they cook with syrup from baking dish.
7. Serve apples in individual dishes, and pour the syrup over them.

> STANDARD: Fairly uniform in shape; soft but not mushy; slightly sweet in taste with a flavor of the seasonings used.

VARIATIONS: Use brown sugar instead of granulated sugar.

Put seedless raisins in each cavity with sugar mixture.

Fill cavities with a tart jelly instead of sugar mixture.

APPLESAUCE
6 servings

8 medium cooking apples
¾ cup water
¾ cup sugar, or more if desired
½ teaspoon salt
½ teaspoon cinnamon (optional)

1. Wash apples, quarter, core, and cut into slices but do not pare.
2. Put in saucepan, and add water.
3. Cover, and cook over high heat until water comes to a boil.
4. Reduce heat, and cook for 10 to 15 minutes, or until apples are soft, depending on variety of apples.
5. Rub through coarse strainer or food mill.
6. Stir in sugar and salt.
7. Return to heat, and bring sauce to a boil.
8. Pour into serving dish, and sprinkle with cinnamon, if used.

STEWED DRIED FRUIT

1 package dried fruit
Sugar
1 or 2 lemon slices (optional)

1. Wash dried fruit.
2. Put in saucepan, and cover with cold water.
3. Bring water slowly to a boil.
4. Reduce heat to simmering, and cook for about 20 minutes, or until fruit is soft.
5. Add sugar to taste and lemon slices, if used.
6. Bring to a boil.
7. Chill in refrigerator before serving.

NOTE: Before cooking dried fruit, check the package label for directions.

CRANBERRY SAUCE

4 to 6 servings

½ pound (2 cups) cranberries
1 cup water
1 cup sugar

1. Look over cranberries, discard imperfect ones, and wash thoroughly.
2. Put in medium-sized saucepan, and add water and sugar.
3. Bring to a boil, and boil for 5 to 10 minutes, or until cranberry skins break.
4. Skim foam from top.
5. Chill before serving.

FRESH FRUIT CUP

4 servings

1 medium grapefruit
2 large oranges
⅓ cup grapes
2 tablespoons sugar

1. Wash and dry fruit.
2. Section grapefruit and oranges, and put in bowl.
3. Cut grapes in half lengthwise, remove seeds, and add to grapefruit and oranges.
4. Add sugar, and mix carefully with fruit.
5. Chill in refrigerator.
6. Arrange in individual servings, taking care that a few of the grapes are on top to give a touch of color if they are red grapes. Otherwise decorate each serving with a bit of mint or half of a candied or maraschino cherry.

HALF GRAPEFRUIT

4 servings

2 grapefruit
Sugar

1. Wash and dry grapefruit.
2. Cut in half crosswise.
3. Remove seeds, if any, with the point of a knife.
4. Cut out core with scissors.
5. Cut around each section to loosen flesh from membrane and skin.
6. Sprinkle lightly with sugar.
7. Chill before serving.

VARIATIONS: Put any one of the following in center of grapefruit: sprig of mint, halves of grapes (seeded), several halves of orange sections, a maraschino cherry, or a melon ball.

BROILED GRAPEFRUIT

4 servings

2 grapefruit
4 tablespoons light-brown sugar
Salt
2 teaspoons butter or margarine

1. Wash and dry grapefruit.
2. Cut in half crosswise.
3. Remove seeds, if any, with the point of a knife.
4. Cut out core with scissors.
5. Cut around each section to loosen flesh from membrane and skin.
6. Put 1 tablespoon light-brown sugar in center of each half, sprinkle lightly with salt, and divide butter or margarine among the four halves.
7. Place in shallow pan, and broil, about 6 inches from heat, for about 15 minutes, or until nicely browned on top.
8. Serve hot as either appetizer or dessert.

SPICED PEACHES,
PEARS, or PINEAPPLE

10 to 12 servings

2 28-ounce cans fruit
3 cups sugar
¼ cup white vinegar
2 tablespoons mixed-pickle spices
2 tablespoons broken stick cinnamon
2 tablespoons whole cloves

1. Drain syrup from canned fruit into saucepan.
2. Add sugar and white vinegar, and bring to a boil.
3. Tie spices loosely in cheesecloth bag, and put in boiling syrup.
4. Add fruit, reduce heat to simmering, and cook for 10 minutes.
5. Remove spice bag, and cool fruit in syrup.
6. Store fruit, covered with syrup, in refrigerator.
7. Serve as accompaniment with meat or poultry.

MEATS

ROAST BEEF

3 servings per pound of standing roast
4 servings per pound of rolled roast

1 6- to 8-pound standing rib of beef
or
1 4- to 6-pound rolled rib of beef
Salt
Pepper

Oven Temperature: 325° F.

1. Wipe meat with damp cloth.
2. Season with salt and pepper.
3. Place meat, fat side up, in roasting pan. If standing roast, rest on rib bones. If rolled roast, rest on rack in bottom of pan.
4. Insert meat thermometer, if used, into center of largest muscle.
5. Roast at 325° F. until meat is rare, medium, or well done, as desired. (See "Timetable for Roasting Meats" on page 472 for roasting time and internal temperature for each degree of doneness.)
6. Place roast on hot platter, and keep in warm oven while making Roast Beef Gravy.
7. Use meat drippings in pan to make gravy.

ROAST BEEF GRAVY

2 cups

3 tablespoons fat drippings
2 cups cold water
3 tablespoons flour
Salt

1. Pour off all fat drippings from roasting pan, and reserve.
2. Put some of the 2 cups cold water in pan, and let heat to dissolve browned bits from roast.
3. Pour this liquid off, and reserve.
4. Return 3 tablespoons of fat drippings to roasting pan, and place over low heat.
5. Add flour, and stir to blend thoroughly.
6. Stir in liquids slowly—that reserved from pan and remainder of the 2 cups cold water.
7. Bring to a boil, stirring constantly, and allow to boil for 2 to 3 minutes.
8. Season with salt to taste.
9. Pour into hot gravy dish, and serve with roast.

STANDARD: Attractive appearance; plump, not shriveled; lean, lightly browned; fat clear with surface slightly crisp; meat tender, juicy, and well flavored.

Rare beef—cut slice has narrow rim of brown surrounding bright-red center.

Medium beef—cut slice has wider rim of brown surrounding pink center.

Well-done beef—cut slice is brown to center.

Juiciness and tenderness decrease with greater degree of doneness.

TIMETABLE FOR ROASTING MEATS*

KIND AND CUT OF MEAT	READY-TO-COOK WEIGHT (pounds)	MINUTES PER POUND (at 325° F.)	INTERNAL TEMPERATURE OF MEAT WHEN DONE (° F.)
Beef			
Standing ribs			
Rare	6–8	20	140
Medium	6–8	25	150
Well done	6–8	30	170
Rolled rib			
Rare	4–6	30	140
Medium	4–6	35	150
Well done	4–6	40	170
Rolled rump	5	45	170
Sirloin tip	3	45	170
Veal			
Leg	5–8	35–40	180
Loin	4–6	35–40	180
Rolled shoulder	4–6	50–55	180
Lamb			
Leg	5–7	25–30	180
Shoulder	4–6	35–40	180
Rolled shoulder	4–6	35–40	180
Pork, fresh			
Loin	3–4	40–45	185
Shoulder	5–7	40–45	185
Ham, whole	10–14	35–40	185
Ham, half	6	45–50	185
Spareribs	3	40	185
Pork, cured[1]			
Ham, whole	13–15	20–25	170
Ham, half	5–8	30–35	170
Picnic shoulder	5–7	35–40	170

[1] For fully cooked, ready-to-eat hams and shoulders, follow directions on package.

* From Meat, How To Buy, How To Cook, Canada Department of Agriculture, Publication No. 571, 1964.

ROAST LAMB

2 to 4 servings per pound of leg
3 to 4 servings per pound of rolled shoulder

1 6- to 7-pound leg of lamb
or
1 3- to 5-pound rolled shoulder of lamb
Salt
Pepper

Oven Temperature: 325° F.

1. Wipe meat with damp cloth.
2. Season with salt and pepper.
3. Place meat, fat side up, on rack in roasting pan.
4. Insert meat thermometer, if used, into center of largest muscle.
5. Roast at 325° F. to an internal temperature of 180° F. (See "Timetable for Roasting Meats" at the left for roasting time.)
6. Place roast on hot platter, and keep in warm oven while making gravy.
7. Use meat drippings in pan to make gravy. (See recipe for Roast Beef Gravy on page 471.)

NOTE: If medium-done lamb is preferred to well-done lamb, roast meat to an internal temperature of 175° F. instead of 180° F.

> STANDARD: Attractive appearance; plump, not shriveled; meat tender, juicy, and well flavored.

ROAST VEAL

2 to 3 servings per pound of leg
3 to 4 servings per pound of rolled shoulder

1 5- to 8-pound leg of veal
or
1 3- to 5-pound rolled shoulder of veal
Salt
Pepper

Oven Temperature: 325° F.

Follow directions for Roast Beef—rolled roast (page 471) except roast to well-done stage, 170° to 180° F.

NOTE: Only high-quality veal should be roasted. Otherwise place about 1 cup water in pan with meat, cover, and cook meat for 40 minutes to the pound.

ROAST PORK

2 to 3 servings per pound

1 3- to 5-pound loin of pork
Salt
Pepper

Oven Temperature: 325° F.

Follow directions for Roast Beef—standing roast (page 471) except roast to well-done stage, 185° F.

BAKED HAM

About 2 servings per pound

1 12- to 16-pound ham (mild-cured)
or
1 6-pound half ham (mild-cured)

Glaze for Large Ham
1 cup brown sugar
2 tablespoons flour
1 tablespoon dry mustard
Whole cloves

Oven Temperature: 325° F.

1. Wipe ham with damp cloth.
2. Place, fat side up, on rack in roasting pan.
3. Insert meat thermometer, if used, into center of largest muscle.
4. Bake at 325° F. to an internal temperature of 160° F. (See "Timetable for Roasting Meats" at the left for baking time.)

To Glaze Ham

1. Mix together ingredients for glaze while ham is baking.
2. Remove ham from oven about 15 minutes before it is done.
3. Cut surface fat into diamond shapes with a sharp knife, making cuts about ¼ inch deep.
4. Insert whole clove into center of each diamond.
5. Cover ham with glaze.
6. Return to oven, and bake at 400° F. for 15 to 20 minutes, or until glaze is brown.
7. Place on hot platter, and keep in warm oven until ready to serve.

> STANDARD: Attractive appearance; plump, not shriveled; glaze nicely browned; meat tender, juicy, and well flavored.

TIMETABLE FOR BROILING BEEFSTEAKS *

STEAK	TOTAL TIME (minutes)
1 inch thick	
Rare	About 10
Medium	About 15
Well done	20–25
1½ inches thick	
Rare	About 15
Medium	About 20
Well done	25–30
2 inches thick	
Rare	About 25
Medium	About 35
Well done	45–50

* From *Food: The Yearbook of Agriculture,* U.S. Department of Agriculture, 1959, p. 528.

BROILED BEEFSTEAK
4 servings per pound boneless
2 to 3 servings per pound with bone

> 1 steak, sirloin, tenderloin,
>   porterhouse, or club
> Salt
> Pepper

1. Wipe steak with damp cloth.
2. Slash fat in several places around edge to prevent curling.
3. Preheat broiler and broiler rack.
4. Grease rack lightly with fat cut from steak.
5. Insert in broiler so top of steak is 2 to 4 inches from heat. Leave broiler door partly open when using electric range.
6. Broil steak until top side is well browned (about one-half of broiling time given in "Timetable for Broiling Beefsteaks" above), and season with salt and pepper.
7. Turn steak, and brown on other side for last half of broiling time.

8. Place on hot platter, season with additional salt and pepper, if desired, and serve at once.
9. Pour pan gravy over steak, if desired.

NOTE: If steak is 2 or more inches thick or if it is to be broiled to the well-done stage, place steak so top is at least 3 to 4 inches from heat.

BROILED LAMB CHOPS
4 servings

> 4 lamb chops, about ¾ to
>   1 inch thick
> Salt
> Pepper

Follow directions for Broiled Beefsteak, using the times suggested for medium or well-done degrees of broiling as given in the "Timetable for Broiling Beefsteaks" at the left.

BRAISED PORK CHOPS
4 servings

> 4 pork chops, about 1 inch thick
> ¼ to ½ cup water
> Salt
> Pepper

1. Wipe chops with damp cloth.
2. Heat skillet, and grease with fat trimmed from chops.
3. Brown chops on one side, and then turn and brown on other side, allowing 10 to 12 minutes for browning.
4. Pour off excess fat, add water just to cover bottom of skillet, and season chops with salt and pepper.
5. Cover.
6. Cook slowly for about 1 hour, or until chops are tender when tested with a fork.
7. Serve on hot platter.

POT ROAST WITH HORSERADISH GRAVY

6 to 8 servings

3 pounds beef, chuck or round
2 teaspoons salt
¼ teaspoon pepper
¼ cup flour
2 tablespoons shortening or salad oil
1 6-ounce bottle prepared horseradish

1. Wipe meat with damp cloth.
2. Season with salt and pepper, and dredge with flour.
3. Heat shortening or salad oil in Dutch oven or other heavy kettle.
4. Brown meat on all sides, allowing 20 minutes for browning.
5. Put horseradish in measuring cup, fill with water to make 1 cup, and pour over meat.
6. Cover, and simmer for 2½ to 3 hours, or until tender when tested with a fork.
7. Place pot roast on hot platter, and keep warm while making Horseradish Gravy.

NOTE: Meat may be cooked in oven at 350° F. for 2½ to 3 hours, if desired.

HORSERADISH GRAVY

Broth from meat
1 cup water
3 tablespoons flour
Salt
Pepper

1. Skim off fat, if any, from broth in kettle, and add water.
2. Mix flour with enough additional cold water to make a smooth thin paste.
3. Stir slowly into broth, and boil, stirring constantly, for 1 minute.
4. Season with salt and pepper to taste.
5. Pour into hot gravy dish, and serve with pot roast.

BREADED VEAL CHOPS or CUTLET

3 to 4 servings

4 veal rib chops, cut ½ inch thick
 (about 1¼ pounds)
 or
1 veal cutlet, cut ½ inch thick
 (about 1¼ pounds)
1 egg, slightly beaten
2 tablespoons water
½ cup fine dry bread crumbs
1 teaspoon salt
2 teaspoons paprika
¼ cup shortening or salad oil

1. Wipe meat with damp cloth.
2. Mix slightly beaten egg and water in shallow dish.
3. Mix fine dry bread crumbs, salt, and paprika in another shallow dish.
4. Dip veal chops or cutlet (cut in serving-sized pieces) into egg-water mixture, and then coat in seasoned dry bread crumbs.
5. Heat shortening or salad oil in large skillet.
6. Brown meat on one side, and then turn and brown on other side.
7. Add boiling water to a depth of about one-half of meat.
8. Cover, and simmer for 50 to 60 minutes, or until tender when tested with a fork.
9. Place on hot platter, and garnish with parsley.

VARIATIONS: Use, instead of water, canned condensed tomato soup diluted with water or canned condensed cream of mushroom soup diluted with milk.

LAMB STEW
6 servings

2 pounds boneless lamb shoulder,
   cut into 2-inch pieces
1 quart water
6 small potatoes
3 carrots, quartered
6 small onions
1 small turnip, diced
2 teaspoons salt
¼ teaspoon pepper
3 tablespoons chopped parsley
2 tablespoons flour
¼ cup water

1. Wipe meat with damp cloth.
2. Put in kettle, and add the 1 quart water.
3. Cover, and simmer for 2 hours.
4. Add vegetables and salt and pepper, and continue to simmer for about 30 minutes, or until vegetables are tender when tested with a fork.
5. Add chopped parsley.
6. Mix flour and the ¼ cup water to make a smooth paste.
7. Stir slowly into stew, and boil, stirring constantly, for 1 minute.
8. Serve on hot platter, and garnish with sprigs of parsley.

BEEF STEW
6 servings

2 pounds beef, chuck or round, cut
   into 1½-inch cubes
⅓ cup flour
1½ teaspoons salt
¼ teaspoon pepper
¼ cup shortening or beef drippings
1 quart water
¼ cup chili sauce or catsup
6 small potatoes
4 medium carrots, quartered
6 small onions
2 tablespoons flour
¼ cup water

1. Wipe meat with damp cloth.
2. Mix the ⅓ cup flour, salt, and pepper on a piece of wax paper.
3. Roll pieces of beef in seasoned flour, and coat evenly.
4. Heat shortening or beef drippings in kettle, add meat, and brown on all sides.
5. Add the 1 quart water and chili sauce or catsup.
6. Cover, and simmer for 2 hours.
7. Add vegetables and continue to simmer for about 30 minutes, or until vegetables are tender when tested with a fork.
8. Mix the 2 tablespoons flour and the ¼ cup water to make a smooth paste.
9. Stir slowly into stew, and boil, stirring constantly, for 1 minute.
10. Season with additional salt and pepper, if desired.
11. Serve on hot platter, and sprinkle with chopped parsley or chives.

NOTE: If you have any seasoned flour left over from step 3, you may use it for thickening the stew (steps 8 and 9).

SWISS STEAK
4 to 5 servings

1½ pounds beef round steak, cut
   2 inches thick
½ cup flour
1 teaspoon salt
½ teaspoon pepper
⅓ cup shortening or salad oil
1 medium onion, thinly sliced
1 cup canned tomatoes

1. Wipe steak with damp cloth.
2. Mix flour, salt, and pepper, and put on cutting board.
3. Lay steak on seasoned flour, and turn to coat both sides.
4. Pound all over surface with edge of heavy plate.
5. Turn steak, and continue to pound until it takes up most of flour.
6. Heat shortening or salad oil in large heavy skillet.

7. Add thinly sliced onion, cook until yellow, and remove.
8. Brown steak in fat thoroughly on both sides.
9. Lay onion on top, and pour canned tomatoes around steak.
10. Cover, and simmer for 2½ to 3 hours, or until tender when tested with a fork.
11. Place on hot platter, and keep in warm oven while making gravy.
12. Use meat drippings in pan to make gravy. (See recipe for Roast Beef Gravy on page 471.)

NOTE: Swiss steak may be cooked in oven at 350° F. instead of on surface of range.

PAN-BROILED HAM
4 servings

1 to 1¼ pounds ham slice, about ½ inch thick

1. Wipe ham with damp cloth.
2. Slash fat in several places around edge to prevent curling.
3. Heat skillet, and grease with fat cut from ham.
4. Add ham, and brown on both sides.
5. Broil for about 18 to 20 minutes, turning frequently to brown evenly.
6. Serve on hot platter surrounded with Spiced Peaches (page 470).

BAKED HAM SLICE
4 to 5 servings

1 ham slice, about 1 inch thick
½ cup fine soft bread crumbs
½ cup brown sugar
1 teaspoon dry mustard
⅛ teaspoon pepper
¾ cup pineapple juice

Oven Temperature: 350° F.

1. Wipe ham with damp cloth.
2. Heat skillet, and grease with fat cut from ham.
3. Add ham, and brown on both sides.
4. Mix fine soft bread crumbs, brown sugar, dry mustard, and pepper with pineapple juice.
5. Place ham in greased baking dish, and cover with crumb-juice mixture.
6. Bake at 350° F. for 1 hour, basting meat occasionally. If fruit juice evaporates, add more juice or water.
7. Serve in the baking dish.

MEAT LOAF
(Beef)
6 to 8 servings

1½ pounds ground beef
1 cup soft bread crumbs
3 tablespoons chopped onion
2 teaspoons salt
¼ teaspoon pepper
¾ cup milk or tomato juice
1 egg, unbeaten
2 tablespoons Worcestershire sauce

Oven Temperature: 350° F.

1. Put all ingredients in mixing bowl, and mix thoroughly, using a fork to avoid packing.
2. Place in ungreased 9x5x3-inch loaf pan.
3. Bake at 350° F. for 1 hour.
4. Pour off any fat that may be around meat loaf in pan.
5. Place on hot platter, and arrange around loaf a buttered vegetable, such as small boiled potatoes, small boiled onions, or carrot slices, if desired.

NOTES: If the beef is quite juicy, slightly less than the ¾ cup of either milk or tomato juice may be sufficient.

The meat mixture may be shaped as a loaf and baked in an open pan rather than in a loaf pan, if desired.

GROUND BEEF AND MUSHROOMS
4 servings

2 tablespoons shortening or salad oil
1 pound ground beef
⅔ cup chopped onion
3 ounces canned mushrooms
1 teaspoon salt
⅛ teaspoon pepper
2 tablespoons catsup
½ teaspoon oregano
½ cup water or milk
2 tablespoons chopped parsley
4 slices thin toast

1. Heat shortening or salad oil in skillet.
2. Add ground beef and chopped onion, and cook, stirring occasionally, until meat is brown.
3. Add remaining ingredients, except toast.
4. Simmer slowly for 10 minutes.
5. Serve on thin toast, or if preferred, in Toast Cup (page 482).

PAN-FRIED HAMBURGERS
4 servings

1 pound ground round steak
1 cup fine soft bread crumbs
1½ tablespoons finely chopped onion
1 teaspoon salt
⅛ teaspoon pepper
½ cup milk
2 teaspoons shortening or salad oil

1. Put all ingredients, except shortening or salad oil, in mixing bowl, and mix thoroughly, using a fork to avoid packing.
2. Divide into eight portions, and shape lightly into patties about 1 inch thick. If patties are packed tightly, they will be hard when cooked.
3. Heat shortening or salad oil in skillet.
4. Pan-fry hamburgers for 5 minutes on each side, or until they are as well done as desired.
5. Arrange on hot platter, pour pan juice over them, and garnish with parsley.

CHILI CON CARNE
6 servings

2 tablespoons shortening or salad oil
1 pound ground beef
1 large onion, chopped
1 green pepper, chopped
1 19-ounce can (2½ cups) kidney beans, drained
2 cans condensed tomato soup
1 cup water
2 tablespoons chili powder
1 teaspoon salt
⅛ teaspoon cayenne

1. Heat shortening or salad oil in large skillet.
2. Add ground beef, chopped onion, and chopped green pepper, and cook, stirring occasionally, until meat is brown.
3. Add remaining ingredients.
4. Cover, and cook over low heat, stirring occasionally, for 1 hour.
5. Serve in hot bowl.

PAN-BROILED WIENERS
4 servings

8 wieners

1. Heat a lightly greased griddle or skillet.
2. Add wieners.
3. Cook, turning frequently with tongs, until well browned on all sides.
4. Serve with prepared mustard, chili sauce, or relish, as desired.

BROILED WIENERS
4 servings

8 wieners
Butter, margarine, or salad oil

1. Rub wieners with butter, margarine, or salad oil.
2. Place on broiler rack in broiler pan.
3. Insert in broiler so wieners are 3 inches from heat. Leave broiler door partly open when using electric range.
4. Broil, turning frequently with tongs, until well browned on all sides.
5. Place on hot platter, and cover with Barbecue Sauce (page 512).

BOILED WIENERS

4 servings

8 wieners

1. Put water in saucepan to a depth that will cover wieners, and bring to a boil.
2. Drop in wieners.
3. Cover, and bring water to simmering.
4. Cook for 5 minutes.
5. Serve with prepared mustard, chili sauce, or relish, as desired.

COWBOY SUPPER

8 to 10 servings

2 tablespoons butter or margarine
½ cup chopped onion
½ cup chopped green pepper
1 dozen wieners, quartered
2 cups chopped fresh tomatoes
½ teaspoon caraway seeds
½ teaspoon salt
1 bay leaf
¼ teaspoon paprika
4 hard-cooked eggs, quartered

1. Heat butter or margarine in skillet.
2. Add chopped onion and chopped green pepper, and cook until onion is yellow.
3. Add all remaining ingredients, except hard-cooked eggs, and simmer for 15 minutes.
4. Place eggs on top of other ingredients, and simmer for 10 minutes longer.
5. Serve on thin slices of Johnny Cake (page 497) or, if preferred, on Waffles (page 498) or crisp toast.

PAN-BROILED BACON

4 servings

8 slices bacon

1. Place slices of bacon in cold 10-inch skillet, allowing space for each slice to lie flat.
2. Cook slowly for about 5 to 8 minutes, or until evenly crisp, turning once.
3. Pour off fat (drippings) as it accumulates.

4. Remove each slice separately, and drain on absorbent paper.
5. Keep hot until ready to serve.

NOTE: If cold bacon slices are difficult to separate, place the number needed in the skillet, and allow them to heat. As the fat becomes warm, you will be able to separate the slices easily.

OVEN-BROILED BACON

4 servings

8 slices bacon

1. Place slices of bacon on cold broiler rack in broiler pan, allowing space for each slice to lie flat.
2. Insert pan in broiler so bacon is about 3 inches from heat, and turn on heat.
3. Broil bacon for about 3 to 5 minutes, or until evenly crisp, turning once.
4. Keep hot until ready to serve.

PAN-FRIED LIVER AND BACON

4 to 6 servings

4 to 6 slices bacon
1 pound sliced liver (calf, beef, or lamb)
¼ cup flour
¾ teaspoon salt
¼ teaspoon pepper
Bacon drippings

1. Prepare bacon in skillet as directed for Pan-broiled Bacon, reserve drippings, and keep bacon hot while cooking liver.
2. Wipe liver with damp cloth, remove any tubes, and cut edge in several places to prevent curling.
3. Mix flour, salt, and pepper on wax paper, and coat liver on both sides.
4. Return enough bacon drippings to skillet to cover bottom, and heat.
5. Place liver in skillet, and brown on both sides.
6. Reduce heat, and cook, turning once, for 10 minutes, or to the desired doneness.
7. Place liver on hot platter, lay a slice of bacon on each slice of liver, and garnish with parsley.

BRAISED LIVER
6 servings

1 pound sliced liver (calf, beef, or
    lamb)
¼ cup flour
¾ teaspoon salt
¼ teaspoon pepper
2½ tablespoons shortening or bacon
    drippings
¾ cup boiling water

1. Wipe liver with damp cloth, remove any tubes, and cut edge in several places to prevent curling.
2. Mix flour, salt, and pepper on wax paper, and coat liver on both sides.
3. Heat shortening or bacon drippings in skillet, and brown liver on both sides.
4. Add boiling water, reduce heat, and cover.
5. Simmer for 15 to 20 minutes, or until liver is tender when tested with a fork.
6. Serve on hot platter.

STUFFED PEPPERS
4 servings

2 large green peppers
1¼ cups Boiled Rice (page 449)
1½ cups ground leftover meat
1 tablespoon finely chopped onion
½ teaspoon salt
1 cup canned tomatoes, strained
½ cup Buttered Soft Bread Crumbs
    (page 482)
⅓ cup water

Oven Temperature: 350° F.

1. Wash green peppers, cut in half lengthwise, and remove seeds and center cores.
2. Cook in boiling water to cover for 10 minutes.
3. Remove peppers, and run cold water over them so they are easy to handle.
4. Put boiled rice, ground leftover meat, finely chopped onion, salt, and one-half of the strained canned tomatoes in mixing bowl, and mix thoroughly.

5. Fill pepper halves with rice-meat mixture, and cover with buttered soft bread crumbs.
6. Place close together in shallow baking dish.
7. Add water to the remaining tomatoes, and pour around (not over) peppers.
8. Bake at 350° F. for 30 minutes.
9. Serve in baking dish in which cooked, using some of the liquid in the dish as a sauce when serving each person.

NOTE: Omit salt if leftover meat is ham.

MEAT ROLY-POLY
6 servings

1 cup ground leftover meat
¼ cup chopped onion
⅓ cup tomato paste
1¼ cups condensed vegetable soup
½ teaspoon salt
⅔ cup milk
2 cups biscuit mix
1½ cups hot leftover gravy

Oven Temperature: 400° F.

1. Put ground leftover meat, chopped onion, tomato paste, condensed vegetable soup, and salt in mixing bowl, and mix thoroughly.
2. Stir milk into biscuit mix, being careful not to overmix.
3. Roll biscuit dough, with floured rolling pin on lightly floured board, into an oblong sheet ½ inch thick.
4. Spread meat mixture evenly over it.
5. Roll up dough from long side with hands, and fasten by pinching dough along edge.
6. Place in greased shallow pan.
7. Bake at 400° F. for 40 minutes.
8. Serve with hot leftover gravy.

NOTES: The biscuit dough may be made from the ingredients instead of a biscuit mix. (See recipe on page 494.)

Omit salt if leftover meat is ham.

BAKED HASH

5 servings

2 cups chopped cooked meat (corned
   beef, roast beef, or lamb)
2½ cups chopped cooked potatoes
1 small onion, chopped
⅓ cup milk or catsup
⅛ teaspoon pepper
Salt
3 tablespoons butter, margarine, or
   bacon drippings
¼ cup coarse cracker crumbs

Oven Temperature: 375° F.

1. Put chopped cooked meat, chopped cooked potatoes, and chopped onion in mixing bowl, and mix thoroughly.
2. Stir in milk or catsup, and pepper.
3. Season with salt to taste.
4. Melt 2 tablespoons of the butter, margarine, or bacon drippings in shallow baking dish.
5. Put in meat mixture, and spread out evenly.
6. Sprinkle coarse cracker crumbs over top, and dot with the rest of the butter, margarine, or drippings.

7. Bake at 375° F. for about 40 minutes, or until cracker crumbs are brown.

NOTE: This mixture may be cooked in a skillet until well browned on bottom. Omit cracker crumbs.

CREAMED DRIED BEEF
ON TOAST

4 servings

3 tablespoons butter or margarine
1 cup dried beef, torn into pieces
2¼ tablespoons flour
Few grains pepper
1½ cups milk
4 slices thin toast

1. Melt butter or margarine in skillet.
2. Add pieces of dried beef, and brown lightly.
3. Remove from heat, and sprinkle flour and pepper over dried beef, stirring to blend.
4. Stir in milk, and cook, stirring constantly, until mixture boils for ½ minute.
5. Serve on thin toast.

NOTE: For variety, creamed dried beef may be served on Waffles (page 498), on thin slices of Southern Corn Bread (page 497), or in Toast Cups (page 482).

Courtesy American Institute of Baking

● Creamed dried beef, arranged attractively on toast strips, can be served for breakfast, for lunch, or for supper.

MISCELLANEOUS

CROUTONS

1 slice day-old bread
Butter or margarine

1. Cut crusts from slice of day-old bread.
2. Cut slice in strips as wide as slice is thick.
3. Cut strips across to make cubes.
4. Melt enough butter or margarine in small skillet to cover bottom.
5. Put in bread cubes, and heat, tossing frequently, until well browned on all sides.
6. Serve as garnish on cream soups or in tossed salads.

NOTES: Small croutons may be made by using thinly sliced bread instead of regular-sliced bread.

The unbuttered bread cubes may be spread on a baking sheet and browned in the oven at 325° F.

SOFT BREAD CRUMBS

Cube fresh or slightly stale thinly sliced bread, or tear slices into small pieces with the tines of a fork or with the fingers.

DRY BREAD CRUMBS

Grind dry bread through food chopper, using fine blade, or roll on wax paper with rolling pin. Sift ground crumbs if very even ones are desired.

BUTTERED SOFT BREAD CRUMBS

Melt 2 tablespoons butter or margarine, and with a fork toss 1 cup soft bread crumbs in it.

BUTTERED DRY BREAD CRUMBS

Melt ¼ cup butter or margarine, and with a fork toss 1 cup dry bread crumbs in it. Stir over heat until crumbs are golden brown.

TOAST CUPS
4 cups

4 slices thin bread
Butter or margarine, softened

Oven Temperature: 400° F.

1. Cut crusts from thinly sliced bread.
2. Spread each side of slice with softened butter or margarine.
3. Press slice into muffin pan, shaping to fit cup.
4. Toast in oven at 400° F. until golden brown.
5. Remove to serving dish.
6. Fill with creamed food just before serving.

DOUGHNUTS
4 dozen

4 cups sifted all-purpose flour
3½ teaspoons baking powder
½ teaspoon salt
¼ teaspoon nutmeg
¼ cup shortening
1 cup sugar
2 eggs, well beaten
1 cup milk

Deep Fat: 365° to 370° F.

1. Sift together flour, baking powder, salt, and nutmeg onto wax paper.
2. Put shortening and sugar in mixing bowl, and cream until well blended.
3. Add well-beaten eggs, and beat until light and fluffy.
4. Stir in sifted dry ingredients alternately with milk to make a stiff dough. If necessary for easier handling of dough, add extra flour.
5. Turn dough onto floured board, and roll with floured rolling pin into a sheet ½ inch thick.
6. Cut into rings with floured doughnut cutter.
7. Fry in deep fat that has been preheated to 365° to 370° F.
8. Brown on lower side, and then turn and brown on other side.
9. Remove doughnuts from fat, and drain on absorbent paper.
10. Dip doughnuts in sugar when cool, if desired.

NOTE: To make "crullers," cut the sheet of dough into 8x1-inch strips. Then fold each strip in half lengthwise, twist several times, and pinch the ends together.

CHEESE STRAWS

16 straws

½ cup grated Cheddar or process
   Canadian cheese
1½ tablespoons butter or margarine,
   softened
2 tablespoons milk
⅓ cup sifted all-purpose flour
¾ cup fine soft bread crumbs
Few grains salt
Few grains cayenne

Oven Temperature: 400° F.

1. Mix together grated cheese and softened butter or margarine.
2. Add milk, and blend.
3. Mix together flour, fine soft bread crumbs, salt, and cayenne.

4. Add to first mixture, and stir until smooth.
5. Roll, with floured rolling pin on lightly floured board, into an oblong sheet about 6x8x½ inches in size.
6. Cut into strips ½ inch wide.
7. Place on lightly greased baking sheet.
8. Bake at 400° F. for about 10 minutes, or until light brown.
9. Remove to wire rack to cool.
10. Serve as accompaniment to soups and salads.

MILK TOAST

4 servings

1 quart milk
1 teaspoon salt
Few grains pepper
8 slices bread
Butter or margarine

1. Put milk in top of double boiler.
2. Cover, and heat over simmering water in bottom of double boiler until tiny bubbles appear around edges of milk.
3. Stir in salt and pepper.
4. Toast bread on broiler rack in broiler or in electric toaster.
5. Spread generously with butter or margarine.
6. Place 2 slices in each of four hot soup plates or cereal bowls.
7. Pour seasoned hot milk over toast.
8. Serve immediately.

CINNAMON TOAST

8 pieces

4 slices bread
3 tablespoons sugar
½ to ¾ teaspoon cinnamon
3 tablespoons butter or margarine,
   softened

1. Cut crusts from slices of bread or not, as desired.
2. Place on baking sheet, put in broiler, and toast on one side.
3. Mix sugar and cinnamon.
4. Spread untoasted side of bread generously with softened butter or margarine.

(Continued)

483

5. Sprinkle sugar-cinnamon mixture evenly over butter or margarine.
6. Replace baking sheet in broiler, and toast until sugar-cinnamon mixture is bubbly.
7. Cut slices in half for serving.

NOTE: The amounts of butter or margarine and of sugar-cinnamon mixture are enough to cover 4 large slices of bread. If the slices are medium or small, use 6 slices instead of 4.

CRANBERRY-ORANGE RELISH
2 cups

2 cups cranberries
1 orange
¾ cup sugar

1. Pick over and wash cranberries.
2. Wash and dry orange.
3. Cut in quarters, and remove seeds.
4. Put cranberries and orange quarters through food chopper.
5. Add sugar, and mix well.
6. Let stand for at least 30 minutes before using.

CRAB MEAT–CREAM CHEESE DIP
1½ cups

1 7-ounce can (1 cup) crab meat
1 3-ounce package cream cheese, softened
1 tablespoon grated onion
½ cup sour cream
2 teaspoons lemon juice
½ teaspoon Worcestershire sauce
¼ teaspoon salt

1. Remove bones from crab meat, and shred finely.
2. Add all other ingredients, and mix thoroughly.

PEANUT-BUTTER DIP
1½ cups

1 cup peanut butter
⅓ cup salad dressing or mayonnaise
½ purple Italian onion, minced

Put all ingredients together, and mix until well blended.

Courtesy Kraft Foods Company

PASTRIES

COLD-WATER PASTRY
Two 8-inch or 9-inch crusts

2 cups sifted all-purpose flour
1 teaspoon salt
⅔ cup shortening
5 tablespoons cold water

1. Sift together flour and salt into mixing bowl.
2. Cut in shortening, with pastry blender or two knives, until mixture is about as fine as small peas.
3. Sprinkle cold water, in two installments, over mixture, and cut it in after each addition, using pastry blender or a fork, until all of mixture is moistened and a stiff dough is formed.
4. Shape dough into ball in mixing bowl, cover with wax paper, and put in refrigerator for about 5 minutes, or until ready to roll for making a pie.

STANDARD: Golden brown in color when baked; many small blisters on surface, indicating a very flaky quality; tender (short) in texture; pleasing in flavor.

HOT-WATER PASTRY
Two 8-inch or 9-inch crusts

2 cups sifted all-purpose flour
1 teaspoon salt
¾ cup shortening
¼ cup boiling water
1 tablespoon milk

1. Sift together flour and salt onto wax paper.
2. Put shortening in mixing bowl.

3. Add boiling water and milk, and beat vigorously with a fork until creamy and thick.
4. Add flour-salt mixture, and stir with a fork until all dry ingredients are moistened and a stiff dough is formed.
5. Shape dough into ball in mixing bowl, cover with wax paper, and put in refrigerator for about 5 minutes, or until ready to roll for making a pie.

STANDARD: Golden brown in color when baked; some small blisters on surface, indicating a flaky quality; fairly tender (short) in texture; pleasing in flavor.

STIR-N-ROLL PASTRY
Two 8-inch or 9-inch crusts

2 cups sifted all-purpose flour
1¼ teaspoons salt
½ cup salad oil
¼ cup milk

1. Sift together flour and salt into mixing bowl.
2. Add salad oil to milk in measuring cup, but do not mix.
3. Add, all at once, to flour and salt.
4. Stir with a fork until all dry ingredients are moistened and a stiff dough is formed.
5. Shape dough into ball in mixing bowl, cover with wax paper, and put in refrigerator for about 5 minutes, or until ready to roll for making a pie.

STANDARD: Golden brown in color when baked; very tender (short) in texture; pleasing in flavor.

TWO-CRUST PIE
(General Directions)

Make pastry by one of the recipes on page 485, and then follow these steps:

1. Flour board and rolling pin, using enough flour on board so dough will tend to move as it is rolled and not stick to board.
2. Divide pastry into two equal portions, putting one on floured board and leaving other in mixing bowl.
3. Roll portion on board as follows: Roll from center toward edges, keeping pressure on rolling pin even and pastry round in shape, until pastry is about ⅛ inch thick and 1 inch greater in diameter than top diameter of piepan.
4. Fold in half, slide onto one half of pan, pushing out air from underneath, unfold, and carefully lay over other half of pan, again pushing out air. Press pastry into pan, being careful not to stretch it.
5. Trim pastry so it extends about ½ inch beyond rim of pan, and set pan aside.
6. Roll second half of pastry until it is about 1 inch greater in diameter than top diameter of pan, fold into quarters, and slash folded edges with a knife to allow steam to escape while pie is baking and to decorate top of pie. Leave pastry on board.
7. Put pie filling in pastry-lined pan.
8. Lay rolled-out pastry over filling, unfold, cut off edge about ½ inch beyond rim of pan, press down onto bottom layer of pastry around rim, turn extended edges of pastry back over top, and flute with fingers to seal and to decorate pie.
9. Bake as directed in the pie recipe used.

APPLE PIE
One 9-inch pie

Pastry for two-crust pie
¾ to 1 cup sugar
1 tablespoon flour
½ teaspoon salt
½ teaspoon cinnamon
 or
¼ teaspoon nutmeg
6 to 7 medium apples
2 tablespoons butter or margarine
1 teaspoon lemon juice (optional)

Oven Temperature: 425° F.

1. Make pastry by one of the recipes on page 485, and set aside in refrigerator.
2. Put sugar, flour, salt, and cinnamon or nutmeg in small mixing bowl, and mix thoroughly.
3. Wash, quarter, core, and pare apples, and cut into ½-inch slices.
4. Cover apples with damp cloth to keep them from discoloring while rolling pastry for crusts.
5. Prepare bottom and top crusts as directed for Two-crust Pie (steps 1 to 6).
6. Add sugar-seasoning mixture to apple slices, and mix carefully.
7. Put in pastry-lined piepan, pack down firmly to avoid air spaces, and make higher at center to support crust.
8. Cut butter or margarine into small pieces, and dot over apples.
9. Sprinkle with lemon juice, if used.
10. Cover filling, and seal as directed for Two-crust Pie (step 8).
11. Bake at 425° F. for 45 to 50 minutes, or until apples are soft when tested with a fork and crust is golden brown. Reduce heat to 350° F. after first half of baking period if crust is browning too quickly.
12. Serve warm or cold, as desired.

DEEP-DISH APPLE PIE

Follow recipe for Apple Pie except for these differences:
1. Make pastry by using one-half of one of the recipes on page 485.
2. Put apple mixture in a deep 8-inch or 9-inch piepan or shallow baking dish.
3. Roll and cut pastry as directed for top crust of Two-crust Pie (step 6).
4. Lay pastry over filling as directed for Two-crust Pie (step 8) except turn extended layer of pastry under and press to rim of piepan or baking dish.

ONE-CRUST PIE
(General Directions for Unbaked Pie Shell)
One 8-inch or 9-inch crust

Make pastry by using one-half of one of the recipes on page 485, and then follow these steps:
1. Flour board and rolling pin, using enough flour on board so dough will tend to move as it is rolled and not stick to board.
2. Roll pastry and line piepan as directed for Two-crust Pie (steps 3 and 4).
3. Trim pastry so it extends about ½ inch beyond rim of pan, fold edge under, and flute with fingers, fastening pastry to rim of pan with a little pressure.
4. Chill in refrigerator for 10 to 15 minutes.
5. Pour uncooked pie filling into pastry-lined pan.
6. Bake as directed in the pie recipe used.

PUMPKIN or SQUASH PIE
One 9-inch pie

1 9-inch unbaked pie shell
¾ cup light-brown sugar
2 eggs, well beaten
¼ teaspoon ginger
⅛ teaspoon cloves
½ teaspoon cinnamon
½ teaspoon salt
1 tablespoon grated orange rind
2 tablespoons butter or margarine, melted
1½ cups milk, scalded
1½ cups hot, cooked, mashed pumpkin or squash

Oven Temperature: 425° and 325° F.

1. Prepare unbaked pie shell as directed for One-crust Pie (steps 1 to 4).
2. Put light-brown sugar, well-beaten eggs, spices, salt, grated orange rind, and melted butter or margarine in mixing bowl, and mix thoroughly.
3. Add scalded milk to hot, cooked, mashed pumpkin or squash, and stir into first mixture.
4. Pour filling into chilled pastry-lined piepan.
5. Bake at 425° F. for 20 minutes, reduce heat to 325° F., and then bake for 20 minutes longer, or until a knife inserted into center of filling comes out clean.
6. Serve pie warm or at room temperature, and garnish with whipped cream, if desired.

BAKED PIE SHELL
One 8-inch or 9-inch pie shell

Oven Temperature: 450° F.

Make pastry by using one-half of one of the recipes on page 485, and then follow these steps:
1. Flour board and rolling pin, using enough flour on board so dough will tend to move as it is rolled and not stick to board.
2. Roll pastry and line piepan as directed for Two-crust Pie (steps 3 and 4).
3. Trim pastry so it extends about ½ inch beyond rim of pan, fold edge under, and flute with fingers, fastening pastry to rim of pan with a little pressure.
4. Chill in refrigerator for 10 to 15 minutes.
5. Prick pastry in many places on bottom and sides with a fork so entrapped air can escape as pastry bakes.
6. Bake at 450° F. for 10 to 12 minutes, or until lightly browned.
7. Cool before filling with a cooked pie filling.

NOTE: Look at pastry at end of first 5 minutes of baking, and if large air bubbles have formed under it, prick with a fork to let out air.

LEMON MERINGUE PIE
One 9-inch pie

1 9-inch baked pie shell
1¼ cups sugar
6 tablespoons cornstarch
⅛ teaspoon salt
1½ cups water
3 egg yolks, slightly beaten
1 teaspoon grated lemon rind
⅓ cup lemon juice

1. Prepare pie shell as directed for Baked Pie Shell (page 487).
2. Put sugar, cornstarch, and salt in top of double boiler, and mix thoroughly.
3. Stir in water.
4. Place over direct heat, and cook, stirring constantly, until mixture begins to boil.
5. Place over boiling water in bottom of double boiler, cover, and cook for 10 to 15 minutes.
6. Stir a small amount of the hot mixture into slightly beaten egg yolks, and then stir this into the rest of the hot mixture.
7. Place over simmering water in bottom of double boiler, and cook, stirring constantly, for about 3 minutes, or until mixture becomes thicker.
8. Cool for about 3 minutes.
9. Add grated lemon rind.
10. Stir in lemon juice gradually so that juice will blend in easily.
11. Pour filling into cooled baked pie shell.
12. Cover with Meringue, and bake as directed in recipe for Meringue (step 4).

MERINGUE

3 egg whites
½ cup sugar

Oven Temperature: 325° F.

1. Beat egg whites, with rotary beater or electric mixer at high speed, until the bubbles in the foam are fine and the foam barely stands in a peak when the beater is withdrawn slowly.

2. Add one-third of the sugar and beat it in, add the second third of the sugar and beat it in, and then add the remaining third of the sugar and beat until meringue is glossy and will stand in stiff peaks when the beater is withdrawn slowly.
3. Spread evenly over pie filling, sealing it carefully to crust, and then swirl top to decorate.
4. Bake at 325° F. for 18 to 20 minutes, or until meringue is lightly browned.

CHERRY TURNOVERS
8 turnovers

Plain pastry
Cherry jam

Oven Temperature: 450° F.

1. Make pastry by one of the recipes on page 485.
2. Roll pastry into two sheets about 10x10x⅛ inches in size.
3. Cut into 5-inch squares.
4. Put rounded tablespoon cherry jam on one half of each square, placing it so pastry can be folded into a triangle.
5. Fold other half of pastry over cherry jam, and seal open edges of triangle by pressing them together with a floured fork.
6. Place on baking sheet.
7. Bake. at 450° F. for 15 to 20 minutes, or until crust is golden brown.

GRAHAM-CRACKER-CRUMB PIE CRUST
One 9-inch pie shell

1¼ cups (18 crackers) fine graham-cracker crumbs
¼ cup sugar
⅓ cup butter or margarine, softened

488

Oven Temperature: 350° F.

1. Put all ingredients in mixing bowl, and blend thoroughly.
2. Press evenly and firmly over bottom and sides of piepan, bringing mixture up to ⅛ inch below rim of pan.
3. Bake at 350° F. for 10 minutes.
4. Cool before filling.

ORANGE CHIFFON PIE
One 9-inch pie

1 9-inch Graham-cracker-crumb Pie Crust
¼ cup cold water
1 envelope gelatin
4 eggs, separated
½ cup orange juice
1 tablespoon lemon juice
1 cup sugar
½ teaspoon salt

1. Prepare graham-cracker-crumb pie crust.
2. Put cold water in small bowl, sprinkle gelatin over water, and let stand for 5 minutes to soften.
3. Put egg yolks in top of double boiler, and beat slightly with rotary beater.
4. Add orange juice, lemon juice, ½ cup of the sugar, and salt.
5. Place over boiling water in bottom of double boiler, and reduce heat to keep water just below simmering.
6. Cook, stirring constantly, until mixture thickens and coats the stirring spoon.
7. Add softened gelatin, and stir until thoroughly dissolved.
8. Place in refrigerator, and chill until consistency of raw egg white.
9. Beat egg whites, with rotary beater or electric mixer at high speed, until stiff but not dry, and beat in the rest of the sugar.
10. Add thickened gelatin mixture, and cut and fold until well blended.
11. Pour filling into graham-cracker-crumb pie crust.
12. Put in refrigerator until serving time.
13. Garnish with whipped cream, if desired.

HOME-PREPARED PASTRY MIX
For 3 two-crust or 6 one-crust pies

6 cups sifted all-purpose flour
1 tablespoon salt
2 cups shortening

1. Sift together flour and salt into mixing bowl.
2. Cut in shortening, with pastry blender or two knives, until mixture is about as fine as small peas.
3. Put in tightly covered container, and store in cool place.

To Use: Use 1⅓ cups mix and 2½ tablespoons water for one 8-inch or 9-inch crust.

Follow directions for Cold-water Pastry (page 485), beginning with step 3.

POULTRY

ROAST CHICKEN
6 servings

1 roasting chicken, 3½ to 4 pounds
Salt
Pepper
Chicken Stuffing
¼ cup butter or margarine, softened

Oven Temperature: 325° F.

1. Singe chicken, if necessary, wash thoroughly under running water, both outside and inside, and dry.
2. Sprinkle inside with salt and pepper.
3. Fill neck cavity with stuffing, pull neck skin over stuffing, and fasten with skewer.
4. Place chicken, breast side up, and then lift wings up and out, forcing tips back until wings rest flat against neck skin.
5. Fill body cavity with stuffing, insert poultry pins at regular intervals, and lace cavity shut with a long piece of string. Wrap ends of string around legs and tail, and tie firmly.
6. Spread chicken with softened butter or margarine.
7. Place, breast side up, on rack in shallow pan.
8. Roast at 325° F. for 3 to 3½ hours, or until leg joints move easily and flesh of leg feels soft when pressed with fingers. (Protect fingers with paper towel.)

9. Baste chicken during roasting with pan drippings. If it browns too quickly, cover loosely with heavy paper, foil, or cheesecloth dipped into melted fat.
10. Place chicken on hot platter, remove skewer, poultry pins, and string, and keep warm while making gravy. (See recipe for Cream Chicken Gravy on page 492.)

NOTE: See photograph on page 286 for another method of closing body cavity.

CHICKEN STUFFING

½ cup butter or margarine
½ cup finely chopped onion
½ cup finely chopped celery
2 tablespoons finely chopped parsley
1½ quarts bread cubes
1 teaspoon salt
½ teaspoon poultry seasoning
Few grains pepper

1. Melt butter or margarine in skillet, add finely chopped onion, finely chopped celery, and finely chopped parsley, and cook for about 5 minutes.
2. Pour over bread cubes, add seasonings, and mix well.

TIMETABLE FOR ROASTING POULTRY*

KIND OF BIRD	EVISCERATED WEIGHT (pounds)	LARGE BREAD CRUMBS FOR STUFFING (cups)	APPROXIMATE ROASTING TIME AT 325° F. FOR STUFFED CHILLED BIRD (hours)
Chicken			
Broilers or fryers	4–5	2–4	2¾–3½
Roasters	5–6	2½–4½	3½–4½
Duck	4–5	1½–4	2½ at 350° F.
Goose	8–10	4–7	3–4
	10–12	5–9	4–5
Turkey			
Fryers or roasters (very young birds)	6–8	3–6	3–4
Roasters (fully grown young birds)	8–12	4–9	4–5
	12–16	6–12	5–6
	16–20	8–15	6–7½
	20–24	10–18	7½–9

* From: *Poultry—How to Buy/How to Cook*, Consumer Section, Canada Department of Agriculture, Publication 1189, 1964.

BROILED CHICKEN

4 servings

2 broiling chickens, split apart
   lengthwise
        or
4 pieces chicken parts
¼ cup butter or margarine, melted,
   or salad oil
Salt
Pepper

1. Wash chicken parts thoroughly under running water, and dry.
2. Preheat broiler for 5 to 10 minutes.
3. Brush all surfaces of chicken with melted butter or margarine, or salad oil, and sprinkle with salt and pepper.
4. Grease hot broiler pan, and lay chicken parts on it, skin side down.
5. Insert broiler pan in broiler so surface of chicken is 5 to 7 inches from heat.
6. Turn chicken every 15 minutes to cook and brown evenly, and baste with pan drippings.
7. Broil for 35 to 40 minutes, or until chicken is tender when tested with a fork.
8. Serve immediately on hot platter, and garnish with parsley if desired.

FRIED CHICKEN
4 servings

1 frying chicken, 2½ to 3 pounds, cut
   into parts
¼ cup shortening or salad oil
¼ cup flour
½ teaspoon salt
⅛ teaspoon pepper

1. Wash chicken parts thoroughly under running water, and dry.
2. Heat shortening or salad oil in skillet.
3. Mix flour, salt, and pepper on wax paper, and coat each piece of chicken.
4. Brown chicken in hot fat, turning to brown on both sides.
5. Reduce heat, cover skillet, and continue to cook, turning occasionally, for 50 to 60 minutes, or until flesh is tender when tested with a fork.
6. Place chicken on hot platter, and keep warm while making Cream Chicken Gravy.

CREAM CHICKEN GRAVY

2¼ tablespoons flour
3 tablespoons pan drippings
1½ cups water or milk
Salt
Pepper

1. Add flour to drippings in skillet, and blend.
2. Add water or milk slowly, stirring to make a smooth paste with drippings and flour.
3. Bring to a boil, stirring constantly.
4. Season with salt and pepper to taste.
5. Serve in hot gravy dish.

FRICASSEED CHICKEN WITH DUMPLINGS
6 servings

1 4½- to 5-pound chicken
Salt
Pepper

1. Cut chicken into serving-sized pieces.
2. Wash thoroughly under running water.
3. Put in saucepan, add hot water just to cover chicken, and season lightly with salt and pepper.
4. Cover, and simmer for 2½ to 4 hours, or until chicken is tender when tested with a fork.
5. Place chicken pieces on hot platter, and keep warm while making Fricaseed-chicken Gravy and Dumplings.

FRICASSEED-CHICKEN GRAVY

1 quart liquid—broth from
   fricasseed chicken and
   added water if necessary
½ cup flour
Salt
Pepper

1. Remove fat from chicken broth, measure broth, and add water to make 1 quart.
2. Put flour in mixing bowl, and stir in gradually enough of the liquid, which has been cooled slightly, to make a thin paste.
3. Heat the rest of the liquid, and pour in paste, stirring constantly until gravy boils.
4. Boil for 1 minute, and season with salt and pepper to taste.

DUMPLINGS
6 servings

1½ cups sifted all-purpose flour
3 teaspoons baking powder
¾ teaspoon salt
⅔ cup milk

1. Sift together flour, baking powder, and salt into mixing bowl.
2. Mix in milk with a fork to make a soft dough, stirring as little as possible.
3. Drop dough by tablespoons into *boiling* gravy.
4. Keep gravy boiling and cook dumplings for 10 minutes uncovered, and then cover saucepan tightly and boil for 10 minutes longer.
5. Arrange dumplings around chicken or meat on platter, and pour gravy over both.
6. Garnish with parsley.

CHICKEN À LA KING

5 to 6 servings

¼ cup butter or margarine
2 tablespoons shredded green pepper
10 mushrooms, cut in thin slices
¼ cup flour
1 teaspoon salt
1 cup milk
1 cup chicken broth
2 egg yolks, slightly beaten
2 canned pimentos, cut in strips
1½ to 2 cups diced cooked chicken
Toast Cups (page 482)

1. Melt butter or margarine in medium-sized skillet.
2. Add shredded green pepper and sliced mushrooms, and cook for 5 minutes.
3. Remove skillet from heat, and stir in flour and salt.
4. Add milk gradually, and stir to make a thin paste.
5. Add chicken broth.
6. Cook, stirring constantly, until sauce boils for ½ minute.
7. Pour a small amount of the hot sauce into slightly beaten egg yolks, and then stir this into the rest of the hot mixture.
8. Add pimento strips and diced chicken.
9. Cook, stirring constantly, to heat and blend flavors.
10. Serve in toast cups.

NOTE: If chicken broth is not available, 1 cup water and 1 or 2 chicken bouillon cubes may be used instead.

Courtesy Poultry and Egg National Board

Barbecued chicken is prepared in the same way as broiled chicken, except that during the broiling the chicken is basted with barbecue sauce from time to time. (See recipe for Barbecue Sauce on page 512.)

QUICK BREADS

BAKING POWDER BISCUITS
(Basic Recipe)
Fourteen to sixteen 2-inch biscuits

2 cups sifted all-purpose flour
3 teaspoons baking powder
1 teaspoon salt
¼ cup shortening
⅔ to ¾ cup milk

Oven Temperature: 450° F.

1. Sift together flour, baking powder, and salt into mixing bowl.
2. Cut in shortening, with pastry blender or two knives, until mixture is about as fine as corn meal.
3. Add the ⅔ cup of milk all at once, and stir together quickly to make a soft but not sticky dough. If dough is too stiff, stir in the remainder of the milk.
4. Turn dough onto well-floured pastry cloth or board, and knead gently with floured hands eight to ten times.
5. Roll dough lightly with floured rolling pin until it is about ½ or ¾ inch thick, depending on thickness of biscuits desired. Biscuits almost double in thickness during baking.
6. Cut into rounds with floured cookie cutter.
7. Lift cut biscuits with a spatula, and place on ungreased baking sheet, about 1 inch apart for crusty biscuits or close together for softer ones.
8. Press extra dough together with hands, roll into a sheet as in step 5, handling as little as possible, and then cut more biscuits.
9. Bake at 450° F. for 12 to 15 minutes, depending on thickness of biscuits and the degree of brownness desired.
10. Serve hot.

STANDARD: Symmetrical in shape with straight sides and almost flat top; crust crisp and golden brown; crumb creamy white, medium fine in grain, and flaky, moist, and tender in texture; pleasing in flavor.

DROP BISCUITS

Follow recipe for Baking Powder Biscuits except for these differences:
1. Use 1 cup milk.
2. Stir milk into flour-shortening mixture (step 3).
3. Drop dough from a spoon onto greased baking sheet, about 2 inches apart.

CHEESE BISCUITS

Follow recipe for Baking Powder Biscuits except stir ½ cup grated cheese into dry ingredients after they have been sifted together (step 1).

SWEET BISCUITS

Follow recipe for Baking Powder Biscuits except add 2 tablespoons sugar to dry ingredients, and sift together into mixing bowl (step 1).

RICH BISCUITS

Follow recipe for Baking Powder Biscuits except use 6 tablespoons shortening (¼ cup plus 2 tablespoons) instead of ¼ cup.

TOPPING FOR FISH CASSEROLE

Follow recipe for Baking Powder Biscuits except for these differences:
1. Add ¼ teaspoon nutmeg to dry ingredients, and sift together into mixing bowl (step 1).
2. Use ½ cup water and 2 tablespoons lemon juice as liquid instead of milk.

TOPPING FOR MEAT PIE

Follow recipe for Baking Powder Biscuits except stir 2 tablespoons chopped parsley or chives into dry ingredients after they have been sifted together (step 1).

QUICK CINNAMON ROLLS
(Pinwheel Biscuits)

Follow recipe for Baking Powder Biscuits except for these differences:
1. Roll dough into an oblong sheet about ¼ inch thick.
2. Spread with softened butter or margarine.
3. Sprinkle with mixture of ½ cup brown sugar and ½ teaspoon cinnamon.
4. Roll up dough from long side with hands, and fasten by pinching dough along edge and ends of roll.
5. Cut into 1-inch pieces, and place cut side up in greased muffin pans or close together in greased cake pan.

SHORTCAKE BISCUITS

Follow recipe for Baking Powder Biscuits except for these differences:
1. Add 2 tablespoons sugar to dry ingredients, and sift together into mixing bowl (step 1).
2. Use 6 tablespoons shortening (¼ cup plus 2 tablespoons) instead of ¼ cup.
3. Beat 1 egg, add milk to make ⅔ cup, and use this as liquid instead of milk only.

SOUTHERN BUTTERMILK BISCUITS
Fourteen to sixteen 2-inch biscuits

2 cups sifted all-purpose flour
1 teaspoon baking powder
½ teaspoon baking soda
1 teaspoon salt
¼ cup shortening
¾ cup buttermilk

Oven Temperature: 450° F.

1. Sift together flour, baking powder, baking soda, and salt into mixing bowl.
2. Cut in shortening, with pastry blender or two knives, until mixture is about as fine as corn meal.
3. Add buttermilk all at once, and stir together quickly to make a soft dough.
4. Turn dough onto well-floured pastry cloth or board, and knead gently with floured hands eight to ten times.
5. Roll dough lightly with floured rolling pin until it is about ½ inch thick.
6. Cut into rounds with floured cookie cutter.
7. Lift cut biscuits with a spatula, and place on ungreased baking sheet, about 1 inch apart.
8. Press extra dough together with hands, roll into a sheet as in step 5, handling as little as possible, and then cut more biscuits.
9. Bake at 450° F. for 12 to 15 minutes, or until golden brown.
10. Serve hot.

MUFFINS
(Basic recipe)
Twelve 3-inch muffins

2 cups sifted all-purpose flour
2 tablespoons sugar
3 teaspoons baking powder
1 teaspoon salt
1 cup milk
1 egg, well beaten
3 tablespoons shortening,
    melted

Oven Temperature: 400° F.

1. Sift together flour, sugar, baking powder, and salt into mixing bowl.
2. Stir milk into well-beaten egg, and add melted shortening.
3. Pour into dry ingredients, and stir quickly until ingredients are just blended and batter is still rough-looking. Overstirring will cause muffins to be tough and have tunnels in them.
4. Fill well-greased muffin pans two-thirds full.
5. Bake at 400° F. for 25 minutes, or until golden brown.
6. Remove muffins immediately from muffin pans.
7. Serve hot.

NOTE: Muffins may also be made as follows:
1. Cut unmelted shortening into sifted dry ingredients, with pastry blender or two knives, until mixture is about as fine as corn meal.
2. Stir milk into well-beaten egg.
3. Pour into shortening-dry ingredients mixture, and stir as directed in step 3 above.

> STANDARD: Symmetrical in shape with slightly rounded top; crust golden brown with pebbled appearance; crumb creamy white or light yellow, even in grain with medium-sized holes but no tunnels, tender in texture; pleasing in flavor.

WHOLE-WHEAT MUFFINS
Follow recipe for Muffins except for these differences:
1. Substitute 1 cup unsifted whole-wheat flour for 1 cup of the sifted all-purpose flour.
2. Stir this into the sifted dry ingredients (step 1).

BRAN MUFFINS
Follow recipe for Muffins except for these differences:
1. Use 1 cup sifted all-purpose flour, and sift with sugar, baking powder, and salt into mixing bowl (step 1).
2. Use 1 cup bran.
3. Add bran to mixture of milk, well-beaten egg, and melted shortening (step 2).
4. Let stand for 10 minutes, and then continue with the remaining steps in basic recipe.

DATE MUFFINS
Follow recipe for Muffins except stir in quickly ½ cup cut-up dates at end of step 3.

RICH MUFFINS
Follow recipe for Muffins except for these differences:
1. Use ¼ cup sugar instead of 2 tablespoons.
2. Use ¼ cup shortening instead of 3 tablespoons.

BLUEBERRY MUFFINS
Follow recipe for Muffins except for these differences:
1. Use amounts of ingredients as in Rich Muffins.
2. Wash, drain, and pat dry 1 cup fresh blueberries.
                    or
Use 1 cup defrosted frozen blueberries.
                    or
Use ¾ cup well-drained canned blueberries.
3. Stir blueberries in quickly at end of step 3.

CORN MUFFINS or CORN STICKS

Fifteen 2-inch muffins or corn sticks

> 1 cup sifted all-purpose flour
> 4 teaspoons baking powder
> ¼ cup sugar
> ¾ teaspoon salt
> ¾ cup corn meal
> 1 cup milk
> 1 egg, well beaten
> ¼ cup shortening, melted

Oven Temperature: 425° F.

1. Sift together flour, baking powder, sugar, and salt into mixing bowl.
2. Stir in corn meal.
3. Stir milk into well-beaten egg, and add melted shortening.
4. Pour into dry ingredients, and stir quickly until ingredients are just blended and batter is still rough-looking.
5. Fill well-greased muffin pans three-fourths full or corn-stick pans almost full. Corn-stick pans can be more easily greased if they are hot.
6. Bake at 425° F. for 20 to 25 minutes, or until golden brown.
7. Serve hot.

> STANDARD: Symmetrical in shape with slightly rounded top; crust crisp and evenly browned; crumb yellow, even in grain with medium-sized holes, tender and somewhat crumbly in texture; a sweet, cornlike flavor.

JOHNNY CAKE

12 servings

> 1 cup corn meal
> 1 cup sifted all-purpose flour
> 1 teaspoon baking soda
> 1 teaspoon salt
> 4 tablespoons sugar
> 2 eggs
> 2 cups buttermilk
> 3 tablespoons melted butter
>   or margarine

1. Sift together corn meal, flour, baking soda, salt, and sugar.

2. Beat eggs well, add buttermilk and butter or margarine, and mix thoroughly.
3. Pour liquid mixture into flour mixture, stirring lightly until flour mixture is just moistened.
4. Fill greased pan (square, round, or muffin) one-half to two-thirds full.
5. Bake in hot oven (400° F.) for 20 to 25 minutes, or until brown.
6. Cut as desired, and serve hot.

POPOVERS

Seven 2½-inch popovers, 3 inches high

> 1 cup sifted all-purpose flour
> ½ teaspoon salt
> 2 eggs, unbeaten
> 1 cup milk
> 1 tablespoon oil or melted
>   shortening

Oven Temperature: 425° F.

1. Sift together flour and salt into mixing bowl.
2. Add unbeaten eggs, milk, and oil or melted shortening, and beat, with rotary beater or electric mixer at medium speed, to make a pour batter that is smooth and free from lumps.
3. Fill well-greased custard cups or popover pans two-thirds full.
4. Bake at 425° F. for 40 to 45 minutes.
5. Open oven door when popovers are done, make a small slit in each popover with the point of a knife to let steam escape, and leave in oven for about 5 minutes longer to dry the interior.
6. Serve immediately.

> STANDARD: Irregular in shape; crust crisp and golden brown; interior almost hollow with only small amount of moist material across it; pleasingly mild in flavor.

PANCAKES

About fifteen 3½-inch cakes

1½ cups sifted all-purpose flour
2 teaspoons baking powder
¾ teaspoon salt
2 tablespoons sugar
3 tablespoons shortening
1¼ cups milk
1 egg, well beaten

1. Sift together flour, baking powder, salt, and sugar into mixing bowl.
2. Cut in shortening, with pastry blender or two knives, until mixture is about as fine as corn meal.
3. Mix milk and well-beaten egg, and pour into shortening-flour mixture, stirring only enough to form a smooth batter.
4. Heat griddle, and grease lightly if necessary. Griddle is hot enough when a drop of water sprinkled on it breaks into small bubbles and sputters.
5. Pour enough batter, from tip of a large spoon or from a pitcher, onto heated griddle to make a cake about 3½ inches in diameter.
6. Bake until puffed up, full of bubbles, and cooked at edges, and then turn and brown on other side.
7. Serve immediately with butter or margarine and maple syrup or Brown-sugar Syrup (page 514).

> STANDARD: Uniformly golden brown in color on both sides and uniform in shape; light and tender throughout; pleasing in flavor.

WAFFLES

4 large waffles

1½ cups sifted all-purpose flour
3 teaspoons baking powder
½ teaspoon salt
1 tablespoon sugar
2 tablespoons shortening
2 eggs, separated
1 cup milk

1. Sift together flour, baking powder, salt, and sugar into mixing bowl.
2. Cut in shortening, with pastry blender or two knives, until mixture is about as fine as corn meal.
3. Beat egg whites, with rotary beater or electric mixer at high speed, until stiff but not dry, and set aside.
4. Beat egg yolks with same beater, and stir in milk.
5. Pour into shortening-flour mixture, and stir to make a batter.
6. Cut and fold in stiffly beaten egg whites.
7. Heat waffle baker, and grease if necessary. (See manufacturer's directions.) Waffle baker is hot enough when a drop of water sprinkled on it breaks into small bubbles and sputters.
8. Pour batter onto center of heated lower grid of waffle baker, but do not fill to edge. Close waffle baker, and when steam no longer comes from it, open, and remove waffle. Close waffle baker, and let it heat until it again comes to baking heat. Pour more batter into baker, and continue until all of batter has been used.
9. Serve waffles hot with butter or margarine and maple syrup or Brown-sugar Syrup (page 514), or use them as a base for creamed chicken, meat, or fish.

NOTES: Automatic waffle bakers have a thermostatic control to keep the grids at the right temperature for baking and usually a signal device to indicate when waffles are done. The temperature control can be adjusted to give waffles any desired brownness.

Semiautomatic waffle bakers indicate when the grids are at the right temperature for baking, but they do not automatically maintain this temperature.

> STANDARD: Uniformly golden brown in color and uniform in shape; crisp and tender throughout; delicate in flavor.

BANANA BREAD
One 8½x4½x2½-inch loaf

2 cups sifted all-purpose flour
2 teaspoons baking powder
¼ teaspoon baking soda
½ teaspoon salt
2 eggs, unbeaten
1 cup fully ripe mashed bananas
⅓ cup salad oil
⅔ cup sugar

Oven Temperature: 350° F.

1. Sift together flour, baking powder, baking soda, and salt into mixing bowl.
2. Put unbeaten eggs, mashed bananas, salad oil, and sugar into another mixing bowl, mix well, and beat, with rotary beater or electric mixer at medium speed, until light and foamy.
3. Add sifted dry ingredients, and stir until well blended.
4. Pour into well-greased loaf pan.
5. Bake at 350° F. for 1 hour.
6. Let bread stand in pan on wire rack until cool.

7. Remove from pan, and when entirely cold, wrap in wax paper or foil, and store in breadbox.

NOTE: Quick-loaf breads are easier to slice when they are a day old.

HOME-PREPARED BISCUIT MIX
For about forty to forty-eight 2-inch biscuits

6 cups sifted all-purpose flour
3 tablespoons baking powder
1 tablespoon salt
¾ to 1 cup shortening

1. Sift together flour, baking powder, and salt into mixing bowl.
2. Cut in shortening, with pastry blender or two knives, until mixture is about as fine as corn meal.
3. Put in tightly covered container, and store in cool place.

TO USE: Use 2¼ cups mix and ⅔ to ¾ cup milk for about 14 to 16 biscuits.

Follow directions for Baking Powder Biscuits (page 494), beginning with step 3.

●Pinwheel biscuits make an attractive crust for a meat pie.

Salads

TOSSED SALAD
4 to 5 servings

1 small head lettuce
½ cucumber
6 radishes
1 small onion
1 medium tomato

Roquefort Dressing
½ teaspoon salt
Few grains pepper
⅛ teaspoon paprika
1 tablespoon lemon juice
2 teaspoons tarragon vinegar
6 tablespoons salad or olive oil
1 2-ounce package Roquefort or
   Blue cheese

1. Wash and crisp lettuce, dry, tear leaves into bite-sized pieces, and put in salad bowl.
2. Scrub cucumber and radishes, and cut into paper-thin slices. Do not pare.
3. Peel onion, and cut into paper-thin slices.
4. Wash tomato, peel, and cut into eighths.
5. Put prepared vegetables in salad bowl with torn lettuce, and toss gently with two forks to mix.
6. Put all ingredients for dressing, except Roquefort or Blue cheese, in covered jar, and shake until well mixed.

7. Crumble Roquefort or Blue cheese over salad ingredients just before serving, pour on dressing, and toss to coat all pieces of salad.

VARIATION: Use a variety of salad greens either with the lettuce or instead of it.

COLE SLAW
4 servings

3 cups thinly shredded cabbage
2 tablespoons finely chopped onion
2 tablespoons finely chopped green
   pepper (optional)

Dressing
¼ cup mayonnaise or salad dressing
¼ teaspoon dry mustard
1 teaspoon sugar
¼ teaspoon salt
⅛ teaspoon pepper
⅛ teaspoon paprika
1 tablespoon cream

1. Prepare cabbage and onion, and green pepper, if used, just before making dressing.
2. Put all ingredients for dressing in mixing bowl, and mix thoroughly.
3. Add prepared vegetables, and mix until well coated with dressing.
4. Let stand in refrigerator for about ½ hour before serving to chill and blend flavors.

DEVILED EGG AND TOMATO SALAD

4 servings

8 halves Deviled Eggs (page 465)
2 medium tomatoes
Salt
Pepper
Lettuce
Dressing

1. Prepare deviled eggs.
2. Wash and peel tomatoes.
3. Cut each tomato into 6 wedges, and sprinkle with salt and pepper.
4. Put lettuce on each of four salad plates.
5. Arrange 2 halves of deviled egg and 3 wedges of tomato on each plate.
6. Add favorite dressing.

TOMATO GELATIN SALAD

(Aspic)

4 servings

1 14-ounce can (1¾ cups) tomatoes or tomato juice
2 teaspoons sugar
1 teaspoon salt
½ bay leaf
4 peppercorns
1 slice medium onion
1 stalk celery and leaves, cut into pieces
¼ cup cold water
1 envelope gelatin
Lettuce or water cress

1. Put canned tomatoes or tomato juice, sugar, salt, bay leaf, peppercorns, onion slice, and cut celery and leaves in saucepan, and simmer, covered, for 10 minutes.
2. Put cold water in mixing bowl large enough to hold all ingredients, sprinkle gelatin over water, and let stand to soften.
3. Strain cooked tomatoes or juice, and measure. If necessary, add hot water to make 1¾ cups.
4. Add to softened gelatin, and stir until gelatin is dissolved.
5. Pour into individual molds or one small border mold.
6. Chill in refrigerator until firm.

7. Unmold (see page 430), arrange on lettuce or water cress, and garnish with mayonnaise. If chilled in border mold, fill center with cottage cheese.

POTATO SALAD

4 servings

2 to 2½ cups diced cooked potatoes
¾ cup sliced celery
1 small onion, thinly sliced
¾ teaspoon salt
⅛ teaspoon pepper
2 tablespoons French Dressing (page 504)
½ teaspoon prepared mustard
⅓ cup Mayonnaise (page 503)
Salad greens

1. Put diced cooked potatoes, sliced celery, thinly sliced onion, salt, and pepper in mixing bowl, and mix carefully with two forks.
2. Add French dressing, and mix again to coat all pieces.
3. Blend prepared mustard with mayonnaise.
4. Add to potato mixture, and mix carefully.
5. Let stand in refrigerator for about 1 hour before serving to chill and blend flavors.
6. Arrange on salad greens for serving.

ASPARAGUS AND EGG SALAD

4 servings

16 cooked asparagus tips, leftover or canned
French Dressing (page 504)
3 hard-cooked eggs
Chicory
1 green onion, thinly sliced
French Dressing (page 504)

1. Put asparagus tips in shallow dish.
2. Pour French dressing over them, and marinate in refrigerator for about ½ hour.
3. Cut hard-cooked eggs in quarters lengthwise.
4. Put chicory on each of four salad plates.
5. Arrange 4 asparagus tips and 3 hard-cooked-egg quarters on each plate.
6. Sprinkle with green onion slices.
7. Add French dressing.

TUNA FISH or SALMON AND EGG SALAD
4 to 6 servings

1 7-ounce can (1 cup) tuna fish or salmon
1 tablespoon lemon juice
2 hard-cooked eggs, chopped
1 cup thinly sliced celery
2 sweet pickles, sliced
⅓ cup Cooked Salad Dressing (page 504)
    or Mayonnaise (page 503)
Lettuce or other salad greens

1. Drain oil from fish, and remove bones and skin.
2. Flake fish coarsely, and sprinkle with lemon juice.
3. Add chopped hard-cooked eggs, thinly sliced celery, pickle slices, and cooked salad dressing or mayonnaise, and mix carefully.
4. Arrange on lettuce or other salad greens.

VARIATIONS: Use 1 tart apple, cut in small pieces, or 1 cup thinly shredded cabbage instead of celery.

STUFFED TOMATO SALAD
4 servings

4 medium tomatoes
1½ cups cottage cheese
2 teaspoons minced onion
1 tablespoon chopped parsley
2 tablespoons chopped pimento
Escarole or other salad greens
French Dressing (page 504)

1. Wash and peel tomatoes, cut out stems, and hollow out centers.
2. Put cottage cheese, minced onion, chopped parsley, and chopped pimento in mixing bowl, and mix thoroughly.
3. Fill centers of tomatoes with mixture, and chill.
4. Place tomatoes on escarole or other salad greens.
5. Add French dressing.

KIDNEY BEAN SALAD
6 servings

⅓ cup Mayonnaise (page 503)
1 tablespoon prepared mustard
1 medium onion, finely chopped
1 cup thinly sliced celery
2 14-ounce cans (3½ cups) red
    kidney beans, drained
4 hard-cooked eggs, chopped
Salt
Pepper
Lettuce or other salad greens

1. Put mayonnaise, prepared mustard, finely chopped onion, and thinly sliced celery in mixing bowl, and mix well.
2. Add drained red kidney beans and chopped hard-cooked eggs, and mix gently.
3. Season with salt and pepper to taste.
4. Chill in refrigerator.
5. Arrange on lettuce or other salad greens.

MIXED FRUIT SALAD
6 servings

2 bananas
1 orange, sectioned
1 grapefruit, sectioned
½ cup grapes (Malagas, Tokays, or
    Thompson Seedless)
1 apple, unpared and cut in thin strips
½ cup pineapple cubes
2 tablespoons French Dressing
    (page 504)
Lettuce or other salad greens
Cooked Salad Dressing (page 504) or
    Mayonnaise (page 503)

1. Slice bananas into mixing bowl, and add orange and grapefruit sections.
2. Cut grapes in half, remove seeds, and add.
3. Add unpared apple strips and pineapple cubes.
4. Sprinkle fruit with French dressing, and mix carefully, using two forks.
5. Arrange on lettuce or other salad greens.
6. Add cooked salad dressing or mayonnaise.

WALDORF SALAD
4 servings

1½ cups diced apples (about 2 small
    apples)
3 tablespoons French Dressing
    (page 504)
¾ cup sliced celery
¼ teaspoon salt
3 tablespoons coarsely chopped
    English walnuts
Lettuce

1. Wash, quarter, core, and pare apples, and
   then dice.
2. Mix thoroughly with French dressing.
3. Add sliced celery, salt, and coarsely
   chopped English walnuts.
4. Toss with a fork to coat all ingredients
   with the French dressing.
5. Arrange on lettuce leaves.
6. Garnish with Mayonnaise (page 503) or
   Cooked Salad Dressing (page 504), if desired.

GRAPEFRUIT AND AVOCADO SALAD
4 to 6 servings

1 grapefruit
1 avocado
Lettuce
French Dressing (page 504)

1. Wash and pare grapefruit, and remove sections.
2. Peel avocado, and cut into long strips.
3. Tear lettuce apart into bite-sized pieces,
   and put in salad bowl.
4. Add grapefruit sections and avocado strips.
5. Sprinkle with French dressing, and toss
   gently with two forks.

Salad Dressings

MAYONNAISE
About 1¼ cups

1 egg yolk
½ teaspoon dry mustard
Few grains cayenne
½ teaspoon sugar
¾ teaspoon salt
2 tablespoons lemon juice or vinegar
1 cup olive or salad oil

1. Put egg yolk, dry mustard, cayenne, sugar,
   and ¼ teaspoon of the salt in mixing bowl,
   and blend.
2. Add 1 tablespoon of the lemon juice or
   vinegar.
3. Beat, with rotary beater or electric mixer
   at low speed, until just mixed.
4. Add olive or salad oil, a few drops at a
   time, beating after each addition until
   about ¼ of the oil has been used and
   the emulsion (see page 242) is quite thick.

5. Add the remaining oil in larger amounts,
   about 1 or 2 tablespoons at a time, beating
   in each addition completely and adding the
   remaining ½ teaspoon of the salt with the
   last addition of oil.
6. Beat in the rest of the lemon juice or vinegar when the emulsion becomes very thick.
7. Store, covered, in refrigerator.

NOTE: If a smooth emulsion has not formed by
the time ¼ cup of the oil has been added
(step 4), the emulsion is curdled. The curdled
emulsion may possibly be made smooth by
beating it (1) slowly into another egg yolk,
(2) into 1 tablespoon water, or (3) into 1 tablespoon vinegar.

VARIATIONS: Fold ¼ cup heavy cream,
whipped, into 1 cup mayonnaise.

Stir ¼ cup grated horseradish into 1 cup
mayonnaise.

THOUSAND ISLAND DRESSING
About 1 cup

½ cup Mayonnaise (page 503)
2 tablespoons chili sauce
1 tablespoon chopped green pepper
1 tablespoon chopped stuffed olives
1 tablespoon minced onion
1 tablespoon tarragon vinegar
1 hard-cooked egg, chopped

1. Put mayonnaise in mixing bowl.
2. Add remaining ingredients, and mix well.
3. Store, covered, in refrigerator.

CONDENSED-MILK SALAD DRESSING
About 1½ cups

⅔ cup condensed milk
¼ teaspoon salt
¼ teaspoon dry mustard
1 egg, slightly beaten
⅓ cup vinegar

1. Add condensed milk, salt, and dry mustard to slightly beaten egg, and beat, with rotary beater or electric mixer at high speed, until fluffy.
2. Beat in vinegar slowly.
3. Store, covered, in refrigerator.

SOUR-CREAM SALAD DRESSING
About ½ cup

½ teaspoon salt
⅛ teaspoon pepper
½ teaspoon paprika
1 tablespoon tarragon vinegar
½ cup sour cream
1 tablespoon chopped chives or
   minced onion

1. Put salt, pepper, paprika, and tarragon vinegar in mixing bowl, and stir until well blended.
2. Add sour cream, and beat, with rotary beater or electric mixer at medium speed, until mixture is thick.
3. Stir in chopped chives or minced onion.
4. Store, covered, in refrigerator.

FRENCH DRESSING
About 1 cup

¼ teaspoon sugar
½ teaspoon dry mustard
½ teaspoon paprika
¾ teaspoon salt
¼ teaspoon pepper
⅞ cup olive or salad oil
¼ cup lemon juice or vinegar
1 tablespoon minced onion
   (optional)

1. Put all ingredients in jar or mixing bowl, and shake or beat, with rotary beater or electric mixer at medium speed, until thoroughly blended.
2. Chill, and store, covered, in refrigerator.
3. Shake or beat again just before using.

VARIATIONS: Omit all seasonings but salt and pepper, and do not use minced onion.

Omit dry mustard. Add 1 2-ounce package of Roquefort or Blue cheese, crumbled.

Use 2 tablespoons tarragon or other herb vinegar and 2 tablespoons lemon juice or vinegar.

COOKED SALAD DRESSING
About 1½ cups

2 tablespoons butter or margarine
2 tablespoons flour
1 tablespoon sugar
½ teaspoon dry mustard
½ teaspoon salt
1 cup milk
2 eggs, slightly beaten
½ cup vinegar
Few grains cayenne (optional)

1. Make White Sauce (page 510) with first six ingredients in top of double boiler over direct heat.
2. Mix slightly beaten eggs and vinegar, and stir slowly into white sauce.
3. Place over simmering water in bottom of double boiler, and cook, stirring constantly, until mixture thickens and coats the stirring spoon.
4. Stir in cayenne, if used.
5. Chill, and store, covered, in refrigerator.

Fillings for Cold Sandwiches

CHICKEN–EGG SALAD FILLING
For about 5 to 6 sandwiches

> 1 cup finely chopped cold cooked chicken
> 1 hard-cooked egg, chopped
> ½ teaspoon minced onion
> ½ cup finely chopped celery
> 1 tablespoon sweet-pickle relish
> ⅛ teaspoon salt
> Few grains pepper
> 2 tablespoons salad dressing or mayonnaise

1. Mix all ingredients together thoroughly.
2. Let stand in refrigerator for about ½ hour before using to blend flavors.

NOTE: Approximately 2 to 3 tablespoons of filling have been allowed for each sandwich made with two average-sized slices of bread. However, the number of sandwiches will vary, depending on the size of the slices of bread used and on the amount of filling desired.

MEAT SALAD FILLING
For about 5 to 6 sandwiches

> 1 cup finely chopped cold cooked meat
> ⅓ cup finely chopped celery
> ⅓ cup finely chopped stuffed olives
> 1 tablespoon chili sauce
> ⅛ teaspoon salt
> 3 tablespoons salad dressing or mayonnaise

1. Mix all ingredients together thoroughly.
2. Let stand in refrigerator for about ½ hour before using to blend flavors.

NOTE: See note for Chicken–Egg Salad Filling.

TUNA FISH or SALMON SALAD FILLING
For about 8 sandwiches

> 1 7-ounce can (1 cup) tuna fish or salmon
> ½ cup finely chopped celery
> 2 teaspoons minced chives or onion
> 2 tablespoons sweet-pickle relish
> ⅛ teaspoon salt
> 3 tablespoons salad dressing or mayonnaise

1. Drain liquor from tuna fish or salmon, and mash.
2. Add remaining ingredients, and mix together thoroughly.
3. Let stand in refrigerator for about ½ hour before using to blend flavors.

NOTE: See note for Chicken–Egg Salad Filling.

CRAB MEAT–EGG FILLING
For about 8 sandwiches

1 7-ounce can (1 cup) crab meat
2 hard-cooked eggs, finely chopped
2 tablespoons minced onion
1 teaspoon prepared mustard
¾ teaspoon salt
Few grains pepper
3 tablespoons salad dressing or
    mayonnaise

1. Drain liquor from crab meat.
2. Remove bones, and cut into very fine pieces.
3. Add remaining ingredients, and mix together thoroughly.
4. Let stand in refrigerator for about ½ hour before using to blend flavors.

NOTE: See note for Chicken–Egg Salad Filling (page 505).

SLICED MEAT or POULTRY FILLINGS

Thin slices cold leftover or canned meat,
    chicken, or turkey
Salt

Optional
Salad green or onion, thinly sliced
or
Catsup, chili sauce, pepper relish, or
    mayonnaise
or
Cheddar or process cheese, sliced, and
    prepared mustard

1. Lay slices of meat, chicken, or turkey on prepared bread slice (see page 324).
2. Sprinkle with salt.
3. Cover with one or more optional ingredients, as desired.
4. Close sandwich.

● Dainty sandwiches with a cream cheese spread are frequently served with a molded gelatin salad.

CREAM CHEESE–DRIED BEEF FILLING
For about 6 to 8 sandwiches

1 tablespoon milk
2 3-ounce packages cream cheese,
    softened
1 tablespoon minced onion
¼ cup dried beef, finely shredded

1. Blend milk with softened cream cheese.
2. Add remaining ingredients, and mix thoroughly.
3. Let stand in refrigerator for about ½ hour before using to blend flavors.

NOTE: See note for Chicken–Egg Salad Filling (page 505).

CREAM CHEESE–OLIVE FILLING
For about 6 to 8 sandwiches

1 tablespoon French dressing
2 3-ounce packages cream cheese,
    softened
¼ cup finely chopped stuffed olives
¼ teaspoon Worcestershire sauce

1. Blend French dressing with softened cream cheese.
2. Add remaining ingredients, and mix thoroughly.
3. Let stand in refrigerator for about ½ hour before using to blend flavors.

NOTE: See note for Chicken–Egg Salad Filling (page 505).

Courtesy Knox Gelatine

OTHER CREAM CHEESE FILLINGS

Cream cheese
Cream, light or heavy
Salt

Optional
Cucumber or radishes, unpared and
thinly sliced
or
Green pepper and onion, minced
or
Water cress sprigs or chives, finely
chopped
or
Jelly or marmalade

1. Moisten cream cheese with light or heavy cream to spreading consistency.
2. Season with salt to taste.
3. Spread on prepared bread slice (see page 324).
4. Cover with optional ingredients, as desired.

NOTE: If a chopped or minced optional ingredient is used, it may be mixed with the softened and seasoned cream cheese.

HARD-COOKED EGG FILLINGS

Hard-cooked eggs
Mayonnaise or salad dressing
Salt
Pepper

Optional
Stuffed olives, finely chopped
or
Bacon, broiled and finely chopped,
and celery, minced
or
Chili sauce and onion, minced
or
Sardines, mashed, lemon juice, and
Worcestershire sauce

1. Chop hard-cooked eggs, and moisten with mayonnaise or salad dressing to spreading consistency.
2. Season with salt and pepper to taste.
3. Blend with optional ingredients, as desired.

Hot Sandwiches

TOASTED CHEESE SANDWICHES
4 sandwiches

4 slices Cheddar, Swiss, or process
cheese, 1/8 inch thick
8 slices bread, 1/4 inch thick
Butter or margarine, softened

1. Lay slices of Cheddar, Swiss, or process cheese on 4 slices of the bread.
2. Place on broiler rack in broiler pan, and insert in preheated broiler so cheese is about 2 inches from heat.
3. Toast until cheese begins to melt.
4. Cover cheese with second slice of bread.
5. Spread with softened butter or margarine.
6. Toast until lightly browned.
7. Turn each sandwich over with a spatula, and spread with softened butter or margarine.
8. Toast until lightly browned.
9. Serve hot.

GRILLED CHEESE SANDWICHES
4 sandwiches

4 slices bread, 1/4 inch thick
1 tablespoon butter or margarine,
softened
4 slices Cheddar, Swiss, or process
cheese, 1/8 inch thick

1. Toast one side of slices of bread on broiler rack in broiler pan in preheated broiler.
2. Spread untoasted side with softened butter or margarine.
3. Lay slice of Cheddar, Swiss, or process cheese on top.
4. Insert broiler pan in broiler so cheese is about 2 inches from heat.
5. Grill until cheese is melted.
6. Serve hot.

GRILLED CHEESE, TOMATO, AND BACON SANDWICHES

4 sandwiches

4 slices bread, ¼ inch thick
Butter or margarine, softened
4 slices process cheese
4 slices unpeeled tomato, cut thin
2 slices bacon, cut across into narrow
   pieces

1. Toast one side of slices of bread on broiler rack in broiler pan in preheated broiler.
2. Spread untoasted side with softened butter or margarine.
3. Lay slice of process cheese on top.
4. Add thin slice of tomato.
5. Dot with narrow pieces of bacon.
6. Insert broiler pan in broiler so bacon is about 4 inches from heat.
7. Grill until cheese is melted and bacon is crisp.
8. Serve hot.

GRILLED BAKED BEAN–BACON SANDWICHES

6 sandwiches

2 tablespoons butter or margarine
1 small onion, finely chopped
1 19-ounce can (2½ cups) baked beans,
   plain
¼ cup chili sauce, catsup, or pepper relish
6 slices bread, ¼ inch thick
6 slices bacon

1. Heat butter or margarine in skillet.
2. Fry finely chopped onion until yellow.
3. Add baked beans and chili sauce, catsup, or pepper relish, and mix thoroughly.
4. Toast one side of slices of bread on broiler rack in broiler pan in preheated broiler.
5. Spread untoasted side with baked-bean mixture.
6. Lay slice of bacon on top.
7. Insert broiler pan in broiler so bacon is about 4 inches from heat.
8. Grill until bacon is crisp.
9. Serve hot.

GRILLED TUNA FISH SANDWICHES

6 sandwiches

1 7-ounce can (1 cup) tuna fish
1 small green pepper, minced
1 small onion, minced
¼ cup finely chopped celery
1 tablespoon minced parsley
Salt
Pepper
Salad dressing
3 hamburger buns, split in half
Butter or margarine, softened
6 slices Cheddar or process cheese

1. Put first five ingredients in mixing bowl, and mix thoroughly.
2. Season with salt and pepper to taste.
3. Moisten with salad dressing to spreading consistency.
4. Spread hamburger-bun halves with softened butter or margarine.
5. Spread with tuna fish mixture.
6. Lay slice of Cheddar or process cheese on top.
7. Place on broiler rack in broiler pan, and insert in preheated broiler so cheese is about 4 inches from heat.
8. Grill until cheese is melted.
9. Serve hot.

HOT MEAT SANDWICHES

4 sandwiches

4 slices bread, ¼ inch thick
1 cup leftover gravy
4 slices leftover meat, chicken, or
   turkey
½ cup button-type canned mushrooms
   (optional)

1. Warm slices of bread in oven, or toast, if desired.
2. Put leftover gravy in skillet, and heat.
3. Add slices of leftover meat, chicken, or turkey, and heat.
4. Add canned mushrooms, if used, with the meat.
5. Place hot slice of meat, chicken, or turkey on warm bread or toast.
6. Cover with gravy, and serve hot.

TOASTED ROLLED SANDWICHES
4 sandwiches

4 slices thin bread
1 tablespoon butter or margarine,
  softened
2 tablespoons cream cheese, softened

1. Use very fresh bread, and slice thinly.
2. Remove crusts.
3. Spread slices lightly with softened butter or margarine and softened cream cheese.
4. Roll each slice with hands, and fasten with skewers.
5. Place on broiler rack in broiler pan, and toast in preheated broiler, turning to toast evenly.
6. Remove skewers, and serve warm.

VARIATIONS: Mix dates and chopped nuts with the cream cheese.

Use any soft sandwich filling.

Spreads for Sandwiches

ROQUEFORT CHEESE SPREAD
About ½ cup

¼ pound Roquefort cheese, crumbled
¼ cup minced celery
½ teaspoon Worcestershire sauce
Mayonnaise

1. Mix together first three ingredients.
2. Moisten with mayonnaise to spreading consistency.

AVOCADO–CREAM CHEESE SPREAD
About ¾ cup

½ avocado, very ripe
1 3-ounce package cream cheese,
  mashed
1 tablespoon pickle relish
1 teaspoon minced onion
Salt
Pepper
Salad dressing

1. Wash, peel, and mash avocado.
2. Stir in mashed cream cheese, pickle relish, and minced onion.
3. Season with salt and pepper to taste.
4. Moisten with salad dressing to spreading consistency.

SHRIMP-BUTTER SPREAD
1¾ cups

1 cup butter or margarine, softened
1 cup canned shrimp, minced
1 tablespoon lemon juice
Salt
Pepper

1. Mix together first three ingredients.
2. Season with salt and pepper to taste.

HAM-BUTTER SPREAD
1½ cups

½ cup butter or margarine, softened
¼ pound cooked ham, minced
2 hard-cooked eggs, chopped
Pepper

1. Mix together first three ingredients.
2. Season with pepper to taste.

NOTE: Spreads may be thinned with milk, sour cream, or mayonnaise, and served as a dip with potato chips or crisp crackers.

SAUCES

Meat, Fish, and Vegetable Sauces

WHITE SAUCE
1 cup

	Butter or Margarine	Flour	Salt	Pepper	Milk	Uses
THIN	1 tablespoon	1 tablespoon	½ teaspoon	Few grains	1 cup	Cream soups
MEDIUM	2 tablespoons	1½ to 2 tablespoons	½ teaspoon	Few grains	1 cup	Creamed and scalloped foods and sauces
THICK	3 tablespoons	3 tablespoons	½ teaspoon	Few grains	1 cup	Soufflés
VERY THICK	3 tablespoons	¼ cup	½ teaspoon	Few grains	1 cup	Croquettes

Method 1
1. Melt butter or margarine in saucepan over low heat.
2. Remove from heat.
3. Add flour, salt, and pepper, and stir until smooth.
4. Add milk *slowly* at first, stirring constantly to make a *smooth* paste, and then stir in the rest of the milk.
5. Return to heat, and cook, stirring constantly, until sauce has boiled gently all over the surface for about ½ minute.
6. Hold sauce, if necessary, by covering saucepan and placing it in hot but not boiling water.

Method 2
1. Follow Method 1, steps 1 to 4, but use top of double boiler instead of saucepan.
2. Place top of double boiler over simmering water in bottom of double boiler.
3. Cover, and cook, stirring frequently, for 10 minutes.
4. Hold sauce, if necessary, covered.

> STANDARD: A glossy appearance; smooth in texture throughout; consistency suited to use to be made of sauce—from thin cream for thin white sauce to thick paste for very thick white sauce; a pleasing flavor with no suggestion of raw starch taste.

PEA SAUCE

Add 3 tablespoons cooked peas to 1 cup Medium White Sauce, using the 1½-tablespoon measure of flour.

CHEESE SAUCE

Add ½ to ¾ cup grated Cheddar or process American cheese and ¼ teaspoon dry mustard to 1 cup Medium White Sauce, using the 1½-tablespoon measure of flour.

EGG SAUCE

Add 2 hard-cooked eggs, sliced or chopped, 2 teaspoons prepared mustard, and 1 tablespoon chopped parsley to 1 cup Medium White Sauce, using the 1½-tablespoon measure of flour.

HOLLANDAISE SAUCE
½ cup

½ cup butter or margarine
1 tablespoon lemon juice
or
½ tablespoon vinegar
2 egg yolks, unbeaten
¼ teaspoon salt
Few grains cayenne

1. Divide butter or margarine into thirds.
2. Put one-third in small saucepan.
3. Add lemon juice or vinegar and unbeaten egg yolks.
4. Place saucepan in a wider saucepan containing hot water (well below simmering).
5. Stir mixture constantly, and as it begins to thicken, add the second third of butter or margarine, and as this thickens, add the remaining butter or margarine, and continue to stir until sauce is thick.
6. Remove from hot water, and stir in salt and cayenne.
7. Serve immediately with vegetables such as asparagus, broccoli, or cauliflower or with poached or baked fish fillets or steaks.

NOTE: If it is necessary to hold hollandaise sauce for serving, it should be placed over warm water and stirred occasionally.

MOCK HOLLANDAISE SAUCE
About 1 cup

1 cup Medium White Sauce (page 510)
2 egg yolks, slightly beaten
2 tablespoons lemon juice
or
1 tablespoon vinegar

1. Make medium white sauce, using the 1½-tablespoon measure of flour, in top of double boiler over direct heat.
2. Stir a small amount of the hot sauce into slightly beaten egg yolks, and then stir this into the rest of the hot sauce.
3. Place over water in bottom of double boiler, and cook, stirring constantly, for about 2 minutes, or until sauce becomes thicker.
4. Remove from heat, cool slightly, and stir in lemon juice or vinegar slowly.
5. Serve over vegetables or fish.

TOMATO SAUCE
About 2 cups

1 19-ounce can (2½ cups) tomatoes
½ teaspoon sugar
½ teaspoon salt
¼ teaspoon pepper
1 bay leaf
1 small onion, sliced
3 tablespoons butter or margarine
3 tablespoons flour

1. Put tomatoes, sugar, salt, pepper, bay leaf, and sliced onion in saucepan, and simmer for 10 minutes.
2. Press through sieve to make a purée.
3. Melt butter or margarine in saucepan over low heat.
4. Remove from heat.
5. Add flour, and stir until smooth.
6. Add purée *slowly* at first, stirring constantly to make a *smooth* paste, and then stir in the rest of the purée.
7. Return to heat, and cook, stirring constantly, until sauce has boiled all over the surface for about ½ minute.
8. Serve over fish or meat loaves or croquettes.

511

CREAM OF MUSHROOM SAUCE
1½ cups

1 can cream of mushroom soup,
  undiluted
⅓ cup milk
½ teaspoon Worcestershire sauce
Few grains pepper

1. Put undiluted cream of mushroom soup in small saucepan.
2. Add remaining ingredients.
3. Bring to a boil, stirring constantly, and boil for ½ minute.
4. Serve over vegetables, meat loaves, or fish timbales.

LEMON-BUTTER SAUCE
¼ cup

¼ cup butter or margarine
½ teaspoon salt
Few grains pepper
Few grains cayenne
1 tablespoon finely chopped
  parsley
½ tablespoon lemon juice

1. Cream butter or margarine until soft.
2. Add salt, pepper, cayenne, and finely chopped parsley.
3. Stir in lemon juice gradually.
4. Spread over hot meat or fish.

TARTAR SAUCE
¾ cup

½ cup Mayonnaise (page 503)
1 tablespoon minced onion
1 tablespoon chopped pickle
1 tablespoon chopped olives
1 tablespoon capers
1 tablespoon chopped parsley

1. Make mayonnaise or use a commercial product.
2. Add remaining ingredients, and blend.
3. Serve as accompaniment to hot or cold fish and cold meats.

SWEET-SOUR SAUCE
⅓ cup

4 slices bacon
1 tablespoon light-brown sugar
½ teaspoon salt
⅛ teaspoon pepper
¼ teaspoon dry mustard
¼ cup vinegar

1. Cook bacon in skillet as directed for Pan-broiled Bacon (page 479).
2. Cut into small pieces.
3. Add light-brown sugar, salt, pepper, dry mustard, and vinegar, and bring to a boil.
4. Serve over hot vegetables.

SAUCE VINAIGRETTE
⅓ cup

½ teaspoon prepared mustard
1 tablespoon vinegar
3 tablespoons butter or margarine,
  melted
½ teaspoon paprika
¼ teaspoon salt
⅛ teaspoon pepper
1 teaspoon onion juice
1 hard-cooked egg, chopped

1. Mix prepared mustard and vinegar.
2. Add melted butter or margarine, paprika, salt, pepper, and onion juice, and mix thoroughly.
3. Add chopped hard-cooked egg.
4. Serve over hot vegetables.

BARBECUE SAUCE
About 1½ cups

2 tablespoons butter or margarine
1 medium onion, finely chopped
3 tablespoons sugar
2 teaspoons paprika
¼ teaspoon salt
⅛ teaspoon pepper
2 teaspoons dry mustard
2 tablespoons Worcestershire sauce
½ cup catsup
⅓ cup vinegar
½ cup water

1. Melt butter or margarine in skillet.
2. Add finely chopped onion, and cook until lightly browned.
3. Put sugar, paprika, salt, pepper, and dry mustard in mixing bowl, and mix thoroughly.

4. Add Worcestershire sauce, catsup, vinegar, and water.
5. Stir into lightly browned onion.
6. Simmer for 10 minutes.
7. Serve on hamburgers, wieners, or other meats, as desired.

Dessert Sauces

CHOCOLATE SAUCE
About ¾ cup

1 cup sugar
⅓ cup cocoa
½ teaspoon salt
¼ cup light corn syrup
½ cup water
1 teaspoon vanilla
1 or 2 tablespoons butter or
   margarine

1. Put sugar, cocoa, and salt in medium-sized saucepan, and mix thoroughly.
2. Stir in light corn syrup and water, and boil, stirring constantly, for about 5 minutes, or until sauce is syrupy and falls in thick drops from the side of a spoon.
3. Stir in vanilla and butter or margarine.
4. Serve warm or cold, as desired, on ice cream, plain cake, or cream puffs.

NOTE: If leftover sauce gets too thick to serve, heat it over hot water.

BUTTERSCOTCH SAUCE
About 1 cup

1¼ cups light-brown sugar,
   firmly packed
⅔ cup light corn syrup
¼ cup butter or margarine
½ cup heavy cream
½ teaspoon vanilla

1. Put light-brown sugar, light corn syrup, and butter or margarine in medium-sized saucepan, and mix thoroughly.
2. Bring to a boil, stirring until sugar is dissolved, and then continue to boil until syrup reaches soft-ball stage (240° F.). (See page 402.)
3. Cool slightly.
4. Stir in heavy cream and vanilla.
5. Serve warm or cold, as desired, on ice cream, plain cake, or cream puffs.

HARD SAUCE
¾ cup

⅓ cup butter or margarine
1 cup icing sugar
½ teaspoon vanilla

1. Cream butter or margarine until soft.
2. Beat in icing sugar gradually.
3. Add vanilla, and beat until fluffy.
4. Chill.
5. Serve on hot desserts such as Apple Brown Betty (page 460) or Blueberry Cobbler (page 460).

NOTE: This recipe may be extended by beating in 1 well-beaten egg before chilling.

VARIATIONS: Lemon or almond extract, cinnamon, or nutmeg may be used instead of vanilla.

FOAMY SAUCE
1 cup

½ cup butter or margarine
1 cup icing sugar
1 egg, well beaten
1 teaspoon vanilla

1. Cream butter or margarine in top of double boiler, and stir in icing sugar gradually.
2. Add well-beaten egg.
3. Place over simmering water in bottom of double boiler, and cook, beating constantly with a spoon, for 3 minutes.
4. Stir in vanilla.
5. Serve on cake-type desserts.

BROWN-SUGAR SYRUP
¾ cup

¾ cup water
3 tablespoons butter or margarine
⅓ cup light-brown sugar

1. Put all ingredients in saucepan.
2. Boil until syrupy.
3. Serve on pancakes or waffles.

LEMON SAUCE
2 cups

1 cup sugar
2½ tablespoons cornstarch
2 cups boiling water
¼ cup butter or margarine
3 tablespoons lemon juice
1 tablespoon grated lemon rind
¼ teaspoon salt

1. Put sugar and cornstarch in saucepan, and mix thoroughly.
2. Stir in boiling water, and boil, stirring constantly, for 3 minutes.
3. Add butter or margarine, lemon juice, grated lemon rind, and salt, and stir until butter or margarine is melted.
4. Serve on cake-type desserts.

Courtesy Minute Tapioca

● A chocolate sauce can make a simple pudding into a special treat.

SOUPS

BEEF SOUP STOCK
About 6 cups

2 pounds cracked shinbone with meat
6 cups cold water
6 peppercorns
2 cloves
1 bay leaf
½ teaspoon salt
1 teaspoon sweet herbs
1 carrot, sliced
1 onion, sliced
1 stalk celery and leaves, cut in small
   pieces
Sprig of parsley

1. Wipe shinbone and meat with damp cloth.
2. Cut meat from shinbone, and then cut meat into about 1-inch cubes.
3. Put all ingredients together in large saucepan, and bring to a boil.
4. Cover, reduce heat, and simmer for 3 hours.
5. Strain off broth, and let stand until cold.
6. Remove solid fat from top.
7. Serve as broth, or use as stock base for other soups, such as Vegetable Soup.

VEGETABLE SOUP
6 servings

1 quart Beef Soup Stock
2 cups water
1 cup coarsely chopped onion
1 cup thinly cut celery
1 cup diced carrots
1 cup diced turnips
1 cup canned tomatoes
2 tablespoons chopped parsley
Salt
Pepper

1. Put beef soup stock and water in large saucepan.
2. Add vegetables except parsley.
3. Cover, and boil gently for about 20 minutes, or until vegetables are tender when tested with a fork.
4. Add chopped parsley.
5. Season with salt and pepper to taste.
6. Serve in hot soup bowls accompanied with crackers, bread sticks, or melba toast, as desired.

515

BEEF BOUILLON
5 servings

1 quart Beef Soup Stock
1 tablespoon water
1 egg white, unbeaten
1 egg shell, crushed

1. Put beef soup stock in saucepan.
2. Add water to unbeaten egg white, and beat slightly.
3. Add to beef soup stock, and put in crushed egg shell.
4. Bring to a boil, stirring constantly, and then continue to boil for 2 minutes longer.
5. Let stand over low heat for 15 minutes.
6. Strain bouillon through strainer that is lined with a double layer of cheesecloth.
7. Serve in hot bouillon cups with a sprinkling of chopped parsley on top.

STANDARD: A brilliantly clear soup with a strong flavor of beef.

FISH CHOWDER
5 servings

2 tablespoons butter, margarine, or bacon drippings
2 medium onions, sliced
2 cups water
2 medium potatoes, diced
2 teaspoons salt
1/8 teaspoon pepper
1 12-ounce package frozen fish fillets, defrosted and cut in 1-inch cubes
3 cups milk

1. Melt butter, margarine, or bacon drippings in large saucepan.
2. Add onion slices, and cook until light yellow.
3. Add water, diced potatoes, salt, and pepper, and bring to a boil.
4. Reduce heat, and simmer until potatoes are slightly soft when tested with a fork.
5. Add fish, and simmer for 25 minutes.
6. Add milk, and heat, stirring occasionally.
7. Serve in hot soup bowls accompanied with large round crackers.

OYSTER STEW
6 servings

1 pint (about 1 1/2 dozen) oysters, shucked
1/4 cup butter or margarine
1 quart milk, scalded
1/2 teaspoon Worcestershire sauce
1/2 teaspoon salt
Few grains paprika

1. Drain liquor from oysters, and set aside.
2. Pick over oysters to remove bits of shell, if any.
3. Heat butter or margarine in medium-sized saucepan.
4. Add oysters and 1/2 cup of reserved oyster liquor, and simmer until edges of oysters curl.
5. Add scalded milk, Worcestershire sauce, salt, and paprika.
6. Serve in hot soup bowls, and garnish each serving with a bit of butter or margarine.

FRUIT SOUP
6 servings

1 tablespoon cornstarch
2 tablespoons water
1 19-ounce can (2 1/2 cups) applesauce
1/4 teaspoon salt
1 19-ounce can (2 1/2 cups) fruit sauce
1/2 tablespoon grated lemon rind
2 tablespoons lemon juice

1. Put cornstarch and water in saucepan, and stir to make a smooth paste.
2. Add applesauce, salt, fruit juice, and grated lemon rind.
3. Place over low heat, and cook, stirring constantly, until mixture boils for 1 minute.
4. Add lemon juice.
5. Serve hot or cold, as desired.

VARIATIONS: Use different kinds of fruit juices in this soup.

Garnish light-colored soup with a sprinkling of nutmeg or cinnamon and dark-colored soup with a dot of whipped cream.

CREAM OF TOMATO SOUP

4 to 6 servings

1 19-ounce can (2½ cups) tomatoes
2 tablespoons chopped onion
¼ teaspoon celery seed
1 teaspoon sugar
½ bay leaf
1 whole clove
2 tablespoons butter or margarine
2 tablespoons flour
1 teaspoon salt
¼ teaspoon pepper
2 cups milk

1. Put canned tomatoes, chopped onion, celery seed, sugar, bay leaf, and whole clove in saucepan, and simmer, covered, for 10 minutes.

2. Make White Sauce (page 510) of butter or margarine, flour, salt, pepper, and milk.
3. Force tomato-seasoning mixture through strainer or food mill to make tomato purée.
4. Stir purée slowly into white sauce, and heat for ½ minute.
5. Serve immediately in hot soup bowls, and garnish with Croutons (page 482), bits of parsley or chopped chives, or lightly salted whipped cream.

> STANDARD: Consistency of heavy cream; smooth and velvety with tiny flecks of tomato showing but no suggestion of curdling; flavor of tomato and the seasonings used.

Courtesy Campbell Soup Company

VEGETABLES

DIRECTIONS FOR BOILING FRESH VEGETABLES

1. Wash vegetable thoroughly, using vegetable brush where necessary.
2. Prepare as directed in the chart on pages 519 to 521.
3. Put in saucepan containing 1 to 2 inches boiling salted water (unless a different amount of water is stated in chart). Use ¼ teaspoon salt per cup of water.
4. Cover, and bring water to a gentle boil.
5. Cook vegetable until tender when tested with a fork, using time given in chart as a guide.
6. Drain off any liquid that remains, and save for sauces or soups.
7. Serve immediately, seasoned with butter or margarine, salt, and pepper or accompanied with a sauce.

NOTES: See the table "Food Buying Guide" on pages 78 to 81 for the number of servings from 1 pound of vegetables.

The amount of butter or margarine, salt, and pepper used to season a vegetable depends on personal preference.

For creamed vegetables, use 1 cup Thin or Medium White Sauce (page 510) for about 2 cups cooked vegetables.

Some suggestions for suitable sauces to serve with vegetables will be found in the chart on pages 519 to 521.

DIRECTIONS FOR BOILING FROZEN VEGETABLES

1. Use the amount of water and salt stated on the package label.
2. Bring water to a boil in saucepan.
3. Drop in frozen vegetable.
4. Cover.
5. Break apart with a spoon or fork as vegetable begins to defrost.
6. Cook until vegetable is tender when tested with a fork.
7. Serve immediately seasoned with butter or margarine, salt, and pepper or accompanied with a sauce. (See chart on pages 519 to 521 for suggestions.)

NOTE: The length of time required to boil a frozen vegetable, after it is defrosted, is shorter than the length of time required for the same vegetable when fresh.

CHART FOR COOKING FRESH VEGETABLES

Cook vegetables in boiling salted water 1 to 2 inches deep unless a different amount of water is given below.

VEGETABLE	SUGGESTIONS FOR PREPARING AND SERVING	TIME[1] (minutes)
Asparagus	Break off stalks as far down as they break easily. Remove scales with a knife. Scrub stalks with soft brush to remove sand. Leave whole or cut into 1-inch lengths. Serve with Hollandaise Sauce (page 511), Mock Hollandaise Sauce (page 511), or Sauce Vinaigrette (page 512).	Whole: 10–20 Cut: 5–15
Beans Green or snap Wax	Cut off ends. Remove any strings. Cut slanted crosswise into 1- or 2-inch pieces or lengthwise into thin strips (French cut). Cook in boiling salted water almost to cover. Serve with Sweet-Sour Sauce (page 512).	Cross cut: 20–30 French cut: 15–20
Lima	Remove pods. Serve with Cream of Mushroom Sauce (page 512) or Mock Hollandaise Sauce (page 511).	20–25
Beets	Leave whole, including root end and 1-inch of stem end. Cook in boiling salted water to cover. Remove skins and root and stem ends after beets are cooked. Or pare, and slice or dice before cooking. (1 tablespoon vinegar to 1 quart water helps to keep red color.) Serve as Harvard Beets (page 524).	Whole: 30–60 (longer if old) Slices or diced: 20–30
Broccoli	Cut off leaves and end of stalks. Slit large stalks lengthwise almost to flower heads. Serve with Hollandaise Sauce (page 511), Mock Hollandaise Sauce (page 511), or Cheese Sauce (page 511).	10–15
Brussels sprouts	Remove imperfect outer leaves. Cut off tip of stem ends. Serve with Sauce Vinaigrette (page 512).	10–25

(Continued)

CHART FOR COOKING FRESH VEGETABLES (Continued)

Cook vegetables in boiling salted water 1 to 2 inches deep unless a different amount of water is given below.

VEGETABLE	SUGGESTIONS FOR PREPARING AND SERVING	TIME[1] (minutes)
Cabbage	Cut into wedges about 2 inches wide on outer edge, and remove most of core. Or shred by cutting head into quarters, removing most of core, and cutting quarters into thin strips with a sharp knife. Serve with Sauce Vinaigrette (page 512).	Wedges: 10–15 Shreds: 3–10
Carrots	Scrub, and scrape or pare thinly. Leave whole, or cut into quarters, strips, or crosswise slices. Cooking time is influenced by age and size of carrots. Serve sprinkled with chopped parsley or finely cut chives.	Whole: 15–30 Quarters: 12–20 Strips: 10–15 Slices: 10–25
Cauliflower	Remove outer leaves, stalks, and any blemishes on flowerets. Leave whole, or break into flowerets. Serve creamed or with Mock Hollandaise Sauce (page 511) or Cheese Sauce (page 511).	Whole: 15–20 Flowerets: 10–15
Celery	Remove leaves and trim roots. Scrub with soft brush to remove sand. Cut into ½- or 1-inch pieces.	15–20
Corn on the cob	Remove husks, silk, and any blemishes. Cook in boiling salted water to cover.	5–10
Greens Beet greens Collards Dandelion greens Kale Mustard greens Spinach Swiss chard Turnip greens	Remove imperfect leaves. Cut off tip of stem ends if any. Strip central midrib from leaves of kale and collards. Wash greens four times in water, lifting them each time from water to free sand. Cook kale and collards in water 1 inch deep. Cook other greens in water that clings to leaves from washing.	Spinach and beet greens: 3–10 Other greens: 10–15

CHART FOR COOKING FRESH VEGETABLES (Continued)

Cook vegetables in boiling salted water 1 to 2 inches deep unless a different amount of water is given below.

VEGETABLE	SUGGESTIONS FOR PREPARING AND SERVING	TIME[1] (minutes)
Onions	Cut slice from root and stem ends. Peel off outer skin. Cook in boiling salted water to cover. Serve creamed or with Cheese Sauce (page 511).	Small: 20–25 Large: 30–40
Parsnips	Cut slice from root and stem ends. Pare. Cut in quarters or in crosswise slices. Remove center core.	Quarters: 10–20 Slices: 7–10
Peas	Remove pods. Serve with cooked mushrooms.	8–20
Potatoes Sweetpotatoes	Do not pare until cooked. Remove any blemishes. Cook in boiling salted water almost to cover.	30–35
White	Do not pare until cooked. Remove eyes and any blemishes. Cook in boiling salted water almost to cover. Serve buttered, sprinkled with chopped chives or chopped parsley.	Medium: 35–40 Small: 20–25
Pumpkin	Cut into 2-inch pieces. Pare. Remove seeds and stringy portions.	25–30
Squash Winter	Cut into 2-inch pieces. Pare. Remove seeds and stringy portions.	25–30
Yellow Cymling Zucchini	Cut slice from stem and blossom ends. Cut into ½-inch slices. Do not pare or remove seeds and stringy portions if squash is young and tender. Serve buttered, sprinkled with chopped chives or chopped parsley.	10–20
Turnip White Yellow (rutabaga)	Pare. Cut into slices, cubes, or strips. Serve sprinkled with paprika or chopped parsley.	White: 12–20 Yellow: 20–35

[1]The length of time required to boil a given vegetable until it is tender differs with the variety, age, and size (either of the whole vegetable or of the pieces into which it is cut). Also, the degree of tenderness of the cooked vegetable is a matter of individual preference. For these reasons, the times stated in the chart should be considered only as guides and the vegetable tested for desired tenderness with a fork.

BOILED POTATOES

4 servings

4 medium potatoes
Salt
Butter or margarine

1. Scrub potatoes with stiff brush, and remove eyes and blemishes with a sharp knife. Do not pare.
2. Put potatoes in saucepan containing an amount of boiling salted water that will barely cover potatoes. Use ½ teaspoon salt to 2 cups water.
3. Cover, and bring quickly to a boil.
4. Reduce heat, and let potatoes boil gently for 35 to 40 minutes, or until tender when tested with a fork.
5. Drain off water, and shake saucepan over low heat to dry potatoes.
6. Peel.
7. Put in serving dish, and dot with butter or margarine.

STANDARD: Creamy white in color; fairly uniform in shape and size; old potatoes mealy in texture, new potatoes slightly waxy; mild in flavor.

VARIATION: Return small new potatoes to saucepan after they have been peeled. Add butter or margarine and chopped parsley, and toss potatoes until coated before putting them in serving dish.

BAKED POTATOES

4 servings

4 medium or large potatoes, uniform in size
Butter or margarine
Salt
Pepper

Oven Temperature: 450° F.

1. Scrub potatoes thoroughly, and dry.
2. Place on oven rack.
3. Bake at 450° F. for 45 to 60 minutes, or until potatoes feel soft when tested with a fork.

4. Remove immediately, cut a 1-inch cross on top of each potato, and then, holding with a cloth, press potato from sides until interior bursts up through slits.
5. Dot with butter or margarine, and sprinkle with salt and pepper.

NOTE: The scrubbed and dried potatoes may be brushed with fat before they are placed in the oven to keep the skin soft.

STANDARD: Dry, mealy, and fluffy; skin crispy unless potato was brushed with fat before baking.

STUFFED BAKED POTATOES

4 servings

5 medium Baked Potatoes
¼ cup butter or margarine
⅔ cup hot milk
½ teaspoon salt
⅛ teaspoon pepper

Oven Temperature: 450° F.

1. Cut slice from flat side of each baked potato.
2. Scoop out contents with a spoon, reserving four of the potato shells.
3. Mash potato with potato masher or in electric mixer at medium speed, or put through ricer or food mill.
4. Put butter or margarine in hot milk, and add salt and pepper.
5. Pour into mashed potato, and beat until fluffy.
6. Pile lightly into the four potato shells, making tops rough.
7. Place on baking sheet.
8. Bake at 450° F. for 15 minutes, or until lightly browned.

VARIATIONS: Sprinkle with grated cheese before browning.

Sprinkle with paprika, dot with butter or margarine, and omit browning (step 8).

PAN-BROWNED POTATOES
4 servings

4 medium potatoes
Salt

1. Scrub potatoes, and pare.
2. Parboil in boiling salted water just to cover for 10 minutes.
3. Drain, and place around meat in roasting pan.
4. Cook, basting occasionally with meat drippings, for 1 hour, or until soft when tested with a fork.
5. Place around roast on serving platter.

NOTE: Parboiling of the potatoes may be omitted, in which case allow 1½ hours for cooking in oven.

MASHED POTATOES
4 servings

5 medium potatoes
Salt
¼ cup butter or margarine
⅔ cup hot milk
½ teaspoon salt
⅛ teaspoon pepper

1. Scrub potatoes, pare as thin as possible, and cut into uniform pieces but not too small.
2. Put potatoes in saucepan containing about 1 inch of salted water. Use ½ teaspoon salt to 1 cup water.
3. Cover, and bring water quickly to a boil.
4. Reduce heat, and let potatoes steam until tender when tested with a fork.
5. Drain off water, and shake saucepan over low heat to dry potatoes.
6. Mash with potato masher or in electric mixer at medium speed, or put through ricer or food mill.
7. Put butter or margarine in hot milk, and add salt and pepper.
8. Pour into mashed potatoes, and beat until fluffy.

9. Put in hot serving dish, garnish with dots of butter or margarine, and, if desired, add bits of parsley or chives or sprinkle with paprika.

NOTE: A little more or less than ⅔ cup hot milk may be required to give mashed potatoes a fluffy texture. The amount varies with the variety of potato.

STANDARD: Snowy white in color; entirely free from lumps; fluffy in texture; pleasingly flavored with butter or margarine, salt, and pepper.

SCALLOPED POTATOES
5 servings

5 cups thinly sliced pared potatoes
⅓ cup thinly sliced onion
3 tablespoons flour
1½ teaspoons salt
¼ teaspoon pepper
¼ cup butter or margarine
1½ cups milk, scalded

Oven Temperature: 375° F.

1. Place about one-half of the thinly sliced potatoes in well-greased 2-quart casserole.
2. Place a layer of thinly sliced onions over them, sprinkle with one-half of the flour, salt, and pepper, and dot with one-half of the butter or margarine.
3. Add the rest of the sliced potatoes, sliced onions, flour, salt, pepper, and butter or margarine.
4. Pour in scalded milk.
5. Cover, bake at 375° F. for 30 minutes, remove cover, and then bake for 30 minutes longer, or until potatoes are tender and the top is lightly browned.

NOTE: The flour, salt, pepper, butter or margarine, and milk may be made into White Sauce (page 510) and this poured over alternating layers of sliced potatoes and sliced onions.

STANDARD: Lightly browned on top; slices tender but retaining their identity; flavor of well-seasoned potatoes.

BAKED ACORN SQUASH
4 servings

2 medium acorn squashes
4 teaspoons butter or margarine,
  softened
1 teaspoon salt
¼ teaspoon pepper
4 teaspoons brown sugar

Oven Temperature: 400° F.

1. Wash squashes thoroughly.
2. Cut in halves lengthwise, and remove seeds and stringy portions.
3. Place halves, cut side down, in shallow baking pan containing about ¼ inch of water.
4. Bake at 400° F. for 30 minutes.
5. Turn cut side up, spread over each half 1 teaspoon softened butter or margarine, and sprinkle with salt, pepper, and brown sugar.
6. Bake at 400° F. for about 30 minutes, or until flesh is soft when tested with a fork.

NOTE: This method may be used for baking large winter squash, but before baking, cut squash into serving-sized pieces.

PANNED SUMMER SQUASH
4 servings

1 quart sliced summer squash
3 tablespoons butter or margarine
2 tablespoons water
1 teaspoon salt
Few grains pepper

1. Scrub squash.
2. Cut in ⅛-inch slices, but do not pare or remove seeds.
3. Melt butter or margarine in skillet.
4. Add squash and water, and sprinkle with salt and pepper.
5. Cover tightly, and cook over medium heat for 10 to 15 minutes, or until tender when tested with a fork. Turn squash often to cook evenly.

NOTE: This method may be used for cooking zucchini (Italian squash) and shredded cabbage.

HARVARD BEETS
5 servings

2 tablespoons butter or margarine
1 tablespoon cornstarch
⅓ cup sugar
½ teaspoon salt
¼ cup vinegar
1 tablespoon tarragon vinegar
3 cups sliced cooked beets

1. Melt butter or margarine in top of double boiler over low heat.
2. Remove top of double boiler from heat.
3. Add cornstarch, sugar, and salt, and stir until smooth.
4. Add vinegar and tarragon vinegar slowly, and stir to make a smooth paste.
5. Return to heat, and cook, stirring constantly, until mixture boils.
6. Add sliced cooked beets.
7. Cover, place over simmering water in bottom of double boiler, and heat for about 15 minutes.

GLAZED CARROTS
4 servings

8 medium carrots
Salt
1½ tablespoons butter or margarine
3 tablespoons light-brown sugar

1. Scrub carrots, and pare or scrape off skin.
2. Cook, covered, in small amount of boiling salted water until almost tender when tested with a fork, drain, and let dry.
3. Put butter or margarine and light-brown sugar in skillet, and cook until syrupy.
4. Add carrots, and cook slowly, turning until glazed all over.

CANDIED SWEETPOTATOES
4 servings

4 medium sweetpotatoes
Salt
2 tablespoons butter or margarine
½ cup light-brown sugar
¼ cup water

1. Scrub sweetpotatoes.
2. Boil, without paring, in boiling salted water almost to cover until almost tender when tested with a fork.
3. Peel, and cut in halves lengthwise.
4. Put butter or margarine, light-brown sugar, and water in skillet, and cook until syrupy.
5. Add sweetpotato halves, and cook slowly, turning until brown on both sides.

NOTE: The syrup and cut sweetpotatoes may be placed in a shallow baking dish and baked, uncovered, at 375° F. for 30 minutes.

SPINACH or PEAS WITH MUSHROOMS
4 servings

1 cup sliced mushrooms
3 tablespoons butter or margarine
3 cups cooked spinach
or
3 cups cooked peas

1. Wash, dry, peel, and slice mushrooms.
2. Melt butter or margarine in skillet.
3. Add sliced mushrooms, and cook until tender.
4. Add cooked spinach or cooked peas, toss lightly, and heat to serving temperature.

SCALLOPED SPINACH
4 servings

1 10-ounce package frozen chopped spinach
12 crisp salted crackers, crushed
½ cup milk
⅛ teaspoon pepper
1 tablespoon butter or margarine

Oven Temperature: 375° F.

1. Cook frozen chopped spinach as directed on package label.
2. Place one half of the crushed crackers in the bottom of well-greased 1-quart casserole.

3. Place cooked spinach evenly over crushed crackers.
4. Sprinkle second half of the crushed crackers over spinach.
5. Add milk.
6. Sprinkle with pepper, and dot with butter or margarine.
7. Bake at 375° F. for 20 to 25 minutes.

SCALLOPED ONIONS AND PEANUTS
6 servings

1 pound onions
Salt
2 tablespoons butter or margarine
2 tablespoons flour
½ teaspoon salt
⅛ teaspoon pepper
1 cup milk
1 cup roasted peanuts, chopped
½ cup Buttered Soft Bread Crumbs (page 482)

Oven Temperature: 375° F.

1. Cook onions in boiling salted water to cover until soft.
2. Cut into pieces.
3. Make White Sauce (page 510) with butter or margarine, flour, the ½ teaspoon salt, pepper, and milk.
4. Place about one-third of the cooked onions in well-greased 1-quart casserole.
5. Cover with one-half of the chopped peanuts.
6. Add another third of the cooked onions, and then the rest of the chopped peanuts.
7. Cover with the remaining cooked onions.
8. Add white sauce, and cut through with a spoon to mix slightly with the onions and peanuts.
9. Sprinkle top with buttered soft bread crumbs.
10. Bake at 375° F. for 30 minutes, or until crumbs are golden brown.

SCALLOPED TOMATOES
4 servings

3 tablespoons butter or margarine
1½ cups small soft bread cubes
1 tablespoon sugar
½ teaspoon salt
⅛ teaspoon pepper
1 teaspoon minced onion
2 cups canned tomatoes

Oven Temperature: 375° F.

1. Melt butter or margarine in skillet.
2. Add bread cubes, and mix.
3. Stir sugar, salt, pepper, and minced onion into canned tomatoes.
4. Place alternate layers of buttered bread cubes and seasoned tomatoes in 1-quart casserole, starting and ending with layer of buttered bread cubes.
5. Bake at 375° F. for 40 minutes, or until top crumbs are brown.
6. Serve in casserole.

CORN PUDDING
5 servings

2 cups cream-style corn
   or fresh corn, scraped
   from the cob
½ cup milk
1 tablespoon sugar
¾ teaspoon salt
⅛ teaspoon pepper
1 tablespoon butter or margarine, melted
2 eggs, slightly beaten

Oven Temperature: 350° F.

1. Add all ingredients to slightly beaten eggs in mixing bowl, and mix well.
2. Pour into greased 1-quart casserole.
3. Place casserole in baking pan, pour hot water into pan to depth of the corn mixture, and put in oven.
4. Bake at 350° F. for about 60 minutes, or until a knife inserted into center of pudding comes out clean.
5. Serve in casserole.

H. Armstrong Roberts

YEAST BREADS

BREAD

One 9x5x3-inch loaf

1 cup milk
1 tablespoon shortening
1½ tablespoons sugar
1 teaspoon salt
1 package yeast
3 tablespoons lukewarm water
3 cups sifted all-purpose flour

Oven Temperature: 400° F.

1. Scald milk.
2. Stir in shortening, sugar, and salt.
3. Sprinkle or crumble yeast over lukewarm water in large mixing bowl, and let stand to soften.
4. Cool milk mixture to lukewarm, and stir into softened yeast.
5. Add about 1 cup of the flour, and beat until smooth.
6. Stir in the rest of the flour, as needed, to make a dough that is soft, but not so soft that it sticks to the bowl.
7. Turn dough onto floured board, scraping mixing bowl clean. (Set bowl aside to be used in step 9.)
8. Knead dough for 5 to 8 minutes, or until smooth and until small bubbles of gas appear beneath the surface.
9. Grease the mixing bowl lightly, and re-

turn kneaded dough to it, turning dough to cover all surfaces with the grease.
10. Cover mixing bowl with towel, and set in warm place so dough will rise until about double in size.
11. Punch dough down in mixing bowl with fist.
12. Turn dough onto lightly floured board, and shape into loaf with hands.
13. Put in greased loaf pan, cover with towel, and set in warm place so loaf will rise until about double in size.
14. Bake at 400° F. for 50 minutes, or until there is a hollow sound when loaf is tapped with fingers.
15. Remove loaf immediately from pan to wire rack to cool.

NOTE: The time required to make bread may be shortened if the amount of yeast is increased to 1½ packages. In this case, increase the sugar to 2 tablespoons in order to provide enough food for the extra yeast.

STANDARD: A symmetrical loaf with smooth, well-rounded top; crust thin, crisp, and evenly brown all over top but with sides a lighter brown; crumb fine in grain with uniformly distributed holes, moist and tender in texture; pleasing in flavor, somewhat sweet and nutlike.

527

PLAIN ROLLS
About 1½ dozen rolls

1 cup milk
3 tablespoons shortening
2 tablespoons sugar
1 teaspoon salt
1 package yeast
¼ cup lukewarm water
3 cups sifted all-purpose flour

Oven Temperature: 400° F.

1. Scald milk.
2. Stir in shortening, sugar, and salt.
3. Sprinkle or crumble yeast over lukewarm water in large mixing bowl, and let stand to soften.
4. Cool milk mixture to lukewarm, and stir into softened yeast.
5. Add about 1 cup of the flour, and beat until smooth.
6. Stir in the rest of the flour, as needed, to make a dough that is soft, but not so soft that it sticks to the bowl.
7. Turn dough onto floured board, scraping mixing bowl clean. (Set bowl aside to be used in step 9.)
8. Knead dough for 5 to 8 minutes, or until smooth and until small bubbles of gas appear beneath the surface.
9. Grease the mixing bowl lightly, and return kneaded dough to it, turning dough to cover all surfaces with the grease.
10. Cover mixing bowl with towel, and set in warm place so dough will rise until about double in size.
11. Turn dough onto lightly floured board, and knead lightly to break up large gas bubbles.
12. Cut dough into pieces about the size of a small egg.
13. Fold sides of pieces under until the top is smooth, and place close together in greased baking pan, 2 inches apart on greased baking sheet, or in greased muffin pans.
14. Cover with towel, and set in warm place so rolls will rise until about double in size.
15. Bake at 400° F. for 12 to 15 minutes.
16. Serve hot.

NOTE: Top of rolls may be brushed with softened butter or margarine before they are allowed to rise (after step 13) or just before they are done (end of step 15).

STANDARD: Uniformly golden brown in color; crust soft and thin; crumb creamy white with smaller holes and more delicate in texture than bread; somewhat sweeter in taste than bread.

PARKERHOUSE ROLLS

Use recipe for Plain Rolls, kneading dough lightly to break up large gas bubbles (step 11), and then shape as follows:

1. Roll dough, with floured rolling pin on lightly floured board, into a sheet ¼ to ½ inch thick.
2. Cut into rounds with floured cookie cutter.
3. Crease across each round down to board with dull edge of a knife. Make crease a little to one side of the middle.
4. Brush smaller side with melted butter or margarine, being careful not to brush to edge.
5. Fold larger side over, and press edges lightly.
6. Place on greased baking sheet, about 1½ inches apart.
7. Cover with towel, and set in warm place so rolls will rise until about double in size.
8. Bake at 400° F. for 12 to 15 minutes.

FAN TANS

Use recipe for Plain Rolls, kneading dough lightly to break up large gas bubbles (step 11), and then shape as follows:

1. Roll dough, with floured rolling pin on lightly floured board, into an oblong sheet ¼ inch thick.
2. Brush with melted butter or margarine.
3. Cut into strips 1 inch wide.
4. Pile eight strips on top of each other.
5. Cut across into 1¼-inch pieces.
6. Place on cut end in greased muffin pans.
7. Cover with towel, and set in warm place so rolls will rise until about double in size.
8. Bake at 400° F. for 12 to 15 minutes.

CLOVERLEAF ROLLS

Use recipe for Plain Rolls, kneading dough lightly to break up large gas bubbles (step 11), and then shape as follows:

1. Cut dough into pieces about the size of a marble.
2. Fold sides of pieces under until the top is smooth.
3. Place three pieces in each cup of greased muffin pan with each piece touching bottom of pan.
4. Brush with melted butter or margarine.
5. Cover with towel, and set in warm place so rolls will rise until about double in size.
6. Bake at 400° F. for 12 to 15 minutes.

BUTTERHORNS

Use recipe for Plain Rolls, kneading dough lightly to break up large gas bubbles (step 11), and then shape as follows:

1. Roll dough, with floured rolling pin on lightly floured board, into a circular sheet ¼ to ½ inch thick.
2. Cut into pie-shaped pieces with a floured knife.
3. Brush each piece with melted butter or margarine, being careful not to brush to edge.
4. Roll up with hands, beginning at wide edge of piece, and fasten point by pinching dough together.
5. Place on greased baking sheet, about 1½ inches apart.
6. Cover with towel, and set in warm place so rolls will rise until about double in size.
7. Bake at 400° F. for 12 to 15 minutes.

BUTTERSCOTCH-PECAN ROLLS
About 1 dozen rolls

½ recipe Plain Rolls
3 tablespoons butter or margarine
1 tablespoon water
1 cup light-brown sugar, firmly packed
½ cup chopped pecans

Oven Temperature: 375° F.

1. Make dough as directed for Plain Rolls (steps 1 to 11).
2. Melt 2 tablespoons of the butter or margarine in small saucepan.
3. Add water and ½ cup of the light-brown sugar, and stir over low heat until sugar is dissolved and bubbles appear around sides of saucepan.
4. Pour this butterscotch syrup into well-greased 8-inch square pan.
5. Roll dough, with floured rolling pin on lightly floured board, into an oblong sheet about 12x6x¼ inches in size.
6. Melt the rest of the butter or margarine, spread over sheet of dough, sprinkle with the remaining light-brown sugar, and cover with chopped pecans.
7. Roll up dough from long side, and fasten by pinching dough along edge and ends of roll.
8. Cut into twelve 1-inch pieces, and place, with cut side down, close together in baking pan on top of butterscotch syrup.
9. Cover with towel, and set in warm place so rolls will rise until about double in size.
10. Bake at 375° F. for 30 minutes.
11. Remove from oven, but leave rolls in pan for 3 to 4 minutes afterward so the butterscotch mixture cools enough to cling to rolls.
12. Serve hot.

NOTE: If desired, sprinkle a few pecan halves in butterscotch syrup, and place cut rolls on them.

REFRIGERATOR BREAD
2 loaves

3 tablespoons shortening
2 tablespoons sugar
2 teaspoons salt
1¾ cups milk, scalded
2 packages yeast
½ cup lukewarm water
6 cups flour
Cooking oil

(Continued)

1. Put shortening, sugar, and salt in large mixing bowl, and add scalded milk.
2. Sprinkle yeast over lukewarm water, and let stand to soften.
3. Stir softened yeast into milk mixture.
4. Add 2 cups of the flour, and beat the mixture until smooth.
5. Stir in the rest of the flour, as needed, to make a soft dough.
6. Knead dough on floured board for 5 to 10 minutes.
7. Cover dough with a towel, and let stand for 20 minutes.
8. Divide dough in half, and shape each half into a loaf.
9. Put in greased loaf pans, brush with oil, cover loosely with oiled wax paper.
10. Set in refrigerator for 2 to 24 hours.
11. Remove from the refrigerator, uncover, and let stand at room temperature for 10 minutes.
12. Bake at 400° F. for 50 minutes, or until there is a hollow sound when loaf is tapped with the fingers.
13. Remove loaf immediately from pan to wire rack to cool.

STANDARD: A well-shaped rounded loaf; crust soft and thin, and golden brown in color; crumb even in grain, and tender in texture; mild in flavor.

PIZZA
8 servings

Pizza Dough
2 tablespoons shortening
1 tablespoon sugar
¼ teaspoon salt
½ cup boiling water
½ package yeast
¼ cup lukewarm water
2 cups sifted all-purpose flour
Olive or salad oil

Oven Temperature: 425° F.

1. Put shortening, sugar, and salt in large mixing bowl, add boiling water, and cool.
2. Sprinkle or crumble yeast over lukewarm water, and let stand to soften.

3. Stir softened yeast into first mixture.
4. Add about 1 cup of the flour, and beat until smooth.
5. Stir in the rest of the flour, as needed, to make dough that is soft, but not so soft that it sticks to the bowl.
6. Turn dough onto floured board, scraping mixing bowl clean. (Set bowl aside to be used in step 8.)
7. Knead dough for 5 to 8 minutes, or until smooth and until small bubbles of gas appear beneath the surface.
8. Grease the mixing bowl lightly, and return kneaded dough to it, turning dough to cover all surfaces with the grease.
9. Cover mixing bowl with towel, and set in warm place so dough will rise until about double in size.
10. Punch dough down in mixing bowl with fist.
11. Turn dough onto lightly floured board, knead, and stretch to fit a greased 10x14-inch baking sheet or a greased 12-inch round pizza pan.
12. Spread top lightly with olive or salad oil, and add Pizza Sauce and Topping.

Pizza Sauce and Topping
1 cup canned tomatoes
1 clove garlic, minced
1 teaspoon minced parsley
½ can tomato paste
1 tablespoon olive or salad oil
¼ teaspoon salt

1. Mix all ingredients together in saucepan, and simmer for 30 minutes.
2. Cool.
3. Spread over stretched dough.
4. Top with the following ingredients in order listed:

> 2 teaspoons grated Romano or Parmesan cheese
> 1 teaspoon oregano
> ½ clove garlic, minced
> Thin slices Mozzarella cheese (half of a small cheese)

5. Bake at 425° F. for 25 to 30 minutes, or until crust is crisp and brown.
6. Cut into wedges or squares.
7. Serve hot.

PART VI . . .

Food

Value

Table

NUTRITIVE VALUES OF THE EDIBLE PART OF FOODS*

NOTE: For an explanation of all footnotes, see pages 555–556.

[Dashes show that no basis could be found for imputing a value although there was some reason to believe that a measurable amount of the constituent might be present]

Food and Approximate Measure		Food Energy (Calories)	Protein (Grams)	Fat (total lipid) (Grams)	Fatty Acids Saturated (total) (Grams)	Unsaturated Oleic (Grams)	Unsaturated Linoleic (Grams)	Carbohydrate (Grams)	Calcium (Milligrams)	Iron (Milligrams)	Vitamin A Value (International Units)	Thiamine (Milligrams)	Riboflavin (Milligrams)	Niacin (Milligrams)	Ascorbic Acid (Milligrams)
MILK, CREAM, CHEESE; RELATED PRODUCTS															
Milk, cow's:															
Fluid, whole (3.5% fat)	1 cup	160	9	9	5	3	Trace	12	288	0.1	350	0.08	0.42	0.1	2
Fluid, nonfat (skim)	1 cup	90	9	Trace	–	–	–	13	298	.1	10	.10	.44	.2	2
Buttermilk, cultured, from skim milk	1 cup	90	9	Trace	–	–	–	13	298	.1	10	.09	.44	.2	2
Evaporated, unsweetened, undiluted	1 cup	345	18	20	11	7	1	24	635	.3	820	.10	.84	.5	3
Condensed, sweetened, undiluted	1 cup	980	25	27	15	9	1	166	802	.3	1,090	.23	1.17	.5	3
Dry, whole	1 cup	515	27	28	16	9	1	39	936	.5	1,160	.30	1.50	.7	6
Dry, nonfat, instant	1 cup	250	25	Trace	–	–	–	36	905	.4	20	.24	1.25	.6	5
Cream:															
Half-and-half (cream and milk)	1 cup	325	8	28	16	9	1	11	261	.1	1,160	.08	.38	.1	2
Half-and-half (cream and milk)	1 tablespoon	20	Trace	2	1	1	Trace	1	16	Trace	70	Trace	.02	Trace	Trace
Light, coffee or table	1 cup	505	7	49	27	16	1	10	245	.1	2,030	.07	.36	.1	2
Light, coffee or table	1 tablespoon	30	Trace	3	2	1	Trace	1	15	Trace	130	Trace	.02	Trace	Trace
Whipping, unwhipped (volume about double when whipped):															
Light	1 cup	715	6	75	41	25	2	9	203	.1	3,070	.06	.30	.1	2
Light	1 tablespoon	45	Trace	5	3	2	Trace	1	13	Trace	190	Trace	.02	Trace	Trace
Heavy	1 cup	840	5	89	49	29	3	7	178	.1	3,670	.05	.26	.1	2
Heavy	1 tablespoon	55	Trace	6	3	2	Trace	Trace	11	Trace	230	Trace	.02	Trace	Trace
Cheese:															
Blue or Roquefort type	1 ounce	105	6	9	5	3	Trace	1	89	.1	350	.01	.17	.1	0

Food	Measure													
Cheddar														
Ungrated	1-inch cube	70	4	5	3	2	Trace	Trace	128	.2	220	Trace	.08	Trace	0
Grated	1 cup	445	28	36	20	12	1	2	840	1.1	1,470	.03	.51	.1	0
	1 tablespoon	30	2	2	1	1	Trace	Trace	52	.1	90	Trace	.03	Trace	0
Cheddar, process	1 ounce	105	7	9	5	3	Trace	1	219	.3	350	Trace	.12	Trace	0
Cheese foods, Cheddar	1 ounce	90	6	7	4	2	Trace	2	162	.2	280	.01	.16	Trace	0
Cottage cheese, from skim milk:															
Creamed	1 cup	240	31	9	5	3	Trace	7	212	.7	380	.07	.56	.2	0
Uncreamed	1 cup	195	38	1	Trace	Trace	Trace	6	202	.9	20	.07	.63	.2	0
Cream cheese	1 ounce	105	2	11	6	4	Trace	1	18	.1	440	Trace	.07	Trace	0
Swiss (domestic)	1 ounce	105	8	8	4	3	Trace	1	262	.3	320	Trace	.11	Trace	0
Milk beverages:															
Cocoa	1 cup	235	9	11	6	4	Trace	26	286	.9	390	.09	.45	.4	2
Chocolate-flavored milk drink (made with skim milk)	1 cup	190	8	6	3	2	Trace	27	270	.4	210	.09	.41	.2	2
Malted milk	1 cup	280	13	12	—	—	—	32	364	.8	670	.17	.56	.2	2
Milk desserts:															
Cornstarch pudding, plain	1 cup	275	9	10	5	3	Trace	39	290	.1	390	.07	.40	.1	2
Custard, baked	1 cup	285	13	14	6	5	1	28	278	1.0	870	.10	.47	.2	1
Ice cream, plain, factory packed:															
Slice or cut brick, 1/8 of quart brick	1 slice or cut brick	145	3	9	5	3	Trace	15	87	.1	370	.03	.13	.1	1
Container	3½ fluid ounces	130	2	8	4	3	Trace	13	76	.1	320	.03	.12	.1	1
Container	8 fluid ounces	295	6	18	10	6	1	29	175	.1	740	.06	.27	.1	1
Ice milk	1 cup	285	9	10	6	3	Trace	42	292	.2	390	.09	.41	.2	2
Yoghurt, from partially skimmed milk	1 cup	120	8	4	2	1	Trace	13	295	.1	170	.09	.43	.2	2
EGGS															
Eggs, large, 24 ounces per dozen:															
Raw:															
Whole, without shell	1 egg	80	6	6	2	3	Trace	Trace	27	1.1	590	.05	.15	Trace	0
White of (medium) egg	1 white	15	4	Trace	—	—	—	Trace	3	Trace	0	Trace	.09	Trace	0
Yolk of (medium) egg	1 yolk	60	3	5	2	2	Trace	Trace	24	.9	580	.04	.07	Trace	0
Cooked:															
Boiled, shell removed	2 eggs	160	13	12	4	5	1	1	54	2.3	1,180	.09	.28	.1	0
Scrambled, with milk and fat	1 egg	110	7	8	3	3	Trace	1	51	1.1	690	.05	.18	Trace	0
MEAT, POULTRY, FISH, SHELLFISH; RELATED PRODUCTS															
Bacon, broiled or fried, crisp	2 slices	100	5	8	3	4	1	1	2	.5	0	.08	.05	.8	—

(Continued)

Food and Approximate Measure	Food Energy (Calories)	Protein (Grams)	Fat (total lipid) (Grams)	Saturated (total) (Grams)	Unsaturated Oleic (Grams)	Unsaturated Linoleic (Grams)	Carbohydrate (Grams)	Calcium (Milligrams)	Iron (Milligrams)	Vitamin A Value (International Units)	Thiamine (Milligrams)	Riboflavin (Milligrams)	Niacin (Milligrams)	Ascorbic Acid (Milligrams)
Beef, trimmed to retail basis,[1] cooked:														
Cuts braised, simmered, or pot-roasted:														
Lean and fat ... 3 ounces	245	23	16	8	7	Trace	0	10	2.9	30	0.04	0.18	3.5	-----
Lean only ... 2.5 ounces	140	22	5	2	2	Trace	0	10	2.7	10	.04	.16	3.3	-----
Hamburger (ground beef), broiled:														
Lean ... 3 ounces	185	23	10	5	4	Trace	0	10	3.0	20	.08	.20	5.1	-----
Regular ... 3 ounces	245	21	17	8	8	Trace	0	9	2.7	30	.07	.18	4.6	-----
Roast, oven-cooked, no liquid added:														
Relatively fat, such as rib:														
Lean and fat ... 3 ounces	375	17	34	16	15	1	0	8	2.2	70	.05	.13	3.1	-----
Lean only ... 1.8 ounces	125	14	7	3	3	Trace	0	6	1.8	10	.04	.11	2.6	-----
Relatively lean, such as heel of round:														
Lean and fat ... 3 ounces	165	25	7	3	3	Trace	0	11	3.2	10	.06	.19	4.5	-----
Lean only ... 2.7 ounces	125	24	3	1	1	Trace	0	10	3.0	Trace	.06	.18	4.3	-----
Steak, broiled:														
Relatively fat, such as sirloin:														
Lean and fat ... 3 ounces	330	20	27	13	12	1	0	9	2.5	50	.05	.16	4.0	-----
Lean only ... 2 ounces	115	18	4	2	2	Trace	0	7	2.2	10	.05	.14	3.6	-----
Relatively lean, such as round:														
Lean and fat ... 3 ounces	220	24	13	6	6	Trace	0	10	3.0	20	.07	.19	4.8	-----
Lean only ... 2.4 ounces	130	21	4	2	2	Trace	0	9	2.5	10	.06	.16	4.1	-----
Beef, canned:														
Corned beef ... 3 ounces	185	22	10	5	4	Trace	0	17	3.7	20	.01	.20	2.9	-----
Corned beef hash ... 3 ounces	155	7	10	5	4	Trace	9	11	1.7	-----	.01	.08	1.8	-----
Beef, dried or chipped ... 2 ounces	115	19	4	2	2	Trace	0	11	2.9	-----	.04	.18	2.2	-----
Beef and vegetable stew ... 1 cup	210	15	10	5	4	Trace	15	28	2.8	2,310	.13	.17	4.4	15
Beef potpie, baked; individual pie, 4¼-inch diameter ... 1 pie	560	23	33	9	20	2	43	32	4.1	1,860	.25	.27	4.5	7
Chicken, cooked:														
Flesh only, broiled ... 3 ounces	115	20	3	1	1	1	0	8	1.4	80	.05	.16	7.4	-----
Breast, fried, ½ breast:														
With bone ... 3.3 ounces	155	25	5	1	2	1	1	9	1.3	70	.04	.17	11.2	-----

Flesh and skin only	2.7 ounces	155	25	5	1	2	1	1	9	1.3	70	.04	.17	11.2	—
Drumstick, fried:															
With bone	2.1 ounces	90	12	4	1	2	1	Trace	6	.9	50	.03	.15	2.7	—
Flesh and skin only	1.3 ounces	90	12	4	1	2	1	Trace	6	.9	50	.03	.15	2.7	—
Chicken, canned, boneless	3 ounces	170	18	10	3	4	2	0	18	1.3	200	.03	.11	3.7	3
Chicken potpie. See Poultry potpie.															
Chile con carne, canned:															
With beans	1 cup	335	19	15	7	7	Trace	30	80	4.2	150	.08	.18	3.2	—
Without beans	1 cup	510	26	38	18	17	1	15	97	3.6	380	.05	.31	5.6	—
Heart, beef, lean, braised	3 ounces	160	27	5	3	—	—	1	5	5.0	20	.21	1.04	6.5	1
Lamb, trimmed to retail basis,[1] cooked:															
Chop, thick, with bone, broiled	1 chop, 4.8 ounces	400	25	33	18	12	1	0	10	1.5	—	.14	.25	5.6	—
Lean and fat	4.0 ounces	400	25	33	18	12	1	0	10	1.5	—	.14	.25	5.6	—
Lean only	2.6 ounces	140	21	6	3	2	Trace	0	9	1.5	—	.11	.20	4.5	—
Leg, roasted:															
Lean and fat	3 ounces	235	22	16	9	6	Trace	0	9	1.4	—	.13	.23	4.7	—
Lean only	2.5 ounces	130	20	5	3	2	Trace	0	9	1.4	—	.12	.21	4.4	—
Shoulder, roasted:															
Lean and fat	3 ounces	285	18	23	13	8	1	0	9	1.0	—	.11	.20	4.0	—
Lean only	2.3 ounces	130	17	6	3	2	Trace	0	8	1.0	—	.10	.18	3.7	—
Liver, beef, fried	2 ounces	130	15	6	—	—	—	3	6	5.0	30,280	.15	2.37	9.4	15
Pork, cured, cooked:															
Ham, light cure, lean and fat, roasted	3 ounces	245	18	19	7	8	2	0	8	2.2	0	.40	.16	3.1	—
Luncheon meat:															
Boiled ham, sliced	2 ounces	135	11	10	4	4	1	0	6	1.6	0	.25	.09	1.5	—
Canned, spiced or unspiced	2 ounces	165	8	14	5	6	1	1	5	1.2	0	.18	.12	1.6	—
Pork, fresh, trimmed to retail basis,[1] cooked:															
Chop, thick, with bone	1 chop, 3.5 ounces	260	16	21	8	9	2	0	8	2.2	0	.63	.18	3.8	—
Lean and fat	2.3 ounces	260	16	21	8	9	2	0	8	2.2	0	.63	.18	3.8	—
Lean only	1.7 ounces	130	15	7	2	3	1	0	7	1.9	0	.54	.16	3.3	—
Roast, oven-cooked, no liquid added:															
Lean and fat	3 ounces	310	21	24	9	10	2	0	9	2.7	0	.78	.22	4.7	—
Lean only	2.4 ounces	175	20	10	3	4	1	0	9	2.6	0	.73	.21	4.4	—
Poultry potpie (based on chicken potpie); individual pie, 4¼-inch diameter	1 pie	535	23	31	10	15	3	42	68	3.0	3,020	.25	.26	4.1	5

(Continued)

Food and Approximate Measure		Food Energy (Calories)	Protein (Grams)	Fat (total lipid) (Grams)	Fatty Acids — Saturated (total) (Grams)	Fatty Acids — Unsaturated Oleic (Grams)	Fatty Acids — Unsaturated Linoleic (Grams)	Carbohydrate (Grams)	Calcium (Milligrams)	Iron (Milligrams)	Vitamin A Value (International Units)	Thiamine (Milligrams)	Riboflavin (Milligrams)	Niacin (Milligrams)	Ascorbic Acid (Milligrams)
Sausage:															
Bologna, slice, 4.1 by 0.1 inch	8 slices	690	27	62				2	16	4.1		0.36	0.49	6.0	
Wiener, cooked	1 wiener	155	6	14				1	3	.8		.08	.10	1.3	
Pork, links or patty, cooked	4 ounces	540	21	50	18	21	5	Trace	8	2.7		.89	.39	4.2	
Tongue, beef, braised	3 ounces	210	18	14				Trace	6	1.9	0	.04	.25	3.0	
Turkey potpie. See Poultry potpie															
Veal, cooked:															
Cutlet, without bone, broiled	3 ounces	185	23	9	5	4	Trace		9	2.7		.06	.21	4.6	
Roast, medium fat, medium done; lean and fat	3 ounces	230	23	14	7	6	Trace	0	10	2.9		.11	.26	6.6	
Fish and shellfish:															
Bluefish, baked or broiled	3 ounces	135	22	4				0	25	.6	40	.09	.08	1.6	
Clams:															
Raw, meat only	3 ounces	65	11	1				2	59	5.2	90	.08	.15	1.1	8
Canned, solids and liquid	3 ounces	45	7	1				2	47	3.5		.01	.09	.9	
Crabmeat, canned	3 ounces	85	15	2				1	38	.7		.07	.07	1.6	
Fish sticks, breaded, cooked, frozen; stick, 3.8 by 1.0 by 0.5 inch	10 sticks or 8-ounce package	400	38	20	5	4	10	15	25	.9		.09	.16	3.6	
Haddock, fried	3 ounces	140	17	5	1	3	Trace	5	34	1.0		.03	.06	2.7	
Mackerel:															
Broiled, Atlantic	3 ounces	200	19	13				0	5	1.0	450	.13	.23	6.5	
Canned, Pacific, solids and liquid[2]	3 ounces	155	18	9				0	221	1.9	20	.02	.28	7.4	2
Ocean perch, breaded (egg and breadcrumbs), fried	3 ounces	195	16	11				6	28	1.1		.08	.09	1.5	
Oysters, meat only, raw, 13–19 medium selects	1 cup	160	20	4				8	226	13.2	740	.33	.43	6.0	
Oyster stew, 1 part oysters to 3 parts milk by volume, 3–4 oysters	1 cup	200	11	12				11	269	3.3	640	.13	.41	1.6	

Salmon, pink, canned	3 ounces	120	17	5	1	1	1	0	167[3]	.7	60	.03	.16	6.8	—
Sardines, Atlantic, canned in oil, drained solids	3 ounces	175	20	9	—	—	—	0	372	2.5	190	.02	.17	4.6	—
Shad, baked	3 ounces	170	20	10	—	—	—	0	20	.5	20	.11	.22	7.3	—
Shrimp, canned, meat only	3 ounces	100	21	1	—	—	—	1	98	2.6	50	.01	.03	1.5	—
Swordfish, broiled with butter or margarine	3 ounces	150	24	5	—	—	—	0	23	1.1	1,750	.03	.04	9.3	—
Tuna, canned in oil, drained solids	3 ounces	170	24	7	—	—	—	0	7	1.6	70	.04	.10	10.1	—
MATURE DRY BEANS AND PEAS, NUTS, PEANUTS; RELATED PRODUCTS															
Almonds, shelled	1 cup	850	26	77	6	52	15	28	332	6.7	0	.34	1.31	5.0	Trace
Beans, dry, common varieties, such as Great Northern, navy, and others, canned:															
Red	1 cup	230	15	1	—	—	—	42	74	4.6	Trace	.13	.10	1.5	—
White, with tomato sauce:															
With pork	1 cup	320	16	7	3	3	1	50	141	4.7	340	.20	.08	1.5	5
Without pork	1 cup	310	16	1	—	—	—	60	177	5.2	160	.18	.09	1.5	5
Beans, dry Lima, cooked	1 cup	260	16	1	—	—	—	48	56	5.6	Trace	.26	.12	1.3	Trace
Brazil nuts	1 cup	915	20	94	19	45	24	15	260	4.8	Trace	1.34	.17	2.2	—
Cashew nuts, roasted	1 cup	760	23	62	10	43	4	40	51	5.1	140	.58	.33	2.4	—
Coconut:															
Fresh, shredded	1 cup	335	3	34	29	2	Trace	9	13	1.6	0	.05	.02	.5	3
Dried, shredded, sweetened	1 cup	340	2	24	21	2	Trace	33	10	1.2	0	.02	.02	.2	0
Cowpeas or blackeye peas, dry, cooked	1 cup	190	13	1	—	—	—	34	42	3.2	20	.41	.11	1.1	Trace
Peanuts, roasted, salted:															
Halves	1 cup	840	37	72	16	31	21	27	107	3.0	—	.46	.19	24.7	0
Chopped	1 tablespoon	55	2	4	1	2	1	2	7	.2	—	.03	.01	1.5	0
Peanut butter	1 tablespoon	95	4	8	2	4	2	3	9	.3	—	.02	.02	2.4	0
Peas, split, dry, cooked	1 cup	290	20	1	—	—	—	52	28	4.2	100	.37	.22	2.2	—
Pecans:															
Halves	1 cup	740	10	77	5	48	15	16	79	2.6	140	.93	.14	1.0	2
Chopped	1 tablespoon	50	1	5	Trace	3	1	1	5	.2	10	.06	.01	.1	Trace
Walnuts, shelled:															
Black or native, chopped	1 cup	790	26	75	4	26	36	19	Trace	7.6	380	.28	.14	.9	—
English or Persian:															
Halves	1 cup	650	15	64	4	10	40	16	99	3.1	30	.33	.13	.9	3
Chopped	1 tablespoon	50	1	5	Trace	1	3	1	8	.2	Trace	.03	.01	.1	Trace

(Continued)

Food and Approximate Measure

Food and Approximate Measure		Food Energy	Protein	Fat (total lipid)	Fatty Acids Saturated (total)	Unsaturated Oleic	Linoleic	Carbohydrate	Calcium	Iron	Vitamin A Value	Thiamine	Riboflavin	Niacin	Ascorbic Acid
		Calories	Grams	Grams	Grams	Grams	Grams	Grams	Milligrams	Milligrams	International Units	Milligrams	Milligrams	Milligrams	Milligrams
VEGETABLES AND VEGETABLE PRODUCTS															
Asparagus:															
Cooked, cut spears	1 cup	35	4	Trace				6	37	1.0	1,580	0.27	0.32	2.4	46
Canned spears, medium:															
Green	6 spears	20	2	Trace				3	18	1.8	770	.06	.10	.8	14
Bleached	6 spears	20	2	Trace				4	15	1.0	80	.05	.06	.7	14
Beans:															
Lima, immature, cooked	1 cup	180	12	1				32	75	4.0	450	.29	.16	2.0	28
Snap, green, cooked:															
In small amount of water, short time	1 cup	30	2	Trace				7	62	.8	680	.08	.11	.6	16
In large amount of water, long time	1 cup	30	2	Trace				7	62	.8	680	.07	.10	.4	13
Snap, green, canned, solids and liquid	1 cup	45	2	Trace				10	81	2.9	690	.08	.10	.7	9
Beets, cooked, diced	1 cup	50	2	Trace				12	23	.8	40	.04	.07	.5	11
Broccoli spears, cooked	1 cup	40	5	Trace				7	132	1.2	3,750	.14	.29	1.2	135
Brussels sprouts, cooked	1 cup	45	5	1				8	42	1.4	680	.10	.18	1.1	113
Cabbage:															
Raw:															
Finely shredded	1 cup	25	1	Trace				5	49	.4	130	.05	.05	.3	47
Coleslaw	1 cup	120	1	9	2	2	5	9	52	.5	180	.06	.06	.3	35
Cooked:															
In small amount of water, short time	1 cup	35	2	Trace				7	75	.5	220	.07	.07	.5	56
In large amount of water, long time	1 cup	30	2	Trace				7	71	.5	200	.04	.04	.2	40
Cabbage, celery or Chinese, raw leaves and stalk, 1-inch pieces	1 cup	15	1	Trace				3	43	.6	150	.05	.04	.6	25
Carrots:															
Raw:															
Whole, 5½ by 1 inch	1 carrot	20	1	Trace				5	18	.4	5,500	.03	.03	.3	4

(Continued)

Food	Measure	Food energy (cal.)	Protein (g)	Fat (g)	Saturated fatty acids	Unsaturated – Oleic	Unsaturated – Linoleic	Carbohydrate (g)	Calcium (mg)	Iron (mg)	Vitamin A (I.U.)	Thiamine (mg)	Riboflavin (mg)	Niacin (mg)	Ascorbic acid (mg)
Grated	1 cup	45	1	Trace	—	—	—	11	41	.8	12,100	.06	.06	.7	9
Cooked, diced	1 cup	45	1	Trace	—	—	—	10	48	.9	15,220	.08	.07	.7	9
Cauliflower, cooked, flowerbuds	1 cup	25	3	Trace	—	—	—	5	25	.8	70	.11	.10	.7	66
Celery, raw:															
Stalk, large outer, 8 by about 1½ inches at root end	1 stalk	5	Trace	Trace	—	—	—	2	16	.1	100	.01	.01	.1	4
Pieces, diced	1 cup	15	1	Trace	—	—	—	4	39	.3	240	.03	.03	.3	9
Collards, cooked	1 cup	55	5	1	—	—	—	9	289	1.1	10,260	.27	.37	2.4	87
Corn, sweet:															
Cooked, ear 5 by 1¾ inches[4]	1 ear	70	3	1	—	—	—	16	2	.5	310[5]	.09	.08	1.0	7
Canned, solids and liquid	1 cup	170	5	2	—	—	—	40	10	1.0	690[5]	.07	.12	2.3	13
Cowpeas, cooked, immature seeds	1 cup	175	13	1	—	—	—	29	38	3.4	560	.49	.18	2.3	28
Cucumbers, 10-ounce; 7½ by about 2 inches:															
Raw, pared	1 cucumber	30	1	Trace	—	—	—	7	35	.6	Trace	.07	.09	.4	23
Raw, pared, center slice ⅛-inch thick	6 slices	5	Trace	Trace	—	—	—	2	8	.2	Trace	.02	.02	.1	6
Dandelion greens, cooked	1 cup	60	4	1	—	—	—	12	252	3.2	21,060	.24	.29	—	32
Endive, curly (including escarole)	2 ounces	10	1	Trace	—	—	—	2	46	1.0	1,870	.04	.08	.3	6
Kale, leaves including stems, cooked	1 cup	30	4	1	—	—	—	4	147	1.3	8,140				68
Lettuce, raw:															
Butterhead, as Boston types; head, 4-inch diameter	1 head	30	3	Trace	—	—	—	6	77	4.4	2,130	.14	.13	.6	18
Crisphead, as Iceberg; head 4¾-inch diameter	1 head	60	4	Trace	—	—	—	13	91	2.3	1,500	.29	.27	1.3	29
Looseleaf, or bunching varieties, leaves	2 large	10	1	Trace	—	—	—	2	34	.7	950	.03	.04	.2	9
Mushrooms, canned, solids and liquid	1 cup	40	5	Trace	—	—	—	6	15	1.2	Trace	.04	.60	4.8	4
Mustard greens, cooked	1 cup	35	3	1	—	—	—	6	193	2.5	8,120	.11	.19	.9	68
Okra, cooked, pod 3 by ⅝ inch	8 pods	25	2	Trace	—	—	—	5	78	.4	420	.11	.15	.8	17
Onions:															
Mature:															
Raw, onion 2½-inch diameter	1 onion	40	2	Trace	—	—	—	10	30	.6	40	.04	.04	.2	11
Cooked	1 cup	60	3	Trace	—	—	—	14	50	.8	80	.06	.06	.4	14
Young green, small, without tops	6 onions	20	1	Trace	—	—	—	5	20	.3	Trace	.02	.02	.2	12

Food and Approximate Measure		Food Energy	Protein	Fat (total lipid)	Fatty Acids			Carbohydrate	Calcium	Iron	Vitamin A Value	Thiamine	Riboflavin	Niacin	Ascorbic Acid
					Saturated (total)	Unsaturated Oleic	Unsaturated Linoleic								
		Calories	Grams	Grams	Grams	Grams	Grams	Grams	Milligrams	Milligrams	International Units	Milligrams	Milligrams	Milligrams	Milligrams
Parsley, raw, chopped	1 tablespoon	1	Trace	Trace				Trace	7	0.2	300	Trace	0.01	Trace	6
Parsnips, cooked	1 cup	100	2	1				23	70	.9	50	0.11	.13	0.2	16
Peas, green:															
Cooked	1 cup	115	9	1				19	37	2.9	860	.44	.17	3.7	33
Canned, solids and liquid	1 cup	165	9	1				31	50	4.2	1,120	.23	.13	2.2	22
Peppers, hot, red, without seeds, dried (ground chili powder, added seasonings)	1 tablespoon	50	2	2				8	40	2.3	9,750	.03	.17	1.3	2
Peppers, sweet:															
Raw, medium, about 6 per pound:															
Green pod without stem and seeds	1 pod	15	1	Trace				3	6	.4	260	.05	.05	.3	79
Red pod without stem and seeds	1 pod	20	1	Trace				4	8	.4	2,670	.05	.05	.3	122
Canned, pimientos, medium	1 pod	10	Trace	Trace				2	3	.6	870	.01	.02	.1	36
Potatoes, medium (about 3 per pound raw):															
Baked, peeled after baking	1 potato	90	3	Trace				21	9	.7	Trace	.10	.04	1.7	20
Boiled:															
Peeled after boiling	1 potato	105	3	Trace				23	10	.8	Trace	.13	.05	2.0	22
Peeled before boiling	1 potato	80	2	Trace				18	7	.6	Trace	.11	.04	1.4	20
French-fried, piece 2 by 1/2 by 1/2 inch:															
Cooked in deep fat	10 pieces	155	2	7	2	2	4	20	9	.7	Trace	.07	.04	1.8	12
Frozen, heated	10 pieces	125	2	5	1	1	2	19	5	1.0	Trace	.08	.01	1.5	12
Mashed, milk added	1 cup	125	4	1				25	47	.8	50	.16	.10	2.0	19
Milk and butter added	1 cup	185	4	8	4	3	Trace	24	47	.8	330	.16	.10	1.9	18
Potato chips, medium, 2-inch diameter	10 chips	115	1	8	2	2	4	10	8	.4	Trace	.04	.01	1.0	3
Pumpkin, canned	1 cup	75	2	1				18	57	.9	14,590	.07	.12	1.3	12
Radishes, raw, small	4 radishes	5	Trace	Trace				1	12	.4	Trace	.01	.01	.1	10
Sauerkraut, canned, solids and liquid	1 cup	45	2	Trace				9	85	1.2	120	.07	.09	.4	33

Food	Measure	Food energy (Cal.)	Protein (g)	Fat (g)	Saturated (g)	Oleic (g)	Linoleic (g)	Carbohydrate (g)	Calcium (mg)	Iron (mg)	Vitamin A (I.U.)	Thiamine (mg)	Riboflavin (mg)	Niacin (mg)	Ascorbic acid (mg)
Spinach:															
Cooked	1 cup	40	5	1	---	---	---	6	167	4.0	14,580	.13	.25	1.0	50
Canned, drained solids	1 cup	45	5	1	---	---	---	6	212	4.7	14,400	.03	.21	.6	24
Sprouts, raw:															
Mung bean	1 cup	30	3	Trace	---	---	---	6	17	1.2	20	.12	.12	.7	17
Soybean	1 cup	40	6	2	---	---	---	4	46	.7	90	.17	.16	.8	4
Squash:															
Cooked:															
Summer, diced	1 cup	30	2	Trace	---	---	---	7	52	.8	820	.10	.16	1.6	21
Winter, baked, mashed	1 cup	130	4	1	---	---	---	32	57	1.6	8,610	.10	.27	1.4	27
Sweetpotatoes:															
Cooked, medium, 5 by 2 inches, weight raw about 6 ounces:															
Baked, peeled after baking	1 sweetpotato	155	2	1	---	---	---	36	44	1.0	8,910	.10	.07	.7	24
Boiled, peeled after boiling	1 sweetpotato	170	2	1	---	---	---	39	47	1.0	11,610	.13	.09	.9	25
Candied, 3½ by 2¼ inches	1 sweetpotato	295	2	6	2	3	1	60	65	1.6	11,030	.10	.08	.8	17
Canned, vacuum or solid pack	1 cup	235	4	Trace	---	---	---	54	54	1.7	17,000	.10	.10	1.4	30
Tomatoes:															
Raw, medium, 2 by 2½ inches, about 3 per pound	1 tomato	35	2	Trace	---	---	---	7	20	.8	1,350	.10	.06	1.0	34[6]
Canned	1 cup	50	2	Trace	---	---	---	10	15	1.2	2,180	.13	.07	1.7	40
Tomato juice, canned	1 cup	45	2	Trace	---	---	---	10	17	2.2	1,940	.13	.07	1.8	39
Tomato catsup	1 tablespoon	15	Trace	Trace	---	---	---	4	4	.1	240	.02	.01	.3	3
Turnips, cooked, diced	1 cup	35	1	Trace	---	---	---	8	54	.6	Trace	.06	.08	.5	33
Turnip greens, cooked:															
In small amount of water, short time	1 cup	30	3	Trace	---	---	---	5	267	1.6	9,140	.21	.36	.8	100
In large amount of water, long time	1 cup	25	3	Trace	---	---	---	5	252	1.4	8,260	.14	.33	.8	68
Turnip greens, canned, solids and liquid	1 cup	40	3	1	---	---	---	7	232	3.7	10,900	.04	.21	1.4	44

FRUITS AND FRUIT PRODUCTS

Food	Measure	Food energy (Cal.)	Protein (g)	Fat (g)	Saturated (g)	Oleic (g)	Linoleic (g)	Carbohydrate (g)	Calcium (mg)	Iron (mg)	Vitamin A (I.U.)	Thiamine (mg)	Riboflavin (mg)	Niacin (mg)	Ascorbic acid (mg)
Apples, raw, medium, 2½-inch diameter, about 3 per pound[4]	1 apple	70	Trace	Trace	---	---	---	18	8	.4	50	.04	.02	.1	3
Apple brown betty	1 cup	345	4	8	4	3	Trace	68	41	1.4	230	.13	.10	.9	3
Apple juice, bottled or canned	1 cup	120	Trace	Trace	---	---	---	30	15	1.5	------	.01	.04	.2	2
Applesauce, canned, sweetened	1 cup	230	1	Trace	---	---	---	60	10	1.3	100	.05	.03	.1	3

(Continued)

Food and Approximate Measure	Food Energy (Calories)	Protein (Grams)	Fat (total lipid) (Grams)	Fatty Acids Saturated (total) (Grams)	Unsaturated Oleic (Grams)	Unsaturated Linoleic (Grams)	Carbohydrate (Grams)	Calcium (Milligrams)	Iron (Milligrams)	Vitamin A Value (International Units)	Thiamine (Milligrams)	Riboflavin (Milligrams)	Niacin (Milligrams)	Ascorbic Acid (Milligrams)
Applesauce, canned, unsweetened or artificially sweetened 1 cup	100	Trace	Trace	---	---	---	26	10	1.2	100	0.04	0.02	0.1	2
Apricots: Raw, about 12 per pound[4] 3 apricots	55	1	Trace	---	---	---	14	18	.5	2,890	.03	.04	.7	10
Canned in heavy syrup: Halves and syrup 1 cup	220	2	Trace	---	---	---	57	28	.8	4,510	.05	.06	.9	10
Halves (medium) and syrup 4 halves; 2 tablespoons syrup	105	1	Trace	---	---	---	27	13	.4	2,120	.02	.03	.4	5
Dried: Uncooked, 40 halves, small 1 cup	390	8	1	---	---	---	100	100	8.2	16,350	.02	.23	4.9	19
Cooked, unsweetened, fruit and liquid 1 cup	240	5	1	---	---	---	62	63	5.1	8,550	.01	.13	2.8	8
Apricot nectar, canned 1 cup	140	1	Trace	---	---	---	36	22	.5	2,380	.02	.02	.5	7
Avocados, raw: California varieties, mainly Fuerte: 10-ounce avocado, about 3⅓ by 4¼ inches, peeled, pitted ½ avocado	185	2	18	4	8	2	6	11	.6	310	.12	.21	1.7	15
½-inch cubes 1 cup	260	3	26	5	12	3	9	15	.9	440	.16	.30	2.4	21
Florida varieties: 13-ounce avocado, about 4 by 3 inches, peeled, pitted ½ avocado	160	2	14	3	6	2	11	12	.7	360	.13	.24	2.0	17
½-inch cubes 1 cup	195	2	17	3	8	2	13	15	.9	440	.16	.30	2.4	21
Bananas, raw, 6 by 1½ inches, about 3 per pound[4] 1 banana	85	1	Trace	---	---	---	23	8	.7	190	.05	.06	.7	10
Blackberries, raw 1 cup	85	2	1	---	---	---	19	46	1.3	290	.05	.06	.5	30
Blueberries, raw 1 cup	85	1	1	---	---	---	21	21	1.4	140	.04	.08	.6	20
Cantaloupes, raw; medium, 5-inch diameter, about 1⅔ pounds[4] ½ melon	60	1	Trace	---	---	---	14	27	.8	6,540[7]	.08	.06	1.2	63

Food	Measure														
Cherries:															
Raw, sweet, with stems[4]	1 cup	80	2	Trace	---	---	---	20	26	.5	130	.06	.07	.5	12
Canned, red, sour, pitted, heavy syrup	1 cup	230	2	1	---	---	---	59	36	.8	1,680	.07	.06	.4	13
Cranberry juice cocktail, canned	1 cup	160	Trace	Trace	---	---	---	41	12	.8	Trace	.02	.02	.1	(8)
Cranberry sauce, sweetened, canned, strained	1 cup	405	Trace	1	---	---	---	104	17	.6	40	.03	.03	.1	5
Dates, domestic, natural and dry, pitted, cut	1 cup	490	4	1	---	---	---	130	105	5.3	90	.16	.17	3.9	0
Figs:															
Raw, small, 1½-inch diameter, about 12 per pound	3 figs	90	1	Trace	---	---	---	23	40	.7	90	.07	.06	.5	2
Dried, large, 2 by 1 inch	1 fig	60	1	Trace	---	---	---	15	26	.6	20	.02	.02	.1	0
Fruit cocktail, canned in heavy syrup, solids and liquid	1 cup	195	1	1	---	---	---	50	23	1.0	360	.04	.03	1.1	5
Grapefruit:															
Raw, medium, 4¼-inch diameter, size 64: White[4]	½ grapefruit	55	1	Trace	---	---	---	14	22	.6	10	.05	.02	.2	52
Pink or red[4]	½ grapefruit	60	1	Trace	---	---	---	15	23	.6	640	.05	.02	.3	52
Raw sections, white	1 cup	75	1	Trace	---	---	---	20	31	.8	20	.07	.03	.3	72
Canned, white: Syrup pack, solids and liquid	1 cup	175	1	Trace	---	---	---	44	32	.7	20	.07	.04	.5	75
Water pack, solids and liquid	1 cup	70	1	Trace	---	---	---	18	31	.7	20	.07	.04	.5	72
Grapefruit juice: Fresh	1 cup	95	1	Trace	---	---	---	23	22	.5	(9)	.09	.04	.4	92
Canned, white: Unsweetened	1 cup	100	1	Trace	---	---	---	24	20	1.0	20	.07	.04	.4	84
Sweetened	1 cup	130	1	Trace	---	---	---	32	20	1.0	20	.07	.04	.4	78
Frozen, concentrate, unsweetened, diluted with 3 parts water, by volume	1 cup	100	1	Trace	---	---	---	24	25	.2	20	.10	.04	.5	96
Frozen, concentrate, sweetened, diluted with 3 parts water, by volume	1 cup	115	1	Trace	---	---	---	28	20	.2	20	.08	.03	.4	82
Dehydrated, prepared with water (pound yields about 1 gallon)	1 cup	100	1	Trace	---	---	---	24	22	.2	20	.10	.05	.5	92

(Continued)

Food and Approximate Measure	Food Energy	Protein	Fat (total lipid)	Fatty Acids			Carbo-hydrate	Cal-cium	Iron	Vita-min A Value	Thia-mine	Ribo-flavin	Nia-cin	Ascor-bic Acid
				Satu-rated (total)	Unsaturated									
					Oleic	Lino-leic								
	Calo-ries	Grams	Grams	Grams	Grams	Grams	Grams	Milli-grams	Milli-grams	Inter-national Units	Milli-grams	Milli-grams	Milli-grams	Milli-grams
Grapes, raw:														
American type (slip skin), such as Concord, Delaware, Niagara, Catawba, and Scuppernong[4] 1 cup	65	1	1	----	----	----	15	15	0.4	100	0.05	0.03	0.2	3
European type (adherent skin), such as Malaga, Muscat, Thompson Seedless, Emperor, and Flame Tokay[4] 1 cup	95	1	Trace	----	----	----	25	17	.6	140	.07	.04	.4	6
Grape juice, bottled or canned 1 cup	165	1	Trace	----	----	----	42	28	.8	----	.10	.05	.6	Trace
Lemons, raw, medium, 2⅛-inch diameter, size 150[4] 1 lemon	20	1	Trace	----	----	----	6	18	.4	10	.03	.01	.1	38
Lemon juice:														
Fresh 1 cup	60	1	Trace	----	----	----	20	17	.5	40	.08	.03	.2	113
Canned, unsweetened 1 tablespoon	5	Trace	Trace	----	----	----	1	1	Trace	Trace	Trace	Trace	Trace	7
1 cup	55	1	Trace	----	----	----	19	17	.5	40	.07	.03	.2	102
Lemonade concentrate, frozen, sweetened, diluted with 4⅓ parts water, by volume 1 cup	110	Trace	Trace	----	----	----	28	2	.1	10	.01	.01	.2	17
Lime juice:														
Fresh 1 cup	65	1	Trace	----	----	----	22	22	.5	30	.05	.03	.3	80
Canned 1 cup	65	1	Trace	----	----	----	22	22	.5	30	.05	.03	.3	52
Limeade concentrate, frozen, sweetened, diluted with 4⅓ parts water, by volume 1 cup	105	Trace	Trace	----	----	----	27	2	Trace	Trace	Trace	Trace	Trace	6
Oranges, raw:														
California, Navel (winter), 2⅘-inch diameter, size 88[4] 1 orange	60	2	Trace	----	----	----	16	49	.5	240	.12	.05	.5	75
Florida, all varieties, 3-inch diameter[4] 1 orange	75	1	Trace	----	----	----	19	67	.3	310	.16	.06	.6	70

(Continued)

Food	Measure	Food energy	Protein	Fat				Carbohydrate	Calcium	Iron	Vitamin A	Thiamine	Riboflavin	Niacin	Ascorbic acid
Orange juice, fresh:															
California, Valencia	1 cup	115	2	1	---	---	---	26	27	.7	500	.22	.06	.9	122
Florida varieties:															
Early and midseason	1 cup	100	1	Trace	---	---	---	23	25	.5	490	.22	.06	.9	127
Late season, Valencia	1 cup	110	1	Trace	---	---	---	26	25	.5	500	.22	.06	.9	92
Orange juice, canned, unsweetened	1 cup	120	2	Trace	---	---	---	28	25	1.0	500	.17	.05	.6	100
Orange juice, frozen concentrate, diluted with 3 parts water, by volume	1 cup	110	2	Trace	---	---	---	27	22	.2	500	.21	.03	.8	112
Orange juice, dehydrated, prepared with water (1 pound yields about 1 gallon)	1 cup	115	1	Trace	---	---	---	27	25	.5	500	.20	.06	.9	108
Orange and grapefruit juice, frozen concentrate, diluted with 3 parts water, by volume	1 cup	110	1	Trace	---	---	---	26	20	.2	270	.16	.02	.8	102
Papayas, raw, ½-inch cubes	1 cup	70	1	Trace	---	---	---	18	36	.5	3,190	.07	.08	.5	102
Peaches:															
Raw: Sliced	1 cup	65	1	Trace	---	---	---	16	15	.8	2,230[10]	.03	.08	1.6	12
Whole, 2-in. diameter	1 peach	35	1	Trace	---	---	---	10	9	.5	1,320[10]	.02	.05	1.0	7
Canned, yellow-fleshed, solids and liquid: Syrup pack, heavy:															
Halves or slices	1 cup	200	1	Trace	---	---	---	52	10	.8	1,100	.02	.06	1.4	7
Halves (medium) and syrup	2 halves and 2 tablespoons syrup	90	Trace	Trace	---	---	---	24	5	.4	500	.01	.03	.7	3
Water pack	1 cup	75	1	Trace	---	---	---	20	10	.7	1,100	.02	.06	1.4	7
Dried: Uncooked	1 cup	420	5	1	---	---	---	109	77	9.6	6,240	.02	.31	8.5	28
Cooked, unsweetened, 10–12 halves and 6 tablespoons liquid	1 cup	220	3	1	---	---	---	58	41	5.1	3,290	.01	.15	4.2	6
Frozen: Carton, 12 ounces, not thawed	1 carton	300	1	Trace	---	---	---	77	14	1.7	2,210	.03	.14	2.4	135[11]
Can, 16 ounces, not thawed	1 can	400	2	Trace	---	---	---	103	18	2.3	2,950	.05	.18	3.2	181[11]
Peach nectar, canned	1 cup	120	Trace	Trace	---	---	---	31	10	.5	1,080	.02	.05	1.0	1
Pears:															
Raw, 3 by 2½-inch diameter[4]	1 pear	100	1	1	---	---	---	25	13	.5	30	.04	.07	.2	7

Food and Approximate Measure	Food Energy (Calories)	Protein (Grams)	Fat (total lipid) (Grams)	Fatty Acids Saturated (total) (Grams)	Unsaturated Oleic (Grams)	Linoleic (Grams)	Carbohydrate (Grams)	Calcium (Milligrams)	Iron (Milligrams)	Vitamin A Value (International Units)	Thiamine (Milligrams)	Riboflavin (Milligrams)	Niacin (Milligrams)	Ascorbic Acid (Milligrams)
Pears, canned, solids and liquid:														
Syrup pack, heavy:														
Halves or slices — 1 cup	195	1	1	---	---	---	50	13	0.5	Trace	0.03	0.05	0.3	4
Halves (medium) and syrup — 2 halves and 2 table-spoons syrup	90	Trace	Trace	---	---	---	23	6	.2	Trace	.01	.02	.2	2
Water pack — 1 cup	80	Trace	Trace	---	---	---	20	12	.5	Trace	.02	.05	.3	4
Pear nectar, canned — 1 cup	130	1	Trace	---	---	---	33	8	.2	Trace	.01	.05	Trace	1
Persimmons, Japanese — 1 persimmon	75	1	Trace	---	---	---	20	6	.4	2,740	.03	.02	.1	11
Pineapple:														
Raw, diced — 1 cup	75	1	Trace	---	---	---	19	24	.7	100	.12	.04	.3	24
Canned, heavy syrup pack, solids and liquid:														
Crushed — 1 cup	195	1	Trace	---	---	---	50	29	.8	120	.20	.06	.5	17
Sliced, slices and juice — 2 small or 1 large and 2 table-spoons juice	90	Trace	Trace	---	---	---	24	13	.4	50	.09	.03	.2	8
Pineapple juice, canned — 1 cup	135	1	Trace	---	---	---	34	37	.7	120	.12	.04	.5	22
Plums, all except prunes:														
Raw, about 2 ounces[4] — 1 plum	25	Trace	Trace	---	---	---	7	7	.3	140	.02	.02	.3	3
Canned, syrup pack (Italian prunes):														
Plums (with pits) and juice[4] — 1 cup	205	1	Trace	---	---	---	53	22	2.2	2,970	.05	.05	.9	4
Plums (without pits) and juice — 3 plums and 2 tablespoons juice	100	Trace	Trace	---	---	---	26	11	1.1	1,470	.03	.02	.5	2
Prunes, dried, "softenized," medium:														
Uncooked[4] — 4 prunes	70	1	Trace	---	---	---	18	14	1.1	440	.02	.04	.4	1
Cooked, unsweetened, 17–18 prunes and ⅓ cup liquid[4] — 1 cup	295	2	1	---	---	---	78	60	4.5	1,860	.08	.18	1.7	2

		Cal.	Protein	Fat	(Sat.)	(Oleic)	(Linoleic)	Carbohydrate	Calcium	Iron	Vit. A	Thiamine	Riboflavin	Niacin	Ascorbic acid
Prune juice, canned	1 cup	200	1	Trace	---	---	---	49	36	10.5	---	.02	.03	1.1	4
Raisins, dried	1 cup	460	4	Trace	---	---	---	124	99	5.6	30	.18	.13	.9	2
Raspberries, red:															
Raw	1 cup	70	1	1	---	---	---	17	27	1.1	160	.04	.11	1.1	31
Frozen, 10-ounce carton, not thawed	1 carton	275	2	1	---	---	---	70	37	1.7	200	.06	.17	1.7	59
Rhubarb, cooked, sugar added	1 cup	385	1	Trace	---	---	---	98	212	1.6	220	.06	.15	.7	17
Strawberries:															
Raw, capped	1 cup	55	1	1	---	---	---	13	31	1.5	90	.04	.10	1.0	88
Frozen, 10-ounce carton, not thawed	1 carton	310	1	1	---	---	---	79	40	2.0	90	.06	.17	1.5	150
Frozen, 16-ounce can, not thawed	1 can	495	2	1	---	---	---	126	64	3.2	150	.09	.27	2.4	240
Tangerines, raw, medium, 2½-inch diameter[4]	1 tangerine	40	1	Trace	---	---	---	10	34	.3	350	.05	.02	.1	26
Tangerine juice:															
Canned, unsweetened	1 cup	105	1	Trace	---	---	---	25	45	.5	1,040	.14	.04	.3	56
Frozen concentrate, diluted with 3 parts water, by volume	1 cup	115	1	Trace	---	---	---	27	45	.5	1,020	.14	.04	.3	67
Watermelon, raw, wedge, 4 by 8 inches with rind	1 wedge	115	2	1	---	---	---	27	30	2.1	2,510	.13	.13	.7	30

GRAIN PRODUCTS

		Cal.	Protein	Fat	(Sat.)	(Oleic)	(Linoleic)	Carbohydrate	Calcium	Iron	Vit. A	Thiamine	Riboflavin	Niacin	Ascorbic acid
Biscuits, baking powder with enriched flour, 2½-inch diameter	1 biscuit	140	3	6	2	3	1	17	46	.6	Trace	.08	.08	.7	Trace
Bran flakes (40 percent bran), added thiamine	1 ounce	85	3	1	---	---	---	23	20	1.2	0	.11	.05	1.7	0
Breads:															
Boston brown bread, slice, 3 by ¾ inch	1 slice	100	3	1	---	---	---	22	43	.9	0	.05	.03	.6	0
Cracked-wheat bread:															
Loaf, 1-pound, 20 slices	1 loaf	1,190	39	10	2	5	2	236	399	5.0	Trace	.53	.42	5.8	Trace
Slice	1 slice	60	2	1	---	---	---	12	20	.3	Trace	.03	.02	.3	Trace
French or vienna bread:															
Enriched, 1-pound loaf	1 loaf	1,315	41	14	3	8	2	251	195	10.0	Trace	1.26	.98	11.3	Trace
Unenriched, 1-pound loaf	1 loaf	1,315	41	14	3	8	2	251	195	3.2	Trace	.39	.39	3.6	Trace
Italian bread:															
Enriched, 1-pound loaf	1 loaf	1,250	41	4	Trace	Trace	2	256	77	10.0	0	1.31	.93	11.7	0
Unenriched, 1-pound loaf	1 loaf	1,250	41	4	Trace	Trace	2	256	77	3.2	0	.39	.27	3.6	0

(Continued)

Food and Approximate Measure

Food and Approximate Measure		Food Energy (Calories)	Protein (Grams)	Fat (total lipid) (Grams)	Fatty Acids Saturated (total) (Grams)	Unsaturated Oleic (Grams)	Unsaturated Linoleic (Grams)	Carbohydrate (Grams)	Calcium (Milligrams)	Iron (Milligrams)	Vitamin A Value (International Units)	Thiamine (Milligrams)	Riboflavin (Milligrams)	Niacin (Milligrams)	Ascorbic Acid (Milligrams)
Breads, continued:															
Raisin bread:															
Loaf, 1-pound, 20 slices	1 loaf	1,190	30	13	3	8	2	243	322	5.9	Trace	0.24	0.42	3.0	Trace
Slice	1 slice	60	2	1				12	16	.3	Trace	.01	.02	.2	Trace
Rye bread:															
American, light (⅓ rye, ⅔ wheat):															
Loaf, 1-pound, 20 slices	1 loaf	1,100	41	5				236	340	7.3	0	.81	.33	6.4	0
Slice	1 slice	55	2	Trace				12	17	.4	0	.04	.02	.3	0
Pumpernickel, loaf, 1-pound	1 loaf	1,115	41	5				241	381	10.9	0	1.05	.63	5.4	0
White bread, enriched:															
1 to 2 percent nonfat dry milk:															
Loaf, 1-pound, 20 slices	1 loaf	1,225	39	15	3	8	2	229	318	10.9	Trace	1.13	.77	10.4	Trace
Slice	1 slice	60	2	1	Trace	Trace	Trace	12	16	.6	Trace	.06	.04	.5	Trace
3 to 4 percent nonfat dry milk:[12]															
Loaf, 1-pound	1 loaf	1,225	39	15	3	8	2	229	381	11.3	Trace	1.13	.95	10.8	Trace
Slice, 20 per loaf	1 slice	60	2	1	Trace	Trace	Trace	12	19	.6	Trace	.06	.05	.6	Trace
Slice, toasted	1 slice	60	2	1	Trace	Trace	Trace	12	19	.6	Trace	.05	.05	.6	Trace
Slice, 26 per loaf	1 slice	45	1	1	Trace	Trace	Trace	9	14	.4	Trace	.04	.04	.4	Trace
5 to 6 percent nonfat dry milk:															
Loaf, 1-pound, 20 slices	1 loaf	1,245	41	17	4	10	2	228	435	11.3	Trace	1.22	.91	11.0	Trace
Slice	1 slice	65	2	1	Trace	Trace	Trace	12	22	.6	Trace	.06	.05	.6	Trace
White bread, unenriched:															
1 to 2 percent nonfat dry milk:															
Loaf, 1-pound, 20 slices	1 loaf	1,225	39	15	3	8	2	229	318	3.2	Trace	.40	.36	5.6	Trace
Slice	1 slice	60	2	1	Trace	Trace	Trace	12	16	.2	Trace	.02	.02	.3	Trace
3 to 4 percent nonfat dry milk:[12]															
Loaf, 1-pound	1 loaf	1,225	39	15	3	8	2	229	381	3.2	Trace	.31	.39	5.0	Trace
Slice, 20 per loaf	1 slice	60	2	1	Trace	Trace	Trace	12	19	.2	Trace	.02	.02	.3	Trace
Slice, toasted	1 slice	60	2	1	Trace	Trace	Trace	12	19	.2	Trace	.01	.02	.3	Trace
Slice, 26 per loaf	1 slice	45	1	1	Trace	Trace	Trace	9	14	.1	Trace	.01	.01	.2	Trace
5 to 6 percent nonfat dry milk:															
Loaf, 1 pound, 20 slices	1 loaf	1,245	41	17	4	10	2	228	435	3.2	Trace	.32	.59	4.1	Trace
Slice	1 slice	65	2	1	Trace	Trace	Trace	12	22	.2	Trace	.02	.03	.2	Trace

Food	Measure														
Whole-wheat bread, made with 2 percent nonfat dry milk:																
Loaf, 1-pound, 20 slices	1 loaf	1,105	48	14	3	6	3	216	449	10.4	Trace	1.17	.56	12.9	Trace
Slice	1 slice	55	2	1	Trace	Trace	Trace	11	23	.5	Trace	.06	.03	.7	Trace
Slice, toasted	1 slice	55	2	1	Trace	Trace	Trace	11	22	.5	Trace	.05	.03	.6	Trace
Breadcrumbs, dry grated	1 cup	345	11	4	1	2	1	65	107	3.2	Trace	.19	.26	3.1	Trace
Cakes:[13]																
Angelfood cake; sector, 2-inch (1/12 of 8-inch-diameter cake)	1 sector	110	3	Trace	---	---	---	24	4	.1	0	Trace	.06	.1	0
Chocolate cake, chocolate icing; sector, 2-inch (1/16 of 10-inch-diameter layer cake)	1 sector	445	5	20	8	10	1	67	84	1.2	190[14]	.03	.12	.3	Trace
Fruitcake, dark (made with enriched flour); piece, 2 by 2 by 1/2 inch	1 piece	115	1	5	1	3	1	18	22	.8	40[14]	.04	.04	.2	Trace
Gingerbread (made with enriched flour); piece, 2 by 2 by 2 inches	1 piece	175	2	6	1	4	Trace	29	37	1.3	50	.06	.06	.5	0
Plain cake and cupcakes, without icing:																
Piece, 3 by 2 by 1 1/2 inches	1 piece	200	2	8	2	5	1	31	35	.2	90[14]	.01	.05	.1	Trace
Cupcake, 2¾-inch diameter	1 cupcake	145	2	6	1	3	Trace	22	26	.2	70[14]	.01	.03	.1	Trace
Plain cake and cupcakes, with chocolate icing:																
Sector, 2-inch (1/16 of 10-inch-layer cake)	1 sector	370	4	14	5	7	1	59	63	.6	180[14]	.02	.09	.2	Trace
Cupcake, 2¾-inch diameter	1 cupcake	185	2	7	2	4	Trace	30	32	.3	90[14]	.01	.04	.1	Trace
Poundcake, oldfashioned, slice, 2¾ by 3 by 5/8 inch	1 slice	140	2	9	2	5	1	14	6	.2	80[14]	.01	.03	.1	0
Sponge cake, sector, 2-inch (1/12 of 8-inch-diameter cake)	1 sector	120	3	2	1	1	Trace	22	12	.5	180	.02	.06	.1	Trace
Cookies:																
Plain and assorted, 3-inch diameter	1 cookie	120	1	5	---	---	---	18	9	.2	20	.01	.01	.1	Trace
Fig bars, small	1 fig bar	55	1	1	---	---	---	12	12	.2	20	.01	.01	.1	Trace
Corn, rice and wheat flakes, mixed, added nutrients	1 ounce	110	2	Trace	---	---	Trace	24	11	.5	0	.11	----	.9	0

Food and Approximate Measure		Food Energy (Calories)	Protein (Grams)	Fat (total lipid) (Grams)	Fatty Acids Saturated (total) (Grams)	Unsaturated Oleic (Grams)	Unsaturated Linoleic (Grams)	Carbohydrate (Grams)	Calcium (Milligrams)	Iron (Milligrams)	Vitamin A Value (International Units)	Thiamine (Milligrams)	Riboflavin (Milligrams)	Niacin (Milligrams)	Ascorbic Acid (Milligrams)
Corn flakes, added nutrients:															
Plain	1 ounce	110	2	Trace	---	---	---	24	5	0.4	0	0.12	0.02	0.6	0
Sugar-covered	1 ounce	110	1	Trace	---	---	---	26	3	.3	0	.12	.01	.5	0
Corn grits, degermed, cooked:															
Enriched	1 cup	120	3	Trace	---	---	---	27	2	.7[15]	150[16]	.10[15]	.07[15]	1.0[15]	0
Unenriched	1 cup	120	3	Trace	---	---	---	27	2	.2	150[16]	.05	.02	.5	0
Cornmeal, white or yellow, dry:															
Whole ground, unbolted	1 cup	420	11	5	1	2	2	87	24	2.8	600[16]	.45	.13	2.4	0
Degermed, enriched	1 cup	525	11	2	Trace	1	1	114	9	4.2[15]	640[16]	.64[15]	.38[15]	5.1[15]	0
Corn muffins, made with enriched degermed cornmeal and enriched flour; muffin, 2¾-inch diameter	1 muffin	150	3	5	2	2	Trace	23	50	.8	80[17]	.09	.11	.8	Trace
Corn, puffed, presweetened, added nutrients	1 ounce	110	1	Trace	---	---	---	26	3	.5	0	.12	.05	.6	0
Crackers:															
Graham, plain	4 small or 2 medium	55	1	1	---	---	---	10	6	.2	0	.01	.03	.2	0
Saltines, 2 inches square	2 crackers	35	1	1	---	---	---	6	2	.1	0	Trace	Trace	.1	0
Soda:															
Cracker, 2½-inches square	2 crackers	50	1	1	Trace	1	Trace	8	2	.2	0	Trace	Trace	.1	0
Oyster crackers	10 crackers	45	1	1	Trace	1	Trace	7	2	.2	0	Trace	Trace	.1	0
Cracker meal	1 tablespoon	45	1	1	Trace	1	Trace	7	2	.1	0	.01	Trace	.1	0
Doughnuts, cake type	1 doughnut	125	1	6	1	4	Trace	16	13	.4[18]	30	.05[18]	.05[18]	.4[18]	Trace
Farina, regular, enriched, cooked	1 cup	100	3	Trace	---	---	---	21	10	.7[15]	0	.11[15]	.07[15]	1.0[15]	0
Macaroni, cooked:															
Enriched:															
Cooked, firm stage	1 cup	190	6	1	---	---	---	39	14	1.4[15]	0	.23[15]	.14[15]	1.9[15]	0
Cooked until tender	1 cup	155	5	1	---	---	---	32	11	1.3[15]	0	.19[15]	.11[15]	1.5[15]	0
Unenriched:															
Cooked, firm stage	1 cup	190	6	1	---	---	---	39	14	.6	0	.02	.02	.5	0
Cooked until tender	1 cup	155	5	1	---	---	---	32	11	.6	0	.02	.02	.4	0

Food	Measure														
Macaroni (enriched) and cheese, baked	1 cup	470	18	24	11	10	1	44	398	2.0	950	.22	.44	2.0	Trace
Muffins, with enriched white flour; muffin, 2¾-inch diameter	1 muffin	140	4	5	1	3	Trace	20	50	.8	50	.08	.11	.7	Trace
Noodles (egg noodles), cooked: Enriched	1 cup	200	7	2	1	1	Trace	37	16	1.4[15]	110	.23[15]	.14[15]	1.8[15]	0
Unenriched	1 cup	200	7	2	1	1	Trace	37	16	1.0	110	.04	.03	.7	0
Oats (with or without corn), puffed, added nutrients	1 ounce	115	3	2	Trace	1	1	21	50	1.3	0	.28	.05	.5	0
Oatmeal or rolled oats, regular or quick-cooking, cooked	1 cup	130	5	2	Trace	1	1	23	21	1.4	0	.19	.05	.3	0
Pancakes (griddlecakes), 4-inch diameter: Wheat, enriched flour (home recipe)	1 cake	60	2	2	Trace	1	Trace	9	27	.4	30	.05	.06	.3	Trace
Buckwheat (buckwheat pancake mix, made with egg and milk)	1 cake	55	2	2	1	1	Trace	6	59	.4	60	.03	.04	.2	Trace
Piecrust, plain, baked: Enriched flour; lower crust, 9-inch shell	1 crust	675	8	45	10	29	3	59	19	2.3	0	.27	.19	2.4	0
Unenriched flour; lower crust, 9-inch shell	1 crust	675	8	45	10	29	3	59	19	.7	0	.04	.04	.6	0
Pies (piecrust made with unenriched flour); sector, 4-inch, 1/7 of 9-inch-diameter pie:															
Apple	1 sector	345	3	15	4	9	1	51	11	.4	40	.03	.02	.5	1
Cherry	1 sector	355	4	15	4	10	1	52	19	.4	590	.03	.03	.6	1
Custard	1 sector	280	8	14	5	8	1	30	125	.8	300	.07	.21	.4	0
Lemon meringue	1 sector	305	4	12	4	7	1	45	17	.6	200	.04	.10	.2	4
Mince	1 sector	365	3	16	4	10	1	56	38	1.4	Trace	.09	.05	.5	1
Pumpkin	1 sector	275	5	15	5	7	1	32	66	.6	3,210	.04	.13	.6	Trace
Pizza (cheese); 5½-inch sector; 1/8 of 14-inch-diameter pie	1 sector	185	7	6	2	3	Trace	27	107	.7	290	.04	.12	.7	4
Popcorn, popped, with added oil and salt	1 cup	65	1	3	2	Trace	Trace	8	1	.3	---	---	.01	.2	0
Pretzels, small stick	5 sticks	20	Trace	Trace	---	---	---	4	1	0.0	0	Trace	Trace	Trace	0
Rice, white (fully milled or polished), enriched, cooked: Common commercial varieties, all types	1 cup	185	3	Trace	---	---	---	41	17	1.5[19]	0	.19[19]	.01[19]	1.6[19]	0
Long grain, parboiled	1 cup	185	4	Trace	---	---	---	41	33	1.4[19]	0	.19[19]	.02[19]	2.0[19]	0

(Continued)

Food and Approximate Measure		Food Energy (Calories)	Protein (Grams)	Fat (total lipid) (Grams)	Fatty Acids			Carbohydrate (Grams)	Calcium (Milligrams)	Iron (Milligrams)	Vitamin A Value (International Units)	Thiamine (Milligrams)	Riboflavin (Milligrams)	Niacin (Milligrams)	Ascorbic Acid (Milligrams)
					Saturated (total) (Grams)	Unsaturated Oleic (Grams)	Unsaturated Linoleic (Grams)								
Rice, puffed, added nutrients (without salt)	1 cup	55	1	Trace	---	---	---	13	3	0.3	0	0.06	0.01	0.6	0
Rice flakes, added nutrients	1 cup	115	2	Trace	---	---	---	26	9	.5	0	.10	.02	1.6	0
Rolls:															
Plain, pan; 12 per 16 ounces:															
Enriched	1 roll	115	3	2	Trace	1	Trace	20	28	.7	Trace	.11	.07	.8	Trace
Unenriched	1 roll	115	3	2	Trace	1	Trace	20	28	.3	Trace	.02	.03	.3	Trace
Hard, round; 12 per 22 ounces	1 roll	160	5	2	Trace	1	Trace	31	24	.4	Trace	.03	.05	.4	Trace
Sweet, pan; 12 per 18 ounces	1 roll	135	4	4	1	2	Trace	21	37	.3	30	.03	.06	.4	Trace
Rye wafers, whole-grain, 1/8 by 3½ inches	2 wafers	45	2	Trace				10	7	.5	0	.04	.03	.2	0
Spaghetti, cooked, tender stage (14 to 20 minutes):															
Enriched	1 cup	155	5	1	---	---	---	32	11	1.3[15]	0	.19[15]	.11[15]	1.5[15]	0
Unenriched	1 cup	155	5	1	---	---	---	32	11	.6	0	.02	.02	.4	0
Spaghetti with meat balls in tomato sauce (home recipe)	1 cup	335	19	12	4	6	1	39	125	3.8	1,600	.26	.30	4.0	22
Spaghetti in tomato sauce with cheese (home recipe)	1 cup	260	9	9	2	5	1	37	80	2.2	1,080	.24	.18	2.4	14
Waffles, with enriched flour, ½ by 4½ by 5½ inches	1 waffle	210	7	7	2	4	1	28	85	1.3	250	.13	.19	1.0	Trace
Wheat, puffed:															
With added nutrients	1 ounce	105	4	Trace	---	---	---	22	8	1.2	0	.15	.07	2.2	0
With added nutrients, with sugar and honey	1 ounce	105	2	1	---	---	---	25	7	.9	0	.14	.05	1.8	0
Wheat, rolled; cooked	1 cup	175	5	1	---	---	---	40	19	1.7	0	.17	.06	2.1	0
Wheat, shredded, plain	1 ounce	100	3	1	---	---	---	23	12	1.0	0	.06	.03	1.2	0
Wheat and malted barley flakes, with added nutrients	1 ounce	110	2	Trace	---	---	---	24	14	.7	0	.13	.03	1.1	0
Wheat flakes, with added nutrients	1 ounce	100	3	Trace	---	---	---	23	12	1.2	0	.18	.04	1.4	0

Food	Measure														
Wheat flours:															
Whole-wheat, from hard wheats, stirred	1 cup	400	16	2	Trace	1	1	85	49	4.0	0	.66	.14	5.2	0
All-purpose or family flour:															
Enriched, sifted	1 cup	400	12	1	Trace	Trace	Trace	84	18	3.2[15]	0	.48[15]	.29[15]	3.8[15]	0
Unenriched, sifted	1 cup	400	12	1	Trace	Trace	Trace	84	18	.9	0	.07	.05	1.0	0
Cake, enriched	1 cup	385	10	1	Trace	Trace	Trace	82	292	3.2[15]	0	.49[15]	.29[15]	3.9[15]	0
Cake or pastry flour, sifted	1 cup	365	8	1	Trace	Trace	Trace	79	17	.5	0	.03	.03	.7	0
Wheat germ, crude, commercially milled	1 cup	245	18	7	2	4	4	32	49	6.4	0	1.36	.46	2.9	0
FATS, OILS															
Butter, 4 sticks per pound:															
Sticks, 2	1 cup	1,625	1	184	101	61	6	1	45	0.0	7,500[20]	---	---	---	0
Stick, ⅛	1 tablespoon	100	Trace	11	6	4	Trace	Trace	3	0.0	460[20]	---	---	---	0
Pat or square (64 per pound)	1 pat	50	Trace	6	3	2	Trace	Trace	1	0.0	230[20]	---	---	---	0
Fats, cooking:															
Lard	1 cup	1,985	0	220	84	101	22	0	0	0.0	0	0.00	0.00	0.0	0
Vegetable fats	1 cup	1,770	0	200	46	130	14	0	0	0.0	---	0.00	0.00	0.0	0
Margarine, 4 sticks per pound:															
Sticks, 2	1 cup	1,635	1	184	37	105	33	1	45	0.0	7,500[21]	---	---	---	0
Stick, ⅛	1 tablespoon	100	Trace	11	2	6	2	Trace	3	0.0	460[21]	---	---	---	0
Pat or square (64 per pound)	1 pat	50	Trace	6	1	3	1	Trace	1	0.0	230[21]	---	---	---	0
Oils, salad or cooking:															
Corn	1 tablespoon	125	0	14	1	4	7	0	0	0.0	---	0.00	0.00	0.0	0
Cottonseed	1 tablespoon	125	0	14	4	3	7	0	0	0.0	---	0.00	0.00	0.0	0
Olive	1 tablespoon	125	0	14	2	11	1	0	0	0.0	---	0.00	0.00	0.0	0
Soybean	1 tablespoon	125	0	14	2	3	7	0	0	0.0	---	0.00	0.00	0.0	0
Salad dressings:															
Blue cheese	1 tablespoon	80	1	8	2	2	4	1	13	Trace	30	Trace	.02	Trace	Trace
Commercial, mayonnaise type	1 tablespoon	65	Trace	6	1	1	3	2	2	Trace	30	Trace	Trace	Trace	---
French	1 tablespoon	60	Trace	6	1	1	3	3	2	.1	---	---	---	---	---
Home cooked, boiled	1 tablespoon	30	1	2	1	1	Trace	3	15	.1	80	.01	.03	Trace	Trace
Mayonnaise	1 tablespoon	110	Trace	12	2	3	6	Trace	3	.1	40	Trace	.01	Trace	Trace
Thousand island	1 tablespoon	75	Trace	8	1	2	4	2	2	.1	50	Trace	Trace	Trace	Trace
SUGARS, SWEETS															
Candy:															
Caramels	1 ounce	115	1	3	2	1	Trace	22	42	.4	Trace	.01	.05	Trace	Trace
Chocolate, milk, plain	1 ounce	150	2	9	5	3	Trace	16	65	.3	80	.02	.09	.1	Trace
Fudge, plain	1 ounce	115	1	3	2	1	Trace	21	22	.3	Trace	.01	.03	.1	Trace
Hard candy	1 ounce	110	0	Trace	---	---	---	28	6	.5	0	0.00	0.00	0.0	0
Marshmallows	1 ounce	90	1	Trace	---	---	---	23	5	.5	0	0.00	Trace	Trace	0

(Continued)

Food and Approximate Measure		Food Energy	Protein	Fat (total lipid)	Fatty Acids			Carbo-hy-drate	Cal-cium	Iron	Vita-min A Value	Thia-mine	Ribo-flavin	Nia-cin	Ascor-bic Acid
					Satu-rated (total)	Unsaturated									
						Oleic	Lino-leic								
		Calo-ries	Grams	Grams	Grams	Grams	Grams	Grams	Milli-grams	Milli-grams	Inter-national Units	Milli-grams	Milli-grams	Milli-grams	Milli-grams
Chocolate syrup, thin type	1 tablespoon	50	Trace	Trace	Trace	Trace	Trace	13	3	0.3	---	Trace	0.01	0.1	0
Honey, strained or extracted	1 tablespoon	65	Trace	0				17	1	.1	0	Trace	.01	.1	Trace
Jams and preserves	1 tablespoon	55	Trace	Trace				14	4	.2	Trace	Trace	.01	Trace	Trace
Jellies	1 tablespoon	55	Trace	Trace				14	4	.3	Trace	Trace	.01	Trace	1
Molasses, cane; light (first extraction)	1 tablespoon	50	---					13	33	.9	---	0.01	.01	Trace	0
Syrup, table blends	1 tablespoon	60	0	0				15	9	.8	0	0.00	0.00	0.0	0
Sugars (cane or beet):															
Granulated	1 cup	770	0	0				199	0	.2	0	0.00	0.00	0.0	0
	1 tablespoon	45	0	0				12	0	Trace	0	0.00	0.00	0.0	0
Powdered, stirred before measuring	1 cup	495	0	0				127	0	.1	0	0.00	0.00	0.0	0
	1 tablespoon	30	0	0				8	0	Trace	0	0.00	0.00	0.0	0
Brown, firm-packed	1 cup	820	0	0				212	187	7.5	0	.02	.07	.4	0
	1 tablespoon	50	0	0				13	12	.5	0	Trace	Trace	Trace	0
MISCELLANEOUS ITEMS															
Beverages, carbonated:															
Cola type	1 cup	95	0	0				24	---	---	0	0.00	0.00	0.0	0
Ginger ale	1 cup	70	0	0				18	---	---	0	0.00	0.00	0.0	0
Bouillon cube, ⅝ inch	1 cube	5	1	Trace				Trace	---	---	---	---	---	---	---
Chili sauce (mainly tomatoes)	1 tablespoon	20	Trace	Trace				4	3	.1	240	.02	.01	.3	3
Chocolate:															
Bitter or baking	1 ounce	145	3	15	8	6	Trace	8	22	1.9	20	.01	.07	.4	0
Sweet	1 ounce	150	1	10	6	4	Trace	16	27	.4	Trace	.01	.04	.1	Trace
Cider. See Fruits, apple juice.															
Gelatin, dry:															
Plain	1 tablespoon	35	9	Trace											
Dessert powder, 3-ounce package	½ cup	315	8	0				75							
Gelatin dessert, ready-to-eat:															
Plain	1 cup	140	4	0				34							
With fruit	1 cup	160	3	Trace				40							

Food	Measure	Grams	Food energy (Calories)	Protein (g)	Fat (g)	Saturated fatty acids (g)	Oleic (g)	Linoleic (g)	Carbohydrate (g)	Calcium (mg)	Iron (mg)	Vitamin A (I.U.)	Thiamine (mg)	Riboflavin (mg)	Niacin (mg)	Ascorbic acid (mg)
Olives, pickled:																
Green	4 medium or 3 extra large	15	15	Trace	2	—	2	—	Trace	8	.2	40	—	—	—	—
Ripe, Mission	3 small or 2 large	15	15	Trace	2	—	2	—	Trace	9	.1	10	Trace	Trace	—	—
Pickles, cucumber:																
Dill, large, 4 by 1¾ inches	1 pickle	—	15	1	Trace	—	—	—	3	35	1.4	140	Trace	.03	Trace	8
Sweet, 2¾ by ¾ inches	1 pickle	—	30	Trace	Trace	—	—	—	7	2	.2	20	Trace	Trace	Trace	1
Popcorn. See Grain products.																
Sherbet, orange	1 cup	2	260	2	2	—	—	—	59	31	Trace	110	.02	.06	Trace	4
Soups, canned; ready-to-serve:																
Bean with pork	1 cup	8	170	8	6	2	2	1	22	62	2.2	650	.14	.07	1.0	2
Beef noodle	1 cup	4	70	4	3	1	1	—	7	8	1.0	50	.05	.06	1.0	Trace
Beef bouillon, broth, consomme	1 cup	5	30	5	0	0	0	0	3	Trace	.5	Trace	Trace	.02	1.2	—
Chicken noodle	1 cup	4	65	4	2	Trace	1	1	8	10	.5	50	.02	.02	.8	Trace
Clam chowder	1 cup	2	85	2	3	—	3	—	13	36	1.0	920	.03	.03	1.0	—
Cream soup (mushroom)	1 cup	2	135	2	10	—	2	5	10	41	.5	70	.02	.12	.7	Trace
Minestrone	1 cup	5	105	5	3	—	—	—	14	37	1.0	2,350	.07	.05	1.0	—
Pea, green	1 cup	6	130	6	2	1	1	—	23	44	1.0	340	.05	.05	1.0	7
Tomato	1 cup	2	90	2	2	Trace	—	1	16	15	.7	1,000	.06	.05	1.1	12
Vegetable with beef broth	1 cup	3	80	3	2	—	—	—	14	20	.8	3,250	.05	.02	1.2	—
Starch (cornstarch)	1 tablespoon	Trace	30	Trace	Trace	—	—	—	7	0	0.0	0	0.00	0.00	0.0	0
Tapioca, quick-cooking granulated, dry, stirred before measuring	1 tablespoon	Trace	35	Trace	Trace	Trace	Trace	Trace	9	1	Trace	0	Trace	0.00	Trace	—
Vinegar	1 tablespoon	0	2	0	0	—	—	—	1	1	.1	—	—	—	.1	0
White sauce, medium	1 cup	10	430	11	33	18	11	1	23	305	.5	1,220	.12	.44	.5	Trace
Yeast:																
Baker's:																
Compressed	1 ounce	3	25	3	Trace	—	—	—	3	4	1.4	Trace	.20	.47	3.2	Trace
Dry active	1 ounce	10	80	10	Trace	—	—	—	11	12	4.6	Trace	.66	1.53	10.4	Trace
Brewer's, dry, debittered	1 tablespoon	3	25	3	Trace	—	—	—	3	17	1.4	Trace	1.25	.34	3.0	Trace

[1] Outer layer of fat on the cut was removed to within approximately ½ inch of the lean. Deposits of fat within the cut were not removed.

[2] Vitamin values based on drained solids.

[3] Based on total contents of can. If bones are discarded, value will be greatly reduced.

[4] Measure applies to entire vegetable or fruit including parts not usually eaten.

[5] Based on yellow varieties; white varieties contain only a trace of cryptoxanthin and carotenes, the pigments in corn that have biological activity.

[6] Year-round average. Samples marketed from November through May average around 15 milligrams per 150-gram tomato; from June through October, around 39 milligrams.

[7] Value based on varieties with orange-colored flesh; for green-fleshed varieties value is about 540 I.U. per ½ melon.

[8] About 5 milligrams per 8 fluid ounces is from cranberries. Ascorbic acid is usually added to approximately 100 milligrams per 8 fluid ounces.

(Continued)

[9] For white-fleshed varieties value is about 20 I.U. per cup; for red-fleshed varieties, 1,080 I.U. per cup.

[10] Based on yellow-fleshed varieties; for white-fleshed varieties value is about 50 I.U. per 114-gram peach and 80 I.U. per cup of sliced peaches.

[11] Average weighted in accordance with commercial freezing practices. For products without added ascorbic acid, value is about 37 milligrams per 12-ounce carton and 50 milligrams per 16-ounce can; for those with added ascorbic acid, 139 milligrams per 12 ounces and 186 milligrams per 16 ounces.

[12] When the amount of nonfat dry milk in commercial white bread is unknown, values for bread with 3 to 4 percent nonfat dry milk are suggested.

[13] Unenriched cake flour and vegetable cooking fat used unless otherwise specified.

[14] If the fat used in the recipe is butter or fortified margarine, the vitamin A value for chocolate cake with chocolate icing will be 490 I.U. per 2-inch sector; the value for fruitcake will be 100 I.U. per 2- by 2- by 1/2-inch piece; for plain cake without icing, 300 I.U. per 3- by 2- by 1 1/2-inch piece; for plain cupcake, 220 I.U.; for plain cake with chocolate icing, 440 I.U. per 2-inch sector; for cupcake with chocolate icing, 220 I.U.; and for pound cake, 300 I.U. per 2 3/4- by 3- by 5/8-inch slice.

[15] Iron, thiamine, riboflavin, and niacin are based on the minimum levels of enrichment specified in standards of identity promulgated under the Federal Food, Drug, and Cosmetic Act.

[16] Vitamin A value based on yellow product. White product contains only a trace.

[17] Based on recipe using white cornmeal; if yellow cornmeal is used, the vitamin A value is 140 I.U. per muffin.

[18] Based on product made with enriched flour. With unenriched flour, approximate values per doughnut are: Iron, 0.2 milligram; thiamine, 0.01 milligram; riboflavin, 0.03 milligram; niacin, 0.2 milligram.

[19] Iron, thiamine, and niacin are based on the minimum levels of enrichment specified in standards of identity promulgated under the Federal Food, Drug, and Cosmetic Act. Riboflavin is based on unenriched rice. When the minimum level of enrichment for riboflavin specified in the standards of identity becomes effective, the value will be 0.12 milligram per cup of parboiled rice and of white rice.

[20] Year-round average.

[21] Based on the average vitamin A content of fortified margarine. Federal specifications for fortified margarine require a minimum of 15,000 I.U. of vitamin A per pound.

* From Nutritive Value of Foods, Home and Garden Bulletin 72, U.S. Department of Agriculture, 1965.

References

Books

BATJER, MARGARET Q., and MIMI ATWATER: *Meals for the Modern Family,* John Wiley & Sons, Inc., New York, 1961.

BERRY, MARY: *Manners Made Easy.* McGraw-Hill Book Co., New York, 1966.

BOGERT, L. JEAN: *Nutrition and Physical Fitness,* W. B. Saunders Company, Philadelphia, 1966.

CARSON, BYRTA, and MARUE CARSON RAMEE: *How You Plan and Prepare Meals,* McGraw-Hill Book Co., New York, 1968.

CHANEY, MARGARET S.: *Nutrition,* Houghton Mifflin Co., Boston, 1966.

CHURCH, CHARLES F., and HELEN N.: *Bowes and Church's Food Values of Portions Commonly Used,* J. B. Lippincott Co., Philadelphia, 1966.

Consumers All: The Yearbook of Agriculture, U.S. Department of Agriculture, Washington, D.C., 1965.

COTE, PATRICIA: *People, Food, and Science.* Ginn & Company, Boston, 1968.

CRONAN, MARION L., and JUNE C. ATWOOD: *Foods in Homemaking,* Chas. A. Bennett Co., Inc., Peoria, 1965.

CROSS, ALEENE: *Enjoying Family Living.* J. B. Lippincott Co., Philadelphia, 1967.

EPPRIGHT, ERCEL, MATTIE PATTERSON, and HELEN BARBOUR: *Teaching Nutrition,* Iowa State University Press, Ames, Iowa, 1963.

FITZSIMMONS, CLEO, and NELL WHITE: *Management for You,* J. B. Lippincott Co., Philadelphia, 1964.

FLECK, HENRIETTA, and ELIZABETH MUNVES: *Introduction to Nutrition,* The Macmillan Company, New York, 1962.

Food: The Yearbook of Agriculture, U.S. Department of Agriculture, Washington, D.C., 1959.

GILBRETH, LILLIAN M., ORPHA MAE THOMAS, and ELEANOR CLYMER: *Management in the Home,* Dodd, Mead & Company, New York, 1959.

GOLDMAN, MARY E.: *Planning and Serving Your Meals,* McGraw-Hill Book Co., New York, 1959.

GUTHRIE, HELEN: *Introductory Nutrition,* The C. V. Mosby Company, St. Louis, 1967.

Handbook of Food Preparation, American Home Economics Assn., Washington, D.C., 1964.

KILANDER, HOLGER F.: *Health for Modern Living,* Prentice-Hall, Inc., Englewood Cliffs, N.J., 1965.

KINDER, FAYE: *Meal Management,* The Macmillan Company, New York, 1968.

LEVERTON, RUTH: *Food Becomes You,* Iowa State University Press, Ames, Iowa, 1965.

MARTIN, ETHEL A.: *Nutrition in Action,* Holt, Rinehart and Winston, Inc., New York, 1965.

McDERMOTT, IRENE E., MABEL B. TRILLING, and FLORENCE W. NICHOLAS: *Food for Modern Living,* J. B. Lippincott Co., Philadelphia, 1967.

McHENRY, EARLE W.: *Foods Without Fads,* J. B. Lippincott Co., Philadelphia, 1960.

McLEAN, BETH BAILEY: *Meal Planning and Table Service,* Chas. A. Bennett Co., Inc., Peoria, 1967.

MITCHELL, HELEN S., HENDERIKA J. RYNBERGEN, LINNEA ANDERSON, and MARJORIE V. DIBBLE: *Cooper's Nutrition in Health and Disease,* J. B. Lippincott Co., Philadelphia, 1968.

NICKELL, PAULENA, and JEAN MUIR DORSEY: *Management in Family Living,* John Wiley & Sons, Inc., New York, 1967.

PEET, LOUISE J.: *Young Homemaker's Equipment Guide,* Iowa State University Press, Ames, Iowa, 1967.

POLLARD, L. BELLE: *Experiences with Food,* Ginn & Company, Boston, 1964.

Protecting Our Food: The Yearbook of Agriculture, U.S. Department of Agriculture, Washington, D.C., 1966.

RHODES, KATHLEEN, and MERNA A. SAMPLES: *Your Life in the Family,* J. B. Lippincott Co., Philadelphia, 1964.

ROBERTSON, ELIZABETH: *Nutrition for Today,* Third Revised Edition, McClelland & Stewart Ltd., 1968.

SEBRELL, WILLIAM H., and JAMES J. HAGGERTY (and

the editors of *Life*): *Food and Nutrition,* Time-Life Books, a division of Time, Inc., New York, 1967.

SPRACKLING, HELEN: *The New Setting Your Table,* M. Barrows & Company, Inc., 1960.

STARE, FREDERICK J.: *Eating for Good Health,* Doubleday and Co., Inc., Garden City, N.Y., 1964.

TAYLOR, CLARA MAE, and ORREA PYE: *Foundations of Nutrition,* The Macmillan Company, New York, 1966.

TROELSTRUP, ARCH W.: *Consumer Problems and Personal Finance,* McGraw-Hill Book Co., New York, 1965.

VAIL, GLADYS, RUTH M. GRISWOLD, MARGARET M. JUSTIN, and LUCILE O. RUST: *Foods,* Houghton Mifflin Co., Boston, 1967.

WALLACE, INEZ, and B. McCULLAR: *Building Your Home Life,* J. B. Lippincott Co., Philadelphia, 1966.

WHITE, RUTH B.: *You and Your Food,* Prentice-Hall, Inc., Englewood Cliffs, N.J., 1966.

WILMOT, JENNIE S., and MARGARET Q. BATJER: *Food for the Family,* J. B. Lippincott Co., Philadelphia, 1966.

Canadian Government Publications

Canada Department of Agriculture
The Queen's Printer, Ottawa
Food—a la Canadienne, (bilingual, 1967, Publication No. 1316, $1.00.
Meat—How to Buy, How to Cook, 1968, Publication No. 971, $1.00.
Poultry—How to Buy, How to Cook, 1964, Publication No. 1189, 75¢.

Canada Department of Agriculture
Information Department, Canada Department of Agriculture, Ottawa. (Single copies only).

MEAT, EGGS AND DAIRY PRODUCTS
Eggs, (folder), 1967, Publication No. 1341.
How to Barbecue Chicken for a Crowd, 4pp., 1965.
Skim Milk Powder, 24pp., 1961, Publication No. 1106.
Turkey Rolls, 8pp., 1963, Publication No. 1204.

FRUIT AND VEGETABLES
Apples, 20pp. 1970, Publication No. 1402.

Home Canning of Fruits and Vegetables, 22pp., 1965, Publication No. 789.
Jams, Jellies and Pickles, 24pp., 1956, Publication No. 992.
Maple Syrup, Sugar, Butter, Taffy, 24pp., 1961, Publication No. 1096.
Potatoes, 28pp., 1959, Publication No. 1058.
Savory Herbs, 16pp., 1963, Publication No. 1158.

GENERAL FOODS
Barbecue Cooking, 12pp., 1966.
Buy by Grade, 16pp., 1966.
Freezing Foods, 24pp., 1965, Publication No. 892.
Salads, 32pp., 1964, Publication No. 1050.
The Art of Making Sandwiches, 24pp., 1959, Publication No. 1053.

Canada Department of Fisheries
Information Department, Canada Department of Fisheries, Ottawa.
Easy Fish Casserole Recipes, 26pp., 1965.
Fish for Year Round Salads, 24pp., 1964.
Let's Serve Canadian Sardines, 21pp., 1964.
Let's Serve Fish for the Weight Watchers, 33pp., 1965.
Let's Serve Freshwater Fish, 1963.
Let's Serve Shellfish, 28pp., 1959.
The Way to Cook Fish, 23pp., 1964.

Department of National Health and Welfare
Information Services, Department of National Health and Welfare, Ottawa.
The Consumer's Handbook, 25pp., 1968.
Food, Drug and Cosmetic Protection for Your Family, 35pp., 1966.
The Label Story, 22pp., 1964.
Why Get Ill from Foods?, (leaflet), 1968.
Quackery, 8pp., 1964.

Provincial Health Departments
Canada's Food Guide, (colored sheet).
Food Guide for the Older Person, 23pp.
Good Eating with Canada's Food Guide, (leaflet).
The Noon Meal, 14pp.
Nutrient Value of Some Common Foods, 6pp.
Healthful Eating, 68pp., 1968, $ .50.
How to Plan Meals for Your Family, 24pp., 1968, 15¢.

United States Government Publications

Food Buying

Convenience Foods in the Grocery Basket, Marketing Bulletin 22, U.S. Department of Agriculture, 1962.

Food for the Young Couple, Home and Garden Bulletin 85, U.S. Department of Agriculture, 1962.

Food Purchasing Guide for Group Feeding, Agriculture Handbook 284, U.S. Department of Agriculture, 1965.

Food Standards, Facts for Consumers, Food and Drug Administration Publication 8, U.S. Department of Health, Education, and Welfare, 1964.

Fresh and Frozen Fish Buying Manual, Fish and Wildlife Service Circular 20, U.S. Department of the Interior, 1954.

Grade "A" Pasteurized Milk Ordinance—1965 Recommendations of the U.S. Public Health Service, Public Health Publication 229, U.S. Department of Health, Education, and Welfare, 1965.

A Guide to Budgeting for the Family, Home and Garden Bulletin 108, U.S. Department of Agriculture, 1968.

A Guide to Budgeting for the Young Couple, Home and Garden Bulletin 98, U.S. Department of Agriculture, 1964.

Hot Tips on Food Protection, Public Health Service Publication 1404, U.S. Department of Health, Education, and Welfare, 1966.

How to Buy Beef Roasts, Home and Garden Bulletin 146, U.S. Department of Agriculture, 1968.

How to Buy Cheddar Cheese, Home and Garden Bulletin 128, U.S. Department of Agriculture, 1967.

How to Buy Eggs, Home and Garden Bulletin 144, U.S. Department of Agriculture, 1968.

How to Buy Fresh Fruits, Home and Garden Bulletin, 141, U.S. Department of Agriculture, 1967.

How to Buy Fresh Vegetables, Home and Garden Bulletin 143, U.S. Department of Agriculture, 1967.

How to Buy Poultry by USDA Grades, Marketing Bulletin 1, U.S. Department of Agriculture, 1966.

How to Buy Steaks, Home and Garden Bulletin 145, U.S. Department of Agriculture, 1968.

How to Use USDA Grades in Buying Food, Program Aid 708, U.S. Department of Agriculture, 1966.

Meats with Approval through Federal Inspection, Program Aid 573, U.S. Department of Agriculture, 1963.

Pesticide Residues, Food and Drug Administration Publication 18, U.S. Department of Health, Education, and Welfare, 1964.

Read the Label on Foods, Drugs, Devices, Cosmetics, and Household Chemicals, Food and Drug Administration Publication 3, U.S. Department of Health, Education, and Welfare, 1965.

USDA Grade Names for Food and Farm Products, Agriculture Handbook 342, U.S. Department of Agriculture, 1967.

What Consumers Should Know about Food Additives, Food and Drug Administration Publication 10, U.S. Department of Agriculture, 1962.

Foods

Baking for People with Food Allergies, Home and Garden Bulletin 147, U.S. Department of Agriculture, 1968.

Basic Fish Cookery, Fish and Wildlife Service Test-Kitchen Series 2, U.S. Department of the Interior, 1964.

Beef and Veal in Family Meals, A Guide for Consumers, Home and Garden Bulletin 118, U.S. Department of Agriculture, 1967.

Cheese in Family Meals, A Guide for Consumers, Home and Garden Bulletin 112, U.S. Department of Agriculture, 1966.

Dry Peas, Beans, Lentils . . . Modern Cookery, Leaflet 326, U.S. Department of Agriculture, 1963.

Eggs in Family Meals, A Guide for Consumers, Home and Garden Bulletin 103, U.S. Department of Agriculture, 1965.

Fruits in Family Meals, A Guide for Consumers, Home and Garden Bulletin 125, U.S. Department of Agriculture, 1968.

Lamb in Family Meals, A Guide for Consumers, Home and Garden Bulletin 124, U.S. Department of Agriculture, 1967.

Milk in Family Meals, A Guide for Consumers, Home and Garden Bulletin 127, U.S. Department of Agriculture, 1967.

Poultry in Family Meals, A Guide for Consumers, Home and Garden Bulletin 110, U.S. Department of Agriculture, 1966.

Vegetables in Family Meals, A Guide for Consumers, Home and Garden Bulletin 105, U.S. Department of Agriculture, 1968.

Meal Planning

Family Fare: Food Management and Recipes, Home and Garden Bulletin 1, U.S. Department of Agriculture, 1968.

Family Meals at Low Cost, Program Aid 472, U.S. Department of Agriculture, 1965.

Food for Families with School Children, Home and Garden Bulletin 13, U.S. Department of Agriculture, 1963.

Food for the Family with Young Children, Home and Garden Bulletin 5, U.S. Department of Agriculture, 1968.

Food Guide for Older Folks, Home and Garden Bulletin 17, U.S. Department of Agriculture, 1963.

Money-saving Main Dishes, Home and Garden Bulletin 43, U.S. Department of Agriculture, 1966.

Nutrition

Calories and Weight, the USDA Pocket Guide, Home and Garden Bulletin 153, U.S. Department of Agriculture, 1968.

Composition of Foods: Raw, Processed, Prepared, Agriculture Handbook 8, U.S. Department of Agriculture, 1964.

Conserving the Nutritive Values of Foods, Home and Garden Bulletin 90, U.S. Department of Agriculture, 1965.

Eat a Good Breakfast to Start a Good Day, Leaflet 268, U.S. Department of Agriculture, 1967.

Essentials of an Adequate Diet, Agriculture Information Bulletin 160, U.S. Department of Agriculture, 1960.

Food for Fitness: A Daily Food Guide, Leaflet 424, U.S. Department of Agriculture, 1967.

The Food We Eat, Miscellaneous Publication 870, U.S. Department of Agriculture, 1967.

Food and Your Weight, Home and Garden Bulletin 74, U.S. Department of Agriculture, 1967.

Nutrition and Healthy Growth, Children's Bureau Publication 352, U.S. Department of Health, Education, and Welfare, 1965.

Preserving Foods

Freezing Combination Main Dishes, Home and Garden Bulletin 40, U.S. Department of Agriculture, 1965.

Freezing Meat and Fish in the Home, Home and Garden Bulletin 93, U.S. Department of Agriculture, 1966.

Home Canning of Fruits and Vegetables, Home and Garden Bulletin 8, U.S. Department of Agriculture, 1965.

Home Canning of Meat and Poultry, Home and Garden Bulletin 106, U.S. Department of Agriculture, 1966.

Home Freezing of Fruits and Vegetables, Home and Garden Bulletin 10, U.S. Department of Agriculture, 1966.

Home Freezing of Poultry, Home and Garden Bulletin 70, U.S. Department of Agriculture, 1967.

How to Make Jellies, Jams, and Preserves at Home, Home and Garden Bulletin 56, U.S. Department of Agriculture, 1965.

Making Pickles and Relishes at Home, Home and Garden Bulletin 92, U.S. Department of Agriculture, 1966.

Pressure Canners, Use and Care, Home and Garden Bulletin 30, U.S. Department of Agriculture, 1964.

Index

(Figures in heavy type indicate recipes. See also Table of Contents for Recipes on pages 431–433.)